I have fought
a good fight.
I have finished
my course.
I have
kept the faith.

REFLECTIONS

**Rumination and Reminiscence
from a Nonagenarian**

P.E. MacAllister

For information on bulk purchases or corporate premium sales, please contact Priscilla Dick at MacAllister Machinery Co. (317) 545-2151.

ISBN 978-1-4507-5163-6

Table of Contents

About the Author

I graduated from Carroll College in 1940 as a "Bachelor of Arts" with a major in history and minors in English and Speech…ideal preparation for the hurly-burly of the business world, right? Well, not really. Though in one sense, it did help. An MBA might have been more relevant, but let's remember in the humanities curriculum, learning does not cease upon receipt of a college sheepskin. "Au contraire!" Learning is lifelong. A fact demonstrated in the computer age wherein facility with the technology itself separates the achievers from the losers. And then requires continual adaptation and growth as the field continues to diversify and expand, forever and ever, amen.

In my world there is an interweaving of the liberal arts' traditions into the fabric of contemporary life. When someone says "Gaza Strip", I don't need a map. I learned Gaza was part of the Philistine Pentapolis created in 12th Century B.C. because "the bible tells me so"; because a study of Hebrew history confirms that fact, and the American Schools of Oriental Research has archaeologists currently digging out those ancient cities. I learned about Ramadan and Zakat and Jihad 50 years ago from Will Durant; know the sad history of the Jews, buffeted and abused for two millenniums before the sanctuary in Israel occurred, etc., etc.

In examining the human condition across the globe rife with bungling, corruption and mismanagement, I know it doesn't have to be this way. Pericles, Caesar, Abraham Lincoln, Napoleon Bonaparte or Peyton Manning teach us differently. Leadership is a marvelous gift benefitting all involved; incompetence is more prevalent but not an unavoidable circumstance.

What this series of essays or lectures, or sermons, or editorials hopes to do is submit analogies, models, anecdotes in the business world or in the political, theological or the scientific worlds interpreted with illustrations from the humanities revealing how incidents from history, the military or theology, literature or politics teach us lessons on how to deal with issues and conditions commonplace in our world today.

Foreword

P.E. MacAllister is truly a prototypical "Renaissance Man," a man for all seasons, even though his golfing skills hardly qualify for such a title. Chairman of the Board of MacAllister Machinery Company in Indianapolis for more than fifty-five years, P.E. is beyond all peradventure of a doubt one of the most articulate, literate, well-informed, and-civic minded business leaders I have ever known.

Where should we begin? Well, the first time I met P.E. was on the golf course in 1963, when he graciously invited me, as a new Presbyterian pastor in town, to a golf tournament he was playing in, and I believe, sponsoring. Passing over his golfing prowess, the place to begin is with P.E.'s devotion to the Presbyterian Church. He is truly a man of faith as well as an astute student of biblical literature. While not always agreeing with the liberal stances taken by his Presbyterian colleagues, P.E. has never abandoned the church. Serving as an elder, deacon and trustee of his own home church, Northminster Presbyterian, Indianapolis, he has also given much of his life to the denomination, with extensive service at the Presbytery, synod and national levels of governance. Additionally, he was Chair of the Board at Christian Theological Seminary for twelve years.

What has always struck me about P.E. is his extensive knowledge of the Bible (especially the Old Testament) and the history of biblical and classical times, as well as the Florentine Renaissance. Challenge him to name the biblical Joseph's brothers, and he will rattle them off. Inquire of him about the fall of Jerusalem in 586 B.C., and he can describe the event and its fallout in inimitable fashion. Make a reference to Herodotus or Thucydides, and he will not only give you a few quotes, but explain the difference between these two great historians in their writing styles and philosophies of life. Ask him how Cyrus the Great, Darius and Xerxes are related, and he will give you a disquisition on their family tree. Mention the Battle of Thermopylae or the Battle of Marathon, and he will describe not only the battle, but the topography on which it was played out, in extraordinary detail. Unusual of course, but not for

William Hudnut III

someone who has been Chairman of the Board of the American Schools of Oriental Research, which monitors and authenticates archaeological excavation in the Middle East. Invite him to describe the architecture of the Baptistery and the Duomo in Florence, and he'll enthrall you for an hour. Never have I met layman or clergyman so well and broadly informed.

Thanks to his success in the world of Caterpillar tractor business, this veteran of World War II has been a generous patron of the arts throughout his life. Google his name if you don't believe me. His philanthropic activities have been substantial. Vice President of the Fine Arts Society, Vice Chair of the Edyvean Repertory Theatre Board, member of the Indiana State Symphony Society Board, President of the Indianapolis Opera Company and the Indiana Opera Theatre, P.E. has had an on-going love affair with opera. Although not a particularly good singer himself (!), he created the largest non-restricted vocal competition for opera singers in the nation, known as The MacAllister Awards.

So it is obvious that he has become a treasured civic leader. He has his own weekly TV show, "On Site." He has been active with multiple charitable organizations, from the Indianapolis Committee on Foreign Relations to the Indiana Historical Society, from Garfield Park to the Guardian Home, from the American Council of Learned Societies to the President's Advisory Committee on the Arts. He has chaired the Board of Trustees at his alma mater, Carroll College, and the Board of the Indianapolis Parks Foundation. He is an inductee in the Junior Achievement of Central Indiana Business Hall of Fame.

Then there's his commitment to the political party of his choice, the Republicans. He has always been a generous supporter of GOP candidates, and put in a long stretch as chairman and chairman emeritus of the Greater Indianapolis Republican Finance Committee, which he helped to found. The current Marion County (Indianapolis) GOP Committee Treasurer, Lesa Dietrick, says of P.E.: "For over 50 years, P.E. MacAllister has been a stalwart contributor to the Indiana Republican political landscape. His genuine willingness to contribute substantial sums of money to support candidates for local, state and national office is outpaced only by his desire to promote the philosophy of the Republican Party through service to the Party." When I ran for Congress, and again for mayor of Indianapolis, P.E. chaired my campaigns. He served as a Republican member and President of the Capital Improvements Board, which presides over the Convention Center and dome stadium. And he was a Presidential elector three times.

One might wonder why such a relatively conservative fellow as P.E. would be such a strong supporter of the Civil Liberties Union, customarily regarded as a bastion of liberal thinking. The question goes to the heart of who P.E. is. He believes in the practice of civil democracy. He respects the opinions of others. He enjoys intelligent discourse. What he understands--and so many people don't—is that the mission of the ACLU is to limit government power, that individual liberty, not any particular political agenda, is the goal. And liberty is defined as the right of individuals to pursue their own life ends, their own moral and religious visions/beliefs, free of the coercive power of the state. Sheila Suess Kennedy, former Executive Director of the Indiana chapter, says: "Too many people confuse the ACLU's insistence upon personal freedom with an endorsement of the ways in which people choose to use those

freedoms. The central insight that motivates civil libertarians is this: if everyone doesn't have rights, no one *really* does. If the government can pick and choose who will get rights, they aren't rights—they are privileges that can be revoked at the whim of those in power or of popular majorities. P.E. understands that. I wish more people did!"

He also understands how the past is prologue and how history has its uses, as this collection of essays makes abundantly clear. Over the years, 135 of these essays have appeared in the MacAllister Machinery's in-house journal. They seem so relevant to issues and principles of business management, and so wide-ranging through history, philosophy and theology in their application of lessons learned to the practice not only of business, but also of life, that assembling them in one volume for a more extensive audience makes eminent good sense. Reading them, one will be struck immediately by P.E.'s depth of knowledge, uniqueness of literary style, and passion for excellence, as he draws on sources from Tennyson, Shakespeare, Socrates, Hecataeus, Oliver Wendell Holmes, Amos, Abraham Lincoln. Paul of Tarsus, Napoleon, Koholeth, John Donne, Kipling, John Masefield, Marcus Aurelius, and many others.

No motto fits P.E. better than the one from ancient Athens: "Honor the Gods. Help your friends. Adorn your city." This remarkable nonagenarian, with his agile mind, lean body, generous spirit, and passionate love of life, has throughout his nine decades epitomized this creed. He has honored the Gods, walking humbly and reverently before the realm beyond human contrivance. He has generously helped not only many people, but also the causes to which he has been devoted in the worlds of the academy, the opera, the fields of archaeology, the political arena, the church, the City of Indianapolis, the United States, and of course, the business office on East 30th Street. Truly, this remarkable man has been an adornment to the city and everything he has touched during his long and useful life.

William H. Hudnut III
Mayor of Indianapolis, 1976-1991
Washington, DC
May 2008

P.E. MacAllister enjoys one of his 90th Birthday parties —
this one included several hundred friends!

Acknowledgements

Sometime in the late '80s our corporate Promotion Manager, Elaine Morgan Bookwalter, decided we ought to be putting out a newsletter, or communication, i.e. some printed piece that would connect our employee family together while simultaneously carrying articles, for and about, both our business and customers, which might be beneficial to each. She called this product *MacAllister Today*; laid out the format, then produced it quarterly for the next several years. A regular feature was a front-page editorial by the Chairman of the Board, while the back-page space was allocated to Chris who is the President and Chief Operating Officer, because observations or reports or advice (even a little nagging from him once in a while) seemed appropriate. We have long since changed Promotion Managers and by now the charge for heading this up falls on Sherri Pettigrew who gets this hummer out seasonally. From startup 20 years ago till now, we have produced a sizeable stack of back issues.

This book or publication is a reprinting of those front-page essays or commentaries. They range widely, never get very technical, recite the writer's bias and though a bit wordy, became a durable feature of the publication. This regeneration was an idea triggered by some gentle nudging from my old friend Bill Hudnut, who many will remember served a term as the Congressman from Indianapolis and then spent 16 years as our Mayor. It was during his administration we brought local ownership to the Pacers, hosted the Pan Am Games, built a new stadium, induced the Colts to move here, and a jillion other things. Bill was a fabulous minister, Congressman, Mayor, and the leading cheerleader for Indianapolis. Bottom line: "This is <u>his</u> fault."

But made possible only through the industry and perseverance of Priscilla Dick, who for the past 22 years has proven to be an invaluable Assistant. She is capable of enormous output, good judgment, a strong sense of order and has kept this material together in such a way it falls in order. If the content might leave a bit to be desired, the technical preparation will be nonpareil. Abetting us in this process is the Managing Editor and publishing expert, Sherri Pettigrew, who has no peer in this field and who responds with cheerfulness and ebullience. She is responsible for getting all this into a final product with production assistance from Mary Breidenbach.

Regarding the quote on the cover of the book —Sherri asked me to come up with some quotes I live by or which I've been inspired. The quote has always inspired me and comes from St. Paul in the bible. (I consider him the architect of the Christian faith). St. Paul wrote this from a prison in Rome while awaiting the disposition of his case by the emperor and "reflecting" on how he had viewed his sojourn in the "vale of tears"… (No person in Western history exerted more influence than he.)

We're not competing for the Pulitzer Prize here nor does this read like Mark Twain, John Steinbeck or Ernest Hemmingway. This is a random commentary about a series of topics usually connected to some phase of the business and proceeds in chronological fashion from the first to the last. Look for some repetition, redundancy and some irreverence as well as irrelevance. Written rebuttals are in order, but you'll have to take a number and stand in line.

Thank you,

P.E.

P.E. MacAllister

1986

Recharging the Light

August 1986

There has been a great deal of discussion in the written *and* broadcast media about refurbishing "the Lady" in New York Harbor replete with a gala celebration commemorating her rejuvenation. Everyone thinks this is great, but most of us are generally vague as to why the French had the statue cast in the first place and made this contribution to the United States. What was it supposed to prove, aside from the fact that we were mutual friends, and mutual admirers, one of the other? But they had it done — or Bartholdi got it done — and here she is. Surely no one at the time of the dedication could have predicted the enormous stature and prestige which would accrue to this striking monument and few could have estimated the international symbolism for the American brand of freedom which the statue has come to represent. It is an emblem and a figure known throughout the world and represents these United States in a subtle though clearly identifiable manner. Half ignored by most of us for years (or maybe "taken for granted" is a better phrase) suddenly at the centennial of her installation we are all a-twitter and celebrating, nationwide, a feminine face lift and a complete renovation.

What we are really celebrating, of course, is ourselves and our heritage. We are reviewing the changing scene which the old gal has viewed for the past century and are particularly sensitive to the 14,000,000 immigrants who have sailed on by in the past hundred years, most of them remembering life-long their first glimpse of that patina figure in the harbor, not for what she transmitted in terms of aesthetic proportions, but for what she *stood* in terms of national character, governmental systems, and democratic spirit. Forty percent of our population are descendants of the folk in the last century who have viewed Miss Liberty on their way in from some foreign land.

Introspection is what this period is all about.

Looking inward at ourselves almost axiomatically as we "do" centennials and measuring the progress made or the change which has occurred. These seem more important than the impact which we have created in that five score years, because although we are a nation with unprecedented power and prestige, we spend little time as a people boasting about how great we are and too much time pussyfooting around, half apologetic for our brashness, buoyancy, or the friends we have chosen or the policies we've adopted. Surely no people has ever used its power more sparingly or its prestige with less self-interest in mind. But the point here was *introspection* and the tendency to look back and remember how (we think!) things were a hundred years ago, then ponder whether that means they were better or worse than now. Would we like to go back a

Frederic Auguste Bartholdi's statue of "Liberty Enlightening the World" was erected on Bedloe's Island in New York harbor in 1885. As an ageless symbol of American freedom, she has stood silent watch for more than 120 years through the Golden Age of American Immigration and welcomed tens-of-millions of passengers en route to a new life in America.

P.E. at Butler University's Holcomb Gardens.

century and reproduce their society? Have we used the period well or badly? Is our reputation enhanced or sullied?

Contrary to what many people think, I was *not* personally present when the Lady was unveiled in 1886. My historic reveries are spun from reading and study, not always from practical experience. Like most who view this piece, I am concerned about the same issues as the rest of America: have we moved onward and upward in the century elapsed? Are things better, are people freer, is opportunity as abundant, have the systems which induced this "refuse from your teeming shores" been examined and found still as attractive?

The conclusion would have to be that the reading, "in retrospection" is a good one, though we have in this statement a very biased editor, writing words colored with his own experience. Meaning, his experience in the business of Caterpillar for the past forty-one years has been a good one; therefore, he applies that lesson to the broader spectrum of mankind. But the proof of the hypothesis (i.e. things are still very unique here) is in the record, i.e. the number of immigrants still flocking to these shores (or across certain southwest water courses), counting the Mexican immigrants, legal and illegal. I'll bet we are looking at *record levels* of expatriates entering this country, lead here by the torch the old Lady still holds in her hand. A torch which illuminates the striking difference between "here" and "there" bringing into full view the heterogeneity which is America, the lack of ancient prejudice, the endless and sundry opportunities at hand (600,000 new businesses last year, a hundred thousand plus millionaires); the freedom of movement, of expression, of political viewpoint, the universal education, the open society, and the free-wheeling nature of its populace.

This all has little — and much — to do with selling tractors, digging coal, crushing rock and spreading asphalt. "Much" because we function under the same guidelines and in the same system which regulates the rest of the country. "Little" because we don't have much to do with immigrants except sponsoring and hiring one or two of them on occasion. But we who work here are proof positive of the power of that loadstone which draws others to these shores. We are models, the living examples of free enterprise capitalism which is the core structure of the incentive system which awards with material and incremental units (called dollars) the efforts of those who strive and best achieve. We are tangible evidence of the age-old maxim that affirms he who risks, invests, produces, works hard, contributes and perseveres is rewarded with the dollars to assure security, the perquisites of life, the things which enhance, ennoble and enrich the journey through this vale of tears. This always proves there is not only hope for a better life, but the wherewithal to achieve it. Restrictions surely exist for those who want to participate, but those restricted are the lazy, the uneducated, the derelict, the goof-off, the timid, and the faint-hearted, never those with the "other" political bent, the wrong name, the obscure race, the untouchable class. For the most part, this says anyone with the courage and the gumption has a shot at the brass ring.

That is really truer today than it was in 1886. We tend to forget our fierce and outlandish discrimination against the Irish, suspicion of Italian and Greek immigrants, the exploitation of Orientals, the disapproval of Catholics. The society a century ago was far more bigoted than ours today, though even then, the intercultural mingling and the gap of a generation or two could see the shanty Irish disbarred from respectable pubs in one generation, yet in the White House two generations later. Our prejudice is never universal or as permanent as that in Europe. We do not institutionalize our pet antipathies and though it took awhile to get the blacks free and the women emancipated, we give it a good run these days, making equality a probable reality. The elements which make us who live here happy are the same ones that draw people to this land, so in a sense, we who make the systems work continue to recharge the batteries which light the Lady's torch. We have been, to a degree, architects of the system in which we function and our own input, character, ingenuity, style and panache continue to flavor and color the machinery which make it all go. ■

Why a System?

October 1986

A friendly editor of a conservative publication asked me recently to write an essay on "The Purpose of Government." Why is it here? What was it created to do? Is it, indeed, faithful to its charge or outstripping practical limits and becoming all things to all men? Tractor people are rarely experts on the nature and purpose of governments, but the topic is a titillating one and surely timely for any thoughtful American. I decided there were two underlying conclusions about the whole subject. One was the fact that government was not necessarily designed to serve the same purpose from one age to the next, nor was it created in all societies to perform the same role/function. Secondly, governments don't work very well. If one looks at history, he finds the first two hundred and eighty-three governments flopped. Collapsed along the road and been run over by someone else's succeeding government, while the people who had fashioned the initial one pass from history. (The Chaldeans succeed the Assyrians, but are conquered by the Persians, who fall before the Macedoneans, who ultimately succumb to Rome, et cetera.) Something goes awry internally; something malfunctions or is badly directed and gets wiped out. The entire culture is obliterated. Wooofff. Gone. Though governance is essential to manage the human society on a perpetual basis, governmental *systems* are disappointingly transitory.

Some of us in business ruminate about that type of history grinding on our little operations as well. We'd like to avoid the bad luck of the 283 kings, chiefs, and emperors who failed to make the cut and we start with less ambiguity about our purpose. It is not different (like governments), but the same. All of us were started to make a profit for the investors, though, *the device* for generating profits will vary. Our way is by selling Caterpillar products (exclusively) and augmenting sales with parts supplies and with a large service operation. In the case of our customers, there are a hundred different ways, all sorts of services performed or materials sold or jobs done or yards moved or coal mined or rocks crushed. But the objective is the same, profitability.

The major impediments to our success are both internal and external: interpretation to our employees, the reason we are here (internal) *and* relating effectively — successfully — to respective markets (external). My job in our shop is to focus on the big picture and keep each producing unit (employee) aware of how he contributes to — imperil — the end result. The objective of most workers is fairly simple. It is, do the work at hand each day, handle the problems or routines which the system has brought to each workplace for processing. The assignment is self-fulfilling; is an end in itself. How that is connected to profitability seems to slip through the cracks. (This is getting very complicated.) The point will be a lot of people in our shop or Caterpillar's plant or on a construction site, figure their responsibility is to do what they have been told to do, period. If profitability is to occur, that is someone else's responsibility and that someone else is a vague and imprecise factor called "management." They (or he) have to synchronize the human resource with the tooling , the facilities, the capital, the inventories, the training, the promotion, the selling, etc. in such a fashion that all come together and we end up taking in more money than it has cost to run the operation.

The challenge of management is to hook people at a work site to the larger picture and to suggest that not only is good workmanship enhancing personal reputations, but it happens to be good business. When a buyer likes what we do, he comes back, and we can do some more for him. We are relying upon repeat business and unless it does repeat, we are all in deep trouble. So that routine function performed daily is an insurance policy. If not, it becomes the malfunction, the misalignment which occurred in the history of governments that spelled doom for

MacAllister's office, 1950.

the enterprise. Blundering or ineptness is not limited to a person's work bench. It affects the entire operation, whether one is a stock*holder* or a stock*chaser*. Profitability is essential to all the employees — the whole group — because when a business fails its purpose, it does not get a special reprieve, it goes down the tube. When there are no profits, like those 283 chiefs, emperors, Caesars and kings, there is no institution left. It isn't just the owners who are in trouble then because the employees can't survive if the business folds. A failure in the sales department will not permit the rest of the dealership to disconnect it and go along without the department. The hooked anchor stops the entire craft, not just the stern.

More in line with this rather contrived analogy about the need for persons and departments to succeed is the necessity of success in *all* markets and among *all* customers. We can't do our job just in the coal fields. There was a period when 75% of our income and profitability came from a single source: highway construction. It was a great going and the sort of times to which we'd like to return, but marriage to one income source has obvious weaknesses. One day it withers and the next day it dies, while all the overhead continues. The danger of putting all the eggs in one omelet then becomes dramatically more evident when market collapse is followed by the worst recession in a hundred years. The source of our revenue is a continuing concern and the lessons of the past vivid in mind today. Our strongest market today is coal and we shall take all the coal business we can get, because it is big dollars and it is hard usage. But again, there is no long-term survival through exploitation of a single market, especially one in which major producers can stop so quickly and sizeable producers go belly up overnight.

Hopefully by now, we are wise enough to spread our involvement and coverage. We love 'em all: black-

toppers, rock and gravel producers, guys laying water lines, contractors, utilities, farmers, public bodies, and people running the county landfill, plus sewer people, loggers, site levelers, truckers, users of industrial power, warehouses, and anyone else who even looks like he might need something. What Caterpillar has done for us in the post-highway era is broaden the line to a point where we have a full basket — would you believe — some 400 separate models to sell. Our job is to get this revolution completely in hand and represent the manufacturer across the board, not just where it is easy or where we want to be.

One of the historic considerations on the viability and the efficacy of governments (going back to my analogy), has to be the capacity to change. Governments must serve the needs of *this* people, not those of the Czar's day or the era of armored cavalry or powdered wigs. The major problem has been dealing pragmatically with those conditions which caused major disruptions — losing the war, creating a revolt, or experiencing a depression. We inevitably deal with them *after* the fact. Government uses experience from past history as the "software" for the present (or future) as though history repeats itself. Fact is, that paying the piper for past mistakes is not the same as negotiating the payment for *this* piper, who is calling a far different tune. The challenge is to get ahead of the pressure and gear to accommodate the future's demands, rather than reeling from the hammer of the past.

Companies, large and small, have the same problem. They know what *happened*. How do they use that in negotiating what is about to happen? The experience from the past may or may not be of much help and none should presume the lesson learned is a safeguard against what is to come. Caterpillar's memory of strikes and foreign competitors and oil prices and world recessions is long and prolix. Its size is large enough so it requires major effort in order to turn its course, but it has responded ponderously and positively, letting the highway era slide by with fond memories, while ascertaining now where the volume will be in the next decade and what sort of product will meet the needs of the new age.

The dealer marches to the same tune, though we can react more quickly. Our job currently as manufacturer and dealer is to look at markets for the '80s and '90s and with our extended line get into newer types of operation by selling the broader line of product. We have some pioneering to do; we have to triple our customer base; we have to get acquainted with a lot of new people; we have to sell to far more buyers to generate the same highway contractor dollar. We shall be — and are — doing some fumbling in the process. Salesmen aren't easily regrooved, nor their orientation completed easily. We have a new rental fleet to manage, more inventory to select. Moving into new markets is not easy because competitors don't welcome us very warmly. Prospects who don't know us, look at us suspiciously and, generally, think we are too high priced and too haughty. They are skeptical of $33 hourly service rates, expensive trucks, big buildings, and lots of investment in tooling. It is our job to suggest that we don't sink this kind of money into a dealership only to price ourselves out of range. Rather the opposite: to make an operation so efficient our services *cost less.* Because the sophisticated and modern tooling does more, does it better and quicker, than the shade-tree mechanic with a sledge hammer and a drift. Our cleaning takes less time, specialization is faster and more reliable, component testing prevents bungling in-field installation. A larger dealer has more people and equipment available. He has parts proficiency as well and parts inventory is a direct impactor of machine availability. Larger customers, who have paid a high price for a big piece of machinery, are not prepared to wait around two weeks while we locate a given part. They want it running *NOW!* Today! Our way of responding to that demand is to stock parts until they are coming out the Kazoo (over $4,000,000 worth) which gives us the capacity to supply 95% of the stuff the first day and *guarantee* any Caterpillar part in 48 hours. That availability doesn't just work for highway contractors or Peabody Coal. It works for everyone. There is only one Caterpillar line of products and one source of parts for all of them irrespective of size. The guaranteed service provided our largest customers holds true for our smallest as well.

In considering either service or parts, the obsession in our place is machine availability, something we call "go time." Larger owners need the whole spread on a job and want each machine doing its share, but when one konks out, it doesn't necessar-

Machine availability is vital to contractors including the initial phase of the Honda plant development. (Greensburg, Indiana, 2007)

ily hamstring the complete operation. For a smaller owner, with a machine out, maybe the whole production stops or is cut in two or is diminished by a third. *That* time waiting for parts and repairs can be relatively more costly than to AMAX Coal or to Rieth-Riley. In essence, this says we provide relatively more value to the smaller operator, the one who needs it most, than we do to the major owners.

Our objective, of course, is to be like St. Paul, "all things to all men." The customer is the customer. He is not graded by size, weight, color of hair or type of pick-up truck he drives. He is deserving of one degree of service, one caliber of product support — the best. We don't always get this done and have the same garbling of communication as anyone else, but deal for deal and call for call, we'll match our capacity to produce in the clutch with any competitor on the continent. The reason is not exactly altruistic. The reason is we *need* the business. We give good service because we do more of it that way. But beyond that, because to maximize sales, we have to have all the bases covered; get every account covered; sell every part we can and every hour of service. If this aim is misunderstood, it ought not to be perpetuated. We're never going to get all of the business, but we're never going to stop short of doing just that — every customer, every deal. ■

Traditions

December 1986

An appropriate theme for a holiday-type editorial is *tradition*, the element that moves Christmas successfully from one generation to the next and gears us annually to experience the anticipation and celebration. Supported, of course, by the merchants who pitch in and extol traditions of this sort in order to assure another go-round next year.

Tradition is as old as the species. It is a way of *thinking* and a corresponding response in subsequent activity. It was more than a holiday or a date to ancient peoples. It was the phenomenon which arbitrated all phases of life: the mode of dress, the menu, vocation, the "pecking order," the way we view our neighbors or strangers, how we worship the gods, bury our dead, plow our fields, cut our hair. It told folks where they stood in society and how they related to it, so each became familiar, if not entirely comfortable *with*, the age in which his saga unfolded. There was no solicitation of individual expression or personal opinion or new ideas. Affairs were ordered, binding society together on through the ages; or maybe sidetracked it periodically until we could get ourselves corrected and reoriented. So, mankind moved in the same traces, in the same groove from one generation to the next. The peasant tilled the same fields as his great grandfather, used the same implements, lived in the same hovel, worked the land of the same ducal family, slept in the same bed, was

bitten by the same strain of household fleas, which might have given a sense of continuity and stability since all knew what would be happening from now on. But they also died of the same diseases, were subject to the same exploitation, were condemned to a system which locked them into a very limited horizon; but when one is stupid or unambitious, "horizons" are of little interest. Safety is, however. Food on the table and protection *are* of interest. The point is that tradition of caste, geography, vocation, and outlooks have governed most of the world for much of the time.

Strong and prevailing traditions continue in our day as the build-up to Christmas proves. But tradition in America, *vis-à-vis*, the rest of the world is a brand-new ball game. We broke the age-old, stranglehold, rejecting those ancient memories which preserve archaic animosities and traditions of hating, often centuries old and no longer explicable. Ours were altered or reinforced or modified on the basis of what was needed now, rather than what used to be. On what is purposeful and constructive, necessary and enjoyable, on what reflects best this *novus ordo seclorum*. A great advantage accrues with updated or new traditions, *vis-à-vis*, what the old ones have done to Europe. Discounting the Soviet Union, the old world has about 60% our land mass in the United States, maintains 25 separate nations, meaning coinage, languages, school systems, postage stamps, police departments and garbage pick up to protect the dubious differentness of 35 separate cultural traditions. They remain suspicious, competitive, harboring memories of hoary wrongs now institutionalized. Count their wars the past 1,000 years…better yet the past 200 years, as contrasted to our record. It ought to speak volumes to the nonsense of a good many traditions. Makes us ask if what people *do* with their traditions has been wise or foolish or merely indiscriminate.

We can't survive in America without them, don't get me wrong, but we've done something different: We have made them *voluntary*, made them subordinate to the rule of laws, made them diverse. They've had to give way through the generations to an overriding sense of what is practical, effective, and what best serves the total good of the greatest number. The result has been the casual incorporation into our

E.W. MacAllister, founder of MacAllister Tractor Co., enjoying his first granddaughter, Heather Leigh MacAllister, daughter of P.E.

national ethos of countless bits of foreign or "other" elements to make our fabric the richest and brightest of them all. Rather than rejecting a garment or a dish or a beverage or a holiday because we remember something bad (we think) about its source or origin, we accept or reject it on its own merits. Allowing those who *do* enjoy full freedom to fast, march, worship, imbibe or shoot off fireworks as they please. The result is a potpourri, a collage of international flavors across the spectrum of our lives. Christmas is an example. The date itself is fixed by the winter solstice; the tree is out of Druid sources with the lights, courtesy of Martin Luther; the wassail bowls, Yule log and plum pudding seem to be English. Our carols come from Hans Gruber, the Roman and Protestant churches, medieval English songs, plus Bing Crosby, Andy Williams, and even Gene (ugh!) Autry. The turkey is American; St. Nick is Dutch; the giving of gifts goes back to the Roman Sauternalia; and the credit card that makes it all possible can be traced to the DiMedici's of 15th Century Florence. The crèche comes from Bethlehem and goes back to "the days of Herod the King" circa 4 BC. All saying, we borrow extensively; oblivious to whether or not we like the peoples who thus contribute to *our* Christmas tradition. We have *done something* with this annual celebration that makes it universal, colorful and exuberant — as we have with many traditions.

So we're an amalgamator, rejector, and modifier of traditions, including those applying to human relations. Check our attitudes of 60 years ago when I was a kid. We had strong prejudices and a place for blacks, Jews, and women, like say chopping cotton, across the tracks, and in the kitchen, respectively. All since challenged and gone by the boards — Poofft. Technically and legally, traditions removed and replaced by new ones. Another generation can recreate more appropriate styles of dealing with these time-honored acorns, uninhibited by lingering whisps of prejudice. Those "programmed" like I was about women and blacks take awhile to get a new software package installed and when you're intimidated by a computer, that's not a weekend's work.

Again, our traditions were adopted voluntarily and are subordinate to our political systems, to a rational approach in handling the affairs of a great republic. The shibboleths rejected, we snort disdainfully at myopic arrogance of the past traditions restricting thought and action in politics, religion, sex, and ethnic issues. A major galvanic transformation! Hasn't our discrimination, ingenuity, checking-of tradition

had a direct effect upon our success as a nation? Can a people succeed in the modern world regulated by fixed minds shaped eons back, and to some extent irrelevant? Were we not wise to relegate tradition to an *option* rather than a mandate?

By now, surely you are asking, "What's all this got to do with business?" The answer is: a lot. Because business has its traditions, old as Christmas, but non-seasonal, i.e., used everyday. I was raised within the MacAllister Caterpillar tradition with certain customs and practices, understandings and premises. To the extent we have succeeded, those traditions which directed our course, need to be managed. The chief one being that of integrity, absolute honesty with both customers and employees, factory and competitor, an obvious ground rule, because people don't deal with folks they can't trust. Second policy is sensitivity to the user, the customer, because we know first pop every day, he's the ultimate arbiter of our destiny. He's why we open up — not Caterpillar, the bank or the stockholders. Our relations have to instill confidence and thus qualify us for more business. The day we put the user on the back burner is the day we begin to see a curtain descending.

The commitment to service is another tradition. We are here to be of professional utility to somebody else, and the payoff is not to *say* all this, but to *do* it. The "doing" is evident through investment in the equipment and machinery, in personnel and systems which provide *indeed,* as well as in word.

The Caterpillar tradition is longer than ours, and more encompassing. It rests upon a superior product, requiring enormous amounts of money ($400,000,000 annually) for engineering and design, but finds no way of getting better without perpetual striving. CAT relies upon independent dealers to sell its product. CAT works with a published code of ethics and in the age of scandals, bribery, fiscal shenanigans and enormous temptations, has never once been embarrassed by the activities of its officers or managers, because traditions demand decent business conduct. CAT is represented worldwide; it has stayed in a defined market (it doesn't build airplanes or mine coal), prices product at the perceived value of the user, etc., etc.

The aforesaid traditions, CAT's and mine, are a mere recitation of what were and continue to be. The annual challenge is assuring, both their relevance and effective utilization. Then their maintenance. Traditions exist only if they are passed to the next generation. A group of 15 employees in a small

A.H. Carlson Co., a customer from earlier times, utilizes MacAllister's field service.

company, 45 years ago using them does not mean 220 people in 1987 are still equally and automatically committed. A Christmas editorial needs to reiterate the point about being a way of thinking as it ordains subsequent action. Christmas has the element of purpose or meaning and the implementing aspect. Traditionally we pass around gifts, eat a lot of turkey, sing carols, go through a shopping binge, and decorate the tree, often leaving the heart of the subject or the motivating premises overwhelmed by the glitter and bustle. The reasons why we celebrate need clearer understanding of this traditions' breadth and origins, lest they end up hollow and empty, spelling ultimate oblivion since we celebrate for a reason, not for simple celebrating.

The point at Christmas is the whole deal — is not about "me" — it's about other people. It's not dropping hints about what we want but is rather preoccupied with what we might do for family and friends. The tradition must maintain a vision of He whose birthday we celebrate, and the purpose of that life was endless service, mostly on behalf of the needy or the empty, the hurting and rejected people around Him. The uniqueness of the Judeo-Christian tradition is recapitulated in that model from the days of Amos through the ministry of Jesus, suppressing the ego — the big "me" — to focus on others, primarily "the least of these." Christmas will be a one-year shot, thus, no tradition, when it focuses only on *me* eating *my* turkey and opening *my* presents at *my* house, Amen. Wouldn't survive until the next election *without* reaching to embrace friends, the community, business associates, the family, and the whole darn clan.

Our job, as business people, at year end (and for the new year commencing) is to examine again our style of operations — our traditions of doing business — and see that they are clear in purpose and supported through structure; are both competitive and user-attractive. Then, be sure the whole bloody company buys *into* both those traditions and adopts them as warmly as each observes his Christmas holiday.

Beyond that, we ought to be aware of the possibility of creating new traditions which give versatility to our operation, a better break to our people, more benefit to the customer and serve better the purposes of our company and CAT. Fixed traditions deserve no protection if they do not serve this day's needs. Traditions that do just that need to be created and added to those we pass on. But in the meantime, before I start working on all *that* whole business, let me take time to wish you the happiest of holidays and a most joyous, prosperous and healthy new year. ■

When To Stop

June 1987

President Reagan made a stop in Indiana on the 9th of April to visit the campus of Purdue University, where he made a speech to an aggregation of 10,000-12,000 people, mostly students, in Mackey Arena. This was of particular interest because I had a chance to meet him personally along with a dozen or so "civic and industry leaders" and do a "question and answer" period for 20 minutes prior to his speech. One is bound to be impressed in such a presence because, irrespective of who the *person* is, the office is somewhat awesome. And that aura permeates the occasion. More so in a small room setting than in a large auditorium, but the impact upon the students was nonetheless electric. College campuses are rarely bastions for conservative thought in any age and ol' Dutch reminisced enough to mark the difference in eras, *his* and *theirs*, so there was no mistaking the age gulf beyond whatever political divergence there might be. The separation was more conjectural than real and the wonder of the whole encounter was the way Reagan's person and office affected the student body. One could feel the empathy mounting as he walked on stage. I mean absolutely continual shouts and clapping. Then the audience interrupted 28 times with applause in the course of a 25-minute pitch, even approbation when Reagan got to on SDI (Star Wars).

Although a supporter of the President and one who admires his tenacity and singleness of purpose, I must confess I have never presumed Ronald Reagan to be an *intellect*, a profound man. Sophistry is not his game. His world tends to be simplistic because, when it gets too complex, we tend to narrow it down in order to fit within our limited range of perspective so we can deal with it. Nonetheless, the President's speech was well-structured and "vintage Reagan," with illustrations from history or out of his White House experience. He proved he's still the best cheerleader for America and its most optimistic propounder/defender. An illustration depicts his outlook and gives me a springboard for my point in this editorial.

The President reminded us that anywhere else in the world "nationals" are pretty clearly identified. A Greek is a Greek and he who is Spanish or Italian remains that; the Irish will always be Irish, etc. But it would be impossible for you or I to become a Greek or a Spaniard. We don't — and can't — qualify. How strange then, that all these nationalities have come to America in waves and have no trouble *becoming Americans*. We have accepted and converted, mingled

P.E.'s sermon message: "We Add Value" is stated while he makes a film for AED to boost the trade association.

and conditioned all peoples to our mode of life and thought, made them participants in our political systems and culture insofar as they want to respond. It's peculiar this traffic is only one way; they might join us, but to be French or Austrian, one has to be born and raised *there*. All of which is part of our history and is precisely what makes the nation unique. Our Anglo-Saxon background and tradition of English Common Law, broadened culturally, artistically, gastronomically, and philosophically by a dozen different influences, strains, and impacts carried here and implanted by other elements of the world. If you don't think so, recall the proliferation of Taco Bell — Chi Chi's — Rosa Corona chains; the universality of pizza; the wine bibbing that has swept our culture the past 20 years; the architecture of the southwest; incursion of the Honda and Toyota and little European cars, etc. The result is a sampling of the entire world's taste and the result of that is sometimes the good old American recourse to Alka Seltzer, especially when one applies this foreign inundation to the economic field. We have the same excitement about things foreign when it comes to goods as we do about food or apparel and, unfortunately, we have the same openness and use the same welcome mat. The result is that people all over the world not only look at the culture that makes us what we are, but the generosity which is part of our national characteristic and along with that, note how easy it is to slip into our markets. This is the greatest dumping ground in the world for products of all shapes and sizes. And why, with corn and hogs coming out of our ears, we are *importing* Polish hams or given the dairy glut, why we are bringing in Dutch and Italian cheeses is beyond me. We practically invented orange juice, yet today, most of that being squeezed in Florida is coming out of Brazil and Mexico. We also invented television and portable radios, but all of them now come out of Japan or Taiwan.

So the flow of foreign influence this time in products rather than people continues its age-old pace. The unique thing, again, is the fact that this is not a two-way street either. I mean *they* can ship it in here by the convoys, but try and get something into their markets (besides dollars or arms). It costs the Japanese ten times as much to raise a pound of rice as it does the American grower, but guess whose rice the Japanese eat? Right! It is Japanese rice, premium and all. Something about not wanting to dissolve or disrupt a traditional industry. Beef in Japan is seven times more expensive than Indiana steak, but how much do you suppose we export there? Zilch! We might trade some tractors for oranges in Brazil? Wrong. They won't *let* us export tractors there, nor into Mexico, without one helluva tariff. The Europeans counteract by more subtle ways, by state support of local industries, by propping up Common Market farm prices with Federal subsidies and, in some cases, by state ownership of the operation itself. It's a lopsided game we are in.

One of these days something is going to have to give. We could handle "the refuge from your teeming shores" for a long while, but finally put a cap on immigration. It's a bit more difficult to put a stop to imports, but we surely are reaching the gag point. It's time to stop shuffling industries and folding up one only to try another. Like letting the shoe industry, textiles, the steel, the oil, autos, the electronics and you name it, sort of dry up (in some places wither on the vine), while we close the plants only to start scrambling to see what else we can do in order to sustain our employment. The amazing thing (as Reagan noted at Purdue) is we have still been able to add more people to the U.S. payrolls in the past generation — or the past ten years — than all of Western Europe or Japan combined. There is something vital and ingenious about our capitalism that gives it this endurability, but isn't there some limit to that as well?

President Ronald Reagan
(Source: Wikimedia Commons.)

What is needed in this baffling scenario is a national policy that deals with international depredation and the lopsided level of international trade, i.e., all from *there* to "here" with no return option. It is silly to support our farmers with the biggest giveaway programs in history and have us blocked out of their markets by our trading partners. It is ludicrous to close down our oil and gas industry with all its jobs and peripheral business in order to import oil from our enemies in the Middle East. It is unwise to emasculate critical American industries, like steel, radios, heavy machine tools, textiles, et al., probably for no other reason than that it jeopardizes national security. Meaning it is surely stupid to be sending $150,000,000,000 a year in American dollars abroad in pursuit of foreign products while we board up our own plants. At some point in time, all the dollars we

have will be owned by someone else, yet there appears to be no program a foot to correct the imbalance or rectify that problem. Aside from waiting to see what will happen.

Maybe it is time to see the complexities of the world as they are, rather than simplifying them so we can understand. Maybe it's time for some sacrifice and some belt-tightening. But first of all we need to get our act together, and someone has to tell us how we should respond. Get some of the brighter minds at work to find an immigration policy for goods that works both ways; that looks at our infrastructure and determines what is best for America, then develop a national agenda and a national game plan for all of us to follow, dealing with the tipped scales and the eternal traffic that seems to travel only one way. ∎

Truth: The Ultimate Responsibility

November 1987

Christian Theological Seminary is the only major institution of its kind in our town and has become a well-regarded fellowship in these parts. Founded in 1925 by the Disciples of Christ, their national headquarters is in Indy and their program is one with which I've had some affiliation the past 20 years. On the 13th of September, we all gathered to commemorate "Founder's Day" this year, replete with a big production which included the dedication of a striking new chapel, the last piece in a 21-year building program — all paid for, by the way — constituting the finest theological campus anywhere in America.

The theme for scholars and sundry guests on this historic occasion examined "faith and the life of the mind," reflecting on the occasional dichotomy between *reason* as it conflicts or coincides with theological beliefs ("faith", i.e., that existing without proof or evidence). The Seminary has never bought that first tractor from us, so working them into this essay is a bit contrived. (Fact is, they don't even own a standby generator, CAT or otherwise, so we can't hook up on that score either!) But the whole affair suggested a titillating theme which might have some relevance to Caterpillar-type people after all.

This school struggles to remind we locals that despite the explosion in buildings and parks here, in domes, zoos, museums, shopping plazas, and all the rest, there's another world beyond the physical or economic with which we must deal. That in the midst of our late-century renascence there are concerns for *people* which must be dealt with or the

city's "growth" is a hollow thing and the character of the community becomes lifeless and shallow. That in the shadow of new ascending office buildings (one the tallest in the state) are desperate folk with lousy housing, no jobs, trapped in the poverty cycle now going on the fourth generation and far too many so functionally illiterate that they are disqualified from the "American dream." That along with an "acceptable" unemployment rate (latest figure is 5.1%) and the plans for a new $600 million City Center Mall, beyond a big, ongoing mayor's race and a terrific political battle to be waged next year, there is, indeed, "the life of the mind" in need of emphasis in order that attention is given to the lot of "the least of these." In short, the conscience of the community needs to focus on human conditions as it flexes its commercial muscles.

Although hardly visible, the nourishment of our spirit needs action as well as in other spheres. While balancing the problems of the poor, there's also need to fund the Symphony (an annual scramble, believe me), perpetuation of opera, support for amateur athletics, ballet groups, the vitality of the church, the major convulsion in our school systems, and 50 other things that come to mind. Saying the character and psyche of a city evolves from "the life of the mind" and how it *views* itself and what it believes itself to be, using the physical surroundings, its economic climate and cultural institutions as talismans, reflect the true character of its citizens.

Nothing new in this. Art reached new heights of excellence or immortality in Periclean, Greece, and in renaissance Florence, not because of mere affluence but because the citizen/amateur commissioned painting and sculpture, gave freedom to architects and poets, and evaluated the product resulting from their patronage. It was their desire for beauty and their discrimination in terms of its quality that produced a Golden Age. These same ingredients, the same search for the best, it seems to me, are present and requisites of this age. Meaning that what gives substance to an era or a community, gives it worth and value, is the attitude of the leadership (the patron) directing its destiny. And the destiny is marked by the comfort of the constituency and its capacity to add momentum to the aesthetic, societal quality, as well as to the economic, political, and commer-

P.E spent about 20 years preaching at Protestant Churches.

cial world. When leadership is marked with altruism, a sense of class and style, has a concept of a mission beyond personal subjectivity, the enterprise is inclined to prosper and does so with a good deal of glory. The motivator/arbitrator of all this is the Seminary's offspring, practical theology — personal conviction about me and my interface with others — that moves people into the arena, defending those overlooked and keeping society or the city council, the agencies of government, aware of the need to serve all of us, not only those strong enough to demand attention. There ought to be some political priorities among us to take into account the enhancement of the community ethos, knowing this cannot be achieved unless there's fairness and generosity and a sense of parity across the board. But more than this, can translate "the life of the mind" into becoming the life of the system.

If there's anyone still with me, I have to pull this rather distorted analogy down to the corporation and figure out what this has to do with MacAllister Machinery Co., Inc., which, incidentally, has to deal on two levels as well, but probably has to be more pragmatic. Because while dealing with the "life of the mind," meaning how it wants to run and handle its affairs and its own employees, has to be sure those conform with the reality of the same, intensity of competition, concerns with the manufacturer, the irritation level of the user, the beneficence of the bank, and a good many other things.

The dichotomy which we experience is inevitable because interests vary and pressures are competing so we have the contest between those as well as the eternal one, that of how we perceive ourselves to operate on one hand and how that translates into reality when it hits the marketplace. What we have in the corporate "mind" often loses a little in reiteration as it moves from one level to another through the business structure, and when it coincides (or collides) with the user, it may or may not be what we conceived initially in the aerie of the front office. So, the problem with your friendly dealer is *becoming* what we *say* we are. What is proposed as corporate policy or established as the mode of doing business often gets deflected in the process of implementation either because the concept itself is impractical or because he, carrying out his instructions, doesn't understand, doesn't care, or doesn't know. Having a "life of the mind" is one thing and it is essential if the operation is to be directed, but delivering what has been conceived then determines *what we are* far

Chris MacAllister giving a speech at the MacAllister 60th Anniversary celebration.

more than what our aspirations had been. The concept needs to be shared across the board in our company with some seriousness, and those who practice their sundry arts in our several departments need to feel some ownership of the undergirding principles.

If that is, indeed, the case, how *loudly* we state our mission is of some import because all need to know, but more than that, *what it is we propose* is also crucial. It needs to be the type of conduct others respect and adopt normally as though it were theirs. It ought to be the sort of policy and practice people are proud of and can support enthusiastically. It cannot be marginal or equivocal, timid or fuzzy; it cannot be tentative, transient or temporary.

Getting mechanics and stockchasers, data processors, and clerks to follow this high-flown oratory is really a lot to ask. They live in a world of specific expertise with horizons defined by the technical area in which they work. Maybe it isn't their job to be stewing about the big picture or get into "the life of the mind." One would hope they do so, however, in other personal encounters, but with respect to the business, those on top who give overall direction, do so across the board and set the policies or patterns that ultimately depict what it is we really intend to be. Like the analogy of the city, several people (things) give shape to whatever form we come to assume and beyond that, give us shape on a couple levels for better or worse. But before any shaping at department levels takes place, we must know what it is we aspire to. The concept comes first. The "mind" gives shape to "the life."

What that is supposed to infer is that businesses and institutions have differing stimuli or impulses nudging them on their course. The one deserving of the least response ought to be the direction imparted by destiny. The easy route, the quickest way, the one least complicated or perhaps least expensive, etc. The course ought not to be directed by mere evolution or simply expediency.

Our business lot is no different than many, but it is more complex. We have to respect the demands of customers, plus the pressure of the factory, the fallibility of subordinates and 230 employees on our roster, plus the vagaries of competitors, the bank, and the economy, all demanding consideration. The responding to all demands and moving in the wild course which *these* pressures direct is a sure route to oblivion. The counteracting need behind this is for some, determined policy or plan or rule which gives proper course and direction, oblivious to outside factors steering us through the shoals and avoiding the reefs. In that program which is often called "corporate policy," the modern company, it seems to me, balances the needs of all constituencies in such a fashion he gets none of them really "ticked" and is

professionally faithful as well to the initiating motive which is profitability. But surely as it proceeds down the pike, it is aware of the community in which it survives and, like the Seminary, is conscious of other elements in its surrounding habitat that allow for response to identified needs. Not because it is an obligation, but because it's "mind" sees business operations as part of a greater totality and because out of respect for the environment which permits it to flourish, reciprocal consideration is a normal trade-off. In short, it too has an obligation to support the civic ventures which make the city unique, positive response to the concern for "the least of these," the arts world, the political process, and a record of outlook and outreach that depicts a "mind" more universal than parochial, a reputation for fairness more enviable than mere success, and a general track record that makes the rest of the community glad it is here. In such a fashion, is corporate "faith" truly depicted? ■

1988

Tradition and Technology

March 1988

This alliterative phrase is sort of a marketing theme for MacAllister during the course of this year and hopes to recapitulate too the major ingredients essential in explaining the dealership. The words are supposed to identify its pedigree while giving direction and purpose to its course down the pike. A topic more philosophic than economic in its scope.

Our "tradition" goes back to my father, whose state of earthly nirvana was reached in 1945 when he signed the Caterpillar contract with Bill Ziegler. Mac had been a highway commissioner in Wisconsin during the '20s when America was roughing out its highway systems (three million plus miles) and in Wisconsin, the County Highway Department built most of the roads. He was using CAT tractors in that endeavor and learned considerable about the technology required in a time when much of the horsepower was still derived from four-footed animals. Thus, his lifelong "tradition", by age twenty-five, was grounded in this industry. His role lead to a job with a dealer in Wisconsin who sold Allis Chalmers tractors and from '30 until '41, he was the general manager, a management "tradition" shaped by the stringencies and severity of the Great Depression. In 1941 he became the dealer in Indiana for Allis Chalmers. That's 90 days before Pearl Harbor, and a new managing "tradition" rapidly unfolded in the ensuing months, fashioned from the shortages of machinery, parts, and manpower. Having survived, and even prospered, by mid-year 1945, 25 years after using and selling machinery, he finally arrived where he wanted to be: owning a CAT dealership. The reason he rejoiced in this prospect was, the quarter century of experience had taught him Caterpillar was without peer in its (his) field — so another

E.W. MacAllister, "Mac", and Bill Ziegler the CAT Sales Manager confirm dealership agreement, June 2, 1945.

"tradition" was to represent the best.

All of this warm-up suggests that whatever the nature of the conviction or the objective in practice, it had better be flexible and adaptable to change, that at a given time a specific governing emphasis may be essential (construction, depression, war), but equally important, let's be sure it deals with contemporary situations and does not stay there merely because it was once valuable. Ergo, if some traditions are eternal, others have to be retailored to deal with altered conditions.

Ongoing cycles of business lead to policies which become institutionalized, but in each case the company style evolved out of the philosophy and personal convictions of those running the enterprise. How one does business reflects how it is one thinks about himself, and then how he thinks of others. It is often the case that he who thinks first of others, and thinks highly of them, succeeds the best. In the shaping of our corporate morés, we carry along the best of those personal convictions established by the original management combined with the persuasion of the current owners. The pervading traditions still want the finest product and along with that, the finest people plus the best in physical equipment so that across the board we have an edge — meaning weakness in tooling or inconsiderate people ought not minimize the strength which CAT's product line give us "going in." Everyone strives for good people, but everyone simply cannot afford the capital investment in plant and equipment — not in several locations — because that is a by-product of size and machine population. The result of these compo-

Parts bins shown in the '50s.

nents, hopefully, is good service. That is something we crowd our people hard to perform because that is the way we like to be served. But beyond that, it is the best way to assure that buyers come back and do more business. We also want a reputation for square dealing because, by mandate, Presbyterians are honest, but also because we do hundreds of thousands of dollars per week on the basis of mutual trust and the word of the customer. If he cannot trust us, purchase is impeded. He doesn't want to play around with all the legal safeguards implicit in so many other businesses. There is a remarkable degree of honor in our industry and we aim to contribute our share to its accommodating utility.

The overarching tradition which holds the rest together pivots around integrity. The temperament of the owners, the nature of our product, and the nagging manufacturer who builds it, imply a standard that has to be a goodly cut above the norms, i.e., our reputation for "dealer-ing" has to be as good as CAT's for manufacturing, since we are what intersects with the customer and becomes the guarantor of service and machine efficiency. If a new machine konks out (euphemistically called "early-hour failure" — and it happens), it is not the factory which has to

reassert the integrity of the product; it is the dealer. So any CAT machine has to be reviewed both from the soundness of the design and the reliability of the service to guarantee that the production potential built in is "worked" out.

Traditions about the customer imply we like him (well, let's say about 95% of 'em) to the degree our interest in his success is a personal one. It requires even-handed treatment — the same service across the board, some knowledge and insight into each business, and all the help we can give in keeping each one healthy. We don't know everyone in our territory, but the intent is to do so and to see each as a personality or a character ("character" fits a lot of them, believe me!) not as a computer number dealt with through automated responses. Our tradition also is to like this business and get some joy out of doing it.

An implied tradition also has to do with contemporary technology. CAT provides the model, spending $400,000,000 a year to develop new or improved existing product. Our job is to keep the support vehicle contemporary as machines get bigger — and smaller — have larger components, more horsepower, higher pressures, and faster speeds. We end up buying bigger and bigger track presses, new welding equipment, oil labs, new hydraulic test benches for larger transmissions, bigger field trucks, more diagnostic equipment with more intricate calibration, another Dyno, and computer terminals by the dozens, add new stores, called "mini branches," new offices, new people, and new specialties. We spend $300,000 annually in capital investment trying to keep pace with the technological requirements of today's sophisticated dealer. A single investment can run $150,000 (the Engine PAR DYNO). All in all, this combination of tradition and technology testifies to our commitment and, of course, without that, the other two are dialectical aphorisms (hot air).

The moral to all this hopes to suggest that there are governing precepts directing our company, many going back to ole Mac, and they are manifest in the product, the people, the attitude, and the ongoing growth of the company. That attitude about each other, joy in the business, respect and regard for the customer, and placing principle before profit gives those of us who work here a pride in our job and a sense of contribution to the system under whose aegis we function. ■

Staying Ahead

June 1988

They tell a story about a Jewish immigrant who came here in the late 1930's and ended up pushing a fruit cart around the upper eastside of New York. Success crowned his efforts, so he bought a second cart and put the kids to work. Then, a third and fourth; finally a store and, ultimately, he owned a chain of 40 groceries in the East. Now, the grandkids are trying to get the old man out of the business before he loses everything he has. It's the same story line applied in 1945 to Henry Ford, he of the first moving assembly line, inventor, entrepreneur extraordinaire, who, when his grandson assumed control, was losing $10,000,000 a month in his management of Ford Motor Company. It's the story of Graham Paige, Studebaker, and Pierce Arrow of the story of Cletrac, Monarch, La Plante Choate or Le Tourneau. Being on top doesn't mean that you stay there. It can mean that, but there is certainly no guarantee. In our system, one has to keep proving himself.

The message is twofold. First of all, the competitive challenge demands continual updates and improvements if one is to stay even with (or ahead of) the field. Meaning, we have put a premium on ingenuity. We encourage it, require it, and give it free rein. Secondly, the same sort of managerial style that creates a company and directs its course through the rough years of pioneering, hard marketing, building staff, getting accounts, and wooing clients, might not be the style best equipped to handle a large operation with lots of people, intricate computer systems, sizeable banking needs, and fifty-five government regulations on who you can hire and how you have to pay them. The problems of cash flow alone in our operation today, oversight of a $27,000,000 machine inventory, balancing five stores, the tax accounting from an IRS that doesn't understand its own rules, plus all the rest, use up an inordinate amount of time in "daily maintenance" before any serious marketing effort is even attempted. I know of managers — guys like my father — who loved the old days when they were out making the sale, knew the big buyers personally and kept "hands on" as the dealership moved through the years, but they finally got tired of the impersonal nature of the business, the lack of human contact, and the continual administrative demands required by bigger operations, bigger commitments, and bigger opportunities. Dealerships which outgrew the friendly "one big happy family" role and ended up instead with "Employee Handbooks," tables of organization, annual marketing plans. Some dealers lost interest because they were people persons, rather than systems managers. Some checked out, longing for the old days when they were on the road half the time, cutting the big deal, when time was consumed handling problems and sales rather than reading reports and fussing with administrative minutiae.

One can ponder the difference in dealerships… or in contracting or in family relations…today versus what they were after the war and pine for the days of Dwight D. Eisenhower, but that isn't going to do much good. Besides, who knows which was the "better" across the board? For some managers, obviously the less complicated, less technical, and less fractious era is the best. But fair scores, the status quo isn't what brought about power shift transmissions, 700 horsepower tractors, exchange component repair, or brought us laser surgery, heart transplants, computers, and 747 jumbo jets. Imagine driving from here to Florida (six or eight times a year) or driving to Las Vegas. Man, I can't. The cutting edge of our society is labeled C H A N G E and those who don't follow the technological pattern need to be in special fields or else get one helluva lot of government aid. (Maybe I should have said, "Or else be in politics.") Meaning, for most of us, there really is no option, if we stay.

Fran and P.E. MacAllister pose in front of a CAT 772 Haul Truck at the Fort Wayne Open House in 2002.

The objective ought to be technological advance. We need to be searching for the latest devices in a given field to do it better, faster, and do more of it, at less cost. Reasons for not doing so are usually: content with the way it is; don't know there is better technology; and more often than not, can't afford to spend the money. We are in the business of oil sampling because we've thought for over 23 years that a good way to anticipate breakdowns is to check oil samples regularly and find out from the particles in the oil what is wearing beyond the normal cycle and by finding too much chrome or iron or bronze in a sample, we can get to a weak-and-weary part before it comes unstuck, taking with it everything around it. What also wore out in the process was our technology in the oil lab and the equipment used to check samples, once state-of-the-art, now a candidate for the Smithsonian. So, in January, it breathed its last and we have ordered a replacement. Again, the latest there is and the most accurate technology we can find. The cost, about $100,000. Again, CAT helps keep us boned up on where to find the best equipment and what has proven most accurate; they, likewise, keep nagging us to be discontent with old methodology. Fortunately, we have the volume and the profitability to afford the expenditure. Most dealers in America do not have the same outlook, the same tradition of keeping updated, and most cannot spend that kind of dough on what is basically a customer service — a user benefit.

If anyone were to ask me what the most important ingredient for success in the tractor business is, I'd have to say, "Good luck". But who controls that? One is better off for the long pull with a terrific product to sell and the best staff he can find, plus the equipment and systems found most efficacious so if his luck is just average, he'll appear at the head of the pack. Chances are the operation that does the best in terms of managing those four elements also turns out making its own "luck". We try to stay ahead in terms of the technology, not merely because it's "hip" to do so, it's more profitable to do so. That means people have to be regrooved continually because in managing the new computer system or oil lab or hydraulic test bench or pin press or even working on new tractors like the 416 backhoe or the D11 behemoth, we are into the latest our science has to offer, all of it requiring skilled people to make them function properly. The systems and the equipment demand the human element move apace and it is virtually impossible given this momentum, to get

trapped resting on the oars.

The past that assures that continuum, however, is not natural evolution or the nine gods, it is the management outlook. It is a conscious decision, a deliberate and sustained effort; it's a conviction and a commitment. We do it in our shop two ways: by trying to keep the grey beards (me) appreciating the late 1980's and secondly, by bringing in young people who cannot look back at "the good ole days" because they have no such point of reference. I loved the '70s when margins were good, when you got most of the parts business without hustling it, when warranties were six months — period, when rental was something Hertz did, and when the Nipponese were fumbling around at the back door trying to find a way in. But I also know that to try and apply that experience to 1988 is ludicrous. It's like presuming your kids are going to pay some attention to your advice or assuming the family farm is the backbone of America's ethos.

The other advantage in terms of relevance in avoidance of that romance with the past is coming into an ongoing operation. My father had been at this business through the war, so when I came on stream, he had done the pioneering, got the CAT account, had the staff and was running the show. He had done the organizing, but that exercise is only preparatory. Different planning is required in phase II and III. He was a tiger, but he'd go nuts today because he wanted "in" on all the action; the word delegation never entered his vocabulary. He liked doing it all, but there is a thing called "span of control" that says a given manager can supervise or direct "X" number of people and beyond that, he "loses it" or the enterprise grinds down to a pace limited by his restricted physical capacity to function. I don't have any particular fixation about the need to "press the

E.W. MacAllister, 1946.

flesh" (an obsession with personal contact) to make the big deals, wanting every problem routed through my office, so the predilection to shape a management style around that mode and era isn't in my cerebral computer.

All of which is wandering a bit but hopes to say, business judgment is a product of the person and his experience, his outlook and basic intelligence, that different skills are needed in different phases of the corporate lifespan. Judgment is augmented enormously when he brings in others more skilled and takes advice which is wiser than his own. To insure against a mental lock-in, relevance and change are axiomatic and required as elements in major decisions, and the flow of new ideas moves the marketing style beyond the fruit-cart by stages to where it deals with the reality of a situation. Because newer people with contemporary ideas and tomorrow's technology are factors in the given psyche of a specific company. We don't do it all right at MacAllister's, but we have never tried any harder or been better staffed or spent so much money on today's tooling and technology. We hope it is good business. We hope it makes life easier for the CAT owner, because that's why we were signed on initially — to take care of his needs — promptly. ■

1989

Summer Thoughts

June 1989

Every spring for the past ten years, I have rented a small plot and begun gardening (on a very modest scale, believe me). During the course of May and early June, the regenerative process performs its ancient miracle as the seeds shoulder through the soil, and start reaching for the sky. Rows soon indicate how steady or unsteady was the planter; gaps also appear indicating the frailty of the seed or the carelessness of the seeder and by July 1st the entire plot has a distinctive character. The required thinning, weeding, cultivating, staking, and tying all become therapy . . . while the "bosom swells with pride." If you like this sort of thing. Unhappily, my gardens look best in early stages with all the green stuff up and growing like mad, but, alas, more "green stuff" comes up than what I planted and grows faster, the weeds picking up nourishment from the fertilizer, and saying, "Hey mate, this is great. Let's replicate." A diligent gardener will be out there every other night checking the incursion with his hoe. But the lackadaisical, well-intentioned-but-procrastinating-type (like me) lets the little buggers get rooted for a shoot upward and outward. Next thing you know the soil is hard and dry, and they are a bitch to get out. Lack of will, preoccupation, trips out of town, or loss of steam all combine and take over.

The philosophical condition at the outset, however, is one which understands there will indeed be some dereliction. It won't be a model of productivity, and the garden will get tacky. But re-joice in the doing of what gets done. Enjoy the corn that perseveres and comes out of a boiling pot twenty minutes after picking; or those fresh tomatoes that make store-bought types taste like plastic. I like the peas and green beans and zucchini, and new potatoes. Granted, the carrots never survive the weed attack and onions get lost in the brush and, for some reason, melons never are worth a damn. So confess, the garden never quite turns out the way I anticipated and, though I enjoy the whole exercise, the time I was going to give to it never materialized. On a scale of one to ten, give me maybe 6.5 for performance.

But we don't have to be a complete success at everything we do in order to enjoy the trial — which helps account for the handicaps in golf (mine is 17). There are plenty of experiences which bring rewards without reaching professional standards. Meaning, the fun in gardening outweighs the frustration at not winning the "prize for most weedless plot" and though I cannot do it all completely well, I can do enough to make the effort worthwhile. Getting by with this attitude on the golf course or a ski run or in Little League or the garden is the same. It says the process is the raison d'étre, the involvement alone makes it worth the doing, whether we win or not. But it's a big mistake to assume all of life can be viewed the same way. It can be ludicrous in the business world to assume success is subordinate to the mere endeavor. Or losing can be tolerated and enjoyed. Amateurism is for personal satisfaction, professionalism is the

P.E. enjoying his garden chores.

result of continual achievement. There is a danger in presuming the attitudes in the two separate arenas are transferable, i.e., that a so-so discipline in hobbies or gardening, or even in school, works anywhere. Any graduate who thinks the business world is like the campus, where a "C" is standard or the norm and that is all that's required of one soon gets left in the lurch. Walking into the competitive system with that naïve mindset is to condition one's self, not for success, but for accommodating failure.

An example of the danger in casual attitudes, nonchalant performance is found in the medical profession. Not the nurse on the floor who gets by with a "C," but, in the surgeon where only "A+" performance is tolerated. When operating on someone's brain or kidneys or even prostate, there is no room for a ho-hum effort and no idea that there are three levels of success with which one might be content. One gets the tumor and succeeds or he doesn't. One gets all the stitching done right in a heart operation or the patient ends up in the morgue. Surgeons perform at maximum capacity and with the utmost proficiency each and every time, day-in and day-out, period. They don't let up, goof off, or give it a half-assed effort.

Somehow or other, doctors are trained in school, or in residency, or by their supervisors, or even their attorneys, to consider mistakes unacceptable.

We need more professions where a demand for perfection exists, and where training sees it realized. Instead, we have extolled the uniqueness of the individual and encouraged him to "do his thing," be his own person. Discipline is not a common or popular thing. Unions limit production to expand hirings; peer pressure sees how far it can stretch coffee breaks; too many people "put in hours" rather than contribute units of productivity. That being the given and the norm, it behooves each of us to teach his own vocational requirement, articulate its demands. If we want good response, we must spend the time explaining the ground rules. Few employees automatically perceive what "service" really means or what it entails.

Ergo, the failure of a workman — salesman, counterman, mechanic — to deliver, is not the fault of he on the line or out in front. It is the fault of the company, the manager, or the institution, whose job these days includes interpreting the assignment. And then cross-checking to see it is clear and, beyond that, it is being respected. In a world of mediocre tastes, standards, and performance, that which is excellent or superior stands out like a beacon on a stormy night. The best way to win in the competitive battle then is

to provide for the user the degree of professional performance which not only pleases him, but simultaneously reveals he who provides it as being unique. Not through his advertising or long, rambling editorials, but through his trial in the field of experience or his response to a given demand that is delivered quickly and correctly. Delivered like it is "the norm," rather than some fluky aberration that won't be repeated again in this century.

People in the Caterpillar family brag a lot about being "the standard of the industry" and the size of the average dealership ($75,000,000 in sales, 300 people), plus the past record proven in thousands of machines in every territory, plus substantial physical plants and capital investment tend to bear that out. But it is not the size or sales or capital assets that create the character of a dealership. It is the philosophy of its owner-managers, when they can inculcate or convert or beat into the heads of subordinates those lofty tenets. All investments we make are only an adjunct to the motivating premises.

In a given field of endeavor, there is usually one agency who is "numero uno" and one, of course, who is "tail-end Charlie" — while "in between in the misty flats, the rest drift to and fro." We'd like to think we are in first place because total volume illustrates it; repeat business affirms it; and 44 years of experience out of a record number of locations ought to prove it. But being number one is not the point. <u>Staying</u> number one is the game now, and the objective of our management and our managers is to find out how one does that. The secret already revealed is simple: provide a quality of excellence in the services which we provide that is so distinctly unparalleled it speaks for itself in terms of supporting the owner-user. Not as we can get to it (like some gardeners I know), but as a norm or a standard or something we do by reflex action. Do it so well, there is no way to improve on it. Having managers declare it or announce it is not tantamount to achieving it because our services are diverse, in variety and geography, and our customers peculiar and distinctive in terms of their needs. The "intent" becomes "accomplishment" when our people respond as though they heard the message and remain "user friendly", which means sensitive to needs or requirements and then have the capacity to respond with true competence, demonstrating the proficiency found in those whose objective, day-in and day-out, is top rate service. We may get a few weeds in the garden of our endeavor, but the objective is still clear and the scramble for increasing excellence is on-going. ■

Moment of Truth

September 1989

Most of us are probably satiated with news these days. We get our first headlines while shaving in the morning (especially those of us who shave beards), and at breakfast scan a newspaper. Later in the car en route to work, another segment unfolds and we finalize in the evening before "the tube" to see it all in living color. It is reinforced by three or four weekly magazines which repeat in editorial and interpretive fashion what we have already heard. Bottom line is we have a full — I mean full — picture. If any society was interested in the world about it, surely this one is and if any was informed about national, local and inter-galactic affairs, our generation is head and shoulders above the rest.

In the midst of today's plethora of headlines and TV commentators, there is a revolution at work and surely we have all observed this. An unprecedented sense of movement in the world, a dramatic, momentous change occurring, and across the globe we are seeing some astounding things. It reminds one of 1848 when revolutions swept one nation after another in Europe (an ongoing bit of turmoil I did not witness in case you are wondering); or the period after 1918 when half the countries on our globes changed names, as the power structure in Europe and Africa altered demonstrably. This year's headlines are numerous: The pull out of Russians from Afghanistan; the Cuban troops leaving Angola and freedom in Namibia; the great unloosening in China and a million students waving banners and erecting liberty in Tienamen Square; the policies of Gorbachov, easing government control, trying to undo the bureaucracy; the election of a lower house representing "we the people" in Poland; dismantling the fence between Hungary and Austria, free enterprise gestating behind the iron curtain; the Viet Cong withdrawal from Kampuchea; Arafat's recognition of Israel and the 1992 deadline for economic unity in Western Europe. More has happened in the past twelve months than has happened in any decade this generation, and more potential benefit exists for the future of the species than all the cumulative results since the end of World War II.

But the qualifier is "potential". Mankind, alas, generally or specifically, has a tendency to bobble its opportunities. The French Revolution on this its bicentenary is a good example of blown chances, a good illustration of bursting bonds and loosing fetters ages old, and destroying a government which was both corrupt and incompetent. Only to supplant it with something worse: anarchy. The French mobs toppled the King but had little positive in mind aside from sort of "getting even" with those who had been exploitive and abusive. They proceeded to revamp the chamber of deputies and bring total representation to the process. Representation, however, is not tantamount to competence. When the new group bungled the job, the republic turned on itself in a reign of terror that executed thousands of victims as though blood cures political ineptness. The King and Queen got the axe — really the guillotine — and the aristocracy was savaged. Mere vengeance or passion, I submit, is flimsy stuff from which to fashion a state. The Revolution stabilized with Bonaparte thus taking it all back to where they started, only with a new sense of pride under a brilliant orchestrator of event. The 1789 Revolution, I repeat, disliked and overthrew its government but was incapable of creating another anywhere near as good.

The pressures evident in Hungary, the Baltic States, Poland and elsewhere are identifiable; a change in government. Not necessarily to a democracy, but a change in personnel or a change in style that permits participation or a reversion to civilian control or maybe a change in the basic form itself. In each case it pleads for more freedom, and in each case it has weakened the totalitarian camp, which is suddenly succumbing as though tired of the role anyway,

CAT D4 tractor demonstration, 1950.

because the system isn't working, especially the economic part. So the time is ripe for great, sweeping, overwhelming change, and the tide is oriented to western democratic styles wherein capitalism and free enterprise are no longer heresies. Republics are studied and liberty is worshipped.

It is a moment, I repeat, of unparalleled opportunity. Question is: Who will seize it? Who will capitalize on it? What will they (he) do with it? There is obviously no plan in place anywhere I have identified above, no strategy for handling the transition. There is no consensus on what should be done and how it ought to go. There is a surging, a sniff of freedom in the air, the prospect of unfettering and a brighter tomorrow. But there is no design to assure we shall indeed realize the prospects now dawning. Some situations may work through to a new era; others will turn to military dictators as the course of least resistance, the rest take refuge in a benign civilian dictatorship. Because the fate of democracies, alas, is not very good as one examines history. Nine out of ten fail to make the cut. They demand too much of unsophisticated constituencies and contingent upon citizen support, find everyone wanting things and services but rarely willing to contribute to the common good. That fact, or mankind's tribalism, its loyalty to my group, to my region, race or sect above national allegiance stoves them in.

History, this says, is not fashioned by mere discontent or human longings or pressures to be free. It is changed by intelligent planning and careful action and though the former (discontent) provokes the later, there is no guarantee the latter — mere change — automatically improves conditions or reflects the dreams or aspirations of those who created the rupture or the revolt.

That all seems a bit heady for a tractor company editorial but the bit about potential or opportunity coincident with timing is as critical for us as it is for Namibia. We have some potential for fashioning our own fortunes in the business world. Each day presents options — opportunities or potential to sell more parts or bulldozers to new customers plus more sales to old customers. We create a climate through marketing efforts and advertising, we nurture it with personal contact by our sales people, plus it occurs through the industry's processes. The critical element is being there when the decision is made. And priced right when we get there or articulate enough to illustrate benefits which justify the cost. If we aren't in on the deal, we have lost one; if it comes and we can't handle it, we have waved "good-bye" to that "potential". Point is the cycle for selling is transitory like maybe it is for governments. It slides on by and when gone, it's forever. There is only one shot at the brass ring and though another opportunity could open up later, it cannot recover that which was lost.

To overwork this analogy, we have already implied one does not capitalize on opportunity by wishing or hoping or figuring a good advertising campaign will convince someone he ought to plunk out three hundred thousand dollars for a loader. Not hardly. Our sales are designed, structured, deliberate, managed all the way through whatever tortuous phases the buyer wants to take us. As much as we can, we have to create our own destiny not become the victim of it. Which means we have to be aware of the period of decision (or else bring it into being), and we have to pounce when the golden moment appears. So potential for success in business as well as other institutions has to be treated with great respect. We are thus reactive to an extent. Meaning it takes outside factors — conditions, time, evolution — to bring it about, i.e., the user decides when he will move; but once the opportunity appears any passive role becomes suicidal. It is time to bolt into action. To be sure effort is properly guided into fruition. The proper resolution for potential is effective disposition. It must be put to bed, its wandering, amorphous or inchoate character crystallized, defined, given form and direction.

Given that sense of the passive phasing into the period of the potential, we can assume that history … called success or failure … is really the result of how it is one deals with potential and that the dynamic which indeed manages — or mismanages — it is the same substance of which history is fashioned. It might be bigger in the Middle East or Argentina than our Caterpillar shop, but one is inclined to see the same balance at work. The key to successful resolution in either may be luck or timing, but for the long pull, it ought to be intelligence, experience and commitment to competence. I don't know how close we get to that, but it is important to know what it takes at the outset, if one is to succeed at the moment of truth. ■

Christmas

December 1989

Christmas is often a time of melancholy because it is a time of reflection. It tends to remember the way we spent Christmas past. As a youngster up before dawn on Christmas morn; trips to 'grandma's house' all jammed with relatives for dinner; coming home at vacation time from college and helping put up the tree; Christmas in the Sahara, in fact, in a tent in the Sahara with so many missions going on the day went unnoticed. Most of all, one recalls how much younger he was and how different the world looked and how easy or leisurely or romantic the old circumstances of Christmas past. Memory has a tendency to refashion experience and the glow around those memories really wasn't there when we lived through them — at least not as I recall them. But maybe it is a time for genuine reflection rather then reminiscing. Stopping for a moment, trying to figure out what it all means, what the holiday says to us — now.

Brought up in a good Presbyterian tradition and thoroughly conversant with the two Christmas stories (which contradict each other something fiercely), one might opine that Christmas is a metaphor. Its story stands for something or has a meaning far different than the mere episodes as reported. If we can adopt that viewpoint, the story is "likened to another" conclusion (if I can use Webster's metaphor definition). The story perseveres because it has a universal charm. In the innocent birth of a youngster under dramatic conditions there is a drama involved that excites the imagination. New life, in any culture, is an occasion of joy and reaffirms the continuity of the species. But more than this, it is the advent of new opportunity and in this case, of new promise. There is something portentous in the birth of Jesus because his pedigree is linked with promises made in the past to be fulfilled at a given time and of such nature it will affect all mankind. What it celebrates in retrospect is change. Because with the birth of the child, a new movement is set into motion and after the death of the same child in 29 A.D. at age 32, western culture begins to pivot and to alter its emphasis totally.

Familiar as we are with western culture, we rarely see its miracle because we don't know what is replaced. And change was legion.

It thought peace more glorious than war; that love was more important than power; that altars and sacrifices empty when compared to feeding the hungry; that women had dignity and other people had value and winning wasn't as important as decency. The orientation of human effort shifted from glorifying the state to tending the person and the nurture of the ego diminished in view of a new emphasis on how to treat my neighbors, especially those I don't particularly like. At Christmas time in 4 B.C. in "the days of Herod the King", a movement was born which would end up reshaping western culture.

Its evidence in the marketplace is rarely considered but is of major value to us. Because we function in a system where trust is important, is paramount, in relationships. We do millions of dollars worth of business a month because we have confidence in the other guy's word; in his honesty because he'll live up to his deal. We do business in groups presuming people will be able to work together irrespective of

P.E. decorating — placing angel on top at
1989 office Christmas party.

P.E. and Fran MacAllister at Christmas 2007.

their creed, background, color or political convictions. We have departments that cooperate with each other and realize the success of the whole depends on the success of each part, which we are committed to support. We get major support from the bank because they have confidence in both our competence and our integrity. We are inter-dependent, and intra-dependent; possible only in an open society, one free of tribalism, of religious myopia, of restricted privilege and unimpeded by grudges created a century ago when forces now indistinguishable banged together in mortal conflict.

Point is what we have, how we operate, would not work in most of the rest of the world. Try this on in Lebanon or Iraq or Iran or even in Israel or in most of tribal Africa or Cyprus in China, etc. *ad infinitum.* It works here because we have high regard for the person, his dignity, value and worth. Because our society respects differentness, insists on tolerance, prizes generosity, presumes equality among its citizens. It works like no other and could work like this no other place. It happens because (I think) it is a product of the Judeo Christian ethic and all year round, in its systems and institutions, reflects — marks, vindicates — the revolution begun the year the "decree went out from Caesar Augustus that all the world should be enrolled".

Merry Christmas from all of us at MacAllister, who rejoice in the season and what it represents on personal and business levels. ∎

Cultural Changes

December 1989

A trip into Egypt (which I made in October) is a voyage into another world. One boasting a civilization some five thousand years old and one scrambling hard to reflect the sophistication of the 21st century — with much of the populace caught somewhere in between. After exploring two dozen tombs and an equal number of temple complexes dedicated to the infinitely complicated Egyptian pantheon, one gets the impression much of the resources and energies of the entire nation went into projects obsessed with dying and the life hereafter. Most of the remnants of the past — and there are a jillion of them — were created to prepare pharaohs for the next world, providing them all the equipment they'd need for about ten thousand more years while most of the umpteen dozen temples take care of another side, i.e., buttering up about 30 gods so they can grease the old boys' ways into the great beyond. The single mindedness and repetitive "monumenting" here and there stretched randomly over 700 miles up and down the Nile is a rather astonishing thing. Not only are the memorials impressive (the great pyramid at Gizeh — 4,600 old — is still the single largest pile of stone ever accumulated by any people for any purpose), not only are they overwhelming, the monotony of the motif is singular.

The style, the form, the incantations from *The Book of the Dead*, the decorations, the inevitable hieroglyphics and cartouches don't change a hands breadth from the time of Cheops and his dynasty to the Greek period. (Alexander got there in 332 B.C.) For some 2,400 years they used and reused the same tomb patterns, same quarrying routine, same mummy wrapping, same style of coffin cases and statuary, same Canopic jars, same double crowns, etc. Change, in those two-plus millennia, was an anathema. There must have been rules against it. Or divine prohibitions about breaking a mold; or some monopoly existed, exercised by the priesthood and the mummifiers who didn't want to bother with new funerary messages or new equipment.

Interspersed with all of this is an even older culture, that of the farmer or fellaheen tilling the land and scratching out a livelihood. In fact, he is the backbone or the supporting element in the state producing a steady and relatively consistent supply of food, fertilized and nurtured annually by the Nile floods. That is what attracted people there in 10,000 B.C. and that is

P.E. in Cairo during WWII enjoying the pyramids while on a whiskey run.

what keeps them there today. So the identical theme is repeated along the river bank on the 4% of land stolen from the desert: sameness; familiar processes, tilling, planting, watering like our ancestors did. The flat pita bread looks like those painted in the ancient tombs; the ovens that bake ditto; the crops are maybe of better strain but are those grown in Abraham's day: leeks, wheat and barley, thus beer; cucumbers, lettuce, garlic, grapes, thus wine; figs, dates, cabbages, a dozen herbs, wild fowl, and wild game, cows, goats, rabbits plus oils and fruits. Field plots are small so they can be ridged or banked for irrigation thus the preparation of the seed bed in limited segments is often by hand, chopping the soil with a mattock like those pictured in the tombs. Plowing is with a wooden share that doesn't turn the soil over but scratches it up a bit, powered often by two cows or steers…as depicted in the ancient farming scenes. Irrigation with the same big wheel-with-buckets-into-a-channel that Moses knew or the long pole with weights on one end and a bucket on the other to dip water out and dump into a trench. In short it is amazing how much the nation still retains of its very ancient institutions and how content it is to preserve them, in fact, to venerate them. As though the system were so hallowed that breaking the mold to simply gain efficiency is unacceptable.

The amazing thing is that the society with its venerable, if often anachronistic, systems has survived and persevered. The reason other customs died is because the invading people who invented or employed them have gone by the boards in the winnowing scythe of history. No vehicle remained to perpetuate the culture. Whether worth perpetuating or whether valid today, the point is that any contravening "creating culture" was not a "sustaining culture".

What strikes us about this all is an ambivalence about change and resistance to it. Obsessed as we are today with the whole business of modernization, up-date, improve, modify, is that efforts to do so or failed to do so, did not save much of the ancient world. One nation after another got overrun by the juggernaut of history to be swept away. The one that didn't change found in its patterns or its consistency or faithfulness to traditions a key to a certain immorality. By hunkering down, anchored to its familiar style, Ancient Egypt let the conquerors flow through or overrun while underneath she retained familiar rhythms and by doing so salvaged her life's patterns like no other people.

We might have to strain this a bit to get it into a quasi business and contemporary illustration, but watching the comings and goings of customers, manufacturers, and competitors over the course of the years; the shifting of accounts from one dealer to another, the tapering of one market or region, the rise of a new one in another place, changing personnel in your company and mine, it is easy to understand the ebb and flow of history, the washing back and forth of influences and personages. We are not merely observers to this drama; we are participants and arbitrators of the same. Empires rise and fall in our world as well, leaders become followers; the mighty relapse into evil times and a German, Italian or Japanese master takes them over, another long tradition departing. The restless flood of product in my field has brought new concepts, enormously larger horsepower, computerization, amazing technical tooling, high sprockets, rubberized tracks, printed circuitry, astounding hydraulic pressures. The only element not involved is pause; there is no period of desuetude or static moment for catch-up. Our age appears to be invariably in motion, often misconstrued as "progress". Sometimes it is; sometimes it is just tread milling. We appear to be in perennial chase and change, trying to catch up. Every time we get a computer paid for around here, it is time to buy another one, bigger and more expensive and just as quickly out dated. When we get our track servicing equipment all in place, CAT comes out with D11's, and we have to buy another order of everything. Liability insurance was a disaster in 1985; by 1989 it was hospitalization insurance instead. The shifting about brings both grief and improvement, but we need to keep our eye on something else.

While all is going on at this frenetic pace above, there ought to be some mooring down below to keep our bearings and retain some benchmarks. Like the Egyptians, keep us reverent of the past; holding fast to practices that have served us well and ought to be preserved. The first tradition of this company when it was founded 44 years ago was the quality of its product line. There is no way to discard that fundamental. The second was the integrity of its manager; the third was the service-oriented nature of its people. Next has to be a genuine commitment to the job and an honest love of the business. One doesn't fake very well if he pines to be doing something else, or his head and heart are elsewhere while he beats time to the measure of a forty-hour week. Losing track of the end user would be a major catastrophe for us. To become obsessed with system or preoccupied with "strategic planning" is losing track of the reason for being here. We really aren't here to sell tractors or loaders. We are here to help build shopping centers or strip coal or lay asphalt plus a hundred other things by supplying the equipment best designed to accommodate the builders, strippers and black toppers. We are a facilitator; we are an intermediary phase of a process; we are not sufficient unto ourselves any more than is a parked bulldozer. We rely on the people behind us who supply the machinery and those in front who put it to use. What makes that all fit together is not horsepower or bucket-break-out-force but human skill in service support, in our interpretation of benefits and productivity; in timely service of sundry sorts. In short, the clue is how we deal with people, not how we process or market machinery. We serve the client best when we sell him the best product available. When we do so for a fair price in open and honest dealing, backstopped by the sort of service expensive and complicated machinery requires. We do so because we like this business and the size of our investment attests the over-excited degree of our commitment to it. But it is the professionalism of a given person brought to play that creates the action; it is people who make things happen. And if our people are as faithful to the conditions that have let us persevere for the past four decades (while most competitors from the early days have floundered), then I guess like the Egyptians we have found those secrets to cultivating our strip of land so we, too, might enjoy a long tenure as well. That part of the past which has been critical to our success needs to be retained and reemployed at the same time we change technology or equipment or product models or tooling. Because what gives us character is not necessarily the commodity we sell but the style and the principles involved in how we sell and support it. What gives us character and continuity is the quality and caliber of our people. ∎

1990

The Democratic Process

March 1990

There is a great deal of ferment swirling in Eastern Europe these days, virtually unprecedented movement in the demolition of political institutions as the practitioners of Communism and their allies look for places to hide or ways to escape the vengeance of the populace they have so long kept in servitude. In the denouement which is depicted in the press and through the tube, we are somewhat amazed at the lifestyle of Communist ruling clique who were supposed to be models of the common proletariat and living in a system where there was no rank or class distinction. We are flabbergasted by the special commissaries to provide food for the party bosses, the lavishness of their homes and hunting lodges, the cars they own, the monuments they have created from the sweat of the peasant population. The wardrobes, the perfumes, the bars stocked with exotic liquors, the servants and conveniences, altogether shocking in view of the destitution created in order to sustain such Sybaritic styles. If there was ever an example provided to expose the hypocrisy or the phoniness of the Soviet system, it is evident here in the way the rulers and their cronies fattened themselves from the people they have suppressed in a fashion that would make the Czars and the Kaisers envious. If the whole system in principle works this way in this model classless society, the "triumph of the Proletariat" (we see at once) was a will-o'-the-wisp, a shadowy figment and bad dream.

The question posed by the unraveling of a system (which has never worked but has survived despite its failure) is how do the Czechs, Poles, Hungarians and the rest get their act together given forty years of total and unmitigated ineptitude? Not the political

"act", how do they create a business base to generate capital and create commodities to trade? A solution posed recently by Dick Judy, who is the Hudson Institute's expert on Russia and the Eastern Block, is "by infusing appreciable increments of capitalism", of the entrepreneur spirit; because when that dynamic is put into effect and begins to succeed, it almost automatically creates and enlivens the democratic processes. The success of the economy vindicates that system which provides success and the free play of the creative spirit solves problems…manages change, creates institutions and provides benefits for others. This is what democracy is all about. The two (entrepreneurship and freedom) go towards open government whether it is a government like ours or a parliamentary democracy like France, Sweden and Israel is to under shore the economic base and the best way of doing that is encourage private enterprise. What it takes to create wealth is not state control but opening a business, finding a commodity someone else will buy, and the marketing skill used by any successful businessman.

MacAllister shop, 1943.

Mechanic working on tractor, Fort Wayne, 1947.

Problems of putting the state (or a business) together are a lot easier if there is a source of revenue. In government it is normally revenue from taxes. But on what? In incomes or on transactions. But who provides the jobs to provide the income to provide the taxes? It has been the state, but that is no longer a prospect because state-run industry in Poland, Russia, Romania and even Czechoslovakia has been so bureaucratized, its business based on barter, overvalued currency and so mismanaged and so criminally inefficient it is no longer an option. It is bankrupt and the process has bankrupted the nations, both the currency going phony, exports shrinking and the national debt escalating. A point of no return has been reached, and it is time to pronounce the whole system dead, some fifteen years after it expired. A good solution for income is developing a national product, like say oil where it comes out of the ground at $12.00 a barrel and sells for $22.00. Or maybe it is vast national timber resource, lumber being in strong demand around the world. Or maybe if one has gold deposits, that will provide a stream of revenue, gold always being a neat thing to have at hand, whether you are a dentist, a collector, investor or just a miser. Alas, however, Eastern Europe is mostly agricultural sans oil or gold and although capable of producing adequate foodstuffs to feed its own population, and maybe products to export, lots of folks in other parts of the world like France or Belgium or the United States, Canada, Australia and South America are also in the same business. The field is a bit congested and highly competitive.

The best answer to developing income is the resort to capitalism. Find some seed money, probably from private investors and go into business. There doesn't happen to be enough timber to export, but the French have gone into building airplanes, designing and making clothes, raise some great wines,

build construction machinery, do a lot of tourism, make perfume and are in the movie business plus a lot of other things. The secret is to provide some incentive to permit he who is clever, hard-working, quality-minded and sensitive to market needs, a chance to make some money and improve his style of life. Let the individual get the idea, manage and market it.

If he can link up with others equally committed to fine quality, at a reasonable price because they have steady jobs and thus the wherewithal to buy a cottage or a car, they not only support the system, they work their buns off to do it better and in greater quantity because the bigger the paycheck the more things the family can enjoy. Finland has a strong economy, look at Switzerland, even Luxemburg is thriving and you think these countries have more going for them than Czechoslovakia or Hungary or Poland? What they have going for them is the dynamic of a relatively free market and the ability of people to create, improve, modify and sell; find something people want and then find a way of producing it profitably at a fair price. What will solve Eastern Europe's problems the quickest might well be capitalizing on enough creative ideas, converted into sundry enterprises, which invade the economic mainstream if the required capital arrives to create them to give material substance to the ideas. If the populace of the countries involved have the patience to let some form of relatively free government get into place and settle long enough to establish the internal political and security apparatus, chances are the operation of a free economy motivated by the incentive system which encourages people to produce or to work or to struggle in order to improve their own personal circumstances, will be the critical factor which saves the day.

All of which might sound far afield from the tractor business in Indiana, an element in the local economy and far removed from struggles for freedom or rioting for rights or revolts against tyranny. Capitalism is a fact of life, and the entrepreneur has been around for so long in this land and does so well he has become a suspect. He has, also, become complaisant if not down right lazy.

We need to recall that premises of free enterprise function inside the given structure. Not only can a certain plant or product bust the market wide open, but inside a designated plant, factory or shop the same sort of entrepreneurial model functions. It permits some guys to rise through the ranks on the basis of their performance, by working harder and faster, catching mistakes before they go out, helping others. Some people in our shop latch onto all the training offered them; absorb all they can get, move up the ladder of proficiency because they learn quickly, like what they are doing and get raises consistently on the basis of merit increases. Trainees become mechanics, become field servicemen, become leadmen or become supervisors. Most of our service managers have risen through our shop; our sales manager hired on as an apprentice salesman; our store managers all graduated through the ranks. The entrepreneur theory is not restricted to systems but operates, I repeat, with individuals. It tends to reward he who works the hardest, does the best job, tries to improve rapidly and enjoys what he is doing. It lets the individual arbitrate his progress and his income and his station. It rewards those who achieve and allows those who are content to coast, ride indolently down the current. And management benefits by using its best and brightest, its problem solvers and innovators; the people who take charge and know what to do next. What it needs to do is view all employees as entrepreneurs.

Because "management" generally does not encourage free thinking or too much creativity or a lot of experimentation in the ranks. It is too obsessed with rules, with 'standard procedures' and grooving the average worker into a mold already established which tends to minimize rather than maximize human enthusiasm and productivity. In short it becomes a bit like Romania where the boss tells you what you will do and how to act, rarely listening to what is wrong or paying attention to ways for improvement. That is a pretty heavy-handed comparison but the irony of the free enterprise system is its record in achievement gained by permitting the creator of the business to do his own thing and knock 'em dead in the marketplace only to insist that employees do HIS own thing too, rather than allowing the personal freedom to experiment, modify or create. It is a puzzlement! What worked brilliantly at one level is then disowned when it appears at another. But there is a revolution afoot in the land, not in Eastern Europe but in middle America, based upon the same underlying premises, i.e., most people get ideas, that people working at a given process probably know better what should be done with it than someone else who sits in a front office and what it takes to break off the shackles is a communication system rather than a production system, to sift out good ideas from the shop and the parts office and the accounting department about how things could be done cheaper and better and more quickly. It is a resort to the Demming principle, or one modified and studied here adapted from Florida Power and Light, both of which encourage all employees to be concerned with all aspects of the product developed. With respect to this company, we have had our first introduction to the idea and have scheduled the first full scale meeting of managers to see how we can introduce it at MacAllister Machinery. We need to take advantage of all the good ideas generated in the company and find ways of using them. We simply have to think better and that really means work smarter and we don't do that 'til all the good ideas are harvested for us to employ. So if we haven't been good at employing the existing measure of internal ingenuity that might be a good experiment to try in. ■

Statement of Ethical Purpose

March 1990

Technically speaking, the obligations of a corporation are relatively simple: Perform the economic function for which it was created; at a profit for the stockholders; operate within the legal guidelines of the pertinent governmental agencies. Our type of business is most successful, however, when as dealerships we meet the demands of the manufacturers we represent and serve well the interest of customer and employee. So to be "legal" and to be "successful" requires two separate standards, the one required by law and the owners, while the second involves human relationships, personal philosophies of management, vested and enlightened self-interest, plus the accommodation of other elements in society.

At MacAllister Machinery Co., Inc. we have always held that our corporate "charter" extends well beyond the minimal legal essentials. It is our practice to operate the business in such a fashion that each party involved is proud of the connection, whether that be the manufacturer we represent, the users to whom we sell, the employees we hire, or the communities in which we are located. We would like to be so regarded in terms of both our business acumen and our operational style that the people who support us in the field of auditing, banking, legal counsel, professional trade relationships, and all other ancillary

groups are, likewise, proud to have the affiliation.

To gain this sort of stature in the world at large, we realize that our affairs must be managed so we stay legal and make profits in a fashion compatible with the Judeo-Christian ethic as we adapt same to our circumstances. We interpret this to mean that we must be absolutely honest in all our dealings, treat people with respect and accord to them a measure of dignity; to be totally fair in each and every transaction; avoid exploitation or abuse of either customer or employee; and handle corporate responsibility to the communities in which we live through support of the political process, the local "betterment" organizations, those who work in arts and education, plus those endeavors which try to make more wholesome our society. We encourage our employees to involve themselves in the activity of the world around us and we intend to give not less than 3% of our pre-tax profits annually to causes in which we have interest and involvement.

At the same time, we must be good business men and women. We intend to sell products of high quality at a price fair to the buyer. We intend to hire people who are — or who become — highly proficient in the tasks assigned and who perform their jobs with professional pride and sensitivity to customer requirements, the end result being user satisfaction to the degree he enjoys doing business with us and plans to do more. It is our policy to reinvest heavily of our earnings in the finest "tooling" and equipment for each department, so that services provided are "state-of-the-art" and efficient. We want facilities that are modern, working conditions that are without peer and managers who are both competent and enlightened. We pay a fair wage for work done and provide a fringe package commensurate, or superior to, that accepted by our age or set as norms within the industry.

In all of this we may not succeed every time in each department, but every manager and employee knows the objectives and is commissioned to support and make real this statement of our corporation ethic. ■

P.E. MacAllister.

Principle Versus Pragmatism

June 1990

Since the age of Thales, philosophers and theologians have explored and dissected the eternal conflict (real or imagined) between good and evil, the war between "the Sons of Light and the Sons of Darkness" (if one recalls the Qumran writings). The old tug of war that goes on between me and the other guy, meaning me in the white hat and he in the black hat, i.e. the bird selling the Japanese product. Complicating the picture is the possibility that maybe "right" and justice are the perceptions or designations of he who articulates the character of his opponent. They are not determinations arbitrated in the lofty realm of some universal, ethereal court. The Iranians are good at this because they declare to us each week who is "the great Satan" this month, and it is usually somebody who confounds their confounded policies.

In the retrospect which is history, however, often the conduct of events or the very actions of a given people when screened through the vision of an international law or traditional norms of human conduct, automatically define the pedigree or the infamy. Good illustrations here might be Hitler's Germany or the regime of Joe Stalin as they shout out loud the brutal repression and the mangling of the human spirit which each contrived. In such cases there appears to be no argument with how wrong it was. It is a gross violation of civilized conduct. In the story of the Civil War, however, there is far more difficulty and some real ambiguity. Generally speaking, we agree that saving the Union and abolishing slavery put Mr. Lincoln on the side of right, and the Confederacy on the side of misguided motivation. Though at the time, states rights and constitutional law augmented by the character of the Confederate leadership made a strong case for their viewpoint. We have a similar confusion with the Vietnamese War, the Contra efforts in Nicaragua, the Israeli attitude and actions against the Arabs, all telling us how difficult it is to find the right course from the wrong. We revert back again to he who views the issue or writes it, knowing impartial judgment is harder to come by since it is almost impossible not to take sides. In fact we even use different criteria and different facts to deliberate a common condition.

The current upheaval across Eastern Europe seems to rehearse a familiar 20th century manifestation of this old seesaw. The forces of freedom bursting loose from the heavy handed, bureaucratic and totally inept system looks like a great victory for the good guys. Those of us rooting for them say, "It's about time. It's unprecedented in the annals of the species, and it was unexpected, but boy, isn't it a great thing!" What happens now as it does with any of us in a lot of situations is the advent of a second phase in another face-off between contravening forces. This time it is the trial between principle and pragmatism. Making the principle newly established, work. Moving from the idealism of the student, the freedom fighters, and the intelligentsia into the concrete reality of governmental forms and agencies, establishment of a market economy which generates capital to provide income, creation of a decent currency, and keeping all the systems running. The principles of right and justice and fairness and equality and openness now have to find expression in institutions or they are merely abstractions, devoid of much benefit. If we can't use them, do they have any reason for being? The principle is relatively easy as long as it remains an idea. When it is called upon to invade the marketplace and begin regulating conduct, it is then we note, "Ah! There's the rub". So until ideas become a reality in the society, their validity is suspect.

The reason for principles is to regulate, enforce and shape human conduct. Its ultimate test is usage. And we find too often that dreamers or thinkers — the cerebral types — are poor practitioners of the schemes they conceive. Karl Marx couldn't operate a filling station, yet he described how the world should run. His pupil, Lenin, had to con-

P.E. MacAllister.

vert the idealized communal state into a tyrannical dictatorship because the principles espoused in Marx were too high flown to employ or else impossible to utilize as governing principles. Remember the Rappites and Owens down in New Harmony? Great idea for a community. We all share in the effort and split up the results, but the thing didn't last a generation. Ancient Athens has been a model for two millennia, but a model for what? Philosophy, architecture, city planning, drama, free speech, dress, and (people will say) "of democratic forms". We got the concept from Athens but forget that remarkable state destroyed itself because of the license involved in a pure democracy wherein all 35,000 free males in the city were called upon to make laws. It proved to be a totally infeasible way to manage a state and thus snarled in its processes with that huge body of lawmakers, Attica fell to the Spartans after about a century of glory. Democracy itself is an inefficient political model.

Democratic forms, I keep reminding you, have been tried a hundred times around the world since the turn of the century but tried unsuccessfully. Nine out of ten go by the boards because they prostitute the principles of freedom and openness and power sharing to authoritarianism. It ultimately becomes apparent that openness, representative assemblies, and free speech don't automatically make the trains run on time, control inflation, or create economic vehicles which could provide jobs and wages. Elections in themselves are not governments. Which might give us the secret to succeeding. Tie the architect of the principles to the vehicle of implementation. Use one element to do both. Find common sense people or committees or agencies so the two are merged. When they arrive and exist as separate forces, however, i.e. principle here and practice there, amalgamation in the process or performance seems to find the weakness in both.

In business we try to unite planning and action by using the dictum that marketing or goal-setting or budgeting "are done with the people involved", meaning plan with those who have to effectuate. He who makes next year's sales budget is he who is assigned the responsibility for generating those sales. This is true for the Parts or Service or Engine or Computer Department budgets and plans. To thrust upon managers targets for achievement they have no part in establishing is to make them either too tough or too easy. Beyond that, it is stupid to ignore a given manager when he has the obligation to know more

about his potential, his competition, the marketplace, the effectiveness of his own department than anybody else in the joint. In any human endeavor including an engine division or a service operation, it is wisest to find the brightest and most capable people you have to do your planning and then to do the job. Which is one reason we have so much trouble with governments. We don't get the brightest and most capable people. We get people who think they are dynastically anointed, those who are television personages, those with glib tongues and generous spirits, meaning generous with your money and mine. We get people who were the best campaigners. Then one day they have to make laws and guide the nation. They end up still being great campaigners though a good many of them alas, peaked out along the trail. But I am digressing.

One of the premises in this essay is that the free market economy itself in the capitalistic society tends to provide a good example of the marriage between the principle and the pragmatic. The principle is the articulation of what we want to do and how we intend to do it. Here's the plan, the dream, the expectation. The pragmatic phase is the implementation. It is making the sale, inventorying the right parts, gearing up with people and equipment to do the service job plus all of the rest, hopefully in the fashion they dovetail and are mutually supportive. The easy part of this is always the design. The frustrating thing is failure to implement, trying hard but falling short. Or implementing and then finding that there was no profit involved. Profits, incidentally, are "principle" in their concept but must be the ultimate pragmatism. Success is measured by the bottom line more than anything else. This is an indisputable verity.

An enterprise such as ours or any other on the scene today has to find a way where its planning and implementation stay in sync and as a result, please the customer. Because the difference between business and government or the church, the school or the family or the trade association, is that business is continually being measured and judged. Daily by the consumer. It's rewarded or punished, transaction by transaction. If it proves unable to either plan or execute well, the buyer whose dollars keep the ship afloat suddenly stops buying, and when there is nothing left to support it, grounds on a sand bar; (or if I could rework the metaphor), it sinks to the bottom joining armadas of its fellows who already suffered the same fate.

All of the above is relatively fundamental to anyone who reads this unsyndicated column, and there is no great mystery or marvel in any of it. The intrigue in the tug of war which still goes on lies in the ability to maintain principle despite the eternal-bending pressure exerted by pragmatism. By expediency. By the lure of short-term goals which are oblivious to the long-term fold. In that dynamic there is a tendency to reshape the principle so the doers can find something which is achievable. In short, it is to move what we can do ahead of what we should do.

Reasons for the triumph expediency over principle are found in human nature. Fibbing about dates or delivery to avoid a bad reaction from your client; giving "the squeaking wheel" the most "grease", i.e. giving the most obnoxious customer the break when the one who treats us decently is the deserving one. Ambiguity about pricing, stretching production or performance figures, fabricating facts about competition all with the noblest of reasons in mind. Complicate that with 250 of our people talking every day to customers and becoming to each "the company", and there is an arithmetic exposure for fudging or corner cutting that multiplies exponentially. Our objective is to state clearly to our people that there are standards involved and for the long pull, people do business with people they trust, especially when talking the kind of dollars we are. That it is to our mutual and total benefit to tell the truth and take the guff. Sometimes it costs, but again, for the long pull and for the total corporate good, that is the only way. The types of people with whom we deal are familiar with the problems and honesty as a criterion that will qualify us for a long time and in most situations. We may not always achieve it, but at least the objective is clear. No one who works here can doubt that MacAllister's honor is every bit as important to us as the CAT name. ■

Of "Time and Chance"

September 1990

There has been a good deal of material produced this summer as we vicariously revisit the Second World War. Articles in Life, newspapers and periodicals about the Battle of Britain. TV shows like a weekly series appeared about the Royal Air Force, decamped to France in the fall of 1939, after the war had broken out, but before Hitler attacked France and the low countries. There was also an on-going documentary about Hitler's era and a television play written about "The Battle of Britain" airing during July, also marking the 50th anniversary of Goering's attempt to bring England to her knees, prior to invading the island itself. Maybe it is all the recollection of events fifty years ago that trigger this outpouring since it is half a century since Dunkirk and the fall of France.

One of the books recently reviewing the WWII land war made a very surprising observation. It said that gun for gun, especially artillery size, the Germans had the superior equipment. That tank for tank, they had us badly outclassed. (The 88's put a shell through our biggest tanks while our shots bounced off German Tiger tanks unless they hit the seam where the turret mounts or some other

vulnerable place.) Moreover, whenever comparable sizes of artillery or tanks or infantry, American and German, met head to head, the Germans usually proved superior. This sort of stunned me, proud as I was of our fighting forces, but the author pointed out that German designers had more time and had taken more patience to build and equip the war machine and that when we got into the fray, we were up against professional, seasoned and battle-hardened troops, and "we" were a lot of recent draftees who had trouble marching in step. Our entry had been hasty and our preparation frantic, starting on the downhill side of the whole business. So unprepared were we, that when the Nazi's were rolling across Eastern Europe, our temporary draft law was running out and were it not for the personal intervention of the President and a Herculean effort by Sam Raeburn, the draft would have expired and our military preparedness been that much worse. (The vote to extend the draft passed by a single vote in the house.)

I know who won the war, despite the prowess of the Wehrmacht. We did. But we didn't do it with superior equipment. Maybe our fighter planes were better with longer range, better fire power and more armor plate, but fundamentally we triumphed because of overwhelming supply superiority, unlimited gasoline and infinitely more manpower.

Maybe too, we had better leadership. Though the German High Command were professional soldiers and very good at what they did, the top echelon of Hitler's political hierarchy was really bush-league. And we aren't too sure that the rigid German discipline did not discourage individual initiative at the lower ranks which tends to wait for orders and inhibit the sort of spontaneous leadership which au-

P.E. in the service during WWII.

Typical flight line.

tomatically appears when the officer or sergeant is killed in the American army. We seem more capable of individual response in crisis than most people. Our system does not limit thinking or leading to a given caste or class.

The biggest mistake was Hitler himself, whose insane decision to start directing military strategy led from one gigantic catastrophe to another, and his troops were wasted in fruitless and stupid assaults or stand-pat tactics when the situation called for orderly withdrawal and regrouping.

If you are wondering where this is going, don't despair. It will say that superb equipment and even excellent personnel do not equate automatically to success. That there are other elements at work which deploy or utilize the product itself. How that is done often arbitrates its ultimate effectiveness. We have seen illustrations of baseball, basketball or football teams which consist of all-star athletes and individual superstars only to take the field and get themselves clobbered with some regularity because there is something lacking in the team performance. The best cars do not necessarily win the Indy 500, and the best drivers could end up in fourth or fifth place when car and driver are not matched. All this goes back to Ecclesiates which observed three thousand years ago, "Again I saw that under the sun the race is not to the swift nor the battle to the strong nor bread to the wise nor riches to the intelligent…but that time and chance happeneth to all." That might be a fairly profound observation, and we know that chance does indeed "happeneth", but we also know that those who wait for destiny or The Nine Gods to arbitrate their affairs are copping out. The Muslim opinion in early summer ascribing to "Allah's Will" the 1,400 people crushed or suffocated in a connecting tunnel at the shrine in Mecca is a lot of hokum. Allah "willed" no such thing. Bad design, frantic people, an unexpected crisis and who knows what else determined the sad plight of those killed in the rush. Napoleon had it right when he said that, "God is on the side of the heaviest battalions", meaning fortune smiles on those most efficient and effective, those who do the best work which means it is not fortune at all who ordains our affairs, but we, ourselves, by dint of our own effort.

In the free enterprise world of tractor dealers, one has indeed the element of fortune or fate to consider, those malevolent forces beyond the area of our control: interest rates, foreign competition, the value of the dollar, the supply of machinery; long,

wet springs; strikes; housing starts and you name it. We have to finesse all these the best we can and negotiate each to minimize its impact. Where most bright tractor people spend their time, however, is not stewing about where they can do nothing, but in that sector in which they do have control. In our corporate situation, aware of the temptation to coast along with the tide, especially when the tide is moving strong, and we are sailing smoothly, the effort is being mounted to examine what we do control and see how well we are about the task of doing it. How well do we match the technical aspects of the business, the machines we sell or rent or repair, the equipment we put to work in our offices, trucks and shops, match these with the human resource secured to operate this business, in order to assure ourselves the troops are not only superbly equipped, but are professionally trained and properly motivated. We understand that to win the war, it takes both high quality, strong logistical support, intelligent command structure, and all-out frontal attack against the competition. But we also know that we not only have to articulate what we intend to do, but gear up and then proceed to execute. That means perform – day-to-day-to-day.

Part of the current strategy to improve what is the existing situation assumes that excellence demands continual nurture. It is not achieved once and then endures for all time. Moreover, it has wide ownership and to gain such requires communication and motivation. Having people in the ranks who know what we are about and how we intend to do our business and the role they play in effectuating the attack are all issues of import and moment. The need for them to respond is elementary; the devices used to solicit their input is highly important and finding a way to let them contribute their expertise in

MacAllister field service technician welding a machine in the '50s.

terms of opinions, ideas, suggestions, shortcuts, new procedures and fixing what is wrong, all become part of the new program our managers are developing to make the customer happy by making the employees more sensitive and aware of user needs and expectations.

We are at the task of designing systems wherein the foot soldier in the ranks (or back in the shop, computer room or parts desk) knows he is supposed to be thinking about his job and how it could be done better. The command staff is not proficient at ground level routine and cannot speak with experience about most of the mundane habits, routines and rituals of each department. They may have authority but ought not be deluded with the presumption that brings wisdom. Most programs that tout the firm's strong desire to please the customer are created at top levels but rarely get that message down through the ranks, and thus said "foot soldiers" remain halfway oblivious to what is being said about the way they are supposed to be performing, even if it happens to be right. Dealing with the same issue of garbled orders St. Paul said, "When the trumpet gives indistinct sound, who can prepare for battle?" One can neither achieve nor sustain excellence until he has support across the ranks and a deliberate program to create such a condition.

One of the secrets which the Japanese have revealed as contributing to their success is both the attitude of the employee and his involvement. They have induced a fierce sense of pride in the worker often because said worker, through his suggestions and ideas, has contributed to making the system in which he spends his vocational life a better, more efficient, more competitive and more perfect one, turning out products that head-to-head in each encounter

out match competition. It does them little good to "borrow" CAT's tractor designs or the engineering of Cummins if they don't have the human capacity to recreate the product as good or better than the American producer of same. Then they are clever enough to "borrow" from Demming the principles of communal problem-solving (quality circles) and then "borrow" from their employees ways of cost cutting, "just-in-time-inventory", assembly techniques, design of tooling and a jillion other things BECAUSE they involve the workers in shaping the systems used to produce the product. It works for them. It will work here…when we get around to soliciting comment and help from those most qualified to do any given operation, the people we have hired to perform each function.

The idea is a sound one, but ideas themselves rarely have much impact on any society until there is implementation. Writing "$E=mc^2$" in 1918 didn't change a thing. It was only when we were able to create the Manhattan Project that the fearful and overwhelming consequences of that theory finally landed in the embattled world with its complete impact. Until then, it was only some goofy formula from this postal employee in Bern. The program we have in mind is at hand here on 30th Street and slowly unfolding. The teams are being set up to do some preparation. The implementation phase follows. Then it becomes, "Don't tell me, show me". That is what the customer wants. Not more promises or programs or good intentions. He wants delivery; he wants to see something happening. And if we are serious about staying number one in our field and dominating this industry in Indiana, we better darn well commit ourselves to assure something is indeed happening. ■

Cerebrally Speaking

December 1990

The eruption in the Middle East has given rise to endless exposition of the area and countless discourses on Arabic culture, character, geography and lifestyles. We have had to sort out the boundaries again and become specific about where Kuwait is with respect to both Iraq and Saudi Arabia. Saddam Hussein laid claim to his neighbor's territory — so we had to duck back into history and find out where he got that idea and when he thinks Iraq "owned" Kuwait. The climate, terrain, sizes and distances, populations and national economies all become germane in an effort to really understand the unfolding drama.

One of our discoveries was the fragmented nature of the Arabic world, divided somewhat arbitrarily by the Great Powers a generation or so ago and still whacked up in a dozen pieces. The second was the aspect of Arabic pride and exclusiveness. We were taken aback by their suspicion of the West, their hostility to Western ideas, culture and even Western presence. In a Germany which has just united two factions; in a Europe breaking down ancient territorial boundaries for a quasi union in '92, parochial animosity seems rather out of place. It's distinctly at odds with the openness and heterogeneity to which we are accustomed.

Given the backward nature of their societies (backward to us when women wear veils, can't vote, stay cooped up, all technology is borrowed), we are hard pressed to wonder what in hell they are so proud of and why they don't want to share ideas, books, friendships or institutions with the West. There is something anachronistic in all of this. If we are both right with respect to our individual systems, how can we function on any common plane in the "one world" of today? What appears to be happening is that the royal families constitute the contact with the Western world to market the oil and collect the revenue and buy the limousines while at the same time living mostly in the Arabic world of the veil, purdah, ambiguity about time, rhetoric instead of action, separation of the sexes, hatred of the Jews, and dreams of former glory. There is a sense of the unreal in all of this as though indeed Arabic thought looks backward in time to the days of Harun al Rashid and Sal ed al din and Avincenna and Sulemin the Magnificent. That somehow by thinking or talking

or conceiving cerebrally, we move into the genuine world and that is where we are most comfortable. Or that by polemical outbursts and passionate speeches and the most calamitous of threats, we create solutions or resolutions to given situations. Fortunately, our politicians are dealing with the war issues. They have a lot in common with Arabs since they tend as well to live in a world where talk is all important and oratory about balancing budgets, solving the crime problem and dealing with the environment is also left largely in the realm of the fanciful and the hypothetical. It appears to bring a kind of therapy to our political types who eschew the real world, thus never grapple with the problems they so eloquently describe. (Got a little bitter there. Sorry.)

All of which is digressing from the main theme of this essay, which is the peculiar nature of many Arabic states. Why, for example, does Jordan exist as it does? Because it was carved out by the British after World War I from the Ottoman Empire as a sop to the Arabs and as a means of keeping an element of control in the Middle East. The Britts set up both Palestine and Jordan (plus Egypt) as "mandates", (client states) with native governments in place but with British Viceroys or some such thing tugging at the rulers' coattails. Jordan's king was Abdullah, the current king's grandfather, and he kept control of his desert people (since he came from Bedouin stock) through the auspices of a British trained-and-lead military component.

Jordan got its freedom from British control after World War II, and the states of Israel and Palestine were created in the same era. But not for long. The

Typical scene from Israel; hard to find the "milk and honey".

Arabs resented the Jews and tried to undo the U.N. arrangement with a massive invasion of Israel only to get clobbered by Jewish heroism and tactical superiority. They have tried again on two occasions only to get their clocks cleaned, ignominiously. Arabs don't really hate the Jews. They hate having a small, struggling, brand new state rack up the combined Arab military might with relative ease because it makes all their loud boasting of Arab glory so much idiotic nonsense. They hate being made to look inferior, and anyone who does that merits their eternal enmity. (It should spark their curiosity. I mean, why not find out what makes them superior so we can correct our tactic?)

But my point was Jordan. The state is there because outside forces put it there, but not because it is a viable "anything". It contains a piece of an ethnic population called generally "Arab", the original Bedouin stock and now a million and a half Arabs known as "Palestinians". Jordan is also geographically defined with an autonomy the greater world acknowledges. It has a royal family, a seat in the U.N., a lot of IOU's for aid, and it has a standing army. But if it is a political and geographic unit in world affairs, it is not a feasible, economic organism. Jordan cannot maintain itself on its own income. Why would anyone create a state which is not self-supporting? That's like creating a business which doesn't — which can't — make profits. Ever. What a future is there for a political unit which does not have the wherewithal to support its people and underwrite their sovereignty?

Egypt is another example. Fifty million people but no economic apparatus capable of producing capital, requiring jobs, which present opportunities and assure incomes. Egypt exists through the largess of the United States (two billion bucks a year), and Saudi Arabia and other friends in the world who prop it up. Like pouring money into a bankrupt company, year after year with no hope of ever getting it out, but obsessed with keeping it going.

Syria is another example, replete with the typical blow-hard dictator, a repressive society, a large army (much of it meddling in Lebanon), and a growing population, but not enough internal commercial activity to provide jobs and incomes for its people.

When you get to thinking about this, there are twenty nations (or more) in Africa in the same boat, tribal enclaves or amalgams, reproducing like mad with no plan or program to sustain the population through marketplace vehicles that generate revenue through hiring and employing the native populace. Meaning how does one feed the people if the state no longer has that responsibility and if part of freedom means the right — and the obligation — to feed oneself, at any vocation he chooses. Right now, there doesn't happen to be many vocational choices, and as we watch all this unfold, are stunned by the number of governments which are economically dependent. A major and confounding enigma when one realizes that the politics of a given people or nation are really incidental to the outgrowth of evolution or revolution. But political systems are concepts, imposed to govern in a given fashion. They are helpless if there are no means around for paying the state's bills or creating marketable products. It is from salaries or profits the state derives its revenue or from taxes on commodities. When little of this occurs, we are hard pressed to pay for the army, the planes and guns, the dictator's mistress and this month's supply of imported wheat. Societies are limited in terms of what they can do by virtue of the discipline and culture of the people as well as the available resources (dollars, marks, pounds, lira — you name it) at their disposal to make things happen.

It is rather shocking to discover that there is no sensible reason for Jordan to exist, or Syria, or Chad or Upper Volta or Niger. They are really too poor and disorganized to qualify for membership among the legitimate nations of the world. It is almost as though they are there because the world keeps them propped up but never asks why.

Ordinarily what happens these days in the world of statecraft cannot happen in our business world. A business has to be fairly specific about what it is here to do and tested with monotonous, inexorable regularity, on how well it does so we cannot coast along merely because we have been around 45 years thus entitled to survival. No one is really interested in how well we did in 1955 or 1987. We have to prove up today and no amount of tradition, aspiration, noble intention or degree of integrity is adequate to assure any business its continuum. Performance assures that. And no perfunctory performance either. Superior or better-than-the-other guy performance, that's what keeps the ship afloat.

Moreover, business is measured and sustained arbitrarily on profits. These occur as the result of good luck, good management, good times, good product and service or being better than your competitors. Those failing the profit test are businesses that fail, vanish from the scene (unless they are incompetent farmers whose profusion and pointlessness the state continues to sustain). The free market economy demands success. It is a circumstance where only winners survive and you can see my point by now: Why aren't states made to run the same way? Take a lesson from us. Succeed across the board or depart. Or amalgamate.

In my business our major competitors have taken the gas or been subsumed by some friendly, often foreign, company (Dresser, all lift trucks, Insley, Clarke, Koehring, Allis Chalmers, Euclid). Our challenge in the CAT family is to avoid that option

MacAllister ad from the '50s

and stay alert enough to meet competition through customer satisfaction achieved with a competitive product sold and served by a competitive dealer. So far we have succeeded. Because internally in both factory and dealer operations, we have scrambled to adjust, adding product line, opening new stores, resorting to extensive lease/rental fleets, changing personnel, improving tooling. We have to provide what this day's climate demands. Why don't we force that sort of tactic on the world political scene? To maintain the superfluous integrity of a tribal society which has no economic validity is ludicrous. There ought to be a matching of ethnicity and tradition with corresponding elements of business or mercantile or agricultural or commercial independence. We ought to merge Jordan with Kuwait, for example so there is a better distribution of rich and poor Arabs. Merge Iraq with its oil along with Syria and its problems. (Beside that Hussein and Assad deserve each other.) Libya's oil could alleviate part of Egypt's poverty. Iran's the deprivation of Afghanistan. I'll bet it is going to work in Germany. It could in a lot of places in the world if we used our heads instead of prejudice. It isn't that it can't work; it is that we won't make it work.

Where it works best is where free enterprise capitalism thrives. Because of the internal dynamic: accountability, measured performance, success or else; stay loose, internal competence, ingenuity, change, incentive. These are not contrived components of a system; they are natural elements arising in a free society. They are normal to human and economic conditions, and they fit and balance. When it all seems so simple it looks like you have to really work hard deliberately to screw it up. And that occurs at the top where dictatorial or repressive forms restrict the nature of the operating economic. If we could provide for entrepreneurial spirit to flourish in any given nation, we could solve the problems of rampant national economic malaise. ■

Christmas Time Editorial

December 1990

Some months ago, Stephen Hawking wrote a book called *"A Brief History of Time"*, an illuminating and scholarly work. Partly because it deals with mind-boggling dimensions, speeds, pressures and temperatures at work in our universe. He is well acclimated to the esoteric world in which he functions, along with Newton, Galileo, Einstein, Hubble and a rare, eclectic fellowship of scientists. But it is impossible for the likes of me to get my bloody head around the incomprehensible system he and his colleagues are beginning to explain. To say I "understood" about a third of the work is an exaggeration; and even when comprehending what was said, the concepts themselves are so far out of proportion to the world in which you and I live, it sounds almost like science fiction. Moreover, it is a science of formulae and conjecture, a system of mathematical equations and laws made up just for this group to employ, and its premises are each contingent upon prior theories and assertions most of us never heard of, so who am I to say he is wrong. All this is not like fixing a tractor or loading a truck full of dirt or backfilling a sewer trench, the good earthy tangible stuff we see, feel, measure and cost out in dollars and cents. It is about how the universe functions and what laws govern what forces, all of which start with Galileo's and Newton's principles…in case we want to chat at cocktail time with Hawking about Einstein's work and his own.

One of its commonly used principles has to do with speed and ole Albert's assertion (now universally accepted) that nothing travels faster than the speed of light. He opined that was about 186,000 miles a second, faster even than Superman. How he measured it is a mystery, but since this has been rechecked for the past 80 years, it must be pretty correct. Happens to be a rather significant discovery because when considering the universe itself, the speed of light becomes a measuring device to indicate the distance heavenly bodies lie from the earth or from each other. (They don't really "lie". They exist as part of some great galaxy or other, cartwheeling through space and ever expanding, hurtling in fixed relativity at some 25,000 miles per hour.)

Ascertaining how far away stars and planets and constellations are is still a function of both distance and relativity. It appears that using miles gets cumbersome; we choke on zeroes. Given the speed of light, we quickly compute that it travels 6,000,000,000,000 miles a year. When you want to talk about doing this for let's say four billion years, we are multiplying 6,000,000,000,000 times 4,000,000,000 and we come up with 21 zeroes. My handy little Hewlett Packard portable computer won't go that high and surely frequent factoring of figures such as this in terms of working out problems accelerates the consumption of paper. So a common measure of distance is the distance light travels in a year and the reversion is to light years. Arcturus is the closest star, and it takes light four light years to get here. Other constellations, of course, take infinitely longer and the remotest galaxies into the billions of light years away.

One bright, moonless night, when the stars were glittering in the clear air, it dawned on me as I made out Cassiopeia, the Pleiades, Orion and the Great Bear that I was not looking at stars at all. I was looking at where stars used to be, the bodies who threw off this light a couple hundred million years ago have long since spun onward in their course, lengthening the distance between us as they went and are now an eon or so down the pike. The rays they emitted have taken forever to get here, whereas our type everyday light-rays bouncing off an automobile or a Christmas tree or stop-sign frame the object so we see the reality itself; we presume what we see is what is there. We can feel it. We have trouble fathoming the fact that what we see in starlight was not manufactured this very second but way, WAY back in time. Because stars are infinitely farther off then stop-signs, so far

The herdsman in Israel is as old as the landscape.

off it takes the pulsations of light so long to get here the bodies that created them are another million, million miles off into the future and what we see is what they were a hundred million or so years back. We can't comprehend distances that vast, speeds that fast, sizes as enormous as exist in the planetary world, nor are we good at dealing with timelessness and a system which has no limits, no beginning and no end (space). We can read about it, understand what it says, but have trouble using this anywhere in the tractor business or in life since we have an altogether different set of criteria.

By now you are wondering what in the world all this has to do with the Christmas season or the Christmas story. Maybe with a bit of mental gymnastics and a good deal of tolerance on your part, we can draw some parallels. What we are seeing in our own Christmas season is a manifestation of something that happened as well in the past, some 1,994 years ago. A star was involved in that episode also "when Quirinius was governor of Syria", a star whose light has illumined the ages with its insight and reaches out especially at Christmas time once again to lighten up our holiday. The event itself, we know well, has moved on down the corridor of history and has put almost 20 centuries of time between it and us, yet the pulsation or the vibrations which it created continue to reverberate in our world.

They do, however, only to a special group of people (not scientists in this case) whose uniqueness and whose special knowledge has bound them into another sort of "eclectic fellowship", one we call, not the Interplanetary Society but an "ecclesia". If most of the world is oblivious to the meaning of Einstein's theory or Newtonian law or Hawking's work on the nature of black holes, too much of the world is likewise oblivious to the radiance which refracts and reflects off the church this special time of the year. Like beams from distant Polaris, the light from the Wisemen's star is a continual emanation, steady through the ages, propelled by a body no longer visible whose energy, whose waves, look so fresh to us we think they are happening as we watch.

If there is a metaphorical difference, it is in the fact that the impulses from the Christmas star are not abstractions or mere theories, dealing in some ethereal element no one can get his hands around. They are connected to the tractor business. And the household, the school room, the athletic field, the oil rig, the hospital corridor, and bivouacs in Saudi Arabia. Rather than hypothetical, if interesting

Sometimes form dominates substance.

theories about worlds we'll never see, the church is so relevant it shapes our environment and has had a good deal to do with how we behave and how we treat each other. Nothing is more important in the realm of human affairs than the observance of its dicta and nothing more tragic than seeing the misery of the world (especially at Christmas time) rife and rampant…needlessly…when we ignore its precepts. Most of us have survived this far without learning Galileo, Newton or Einstein. Their theories pertain to what already exists, meaning they are not changing anything; they are helping us describe what is. But in terms of our faith and this Christmas and the year ahead, we are helped a lot more by "hands-on" type of instruction, by lessons which take us from day to day through the valleys and shadows of life. We need light created in our world and for our circumstances and dealing with our problems rather than abstract speculation. Seems to me "the light of the world" is suddenly more germane or at least more topical and for a few moments at holiday time we are better served in examining it than trying to imagine what it means to have a system with no time or space dimensions. The mind-boggling fact about Christmas is that it too, rejects time-space restrictions and though it happened also an eon ago, is a reality this year, maybe more so (since it impacts more lives) than when it occurred in 4 B.C. It is not a reflection of the first incident since "the first incident" transcends history and refuses to die or depart. It exists and the very fact of Christmas, annually, reaffirms its validity and its existence. There are miracles and surprises in the theological realm as well as the galactic. And for my part, they tend to be far more helpful and more comforting, especially at Christmas time. ■

1991

A New Beginning

March 1991

Whether or not you have noticed, this publication comes out on about a quarterly basis (March, June, September, and December), neatly seasonal, and is spaced infrequently enough to get us charged up to create something different each issue. Since this is the spring quarter, it is not inappropriate to deal with that subject…that welcome topic…as a means of launching this editorial.

Great season, spring, in fact, it has been great since time immemorial. First, because there is more daylight for daily chores; secondly, because the spring rains, in much of the ancient world, brought stimulus to the grain crops and thus assured nourishment from the soil that sustained the population. (An ancient Jewish prayer in Jesus' day went something like, "Blessed be thou, Lord God, King of the Universe, who causeth bread to come forth from the ground", reflecting the gift of grain, and thus, the gift of life for the people.) Beyond that, spring's warm breezes announce the advent of summer, following leisurely on zephyred wings. But more than all of these, was the miracle that saw the sullen landscape metamorphize into colors, and then blossom and rejoice. Almost overnight, the flowering fields, green trees, meadow, vale and swale freshening in the sun and reaffirming the marvelous cosmic rhythm of the universe are the proof of divine blessing as the world of nature becomes downright bountiful.

Christians equate the spring, as did most ancient peoples, with the time of rebirth and saw it replicated in The Resurrection, the metamorphosis from death to life. Like many other cults and sects, the movement in nature was coincident with, or dependent upon, some divine force (god or God) making his (her) annual assurance that the earth

will cooperate again this year, and mankind is thus the beneficiary of the divine largess. So our systems change in the spring (especially in agrarian cultures), our outlook and attitude; there is different activity possible and more "cups runnething over".

The rebirth in nature pertains to new life: New leaves on the trees, new heads on the barley and wheat, new blossoms to produce new fruit on the grapevines or olive trees. The concept of rebirth in nature, it is dealing with a new crop; it might be the same basic plants each year, but they bring new produce in proportion to the health of the roots, the degree of moisture, the amount of sun and all the rest. What is born each year is the fruit. What is this, an agricultural essay or a discussion of ancient farming practice? Nope. It is really about people and contemporary institutions, wondering how (or if) renascence…rebirth…works with them. We view the spring and see the new shoots, but we are the same people who viewed them last year and the year before. All that is new with us is our seeing it unfold,

Chris, Dave and P.E. MacAllister break ground for the new facility at Indianapolis, 1965.

marked or appreciated with the same mind that went through the exercise last year. There are new blossoms on the daffodils, but the same old householder who planted the bulbs five years ago sees them from the same vantage point (which is really why he put them where he did) with the same eyes, and sipping his nightly martini from the same chair in the same kitchen. What is not reborn in the spring is me (is I), the observer, testifier, enjoyer, marveler and all the rest but I am seeing rebirth, I am not experiencing it. Personal regeneration does not occur on a seasonal basis if at all; is not automatic; is difficult at anytime to both contemplate and execute.

How Medusa lost her head sculpture.

Partly because it means change, and that makes us uncomfortable. If it is so crucial and inevitable in nature, makes us wonder why it isn't important with people and their aforementioned institutions. On rare occasions when it occurs, it can work miracles. Best proof of that might be a type of city-state rebirth which occurred in 14th–15th century Florence, and incidentally called just that by subsequent generations: "Renaissance".

Cosimo and Lorenzo de Medici inaugurated an age of rediscovery, which encouraged a study of the past in order to inspire the present. They sponsored scholars to translate works of ancient writers, especially Greece and Rome, in order to better understand those governmental vehicles, manners, that architecture and literature, those sculptors, philosophers and whatever else seemed of interest. By making available hundreds of ancient texts on the glory-period of Greece and Rome, they reeducated a whole society to the cultural ambience spawned in each society and before too long, recreated much of it in Florence. By studying Vitruvius, new styles in architecture appeared; learning Myron and Praxiteles gave rise to the first great bronze and marble sculptures since ancient Rome; the first non-religious themes were extolled and ancient heroes or divinities became endless subjects. A shift in writing from Latin to Italian occurred, and more people than ever became literate. Through the sponsorship of artists who were suddenly permanently employed, paint-

ing exploded, and dramatic styles gave color, movement and perspective to dozens of canvases, soon present in every ducal house in Italy. Commerce flourished in Florence, and at the base of this cultural revolution was the vast resource of the de Medicis who singlehandedly created this watershed of curiosity, new knowledge, boldness, celebration of the human spirit and freedom from the long inhibitions enforced by the Medieval Church.

What is interesting is the fact that Florence did not change its location, its government (although the de Medicis were "gonfaloniers" year after year) its booming cloth industries, its banking prowess, its brand of wine or its battles with neighboring city states. What changed was the motivation, the inspiration, the direction, the leadership and what that did was employ the existing, familiar resources or vehicles to do something marvelous with them. To support a new burst of energy, directed in exciting and strange directions, producing an age of discrimination and taste, an educated mercantile aristocracy whose sponsorship of art and architecture still dazzles the world. Using the materials at hand, a gifted and public-spirited family, induced by example and persuasion, a revolution in human endeavor which swept the peninsula, filtered across the Alps to Northern Europe and soon infected all the continent with its charm and wonder.

The message: rebirth, newness, awakening, can occur under proper conditions and through proper stimulation and can rejuvenate old forms and systems. But the momentum of familiarity and the comfort of the status quo conspire against innovation, even when those tried and true patterns once successful, suddenly prove barren of acceptable results. We are a great study in consistency as a nation when we should be wondering seriously about "reawakening" our vast potential and getting it redirected along new lines. It is time for a new season in America. Anyone who has watched the Congress last fall as it failed with determination and steadfast resolution to deal with our disgraceful budgetary and fiscal crunch almost despairs of a society or a body or people unable to "awaken" to the reality. Or at least change their own pace to accommodate the nemesis so obviously breathing down our backs. Does it raise questions about the validity of the system which extends or ignores or accommodates those problems it was constituted to solve? Can people whose primary objective is reelection deal effectively with social challenge poised by the age and the multiplicity of demands spawned by the American culture?

We can ask the same questions of business and commerce in America. Or at least we can ask those questions to the companies still around and able to respond. When business fails, it goes out of existence — unlike governments who continue to mill around. I have been struck by the fact that the major competitors in my industry have all made painful changes in ownership the past ten years in order to survive, changes thrust rudely upon them by the intense competition and vanishing margins. Ten years ago Allis Chalmers was a major factor in our market, so was International Harvester, ditto Clark Michigan, plus Le Tourneau, Terex, Adams, Galion, J.I. Case and a dozen crane and shovel manufacturers. Every single one has been taken over by foreign owners or merged with other U.S. manufacturers. Very few remain intact, among them John Deere and Caterpillar, and our dealer family has dropped from something like 95 members in its heyday to 68 or 69 today. Why? One reason could be we like "the good old days" and the good old ways better than any "rebirth" or renascence. We have rejected the New Testament concept of being "born again", and in the process continue to use tactics, marketing, personnel, motivation and you name it that put us in such good stead back in the '70s.

The rule in our capitalistic society is that you succeed or they cart you off to a place called "Oblivion". We don't tolerate failures in our entrepreneurial business system. And the ones still around got very lucky or got very good at what they do or the Japanese overlooked them or they are a utility while an appreciable number also decided the way to survival and success was to awaken, to regroove, recreate, and recommit. Although a great idea, the design for doing so becomes the problem and the pathway to hell, as you know, is littered with good intentions. The tactic is the same one dwelt upon in such detail earlier. By using the same people in the same market, battling the same competition and generally playing on the same field, how do we

retail our approach so the troops are revved up, the customer gets new levels of attention and proficiency, the house makes a little money, and the team pulls together in such a fashion that synergism results, and MacAllister triumphs? Classic examples of building a team adequate to these times are found all over Japan, thanks to the Demming principle. In this country one of the most successful strategies and programs has been developed by Florida Power and Light. The objective is ever higher quality output, and the key to achieving it is by getting all of the employees on the team to adopt the same objective. Elementary, my dear Watson.

Question is, how do you pull it off? In our case you sign on with a major company who has already succeeded in the endeavor and is able to translate its secrets and successes into your format. So along with Eli Lilly and Company, the City of Indianapolis, Citizen Gas and a few others, worried about quality, about customer satisfaction, about internal cooperation, about training and about getting the employee to help in cost-cutting and more efficiency, we have taken the pledge and are full blown in a program which we hope speaks to the weaknesses in the contemporary corporate structure, the need for dramatic new styles of management, the desirability of having everyone in the place looking for better ways to do things quicker and cheaper.

We are not celebrating our achievement or the high-water mark in our 45-year corporate record, but we are celebrating this spring with a corporate reawakening, with a program for corporate renewal and new growth which will extend two or three years down the pike before we get it all done. Chris wrote an article about this in the winter edition (Q-Max) to explain what it's all about. The proof is not in the literary effort, but in the internal effectuation of all the things we need to do in order to get the next generation properly equipped so we are surviving 20 years from now. Get in step with the demands of the time and stay there. We are in the springtime of our effort and will be busting our butts to bring it off. This is the eternal challenge of bringing our do-how to our know-how. Don't tell me, show me. Our customers will ultimately make the judgment about how well we succeed. And their judgment is irrevocable. We intend to make it favorable as well. ■

I Am Proud of My Son!

March 1991

It is time to pass the baton. After an eleven year indoctrination and apprenticeship, Chris MacAllister has been elevated to the office of Corporate President and Chief Operating Officer. In a meeting of the Board of Directors on March 5th, the long anticipated move was made official as he was unanimously elected to serve an unlimited term, the fourth President, by the way, in his family to do so. (The first was the founder E.W. MacAllister, the second was P.E. and the third was D.W. MacAllister when P.E. moved up to Chairman for eight years.)

The process to this moment has not been an easy one since the times themselves arbitrate to a large degree how fortunate or how difficult will be the market and thus the job. Chris signed on after graduating from Ball State in 1978 and began working in the Service Department though he had worked summers all through college. As a matter of fact he began cutting the grass and haunting the premises when he was nine years old. Although he saw a couple of great years, as we opened the '80's it began getting tougher and tougher so that by the end of '82 our industry, world wide, was suffering from a recession greater than that inflicted upon it in 1932. From the best year in our history — '78 — to the nadir of our fortunes — '82 — Chris quickly experienced the best and worst. The 'worst' took a

long time to get over and while we were riding the waves of whatever "recovery" there was, he was 'going thru the chairs'. In his career he was worked in the lift truck operation, did a long stint in the service department, worked as our demonstrator-operator in the sales operations, delivered and did "call back" on new machines; even served a stint as salesman in the Ft. Wayne area when a vacancy occurred. He became Parts Manager in 1984, moved up to Product Support Manager, and in 1988 became Company Operations Manager. Result is he has more first-hand knowledge of departmental operations than any of his predecessors.

Thus having been through the sundry departments, getting first-hand experience, he has learned most of the idiosyncrasies of a CAT Dealership. Although I have done most of his mentoring, Larry Hannah, who is a professional manager, laid out a formal course to pursue which took him through the above departments one at a time, finishing in Accounting/Treasury/Data early last year. Always fascinated by business and being a reasonably bright kid, he learned quickly and knowing what was at stake, was dead serious about his professional preparation. But there is another factor in qualifying for the role and that is the scrutiny of Caterpillar who holds the prerogative of appointing its dealers. Since most existing CAT Dealerships in the country are family owned and most of these are second and third generation operations, the development of son/daughter successors has proven a fortuitous device. It leaves a respected name in place, the same management team, most of the capital, the buildings, tools, et al. so the flow of business affairs and the flow of continuity are imperceptible to the outside. It avoids the convulsions of new owners, new locus, new bank, new people and you name it. But CAT has another advantage in this approach, it knows with what sort of management talent it is dealing. It helps monitor and abet the training of the next generation and can examine the credentials. When the stuff isn't there in a family candidate, they are candid enough to say so. After all, as long as the dealer organization is their marketing arm, they have the right to find the best option they can and in most cases, it works like this one: the heir is well trained, well known as a commodity, comes well equipped and is dead serious about his job.

Chris becomes MacAllister's President in 1991.

Along the way over the past decade we have done considerable sorting in our own staff and the major managers today are those who have come here under Chris's initiative. He has interviewed, screened, checked credentials and when satisfied with what he has found, signed on all the major departmental managers. Point is the team as it now exists is pretty much Chris's product and his design. It's a good one, let me tell you. Key to success in the next decade and the next century is the capacity to both understand the contemporary marketplace and to respond properly (and profitably) to it. So giving the reins to the generation shaped by the age is the best way (we think) to keep the momentum going.

It is hard for a father to judge his son impartially. He is usually over tolerant or hyper critical. Mostly he doesn't judge fairly a style different than his own. And I won't do much better than others. But fundamental to our understanding about his ultimate management of the company has been the mutual agreement that first of all he had to have the capacity, secondly the desire and third the energy. Now that he has proven himself in all three categories, a little luck won't hurt one bit.

From my standpoint, he has done well in whatever job we gave him. From what I can tell, his managers respect him and are guided by his design; the employees in general like him and our customers relate well and easily to him. He is well organized, a meticulous planner, can be a bit demanding, and always would like it done a bit better; is obsessed with serving the customer and knows where his head is. Practical!

Clan MacAllister Arms.

This is a proud moment for me. Mostly because he has succeeded and proven his ability as a manager of a decent sized Indiana business venture. (Thanks to the diligence and commitment of 285 employees.) But beyond that, and even more gratifying, is that his character is right not only for Caterpillar, but for the MacAllister name. Chris is honest, fair, judicious, open minded and decent. I couldn't have asked for a better President. Nor could I hope for a better son. ■

Conflict

June 1991

Perhaps our earliest piece of western literature is a long classic poem called "*Enuma Elish*". It was written some time around 3200 B.C. in ancient Sumer and like much that type material was rehearsed, revised, and refined for a millennium before it got into the shape we have today. It's a creation narrative, telling how the world came into being, but before that, how the gods came about, and beyond that, how well they got along with each other. Without beating this to death, the key figures are Tiamat, the mother-type goddess, and Aspu, the male head god. From their union came the other gods and god-ets, ultimately a sizeable though not altogether happy family. The younger, lesser gods did the work, and their elders enjoyed life generally in whatever ways were possible in 3200 B.C. — but not totally. Turns out the younger gods made so much racket it drove Aspu up the wall. He decided to chastise them in a rather formidable fashion, but was held back by Tiamat who objected "because they are our children. They are part of the family." The kids eventually rebelled, and one of them, Ea, killed Aspu at which point Tiamat had to change her opinions about how one deals with this insubordinate insurrection. Her vengeful reversion to force was thwarted in battle by Marduk, the champion of the younger set, who slew Tiamat and split her body down the middle like a clam shell (the text notes). Part of her he thrust upward to become firmament and part he used to dam up the primordial flow, thus creating the land.

The leit motif of the story is the eternal existence of conflict, both within the family and within the so-ciety. The creators of these stories lived in a vast, tree-less, alluvial plain exhibiting struggle first hand: land and waters which had to be managed, measured and controlled to make them productive; conflict with the cold of winter, the baking sun in the summer (Sumer is in Iraq. Our recent TV acquaintance saw it hotter than hell, then colder than the dickens.). There is paucity of resources — no stone, mineral or wood; there are torrential rains which flood and shift the life-giving rivers (Tigris and Euphrates); there is disease, famine, pain. Beyond that, conflict with the mischievous gods, who were disdainful of men, created ultimately to do the work so the gods could loaf and consume the endless sacrifices of meat, oil, wine and grains. In addition to all this, the scrapping between twenty petty states elbowing each other aside for position. Point is, that amazingly the confrontations depicted in the creative myths of Tiamat and Aspu reflected a basic theme of life itself, the diverse ubiquity of conflict…of struggle.

When the Hebrews created their story (and ours), "In the beginning" ("Bereshit" or Genesis), they were privy to the Babylonian yarn and borrowed extensively to give history a background, explain the cosmic systems, identify the procedures of creation, and in that recitation define and describe the God. The battle of Elohim or Jahweh with primordial chaos (tehom in Hebrew) dividing waters, separating land, establishing the firmament, echoes a bit of the other story, but gets more specific when Adam is pitched out of the garden where he is then up against the same warfare his Sumerian counterparts encountered, one against weeds, pestilence, thistles, drought and pain. It's an endless battle with (a now malevolent) nature. The first sacrifice recorded in Genesis introduced another form of struggle and the only two offspring in all creation end up in a duel — one between the farmer and a herdsman. The god by selecting the sacrifice of one (the herdsman — this is a southern story) and turning up his nose at the offering of the other, created enough enmity to produce the first murder in history. Conflict can take no more dramatic form than this.

The biblical story recounts tribal warfare, so bitter it ultimately split the state in two (like a clam shell). Bloody encounters with neighboring people (particularly the Philistines); the age long trial be-

A bit of the Roman forum.

tween the worship of Jahweh and "the whoring after Baal" echoed in the voices of the prophets. One gets the impression if all the struggles were removed from the Old Testament, there wouldn't be enough left to fill out one scroll sized for "Genesis". Note that both epics are allegorical teaching us that species is condemned to eternal hassle, one which will be going on among men like the competition between Marduk and Tiamat or the nomad and the farmer.

The New Testament isn't any better as we encounter Jesus' battles against the priesthood, the Pharisees, the caste system, against ignorance, brutality, oppression and superstition. His mission seemed to have been "taking on" one force or another. His early church reillustrated the point when Christianity split almost from its inception (like a clam shell). The anxiety of the Hellenic Jews subsequent to the death of Stephen and their scattering; the differences between Peter and Paul about Gentile conversion, the fracturing created by early heresies, trying to remember what Paul taught — of what he may have remembered of the Jesus story and how he applied it to his world. And then "remembering" differently with different answers from one community to another. The revisions of Marcion, inroads of Neo Platonism, Gnosticism, Manicheism, the Arian-Athanasian controversy and you name it. Three centuries rife with disagreement and discord settled with recourse to warfare and execution.

But what it did was hammer out (and here is the point) Christian doctrine, dogma, creed through trial in the marketplace and tempering in the heat of conflict to fashion a system which will make sense, will attract converts, heal their wounds and ultimately change their way of living. Hoping as the individual changed, the nature of society would like slowly swing around. This is not necessarily a happy record and to the embarrassment of the Christian church, sees about as much battering and banging-about in the "A.D." world as it did in the "B.C." world, making us wonder what differences it all made.

The answer is considerable. Though this is not a theological essay. A difference in the way people treat each other, regard women and children, view slavery, promote education, respect human life, appreciate and tolerate different viewpoints, succor the weak, care for the handicapped, and a jillion other things commonplace in our society. We've done most of it in the past hundred years, and the biggest piece in my lifetime, saying the world (or at least America) is vastly different. Do not presume this is merely part of the evolutionary process. It is a result of the humanizing process finally inculcated by the Christian ethic, which came only through trial and testing, blood and blunder, struggle and striving. Through conflict!

But it took centuries of battling and digressing and crabbing sideways to get to where we are. It's no news that conflict is alive and just as evident as it was "in the beginning". So be it. But let's appreciate it can be constructive, maybe essential, a part of the growing cycle since we are always at the "creative" task — families, products, neighborhoods, entertainment, forever building new mouse traps. Creative conflict is that which bloodies us, but also improves the system, the tribe, the enterprise, the nation, the tractor business or the campus. It occurs because people need to belong, to own part of the on-going process. They need to have roles to play, and the battles occur in sorting out who plays what parts and by what rules. The shuffle is to get in the game. There are winners, of course, and losers, but unlike Marduk or Ea or Caiaphus, the defeated is not destroyed and disposed of. In our world of work and worry, the conflict goes on in a less mortal venue. It is a contest of ideas or of principles or of positions or viewpoints. Not altogether evil, this conflict brings about adjustment so that pieces which haven't fit very well before now have some of the edges rasped off and come more neatly together. Its accommodation is the art of compromise, the middle ground — two partial winners.

Most of my conflicts come with competitors, with customers, with employees, the bank, the government and even, yes, on rare occasions with Caterpillar. Because each has his own interest to serve as he deals with the other, and each sees his share as being larger or more important or more generous than the other wants to allow. The fact that

Photo taken before skyscrapers.

disagreements exist is hardly a bad thing since it is as old as first civilized community and is described in our first written records. It is produced by, or native to, human kind as part of a mechanism to fashion society's system. The secret comes not in resisting it or even resenting it, but in managing it, directing or using it. Comes in making it productive. Converting it to become a standard for the future; a way of getting the opponent to buy into an agreement; resolving a problem which is blocking progress. One has to get pretty philosophic in keeping down the old ego and remaining good natured about having his convictions squashed or altered, but he ought to be helped by knowing this is the only way society can function. It cannot eradicate the struggle. It must be endured, the question is how. How to cope, how to profit by it, anticipate it long before it rankles our nerves, prepare. How to use it?

What makes this tougher for us to handle is our competitive nature. We like to win and our society pays the winners big bucks. It ignores the loser. But perennial winners, monopolies, single-style systems have not been all that attractive in human history. When there is no legitimate opposition or resistance or conflict to the status quo, unhealthy conditions arise. Look at the monolith of communism for forty years and see the mess it leaves in its wake. Recall the Roman church in the middle ages and its control over the lives and systems of medieval Europe and what stifling there was as a result, what venality and what corruption (before Ignatius of Loyola). But people get monopolistic as well as institutions, obsessed with their own viewpoint and resistant to new idea objectivity. A dozen dictatorships

you can name (Duvalier, Idi Amin, Hitler, Ho Chi Min, Ceausescu, et al.) gave us "not fun" societies, gave us nightmares, driving whole nations back to the caves. So to keep from totalitarian infallibility — which ultimately is myopic — whether in the church or state or business or university or police force or Chamber of Commerce there needs to be the opposition, the room for ideas and disagreements, especially when the attack is wrong. There needs to be objection and resistance to examine the underguarding premises. Questioning it is proper; it is necessary to challenge and battle such situations, and through the conflict either get them turned around or modified or consensual.

Basic problem in business is the fact we have to use people to get it done. Causes 90% of our problems. And often the problem is disagreement; caused by the strange fact that each of us knows how well we do things and how much better ole George would perform if he would follow our advice. We invariably know more about doing his job than he does, and it is our duty to point out weaknesses. Why does he resist or get red in the face when we try to "help" him? He does because he feels the same about us. And until there is some sort of interchange between two opposing opinions — there can be no amelioration, sometimes no program, no team effort. It takes head-on facing an issue and candid airing of views before mutually joining ranks and moving forward. Conflict can thus be a critical essential element to success. Conflict it seems is the action of splitting us apart (like a clam shell), but it is also the element that allows us to get back together and move on united. ■

What Is Important?

October 1991

One of the problems in our "media-oriented society" is an escalating confusion about what is important in life and what is inconsequential. The information deluge with which we are all inundated is remorseless, and though we applaud the insight it imparts and the recounting of national and global affairs which make us the best educated people in history, we also need to look at quality as well as volume produced. Newscasts last anywhere from a minute to an hour, and they come with inexorable regularity. Time is blocked out, the sponsor is paying the bill or the station is competing for ratings and come hell or high water, the newscast…or the newspaper or the weekly magazine "Must go on". Whether it has anything to say or not, it will go on. And whether there is five minutes worth of news or ten, we are gonna have to use up the entire time allotted…or column space…so find the "filler" to deliver "X" amount of material. The result is a lot of stuff gets included that really isn't earth shaking; or else a lot of news gets coverage so detailed it is exhausting.

The result is achieving a quantity objective with quality becoming incidental, and the oversupply gorges us with data. We conclude headlines indicate importance forgetting that even when nothing important has happened, there is going to be a headline anyway. Certainly television, the radio, newspapers or news magazines perform a function. And their objective appears to be "all the news that is fit to print" (or some such similar high-flown aphorism). Not quite true. Don't let's be naïve. News is the commodity, but PROFIT is the objective. Achieved through readership, through people buying (or viewing) what each has to produce.

What happens in that scramble is curious. The news (or the content) is then tailored to the popular taste because each wants all the public attention it can induce. To secure same, each vehicle gives "them" what they like, so to a degree you and I end up shaping or skewing the news to that which best titillates us, the buying public. Ergo, we, the consumers, arbitrate what we read-hear-see. Because the dogs have to like the dog food or there is no repeat purchase.

A friend of mine started a publication several years ago for the business community. His idea caught on, intrigued the reading public and became a financial success. The owner was a die-hard conservative, and I began to wonder at the tone of some of the editorials and all the stories about bankruptcy, divorce actions, this firm's failure to make bond payments or that character's exorbitant salary, etc. I saw a negative trend; asked why he didn't talk about the good things. A professional editor managed the paper and though the owner agreed with me, said if he ran his sort of stories, the paper wouldn't last three weeks. The professional knew what the public wanted to read, and though there is a way of moderating, in the end what sells (unhappily) are problems, misfortune, failures, management screw ups, et al. The objective was to create a successful new paper to keep selling. It had to be balanced with what the public wanted to keep subscriptions coming.

So what's the beef? The job is to sell papers — or magazines or TV time. The news is a by-product. How it is handled, what is reported are keys to success and the journalistic integrity or objective reporting or balancing news coverage is important only insofar as it attracts the public. There is no overall standard of excellence or guidelines for public good or concern for general well-being as criteria.

What happens in this venue is the tendency to confuse priorities and while we presume headlines or TV time equates to import, underneath producers look for that which will attract popular attention. When national policy gets the same treatment flowing along lines impacted by the media, searching for popular opinion, we are doing our nation an injustice. The public rarely stews about topics of complexity, strangeness or substance, but opts for voyeurism and enjoys gossip if not scandal in its taste. In that scenario we are what King Arthur called "following wandering fires", pursuing the tangential, ignoring the important. An example in my mind of obsession with a phantom was Watergate, reawakened for me with the President's visit in July to Greece and Turkey, promising negotiation on the Cyprus issue. That big rift occurred on Nixon's watch, though after he had been hounded into ineffectiveness. Nixon may have been the best equipped man in this century to serve in the Oval Office because he understood well the use of power and the role of the Presidency. The insignificant nature of the crime, his blindness about tapes, the defection of aides, all got badly blown out of proportion. It was not sufficient reason — in my mind — to dismiss a president, hamstring a government. Nixon was badgered out of office because he was unpopular with the press and public, because he was slightly paranoid, and because he handled the situation without proper humility; not because he was a bad president. Watergate was of no consequence as a world crisis, but during Nixon's unavailability, Cyprus erupted, unchecked, with the one person in the world who could have handled it, mired down in a mortally ridiculous unimportant struggle. For more significant to us than the fate of Greece and Turkey were endless tapes, righteous judges, breast beating about honor and purity. In my book, keeping the Greeks and Turks on an even keel should have been more critical than getting even with an unpopular, unloved public figure, who generally speaking, did his job well.

It still goes on: Ollie North goes through the ringer for doing what Dutch (right or wrong) wanted him to do and spends a fortune on lawyers' fees, while you and I spend millions persecuting (excuse me, prosecuting) him. What good has been done for anyone? Ollie North is a puff of smoke, a summer zephyr. The Federal deficit and the fiscal irresponsibility of the Congress are a national travesty of monstrous proportions, a crime far more inexcusable than some poor Lieutenant Colonel completing a politically unpopular assignment. Why doesn't Congress determine what is important and spend its time — and our dollars — there? Why pander to the press creating news but neglecting duty? They might try dealing with the nation's infrastructure, confirming presidential appointments, improving education, housing and governmental efficiencies for starters.

I think abortion is a non-issue in the scope of the world problems. It is an emotional opinion about an esoteric option neither right nor wrong because "my thinking makes it so". It is thus insoluble. It is news, and those heavy into support of one side or another deliberately make news in order to reflect upon — not solve — the dilemma. News becomes the objective, not resolution.

The Smith affair in Palm Beach is a non-issue yet a major news item. We shall be digging up everything we can find about him because he's also a Kennedy and because the public likes this crap. Compare that with the minimal news we read about Ethiopia trying to create a new government, status of the oil spills in Kuwait or the desperate plight of Cuban and Haitian peoples, the conundrum of

Iraq, our trade imbalance. Why a national paroxysm about some bimbo drinking in a bar at 3:00 in the morning, then going home with "the boys" for what purpose God only knows. Now, if we had the same amount of ink spilled on daily pork barrel projects loaded into our fiscal deficit, I'll bet we'd get some action. The media might serve a more constructive purpose. But we'd sooner read about alleged sexual escapades.

Distinction between the important and the tangential lies at the root of a lot of business and personal problems as well. The diffusion is not restricted to "those people" or to "they" and "them". Fact, it is more pertinent if it involves "you" and "me" because we can do something at our level. It is no longer a spectator sport; we become then "we" as well. The diffusion is not restricted to "those people" or to "they" and the players, we are on stage. A good many of our managers got there, like leaders in any organization, body, etc., rising to the surface because of how they do their jobs, meaning how well they solve problems. Our system itself whether political, societal or business looks for leadership and has provided the vehicle for identifying and then employing it. Our corporate department heads or CAT's managers rise through the ranks on their capacity to figure out what is important and what is "routine". They don't sweat the small stuff. They look for the key issues, core problems. A battle against "the system" which in all institutions seeks to conform and loves anonymity in "corporate policy" is a side issue. The customer doesn't care about internal friction which does nothing to help his function or vocation. He wants us dedicated to the number one topic, his

MacAllister's manager meeting; Bob Drummond, a young Doug Clark, and Norm Hale.

own efficiency and profitability, as our equipment (or service) augments his role. Our better managers need to see the distractions of the office and departmental linkage and factory ambiguity as part of the process, but apart from the bottom line concern: serving, performing, producing to vindicate our role. It is not in the mechanism of the corporate vehicle that we perform our function. It is in the field involved with the user on one front or another.

A key factor in hewing the line on this distinction is not merely determining what's critical and what is not, but moving to redress it, which is the job of management anyway. Irwin Miller once observed that this is the chief function of leaders: hunt for problems, look for trouble. Ferret it out, try to find it because your job is to get it corrected. We don't need a lot of brilliance to direct a smooth humming enterprise. Tables of organization, company statements of ethical purpose, annual business plans, new slogans about "Customer First" are not guarantees of anything and change nothing unless those committed to the enterprise are not only aware of where we are going, but pledged to go along and support. The tractor business involves a lot of factors and a great many interconnected components, some are important and some are merely there. Knowing the difference is what makes the difference. ■

1992

Real Freedom

April 1992

We spend a lot of time (it seems to me) living in a "what if" world. A world of planning, hypothecating, presuming, projecting, assuming, all of which — I grant — is an essential process if we are to prepare for the future or gear up for what is to come. It is that recourse to the mind the Greeks taught us to employ so we could solve problems in the abstract. This means creating conditions mentally which envision all the contradictory or impinging circumstances were this the real thing and thus permit "living thru" a given exercise or experience, so we can find the weaknesses, possibilities, potential, success or failure and thus avoid beating our heads apart in the empirical world where the only prospect is reality, and the only way to succeed or fail is to launch forth and find out what might happen as we go. What occurs is the interlink between the mental or conceptual and daily reality.

What distinguished society in the West from that in the Orient (after 546 B.C., i.e. after Thales) was the recourse to accumulated knowledge, analyzed to provide wisdom, which now lead to truth through journeys of the mind rather establishing truth through bitter recourse to experience or delivered oracles from The Nine Gods. Reasoning became an endemic component of Western culture, invaluable as a process and one now common to all of us whether planning a trip, building a budget, adding a product line, Christmas shopping, negotiating with the union or preparing for the hereafter. It is so commonplace we take

it for granted, i.e. we do it all the time. Wherein "lies the rub" as ole Hamlet used to say. We do it with such frequency and such abandon, we begin to lose track of whether the cerebral world, the world of concepts and ideas, that of plans and prospect, is more important than reality, the arena in which we do battle day by day.

Reflecting this ambivalence, the Greeks themselves became too enamored of thinking processes per se and the limitless realm of the abstract, they designed a thing called "sophistry" which had as its objective complex journeys in the mind pursuing hypothetical situations all largely theoretical. Like trigonometry or geometry, these were patterns of logic and reason, dealing in contrived circumstances which worked through to find ultimate conclusions and enjoyed for the mere exercise itself. Before radio, TV or movies, merely thinking or mediating on the give and take in imagined situations was justifiable and probably common course in Plato's academy or the schools of other Hellenic philosophers, the mental wandering unlinked to any proposed action. As though the mind ought to have a period of aerobics all its own.

The reason I'm beating this to death is because the practice or the science (as noted earlier) has not lost popularity, mental projection still being essential to the health of our systems. The most famous postulation is $E=mc^2$, a premise of Einstein, first stated in the '20s and ultimately fulfilled in the Manhattan Project of 1942-44. That's an example of thinking something

Albert Einstein during a lecture in Vienna in 1921 (age 42).
Photographed by Ferdinand Schmutzer.
(Source: Wikimedia Commons)

through and then later implementing same (a partnership between thought and action). All of which will lead us to the conclusion that a good many cerebral experiences lead to fruitful and productive action later on, but will also tell us that often we also get carried away in terms of our dreaming or planning or hoping or wishing and begin to find the thought so intriguing we overload the program and the huge unused surplus drifts into sophistry…or idea dreaming.

There was a bit of both thought and action in our early history. It became more pertinent when we had to articulate our reasons for the rebellion against King George, an assignment completed for the Continental Congress by Jefferson in his "Declaration" spelling out the principles underlying our philosophy vis-à-vis governments. Subsequent to the War (1787), the Convention had the task then of shaping a vehicle which would implement or in a more accurate sense, would reflect and make real the principles so boldly stated earlier. It was time to stop cutting bait and start fishing. We have done the dreaming, now to see them realized.

Turned out there were again more dreams or aspirations involved than could be reasonably accomplished given the regional-cultural-economic-

and-philosophic divergence of the group, so they did what they could, meaning, got most of it institutionalized. We are celebrating the follow-up work in this Bi-Centenary of the Bill of Rights, i.e. the first ten amendments to the Constitution, provisions that many thought were not needed earlier, were covered by state constitutions or were too hot to handle when the Constitution was drafted. So hopes for freedom of speech, of assembly, of worship, from unwarranted search et al. were now also moved from wish to reality. And more would follow. Reflecting again the fact that an idea or vision or need precedes the action and telling us too, the ideas keep coming. It is ideas that lead us along, and this province of the mind that continues to regulate action.

If I can stop repeating and get to the core of this essay, it will be to suggest that a lot of political thought is inevitably converted to oratory and occurs today in such abundance there is still a major overload of ideas. Aspirations articulated, but no fruitation following. Partly because we begin to impute to our constitution, or to our "principles of governance", handfuls of whimsy, fluff from Utopia that was not designed in the system. Ideas that maybe sound good and so must therefore have value. Ideas that intrigue and romance the public but are sounder in theory than in practice.

For example, it is good Christian thinking to be concerned for people who are unemployed, and their succor is a noble idea. I think it is very bad politics, however, to presume their predicament requires a Federal "fix up" or rectifying programs. For several reasons. There are first of all a lot of "unemployed" whose spouses still work, so there is no genuine destitution. Next, we are over-spending like mad in America and have been profligate with our substance, buying and charging and committing for more things instead of saving for a rainy day. Using Federal dollars to support that practice is the wrong move as is bailing out people who live beyond their means. Moreover, I still see "Help Wanted" signs every time I go out, employers looking for ready hands and someone to work. Not at $30,000 a year, but for some income, and placing one back in the economic system. Last of all and most important, it is not the purpose nor the obligation of the state to keep people employed. The government does not owe people jobs or a livelihood. Its role is to assure a level playing field so that both democracy and free enterprise flow naturally, that the conditions exist for society to function freely. What we want is an environment that permits the creation of jobs. We want opportunity for decent wages, freedom, rewards for excellence, incentives to encourage effort and investment. In short, systems that produce and create and employ because there are merit and rewards for doing so effectively. And within the system, encourage each to manage his own life and career allowing the person total flexibility dependent on his own preparation, contribution, intelligence, competence and good luck. Now that is the way the system was established, and the dream of the founding fathers was that people had gained independence for the express purpose of handling their own destiny under new rules that assured personal freedom and abundant opportunity. It was not particularly easy in that society, much of it strung along the frontier, to achieve the good life, but the land and the systems attracted those with free spirits and a sense of adventure, and their seizure of opportunity established a momentum and created traditions that carry us along to this day.

But in the meantime we have found inadequacies, have been careless with the way we handle our resources, dramatically altered the role of government and have minimized the obligation of the individual while accentuating the role of society. In dreaming about the equality of men and their freedom, we have forgotten Will Durant's unnerving observation that freedom and equality are sworn enemies. That freedom to invent or create or produce or organize or educate automatically raises to newer levels some men while the slothful, indolent, less ambitious or the luckless drop below the norm and *voila*, we are drastically unequal in a single generation. (But our own efforts, you see, are what determine that difference!) Having done that for several generations, the penchant in my time has been to try and get those behind in the "equality" scale caught up and by impeding the progress of the more adventurous through several devices (i.e. taxes) to try and rearrange the new order that freedom has permitted, making it now unfree.

We do all this because we are into the "what if" business, and we are into the dream world because the world of day-by-day reality turned out different than many people want it to be. What economic or societal or educational evolution has ordained is not Utopia after all. It does not give everyone the same rewards. And in this country, we dream, to a degree, everyone should have them. So we began several presidents ago legislating to try and get every working American a decent wage, a retirement income

at 65, health insurance, single parents ought to have subsistence payments if he/she can't work, ought to have an education and a lot of other things we once did for ourself. The nation can't afford it; we have not ruined the whole experiment in modifying the initial contract between the person and the state; our standard of living remains the highest in the world.

What's the beef?

The beef is we are on a slide which like most slides you know, go only one way. Maybe it is inevitable and necessary, but it is different, and we ought to ponder the wisdom or the ultimate value of the continual movement along its course. What is now occurring is that the ideas which are becoming rhetoric are ideas expounded to titillate and to induce. They are the dreams of our political theorists lofted to attract public attention and induce support more than they are constructive elements of a national agenda. They are usually amplified in election years to garner votes. It is their sound which is important because they are in essence sophistry.

What happens is we get back into the dream world; we want to line up with Thoreau and build the idyllic society. Unhappy with what we have, we dream of a situation where there is no unemployment, where all babies born have two identifiable parents who even hopefully are joined in holy wedlock. We want everyone who is ill to have access to doctors and hospitals; want those ready for retirement with comfortable incomes; we want everyone living in a decent house; want kids educated so everyone can at least read and write. We want a lot of things, and in our early history we got a lot of things because we were tough enough as a breed to utilize the resources available and convert them into securing us a decent situation. As a matter of fact, at the time of the Continental Congress, we had the highest standard of living in the world, not very sophisticated or polished, but robust and well fed. What we are doing now is changing the rules and instead of affirming a system which encourages personal initiative and participation, we create first the "wish list" — income, housing, medical, educational standards — and we warp the system from its guarantee of opportunity to guarantee for unlimited benefits.

The fact that there is enough to go around and the wherewithal exists to provide all Americans with the good things of life does not mean we are authorized to redistribute same from its current channels and give everyone everything he wants just because it is here. It is hard because the existing system made it all happen. To modify or tamper or dream away what were fundamental principles is to mortally wound the goose which has been laying the golden eggs. Utopian dreams or the ideal societies of Plato, Sir Thomas Moore, George Orwell, Thoreau, and others belong in the dream world. To convert them to reality by rejecting our history and diddling with the system is to confuse sophistry with pragmatism. The President has no business diddling with the economy, and the cries to do something about employment ought to be cries that declare employment is the province of business, free enterprise, not the obligation of the government. If we could get regulations off our back, get unions back in line, get competitive in the workplace, we would also solve simultaneously the unemployment problem. To blatantly create jobs or finance artificial interest rates or erect trade barriers by governmental fiat is to treat the symptom, not the malady. Unless American business is strong, the American system is in jeopardy. The best antidote at the moment is to try and restore a bit of independence — not dependence — and a larger measure of personal responsibility to the national fabric. Applying experimental legerdemain to the marketplace is sheer gimmickry. Changing governmental policy to accommodate what people want or think they should have or by now feel they deserve, is a protracted form of national suicide. Kipling once advised it was o.k to dream, but "not make dreams your master". We need to heed his advice. ∎

History of Construction
April 1992

Those of us who think philosophically about this business (in those periods between economic malaise, foreign incursions, bouts with the IRS, unions and other malefactors) are inclined to think proudly that there is something very unique about what we do or what we provide. Meaning, we rehearse with some pride the fact it is our industry which furnishes the nation — and always has — with its capacity to build, expand, improve, renovate, and to a degree, produce. We are the stuff of which cities are built, great national projects come about, shopping centers develop, gigantic dams and resulting lakes come into being, highway systems unfold, airports are possible, and all the rest. We aren't "on the cutting edge" of expansion, we are the suppliers, the enablers to those who build. So venerable, by the way, is this profession that my major premise will aver we are essential to human progress and have been since the dawn of civilization. Without those fundamental processes which involve earth moving, trenching or channeling, transport, communication, agriculture, mining and logging, there is a good chance we would still be living in caves (and if we were Picts, painting our bodies blue).

The "cradle of civilization" evolved in "the land between the rivers", i.e. Mesopotamia (modern Iraq). Here man developed his first major cities, produced written records, major temples, palaces, trading ventures, large scale sciences. But all was based upon the fact that men could plant wheat, barley, spelt, and other crops, irrigate them, and in the process provide (at long last) a steady supply of food without wandering hither and yon in search of same. Along with the hundreds of thousands of irrigated acres came naturally the development of large herds of domesticated animals, primarily sheep and goats, but also cattle, pigs and sundry wild fowl, mostly ducks. Out of the steady supply of food, a whole culture was created and with the creation of a universally needed commodity (grain, meat, wool) also came the development of wealth and with that (as Will Durant has reminded us) the creation of government, arts, religion, science, commerce, in short, civilization.

In case you think I have lost track of my point, rest easily. All of this came about only because primitive engineering was able to build water channels to direct the life-giving liquid from both the Tigris and Euphrates into a thousand, thousand fields, and because in the nature of this peculiar drainage basin (flooding) and climate (hot and freezing cold, replete with blowing winds and with torrential cloud bursts), there was a constant requirement for repair, maintenance, and alterations in the network of canals, sluices, maybe locks, dikes and dams. The creation of this system which was an inter-connection of huge, merely large, and small water courses, channels, and ditches not only laid out an agriculture grid, but established a transport system that encouraged traffic through a vast connective water link throughout the whole region both for commerce as well as political and social intercourse. Without earthmoving, without engineering and planning to reshape the land, I'm saying to you, no civilization in Babylon or Nippur or Larsa or Ur of Nineveh. Without earthmoving, no water system of highways or transport system. Man's ability to alter the earth as it suited its purposes and thus served the noble cause of both progress in the public good, permitted and augmented the first great civilization.

All this was full blown by 3000 B.C. The systems lasted as long as the great Semitic empires in the area lasted, which was close to 3,000 years. But, still important to this thesis, when power shifted from those astounding experiments to the west, i.e. to Alexander and then to Rome, so did the focus of interest and the wealth and the engineering emphasis. When the venerable eastern society was unable to maintain those canals, repair the damage, lay out new fields or regions for development, meaning when the earthmoving contractors of the Fertile Crescent were no longer brought into the picture to apply their trade, then the whole society began literally to dry up and as it does to this day, blow away. The countless thousand acres of waving wheat and barley or groves of date palms returned to the encroaching desert from which they sprouted. In our time, most is a trackless waste. The society which our progenitors in moving the earth permitted and helped fashion returned to desolation when its ministration and skilled expertise were no longer applied.

Now all of this comes on as a bit strong, but in ruminating about our profession, I can make the same application in Egypt, which is the next great power — and perhaps the longest living empire in man's history

Some architecture lasts forever — this is 2500 B.C.

— because to a degree it was based upon a similar principle. The Nile flooded annually, commencing on the 19th of July every year and spread a blanket of water over the arable land, rising in a good year from 10-16 feet over the banks. But to get all of this aqua fresca where you really want it or to take it further than its natural flood stage or to build ponds or re-taining walls to keep it trapped so it doesn't flow back into the river when the crest is gone, what do we have to do? We should have shaped the land, rearranged the contour of the earth to exploit the gravitas po-tential, build banks and dikes to take advantage of all the water that is there because when it subsides (takes about three months as I recall) "that's all she wrote" for this year. There is no rainfall to speak of in Egypt. Beyond that, when a quarter of the year our inhabited area is under water, it says something else about local contractors. It says we better get our houses above ground level so we aren't sloshing around inside, night and day forever, and it says there are other functions like baking or metalwork or milking or teaching or embalming or tavern-keeping that has to somehow be lifted on pads or foundations so the processes can go on during the soggy period. Agriculture in the Nile Valley was as effective as the skill and industry of the Pharaoh's engineers and his earthmovers.

Not as critical to us, but sometimes far more interesting is the creation of the great national monu-ments in Egypt. We are all familiar with the pyra-mids, especially those at Gizeh (there are really some 80 altogether, not just the three in the lithographs), and all of us have seen (or seen pictures of) the huge statuary, the mammoth temples and the obelisks plus who knows what else in that protracted and phe-nomenal experiment. How do you suppose they got

2,300,000 stones weighing something like two tons a piece, 100, 200 finally the last stone, 470 feet in the air, and got them in the right place in the pyramid at Cheops? They did it with gigantic earthen ramps. They rolled those hummers up part way or maybe dragged them on huge sledges, greased underneath with mud or with fat and oil to let them slide. But the pyramids of Cheops, Chephren and Mankere (2500 B.C.) must have been the first great public works program in history, and it required millions of tons of earth to be picked up from here and transported to there, ever-growing, ever-rising, probably always maintaining the same slope. You get the point. There would have been no pyramids without a way to get those bloody stones up and up, one course at a time, and there would have been no "course at the time" without a government contractor using volunteer, conscript, and slave labor to engineer and design them and then the bags and wicker baskets to move all hundreds of thousands of yards of dirt. And then, of course, when we are finished and have a big week-long, ribbon-cutting celebration, we have to put the ground back into about the same condition in which we found it. (EPA started early in our ontogeny as a species.) So here are a couple million yards to move again. Big cut, big fill!

In the case of Egypt, the Nile retained its rhyth-mic cycle, replete with the fertilizing silt spread each time it flooded the 700-mile valley from Aswan to the sea, but the political system which sustains society for so long ultimately eroded and finally collapsed. In my mind, another example in history where a venal, an exploitive priesthood, ended up with far too much property, wealth, and power and had as a major objective the modest goal of getting it all. They blew it, of course, and Egypt fell to a series of conquerors, finally for good to Alexander, a subject status retained by Ptolemy and his line. Then the colony or the sub-ordinate status was reinforced by Caesar, Anthony and Octavian, in that order. Before ever getting loose in the aftermath of the Roman crackup, a new tide rolled in, via the Arab conquests — 7th Century A.D. — and settled any questions of regaining former Egyptian grandeur or power. But despite the unfor-tunate political circumstances, underneath it all, the seasonal pulsations of the river ordered Egyptian life and the maintenance or an agrarian economy, based still on the wise use of available water permitted our digging and dredging and baking and channeling forbearers to unobtrusively, yet inexorably, carry on their craft and preserve life's fundamental process, that of providing food. That they succeeded — captive or free — is evident in the historic fact that Egypt was "Rome's breadbasket", and when crops failed in Egypt, riots broke out on the Tiber.

All of which turned out to be a lengthy harangue indeed. We aren't going to get a complete historical reflection done in a single episode, not one this rambling or not without taking up the whole paper. Maybe we can do more in the next installment (that is if anybody is interested) and the role construction played in developing the ancient world's greatest and most productive empire. ∎

What's Wrong with the System?

July 1992

There is a great deal of introspection going on in America these days, due in part to random, rambling political oratory rehearsing and reviewing the weakness and error of the Bush Administration; part is the calamity in Los Angeles and the recognition that racism and savagery exist in a startling fashion, unexpunged; part is the mounting debt and the realization the Congress has not solved our problems; weekly we warm over the environmental hassles, etc., etc., etc. The ongoing inescapable litany points out what is wrong with welfare programs, how badly we are losing the drug war, how poorly we are educating our young, how much healthcare costs will rise this year, etc. (again) ad nauseam. We are a people who recite our sundry, separate weaknesses as one droning through a daily rosary.

The disturbing thing is not the range or extent or nature of our problems, it is the resolute way we resist solving them. Because the truth is, what happens to us is not what really matters most. It is what we do about what happens to us that ordains our destiny. Defining the problem is surely critical. Amplifying, redefining, modifying, extending and clarifying the same as not (repeat not) ends in themselves despite the fact we have made them so. So, the obvious question is, why don't we plow into the stack, sort out the sticklers one at a time and create remedial problems to deal with each? What is the hold up? First hold up is finding a scapegoat. Just who the heck is at blame? Let us call him to account for starters and demand recompense.

At about this point, we get a lot of nominated candidates for chief culprit. One is the inert Congress who has given lip service to one position while voting another. Andy Jacobs has a favorite acorn about an old congressman's advice. "Son", he said, "I've succeeded here for 32 years because I never voted for a tax increase…and never voted against an appropriation." Or maybe the President is to blame. He is supposed to outline a program for the nation annually, one eschewing deficits, correcting shortcomings, and raising the standard of living for all of us as he eliminates poverty, ignorance, greed, and avarice. Or, take the urban mess, refocused for us as a result of the L.A. riots. Here, I blame the mayors. Their job is managing whatever jurisdiction they fought so desperately to control, and now

their only solution is to whine for money from the Federal Government. Wrong move! Running a city is the job of the local administration, not the Feds. Funding urban renewal, job programs, education, toxic cleanup, infrastructure repair, garbage pickup, and you name it, are all functions of the mayor and council. Now they suddenly turn gutless before a tax-sensitive constituency, leaving us with sagging services, shrinking budgets, and wails of alarm instead of honest appraisal of required costs and appropriate taxation to meet the needs. Downtown L.A. is not the business of the President nor is it your responsibility or mine.

Another factor for failure is the breakdown of the family replete with its bifurcation into a working father here and a working mother there getting the good things of life for the kids, but sparse in terms of parental tutelage, modeling, and discipline. Add the proliferation of single parent family, disgraceful ratios of illegitimacy, and third or fourth generations on the public pap. There are far too many parents who don't know the parenting role and don't propose to learn. They are too interested in the breeding process.

Other whipping boys are the educational system, or maybe big business which divides us between the haves and have-nots, a growing disparity between rich incomes and poor. We can blame the budget deficits, the S&L scandal that sucked up 400-500 billion dollars to correct mistakes made by greedy speculators and dumb-ass bankers, blame the Japanese, racism, the recession. In short, we can find a lot of people to blame.

Bottom line, however, says the real culprits are you and I. We are responsible. Because it is also we who take the system for granted and want it functioning without any semblance of personal support for its maintenance and upkeep. It is we who fracture ourselves into vested interest partisans and squabble over incidental issues which make mountains out of mole hills. It is we who vote in the government, whether at school board level, at county or city stage, whether governors or presidents, and it is we who elect those who promise us the most, often unobtrusively robbing the republic of courageous leadership who happens to be right, but personally unappealing or misunderstood. But most of all, the blame falls on us because we want our special interest protected

Indiana Senator Richard Lugar and P.E. MacAllister.

first, and maybe the total good attended to later on. We are not ignorant of major needs, of right and wrong, of priority sequence, but it is just that our personal hot buttons are emotional issues, compelling us to stands that work to the disadvantage of the enterprise, emotion being far more compelling the logic.

I have watched a number of political campaigns here at fairly close range wherein our candidate starts by "taking the high road". You know, the noble and lofty route to a given office by discussing issues and proposals while the dirty-minded opposition goes on attack, tearing down our guy, smearing and misrepresenting him with savage 30-second commercials on TV. What do you suppose happened to our torch bearer, riding proudly ahead with the white plume flying? He was clobbered in the polls. He dropped week after week. So being pragmatic, finally decided to go on the attack. And after getting nasty, he shifted the trend and began to move up. The great Hoosier unwashed, the spectator and media consumer, was turned off by discussion of issues or program or qualifications and tuned on by dirt, smear, mud, and slander. Unhappily, this is what campaigns are all about; taking their tone and tempo from what? From what the American public wants to see. From what impresses you and me; what turns us on.

This is a pretty sorry commentary on the process of selecting candidates or criteria for public office — who can throw the most filth the hardest and make the most stick, but men and women who have been this route know a discussion of how we solve our major problems is not what revs people up. It is cutting up the other guy, sad as that may be.

Part of the point here is that polls indicate what kind of a campaign a given candidate uses. Which

means he samples the public's pulse to see how he should shape his run. Know what? This is the way national policy is also run. When it becomes apparent we are up in arms about the plight of the cities and Gallup lays his figures before the lawmakers, *voila*! We earmark a couple billion dollars overnight for the plight of the cities. No coherent program, no major strategic initiative, no balanced partnership with the state. A hurried response to the pollster, meaning the populace, who says, "Throw some more money at the cities", even though the last trillion did no good and even though using federal dollars in city budgets once again allows the mayor to cop out with no resolution to his problem. When the federal dole is ended, he — and his city — are back in the same stew.

Polls are really wonderful. They repeat the attitude of Robespierre who said something like, "Excuse me. I have to run. There go my followers. I must hurry up and catch them because I am their leader." We are still confused 200 years later as to who follows and who leads. The people tell the pollsters and these in turn tell the Robespierres (i.e. politicians). Those polled through Roper or Gallup or Harris send the signals, and the political reception on the other end is a large knee jerk. That is a bad dynamic to have evolved since in a republic we send people to Washington to learn the job, stay boned up, and do what is right for all of us. They ought to be doing that…doing what is wise and proper, not what I want or what is popular. The point again is the root cause for so much of our travail happens to lay out here with the "we the people", who do the nagging and badgering, thus shaping national policy.

Reason this strikes me as unfortunate is the vested interest nature of most American. It is unwise for a group, whether pro life or pro choice to land on a candidate and see nothing else about him except his stand on a single issue, one upon which he may never have a vote. In the spectrum of today's national concerns, there are surely a jillion other positions to evaluate and when the best possible candidate for a congressional or gubernatorial office get broadsided because he is not on the right side of the sole abortion thing, is not serving the interests of anyone.

My industry had an apoplectic seizure two years ago when someone sent a trial balloon suggesting we add 50 cents or a dollar a barrel to the price of oil and use it to reduce the federal deficit. My trade association erupted with a series of memos and official positions of the board explaining why this was heretical, unpatriotic, sacrilegious, and heinous. "Why?" I wanted to know. "Well, because gas tax money has always gone to roads and streets." Meaning, since motorists paid the tax, it is their dollars we are dealing with. "Aren't we putting our industry's interests ahead of those of the nation?" "Tough."

I'll bet most of us are in the same boat. What if we ended subsides for the tobacco growers, a product which kills a couple hundred thousand American a year? The growers would yank the chain of their congressman, who would argue damage to the economy, loss of experts, tax revenue lost, and simply back reason, logic, and common sense into a corner making the benefits to a special group more important than a fortune of the rest of us. Senator Dick Lugar has been trying to consolidate a lot of local Farm Bureau offices for the sake of economy and efficiency. He gets all sorts of flack. What will happen if he recommends ending the $28 billion annual farm subsidies, supporting the American farm which can only compete by virtue of its subsidy program? There's be a parade of farm tractors storming into Washington, not because we couldn't buy cheaper grain and tomatoes elsewhere, but because we have another group whose personal interest exceeds that of the vast majority.

The only way to get on top of the national debt — and deficits — is to cut entitlement programs.

The second you touch Social Security, AARP comes out of its offices like a rocket and says, "We have 65 million recipients. Cut off their handout at your peril. We are far more important than the rest of America". But Social Security was not invented as a retirement program. Handing a family who doesn't need it $21,000 a year is typical bureaucratic profligacy. Try a cut on the education budget and see what happens; closing military bases is a rear-guard action; tamper with food stamps or ADC grants or welfare funding or even National Endowment for the Arts and people get exercised to the point of screaming. They don't get outraged about four trillion in national debt or the 52-week unemployment handout or the imbalance of payments, but get into my pet program, and there is hell to pay. The solution is to get the same ardor, the same passion, and the same interest in America's problems and see if that wouldn't help the cause. Not merely of the nation, but of all the special interests now scrambling for their share of the pie. It is time to see that my best interests are better served when the national problems are solved and "the invisible hand" which strengthens the general good also creates a more wholesome climate for the person or local interest. ∎

Hilda L.E. MacAllister
July 1992

My mother was born on a farm in Oconto county, Wisconsin, the 17th of March in the year of our Lord 1897, the first year of William McKinley's presidency. Her father was Herman Yakel, a dairy farmer who had rested his land from the virgin timber with great sweat and strain, meaning cleared the bloody thing without bulldozers. His livelihood from this clay loam soil came from wheat, barley and oats plus lots of corn to feed a herd of about 15 or 20 Holstein cattle whose milk provided the household cash.

Herman's wife was Wilhelmina Rader, originally from Berlin, and more recently, from a homestead just up the road a piece. My mother was the ninth child in a family topping out at twelve, and, for reasons unbeknownst to me, christened — in German of course — Hilda Lydia Elsie.

Reflections from her early life, reconstructed from what I recall of her family, the farm and the age in which they lived, point to the enormous self-sufficiency of that generation, a spirit of independence. Proven in a lifestyle. From their sheep, my grandmother carded wool for a later separation into single strands, a process accommodated by a spinning wheel. I think my brother Dave still has that same spinning wheel. Grandma then knitted the winter long, making mittens and stockings, with an occasional sweater or scarf thrown in. She made her own soap, grew her own vegetables and fruit, canned, and stocked the shelves with beans, peas, venison, horseradish, rhubarb, sauerkraut, pickles, and you name it. She dried apples in the oven in the fall, baked fresh bread several times a week, baked pies, tarts, apple strudel cake, animal cookies; kept chickens and geese, and thus eggs, and meat; churned butter, made quilts, made noodles, dumplings, sausage, mincemeat, etc.

The cellar was stocked with four or five kinds of apples, with carrots, beets, potatoes, cabbage, rutabaga, and onions. Ol' Herman hunted and fished to broaden the bill of fare, so we had venison oc-casionally, squirrel, trout, pickerel, and rabbit, along with beef and pork, including hams, sausage, and bacon smoked on his own farm.

He had built the house and barn personally with help from the neighbors and constantly improved it. My grandfather was the first in the community to get electricity, then to have a pump and running water, owned the first automobile, the first big iron-lugged Ford farm tractor, and the first telephone. Unhappily, the confused ol' guy was a Democrat but happy nonetheless. Fact, was a half-assed politician, serving at times as township clerk and as a member of the county's Board of Commissioners.

So my mother was raised in a busy family, with each having lots of work to do, this being the age of hand labor, before washing machines, hot water heaters or water softeners, dishwashers, gas or electric ranges, microwaves, mixers and blenders, electric irons, or hair dryers. There was no central heating system aside from the pot-bellied stove; we used outdoor privies, baths came once a week whether you needed it or not, chores assigned to everyone. It was a hard life, with work year-round, regulated by the bloody cows that had to be milked twice a day and ordered by the farm cycles which ebbed and flowed with the seasons. This is the environment into which my mother was introduced, and which disciplined and developed her character. This environment also had definite religious overtones, with church every Sunday and often sermons both in German and in English. The church was St. John's Evangelical Lutheran, down the road just a mile or so, beyond the cheese factory. Incidentally, Herman and Wilhelmina live to this day in their long sleep in the adjacent cemetery. Hilda reminded me that I was baptized in German by a Lutheran pastor with my grandfather as my godfather — after which, the parson collected a small fee (like would you believe a half bushel of oats?), climbed into his surrey and clomped on back to the parsonage.

Hilda MacAllister.

My father was raised on a similar-type farm, fifteen miles away, and he was two years older than Hilda. Ole Bull MacAllister likewise served on the Oconto County Board, so obviously the two fathers knew each other. At seventeen, Hilda had gone to work for the local telephone company in Suring, two and a half miles away, while my dad was simultaneously joining a construction crew, building roads in Oconto County for a new

1890 Herman Yankel (P.E.'s grandfather) and family on their farm.

and proliferating gadget called the automobile. They usually called it the Model T. Fact, Ed MacAllister found himself on Wisconsin Highway 32 outside Suring, bending south and west around the farm of Herman Yakel. It was during a process of buying gravel for this road that my dad got acquainted with the Yakels, particularly Hilda Lydia Elsie. The romance blossomed and though something about the relationship did not please one or the other of the families, the course of true love managed itself to run smooth. They took the ultimate step the first week in January 1917 by hopping on a train, eloping to Green Bay, and settled in Stiles, Wisconsin, not five miles from the MacAllister farm.

Three years after the wedding, my father, age 25, was hired as the county highway commissioner at a salary of $3,600 bucks a year, which in 1923 was big bucks. We moved to Oconto, the county seat, and by now we were building roads using crawler tractor power and whatever graders, elevating scrapers and steam shovels were available. It was easy to make the transition from using the equipment to selling same, and in 1929, Paw went to work for the Caterpillar dealer in Milwaukee. In two years, he was sales manager and then general manager, so in 1930 we left Oconto to move to the headquarters town, Milwaukee. And left the farm connections forever behind, the frequent trips and the relationships slowly slipping from view. By now three of the four grandparents had died, and Herman Yakel was retired. Beyond that, the farms themselves changed hands, no son being able or willing to make them

go. Times and economics changed, markets dropped, technology appeared, and the era we call the "Great Depression" descended.

Despite the years and the changes, my mother never lost that early conditioning. Though she forsook the Lutheran Church to become a Presbyterian — hardly a very passionate one. My parents were not very active, nor very regular — alas — in attendance, not 'til Dave and I went into the service. They figured religion was really a way of life rather than an exercise in theological speculation, and both had exemplary moral habits and attitudes, which may account for the good marriage — a very good marriage — part of that strict Lutheran tradition. People stayed married in those days, which means they were more committed to the family than shifting interests or change in preference or "what turns me on now". My mother retained a lot of things out of her era, the age of McKinley and Theodore Roosevelt, of Taft and Wilson, Harding, Coolidge, and Hoover, maybe because she was not a very complicated person. Life was simple on or off the farm. It was practical, utilitarian, and my mother stayed that way most of her life, straight forward and unambiguous. She was a poor dilettante, and dialectics did not interest or amuse her.

Her attitude toward our family was one of total commitment. That is where she spent her time. She fed the four of us — she claimed — on $10 a week; augmenting with a vegetable garden in Oconto, grew flowers and raspberries. She learned to drive our Maxwell, bobbed her hair like Irene Castle when the time came, and was her own housekeeper and a fabulous cook, especially talented at stretching a meal prepared for four to accommodate five, six or seven. When my father or Dave or I brought unexpected guests along for dinner "FHB" was the secret code word ("family hold back"). Our kids today still use her recipes for Christmas cookies; in fact, still use her cookie cutters; we still bake her type beans; my internationally-famous chili recipe grew out of her first experimentation; and she had the reputation of being the finest producer of potato pancakes in the State of Wisconsin.

Her family had survived because of discipline…and no nonsense from spoiled children. Dave and I were introduced to the same treatment, and Doctor Spock would have gotten short shrift. When she got maternal and sentimental about her record as a mother, I'd say, "Hilda, that all sounds pretty glowing, but truth is I can't recall a time when you weren't on my case, nagging me about something." Without batting an eye she'd say, "Well, it paid off, didn't it? You didn't end up in jail — fact you might turn out all right." Inferring if I were honest about it, she made me what I am today, took full credit. Who knows, maybe she did and maybe she should.

1921 E.W. and Hilda MacAllister
with Dave and P.E.

There was a degree of transition to make when she moved into a sort of executive circle in Milwaukee and then a larger role to play when my dad created his own dealership in Indiana. September 1, 1941. A role expanded when he became the CAT distributor, and thus, the largest dealer in the State of Indiana. Meaning, it is a long way from the farm in Oconto County and the narrow horizons of those 240 acres or from a 50 cents-a-day telephone operation to a millionairess by 1980. But it never bothered her a bit, or if it did, she never showed it, because she had a unique advantage. She had only one personality. She didn't play different persons contingent upon the audience or conditions. She made the circumstances accommodate her or it was tough luck.

Anyone who knew her would tell you something else: we didn't have to wonder what she felt. She'd tell you. In crisp, succinct syllables. I almost said, "tell you what she thought", then recalled she might even pop off before she thought. She judged people and conditions intuitively and delivered an opinion, I mean right now.

Recalling her own background with a bunch of kids around and the universe orbiting around the family, we all stayed pretty close together, especially at holiday time. So for 35 Christmases in a row, 35 Easters, Thanksgivings, and you name it, we all bundled up and descended on Hilda 'til there were (at full count) 13 of us around the board, eating turkey and dressing. She made fresh bread for each occasion and both cherry and apple pies. We cleaned out the leavings as we left. Holiday traditions in my mind are fixed around the family, and the familiar pattern established when my mother was matriarch of the house, a memory that will last me as long as Christmas endures.

Like her mother, fixing for large groups was no big deal, and she was capable of providing the whole nine yards…gravy, stuffing, rutabagas, mashed potatoes, Christmas cookies, the bread and the pies, the bird…everything. Having 40 sales people on her patio annually was taken equally in stride. And she made bread for that gang. Pies, fresh corn, salad, steaks and homemade baked beans. No panic, no screw-ups, no strain, just stay in the kitchen 'til it is done. The company was really an expanded family, and it is interesting to me that until my father died, her entire circle of friends was the neighbors next door, relatives, and people from the company. Her life still orbited in a fairly fixed area and within that unit was contained whatever psychic nourishment she needed.

Chief among her joys was travel. She loved to go. I used to kid her about foreign tours. Between us we had taken her on at least 25 junkets all over the world. When someone said, "Hilda, we are taking a trip. Would you like to go with us to…" and she'd start packing even before she learned the destination.

We are not talking about a paragon here. She had some weaknesses. One was being judgmental. Wow! She was a black or white type gal. Next to that, she might be the second worst gin player in the world. Bill Diehl used to stop by and play with her, half a cent a point, every month or so and used all of his wiles including keeping score to make her look good, and for Bill Diehl, letting someone else win is a sacrifice of monumental stature. She was always ready to deal and enjoyment was the game, not the winnings. She played bingo at Marquette Manor every Thursday for years. Winning three dollars was really a triumph. That was great.

Her other frailty was nonchalance about checkbooks. She paid her own bills 'til about six months ago, but never bothered to retain an indicated balance. She'd record the check but never have the faintest notion of what she had left in her account. Reconciling with a bank statement was out of the question, strange for someone who wanted the bills paid right now. Every day. She did not like owing money and not understanding the statement, was never quite sure she could cover what she had written, and despite my weekly lectures asked, "Can I afford this expense?" When she died, she was down to $61,000 in her checking account. I'm glad indeed she could be that casual about money and never had to fuss with figures. That, in her world, was a man's job, and she happily relinquished it to Dad, then to Dave and I.

Given the vagaries of her early life, the uneven weather, the frequency of disease and death, the severe winters, economic ups and downs, conditions, she was schooled to go with the flow. Adaptable is the word. Adapting early in her marriage, in changing stations in career, adapting later on when my dad got sick, and she became a practical nurse, then in a big house all alone, and finally moving into Marquette Manor with its bustling agenda and crowds of people. Adapting from robust health to increasing infirmity. The bitter with the better at each juncture, she took life as it came and never did much whimpering. She had been raised that way and figured some jolts and disappointments and even tragedy along the way were part of the contract. Her

last years saw the activity tapering, but when you are still packing your bags to see Panama and the Galapagos at 90, it says maybe it's "tapered" but not "stopped". She kept going as long as her body would allow her to travel.

And when the body made life no longer pleasant or even endurable, she felt it was time to retire same and make one more move. She greeted death with equanimity, even welcoming it because the life she had lived was no longer possible nor much fun, and she was ready for the last, the final change. And slipped away a week ago, unafraid. Sustained by a fairly practical kind of theology, the one she had learned in German, at St. John's Evangelical Lutheran Church when she went through the catechism and was confirmed at 12. It was the kind that used to drive me up the wall, but like sticking to her principles or her convictions, she stayed fast on her religion. She believed in God, the Bible, and the hereafter. Believed the Bible verbatim, even when I'd tell her it made no sense. It amounts to having faith in her faith. Believing would make it so, which is far profounder than might appear at first glance. Which allowed her to move into the next world with perfect confidence and a measure of peace.

Like St. Paul, she was a scrapper and had fought the good fight, had finished the course and had surely kept the faith as she understood and believed it. With this ceremony we bid her a final farewell, grateful for what she was and what she has done for us, each in the family remembering her until our dying day. What a gal. So long, Maw, we'll really miss you. But none of us will ever forget. ∎

Accommodating an Imperfect Society

September 1992

One of the confounding things about our world, whether in the field of athletics, the tractor business, politics, the United Way, or the highway system, is the inevitability of inadequacy — the fact that few elements in our society are working as well as they might. We are confronted nightly with imperfections of said world, as represented in the Yugoslav outrage or the fragmentation of the Russian empire or the misery in Afghanistan — all ironically suggesting it used to be better under iron dictatorships. Yet these were thought so bad, people struggled long and hard to overturn them. Then from an imperfect system, they went into one of confusion, chaos, and insecurity where practically nothing worked, including a way to elbow back onto firmer ground. All the while holding up the glimmering mirage of the political system developed in the United States as the model to achieve affluence, stability, opportunity and another color television set. It is the problem of knowing where you want to go, but like some confounding bad dream, never being able to run fast enough or find the right route to get there. And then, in the interim — which may be a lifetime or three generations — having to put up with what is less than satisfactory.

We look for perfection because we are mostly Calvinists at heart, aware of life's weakness and failure, but dedicated in our working, waking hours to addressing identified problems. The church, for example, rarely commends us on our conduct, but rants instead about how much sin there is, how much backsliding, how rampant the forces of evil. It is obsessed with human and societal weakness because its purpose is to challenge sin and eradicate it (or at least as much as can be reasonably expected). This model (harping about what is wrong) is not restricted to the theological field; it is replicated in social, economical, athletic, et al., institutions and populations as well. In business, we don't look at the monthly statement to see how much comfort we might take, but to find out where the expenses got out of line, margins slipped and what went wrong this month so we can address our business transgressions. We look for trouble in order to correct it. And if that Calvinistic practice is applied to the big wide wonderful world, there is a lot of trouble thus to confront and a lot of work to do. The process again

assumes evaluating the frailty and failure extant in the given system, and assuming when corrected, a measure of perfection is achieved and conditions improve. But it's a continual grind. Mankind itself is imperfect, so inevitably produces institutions or circles, communities or enterprises reflecting endemic shortcomings and the result is a world in general which is sorely in need of a major ministry — or surgery, or transfusion, replacement, redress, or redirection. More than just slightly overwhelming.

It won't surprise anyone to note the tractor business is also eternally concerned with the nature of the oversights and the weaknesses extant therein. Because when something goes wrong, relationships are impacted adversely and the end product suffers. And we are on trial with not only every deal, but every transaction. Like the Bosnians or the Moldavians, however, the impact is realized after the fact, not before. Our existing weakness is rarely identified until after the mistake is made and the damage already done. So the corrective action now deals with repairing whatever the bungle, hat-in-hand, before the transgressee — whether customer, banker, other department, tax agency, lessee, neighboring dealer, manufacturer, or whatever — he against whom we have "sinned" and then correcting the factors which created the miscue.

The tractor business, of course, is analogous to human society, since the same dynamics apply; when an eruption appears (in Yugoslavia, the S&L's, Indiana's lottery mirage, etc.) there are out-of-sync root causes that lead to the breach on one hand, and the clean up of damage on the other, and the program of preventative maintenance to shortstop the defect. It's the Serb attack against Bosnia, prompted by ethnic rivalry, religious intolerance, wounds created during the Nazi occupation, plus whatever economic or territorial greed is involved as the trigger device. Then — if possible — the repair of attitudes, of the enormous damage done to property and systems, the recreation of some political vehicle to manage the surviving society, the need for establishing an economic stem, and all the rest.

As one surveys what is wrong in his world, the appreciation dawns that the mound of ills in society is enormous and the task at hand is almost hopeless. There is thus the inclination to say, "It is all too much to handle," or to say, "Not my problem," or most often, "There is nothing I can do about it," which lets most of humanity cop out. The problem-creators in our human fellowship are, of course, legion, while those doing the repair work far too few. Bad imbalance here.

Complicated by another dilemma: the fact that there may not be solutions to all of life's shortcomings, inequities, aberrations and injustices. A matter of not merely "unwilling to change", but also "unable to change". It is very hard in the business world to do much about over production, about a manufacturing society that worldwide produces far more cars, television sets, tractors, backhoes and motor graders, more shoes and computers and soft drinks than the world can utilize or consume. Unable to correct that condition, we live with intense competition which drives down margins, requires rigorous expense control, and curtails expansion prospects or addition of capital investment. On the users, where a similar condition of too many contractors, too many coal mines, et al. exists, it leads to hard bargaining, tentative buying, short-term commitments, extensive leasing "'til we see how things work out," and high expectations from the supplier. Over supply also leads to fewer manufacturers, fewer dealers, fewer contractors, fewer coal mines. Their departure, however, did not correct the imbalance, so great is the output of the remaining industrial world. The point in all of this being the fact that, despite our desire to eradicate life's harsher circumstances, many will exist because we cannot, within our systems, do so. Reinhold Niebuhr is said to have dealt with all this in a slogan that pleaded: "God grant me the serenity to accept the things I cannot change, the courage to change the things I can, and the wisdom to know the difference."

Apostles of the philosophy are inclined to do all three things both rightly and wrongly including "serenity to accept" when in reality, it is a situation in which change indeed could be made. I'm not an expert on Islam, but sense a great penchant there to credit a good many injustices, inequities, misfortune and hard living to destiny. He is a beggar and blind, while I am rich "because Allah wills it." If that is the case, should I be meddling with his condition? If Allah wants him broken on life's rack or wheel, do I dare intervene, beyond the requirement to give alms? I can't push this too hard, but the point will be using the impossibility of change as an alibi for not trying. In talking about the poor folks of Galilee in one of

his observations, Jesus is reported to have suggested that he was there but a brief time, but "the poor you will have with you always." Oh? Why?

With respect to Niebuhr's three options, seems to me the business community offers a decent model to consider because its very survival depends on avoiding too many "transgressions," "changing the things (it) can" and then continually improving its processes. It does so partly because of professional pride, but ultimately as an element of necessity. Competition, the user, the friendly folks at Caterpillar (in my case) all call us to account and measure us continually. The closer to perfection, the nearer to success; the farther from perfection, the more proximate is failure. And like other institutions, this is not a narrow band measured on a single element; this is a spectrum of judgments made across all our stores and departments, not periodically, but hourly; not on the machinery, but on the product support, financing accommodation, promptness of service, employee attitude, price, et al. What this sort of scrutiny does is keep us on our toes and make us wish the federal government had such a simple and arbitrary measure of success and the same accountability: get it done right or we'll do business with someone else. Or makes us wish the church were evaluated weekly on the quality of sermons, condition of the buildings, service to the member; or the U.N. or the bank, or the Middle East, or the factions in Somalia all ordered to shape up or ship out.

The problem is that copping out and yet surviving — adopting the "What can I do?" attitude — creates and sustains whole battalions of losers who we tolerate as part of the system, who, like the poor, become inevitable in our society. They exist because the discipline all of us applied to the marketplace is rarely exercised elsewhere in society. How strange that Calvinism affects my tractor operation more directly and more wholesomely than it does the school system, the Republican party, the governor, or Medicare. No one likes the rigor involved in our competitive industry, but who can deny its benefits or who says that element of continual evaluation from the user is not the best thing that ever happened to us? It makes us do things we might consign to "the things I cannot change," instead of being about the job of providing a new service or finding another way to attack a problem.

So on the business front, we adopt the attitude that every day is another occasion to either "prove up" or fail, on some fronts, on most, or on all. We stay vigilant because we know that systems and people are imperfect and the objective is to minimize the frequency and extent of error, not necessarily to achieve some sublime perfection. The objective is to do the best we can, knowing full well that we may fall short of "the golden mean", but given what's available in the marketplace, supply that which is both reputable and sufficient for the time. In society, it is disappointing that there are so many worried about conditions and so few at work to bring redress. In business, the same worry exists about the same relative situations, but it is not our option to plow in or take a pass. It is mandatory that all of us stay at work in search of the best performance as a necessity for survival. As long as the user demands an accountable performance, our success depends upon meeting their standards, which are achieved only through the very best effort we can sustain. ■

P.E. hosting annual employee awards.

History of Construction II

September 1992

There are few treatises in the Ancient World on the technical science of construction in any of its manifestations — buildings, roads, canals, monuments, residential projects, aqueducts, theatres, public baths, etc. But the prospect did exist for surveying, for measuring, leveling and compacting, for gravity feed of water (sometimes even uphill), for the construction of reservoirs, channels for draining swamps, terracing fields, etc. Knowledge comes from references or accounts, from archeology, from pictures on walls or in mosaics on floors, in tombs or on monumental stellae, sometimes even from the scriptures. The Prophet Isaiah, Chapter 40, talks obliquely about earth-moving trade in 500 B.C. It tells us when the King of Kings (Persia) traveled in state, construction crews preceded him to assure a smooth road. In Verse 4, we read of making "straight in the desert a highway", i.e. "Every valley shall be lifted up and every mountain and hill be made low and the uneven ground shall become level and the rough places a plain". We are filling in the low areas, cutting through the mountains, grading the chuck holes, and giving the monarch a level ride. The art of cut and fill, the science of compaction and drainage, the recourse to borrow pits and engineering are at least 2,500 years old.

In the succeeding empire of the Greeks, circa 335 B.C., we know of extensive port and city building, the creation of temples and monuments, but since the tenure of Alexander was relatively short, great international projects were sort of put on the back burner until his successors, three or four generations later, were replaced by Rome. And here, of course, the grandest builder of all times.

Anyone who travels in Europe, the Middle East or North Africa is well aware of the fantastic skill of those engineers and builders. From Hadrian's Wall on the Scottish border, south to Aswan in Egypt, the Roman dominion moved: eastward from Britain, following the line of the Rhine, Danube, and Euphrates to the deserts, east of modern Syria and Jordan. Most of the major cities within this line are expanded Roman camps or products of Roman auspices, marked to this day with ruins in varying stages of disintegration, attesting the long, durable impact. Founded in 753 B.C., the Roman Empire fell officially to Odoacer in 476 A.D., a total span of 1,229 years. But a lot of this was "warm up" or "cool down" time. Appius Claudius completed a road we call the Appian Way (about 350 miles), linking Rome to the heel of the Italian boot (Brindisium) in 312 B.C. So there is a fairly cohesive political unit at this point and already building solidly. At the twilight stage, Constantine "hung it up" in 335 A.D. and after his departure, although periods of strength and hope, for the most part it is a badly managed enterprise on the way to "Chapter 11" and then total bankruptcy. But that's still some 650 years of world domination.

And since we have introduced Appius Claudius, we have also broached the subject of road construction, carried on by he and successors with slave labor, by individual contractors, by recruited paid labor and, of course, by the Roman legions. The Roman Interstate Highway System totaled some 50,000 plus miles of highways linking up all the major centers of her domain. We have 40,000 miles in our system called "Interstate Highway Defense System", Rome also built hers for defense reasons: to supply and reinforce the 30 legions which were strung around the periphery of the Empire (in Augustus' time) assuring the pax Romana, and the myriad activities, thus fostered.

Roman roads ran straight as a die since Roman axles were affixed to the body of the cart and could not turn. They ran up hill and down with appropriate minimal cutting and filling and were painstaking in design. The construction commenced with an engineer-surveyor laying out the course, giving care to alignment and levels. When the stakeman had marked it as ordered, a plow furrowed a delineated

This style and symmetry define the culture that produced it.

outer edge and then loosened the soil in between. The excess fill was removed (by baskets) and carried away or more likely dumped into a low spot. Tampers beat down the bottom layer, preparing it for the first course, one of sand or lime mortar followed by an 18-inch layer of fist-sized stones cemented together. Then a 10-inch layer of limed concrete and broken stone, then followed by another foot of mixed gravel, compacted with a roller, but swelled to 18 inches in the center so the surface was crowned. Finally, the *sumum dorsum*, the wearing surface, often made of crushed sand and gravel compacted into place, but usually replaced (or originally furnished) with 6-8 inch polygonal blocks, fit into place like a jigsaw puzzle, and socked into wet concrete. The whole thing, despite its painful construction, was four to five feet thick and lasted maybe 20 to 40 years before repairs were necessary since such a locked-together mass was not as flexing as it might be. Roads were from 16 to 24 feet wide; curbs were two feet each and 18 inches high, often with paved footpaths alongside; milestones marked the distance from Rome, and the name of the emperor who last worked on a given stretch.

Which suggest to us that construction of a massive highway system was not the only work for contractors. Periodically, sections had to be resurfaced or rebuilt, and although there is extensive use of concrete, alas, no blacktop that I know of. In its entirety, a marvelous system, linking the empire and facilitating its sundry functions. Some of the bridges built in those days still carry traffic today. So effective the entire undertaking and so smooth the travel, Tiberius (in a given mission) moved along those roads 180 miles in a single day, a feat not surpassed in terms of expedition until the middle of the 19th century. (I suppose the advent of railroads.)

Three other major elements of Roman construction which kept our predecedents occupied were a system of aqueducts, great public buildings, and the city baths. We all have seen pictures of the Roman forum and the great glistening temples to the gods of dedicatory edifices to emperors and heroes as well as remnants of the Senate building, the Roman courts, markets, etc. Hadrian's tomb is virtually intact, and the forum of Trajan, the commemorative arch of Constantine, and the Flavian theater called the Colosseum, and the remnants of the emperors' homes in the Palatine, all remind us of that period. But the most striking building of the lot is the Pantheon, first built by Agrippa (Octavian's colleague and commander) in about 27 B.C. and remodeled by the architect-emperor, Hadrian, around 128 A.D. Unique because in that world of rectangular structures, this was a combination of box and sphere. A great round dome mounted on a quadrangular base with the orb itself measuring 130 feet from side to side and 130 feet from the top to the floor of the building. Amazing to me because the vast dome is made of poured concrete. Talk about a "forming" miracle and the painstaking ingenuity involved in getting all that concrete up there and into the wooden forms, and you are talking about some real craftsmanship. This is the oldest, intact, roofed building in the ancient world and unique for both design and construction.

Aqueducts tell us something about Roman discrimination, along with Roman engineering because this people was not about to dip into the Tiber or the Arno or the Po for drinking water as the Egyptians or Indians or Chinese today. Water came from fresh springs carried in stone ducts or lead pipes to the great cities. Thousands of miles of channels bringing fresh water to fountains, baths,

Unique because an inscription credits this aqueduct to Pontius Pilate.

Hadrian's Cenotaph-World's most enduring and monumental tomb.

even the homes of Roman citizens. There were 1,300 miles of aqueducts serving the City of Rome alone, delivering 300 million gallons of fresh water each 24 hours. That's 300-400 gallons per citizen, per day, which is twice as much as we used in Indianapolis in 1992. A good deal of this went to the public baths since many Romans bathed daily, usually in a public facility, but private homes also had tubs replete with taps. In 33 B.C. there were 170 bathing facilities in the city; three centuries later, 856 of these plus 1,352 swimming pools. Nine different emperors erected new and loftier accommodations. The baths of Caracalla and Diocletian accommodated 3,000 bathers at a single time or 30,000-40,000 a day — each. The complex which housed the cold, warm, and hot water services was 270,000 square feet in size (six acres under roof) and was a virtual shopping mall with places to eat and drink, to gossip and shop, to politic, and romance. I suppose joggers in those days could get their morning exercise by making a couple of laps, and if one wanted a bath at the end of the run, the cost was 1½ cents — one quadran. Built of Roman brick, niched and arched and decorated with hundreds of busts, statues, urns, and decorative pieces, these things reared up 90-100 feet high and so mammoth were the proportions, one became a model a century ago for the Union Station in New York.

The glory of Rome is not simply the glory of her military commanders or seasoned legions or administrative genius, but work as well of her architects, designers, engineers, and contractors. There was no fresh water without the construction of aqueducts, no baths or great buildings without the skill of the designer, the techniques of the masons, the art of the earthmover, the builder, and their inevitable services. I've always been proud of my particular vocation for this very reason. Since time immemorial, it has been dedicated to the building or the rebuilding or the reshaping of society. It was — and is — critical to man's comfort, security, internal political processes, and societal patterns. We don't expand or facilitate or accommodate or improve or revitalize very much of our American systems today without construction being involved, and I submit this is as old as Rome whether 312 B.C. or 335 A.D. ■

Christmas Past

December 1992

It is difficult for me to write a "Christmas-sy" piece without getting theological — or at least quasi-religious. But it is that kind of holiday after all, right? And though I never got far off the curbstone in my theological development, there is enough lingering orientation to understand the Christmas event in terms of its identified context. One content historical, the other religious. The historic frame was a watershed period in history, i.e. the early stage of the Roman Empire, 23 years after Octavian had become "Princeps", then Imperator; was named Augustus and also Pontifex Maximus; the era during which he overhauled the Roman vehicle after a century of civil war and gave it a structure and momentum to carry it on through more than three and a half centuries of greatness. The birth of Jesus is identified more precisely as taking place "in the days of Herod the (Judean) King", which translates in Indiana to something like 4 B.C. (Always seemed strange to have Jesus born four years "before Christ"), but blame that on Dionysius Exiguus whose incredible sorting of "B.C.'s" from "A.D.'s" established through listing the tenures of consuls, the reigns of kings, the spans of pharaohs, number of Olympiads, et al., laid out a timeline, so we know who lived when and how long. Missing it all by only four years is great work, believe me. All sans computers. And using those numbers that dated Moses at MCCXI, B.C. or Solomon at DCCCCXXII or was it (CMXXII?).

That was the historic context. The "religious" relevance is less complicated. It says simply that though the nativity — and thus the first Christmas — might have occurred in 4 B.C., it is not about 4 B.C. or the world of Caesar Augustus. It is about today and each day since then. It is a metaphor used by Christians to get the concept of God into a form whereby they can begin to deal with Him (It?) on a basis which has some utility. In short, it followed that as long as gods remained aloof on Olympus or Sinai or even heaven, they remained disdainful of the human partnership. What's the point in creating the world and then taking off, to reside elsewhere as though this planet were simply inadequate and the creation undeserving of attention.

The nativity was ultimately reinterpreted as a phenomenon called "the incarnation", which is really too esoteric to dwell on, but ends up bringing God to earth. Christians feel He is part of this day's dynamic

Izmir, Turkey.

because the church is His indwelling, ongoing, perpetual vehicle, manifesting His love and power. I'm not trying to convert anyone; I'm trying to deal with the religious relevance of Christmas in terms of those historic and theological perspectives and saying the point in time when this shift took place was maybe 4 B.C., though no one knew it or understood what was really happening 'til Paul declared it, maybe 50 years later.

There is a bifurcation, a duality at work here. I journeyed back into that age, figuratively, kicking around Western Turkey recently visiting Troy, Nicea and Miletus; roaming through Smyrna, Ephesus, Halicarnasus, and a dozen other cities, all mutely outlined in the tumbled columns and capitals, overturned altars and tilting walls, the stone remnants of a thousand small shops along miles of still intact flagstone streets. Went there to observe and marvel at the monumental buildings which our forbearers reared into place, awed with the protean stature of their baths, the silent theatres, the ubiquitous temples, all abundant in Turkey. The old forum or agora there is less cluttered by modern city development, less encroached upon, is grander in scale, richer in terms of artistic achievement and far more profuse than Greece or Rome. All this priceless, orderly classical debris, once the bustling, glistening, overwhelming evidence of the power of the empire — or the city — or the state — "in the days of Herod the King".

But, remnants from a culture long gone, whose institutions are mostly forgotten. We saw the melancholy residue of a society dead for 16 centuries. How strange to visit a land only to view what the ancients produced, what former generations created, because that legacy far outshines the contribution of this day's population. People come to our world to see what Disney has done in those two intriguing experiments; or try Hollywood to look at handprints in concrete or ride up the Sears Tower to dine atop the world's tallest building, or maybe even stop in Peoria to see a tractor

Looks like a project where architects disagree.

three stories high that sells for a million dollars. But who would go to Greece today if you eliminated the remnants of the past? Italy would be a basket case if we removed from her landscape the glory of either the empire or the Renaissance. How strange to still be coasting on the momentum created ages ago, the shell remaining, but the spirit departed.

So the historic world vibrant and burgeoning at the time of the nativity is today little more than a relic, a souvenir of the past, a reminder of what once was, now without utility or practical value. But the religious product of the nativity event retains a vitality and a stubbornness which continues to function and influence with a force, unabated. It was not the product of an age like the religions it replaced, but out of man's long search for cause and meaning and purpose, bringing a new inspiration, universal in character, limitless in scope which continues to shape western society. It is as though the temporal/physical and the spiritual are contrasted: that which was the architectural milieu, left behind in its glamorous yet impressive wreckage harbors history and memories while that which is the theological, became virtually eternal and pulsates with life yet today — Christmastime and beyond.

So this particular season in the liturgical calendar reminds us of our long tradition of change as well as the need to hold fast to that which is good. With one hand governing the psyche and the soul, the other altering the physical universe, whether hearthside, city or nation as history bends us (or is bent) to accommodate the rolling years. It says that certain truths are eternal, certain principles irrefragable, some precepts and tenets forever relevant. Within that state of ambivalence, a subtle message appeared telling us that the evolving religion which would flourish within a century of Herod's or Augustus' departure was to reveal or enunciate imperishable truths and in the process fashion a new society. One better than the social systems it supplanted, possessing an equanimity which

both changed our way of thinking, and when it could not, worked within the residing structure and continue to pulsate and to function. Change when we can; minister, heal, commiserate and console when we cannot.

We don't think about this (being generally a bit ignorant of the 1st Century Roman World), but there wasn't much love around before Jesus got here. A mother's affection for the family and a guarded sympathy between siblings, but tradition, duty, the state and the gods encouraged a stoic sort of discipline with no room for weakness. And none for those outside the caste or clique. Outpourings of sympathy or concern or empathy for those suffering, in trouble, diseased or starving were not a normal thing. We have to be tough and endure life's vicissitudes; we don't spend a lot of time short-stopping or eradicating or eliminating them before they get here. Courage, not compassion, is the order of the day; fortitude before friendship; power is the secret, gentleness or collegiality is too expensive to try.

The first Christmas went largely unheralded. Truth of the matter is, the "mass of Christ", i.e. Christ-mass doesn't appear in the Christian calendar 'til the 5th Century. It is a very subtle event, and its impact is still inclined to misunderstanding. Only in retrospect did the whole drama become clear, only to thoughtful people today is its import perceived. We have to ask if Christmas is really about wise men and shepherds and angel choirs. If its true symbols are lighted trees, gift packages, plum pudding, caroling and Santa Claus. This surely is not its substance. We are inclined to read into things…political candidates, the stock market, biblical texts, current morality and holidays…what we want to find there, creating verities where none exist because we like to be comfortable, we like happy situations. Ergo, the shopping and the stuffed turkey, the holly and mistletoe. But in my mind, these only identify the holiday. At its core Christmas is about other people. It is not about me. It is rededication to the ethnic which sees service to those in need as true replication of its underlying principles. It is remembering there is partnership between the human and the divine. It is about love, and it is about grace and gratitude and selflessness, stuff sophisticated adults don't discuss very well or very often. It's a moment of recommitment to the family; it's a remembrance of seasons past; friends and relatives of long ago. It is reflection, introspection and charity. It is a moment for refurbishing the elusive element of love that appeared when Herod was king and struggles yet for control and a direction of the human spirit. ■

1993

Hope? or Hope!

March 1993

Not only are most Republicans watching the unfolding strategy of the new administration, the entire planet is tuned in to view the early direction President Clinton is taking. We are anxious to see how much of his campaign oratory converts into substantive agenda and how many changes he thought so important in terms of America's future will not be made; campaigning being one exercise; governing another. The rubber has now hit the road. We have spent a year proclaiming, expounding and illustrating our national weaknesses and defects. Now that we know, do we have the skill or courage to fix them?

As the Administration begins to change America, we shall encounter a rarely discussed aspect of the system itself. Familiar as we are with the original struggle to get this confederation into a federal state, we have often missed a nuance in that early dynamic… the one of both 1776 and 1787. We have missed the fact that there was no single vision for America nor ideal system, universally saluted. There were

differing viewpoints, one of which became orthodoxy. The others did not dry up and blow away; they stayed submerged and remain, reminding us that societal unanimity was not achieved under our Constitution. A major theme prevailed and dominated while those who were unenthusiastic reluctantly acceded, but never concurred with all its premises.

Which I'm sure is anything but clear. What happened to us as a people in the 18th Century was a protracted exercise in autonomous government. Though we were colonies of Great Britain with mixed nationalities and under sundry auspices, there was a good deal of self-rule. O.K., so George First, Second, or Third was the sovereign and the parliament governed ultimately, but at colonial levels each town, county or colony did fashion constitutions or ordinances, laws and governance vehicles. Particularly

Howard Chandler Christy's *Scene at the Signing of the Constitution of the United States* in Philadelphia on September 17, 1787. (*Source: Wikimedia Commons.*)

after July 4, 1776, when each became self-governing.

When the time came in 1787 to write a new constitution which realized the newly won freedoms, every single guy sent to Philadelphia had previous experience at elective or appointive office…in elected assemblies, as officers of the state, appointed positions representing a given body and often had helped fashion the documents under which he served. Each understood "the drill" a lot better than most of us do today since each was experienced in managing the state (or parts thereof).

But who were these men…the Masons, Rutledges, Gerrys, the Randolphs, Wilsons, Franklins, Morrises, and Hamiltons? In the first place, they were all male, right? Right! In the second place, they were all property owners because under the Articles of Confederation, only property holders could vote. In the third place, they were leaders in their own communities. They were people of influence. And, of course, all were free. They were educated; they could speak, think, debate; most could write well, and they knew political reality. It's unique that at this moment, we probably sent the finest brains we had to do a given assignment, a fact of history probably never achieved before and never replicated since.

So what kind of a document did they write to create what kind of system? They created a body of law and a system which could be used by such men as they were and which presumed men could reason independently, were Americans because they wanted to get ahead, would be able to start farms, cut timber, run plantations or sailing vessels or shops or small plants. A governance apparatus which would appeal to the enterprising, would facilitate the settling and exploitation of the frontier, compete in the world of trade with Britain, France, and Holland by protecting the formation of businesses, including contracts for labor or materials and generally convert the raw materials of the nation into capital. They assumed that independent men would want as little government as possible, but wanted instead the shelter of government to support and protect their fishing, farming, trapping, wholesaling, their inventions, their beef, cheese, and shops. Would assure their rights to import silk and tea and porcelain for sale here, their contracts with merchant agents in Amsterdam, London and Paris for the distribution of cotton, tobacco and indigo, et al.

So the emphasis was to accommodate the doers, support those anxious to create or build, enable those who would acquire the good things of life, all under the protection of the law. Nothing wrong with all of this because they saw the greatness in America blossoming as the result of human initiative and endeavor, building a society wherein freedom under the law meant opportunity to expand, experiment and produce. For ourselves and for profit. The incentive to achieve was thus engendered by protecting those anticipated rewards which had first triggered the quest, plus the investment, the effort or the risk. Equal justice before the law thus laid a continent open to exploitation by those who wanted to either search for the Grail or grab the brass ring.

Only trouble, of course, is that a lot of people found themselves at a disadvantage in seeking the American dream. A quarter of the population in 1776 was slaves. Fat chance they had to get rich or to become entrepreneurs. Half the population was female and had no role in governance, exploited as they were by the chauvinism of the 18th Century males in a fashion different than Europe, but still repressive. The lack of incentives or encouragement blocked out most of life from female participation. What this is saying is that had the women or the slaves written the Constitution, it would have been a dramatically different document, one instead securing <u>their</u> rights and potential. The two viewpoints — theirs and Madison's — were vastly different.

Beyond is another group in the common man, the "great unwashed" to which this applied in varying degrees. The immigrant without connections or education, the freed indentured servant, the grown children from the large families, laborers, the settlers

P.E. still types all of his articles on a typewriter.

along the frontiers, and the trappers, all scrambling for a living, and not generally knowledgeable about the opportunities provided through the phenomenon of commerce. The rights of free speech or freedom to assemble or to worship were hardly hot button items with them. They would hardly care in which house of Congress spending bills originated or whether foreign soldiers could be quartered among us, whether or not we created titles of nobility or whether search warrants were a necessary thing. What might be high on their list of needs from the government would be good roads, protection from the red varmints, maybe education for their kids, medical help in time of trouble, some instruction in building houses, clearing forests, tilling fields, harvesting and storing crops.

There might be some commonality between their constitution and that fashion by the slave/female sector, but there would be differences too. Homesteaders became owners and could vote, had vested interests to protect, and when successful, moved from one class up to the next whereas the slave/female segment was locked in place.

You get the point by now: we tend to take care of our own, and the early framers (of the Constitution) did that pretty well. But wisely. Because the ensuing scramble would be for all to achieve full privilege and status, enjoying the benefits of the Constitution. As it turned out, that did work. One day, *Voila*! Slavery was gone; women were emancipated (some of us think) (well, at least they can vote and they do own most of the wealth in the nation), and the system applies far more universally. What was conceived and implemented, lopsided as it was, did form a broad enough umbrella to gather most of society under its shelter over time and provides now not for a minority of the powerful and educated, but to an extent for the vast majority of Americans.

But not all. There are still countless millions who do not agree with the way the system works and who do not share in the opportunities provided. There is still racial prejudice, equating to disenfranchisement. There are still those ignorant and uneducated (16.5 million) who cannot compete because they cannot read and write and are not skilled enough to grab the brass ring, no matter how long the carousel keeps circling. Thirteen percent of Americans fall below the poverty level. Beyond that, the system of equality which is so proudly proclaimed as our founding premise means all citizens are equal before the law when they can afford a lawyer. "Equal" — when the bank account and political savvy are equal".

The conservative argument to all this is simply that the governmental apparatus in America is constituted to encourage options and opportunities; it is not mandated to furnish them. The poor, the homeless, the "great unwashed" or the unfortunate ethnic element say, "Wrong, the nation is wealthy enough to supply the needs of all. If for some reason I cannot compete in the system set up, who says the government should not serve my needs just as it does those who scramble, get lucky or inherit." They say the system as established is still rigged for a certain category of people and ignores or disenfranchises or loads against the dumb, the lazy, the luckless or those lacking a lot of drive. Just as the original one did.

It is to this element, those somehow "looking in", that Clinton has made his appeal, and it is to those serried ranks of gainsayers that he must shape some response. The group includes, of course, those who backed him in the campaign, meaning blacks, the unions, the urban populace, the freedom of "choice-ers", the poor, gays, and women, among others. Banding together because they want their piece of the pie. Whether or not cutting it for them is good for the future of the nation, President Clinton, will have to sort out. It was great in campaigning because it helped get him elected. How about the long haul?

The Virginia Constitution, the one built for the enterprising, the gifted, the landed-or-commercial-aristocracy, has served us well for the past two centuries, though it has not served us equally. Not if we cannot capitalize on its options or its opportunities. That "other" half, those ignored early and more recently failing to qualify or benefit, have now raised the issue of cutting them in. At the expense of guess who? If somehow successfully shunted aside with occasional eruptions from time to time and some progress on their agenda under Kennedy, mostly Johnson and Carter, it is now a different ball game. We now have a chance to shift our priorities and our budgeting in response to the clamor raised by those who elected the President. It is one thing to be hoping or wishing vainly when we are on the outside, but it is a far more interesting matter when "our guy" is not in the White House and has promised to cut us in to the action. All of which will challenge the power structure because of the very size of the undercurrent now mounting and because of the attitude of the new administration. How he deals with this, and how the whole engagement affects the rest of America will be interesting to see. ■

Which Generation Is Right?

June 1993

There is a growing suspicion that I'm going to have more trouble with President Clinton than I originally suspected and though content to give him all the rope he needs, there is a bit of irritation building up. Most of the dissatisfaction stems from our divergent viewpoints about what the role of government is and isn't, and what we ought to be doing about national problems. I'm a great believer in the prospect that sometimes when confronted with a dilemma, the best possible course for ultimate resolution is to do nothing and let existing forces (e.g. the economy) work through the established process. One has to also believe that dilemmas — unsolved problems, given weaknesses or shortcomings — are part of the equation, are inevitable, their existence integral to the dynamic, and they are endemic in any given system. A society or institution or business (or family, for that matter) that doesn't have problems is not normal.

We are parting ways for starters on one of Mr. Clinton's favorite acorns, on what he views to be a major national dereliction: the standard of living in the good ole US of A. The particular philosophy that thinks it is a crime because "this will be the first generation of Americans who will not live as well as did its parents" to paraphrase his contention. We need to look at this and wonder what is so gross about it. I mean, "So what?" Or if it is accurate, is it analogous? Is it important?

My parents only married once and had two sons, Dave and I. Luckier than most, we were considered "upper middle class". My father's income was always well up into the top 20th percentile so we weren't ever hungry or wanting life's necessities. Mostly, because that was a different age with the nation still expanding, building, inventing, exporting and creating the structure from which we'd double our population, i.e. 120,000,000 to 240,000,000. Despite that, we **over** grew and corrected dramatically in the '30s.

A long correction, devastating in its economic and social impact through a thing called "The Great Depression" which lasted from 1930 'til the war broke out at the tail end of 1941. People have forgotten that the unemployment rate on Pearl Harbor Day was down to 17%, without riots or a wave of wrist-slashings and suicides. In those days, before or during the depression, we managed without school lunches, un-employment compensation, Social Security, Medicaid or Medicare. There was no Aid to Dependent Children; welfare, if ever received, came from the county. This was prior to pensions for retirees, and there were no farm subsidies for the great numbers struggling on America's farms. There was no SBA or Fannie Mae; no federal aid to education or student loans; no minimum wage; no UDAG grants or distribution of highway funds for county roads and city streets. Expectations were low; pride was high.

We haven't clearly defined what President Clinton specifies to be the precise "generation" which lived so much better than this current one, but I'd submit he could help them a lot in his rhetorical analogy if he'd keep in mind the detail that marked and identified my generation. If he thinks it's a lot tougher today because of what our kids or grandkids don't have, he might check the current federal budget and he'll find so many give-away programs for people it will make his head swim. From a society that practiced individual responsibility and taught self-sufficiency, we have shifted to one whose greatest societal expense is payments to people. Seven or eight hundred billion passed out to old people, poor people, farm people, sick people, homeless people, racially oppressed people and lazy people, even dumb people. My generation which had it so good shifted for itself; solved its problems at state and local levels or simply went without. If he thinks that was easier than today, he's nuts. If he thinks all this is necessary, he's wrong. If he thinks it gets votes, he's on target.

Maybe he's referring to the post-depression gang, my kids, who caught the cycle on an upswing. They got the standard up — but high. When I was a kid, we had one car in the family, the Maxwell my father drove as County Commissioner and then as a salesman. One car for four of us! Becky and I had four children and by the time each had reached the age of 16, he/she had a set of wheels. And, of course, my suburban wife needed one, so we had six cars in our family. Six hundred percent increase in one generation. Looks like we switched from necessity to profligacy.

Our old home had one radio, an Atwater Kent console in the front room which gave us our last minute news and also gave us "Amos and Andy", "Graham McNamee" or maybe "Jack Armstrong".

Today, my kids (and I) have a minimum of three colored television sets per family plus probably all-tolled, four radios each (counting the car and the Walkman). Some real deprivation here. We no longer settle for what we need, but make judgments on what we want. Beyond that, seems to me he is using "things" as a measurement, presuming that the central issue in society is accumulation of properties or substance.

The rat race to acquire tends to shift the focus. The somewhat primitive conditions under which I lived and the chastening discipline of the depression did something to our degree of expectation, self-reliance, spirit of community, family concepts. Maybe — no longer relevant because in certain respects the current generation is the darling of history; most blessed (at least) from the standpoint of its diet, medical benefits, comfort, lifestyle, leisure options, income, etc., etc. How much they **have** compared to mine or that of my children is a specious comparison.

Because it is apparent to me that the higher our standard of living is extended and the more sophisticated our gadgetry, the deeper becomes our dilemma and more exponential the growth of societal problems. The faster we scramble for things, the more we become vassal to the bank, the mortgage company, peer pressure, and the plastic card, the higher the illegitimacy, the larger the drug culture, the faster the school drop-out rate, the bigger the unemployment line, the more diverse and profuse the crime rate.

Mr. Clinton ought to be hammering us on values rather than material blessings. He ought to be looking at morals and ethics between the two generations and wonder if the scramble to get a new house in the suburbs is not directly connected to individual value systems and fundamental motivational urges. I'm not sitting in judgment on one generation at the expense of another, but I'm saying the emphasis on things is the wrong one, because how much more one has than another is exactly what has been wrong with the governmental philosophy for the past 45 years. The idea that all should share equally in the nation's wealth through same number of TV's, cars, homes, a guaranteed job, and a pension is a fantasy, born of some bad "trip" or mental aberration. What we ought to be passing around and pressing to make universal in this free land are traditional values. And the first one of these ought to be a re-emphasis on personal responsibility as the key element in fashioning a successful or fruitful life. It is outrageous the way we hammer on the school system because one-fifth of our kids graduate from metropolitan schools as functional il-

literates. It is a disgrace that school grounds are dangerous and the timid are browbeaten by the bullies. Because the system has broken down and is not doing its job.

The institution at fault here, however, is not the school system, it is the family system. When did we conclude that manners and morés are the responsibility of the teacher rather than the parent? That a kid carrying a knife into the classroom is an indication of **teacher** dereliction because it wasn't discovered? Why in the hell isn't the parent of such a menace hauled before some tribunal and required to account for such flagrant misbehavior? Illiteracy is a major reason for failure in the job market. Thus, failure in creation of the family, and, in fact, failure as a participant in the game of life. It is hard to understand how any parent can stand around nonchalantly watching a youngster slowly disqualify himself from full membership in this society because said parent doesn't want to bother with some home-style tutoring or demand minimal standards of obedience. Not only for the benefit of the child, but because it is patently unfair to dump onto society the neglect and nonchalance of far too many parents who have copped out and are laughing all the way to the food stamp window.

What a change! When I got smart-alecky in school, I could look for trouble on two scores. First was the teacher who gave me half a dozen whacks with a ruler on an outstretched palm, and then the encore when I got home and my dad found out about

it. He didn't go back and raise cain with the teacher, he automatically took her side and gave me another bit of insight into correct deportment.

But back to the subject at hand which is generational disparity. And the irony of the situation wherein there **is** enough of the good life for all in America and it is each person's dream to acquire it. The potential exists to do so in the free market economy. Those who don't seem to share the benefits might want to look at their whole card. And remember Shakespeare… "The fault, dear Brutus, lies not in the stars but in ourselves." The formula for securing the good life is no secret and has several answers. One is simply luck, get the breaks; another has to do with birth and inheritance; the most common route, however, is hard work, performing, risking, and persevering. I don't know that any of the traditional modes includes one that says, "Wait patiently and vote Democratic because when they get cracking, they'll provide for us as part of our birthright."

If the most popularly accepted way is to work with some industry, stay creative, out produce or perform the competition and hope for a break, then one needs some internal conditioning. He needs to be literate, diligent, do more than his share at the workplace, do things right the first time, follow instructions, initiate, enjoy what he does. I would guess if we had a national program to suggest that preparation for life in suburbia is an option which we can choose or reject by how we discipline and condition ourselves, our outlooks, and those of our children, we'd go a long way toward evening out any generational disproportions. We'd also go a long way in getting a lot more people into the middle class and out of the welfare cycle now three generations old. People who can't hack it need to be taken care of; people who won't prepare and set their sights no higher than a relief check need to be counseled by William Clinton in terms of what their opportunities are what it will cost to realize them. They ought not be relegated to a poverty existence because they don't know or because a benign but blind bureaucracy supports them there, so no change is required.

The key is in the old story about the high-powered motivational consultant dealing with a room full of aggressive, ready-to-go salesmen and a blackboard full of stages and steps to become successful in their fields. A janitor came in, looked at the acres of verbiage and wiped most of the board clean. "This", he said, "is all far too complicated. The secret is in these three words", and he wrote on the board, "Ya Gotta Wanna". Let's talk about jobs, opportunities, education, and societal benefits as prospects, not as rights, and let's teach they are results of personal endeavor, not governmental largess. ■

Dave MacAllister

June 1993

My brother Dave was born on the 29th day of August, 1920 (which incidentally was one day before my birthday, but two years later). So we were both Virgos according to the calendar and the zodiac, but were not really all that much alike in terms of temperament, style, tastes, outlook, and general philosophy. Which was never very apparent since our lives were linked pretty closely together, and we got along famously as kids, each developing in his own way. Our career paths, moreover, bore striking similarities.

We were both raised in Oconto County, Wisconsin, which lies directly north of Green Bay, located where the Oconto River empties into "the Bay", a convenient site for a logging/lumber town. We had early schooling in Lincoln Elementary School and by the time Dave was ready for junior high, had moved to Milwaukee where our Dad was employed by Drott Tractor Company as a salesman. In 1930 he became Sales Manager, thus requiring our sad departure from Oconto. Dave matriculated successfully — and successively — (as had I) — from Steuben Junior High, from Washington High, and thence from Carroll College, getting his B.A. in the spring of 1942. He was an average student in what was a good school system, so had a better than average education and of course, in his day, only one high school graduate out of 12 finished college. In the course of his collegiate experience, we pledged the same fraternity (Phi Theta Pi). Dave became editor of the school paper, worked in the Athletic Department issuing equipment, and was the creator of Carroll's first wrestling team. He worked on the side at Drott Tractor, Waukesha Motors plus occasional duty at Goff's Restaurant. While at Carroll, he fell in love with the cute little gal across the alley from us in Milwaukee named Evelyn Kreuger who spent a year or two at Carroll and beginning in 1942 commenced a full-time career as Dave's wife. Their Golden Anniversary was last August 29th. Three sons blessed their union.

Our home moved to Indianapolis in 1941 when E.W. started the MacAllister Tractor Company as the Allis Chalmers dealer for Indiana. Dave spent what time he had after graduation working in the tractor business…pending a call from Uncle Sam. When it came, he shifted his attention to the military and ended up as a First Lieutenant in the Quartermaster

Dave MacAllister.

Corps with an overseas assignment in Paris. By the time of his return, E.W. had organized MacAllister Machinery Co., Inc. to accommodate the Caterpillar franchise which he landed in June of 1945. Part of the contract with CAT involved taking over an ag dealership in Fort Wayne owned by John Cockrell, and Dave was assigned to the new store when he got his "land legs" back in January of 1946. He knew a bit about the business from his former exposure and dove right into the race, in those days running at a brisk pace because demand was heavy and machinery in short supply. Parts and service made up a good deal of our volume.

In a year or two Dave was running the operation and looking for a better location, available rental property in 1946 being rare indeed. So he negotiated for four acres on California Road and began planning for a new store, going up in stages with the final addition (the office and parts area) opening in 1951. That was the year our father had his first stroke and when a second one hit him hard in January of 1952, it looked like we were on our own. (E.W. lived 'til January 1977.) Dave and I owned equal shares of stock, had the same salary and perks, each his own corporate responsibilities. Although the Fort Wayne Store continued to do well and although Dave loved the city and its great restaurants, Caterpillar finally nagged him a couple years later into moving to Indianapolis where as Vice President he managed the parts and service operations, meaning 85% of our people and 95% of the problems. Along with Bill Diehl in Sales and Rollo Ramaker, an old roommate from Carroll, the four of us ran the operation as a team for the next 25 years.

And they were great years. Contractors waxing

and waning as we geared for the Toll Road and got it done; re-geared for the interstate system, which over the next dozen years was completed as well. Coal was big in the early days; then sank to almost nothing with prosperous mines slowly folding and that market shrinking as well. Only to revive again in the '70s and end up constituting half our volume. The product line exploded; we tried (unsuccessfully) to add to our opportunity with lift trucks; opened branches in Plymouth, South Bend, Elkhart, Bedford and Washington to accommodate surges in demand only to fold the first four when things went sour and the markets dried up. The Washington venture hit the jackpot. It was a process of ebb and flow, flex and stiffen, expand and contract, as the situation demanded and the months rolled on 'til one day we looked around and we were all getting "long in the tooth" and began talking about a "sequential withdrawal" from the company…Bill first, then Rollo, and finally Dave in 1984. But what a great ride it was and what a terrific experience.

Dave had his own unique operating style, one a good deal like our father. It was "hands on". Being in the middle of all the action. Directing things. He was people oriented because he trusted people and his instincts more than systems. Being himself personable, he had a horde of friends in the industry both on the customer side, in the ranks of competitors, and of course, among our employees. He was popular and greatly respected. Despite his gregarious outlook, he was not a great "joiner", meaning the C of C or the NAM or partisan politics did not turn him on. His attention was focused first of all on his family, who did a great many things together and stayed extremely close. This seemed to be his major preoccupa-

tion and a priority concern, and of course, he dearly loved this business. Passionately and profoundly. He enjoyed travel to a modest degree, and England was one of his favorite destinations. He got a real kick out of Claridge's, a contrast to the rustic charm of merry England.

A prime avocation was spectator sports which saw him most of the time at Pacer and Colts games as well as frequent trips to watch the Indians. He saw a jillion World Series games and an occasional Super Bowl. He puttered with roses and grew tomatoes; was an indifferent golfer. Dave also knew and loved the good life. Good steaks, fresh steamed or broiled lobster, J&B Scotch (with a generous dollop, please), the best beers, and the inevitable El Producto cigar.

He was more than solicitous of our mother when she finally lost much of her ambulatory capacity. For years, Dave went to Marquette Manor every single Saturday with her groceries and stopped every Sunday with a hamburger and a bit of gossip. They'd have a J&B shooter and talk about old times or the weather or what the kids were doing now or maybe watch the tail end of a ball game. He never missed those weekend visits when he was in town.

Dave got waylaid by cancer and left us on the 15th of April, ten months to the day our mother departed, leaving an imprint which is surely indelible on both his family and our business. What have become fixed in terms of our operation are bits of D.W.'s philosophy and his concept of customer service. In his early days at Fort Wayne, scrambling to make a new store go and to generate all the volume he could, his guys busted their butts to take care of the owner looking for parts because once well served, he was bound to call back again. When other dealers had gone home at 5:00 PM, our store was still humming and available for service into the night. That factor of going the extra mile and working the extra hour became a talisman of the Fort Wayne operation. The concept of keeping the "Customer First" is hardly new around here. Dave invented it.

The other thing he taught us is that you don't make your money with buildings; you do it with people and with service. Dave was in the rattiest buildings in town, two stories in his parts operation and a dingy, dark, dilapidated shop four doors down the narrow street. But they were simply loci for what we do: take care of the user. It is really a matter of people skills, people attitudes, and the company's ability to do the job that built the business, not the style of the monument or the architectural purity.

E.W., Dave and P.E. MacAllister.

The other element he left was a cordial relationship with the customer. We are not IRS agents; we are in the business of selling to people who do or don't buy a product. To succeed they have to like us, trust us, depend on us, understand us, and want to do business with us. No one had a better capacity for making the owner feel important than Dave or was better at proving the value of strong personal relationships as an adjunct and benefit to our success.

In his last phase, which was not an easy one, he met it with courage and equanimity. We might observe that like Paul, he fought the good fight, had finished the course, and had kept the faith…with his family, his friends and his business. We could — and did — all learn from Brother Dave. ■

Dave MacAllister.

Politics or Policy

September 1993

The antics of politics and politicians continue to intrigue, infuriate and even confuse us. Partly because there are too many balls in the air and so many problems under foot to stew about. We feel our pattern of life is practically hopeless. All of it arising out of perceptions conveyed to us by politicos through the media about what is transpiring. Information sources invariably relate their version of the world and what they relate is the dramatic and outrageous, rarely the quiet success, the orderly society; the well-functioning institution. Beyond that on a personal level, we all tend to depict things in a fashion that serve our own purposes, imbued with a natural subjectivity, even in trying to be objective. When a major issue surfaces on the scene and sides begin to form, pro and con, this bias escalates to deliberate dissimulation while the effort is mounted to portray things, not as they are, but in a fashion to support my viewpoint. Result is, we build a case for and against what is seen and heard, supporting our viewpoint with argument and conclusion which may turn to flimsy whimsy under the dispassionate scrutiny of the rational process.

There is really nothing new in all of this. Mankind has been eternally informed by sources which are biased and have been mislead (inadvertently or deliberately) by historians or biographers. Tacitus (The Caesars) and Procopius (Theodora) wrote more slander than history. We haven't been treated much better by prophets, priests or kings either, by the way (they being the arbiters of human conduct). Again, not always deliberate or devious, but the result of a given person's impression of what ought to happen and how he interprets subsequent events to future generations. Ergo, one biographer of the late JFK can depict him as a rascal while another sees him as a visionary of great promise and charm. Same subject, two different viewpoints. But maybe a better example of converting viewpoints into history or creating perceptions that lead to misleading conclusions involves a character named William Shakespeare and the printing process.

Gutenberg is accredited with creating the first printing machine and almost at once produced a Bible (in 1454) which became a powerful prototype of not only the technique to be used for communication, but also the precursor to a revolution which would soon shake Europe through the massive availability of the world's great wisdom. Knowledge no longer belonged to the nobility and the church, it became (especially after Luther and Erasmus) widely available to any who learned to read and who sought knowledge. Ole John Knox in Scotland took it so far that he not only broke his Presbyterian Church loose from dependence on the crown by creating the Session and giving it jurisdiction over the management of the Kirk, he insisted every parish create a school so kids could read the Bible for themselves. He insisted upon educated members, and surely this model played itself out across the rest of Europe to some degree, albeit the agent for schooling elsewhere may well have been the prince rather than the church.

Only place this did not explode was in Great Britain where learning failed to accelerate very much. It existed in its great universities, but did not replicate the sudden plethora of new wisdom cascading across Western Europe. Because the vehicle to expand knowledge, namely the printing press, was not widely employed. It was not permitted. When France, Italy, Germany, and the Low Countries were going like gangbusters, England had no more than seven presses in the land, the licensing of same being controlled by the crown. What happened after Gutenberg's first works appeared was a civil war which saw the City of Mainz (where the Gutenbergs lived and worked), sacked and the town torn apart; the printers themselves fleeing for safety, taking their knowledge of presses and printing to other locations. A year after the big ruckus (1463), there were presses in Strasbourg, Cologne, Basil, Augsburg, Nuremberg, Ulm and Eltville. The following year saw them opening Rome (two of them), Venice, Paris, Holland, Milan. By 1472 Switzerland was in the printing business as were Hungary and Spain: four years later England as well as Denmark, Sweden; Constantinople and Florence. With this marvelous new device, the knowledge of the past was made readily accessible in virtually all languages, not merely Latin, and came pouring out in a vast inundation which engulfed the civilized world. Except England. Estimate suggested there were about 100,000 manuscripts in Europe prior to 1450, the literature, theology, science and history of the known world, exclusively held in this minuscule body of scrolls or books and inaccessible to 95% of the populace. Now all of this learning comes gushing forth. By 1500 Venice alone had printed 2,835 separate works and the rest of Italy another 4,987 editions with how many thousand copies of each. Jackpot!

All this, of course, made knowledge available and gave to those who searched, evidence or data which they could personally evaluate. Knowledge multiplied exponentially. Except in England. There Henry VIII sort of kept his thumb on the process of printing, limiting it considerably and moving his nation into the back rows of the growing literate countries. Not held up forever, but there was a lacuna there, a vacuum, and a very slow start. Which is where Bill Shakespeare comes in.

He wrote in Elizabeth's time, not Henry's, but England had not gotten caught up, and what Shakespeare did with his talented pen (quill) and clever mind, was give the British their history lessons. Fact is, he gave them to many of us as well. People then (now?) learned all they ever would know about Julius Caesar, Macbeth, the Montecchi and Capuletti (Romeo and Juliet), Henry IV, Richard III, Anthony and Cleopatra, about Renaissance Verona and Capua or Venice, et al. from Shakespeare's plays. Mr. Shakespeare was a good teacher and his characters ring fairly true or so they seem to us. The reader, caught up in his spell-binding drama and portrayal of the human condition, absorbs the historical texture of the play. His account is our perception of those people and societies. A case in point is that of Macbeth, who Shakespeare recounts, murdered Duncan and stole the throne of Scotland only to be removed shortly by the son of the late King.

Although we empathize with Macbeth we view him as a ruthless, regicide nagged by an ambitious, power-seeking wife whose counsel brings about his ruin. He does not come off well in history and his brief reign is a black one. That is what I recall of Macbeth and if asked to summarize his reign in Scotland, I would have quoted Shakespeare's depiction of that era. My hunch is you'd agree. We have this perception of a historic figure, not very kind or flattering, but true to life, right? Not really.

Truth is, Macbeth did kill Duncan, but on the field of battle fighting for the crown, and history suggests he had a better claim to fame than did the loser. Because Macbeth was the grandson of Kenneth II and strengthened his rights by marrying the daughter of the next king, Kenneth III

Venice, Italy.

who died without male heirs. Duncan also claimed through the female line, but in duking it out, lost at Eglin in 1040 and passed from the scene. Macbeth then proceeded to rule Scotland for 17 years, and records indicate the land was secure enough for him to make a pilgrimage to Rome in 1050. The son of the out-shuffled king, however, still schemed to avenge his father and regained the throne in 1057 with the help of the hated English, killing Macbeth in battle. Macbeth was no worse than most kings of the day, or any more a nefarious figure than his counterparts, fact was probably a lot better, Will Shakespeare notwithstanding.

Point is, that the immortal bard was far more popular than history and thus, more widely read and thus influential well beyond normal because of the paucity of scholarly data and the general level of education in Britain. It took a couple of centuries to bleed out some of the misconceptions Shakespeare inadvertently imparted to the western world where assumptions of his accuracy bent a good deal of certain history out of shape.

All of this business about perceptions is especially pertinent these days as we have anguished through the Congressional process of creating a budget. The legerdemain foisted off upon us has been classic in terms of its misrepresentation. For example, why do we keep talking about "a $500,000,000,000 reduction in five years"? Why don't we say a hundred billion dollar reduction next year or two hundred billion in '94 and in '95? Why five years? You guessed it. There are no cuts the first three years. There are increases, but they become cuts when viewed for five full years if we are lucky. Then, cuts from what? The existing budget or from what we are spending? Of course not! Cut from what we would have spent had we escalated the budgetary expenditures 3% per year compounded. We are only gonna increase spending by 2 ½% and therefore, we consider that increase a "cut". I mean, give me a break.

There is no point in climbing on Bill Clinton for this hucksterism nor is the issue here necessarily this slight of hand, recited daily on the airwaves about what a revolution this tax package and these spending cuts are. Nor is the point all the bold-face lying certain members of Congress have been doing in a deliberate obfuscation, if not downright misrepresentation of the facts. What is most reprehensible is disguising the truth from the general public so they are unable to know the facts. Ergo, there is no way we can react wisely or properly. Though I don't necessarily believe that "vox populi, vox dei" — the voice of the people is the voice of God — I do agree with both Lincoln and Jefferson who thought if the American citizen was properly informed, he would come to the right decision. It is patently dishonest to posture as the "servant of the people", poll endlessly to see just where the mind of the constituency is and then so torture the components of a given situation no honest reading can be made of it.

If the course is the right one, the proper one, there is no need to play games. Dissembling occurs only when the truth will not succeed, then we decide John Q. Public is so dumb that if we lay this out for him, he will make the wrong choice; therefore, we've got to disguise the package through legal complexity so he can't understand it, and we shall then decide what's best for him. We do it through misrepresentation fashioned to induce his support though it is support for a totally different animal than he thought it was. We all need to be asking more questions about major issues, get separate opinions, know going in that impartial depiction is not normal and assume what's happening politically in America today is too serious to relegate totally to politicians. An informed constituency is needed to assure its own ultimate fortunes and one that sorts the truth from the ambiguity and doubletalk. If we can't get our Representatives to shape up, isn't it time we started shouting and got them back on track? ∎

What Child Was This?

December 1993

The Advent season is upon us again and provides a new opportunity to talk about a very old subject. Mindful at once that Christmas is about concepts and ideals and meaning, despite the heavy burden of tinsel and gaily-colored paper wrapping up the whole event. The holiday season, of course, closes the calendar year, which is curious because in the liturgical calendar of the church (at least the Presbyterian Church), the year commences with Advent. The significance of this might be really zilch, but it reminds us that some aspects of Yuletide have shifted with the moving tide. Fact, much of the world might make the cynical observation that Christians make a great deal of to-do over the birth of the Christ Child but spend little time thereafter remembering the life and mission of Christ Himself. As though this were a one-shot deal or a life wherein the climax comes in the first part of the story while the theme development comes later with a wavering, wobbling end.

The relationship of beginning and end reminded me of a trip to Germany and the dozen great cathedrals visited. Marvelous buildings and older than those in France or Britain. Amazing enterprise on the part of our western forbearers who, without that first bulldozer or hydraulic crane or OSHA office, fashioned countless thousands of stones, hand cut from the quarries, shaped them perfectly and with rickety wood scaffolding and primitive block and tackle, hauled them miles in the air to put them in place with a jillion counterparts. The spire of St. Peter and St. Mary in Cologne is up there 157 meters, like 480 feet…taller than the Pyramid of Cheops, higher than the AUL Tower in town. Wow! Or in checking out the cathedral in Aachen, which is the most ramshackled, built on-to and added-on-to structure I ever saw, we are looking at an edifice ordered built by Charlemagne in the early 800's A.D. Man, this is old. Eleven centuries ago the creator of the Holy Roman Empire and the first leader tough enough to induce the Saxons, Franks, Alemanae, Angles, Burgundian, and a dozen other tribes into one jurisdiction, not only Christianized his conquered or subdued people, he built a royal basilica to mark his faith which stands now as testimony to his age. (Charlemagne didn't pussyfoot around in his proselyting campaign, timid about preserving ethnic rights and status. He told the Saxons it would be nice if they gave up the pagan gods and adopted Christianity, but they didn't have to. They could have their heads chopped off instead. His logic was most persuasive.) (I, personally, never found much value in dead martyrs.)

The cathedrals of Europe, however, their glory and the memory of the faith they have kept alive, are now a great piece of irony because they are mostly what is left of "the church" today. That and the memory of an age when it was the most dramatic and powerful force in the world. The church today has become synonymous with a "building" not a vibrant, influential movement changing lives and improving conditions. The faith itself somehow has surreptitiously slipped away and is practiced elsewhere, perhaps inculcated into the society, leaving in its wake a monument to what it was and the power it once wielded. Today, its prime concern is maintenance. Not of the faith, nor of the people or the congregation. Maintenance of the building. The vehicle has outstripped the institution. The cathedral at Cologne requires about $10,000,000 a year to keep in shape and its shape, by the way, is very good indeed. Is it fair to wonder, however, what $10,000,000 a year would do in the field of foodstuffs, education, housing or medicine either in Cologne or in Somalia? And wonder whether the church today is about buildings or people? Great and glorious beginning, baffling, unheralded end.

Business institutions might follow a similar course or sequence. Created in one era by those with a given mindset, over the years forces (induced or inadvertent) creep in and change the method (which is technology), the style (management)

Cathedral in Cologne.

which could result in changing the product. Change is no surprise. So not unique that over the years in our company, a single building on Daly Street in Indianapolis at Christmastime in 1941 constituted the old MacAllister Tractor Company, smaller than our Engine Power Parts Department. Today, the successor company has ten buildings with five different locations, employing 20 times as many people. What has not changed, however, is our purpose, our reason for being. If much of what the church did for the medieval world has been subsumed by the state (education, protection, legal counsel, banking) and if it has lost importance in the process, we would hold that has not occurred in our business or market economy. If the church suffered from bad leadership and failed to appreciate the value of its mission, we work hard at professional competence and rewrite mission and vision statements regularly.

The church is not, however, a free enterprise institution required by its discipline to vindicate its value or departure. It is locked in the tradition of a culture and is wet-nursed for reasons sometimes too arcane to explain, but most of all remains to remind us of the source or the moral well-spring from which Western civilization got its ethics and its morés. A shame that its teachings outstrip its institutional competence. Which I think differs from the tractor business because what we provide has utility and in a given segment of our economy is virtually indispensable. Construction in general would suffer grievously were we to depart or revert to merely maintaining our property. Because we are not just buildings (or computers or shuttle deliveries or lease and rental inventories available upon demand). We are a concept, a resource, an initiative, a competing unit created to provide a service and to perform a role as well as a function.

Which then requires buildings and people and parts stock and machine inventory, and Caterpillar looking over our shoulder from time to time to complete the purpose. Buildings are integral and necessary to our operation, and they too require a lot of maintenance, but the difference is that we have not lost our functional importance nor relegated our role to the user or dumped it on the manufacturer or the state. Instead of resisting or retrenching, we have expanded what we do — not a bad concept for the church to consider.

In all fairness, however, we are not just high-minded or all that noble. Truth is we have to compete to survive. Compete and succeed to survive. We do not have a lock on the market like the church has a lock on salvation. Without the check of either the competitive threat or the internal scrutiny of the membership, the church became corrupt. Meaning, distracted. With estates to manage, armies to raise, whole cities and towns to tax, crusades to mount, great cathedrals to erect, and all the rest, its purpose changed and the salvation of souls or service to mankind slipped back into fourth place. After all, where else could humanity go to get saved? Without someone calling it to account, it lost accountability, validity, and altered its pursuit to worldly rather than celestial affairs. Then one day its dynamism and impact were gone.

Destiny is a dangerous manager. Fact, it probably implies there is no manager at all or there would be no such forces prevailing. And mere momentum is not the chief ingredient for successful institutions or successful lives. Christmastime after all is about people, human beings who function within and who constitute, most institutions and who either surrender to destiny or momentum or who take charge. Surely we know that just "being there" oblivious to any reason for being is not the stuff of which great churches are made, successful tractor companies march forward or human beings make life significant. There is a spirit involved and that has to be motivated and directed since that is what gives life to the church, company or individual. Of consequence for the moment because the need for inspiration is often fulfilled at this time of the year. A time for taking stock. A systematic ritual, time ordained by the calendar annually for examining what the rejoicing is all about and finding it has theological roots. That is also a period for reflection. Concluding eventually that within the Christmas event a spirit was born which not only created the church, but fired and ennobled the human psyche in a fashion which is unquenchable as long as it is annually recharged and recalls its inciting incident.

Lives change just assuredly as churches or companies and as they do, can become as empty or unused as abandoned buildings. The purpose sometimes departs; the function vanishes; the driving force runs down. Persons need reasons for existing just as does the church or the tractor business, and it is interesting that on this score the two become partners. The church can help in responding to the eternal questions about being and ceasing to be, can deal with the dignity and value of the individual as a product of the divine hand while the business finds employment for talent, ways of engaging the individual in a corporate activity which produces and creates and, hopefully, along with a livelihood, provides some sense of vocational pride. Each tends to vindicate and to utilize the human unit and shore it separately in the adventure which is life. It replicates the major functions of the species, i.e. thinking and doing. Though it reminds me that in the tractor business we have to utilize both components, the planning, budgeting, marketing, administering as well as fixing broken machines, financial accommodation, inventorying and supplying parts, guys in the field demonstrating. There is as much doing (performing, acting, working) in our sphere as there is considering or planning. Without being sacrilegious, it would not be all that bad if the church got off its haunches and found ways to do more and talk less; measure the talk by the scope of the action; wonder how it can be more successful in its own mission that nagging another institution about how it ought to be running its shop. In short, role-modeling might not be a bad tactic and adoption of the phrase, "Do not only as I say, but as I do."

Which might have been a cheap shot but what most of us understand best is evidence, is example, demonstrated achievement. What we produce abundantly in America are words, promises, good intentions (never fulfilled), knowing what to do but baffled by how to do it. All part of the human pattern and human weakness as old as the species. What Christmas ought to be about is breaking the mold and doing for a month or for a quarter (if we can't do it all year) what we honestly do at Christmastime. We get outside ourselves and try to live differently in terms of our respect for others. For family, for neighbors and friends, for people we don't know, often for people in need. This comes in the ritual of celebration, gifts to others, gestures of love, fellowship and

Lake Galilee showing Syria on the far bank.

appreciation. But it comes also in special church offerings for the needy; the Salvation Army, clapping bells to raise dollars for drifters, the luckless and the homeless; it is companies, people and churches by the thousands clothing children, delivering baskets, serving meals.

It is for a moment, remembering not merely the birth of the Christ Child, but the emphasis found in the mission of the Rabbi who walked through Galilee talking about love, encouraging the desolate, healing the ill, feeding and ministering to the hopeless, demonstrating what the divine love was. Declaring these were not isolated dust particles in the vast universe, but loved and respected units in an eternal program only part of which was unfolding for them now. Hope was the message; friendship the evidence; love the consolation. Almost everyone leans this way at Christmas, but for some reason it is hard to sustain. Maybe we should not despair that it eludes life's total pattern, but rejoice instead that it does appear annually and proves again the value — and the potential — within the human soul.

A joyous Christmas to you all! ∎

Good Leaders ... A Necessity!

March 1994

Every red-blooded American tractor salesman knows about our Colonial origins and that the first English colony planted on these shores was a land grant 200 miles north and south of Point Comfort (and westward ... forever). A plat on which 105 settlers landed in May of 1607 and began hacking out plantations, creating the first town, worshipping congregation, first representative assembly in America, i.e. roots from which the Virginia Colony evolved. A romantically courageous and dramatic move. But at a very dumb location. There is no Jamestown, Virginia, today because the site picked was a bummer. It was surrounded by malarial swamps, fetid and stagnant water, and was a sauna bath all summer long spawning malaria, pneumonia, dysentery and starvation. It struggled, bled, burned twice, and finally moved to reassemble at Williamsburg.

Thirteen years later in Massachusetts, another experiment in courage and lack of wisdom unfolded when 102 pilgrims landed on Plymouth Rock, 600 miles off-course, striking a blow for religious freedom. Ever been to Cape Cod? It's picturesque and the landscape bustles with summer tourists, but mostly it is also barren, windswept, infertile and bleak. The Mayflower anchored, wrote the famous "Compact", suffered horribly through the winter and set up a theocratic state, demonstrating how stubborn Calvinists can be as though perseverance in itself would overcome poor judgment. Why in the world choose a barren, harsh, and sterile tract on which to build a colony? Who in his right mind would set up housekeeping in Massachusetts on the 21st day of November with no shelter but a boat, and the roaring winds out of Canada blasting snow, sleet, and savage temperatures on them for the next five months?

Why not start, say in April? The lack of forethought cost the lives of one-half of their colleagues that first five months in the New World. This colony never prospered either and was salvaged from total extinction when subsumed 20 years later by the Puritans who settled more wisely and more timely.

Each group had to negotiate life in the impenetrable forest, deal with unpleasant Indians, and bereft of pioneering or frontier skills, likewise endure the needless locational vicissitudes brought about by their own blundering. All of which, by the way, (philosophically speaking) replicates the long trial of the species as it struggles against adversities (each in its own day), often self-generated. Is not much of life's travail like those of our Colonial forbearers, self-inflicted? Like Pogo, we have met "the enemy", and guess who it is? Not the IRS or the competition or the do-gooders or Nemeses. It is us.

I think of this little axiom as I watch the Colts play football. They have been great for the city; we

French Cuirassiers charging onto the British squares during the Battle of Waterloo as depicted by Felix Philippoteaux.
(Source: Wikimedia Commons)

are lucky to have them; they still draw respectably well. But how many times this past season were we really "in the game" and could have won, only to blow it…thru a run called back because of holding, a dropped third-down pass, a 15-yard gain ending in an unrecovered fumble? What beats the Colts (for my money) is, of course, the other team. But only about half the time.

Anyone who reads military history is continually appalled by the variety of blunders which resulted in disaster. Typical is Marshall Grouchy, wandering about the Belgium countryside on the 18th of June in 1815 with 35,000 of Napoleon's troops ordered to "march toward the sound of the guns" booming away at a place called Waterloo. A Marshall of France who cannot find the battlefield is not much help to his commander. Grouchy held in his hands the key to a French victory had he gotten there in time, yet here's a man who can't figure out where the action is. Grouchy was partly responsible for the Allied victory.

My favorite illustration of contemporary self-destruction is the fate of the mainline church which sees relentless decreases in its membership year after year. Early on (1770-87), the church shaped our nation through the founding fathers who wrote into our Constitution elements new to political documents, most of which came out of their religious backgrounds. Today it is more likely that the culture influences the religion. Typical of the deterioration is my group, the Presbyterians, who in the course of the last three decades have lost probably a third of their membership and by the year 2000-and-something will become an extinct species.

One reason (in my book) is our resort to the quota system for representation. We run our show like the republic, i.e. we elect the persons to do our business at our different levels of governance. And in selecting people for any working elements, we are caught up in the "enfranchisement binge" of the '60s and '70s. Each committee, council, plenary body, et al. must "represent" old, young, ethnic types, poor, left-handed, ambidextrous, et al. Everything in short, but competence. So when we get into a crunch at any level and need some muscle to get a camp built or conduct a campaign for funds or decide to support some missionaries, we appoint the inevitable committee, to which we send (you got it!) young and old, rich and poor, black, red, and white, experienced and naïve, to do the job. We are truly homogenous. But how do you suppose we fare when it comes to building the camp, raising the money for the budget or putting two more missionaries in the field? Or gaining more members? We have the most thorough and protracted discussions you ever heard, but when it's time "to bell the cat", we learn that problems are not honestly solved or great endeavors effectuated by heterogeneity. They are best attacked with ability, leadership and people capable of raising money for camps or budgets or missionaries. The cause of the kingdom is rarely advanced with bush-leaguers. Even in the divine mission we opt for doing things the hard way.

The process, as such, carries on across the spectrum of society. Who creates the welfare problem in our midst, eluding resolution for four generations now? Is it slave owners, sweat shop operators, a class of medieval land barons locking people to the soil for centuries or a repressive society which ghettoizes identified classes for special persecution? Hell no! It is the self-induced breakdown of the family unit which has loosened its discipline, unable then to compete with the siren song of the boob tube and the culture of violence and promiscuity which is our fare these days. So peer pressure, single parent families, too much available dope, gangs and guns, fill the void created when the center collapses. Any society which tolerates rampant illegitimacy and absolves parents from the task of parenting after all the fun of sex, spawns in exponential fashion, a humongous problem to which there is affixed an enormous price tag, both in dollars and social agony which assesses the innocent to sponsor continuation of the outrage.

We exempt people from assuming the responsibilities for their own actions. We have taken away the tempering element, lifted the cost or the charge which should apply and removed the factor which could restrain transgression. Society, we complain, not the individual, is the culprit, forgetting the composite of individuals is "the society".

Baalbeck-Valley of Tears.

Which sort of leads into the over-arching premise as these proposed hypotheses are applied to history. The point is obvious, I'm sure. It's the old model of the Roman Empire which was not taken apart by the barbarians UNTIL it had collapsed from within. The self-inflicted ruins from haphazard election of emperors, the cop-out of "we, the people" from assuming civic responsibility, the attempt to rule too wide a region with too many conflicting people, and the dilution of civil pride by giving citizenship to hundreds of thousands who had no idea of what the word "Roman" meant. No national power on earth could have crushed the Empire in the day of Augustus or Trajan. The unraveling came not from the Visigoths or Vandals, it came from within.

Should we take a guess at how that all applies here? Corporations and governments are really organized to function in perpetuity.

There is no specific time frame for the life and purpose of a given institution (unless you are Hong Kong). Yet despite the long-term objective, history says governments do not work for the long pull. We can find some 80 major powers in the business since 3100 B.C. What happened to most of them? Whether it took 40 or 800 years to reach dissolution, they ultimately collapsed. Same thing that happened to over 20 carmakers who once made Indianapolis their home but didn't make enough money to stay the stride, or the jillion breweries that once existed in every town of 10,000 or more in America in the '20s, all succumbing to Bud or Miller.

Given the pattern which is finally internal incompetence in the form of bad judgment, blundering or an inability to meet new conditions with contemporary solutions, the odds seem to be against survival. Time is an exacting arbiter. So maybe the real point is not Waterloo and Grouchy's aimless search for the battle, maybe it's the fact that Bonaparte did create an empire out of the French Revolution because for the most part he knew what to do with it. Though he fared as badly in Spain and Russia as he succeeded at Austerlitz, maybe the point is that in 15 short years he altered for all time major institutions of France and had a dramatic, permanent effect on the thinking of Western Europe. Maybe the successes between failures are the talisman, the real benchmark.

Much is written about "the fall of the Roman Empire", but maybe the important fact is not the fall, rather that it existed as the most significant influence in the world for 500 years and its legacy is built into most of the systems of Western Europe. The church about which I ranted at some length is having its problems, but again, the point is that Mr. Clinton's budget this year has over $690 billion for Health and Human Services. That concern for people, especially those in need, exists in this nation not out of Roman or Hellenic influence, but out of the Judeo Christian teachings which have worked their way deep into our psyche as a people, a direct result of that very church now suffering such heavy weather. Again, it is the achievement that altered affairs, not the self-inflicted wounds.

The analogy in business is readily apparent. We have a lot to do with our own success or failure through choices we make (called "executive decisions"). We cannot build a better team than exists in the quality extant in the individual human component assembled to do our job. Hiring is always a corporate choosing process. A product and a market are also critical. Evaluating those three in operation the past ten years, the impact is obvious. My competitors have fared badly because they represent manufacturers who "backed out from under them". Caterpillar and the Nipponese have taken most of the market because they have better leadership, and in our case, because CAT has spent $400,000,000 a year on research and development. Once again, an internal decision not to stay where one is and sells what he sold eight years ago. Those whose corporate choice was no product improvement saw the arrows pointing into oblivion. He who picks up one end of a stick picks up the other end also.

Is the message clear? First place to look for "reasons why" is in the mirror. In our world, individual, personal, i.e. corporate decisions arbitrate our future, which will unroll on the basis of how we decide to staff, market, finance, inventory and train, more than the determinations made by those with whom we butt heads. If we do right with the opportunity we have, let the enemy do his damnedest. Our greatest jeopardy is making wrong calls, making no calls, letting things "work themselves out" versus making things happen. Product is absolutely essential. But so is clear thinking a lot of luck, aggressive management, good staffing and professional competence across the board. Much of this is implicit in the term "leadership". Since that is what assures making the best choices and avoiding bad timing, a poor location, unqualified generals, internal malaise.

The objective then is to achieve and survive, not die a martyr's death in a noble cause. ∎

The Gift of the Wise Men

Carroll College Commencement given May 15, 1994
June 1994

Editor's Note: P.E. MacAllister graduated from Carroll College in June of 1940. He joined the Board of Trustees in 1963, serving as Chairman for 17 years. He handed over the gavel to his successor on May 14, 1994. On May 15, 1994, he was awarded an Honorary Doctorate of Humane Letters by the Board of Trustees and Faculty. Following the presentation of the award, he made the following address to the graduates of the Class of 1994.

My wife tells a story about a middle-aged guy walking across the campus and encountering a frog. A frog who said, "Please sir, a malevolent force has transformed me into this wretched creature, but if you will kiss me, I shall be metamorphosed immediately into my former self. I'm really a 23-year old blonde with a shape that will drive you nuts. One kiss and we can spend the rest of the afternoon frolicking in the tall grass." The old guy was stunned and for the moment speechless. The frog repeated, "Did you understand? If you kiss me and transform me back to normal, you'll get one of the most erotic experiences you've ever imagined." After a long pause the old gentleman picked up the frog and carefully placed it in his pocket saying, "All things considered, maybe I can get more mileage out

P.E. addressing the 1994 graduating class of Carroll College after receiving an Honorary Doctorate of Humane Letters.

of a talking frog." Which is a pretty corny way to begin a serious address, but with a little give on your part, I can hold it illustrates that viewpoints may differ on courses to pursue, dependent upon outlook and vantage point. The Presbyterians say it more pedantically: "There are truths and forms with respect to which men (and women) of good character and principle may differ." You have encountered this condition the last four years when you took exception to viewpoints of a particular professor. And it might even apply now to what I'm going to say. But if your professors could nag at you for a year at a time, maybe a Trustee can thrust his opinions on you for 15 crummy minutes.

Starting not on differences, but something we have in common — a commencement exercise at Carroll College. Two generations ago, I sat where you are, listening to a commencement speaker regale me with platitudes in what was the last official exercise of my college career. There will be more in common if some of you find the moment not one of supreme joy, but rather one of melancholy, one weighted with some vague sadness. It certainly was for me. Because the smooth ride I had enjoyed for so long was now over. My father had spent the outlandish sum of $2,400 getting me educated at Carroll, so I had a leg up on life. Since only one high school senior in 10 or 12 went to college, surely this should have been an advantage in the job market. Surely, I was now impatient for life on my own and raring to go. Wrong! I was not ready for the cold, cruel, inimical world, and moreover, said world was not very cordial to me. A college degree or not. The unemployment rate was about 20% in those days and inexperienced help was not in big demand.

Beyond this private and depressing introspection about lack of preparedness, the news headlines had just recounted the British evacuation of Dunkirk and surrender of the French Army. Western Europe had fallen ignominiously to Hitler's blitzkrieg and accompanying Teutonic arrogance. Which war-like environment, tragic as it might have been, was the very factor that solved my problem. The day before my 22nd birthday, I joined the United States Army Air Corps and shipped off for military service which lasted exactly five years. The war ended the Great

Depression, enhancing civilian opportunity, even in the great State of Indiana where my father was signing a contract to become a Caterpillar dealer just as I was being discharged. He invited me to join him, thus, solving my "career" problem. But less than six years later, my dad had a slight stroke which took him forever out of action, handing me the ball and voila, déjà vu. I was no better prepared to run the tractor company than I was to find a job after graduation. My dad was almost a legend as a salesman and as a personality, but he was a nonchalant administrator and a poor teacher. Our corporate learning program was based on osmosis and capillary action, which really works better in plants than mental processes. Ergo, my credentials for directing the affairs of 60 people were somewhat limited. Or so I thought.

In 1951 you had to be pretty stupid to screw up a Caterpillar dealership, so it's not phenomenal that 43 years later, we're still around, now employing 350 people. My son (better groomed than I) runs a very successful operation. Maybe we lucked out. But not altogether. Luck will always be a major factor in human affairs, e.g. there is no way in a thousand years I would have qualified for a CAT dealership. 100% luck. But let's realize, too, that equally important is inevitably the manner in which luck is handled. Good luck, badly managed, leads to failure. Bad luck can destroy the will or demolish hope if we let it. "What happens to us" is not the ultimate arbiter. What *we do* with what happens to us is the key. Fortune has to be managed.

My adventure in the bulldozer world brought another element into play. It was my random education. With a major in history at Carroll, minors in speech and English, it's hard to think this was ideal preparation for the business world. The long exposure in the classroom, however, introduced me to something else: The wisdom of three sages whose impact across the centuries had invested the educational apparatus on the Carroll campus. They were precursors of a revolution in thinking that stood the ancient world on its ear and changed forever the way Western Civilization would view the person, the state, the universe, would think about justice and honor, about the gods and about human capability. About everything. They were from Ancient Miletus and were named Thales, Anaximander and Anaximenes.

About 600 B.C., Thales brought from Egypt the rudimentary principles of geometry and the beginning premises of astronomy. Geometry deals as you know with hypothesis and theorem, a system of rules and ratios which postulates certain conditions existing and creates extensions of these into different configurations to see what sort of outcome the application of a given formula might create. It unfolds in a world of ideas and theories, which can be applied in many cases to physical situations, but can exist simply for the purity of the cerebral exercise. Astronomy is largely a matter of recording celestial positions, accumulating data, marking courses and orbits. The practical application of this came into focus as proof of the value in the system when Thales, analyzing collected lunar data, seeing the pattern and rhythm of the heavens, predicted an eclipse on May 28, 585 B.C. because he could project the moon interposing itself between us and the sun. Studying collected data and applying critical thinking to it evolved to a thing we named "science."

By virtue of the extension and expansion of these new techniques through Socrates, Plato and Aristotle, et al. mankind developed an ability to find truth through exercises of the mind. It, likewise, amplified the element of beauty, sophisticated all human institutions, became a major source of wisdom and had a dramatic impact on theology, politics, mathematics, and social systems. Where the Semitic culture found truth from empirical knowledge and announcements from the Gods, we now added the recourse to <u>reason</u>, a factor which soon became the driving force in history.

What we have in common is an exposure to the gift of these wise men whose premises we employ and whose processes have become second nature to us. For the past four years you've been practitioners of this art, of accumulating data through notes and reading, and through discussion and dissection have been analyzing the nature of the material trying to understand what it means, how it works, why it is important. In a more pragmatic vein, you have developed the key to solving problems, which is finding out all there is to know about a given instance, studying to understand its frailties and why it is a bummer. When all the detail about a given situation is assembled and considered, nine times out of ten, the course to pursue is obvious.

Let me illustrate, reverting again to the tractor business. The continual objection to buying our product is invariably its high price. So when the casual salesman is confronted with this challenge, his plea to us is lower ours and meet competition. The casual salesman is not thinking; he is reacting. Price is what the competitor is selling because that is all he has to offer. Anyone exposed to the training we give at Carroll goes back to facts and analyzes information pertaining to a given dilemma.

He will start by comparing hourly, owning and operating costs from 40 years of data, often proving "Brand X" does not even provide such statistics. He will talk productivity which means earnings, press hard on "downtime" and the costly lag in getting parts for machines few in number and note that we have five times more units in the field than all competition combined. We guarantee parts, service in 48 hours. Multiply lost production at $2,000 a day waiting for parts and what do you waste? We can whip out an auction record of used machinery sales and illustrate the buyer will get 40-50% less for "Brand X" than he will for ours when he trades or sells it. Enough to wipe out the so-called savings at purchase time. When all the material is summarized…and our guys do this on a portable computer just to show how sophisticated we are…the conclusion is "Mr. Customer, on the basis of this data, there is no way anyone owning "Brand X" can compete in a competi-

tive market against he who uses a CAT." What the good salesman does is relate cost to value; he sells benefits; he insists on looking not at this moment of purchase, but costs during the life of the machine.

We want to see the whole ballgame, not just the first inning. Which is recourse to the same dynamic employed by Thales and by you in many classrooms. And is applicable in banking, manufacturing, a bakery shop, a restaurant and almost any other institution we know. Everyone *reacts*; far too few people think critically or analytically.

Skill in this particular exercise is the key to leadership. Always of major importance in human affairs because the solution of problems is what life is all about. Those who excel in the resolution of the problems existing across the spectrum of our systems are the ones we want in positions of authority. In a society where most don't know how to be followers, leadership is a commodity always in demand.

My own personal experience finally revealed that although history and English may not have prepared me technically for reading a balance sheet or computing inventory turn, my education at Carroll equipped me to learn to do what a CEO does. Moreover, taught me how to get along with people, tolerate differences of opinion, view situations with objectivity, and think about problems rather than emoting about them. It declared learning is a function not a fait accompli. It should not stop with commencement. The techniques for learning are now at our fingertips for the rest of our sojourn in this vale of tears. Success is paced by improving competence and the ability to assume more responsibility, to do more things. Both of which are conditioned precisely on how well we assimilate and employ new knowledge and different skills. He, who learns no more, advances no farther.

The message here is that you are equipped with the same delayed reaction potential as are your liberal arts peers, which is the same equipment delivered to my generation. It takes awhile to kick in because the first job is rarely the one which will see you in position to do major managing of an enterprise, but it will equip you to do well that portion of the assignment handed to you. What brings true leadership is both the capacity to think and then to respond, to act. Both of which are sharpened, enhanced through the leverage of experience. It takes awhile to learn the drill in any business, any school system, hospital, trade association or whatever calls you into its service. Seems to me, the first priority is to get connected

P.E. playing golf with Larry Hannah.

somewhere, understanding that if you start out cleaning tables in McDonalds, it's on a course toward owning a string of them ten years later. The object, wherever it is, must be to succeed. Few of us in business promote on the basis of past failure. That works only in politics.

Another observation advises there is a lot more to life than selling tractors or keeping ledgers or examining patients or selling life insurance or preaching sermons. The lesson learned in the marketplace becomes a post-graduate course itself, when combined with what you already have assimilated from the wise men of Miletus, and is a capability applicable anywhere. In this country we elect persons to manage … or maybe mismanage … our political affairs. Has it occurred to you that most other institutions are constituted the same way? A volunteer group created Prairieville Academy 148 years ago; a representative body called a Presbytery took it over four years later; people elected to boards or councils or committees run the symphonies in America, the United Way, Little League, Red Cross, opera, the Protestant Church, colleges, seminaries, hospitals, etc., ad infinitum. One hundred thirty billion dollars supporting volunteer action in this country every year, making us the richest society in history in terms of services and amenities, all managed by those we select to run them.

"X" number will be elected to serve on the school board in your community, represent you on the city council, keep the museum going or a zoning agency, run the symphony or opera company, set policy for the hospital, be appointed to serve on a park board. It represents us all better if such people know how to think rationally, understand what is really important and what is a smoke screen, are bold enough to see the big picture and deal with the total good, rather than protecting the parochial interest. It helps if they are judiciously impassionate and avoid becoming infallible. Those equipped for leadership positions ought to be sensitive to this aspect of our life in America and realize it is hard to enjoy even as great a vocation as Caterpillar if the community in which ones lives is nondescript, inefficient, and bush league. Because no one in the leadership cadre cares enough

about the total good to lend his efforts or gets too busy to try. Again, those who can learn the best way to direct a theatre operation or a private school or an art museum or a volunteer fire department are those conditioned such as we are. Both the New Testament and, of course, the ancient Athenians had admonitions about this. The first suggests that "to him who is given much, much is required," and Pericles admonished his citizens to "honor the gods, help your friends, and adorn your city." Our communities should be as wholesome and efficient as a successful business and if those who have achieved the latter apply themselves to the former, the same results will occur.

Sad thing about life in the big world, as I close this discourse, is the needless pain, bungling, wasted effort, shattered dreams, incompetence, inequity and injustice on every hand, not because we don't know how to redress or correct, but because we have the wrong people in charge. We know what is wrong, but we don't bring the resources for resolution properly to bear. We don't bring our "do-how" up to our "know-how". You have within you, because of the last four years, potential for both knowing and doing, each developing as experience sharpens your capacity. The degree to which you will apply talent beyond the job and the family will determine, to a modest degree, what your impact will be on society as a whole. If, indeed, any. That is a personal choice. But make it a pragmatic choice. Don't waste options by trying to stop tribal warfare in Rwanda or suppression of rights on China. Your influence will be at home. Your knowledge, interest, leverage is where you live. Carroll would be proud indeed if when the time comes you set about making it a better place to live. We hope all of you find Maeterlinck's "bluebird of happiness," but remember, please, happiness is not what life is all about. Achievement is the name of this game. Leaving something a bit better than you found it. Especially to those of you who have not been merely exposed to learning, but who have received an education. From Carroll College. Preparing you for leadership and responsibility. May the shade of Thales of Miletus go with you and his example guide your course as he has the past four years. ■

Essay on Freedom

September 1994

The Fourth of July has come and gone so this might be a strange sort of editorial, but to a people who take too much for granted, the topic of freedom needs more visibility than some fireworks once a year. Watching the way Central Europe, the former members of the Soviet block, Latin America, almost every nation in Africa (would you believe 49 of 'em), and the Arabic world bungles, stumbles and mangles democratic experiments, we need to conclude making a republic work is no piece of cake. Most efforts fail. They revert to dictatorships because most citizen constituencies are ill-equipped to make one function. We are different here on several accounts, the first being the English origins of the colonies and their "enlightenment" concepts replete with their concept of common law and parliamentary process. The caliber of our founding fathers was likewise unique, but over-arching all of this was the religious impact so deftly and so definitely implanted in our institutions. There was never any doubt that our Constitutional framers were Christians and figured "Divine Providence" had a hand in shaping our affairs. Ergo, those tenets, when properly applied and subtly used can make the difference between success and failure. The tradition of marrying state and religion is an ancient one... goes back to early Biblical history.

Back to the emancipation of the Hebrews from the enslaved conditions of Egypt, a struggle for independence well known to 18th Century Americans. They knew how Israel came into being as an ethnic unit and got committed to the worship of the God Yahweh, who gave them their covenant, the ritual and legal codes of law, then guided their occupation of Canaan and creation of a federal state. The colonial leaders saw the rescue of Israel as a fitting parallel for the exercise in which they were then engaged. Each people saw itself suppressed by a tyrannical monarch. Each recited increasing

The Minute Man, a statue by Daniel Chester French erected in 1875 in Concord, Massachusetts. *(Source: Wikimedia Commons.)*

harshness in the terms of their conditions. Each had a single dominant figure whose leadership would make liberty and nationhood possible. Each had 13 separate units, each united through a distinct legal document creating their political and social institutions.

Americans then felt they were inheritors of a tradition which mixed together harmoniously elements of church <u>and</u> state. If an anomaly to <u>current</u> America, it posed no difficulty to our forbearers. Implicit in their theme, moreover, was the hand of God guiding a people to freedom, a circumstance highly improbable without divine sanction. Thus, familiar mottos or phrases: "In god We Trust"; "Men are <u>endowed by their creator</u> with certain unalienable rights"; "With a firm reliance on the protection of the Divine Providence"; "Appealing to the Supreme Judge of the world", etc. These men unabashedly confessed their reliance upon the same Yahweh Moses worshipped and were likewise convinced He guided and justified their actions.

God wanted his people free; servitude was not the divine institution so those who fought for liberty were crusading on God's side. Moses repeated God's demand to Pharaoh at least three times; "Let my people go that they may serve me in the wilderness", and this meant out from under the jurisdiction of Egyptian gods, away from Egyptian influence, culture even Egyptian geography.

Ironic thing about both stories is the fact that <u>the process</u> for securing freedom seemed more exciting than the end results. In each instance there is a long story of the steps taking place before liberty was achieved, but once the peril has past, neither people really knew what to do with it. According to "Judges", the Hebrews spent their first 200 years in the land, battling each other as separate tribes or repelling foreign incursions. Our 13 colonies milled around from 1781 till 1787 with no idea in mind as to how they would structure the new situation, and only lucked out when a fellow named James Madison used a colonial political gathering to create the Constitution. Makes one wonder: If there is no compelling reason to secure liberty, or if no one knows what to do with it, why bother in the first place? Do we just know what we don't want? Rebellion and revolt are exciting and easy. Making a free society function politically is the real bear. The battle has to be seen as the <u>means</u> by which the <u>end</u> is achieved, it is not sufficient unto itself. Nor is freedom established with an abrupt decree; it is an evolution. It has stages. But most important, one needs to be free for a reason. Liberty has to empower him to act in a fashion not possible in servitude or it is pointless.

Good example of bungling newly-won freedom is the French Revolution. Out with the king and off with his head. Dispossess the aristocracy and emasculates the church, make big banners reading "Liberty, equality and fraternity". The people take over; big ruckus, blood bath, active guillotine, and great churning around in the Estates General. <u>But not a clue as to how we make a state work.</u> After seven or eight years of mismanagement, order finally returned; the guillotine was put away, and all systems made operational. Under a young Corsican named Napoleon Bonaparte, Consul for Life. That's what happened to the French Revolution.

That pattern is repeated monotonously in <u>our</u> time? Haiti, Cuba, Ethiopia, Sudan, Kenya, Nigeria, China, North Korea, Iran…50 nations in 50 years. The process continues in the Ukraine (which is a basket case), Bosnia, Slovakia, Bulgaria, Georgia, and most of the former members of the Soviet Union. Ardor and anger which support the revolution rarely provide the competence to fashion a responsible society. So the trick is not only secure freedom, it is also institutionalize it in a fashion which generates popular support. The first without the second is pointless.

But both Israel and Colonial America succeeded in gaining freedom <u>and</u> creating lasting institutions. Is it a coincidence or a fluke that both are free <u>and</u> products of the same God? Could that indeed have been the redeeming factor in the salvation of each when nine out of ten revert to autocracy? Why do nations "whose God is the Lord" survive with free institutions and the Philistines fall by the wayside? There is some freedom in Islam, but rarely for other creeds. There is mostly tribalism in Africa. Asia is riven with a caste system or totalitarian states. Does indeed God vindicate himself through partnership and presence among the greatest nations of the world and through their power and influence proclaim again that freedom is the divine plan and the divine recommendation?

It is dangerous business, however, determining which is "the Lord's side", recalling the slogan of the Kaiser and his German armies in 1914. "Gott Mitt Uns"; "God is with us." Like the Crusader slogan, "Deo Volente", meaning "God wills it." Both wanted the sanction of God, but our guess is before any confirmation, both were fighting and killing in God's name. As the bleeding Belgians and the Dutch could testify in 1914, while stacks of slaughtered Jews and Saracens marked the crusader course. Was the Lord indeed blessing such actions? Hardly! Maybe our colonial forbearers felt the same divine approbation, though our picture of Washington sees him on his knees trying to <u>find</u> rather than assume, divine guidance.

Our hope today should be that our land and people are blessed <u>insofar as they merit divine sanction</u>. Which puts us back to the unavoidable issue of church and state, since it is the church, not the state that can define goodness. The state is not good at shaping character as Hitler and Mao have proven. I figure a <u>partnership</u> is best, a nation under the Christian aegis. We are not unanimous as Christians on the precise formulae for salvation or timing of the millennium or the exclusivity of the New Testament covenant, but it is hard to deny the impact on American society, of the Pauline themes of love, and Jesus model of concern for "the least of these". If we have technically separated the two entities, we have long ago subconsciously merged them. The conscience of America is a Christian conscience, nothing less, and we are respected for it worldwide; respected for our generosity, our treatment of conquered nations after WWII, our food shipments to Bosnia, our water-treating devices to Rwanda, our bail-out of Kuwait.

Our arena for battle is usually on athletic fields; or fighting political campaigns where, by the way, we lose with equanimity, rather than responding in revolt. Our ability to merge cultural, ethnic, religious, racial, regional and vocational diversity into a single fabric has no parallel in the world. Our educational system is much belabored these days, but who wins 90% of all the Nobel Prizes? What other nation provides universal access to all classrooms such as we provide our people?

I got a foreign opinion about America recently. Becky and I took our two daughters and husbands to Rome in June, went kicking through old ruins, visiting galleries, checking out the papal diggings in Vatican City, and inspecting Michelangelo's refurbished art work in the Sistine Chapel. On the 5th of June, we were visiting the Dori Pamphilli and got into a random discussion with our guide about crowds, Rome and D-Day. She reminded me that "50 years ago today" (the 5th of June), the city of Rome was liberated by the allied forces and part of the crowds were old soldiers who had played a part in that event. I told her that I, too, was in Italy "50 years ago today" in Foggia with the Air Corps and remembered the event. She was surprised and delighted. Fact, she stopped our tour in mid-step and recalled she had been a child of five at the time. "*I will always remember that day*", she said. "*We had not been able to get food for weeks, people were starving, the conditions were desperate, and we were ravenous with hunger. Then we saw the trucks coming in, the Americans, in convoys, rolling into the city. And do you know the first thing they did? They passed out bread! Bread! The Americans were handing us bread left and right. They were feeding us. Free. Everyone! Those of us who were there will always remember the Americans. And what they did for us — total strangers. Especially a child of five who had been through some very grim years.*" She choked all of us up with her account. "*You left a lot of bodies here in Italy giving us back our freedom, Mr. MacAllister, and there are a great many of us who will never, <u>ever</u> forget what America did.*"

I have seen the American cemetery outside of Florence where a good many of my comrades in the First Fighter Group are buried or listed in the accounts as "so-and-so Killed in Action" or "Missing in Action". Two years ago we ended up in Normandy, above the D-Day beaches at the American cemetery there. The feeling is hard to describe, but Americans have designed these sepulchral installations with

American cemetery.

great care, balanced proportion and solemn symmetry. There is a measured dignity about the rows upon rows upon rows of white crosses. In these sober, compelling and ordered precincts, one finds the character of America represented and enshrined. Not in building empire, but in safeguarding the rights and freedom of others. These men lie there eternally attesting mutely to American principles of honor, right and justice.

Because we know as Christians the companion element of freedom is responsibility. First for ourselves, and then for others.

As the inheritors of both legacies, we do not have the revolutionary battles to fight, but we do have the charge to maintain the progress gained, and by virtue of what it has allowed us to do, vindicate the blessings accorded us as we utilize the opportunity. It would be a hollow sort of faith, if having gained or inherited it, <u>we</u> do not know what to do with it; if we think citizenship, like the Declaration of Independence is "completed" rather than an ongoing process, something we spend a life <u>doing</u>. Because we are in an <u>evolution</u> and as the world spins on its course, we need be ever mindful of our response, finding new solutions to the new problems in our laps.

The issue of political strength as a by-product of a Christian people was interpreted in a quote by Alexis de Tocqueville. "America is great because America is good." "Goodness" did not originate here among the Aborigines, much as we are kowtowing to them these days. Goodness arrived with the Puritans and with the other immigrants from Western Europe who brought along the Bible, inculcating into our system the concepts of liberty proclaimed in our official documents and installing the church in every community. de Tocqueville found a people who made do for themselves and created much of what they needed with their own hands; he found them helping each other; respecting property rights; serving in the vehicles of governance and in the militias. He found them hard working, tough, God fearing, respectful of the rights of others. He saw active, aggressive, successful parishes, and a thriving religious community which in his mind shaped the moré and ethic of this people. At the base of America's strength was this major issue, monitoring and molding the rough, hard, hazardous and primitive life on the frontier. The "greatness" was a greatness of the soul, not of the Army or the industrial sinews.

And he predicted we would stay vibrant, powerful, dominating just as long as we stayed good. But when we lost our character or patriotism or our faith, we would cease to be a factor in world affairs.

If we wonder about the validity of the church in today's world in an increasingly secular society, we might ponder de Tocqueville's premises and recognize that in our hands lies the key to America's decency and integrity, the very elements which arbitrate her goodness and, thus, her future. What will save this people is not another NAFTA treaty or GATT or more EPA regulations or Clinton's do-good programs; what will save this people is its allegiance to the tradition which released <u>us</u> from bondage and calls us in this age to keep the torch alive, witnesses and practioners of the democratic forms bequeathed us by our forbearers. ■

Christmas Time Again

December 1994

The Christmas season is often approached through a linkage of retrospection with longing. We remember "Christmas past" and see it in a sentimental light, recalling the youthful joys and anticipation, the long holiday filled with delight. It was a special day because it was a family time. The "clan" (appropriate word in my case) gathered in early morn at individual hearths and opened parcels, then descended with other septs at the home of the patriarch where we celebrated with broader intensity and a larger unity. As a youngster, my major gathering was "Granma's farm" with my cousins. In later years it involved Brother Dave and his family at my parents' home. Today, it's the same formula when the three kids and their families gather Christmas day around <u>our</u> tree and table.

Familiar traditions tend to add a sense of comfort and reassurance. One likes circumstances wherein he is acceptable, respected and secure. Despite the fragmentation of society, reinforcement of the family unit is still critical to the psychological well-being of many people. And along with that factor at

P.E. with his granddaughter, Casey.

Christmas is the enhancing magic of memory; not always accurate, but inclined to be consoling. What many of us remember about Christmas past is the lack of care or concern — a sans-souci of sorts. As though that forgotten society which had fostered the Christmas event was better disciplined than now; in better order, less fractious and disheveled than the one depicted nightly in our news or each morning in the paper. It was a world before crack and heroin, before AIDS, and the waves of illegal aliens; before the racial frictions, and the disgraceful rate of illegitimacy. It was pleasanter, too, before we made atomic weapons, put holes in the ozone, spilled oil so frequently and indiscriminately, jammed our cities with traffic.

Saying Christmas past is pleasant as a memory because in the mind's eye it was a different world. But most of all, a world in which we were young. Young and probably uniformed, seeing what we wanted to see, aware of only our side of the picture, the good part. If a seamy, unpleasant side existed, we didn't know about it and probably ducked opportunities to learn. "When ignorance is bliss, 'tis folly to be wise", Mr. Pope once observed. Our joy and contentment are conditions <u>un-impacted</u> by anxiety, frustration, worry and apprehension. At seven, ten, fifteen years, the harpies of discomfiture had not yet intruded upon the consciousness, and our minds were light in this season of light. So, it is Mr. Pope's "bliss" that we recall around the tree, that and the security of the family through the eyes and impressions of a younger time and person. It is that transcendent condition we'd like to restore.

Which is why Christmas can be a melancholy season. Not sad; just melancholy. But, honest reflection must confess this is a pretty silly way to feel. Because in the first place, the things we keep in memory are mostly the good things. We have sifted out and discarded the bad. Christmas is almost an ethereal situation for the retrospective; one carefully nurtured, doctored and massaged after we have scrubbed off all the warts and blemishes. We have <u>impressions</u> of Christmas past, not accurate records. Then, too, we saw a world biased by our perspective and through the conditioning of our individual culture. We didn't know then (when things were so great!), simultaneously, we were building toxic environmental booby traps, wasting natural gas, polluting our lakes and streams, repressing and exploiting 20 million Blacks who couldn't vote in elections or buy a room in 98% of our hotels. I look back at my days as a kid and recall what my WASP society thought about Jews and how my town viewed Roman Catholics, much less minority peoples with different hair, skin color, and accents. Without even considering it evil; in fact, we presumed it was normal. We were the superior group, and the rest just didn't belong and could never join. Such naiveté, ignorance and prejudice, casually practiced, especially at Christmas time must have made the whole season an outrage to those not Anglo Saxon or Protestant. And we never realized we were doing it. That was "Christian"? Christ-like? Wow!

The second major weakness in this nostalgia over "the way the world used to be" is the inaccuracy of our perspective on the <u>present</u>, i.e. everything has gone to hell. Many of us are Calvinists, which is not altogether bad because among other things, Reverend Calvin himself was up to his neck in politics. While writing his "Institutes", he was also running the City of Geneva, Switzerland as its City Manager, Mayor and Chief of Everything; plus running a seminary; plus creating the Presbyterian Church which he also directed from Geneva. Ole Jean was not a very happy sort of guy since totally committed people rarely are. Dedicated and fanatic, he was also infallible … a hard guy to live with gracefully. He spent a lot of time finding what was <u>wrong</u> with things. Like the city water supply, its economic base, Geneva's drainage, conditions of jails, inns, the hospitals; plight of alcoholics, the gambling joints, and the shabby whorehouses. All of which he regulated, cleaned up, brought to standards.

In our time Calvinists look for trouble in the economy, with illegal immigration, balanced of payments, the church, street gangs, the Republican Party, the tractor business, etc., ad infinitum. Not because we are bitchers, but <u>so we can fix 'em</u>. The way to make something better — here or in Geneva, now or in 1560 — is to find the weak points and make them stronger. We complain about margins in the machinery business in order to focus our attention and see how to make them better or at least as good as our competition.

But modern-day Calvinists have gone overboard and a bit cockeyed. We spend a lot of time trashing Bill Clinton or exploring O.J.'s marital problems; or the welfare cheaters; chart the rate of AIDS in

Judea.

Indiana or who hasn't paid his nanny tax on illegal housekeepers. The stock market is terrific at this. It works to anticipate <u>what can go wrong</u>. Each time unemployment drops, the market has a spasm. If business gets better, we could have inflation. Oh, my God! But what is happening is that we have become so fixed on "what is wrong now with America" or "with teenagers" or with "the administration" or "the school system", we have made finding fault, not a means to a corrective end, <u>but an exercise sufficient unto itself</u>. Bad news, weakness, error, frailty, falling short et al are all items that stand on their own as deserving of attention so we can "Tsk Tsk" some more. Find fault and bewail the times. Not helpful.

Since this is a Christmas-type editorial, maybe a "Christmasy" quote on a sunnier note would be appropriate, one from the ancient prophet, Isaiah. Because it also has a sort of "longing" theme. But not for the past, rather anticipating a future which will dawn brighter and better If I recall the halcyon past, this bird anticipates the same glory in the future.

"A shoot shall come out from the stump of Jesse, and a branch shall grow out of his roots. The spirit of the Lord shall rest on him, the spirit of wisdom and understanding, the spirit of counsel and might... with righteousness he shall judge the poor, and decide with equity for the meek of the earth; Righteousness shall be the belt around his waist, and faithfulness the belt around his loins. The wolf shall live with the lamb, the leopard shall lie down with the kid, the calf and the lion and the fatling together, and a little child shall lead them. The nursing child shall play over the hole of the asp, and the weaned child shall put its hand on the adder's den. They will not hurt or destroy on all my holy mountain; for the earth will be full of the knowledge of the Lord as the waters cover the sea."

What a glorious dream! A popular opinion is that this "hoped for" age would occur under a new Judahite king, perhaps Hezekiah, whose brilliance and superb leadership will right all wrongs, bring in new prosperity, and create such a reign of peace and tranquility all the east will marvel. It is longing for harmony, happiness, well-being, and it's a hope that extends benefits to all mankind (or at least all Hebrews). It is an idealized society he depicts…a perfect world.

As the year winds down and we look to <u>the future</u>, wanting a great many changes in Congress, society, business et al, maybe it's more helpful — again — to take a look at <u>the present</u> and wonder why in the world we are complaining. Let's get real, Isaiah; life is not perfect. For a great many of us, it has never been better. For the species, especially for the American species, there is no moment in all of past history that can hold a candle to this one. We Calvinist can continue to look for the glitches and hold aloft human frailty and economic complexity; a world thrust into conditions and opportunities it is unable to exploit because it cannot get its act together. But tell me at what other point in history would we like to have lived? It won't get much better than this, sports fans. Not if we want an open society; not if we have to manage the lives and provide the services to 255,000,000 people with a governmental vehicle designed to govern 4,000,000; not if we have to affluence to cram the traffic of 7,000,000 people onto streets designed for 700,000; not if we want freedom of speech and assembly; not if we support free enterprise capitalism, yet still want equality for all of our citizens.

There is no system <u>designed</u> which will bring Isaiah's kind of peace and prosperity to a complex, interlocking, hopelessly snarled system like this one and permit us the freedoms we enjoy. We can get fairly close, but the technology, the politics, the pressure groups, the sheer mass and volume of everything is frightening. We ought to be grateful it holds together and doesn't explode in another "Big Bang". The fact that it is not perfect — could be made better — doesn't mean it isn't still functioning.

In my lifetime we have achieved amazing things and taking stock brings new perspective. My grandfather would look at my Cadillac or a 747 jet with his eyes agog. It would have taken him a week to drive to Naples, Florida, a trip we made from Indianapolis in two <u>hours</u>. What would he have said if I told him we can put people on the moon? He'd have called the county asylum. He'd react the same way if we explained heart and liver transplants; how to eradicate diphtheria, polio and smallpox; told him how telephones now work by bouncing signals off satellites circling the earth. He would think the modern computer was black magic; atomic power unfathomable; and the minimum wage an executive's salary. The simple convenience of hot and cold running water in the house, central heating and air-conditioning; refrigeration; trips to any part of the world nightly … the Serengeti, underwater in the Great Barrier Reef, climbing Mount Everest; monitoring a California wildfire; battlefield views of the fight in Bosnia, and a jillion other places by virtue of the television would be out of Sir Thomas More or Nostradamus. All commonplace to us, all routine and none of it properly appreciated.

Yet, most of the world today lives like my grandfather. It thinks a drink of fresh water a blessing; three squares a day; wunderbar; a warm (or cool) dry home, nirvana … miracles. Looking back at how it used to be or forward to what it might become are fantasies of the mind and perhaps enjoyable. But unless helpful in terms of meeting tomorrow's problems, they are pretty empty. We might be grateful indeed to the Almighty for what we remember and be optimistic about what we might see for the future. But we had really better be on our knees in the profoundest gratitude for the blessings of this Christmas, in this society, and rejoice in the entire American experiment as it looks down from the mountaintop on all of man's previous toil up the painful slope. ∎

1995

It Seems Like 50 Years

February 1995

Because that is what it is ... a half century! On the 2nd of June, 1945, E.W. MacAllister signed an agreement with Bill Ziegler, Caterpillar's Eastern Division Sales Manager, to become the dealer for 68 of the 92 counties in Indiana. I made the trip to Peoria with my father and being still in uniform, must confess I cut a dashing figure with six campaign ribbons, three presidential unit citations, five service stripes and silver Captain's bars. Only problem was, all that didn't make much of an impression on E.W. He may have been impressed enough to offer me a job when CAT asked him to

take their account, but he failed to give me commensurate rank in the new company he was forming. Fact is, he started me off where he thought the company needed me, and about where my machinery talents lay. That was close to the bottom of the heap: a stock chaser in the Parts Department, working for Lee Henderson.

Point is, I was on deck with the old company, MacAllister <u>Tractor</u> (who had done nobly with the Allis Chalmers account during the war) the last three weeks of its existence and helped pack up to move from 802 Daily to the diggin's of the replaced CAT dealer at 2118 North Gale Street. It was there we prepared to do battle for Caterpillar and righteousness, a locus that served us for the next 21 years. Unhappily, the records of that era, the photos

Above: Bill Ziegler, E.W. MacAllister and P.E. MacAllister on June 2, 1945 signing the Caterpillar contract.

Left: Caterpillar contract with MacAllister, 1945.

and the memorabilia have long been checked out as "junk" and aside from a few fragments, most reconstruction has to come from memory. At which point I'm reminded of John Masfield,

"I am last alive that knows it,
All the rest have gone their way" ("Spanish Waters")

(A destitute old pirate recalling buried treasure with no way to retrieve it.) Like he, there is no one to help <u>me</u> remember what's buried in the past.

The history of these 50 years has been exciting, especially when engaged in a thing called "free enterprise" where there are not merely certain rules (multiplied now by Πr^2, thanks to the federal government), but there is a continual testing and reaffirmation of competence. There is no such thing as "failure-to-perform" for very long. We might get by — we <u>do</u> get by — with marginal lawyers, teachers, housewives, mediocre ministers, a politician here and there, a so-so postal employee, but giving lousy performance <u>in business</u>, I keep saying, is a temporary condition just prior to failure. Surveying my industry over the course of that half century, one sees a lot of changes, which fact continues to impress me; more specifically, the realization that every major competitor has departed. And the manufacturers they represented are all totally "reoriented". All have been merged, amalgamated, bought out: none has the same ownership it had in 1945. When this convulsion improves the product or the distribution and the customer is better served, then "Hooray"! But when it is the result of failure to deliver, an artificial device to shore up the enterprise, then "O tempore, O mores" as Cicero used to say.

After 50 years one is entitled to a bit of retrospection. And then to some philosophical musing:

1960 Stockholders meeting: E.W. and Hilda MacAllister (front), Stan Emanuel, Norman Williams, Bruce Beckley, David MacAllister, Rollo Ramaker, Gene York, Howard Taylor, Becky and P.E. MacAllister, Lee Henderson.

Which ponders the secret to survival and wonders what 50 years on the line means.

Without preening or breaking an arm in an effort to pat one's self on the back, the fact of survival is not commonplace. Sixteen out of 17 businesses in America fail; the average life is 7.5 years. Only one in 29 who survives, makes the generation-continuity transfer which puts the odds of a business starting and sustaining, at 493-1. The odds in making the transfer of ownership and management to the third generation, I need a mathematician to calculate. Our manufacturers felt the pain as well. There were 94 CAT dealers when E.W. passed the baton to me; today there are something like 63. Continuity in our system is not automatic. It is achieved only with considerable — and successful — effort.

"So what does hanging around for half a century prove?" In my opinion, several things such as:

- We had the <u>right account</u>, the right product, and successfully battled competition not only to preserve, but to triumph. Our machine population in this territory is greater than all competitors combined (in the larger/medium machine category. We got into the loader-backhoe business late, remember?)

- We have managed to find the <u>right people</u> in critical spots to do the job which was acceptable to the manufacturer. As an example, last year <u>our</u> salesman, Tony Reisman, was rated by Caterpillar as "the best CAT machinery salesman in North America". We think a lot of "Tonys" work for us.

- We have been able to handle luck: take advantage when it's good luck, finesse it when bad.

- We have learned "the drill". Elsewhere in this issue an article suggesting Caterpillar — recently — rated us the "Number One Dealer in the United States" in dominance of CAT parts sales to CAT customers.

  Our <u>Service</u> Department's DCAL (percent done of total available) was second in the nation in 1993 (last figure available).

- We have learned how to learn. Which means how to teach, to change, to structure, to relate, to communicate, to market, and to manage. And like the "Energizer Bunny", learning had better go on and on and on.

The significant element of 50 years has been the capacity to respond to a necessity, the necessity of doing better that which we <u>have</u> to do, in the performance of our sundry functions. The program which Chris instituted almost four years ago now called

"Q-Max" is another phase, one that seeks to involve all employees in this process and make sure they understand how important is their role not only in serving the user, but in improving the processes of their own dealer; how to make the workplace more efficient, safer, more attractive; make the job easier to do.

A fortuitous generational succession is critical in this search for survival because younger managers bring new relevance, and they bring a flood of new ideas. A typical problem of old fogies is a mentality programmed to a "bye" gone era. Remembering how things <u>used</u> to be, what elements <u>then</u> gave us success, and measuring by the yardstick we employed 25 years back. Some of it is surely still appropriate, about as much as is now obsolete. But tolerance of any error in the capitalist system is dangerous and sustaining or institutionalizing an archaic or invalid premise as a corporate practice automatically orchestrates severe difficulty, if not ultimate failure. Errors are part of the human equation, and we have certainly made a bundle of them. But thank goodness we have seen them in time and got them neutralized or been able to pay the price of error and learn. Blundering isn't what is fatal; failure to redress or correct is what causes the problem; so to leave in place ineffective policies because you don't see their weaknesses courts disaster. Younger people are critical to the present and future because once fitted to the discipline and dynamic of the dealership, they keep it pertinent to the buying market which is likewise refreshed with continuing management changes within the same generational pattern. Our young guys likewise deal better with bankers, factory people, competitors and IRS agents than I do because these, too, are of the new generation. A parallel rejuvenation permits a better relationship because each uses the dynamic and system of 1995.

We all know change is essential. <u>How it is negotiated</u> is even more essential. History has a thousand illustrations of superb institutions that ultimately become obsolete. Will Durant provides an example in his accounts of Greece and Rome through their intersection along a number of lines…mostly military. Hellas dominated the eastern Mediterranean two and a-half centuries after the golden age of Pericles, thanks to military genius of Philip II and a professional army curiously structured around the phalanx. In case you've forgotten, this was a body of soldiers (hoplites) formed with 256 men across the front, 26 rows deep, a body of 4096 men. The chief weapon was the sarissa, spear or lance 18 feet long thrust

Now 3 generations of MacAllister dealer principles' — Chris MacAllister (left), P.E. MacAllister (middle) with upcoming future Alex MacAllister to be the fourth.

outward to present a battlefront like an uneven porcupine. Drilled like a color guard, it moved behind four rows of steel points; disciplined, functioning with methodical and devastating precision. So effective was this army, Alexander could confidently land in Asia with 37,000 men and fight forces five, even <u>ten</u> times larger than his and never lose a battle — from the Danube to the Indus. Here was an indestructible vehicle for warfare.

Until Pyrrhus took the phalanx to Italy against the Romans in 295, however, and ran into a buzz saw. What he ran into was the Roman Legion, large as a phalanx — 4300 troops — laid out in checkerboard fashion with its blocks of legionnaires grouped in 30 separate squares (maniples), ten wide and three deep, with distance between each the size of the maniple itself. What this provided was remarkable versatility. Instead of wheeling 4096 men, we can move 750 or 1750 where needed — quickly. If there was a break in the enemy line, ten units could slide up through from the rear and go clanging into the breech. Cohesion, rapidity of movement, mobility and new formations made the phalanx obsolete. Unsurpassed in its day, by 250 B.C., it's utility was all but zilch. Not so because of weapons, armor, climate, elephants or bran flakes. What singled its demise were new battle formations, fluidity, versatility, greater options.

So it isn't how good you <u>were</u> for 200 years, or in our case how good for 50, it's how good you are <u>now</u> on each new battlefield. Achieving success in the good old days of Dwight Eisenhower is a fond memory, but it really doesn't prove a lot about now. It says we could handle it all then, but we are fully aware the competition has changed, products and markets are different, and we have Bill Clinton (Hooray!) plus an army of federal regulators, taxers and inspectors to deal with now. The same tactic that won the day in the '50s, when the toll-road was finishing and the interstate beginning is of little relevance now. The secret for us and our owners is surely supplanted by the experience of the past in two areas. One has been mentioned, it is looking for trouble in order to control it. We need to not only find our problems, but to solve our problems. Beyond that, on a different level, the traditions of the past are still important…especially commitment to integrity. We are in a business that does over $140,000,000 a year on the basis of mutual trust. We have to take our customer's word and trust in his fulfilling obligations, and we have to set the example by square shooting with him. They have to believe in the quality of our product, the fairness of our pricing, the decency of our people, and know that service is not a slogan, but a fact. That our "people skills" are what ultimately arbitrates success just as much as the quality of our product. If we can succeed in teaching this generation the ethic and moré of the distribution business which my dad imparted to me as surely as we train them in the technical aspects of its demands and opportunities, we can look with confidence toward the next 50 years and make it work as well as we have in the past. ■

Looking Back

February 1995

As one looks back 50 years, he can't help recalling the age or era in which our new company functioned, vis-à-vis the environment it negotiates today. He both shudders and rejoices, depending on the image coming to mind. He recalls the primitive shop conditions, the sledge hammer power, the lack of safety precautions, the number of accidents occurring (both with us and within our industry), and he is somewhat appalled. Part of that problem in our service operation was due to the relatively primitive building, originally constructed to warehouse lumber and, thus, oriented to general rather than specific purpose. It occurred, too, because much of the power supplied anywhere in that day was supplied by human muscle and more lifting was done with the arms and shoulders than winches or automatic hoists. Jacks were mechanical; hoists were "A" frames avec pulleys, hand-operated through chain power. No specialization equipment, no engine stands, no washing or cleaning tanks, no torque wrenches, no pneumatic tools.

We live, however, as a species within the culture provided by our age, whether the "culture" is social, economic, financial or technological, assuming that human ingenuity and initiative will supply the effectuating momentum. Meaning, we worked with what we had at hand, but got the job done just as effectively as we do today, if one could compensate for the elementary shop equipment. And maybe done just as quickly. Our tooling was simpler, but the equipment on which we worked was far less complex, and there were limited number of models in which to gain technical proficiency. The element of shop equipment is, of course, critical, but the key element, the one that makes the difference, is the human skill. The professionalism achieved. The degree of proficiency we were able to develop or inculcate. Dumb people can make humongous mistakes with the world's most advanced equipment and careless people today still constitute the chief source for our service rework account. The quality and caliber of tools supplied cannot eradicate human bungling.

Reflecting on the personnel effect of a shop workforce leads to the type of mechanic we attract to our business. He may come from anywhere, but to a large extent, many of ours have come out of rural Indiana where maybe so-called polish, or modern social sophistication, is minimal. More specifically, many have come out of Southern Indiana and since the degree there of gentility has little impact on manual dexterity or understanding the mechanical principles, background checks are primitive, if not totally superfluous. What he usually brings from his environment is a strong work ethic; a conditioning to manual labor and a desire to learn, a tolerance for some rough going and some hard work. "Rough going", meaning, he is not intimidated or threatened by crawling under a tractor stuck in the mud somewhere back in the boonies that isn't gonna move until he gets it fixed. It also means working at night, weekends, in the heat of August, and the blast of January; means working not only in mud, but in grease, oil and hydraulic fluid. With respect to mechanics, then and now, the challenge is the same and, frankly, the prototype has not changed. I have never been convinced that young people in this generation are less ambitious or less dependable than young people in my generation. They work just as hard and just as seriously today as they did 50 years ago, and our turnover of employees (forever a problem) is no greater — relatively — than it was when my Dad opened his new company in June of 1945.

Although this has dealt with shop conditions, the environment in which our mechanics worked, the same element of "tooling" is an item which impacted us across the board. The whole building was a lumber warehouse, not just in the back "L" where the service operation functioned. All functions were rudimentary — because the age, not just the build-

MacAllister Machinery's first Indianapolis location at 2118 North Gale Street.

ing was simpler. Ledgers and records were kept, of course, by hand and with a finely sharpened pencil. Statements were taken monthly with an adding machine and more ledger paper. Accountants, clerks, even parts pullers could add, subtract and multiply without a hand-held computer back in those days. Copies of anything we wanted were produced with a thing called carbon paper. The second sheets were cheap yellow paper and one could maybe get three copies if he wasn't too fussy about the quality on the fourth sheet down. When a mistake was made, out came the eraser...to deal with the original <u>and</u> the three copies, one at a time.

I went nuts, given the mistakes I make in typing, but this is the only way it was done, and stenographers adopted and complied with the current mode. And they typed in offices with so-so lighting and in offices without air-conditioning in the summer. Relief was provided through a fan which blew the hot air around. Early duplication was achieved with stencils and a mimeograph machine and that was about it. You'd be surprised at how much the given techniques for communication curtailed the amount of papers we had to shuffle. And to read; and to file; or to pitch.

The parts operation in that old lumber warehouse on Gale Street occupied the south end of the longitudinal stem of the "L", right where the shop joined the building at right angles. It functioned in principle the way it does now; meaning, we ordered parts from CAT probably once a week, typed them out, mailed them in. We used "Partsgram 106" which has been arbitrating parts operations since time immemorial. It said among other things if we get two sales for a given part in six months, we ought to be stocking one. We establish how many on the basis

P.E. working the parts counter.

of our volume in each part, the <u>maximum</u> number we want to carry and the minimum (that being the trigger). Meaning, when it gets below the minimum number, we ought to order to bring up to maximum. Parts shipments came in through the course of the week out of Peoria (though we finally bought our own truck to facilitate delivery since we thought it would cut down on freight and save us a day or two each week). When they arrived, I'd open the boxes, take the packing list, sit down at the inventory cardex and put down bin locations for each part shipped, then go back to the shipping area and start wheeling the stuff to where it belonged in the warehouse bins. Our records were kept on cards in a series of umpteen file drawers, each with maybe 25 or 30 cards over-lapping each other so one could see the part number at the bottom of the card, flip up the rest on top and enter figures on the part number processed or restocked. In this case the number he just put in the bins was added to the number in stock already, arriving at a new total inventory count.

Point is, it was all manual and was labor intensive. But it was so critical in terms of good service to customers; this is where <u>I</u> was assigned to work on opening day as I began my career with MacAllister Machinery Company. It was a vital role. The entire shop operation depended on it, did it not? On <u>supplying</u> parts for every tractor torn down and being repaired in our shop. In fact, every machine in our territory which was down with mechanical trouble was dependent upon my ability to supply the right parts in order to get them back in operation and making money for the owner. It might have been the critical function in the whole company...maybe the whole Indiana economy. (It <u>might have been</u>, but it wasn't. The <u>system</u> was what made it work, and still does. Any dummy can open boxes and locate where we are storing '4A332 filter', and if it is in row 6, location A-41, and if he can read, now takes the new stock back to that location. Any dummy can pull parts by reversing the order and it does not take a rocket scientist to put a carton together and pack parts in it for either shipment or for pick up. Truth is my Dad found the simplest job in the joint for me when I signed on, one so fundamental and elementary even I couldn't blow it and disgrace myself.)

Fact is, though still utilizing the same principle, the current parts operation is so complicated with its microfiche, its computer search, with daily stock ordering, automatic pricing, extensions, and inventory, I am now no longer qualified to function there. Technology has passed me by.

Maybe the selling phase of the operation in 1945 was the one which changed the least over the span of the years. E.W. MacAllister was a super salesman and <u>loved</u> the craft. Fact, his skill there and general reputation is what attracted CAT to his potential and invited him to consider the Caterpillar account. So he did a lot of the selling himself and probably could have done it all alone the first three years since machinery was tough to get and people lined up for the number of units we were allocated from CAT's short supply. But to cover the territory and to prepare for days when the tables would turn, he secured four new salesmen and added them to Tommy Thomas, his old salesman through the war years. Five guys in the field meant five separate territories, and each represents the company there. George Bowman was an ex-school teacher who had worked for Jack B. Haile; Walter Zarnekow was a German immigrant and had cut his eye teeth with Jake Rose up in Northern Indiana selling machinery of sundry sorts. K.C. Cawood had been a state highway engineer, and Al Hipskind had also been with the State Highway Department.

The deal with these people was simple: We shall pay you one third of the commission we make on each deal, and you in turn will take care of your own expenses, period. What could be simpler? A hundred thousand dollar sale at 20% profit (which was what we should be making in those days) meant the company made $20,000. The sales commission is, thus, about $6,700. This illustration is contemporary and it is illusory. A D8 in those days sold for about $8,000 with a bulldozer blade on it. Profit would be $1,600 and the salesman would then get about $550. If a guy made $15,000 a year and it cost him $5,000 to travel, he was netting something like $10,000 before taxes. That was six or seven times greater than the average Hoosier made in wages that year. In short, it was a good — in fact it was a handsome — living.

Since I'm making comparisons, then and now, this is not a tough one to make. Selling in 1945 I noted was no problem. <u>Getting</u> machines to deliver was the sticker. And it stayed that way for three years or so. But when the day came wherein I had to manage the sales force, I turned the job over to Bill Diehl, a contemporary of mine who was a superb salesman himself. Between us, we learned that one of the five was the best and one, of course, the worst, a typical situation in any sales force. As times changed

and the challenges posed new problems, we encountered some trouble shifting to accommodate new demands. I have no hesitation in saying that none of the five we had, then, could have made our sales force today on the basis of his selling skill and analytical ability. My Dad was a great guy and a powerful personality, but hiring was not his chief forte nor was he the world's best teacher. Maybe a great salesman is reluctant to relinquish that role and maybe subconsciously he was content to be the sales star. With this team, although good enough to dominate the market, it would never make the playoffs today.

Speaking last of all more generally, in terms of the local, state or national conditions, there are likewise considerable differences. There seemed to be a lot less regimentation and far less regulation or governmental kibitzing in 1945 (despite Franklin Roosevelt's new style of intrusive governance). I don't even recall a sales tax back then; Social Security was maybe three or four percent and was construed to be a modest kicker upon retirement to augment the savings each of us had accrued to make more graceful the twilight years. There was no "profit share" in those days and, thus, no 401K nor did we have such a thing as hospitalization insurance. That did come along maybe about 1951; but when somebody got sick in 1945 he paid his own doctor and hospital bill. Course he was probably only paying $25 a day for a hospital room at that time. We had the traditional holidays, though no one knew who Martin Luther King was yet, and Memorial Day, Washington's Birthday and Armistice Day were celebrated when that fell on the calendar. All this happened before OSHA and ERISA; before Equal Opportunity

Bill Diehl

E.W. MacAllister (right) with customer.

Employment, before ERA; before unemployment compensation, drug testing, environmental testing and hiring quotas. Our work hours were about the same, and we did stay open on Saturday, at least till noon though few of our competitors cared to.

Management was simpler as a style as well. We were, like most CAT dealerships I know, a "benevolent dictatorship". My Father was a strong central figure and liked things done his way. One gets the idea Ross Perot has similar tendencies and even Bill Clinton has the same sort of style, except he doesn't "stay put" very long and his convictions varying from one week to the next on given issues, drive the rest of us crazy. For our operation, E.W. told us what he wanted done, and this was the way we were supposed to function. When you are an unimaginative manager that is not a bad way to find things since it takes much of the responsibility for planning off your shoulders and lets it shift to the boss. When problems arise, we chat with the ole man about it and he tells us how to solve it. Which says that this was also before the age of Edward Deming, Peter Drucker, Tom Peters et al. This is also before "management by

objectives"; it was before written departmental operating procedures, job descriptions, employee testing, before business plans, before training programs, and before drawing up budgets. We sort of managed what came our way and since that had always been adequate, there was little reason to stew or to fret. When things got tough and didn't reach norms or expectations, we'd worry about them. My Dad had lived through the Great Depression and was no stranger to adversity. He was supremely confident in his ability to solve our problems, and if he was confident, why should we worry.

There was nothing wrong with his style and his outlook if business continued steady and strong. So for several years we went sailing merrily along our way. But underneath us, America was changing and along with it America's people, its system, its fundamental concepts, and its economic texture. The control and discipline forced upon us by the depression years, then by the war years, then by a couple years of shortages, were suddenly released in the last years of the '40s and the early '50s and a new age swept in with a lot of looseness, a lot of ideas about how we should think, live, work, play, educate ourselves, constitute our political systems, and represent the will of this republic. No one really saw the early years as a warm-up, as a conditioning, as a preparatory period for circumstances far different and for opportunities or threats which lie ahead. MacAllister Machinery Company was off on the first stage of a long ride, one extending now for 50 years in terms of its duration, and one which has taken us through some hard years, some so-so years, some desperate times and some great times. The pride and the dreams of E.W. are transformed and preserved in an institution, still trying to reflect his better ideals and his strong principles as it endeavors to fit into this day's regiment of demand and still hopes to seize every new opportunity for sales and for service. ■

50 Years on the Fast Track with CAT

June 1995

This, of course, should be designated "The Official Anniversary Issue", commemorating our 50 years in business. And as we proceed with an employee party on June 3rd; five branch open houses, the inauguration of a new building in Washington, the publication of our corporate history and distribution of miscellaneous commemorative memorabilia, it might pay to point out we are not celebrating just to have some fun, we are acknowledging or consecrating a milestone along our course. The sundry activities, the events and accompanying hoopla have at their core some basic reason or some principle which is worthy of highlighting. Said another way, the fun part or the socializing or the speeches and feasting are not self-justifying. They represent an underlying condition or situation which now takes on physical manifestation. This will not be self-evident, since not everyone who "parties" stops to ask "Why," pauses to sort out causes for the merriment. Fun is not all that complicated; it is having a good time, which is sufficient for most people to pitch in and enjoy.

I'm suggesting, however, that we are going through all this trouble and getting everything decorated because we are proud to have survived. Prouder still of the people whose efforts have sustained our half-century of service; and in the process permitted us to stay the course where others have failed. We have made a contribution; we have vindicated my Father's founding purpose: represent Caterpillar with distinction in Indiana. So what we are marking is the success of the company. "Success" because in terms of free enterprise, when it survives the competitive process, the machinations of the government, the vagaries of the market, occasional road blocks by organized labor (CAT is still on strike), and the uncertain hand of fortune which from time to time afflicts — or propels — us all, it is pure and simple: AN ACHIEVEMENT.

I think naively enough that running a business in America today is still an adventure. It has elements of the unpredictable on every hand (like almost daily); there is major risk and ample opportunity to mishandle one's affairs leading to disaster; there is the heady aroma of success when Lady Luck lends a hand; or super satisfaction when personal — and corporate — effort mount adversity

and triumph. In case you haven't thought this through, success is not all that commonplace. We create something like 600,000 new businesses each year in America; have about 9,000,000 of them chugging away now across the land. Right now! This number might remain constant, but each roll-call will see different faces. In three years, 27% of 1995's crop will have gone by the boards; in five years, 44% who answered today will be gone, and by year ten — 2005 — 69% of those started will have collapsed along the way. Or been so successful the owners sold out and retired to Naples, Florida. That record, of departure, seen out of the corner of one's eye, is what adds intensity to this endeavor and keeps us deadly serious about nonchalant performance or bad guessing. No company I know was created to last for 5 or 10 or 20 years and then automatically self-liquidate. Yet 16 out of 17 depart the scene in 20 years. Inadvertently. Reluctantly. Often painfully. Which is why I say this whole gambit is an adventure.

It is a contest — on going — of one's skill against the odds, and it is risking, not necessarily his life, but his life's savings and his reputation. This isn't rolling the dice with outcome completely contingent upon luck, but when you have $50,000,000 in machinery inventory, betting that it will be sold in due course and have borrowed $25,000,000 to pay for it, it is gambling. One could equate rolling dice at Caesar's Palace with pitching pennies. So it is that sort of dynamic, that movement of substantial investments, requiring lots of people whose individual judgment from time to time has a stack of your chips in the game, that keeps the adrenaline flowing. Which is why doing it right for half a-century seemed like a good reason to celebrate.

Beyond that is the recollection of that long span of time and what it has contributed or what it has taught or what it has achieved. Hopefully, it has represented the product adequately and sometimes even excellently over the course of time. It has delivered into the state of Indiana 7,521 Caterpillar new machines worth $839,000,000 plus thousands of tons of parts, which replete with service billing brings our total sales to $1,400,000,000 the past one-half century (looks like a federal number). All were taxable to the sovereign state of Indiana and to the Federal government while our inventories generated as well astronomical personal property taxes to Marion County. Last year it was $265,906. It has, likewise, provided employment for some 2,017 people over the course of time, 360 of them still supporting their families (or their hobbies) as a result of their role with our company. Said folk coming over the years from Indianapolis (of course), Fort Wayne, Plymouth, South Bend, Elkhart, Bedford, Lafayette and Washington, Indiana, as we have opened and closed stores to accommodate an undulating market fluctuation. We have built ten separate structures over the course of the years; owned or rented seven more; end up with our roots down permanently in four of the five cities out of which we currently operate.

What has been the dominant theme over the course of the years, of course, is the restless element of change. We have yakked so much about that, no one needs to build a case for its inexorable inevitability. What successful folks do, however, is see it as an ally and not an enemy. Because it is changing models and product, changing factory lines, even changing structure that has kept Caterpillar — and its dealers — ahead of the field. The objective is not merely to accommodate, it is to become the <u>instrument</u>, the originator of change. Get on the cutting edge. Be the first one in the field with a main frame computer, parts shuttle service, segmented billing in the shop; daily parts ordering; instant inventory entries with every order; lap-top computer-equipped salesmen with ready access to pricing, specs, delivery data on anything we own, a truck engine dyno, etc. If movement is the name of the game, plans are probably always in the making and little that we do is static or anchored in place. We ought to be looking for a better way to do everything which is why we try to involve the whole place in constructive analysis and consideration of our systems and processes. Don't always succeed and can't get everyone really engaged, but compared to the old days when my Father was <u>THE</u> instrument and the rest of us waited for instructions, it has become a genuine democracy around here. Everyone votes. Only trouble is that for some reason or other, when his era kicked in, so did inflation and prices changed.

Ruminating about the old days, I marvel how

they have moved and how we've accommodated to them. I went to a movie as a kid for five or six years, and it cost a dime. When I got to be age 12, the price went up to a quarter, and there it stayed for 20 years. Today, movie Coke is $2.25. UMPH! Then, Coke was a nickel; from 1928 till the '60s. Candy bars ditto, a stick of gum for a penny, and for 25 years an ice cream cone was 5 cents, often with two dips. How did we manage that? Why can't we get back to that static sort of costing? Why doesn't improvement mean more for less? Maybe too much change. But to some degree what hasn't changed is the basic character of our people. Despite the remarkable and astounding fact that what brings about most <u>of our</u> change (before I wandered back to "the good old days") is those same people...or let's say a <u>person</u>, who found a better way who did something new. What has amazed me about these people, hired on at some point in time to do a rudimentary job and work on through the ranks is the way private enterprise develops leadership through its on-going routines. The counterpart to that will be the general reluctance on the part of most people to duck responsibility; to do my job and "leave" the company at five o'clock, not take it home. Not surprising, fact, it's normal. The phenomenon (again-for emphasis) is the talent we do generate in this country which waits for an opportunity to mature, bloom, to be given a chance. Our branch stores are managed by people who sought more responsibility (or maybe <u>it</u> sought <u>them</u>) and who simply worked their way up to managerial slots. And in the process and maybe only by <u>this process</u> are able to fit our peculiar brand of service to a given geographic region or market constituency. Washington is a good example. The service operation is run by Donnie Shelton and out of what was almost a makeshift sort of shop. He has painstakingly developed a capacity for our people to work on gargantuan machinery units there or en situ (in place); meaning, down in the bottom of a box cut in a coal mine (and probably in the mud), sorting out various problems and pulling apart machines that are three stories high to get them fixed. Twenty-four hours a day, summer and winter, daylight and dark, whenever you need it. He runs 22 field service trucks out of his office, says grace over 29 in shop mechanics plus five under carriage men while Jerrel Blackburn runs his parts people in parallel tracks, indicating scope of operation by dollar sales. Last <u>month</u>, $1.5 million in parts sales. Mecastor! As Tacitus used to say. (Holy moly!) These two men do not achieve a genuinely remarkable level

Chris MacAllister (left), P.E. and Donnie Shelton at the 1994 Washington branch ground breaking.

of success because of superb facilities and protracted training. They did do it because they are leaders, self developed, home grown.

The point here is that we could not hire someone from MIT or Wharton for any price who could generate the results these men and their counterparts have. For the simple reason this is Southern Indiana, and its coal and contracting market. Decidedly demanding and unique, learned first hand not vicariously. Local people know the drill. Securing and training others is the key. The application, the demands, and the servicing capacity have to fit together, all part of the milieu; of the circumstances created by the application environment.

The genius here as we cultivate managers is conditioning people in their given sphere of influence to meet the distinct requirements peculiar to a particular store. Since they are part of the culture, honed by practice and the customer needs, they automatically and axiomatically transform our corporate response to fit the given situation. It can't be done with directives from Chris' office or mine because we are not in the middle of it and don't know precisely what the proper reaction should be from one, to the next, to another, and to this bird. But our managers and employees do know and deliver the company's penchant for service, extending it to each occasion which arises because all are taught the same sense of urgency. If we've achieved success the past 50 years, it's really great for the company and its owners, but it's the result of the esprit de corps developed naturally out of a given circumstance and shaped by clever and perceptive managers in each of the last five decades.

Behind all of it is more than homespun routine, there is a decided type of supervision which when replicated across our company tries to see our role performed in all the departments and in each location. Again, we don't win them all, and we have personnel turnover, but generally speaking, most of the direction, the drive, the momentum on-going this, our 50th year, is generated by people whom we have trained, and in the American tradition know what initiative and responsibility are all about.

It is evident in the two guys down south; in Paul Fuhrman at Fort Wayne; in Randy Manning in Lafayette; or Bobby Saint; or Eric Reimer and Bruce Zupancic up there in South Bend; Roger Woodruff in Truck Engines; and to a degree in Chris, since he came thru the ranks. A step at a time. It was evident, too, in Bill Diehl, in Ruth Booker, Dick Hagen, and a generation or two of former managers and colleagues. It was evident in my Father whose management style fit perfectly to his age and element.

Over the course of these long years, I have learned something else and said it earlier: The hourly people who work for us don't change all that much as prototypes. We don't stew much about "work ethic." We worry about what the government is doing for folks who <u>they</u> used to do for themselves and see a continual incursion into our lives and institutions with more and more regulation and general meddling. We have a lot of homeless people, have too many on welfare avoiding work and a preoccupation with television and the sitting-room couch. But the young people here in the tractor business work just as hard and just as long and just as diligently as they did 40 or 50 years ago. We make a mistake of watching the newspapers, reading of those who make the news. Invariably <u>characters</u>, wild, eccentric or troublesome, as though this minority were indeed the pattern or the norm rather than an aberration.

Left to right: Bob Poorman-Machine Sales Manager, P.E. MacAllister-Chairman, Jim Bernhardt-Manager Engine Division, D.W. MacAllister-President, 1990.

Roger Woodruff (left) and Doug Friddle in 1981, diagnosing an engine.

We don't have any more idlers, dummies, coasters or hitchhikers today than we had then, and our output from the American workforce is still the highest in the industrial world. So I give kudos for all the overtime put in and the night shift and the employees available on-call around the clock, and the steady slogging through the years. Fact is, they are called upon to do more. There is a demand on today's employee for a far greater degree of sophistication than he needed "way back when". A technological revolution was spawned by the war and propelled by accelerated usage those three and a-half years, one which continued into peace time and has not rested since. For example — to illustrate my point - today's mechanics, salesmen, secretaries, clerks, accountants, and everyone around here (but me) has become to some degree computer literate. Meaning, they learned something new — something <u>else</u>. The gadgetry does amazing things in trouble-shooting, performance analysis, production of graphs, delivering untold data, spitting out financial statements, credit info, giving us all three times the information we employed back in 1945. We developed more paper than we use or need, but the key to success anywhere is <u>information</u>. Without it, we are in a guessing game. The surer we are of the facts, the better should be the call and the more precise and constructive the management. But what this does is thrust upon the average employee another demand in terms of training and another function aside from that required by his job. I'm saying workers and managers have to be better equipped and generally smarter than they were then. It is typified further in terms of being much "a broader company" because a mechanic now has to work on 50 different models of machinery versus he who had only 20 to worry about when I was your age.

I just wrote a history of the company, beginning with 1945, and was reminded that America had a great deal of building to do when we ended hostilities in August of that year. The nation had been through 3½ years of war on top of 11 years of nasty depression that put a damper on most public and private construction. The major urban areas were eroding, and the infrastructure was pretty well hammered out of shape, leaving much to do across this wide and sunny land. In responding to this pent-up pressure, there was a stuttering splurge which "splurged" very slowly, because there was a paucity of materials. But gradually we began to re-order most of our society, urbanizing it, and scattering our cities out into suburbia. A great building boom resulted as we discovered the subdivision, prefabricated housing, the shopping mall, and all the leisurely accoutrements to edge-of-city life. Then we built great dam projects for water conservation, the toll road and the interstate, airports, campuses, subways. We did all of this ... and continue to do it ... <u>only when our equipment prepares the way</u>. Have you ever thought about that? Only when the dozer could clear the trees, the scrapers move the dirt for building sites and highways, the excavator can dig sewer lines and bridge footings, and all the rest. This might sound a bit strange, but progress flows only insofar as the construction element of society can facilitate it. Which is the reverse spin on what I have concluded, long ago, about "life on the fast track with CAT", and that is that we make our living as facilitators. We are in a business that helps create, build, renovate, maintain, and stretch out the living-working areas of American life. It is different than recreation or leisure or wholesaling or accounting, all of which are totally respectable. But to be <u>building</u>, renewing, and creating is a nobler endeavor, and there is some small pride in participating in that peculiar, but essential exercise, a fact of our dealership life every year for half a century.

So in closing, we are celebrating 50 years because we have survived, succeeded, achieved where our competition has faltered and failed. We have vindicated my Dad's reason for coming into the CAT family, i.e. get out the CAT product, serve the customer, and maintain a modern well equipped plant with professional employees. We have recruited and developed leadership; serviced an undulating and temperamental market, and have facilitated the nation's growth, expansion, regeneration and structural maintenance. And done so for 50 years! Hallelujah! ∎

50 Years of Service — Any Lessons Here?

June 1995

One would think, after fifty years of careening around this industry as a machinery dealer, he would have learned something for his pains. Or perhaps something from his successes. Invariably what we learn is personal and derived out of individual experience and seen to be important or inconsequential, as a result of one's own value system. There's a saying that too many of us "see" not with the eye but with the "I" so here's a bit of what I've learned over the past five decades.

1. Neither contractors nor farmers are ever satisfied with the weather.
2. In our company, every day, a hundred times, an employee dealing with a customer is MacAllister Machinery and represents all 360 of us.
3. It is very hard to keep deals profitable when the buyer is smarter than we are.
4. Product improvement in our field never stops.
5. Long-range planning, beyond two years, is an impossibility because this industry is very poor at forecasting, even a year out.
6. Turnover is inevitable, sometimes desirable, inadvertently can be an advantage but, each time presents a great opportunity to upgrade.
7. Sales Managers and Caterpillar guys are never content with unit deliveries, no matter how high the PINS.
8. The more our salesmen make in commissions, the better the company is doing.

Beyond that, there are a couple of other nuggets I think are fairly important. One comes from the Book of Ecclesiastes, the 9th chapter, 11th verse and goes as follows:

"Again I saw that under the sun the race is not to the swift, nor the battle to the strong, nor bread to the wise, nor riches to the intelligent, nor favor to the men of skill; but time and chance happen to them all. For man does not know his time. Like fish which are taken in an evil net, and like birds which are caught in a snare, so the sons of men are snared at an evil time, when it suddenly falls upon them."

Is this too complex? Or is it unfamiliar? Koholeth, he who has provided this book of ancient wisdom, says simply that winning isn't always the result of speed nor of strength but that Lady Luck, destiny, Fortuna — "time and chance" — arbitrate our destiny. In short, luck has an awful lot to do with personal as well as corporate affairs. And given either, progress or success is contingent upon how well we finesse it. How we handle given conditions, surprises, opportunities, major threats. And parallel with this is the old acorn about Arnold Palmer who had just won one of his matches and was wending his way back to the clubhouse. One of his admirers popped up and said, "Great game Arnie but man, you were really lucky with that 18 footer on the third hole." Palmer looked back and said, "You're probably right friend, but you know something? It's surprising that the more I practice, the luckier I seem to get." Successful people — and companies — surely know how to handle luck whether good or bad when it arrives. More than that, like Palmer, create their own. They do if they have people who know their jobs and keep thinking about how they might do them better. Which brings to mind an illustration instantly from our business and the reason we have dominated the coal market in southern Indiana.

When we first entered the fray, Allis Chalmers had been a major player, Komatsu was obviously evident and there were a lot of Terrex units working busily, excavating coal. None of these people has abandoned the chase but in the last eight years, have decreasing luck in terms of penetration. One reason is the yen/dollar situation; the second is the shifting and change of dealerships and the third thing is a matter of our "corporate luck." That first break came when Doug Clark responded to a major owner who was growling each month about his parts expense.

P.E. and Chris MacAllister in the '90s.

They were indeed humongous. We agreed. Six figure statements each month was really a lot of dough but something hard for us to regret. Our salesman said it was a fact of life but followed up with, "Has it occurred to you that those machines now have over 40,000 hours on them? That old stuff gets expensive to keep around? Why don't you rent a couple of new ones and see what happens?" They proceeded then to rent a big loader and four trucks and *voila!* Parts bills, at least on five pieces, stopped immediately. But then they said, "Hey, the rent's too high." "Right, but you're renting these from month to month. Why don't we look at a 36-month rental deal and see what can be done?" Of course, it did wonders to the rate and in another three months they said, "Hey, can we get some more of these machines on the same basis?"

In the next three years, we traded them out of all the old and off-brand stuff and put in a fleet of brand new Caterpillars, at one point numbering over sixty units. Part of the deal was that we could roll them out and resell them to somebody looking for a bargain, replacing same with brand new units and thus could guarantee machine availability. All this built a larger population which would give us ample records to store plenty of parts, likewise justify a fleet of new field service trucks and simultaneously building a huge inventory of exchange components, all enhancing our service capability enormously. We likewise could now offer the same deals to other owners and had six or eight people in the same mode. It was really a lucky break for the company. But it certainly didn't just happen. Our salesman engineered it, created the dynamic, and did it one step at a time.

Sales team in 1960.

Maybe the lucky thing is living in a territory that has coal but given that prospect or market to start with, the true entrepreneur begins to create his own strategy in one stage after another. In the process, he finds luck builds upon itself and extends stage after stage beyond the original scope.

Maybe a second lesson is revealed in this anecdote and that's the importance of good people. There's a case where a bright salesman saw the opportunity, created a whole marketing strategy. We are all familiar with given persons in history who find a confused and chaotic situation which others have failed to understand or manage. Hitler is one example, someone who knew what to do with a catastrophic German economy during the early '30s and converted an aimless, demoralized German people into a major world threat in less than a decade. When we reflect on Bonaparte's "exile to Siberia" because he was too popular in Paris and shipped off to the army of Italy where it was presumed he would slowly waste away. But almost instantly, he stopped the years of pointless milling around, shaped up the shabby and listless soldiery, sacked a couple of commanders and even dissolved a division in the blink of an eye. In a matter of months, he was ripping apart the Italian and Austrian forces and changed the focus and the face of Europe virtually overnight. The right person is what we need in any human situation if we want it ordered, functional and performing its purpose.

The key to this is not understanding this fact, the key is finding said person which may mean recruiting or it may mean promoting from within but it assumes, of course, we know what we require in terms of talent in each situation. Then having defined it, what we had better know is how to interview in order to ascertain the potential which is repose in each candidate being considered. We spent about fifteen early years getting along fine in the Caterpillar world when there was plenty of business for everybody. But slowly when the job got tougher, more complex, the line got more diverse and moved from ten units to twenty units to forty units in the CAT Sales Manual, the load carried by each manager got heavier. At that point we had to learn how to manage better, how to screen and analyze, how to either train or locate legitimate, bona fide managers. A simple business ritual that's not done easily or thoroughly or reliably, simply through gut reaction or praising the personality traits evident in a given applicant. One has to build a management team or it doesn't occur and he builds it one person at a time with some care. It took a lot of trial and error, a lot of bad calls and traumatic exit interviews before we got it mostly right. We have survived, to a large extent, for a half century because we have "lucked out" with people and, just to be sure, we work hard and carefully to find the right person for each spot.

Third lesson might be simply one of listening. We have to please a lot of constituencies beginning with the customer, with Caterpillar, the employees, the banker, and several governmental agencies. The way we please them all is to find out what each needs then what it is he wants and since we are in the serving business, see if it makes sense. To serve them all — at a reasonable profit because the stockholder has his demands too — is a reasonable objective. But we are directed by what each tells us; our assignment is to respond favorably and judiciously. No one says this is easy but as a professional, it's critical to success.

Maybe another verity I've learned is that people are basically honest. I stay continually amazed at the amount of volume we do on the basis of mutual confidence between buyer and seller and seller and buyer.

Time after time, somebody can call and say he needs X number of pieces of machinery and without signed orders or an attorney standing by your side; we're on the phone to CAT ordering same because we can trust he with whom we're dealing. This is certainly hundreds of thousands of dollars in many instances and as a matter of fact, it's $150,000 a day worth of parts sales — on the telephone — billed next day and expecting payment the next month. We seem to take all this for granted and that is really a shocker. Never counting unusual this trust and confidence existing in the commercial apparatus of America. OK, there are people out there we have to watch and there is a thing called C.O.D. There's also bad debt write-off each year, maybe two to three-tenths of one percent of sales. But even most of these are mismanagement, bad luck, or stupidity. It is rare we encounter one who is deliberately out to snooker us.

The degree of integrity, I'm saying, is surprisingly high and maybe along with a couple of other lessons, is something I recount with pride when reflecting on my fifty years in this fascinating location. ■

Perception — Old and New

September 1995

History, like beauty, to a large extent lies "in the eyes of the beholder". Because in the very process of recording events we inadvertently "record" what it is we perceive. Unhappily, we see as much with the "I" as we do the "eye". We tend, as we write what has happened, to simultaneously <u>interpret</u> it, and thus, we give to accounts (sometimes inadvertently) our own personal spin. Incidents, persons, conditions, degree, import, all come into print as a result of our perception of not only how they occurred, but what they might mean. There is nothing profound in all of this, but there is something unnerving. Because first off a record of "indisputable facts" turns out to be someone's impression of same and can turn out to be neither indisputable nor, indeed, "fact". The other aspect, or the circumstances (or maybe it is merely a parallel aspect), is the probability that two or three of us can see the same incident or look at the same battle or event and see different things in it. So whatever the condition or occurrence, our interpretation of it probably skews from the simple purity of the act or situation itself because of the necessity of describing it and, thus, recourse to how <u>we</u> have seen or viewed it.

In the course of writing a history of our company this past 50 years, I have been a prime example of delivering to prospective readers not only an account of what happened, but also an interpretation — a perception — of what happened. Often the opinions about a given situation dominate the facts and history is submerged beneath personal reaction. But beyond that, it became very apparent that a good many things which tumbled out of the archives during the course of our research are seen in a far different light <u>now</u> than when they happened. The perspective of time, I discovered when the opus was finished, had me seeing day-to-day routines, relationships with my fam-

E.W. MacAllister.

ily, the on-going war with competitors all far more nonchalantly than I remember them <u>being</u> as I lived and reacted in the midst of this eternal conflict which is free enterprise entrepreneurship. Maybe after one wins the battle, he is inclined to far more leniency and generosity than is allowed him in the middle of the campaign as though the intensity and passion are needed <u>during</u> the encounter, but can justly and reasonably subside once the laurels are won.

My father was a problem to me as a novice in this business because he was exacting, he was very good at what he did, an indefatigable worker, and loved his vocation. He was also scared to death he would spoil me which lead to over-zealous correction. Sometimes publicly, which, of course, infuriated me. Beyond that, although exposed to a good many facets of the business (successively in parts, mechanizing, promotion, and then sales), there was little sharing going on and not a lot of teaching. Capillary action, maybe or else osmosis, was the teaching recourse. So there was some bitterness and disappointment, and I was not exactly a happy camper. In retrospect, however, there is mostly gratitude in my mind. It finally became apparent my father was a product of his generation, and he was not only ignorant of Dr. Spock, he probably would have considered him irrelevant. Dad was a busy guy and a successful one. Educated in a one-room school for eight grades, all taught by one teacher, he learned enough there to "learn how to learn" the rest, and by age 25 was the Highway Commissioner in Oconto County, the youngest ever lived in the state of Wisconsin. At age 35 he was the General Manager of the biggest machinery distributor in the state of Wisconsin, and ten years later had his own dealership.

What I perceived in the relationship was slanted toward how all this impacted me, since I was the center of my own universe and took for granted a stable family life, always respected in the community, plus my father's leadership role in the other life he lead. The opinion was based far too much on selfish, quasi-emotional reasons, and ignored the breaks I got because they were assumed, not unique. What arrogance! I got my first corrective lessons about my dad in the months following his incapacitation when I was thrust into his role of directing the company and learned what the industry... customers, influencers, colleagues, competitors, and associates...thought about him. They thought he was a tiger; a giant, and lauded his impeccable integrity.

On the other hand, my dad was disappointed I was not more like him. I didn't have his excitement about the business; was not much of a salesman; my judgment was probably not very mature, and I wasn't a very good back-slapper. My hunch is that he thought I was a trifle mis-assigned, and there was no way I would ever run this operation. He may have been right. But what I couldn't do <u>like</u> him, I got done by finding enough of the right people, who <u>could</u> do it like him and, thus, got the job done. The happy ending is the fact that through the years as the company succeeded, he became very proud of what was happening and was a great bragger about my modest achievement. By this time, personal friction absent, I learned to appreciate what a remarkable man he was. But you can see the point here: Each of us to a degree mis-appraised the other and our perceptions, seen too much through the "I's" prevented a rapprochement which could have served both of our purposes — and our destinies — infinitely better.

In reminiscing about our competitors, the same dynamic is present. Our feelings were often fairly intense "back when". We held the CAT price line fairly well for a great many years, and our guys always felt disadvantaged because we weren't into heavy discounting. Stands to reason if all of us cut 15% off our margins, we are back to the same position we were holding the line at list. So to see competitive sales managers not only cutting prices, but cutting $10,000 and $15,000 more than they needed seemed like an unfair tactic which escalated my blood pressure more than once. Seemed like cheating to me. Today, however, the guys I bitched about so vociferously are no longer around, and it is hard to stay "ticked" at people who have folded. What stayed, of course, was the discounting. <u>We</u> may have survived, but <u>they</u> converted the marketplace. Ugh! Sitting down now with any of those old timers who used to bang heads with us is no longer an exercise in hypocrisy; it is an exercise in nostalgia. It is joining hands with someone who can remember the nature of our trek through the last generation and help explain how it is we got here. The facts of the history have not changed, of course, but the personal opinions and perception of these competitive people and their practice no longer galls me.

Changing outlook is not only a function of time and distance; it is a product of mood as well. We can look at a given set of circumstances one day and see them as real problems; yet two weeks later, after the old sub-conscious has a chance to work, view them as opportunities. It is common in large corporations, for example, not to let agents on transatlantic flights go into a heavy, complex business transaction upon arrival. A thing called "jet lag" has done something to the circadian cycle. We do not think as clearly when we are tired or discombobulated. We don't think as well at home either if we are fatigued, or have had a problem with the kids or experienced some tragic or frightening experience. We have more courage; think with more clarity when fresh, energetic and optimistic. Saying, again, that viewing the same problem, we can come up with different answers contingent upon how we feel personally. Perception changes as does the person.

The element of perspective, as considered in our business world finds similar patterns. The problems we encounter are both exciting as well as confusing. We pride ourselves on our dealer parts service, and the record indicates that with the CAT depot here in town, it is a rare order that does not have the parts in your hands or on the way in 24 hours. There is an edge given a dealer or manufac-

D.W., P.E., D.W. Jr, E.W. and Hilda.

turer who has a jillion units in the field and ten years worth of demand in his files versus the Rolls Royce Company who sold 400 units in the United States last year. But what happens is the user or customer gets conditioned to this sort of service and considers this to be normal...for Caterpillar dealers. He expects 24-hour service. If you are running Komatsu or Link Belt or Wabco, however, and the delay is a week, two weeks, no one is foaming at the mouth.

There is another curious perception, and that's about the high <u>cost</u> of Caterpillar parts <u>and</u> the astronomical cost of today's machinery. A perception that needs to be examined from a vantage point other than model number and dollar list. In doing some investigation on pricing as part of my recent research, discovered that the 1945 dollar which was the medium of exchange the year we came into business, had a purchasing power 8.2 times greater than today's. Ten cents then is equal to 82 cents today. We ought to factor the high-priced dollars we are complaining about so that they relate to some universal. A $100,000 machine today was a $12,200 machine in 1945. Which also said that anyone who had $120,200 in 1945 and kept it in a bank where it grew with inflation would qualify now to be a millionaire (which is why there are so darn many around. They are in 1945 terms "hundred thousandaires".) But moving on to the point, the horsepower cost in today's machines surely costs a lot more than it did then, even in weighted dollars. Maybe, fact is, today's D4 and D6 tractors, actually cost less per single horsepower than was the case when we sold our fist D4 in August of 1945.

But look beyond that at the units now and then. When we say "D4 or D6" and the tractor he is now considering is infinitely more complex and far more technical than the "same" tractors of yore. There is no way to make a proper comparison so rattling off the mantra that "today's machinery has gone out of sight price wise" one needs to look at said machines and see what he is buying. The old D6 and dozer was a

pretty straight machine with no frills and ran forever. The current D6 has a high sprocket final drive, comes equipped automatically with a cab and roll-over structure, the seat is now an "operator's station" with an adjustable contour seat, instrument panel with an electric monitoring system; has an automatic transmission, differential steering, a single small lever to steer; modular components and a plug-in diagnostic tool connector to trouble shoot and locate electrical problems. It runs forever - and a day. Which might sound a bit flip, but the truth is the current unit will last 50% longer than its tried and true predecessor. The reason: better parts and components. If parts prices are high (though they are less than most competitors who manufacture infinitely fewer), they are killing your friendly dealer because they last so long.

When I worked in the shop back in the '40s I recall a #12 motor grader coming in from Raleigh Burke. It was time for some engine work and the amazing thing we discovered was the engine had run 6500 hours and no one had ever taken the heads off. It was phenomenal. We all came over to take a look at this marvel of CAT durability. Now just between us girls, a motor grader on housing projects is not what you'd call the purgatory of machine pain and trauma. Fact, it's pretty light usage. But relatively speaking, 6500 hours was unique. Today, we stick a motor grader in a coal mine and expect the engine to run 10,000 hours without staining a gasket in hard going. We have units in the coal fields with 35,000 and 40,000 hours on them (a fact which in 1945 would have been declared impossible), and we are able now to bring them in the shop, give them a "certified rebuild", assign a new serial number to them, a new machine warranty, and run these suckers another 30,000 hours. A CAT tractor with 65,000-70,000 hours. I tell you, all this durability is ruining new machinery sales. But the point, again, was first of all quick perceptions of machine cost compared to "something"; and the sub rosa reality which kicks this perception into a cocked hat. ∎

... And Peace To His People On Earth

December 1995

Anyone familiar with the Biblical Christmas Story knows there are really two accounts (one in Matthew and the other in Luke) and surprisingly enough they don't have a lot in common. As if that weren't tough enough, we then get into the issue of ancient language, an evolutionary science, and discover something disturbing in Luke's story (the one with the shepherds and the angels). Time and contemporary epigraphy have changed the darn wording on us. When I was a kid, the shepherds heard the angel "*Gloria*" announcing the birth of the child and the information on where he might be found. The song in my day was "Glory to God in the highest, and on earth, peace, good will toward men". That is the old "King James Version", though, of course, I'm not as old as James, who had nothing to do with translating and little interest in epigraphy itself. Disturbing because The New Oxford Bible uses the same shepherds, same fields, same angels, but puts slightly different words in "*Gloria*": "Glory to God in the highest heaven, and on earth peace <u>among those whom he favors</u>". Do you see the difference? One seems to say, like Tiny Tim, "God bless us, <u>everyone</u>", while the second seems to be far more selective as though God wants to bless some and not others. Curious sort of circumstance and leads to all sorts of questions like, "Why part and not all?"; "What must <u>I</u> do to qualify?" or "Why bother creating people in the first place if you are going to turn your back on them?" Etc.

Like it or not, that sort of eclecticism which sees good fortune for part of us, bad luck for others, turns out prophetically to be the uneven condition of mankind at Christmas time 1995. God has not blessed us all; he has singled out only some for his largess. So, we shall spend the holidays in far different fashions. My family will gather around a groaning table which Becky has prepared, and we'll stuff ourselves on turkey and dressing, mashed potatoes and gravy et al with a braver minority even taking a helping of rutabagas. At the same time in other parts of town, there will be a long line of folks at Wheeler Mission waiting for a Christmas hand-out. And out of sight there will also be homeless people, huddled in cardboard boxes half doped up on cheap wine or drugs who won't even know what day it is. With gradations of status and fortune up and down between two extremes, dependent on health, on affluence, luck, circumstance or some divine — or perverse — destiny.

It is hard to understand why heaven's peace and blessing gets so unevenly distributed, if indeed the Creator is the dispenser of love, compassion, mercy and generosity. Maybe the key to this disparity lies in the phrase "peace on earth" (or "on earth, peace"). Maybe it suggests that God's "favor" or His "good will" can exist <u>only under conditions of peace</u>. That in Bosnia or the Sudan or Sri Lanka it is impossible to distribute any favor, each nation being torn apart in civil wars and awash in violence and hatred. That in many other parts of the world, the furious passion and tribal frenzy so dominate and drive the masses, fury is all consuming. Like the tribal conflict in Rwanda or Somalia; the terrorism in Algeria and Palestine, the oppression in Iraq, North Korea and Iran; the violence in Chechnya.

In other words the systems and frailties and violence of men make peace impossible whether the disruption is physical, political, emotional or psychological, creating an environment hostile to the nurturing of peace. One cannot really have estrangement and "good will to men" simultaneously: one has to dominate the other and unhappily for much of the species, violence and battle are triumphant. Luckily for us, in America, however, our basic heterogeneity and multi-cultural society see most allegiance pledged to the common good and far less to the tribal or sectarian interest. Our political battles are fierce and the oratory vitriolic, but fought with words and ideas not guns, rockets and terror. There is, by comparison then, blessed peace in our land...of long standing. Because we have learned to resolve most differences like "gentlemen". Or maybe "like Christians" is better word though it is a simile and in spirit includes Jews, Islam, Bahia's or other folks harboring sentiments of toleration and kindness.

Know what this gets down to? The simple fact that "peace on earth" and any "goodwill" generated is <u>not</u> a divine condition, but a human one. That <u>we</u> have the capacity to accept a universal blessing to all mankind when we decide peace, fellowship, and compassion are more important than <u>my</u> vested interest, <u>my</u> tribal rights, pocketbook, turf, pride or my way of doing things. We'd like to think that if everyone adopted the teachings of Jesus (it is his birthday we are commemorating after all), or parallel codes of universality, kindness and brotherhood, we could assure peace and good will as the blessing and the condition of all peoples. But without a change in heart which leads to a change in conduct, there will be no total enjoyment of any human celebration. ■

The Long and Winding Road

December 1995

Editor's note: P.E. recently made a speech to the American Production and Inventory Control Society which I thought belonged in MacToday. *Too long for reprint here so I have edited it. The subject in essence was "How does an old geezer like you successfully handle change?" The speech opened with a brief corporate history, the exploding market of post World War II and his dad's illness in 1951. Then goes on as follows:*

But this is a personal as well as a corporate odyssey and might segue here to a day in early May of 1951 when dad called me into his office and said he was not well. "I'm going to take off for a couple days until I get to feeling better. Do you think you can handle things till I get back?" I opined as though it were no big deal and moved down into his office. Permanently! He never returned.

Then I had a new role and the <u>company</u>, a new management style. One not <u>learned</u> but intuitive. The first rule was <u>recourse to delegation</u>. My dad was a hands-on manager, involved in all that happened. Not me. First morning on the new job the Service Manager came up to lay a problem on my desk. I heard him out and finally had the sense to ask, "What do you want to do about it?" He told me, I concurred, and the issue was resolved. Many "problems" turned out to be similar in nature and should have been routinely handled by the Departmental Manager. It may have been a tactic of self-defense, but truth of the matter is, any functional concerns of a given section of the company, which they are constituted to perform, ought to be routinely done there.

Aware of my own limitations, it was easy to delegate. Having been a salesman, knew bloody well this was not my ball game. If dad was his own Sales Manager, I had no desire to assume that role and no credentials to undertake it. So, delegate. But, of course, — next key — find someone <u>qualified to perform</u>. And we lucked out in a guy named Bill Diehl, working for us as a specialist in Caterpillar Engine Power and in crushing equipment. He was an All American from Iowa; was 6'4", good looking, scratch handicapper on the golf course, confident,

P.E. MacAllister, 1952.

poised and impressive. He jumped at the chance to take the job, and within days he was the new Sales Manager. Important to me because when you get your manufacturer's product out and made decent profits, you can get by with a lot from CAT. Bill Diehl, for the next 25 years dominated the heavy machinery sales game in Indiana and carried the ball for the whole company. Which is the third point to survival: <u>represent your line professionally</u>. It was luck for me that we had a person around who had the capacity, and incidentally, never disregard <u>luck</u> as a factor in success. It's better than being smart.

We delegated to an ole Carroll College colleague of mine who had come up through ranks the past five years the title of Treasurer, replacing my dad's old guy who was forever three months late getting out a monthly statement. And, my brother, Dave, took responsibility for running the parts and service operation. Voila! A four-person management cadre which worked, managing the show till the late '70s with considerable harmony. But man! Did the months and years roll by! Some good, some anxious, some exciting; many normal.

Then something funny happened. In 1976 after a quarter century, the four of us owned 80% of the corporate stock. When 90% of <u>your personal</u> net worth is tied up in a tractor company and you are reaching 60 years old, what do you think happens to your taste for adventure? I'll tell you what happens, it shrinks dramatically. In the mid-'70s we started looking for a small store in southwest Indiana to get closer to our coal mines. It took us two bloody <u>years</u> to finally agree on <u>renting</u> a small, truck shop in Daviess County about as large as Chris's garage. The darn thing took a couple years to shake out, then ascended like a rocket. We now have a 40,000 square foot branch, suggesting how good the coal business was and makes you wonder why we blinked so long and why we weren't there five years earlier. Answer is obvious. Old guys don't have the same guts as young guys partly because most young guys don't have much to lose. Or maybe it is because opening an operation <u>which I will not be running in a few years</u> is of less interest to me. Or maybe it is simply, "We could lose a bundle of dough on this sucker, and I don't want to jeopardize <u>my</u> retirement stake".

There is more than an element of courage involved in this sort of decision; there is the element of culture. Because when the four of us came into power we were in our early '30s, and we were part of our own generation. Twenty-five years later, things had changed dramatically in the market explosion in coal, the number and type of product we are selling; we had new players in the game (all of them with Japanese names, building good products at a cheaper price); we had substantially greater demands to inventory parts and expand service resources; selling had become odious indeed through an ubiquitous demon called "discounting". It is déjà vu. We are a bit like my dad, not liking too much what is happening; happier with the old days, discouraged about margins and the requirement for carrying more inventories, scrambling to stay ahead of the Japanese. We were playing catch-up ball.

I think you get the point here. Whoever successfully runs the business needs to be a member of this generation ... with one foot reaching for the next; either mentally and psychically or physically attuned and comfortable with the reality of <u>this</u> market place. My solution was to talk to my old friends about exploring a sequential retirement because if all four checked out at age 65, in two years 80% of the working capital is gone. And over the next six or seven years, my three colleagues voluntarily departed, and we were able to bring in the next generation. Like it or not, a new game needs new players. So a player at a time, one here and one there, some trial and error, we restaffed the supervision grid. By now our dozen major managers are all under 40, and all carefully selected. Important to the future because it <u>belongs to them</u>. They talk the same language as the guys at CAT, as the people at the bank, as the customers buying, the users renting, the association types with which they affiliate. Their life and careers are ahead, the focus is on the future, and they are not lead by experience gained over the long years which today

might well be totally irrelevant if not down-right misleading. They are more daring marketers because they have little personally to lose and much to gain through good results.

It is hard to wonder in all of this how I can sort out what is different about my personal style or my own experience that would make me particularly unique. Maybe some personal reflection would help.

In terms of any relationship, nothing is more important than fairness, and that requires an open mind, and nothing these days is less easy to achieve than an open mind. It is usually cluttered with prejudice or opinions. It takes a deliberate effort to listen to someone you don't like, or to some<u>thing</u> with which you disagree. It is harder even to <u>hear</u> what is being <u>said</u> under these two conditions. But the truth is rarely found rehearsing old prejudices. That is exactly how Yugoslavia is dealing with its problems. So I think we have to strive for objectivity. To gain this, I think it helps to be engaged in outside activities. The narrower a person's interests and hobbies, the more parochial his mind and the more limited his vision. And inevitably the more tedious and downright boring. I learned endurance, tongue-biting, and listening from the Presbyterians where I spent a lot of time, six years in particular, on the National Council, 40 persons that ran our church between its General Assembly meetings. We are great at breast-beating and interminable in our oratory, as you know, in the Presbyterian Church. And we spent a disgraceful amount of time absorbed in esoteric causes guaranteed to drive our membership up the wall in outrage. A premier exercise was giving all our money away to disenfranchised people — American Indians, kookie multi-racial ministries, kocked-up organizations creating jobs; to Grey Panthers, minority education etc., etc. We were single handedly making up for 300 years of slavery. I'm sorry, but no one in my family ever owned any slaves and had a hard time feeling guilty for those who did so.

I didn't fare well in these bitter, gut wrenching, perennial hassles. Always got beat, always in the minority when it came to supporting draft dodgers, harboring illegal aliens, South African stock proxies, peace protests, anti-establishment, anti-war, and anti-business resolutions. I'm pretty successful in the business field, but I never got run over so many times with such ease and such abandon as was my experience with the church.

But nonetheless used to say to my wife as I poured my third martini, "It is really ludicrous the way we are pissing money down all the rat holes we can find, but I must confess to you, there is no other forum in which I serve, no business council, no college board, no trade seminar, no political caucus...no place where I hear reasoned arguments as cogently presented as this; hear people who can talk as clearly and articulately, who have thought things through, and who are as persuasive and simply as bright as these wrong-headed sons of bitches from the liberal left." I have never forgotten the quality of argument and debate. It puts fighting with Caterpillar to shame. Often compelling enough in sheer style to make me consider. Got me to changing opinions, required me to publicly defend my stance with logical argument, and to consider not pet prejudices, but a broader, total good. It was painful, but very instructive. I learned to cooperate and work together even while disagreeing. We had a common objective: the agenda of the church.

I have also found a great deal of satisfaction by participating in cultural and community causes, again, because it helps expand one's horizons. Working with a variety of non-tractor people, some who are strangely artistic, many who are young, some gay, all represent our society in a different guise, and which takes a different mind-set if one is to participate as a peer. In the course of outside interest without sounding officious or arrogant, for 17 years I was the Chairman of the Board of Trustees at Carroll College, for 11 years Chair of the Capital Improvements Board, for seven the Chair at Christian Theological Seminary, and for nine years my condominium Board Chair, plus currently Indiana Opera Theatre, Indianapolis Parks Foundation, and whatever else. In a position of moderating a meeting, one's objective is to complete the work set out in an agenda, it is not to fill the hall with his own rhetoric or to tell people what <u>he</u> thinks. The objective is to guide the debate so there is a discussion of issues, hammering on a given topic so every element impinging on it is explored because then one has the best chance of coming to a resolution. That dynamic of working

with people, being obliged to listen to others in a forum that <u>disallows him</u> <u>expression</u> in the process, is good training.

So learning how to listen is important. And so is <u>what</u> to believe. In my first ten years as CEO, I spent a lot of time eating crow because I automatically believed what a customer told me or what an employee said. Leaping to conclusions on the basis of one viewpoint was a major part of my daily exercise. I finally got tired of back-tracking and decided it is a rare circumstance that does not have two or three sides to it. One is better prepared with <u>all</u> the data in mind than a slanted portion of same. Listen. Listen carefully, <u>but withhold judgment</u>. Being right is much more comfortable than being quick. But further experience taught that being right might not be the objective. My dad used to say that one could "win the argument, but lose the sale". When you have a manager or a customer or a traffic cop who is edgy about his own infallibility, it's time to finesse, to persuade, not to win the argument. To tolerate other viewpoints is not to adopt them...but to tolerate is to continue the contact, discussion, and maybe win the case.

Mr. Holmes once observed that "Each of us is an omnibus on which all of his ancestors are riding". So I am a product of a decent upbringing, middle-class morality, and fantastic genes. I am also a product of a liberal arts education wherein the objective

P.E. MacAllister, 1994.

is to teach one how to learn, to encourage the accumulation of evidence or data in order to make decisions and to solve problems, but beyond that to get a grounding in the humanities so he does not terminate his interest on graduation. He should be prepared to continue learning the rest of his life. In my case, I was a nut about ancient history and still am. My contention is that today I know more about the civilization of classical Greece and Rome, of Egypt and Mesopotamia, more about the Renaissance and Reformation than any other tractor salesman in the entire state of Indiana. Having an interest in the Bible and the church since a youngster, I continue to study and to read. I have traveled to the Holy Land five times and belong to the American Society of Oriental Research, America's oldest consortium of scholars, archaeologists, epigraphers, and historians, which contact keeps me up to date on new discoveries and new theories on ancient cultures in the Middle East.

Taking music appreciation in school and playing a clarinet, I developed an appreciation for classical music which is manifest today through infinite convolutions, resulting in the MacAllister Awards for Opera Singers, now 15 years old. It is considered by singers and the judges who come here annually from the St. Louis, the Met, Houston, San Francisco, and Dallas opera companies among the most prestigious in the country. Its <u>purpose</u> is to help aspiring young singers and its <u>joy</u> is represented in Michael Sylvester who had 13 lead roles at the Met last year and says, "I wouldn't be here today without your help."

On a less artistic or humanistic vein, some of you know I do a couple television shows, maybe five or six each month. Which, again, is bent upon teaching the viewer some new things and surely informs the host as he draws out whatever guest has come aboard ... the School Board President, the former Ambassador to Red China, Dick Lugar, a translator of The Dead Sea Scrolls, a balloon ride, Jim Henderson, the CEO of Cummins Diesel, a trip on a paddle-wheel boat, a young man dying of AIDS, the Iraqi Ambassador, the settlement at New Harmony. All cerebral adventures, varied in nature, of contemporary interest, and a schedule that keeps me committed to this experience almost unrelentingly as though I am going to have to keep learning whether I want to or not.

1983 P.E. shooting weekly TV show;
Cathy Kiesling, modeling.

I think also in my life there are a lot of younger people, not simply working for me, but in my range of friends. People who keep ragging me about my anachronisms, chauvinism, and my fast golf swing. Talking about what interests me; but more so, about what interests them in the field of politics particularly, then theology, then morès and manners, things business sometimes, things artistic, cultural, and of international consequence. I think, my contact with them helps me stay toe-to-toe and on an even level; lets me in part of their world, without totally leaving my own.

Now all of this, along with another litany of the same ilk, has never sold that single cotton pickin' tractor. But it does something: it keeps your head working. It keeps your interest alive. It keeps you learning new things; it gives you a broader vision of man, his travel and travail through this vale of tears. What is critical to me is, of course, my good health, my family, my integrity, but of equal import is using them to stay involved in life's affairs. Stay clued in. My memory is not what it was and learning is tougher, but I am convinced that <u>what is IN the mind, does not have to grow old</u>. Not if you keep it refreshed. Learning new things in old Biblical manuscripts or new arias from old operas, or new theories on Constantine's centering Roman power at Byzantium or contents of new tombs just discovered in Luxor, helps keep you learning new things. The process infers you are learning new things in the tractor business, too.

It is not the tractor business that keeps society bubbling around me, it is this amazing system of ours that lets us participate on so many fronts and do so many different things, one of them being the business world which helps us bring discipline, order, results, orientation to a cause. It is important for me to stay busy, stay interested, and stay involved because, hopefully, it tends to keep one relevant. Or maybe just confidently irrelevant. Continuing to learn is important in determining how one views his status here in this vale of tears and how he relates to the forces which whirl about him in this fantastic age. It would be well to see them all in reasonable perspective and each of us as a part of the effervescence that bubbles around us.

Let me summarize in closing with a familiar passage from Tennyson's "*Ulysses*". It visualizes the old wanderer back in Ithaca, where as "an idle king", he rules his pastoral people and after five or six years is bored to death. Watching life go by, he resents it and decides to get back into action with the passage that says:

"Come my friends,
Tis not too late to seek a newer world.
Push off and sitting well in order, smite
The sounding furrows; for my purpose holds
To sail beyond the sunset and the baths
Of all the western stars until I die.
It may be that the gulfs shall wash us down;
It may be.
We shall touch "The Happy Isles"

And see the great Achilles whom we knew.
Tho much is taken much abides. And though
We are not now
That great strength which in the old days
Moved earth and heaven that which we are, we are;
One equal temper of heroic hearts,
Made weak by time and fate but strong in will;
To strive, to seek to find; and not to yield." ■

About Government Shutdowns

February 1996

Anyone who writes an article about Congressional deliberations on budget is really dealing with a transitory subject. Not that the Congress or the budget is about to leave for regions as yet unknown, but rather that given positions change rapidly, public interest waxes and wanes, things accomplished get put away, and new issues arise so that what is of prime interest at the time of writing, a month or so later is not only inaccurate, it is not even interesting. So this article is <u>not</u> about the monumental struggle between the President and the Republican Congress, but rather it merely <u>evolves</u> out of that see-saw battle which seemed a bit long on legerdemain and relatively short on statesmanship.

In the course of the budgetary see-sawing, an article appeared about how the shutdown of government had damaged us. Several hundred thousand federal employees were furloughed because there had been no appropriation of funds to pay them any longer. The caption said "Shutdown Effects Are Widespread", and then it listed 14 different areas of life in this broad and beautiful land, adversely impacted by the fiscal crisis. You saw them all rehearsed on the evening news with copious tears, rending of robes and gnashing of teeth as the commentators interpreted the grievous impairment to the republic. The suspended programs were drugs to veterans, "Meals On Wheels", "Head Start", "Disease Control Prevention", trade laws safeguarding U.S. workers, EPA and toxic waste shutdown, Medicare contractors.

Next, surveillance of 95% of all workplace safety activities. (Tsk, tsk. I don't think we stopped being "safe" here at MacAllister Machinery or told guys they could work without safety glasses, etc.)

Medicaid money was also stopped for nursing home care, pregnant women, disabled and poor children. Finally, mortgage insurance applications are held up, education benefits to 170,000 veterans ditto, money to provide food and shelter for disaster victims. And, last of all, 260 small businesses can't get capital (loans) for their operations.

I'm trying to come up with some feeling of national calamity, a mind's eye image of major catastrophe revealed in this list. Instead I thought of something else. Namely, was overwhelmed at the enormous range, the endless scope of activity supported/underwritten by the federal government. I can't believe the sundry — and pointless — ways Uncle Sam supports us — need it or not; like it or not. I thought about it reflectively. "Reflecting" on how this would have "played" in America when I was a kid; namely, how long would the list have been? "One line long" is the answer. It might have affected some of the veteran's benefits. Beyond that, zilch! How would we have reacted <u>then</u>? We would have hitched up our jeans, said the same nasty things about the Congress and gone about our business. Because we didn't <u>provide</u> "Meals On Wheels", had no "Head Start", <u>hadn't created</u> "Centers for Disease Control"; we let free enterprise battle the balance of trade thing; <u>had no</u> EPA and no Medicare. Nor was there any unemployment insurance or safety czar in industrial plants, no Medicaid or college help for veterans or financial aid to business; federal dollars going to disaster victims.

Yet, I don't recall my childhood as being one lived in a heartless society, which didn't "care" and which left its derelicts indiscriminately in the streets.

We had the same needs then as now, most of the same problems and in spades. Some we solved, others we endured. Imagine where we'd be today if <u>on top</u> of existing problems we imposed an unemployment rate of <u>25%</u>, which was the 1932 depression level. You wonder if today's citizenry could withstand the trial, whining as we are now.

Somewhere along the way, we have lost a great deal of our self-sufficiency. We want someone else to solve our problems. In our effort to be compassionate and extend a hand to the needy, to "the least of these" we have gotten carried away, and we have built into our national consciousness a dependency which is not serving us very well. It is great to be able to take care of the blind and the afflicted, the indigent and the elderly, the unwed mother and the abandoned wife, and I suppose even the unemployed and the veteran. But in the process don't we have to wonder whether all this is a good thing or a bad thing to be doing? Shouldn't we examine the long range implications? Wonder if creating Social Security, e.g. has not negated — made superfluous — the need for personal retirement planning.

I don't care much for many of my youthful prejudices against Catholics, Blacks, and Jews. I'm sure there was a lot of contamination occurring, polluting the atmosphere, lakes and streams. Working conditions were surely dangerous in some mines or manufacturing plants, and women weren't regarded as being qualified for much or very capable. (Dumb men were part of the equation.) But the battering of the depression and the discipline of our society had developed a tough moral fiber and a sense of personal responsibility I don't think we have today. Illegitimacy was a scandal, thus, comparatively rare; the church was a major institution in American life with respect to acceptance and influence…because it conditioned our leadership with moral integrity.

Roman Forum—center of the civilized world for 500 years.

There was respect for the government and the law, for the military and the police, for the courts and the justice system. Kids obeyed their parents, behaved in school, could read their diplomas when they graduated; all part of our ethos and integral to the success of the system. Wasn't all this of any value? Was it not worthy of preservation? Is society better today because we take care of so many people, so many ways? Is it as good?

Every society in history has had its share of the indigent, unemployed, poor, aged, and disabled. Fact, Jesus told his disciples we would "always" have them, so the issue narrows to how we deal with them. A typical response is to give them free grain which is a fix for the moment, but never really brings honest resolution. The Romans had one of their annually-elected officers (praetor or aedile, I've forgotten which) tend to this matter, and the emperors, or dictators, added entertainment to keep them from massive mischief, thus, "bread and circuses". Marius added another device. He needed soldiers after the incompetence of the aristocratic generalship had bled the reserves white, so he went to the slums of Rome and opened a recruitment drive. The populace was shocked. Only aristocrats and the class of knights were fit for, or qualified, to serve in the army. Marius decided this was nonsense and by the thousands he enrolled idlers and wastrels into cohorts and legions, providing discipline, purpose, employment and created the professional army. Point here is that he <u>gave them something to do</u> and at the end of service a retirement program.

When at the end of that century (27 BC) Augustus created the empire, he instituted another tack: massive public works projects. Like 50,000 miles of paved roads; enormous public baths, 13 aqueducts alone in the city of Rome providing fresh water, public theaters; senate chambers; imperial headquarters; a jillion shrines and temples, several forums, etc. This sort of building for centuries — and all over the empire created extensive and extended employment. This did not totally solve the problem, but keeping 30-36 legions for security around the periphery of the empire and providing them with camps, with water and roads — providing Europe with infrastructure so marvelous we stand in awe today of its extent and its scope and magnitude, simply kept a heck of a lot of people off the street. It kept them fed; it occupied their time; it gave them a livelihood, and in hundreds of thousands of cases, gave them a career.

The pop-off valve to the poor and the unemployed was constructive work. Or was soldiering if you are squeamish about semantics. The value was <u>employment</u>. That ought to be the valve today in the good old U.S. of A. The engine is not the emperor, it is private enterprise. With America's ingenuity, its system of communication, access to raw materials, organizational skill, marketing record and the stimulus of the incentive system, the fix here ought to be loosing any restrictions now in place to expansion of free market capitalism. But even that has glitches. There <u>are</u> jobs out there, unfilled; 15,000 in Marion County. I see "Now Hiring" signs everywhere I go. Probably in the service area, which don't pay as well as mine, but each is a rung on the ladder and access to better conditions and future prospects if utilized. There is <u>no</u> future in welfare hand-outs except more welfare. There are also 15,000 able-bodied people in Marion County doing nothing. We have to marry the two by some sort of pressure. Find a climate beneficial and encouraging for business and let's see if it won't soak up the unemployment.

I guess the gut aspect to "fixing" this situation, which Congress is committed (again) to doing, is encouraging the end of the welfare system for those healthy enough to work. Let the states crowd people into the jobs available and let private enterprise teach them how work is managed in our economy. As a fall back, harkening again to a bygone era, reconstruct some sort of national service program. Maybe again the states end up doing this. Remand the unemployment or welfare or ADC money to 50 different capitals and suggest that the able-bodied either go to work in a business or else to a public service program. Planting trees, correcting erosion, cleaning-up dumps and toxic spoliation, they could build some bloody sidewalks in most of Marion County which is still without 'em, could paint public buildings, could maintain our roads and highways, fix up our parks, build nature trails, clean the junk out of our rivers and streams, help breed and release fish and wild life, etc. If the problem to this is a plethora of functional illiterates, they have to be drafted for remediation and start by going back to school.

Objective ought to be creation of a government so efficient and so constituted that when it shuts down, virtually nothing happens to the rest of us. The government ought to run <u>its</u> business like the national defense, the mails, the departments of state, commerce, attorney general, courts, etc., and it ought to get out of doing things for us we do better ourselves. There is no need to get into plant safety, toxic clean-up, Medicare, "Meals On Wheels", "Head Start", and the rest because it is the least caring and lest efficient element in society. Does it occur to anyone that the reason Medicare costs so darn much is the simple fact that the government is indiscriminately, willy-nilly, paying the bills? Anyone figure out that college educations are outlandishly expensive <u>because</u> Uncle Sam is pumping money into it? When the day comes wherein you and I ask a doctor, "What is <u>this</u> gonna cost me?", and then fight about the bill or get some other quotes, that's the day everything stops going up and up. When we negotiate our own relations and determine what we are willing to pay, we do a far better job than presuming there is no limit, and he, providing the service, has a blank check to fill in. ■

Hooray for the Sales Department

February 1996

In this information age we seem to be developing and displaying more data than it is possible to utilize productively. So qualifying criteria for any proposal to "share" even more data lies in its relevance and utility. Is this batch necessary? Is it interesting? In my case is it even wise? I was thinking here of providing some year-end corporate statistics despite being raised in an atmosphere where one never told his employees, the public, or competitors anything. After all the competitor was the enemy; he's out to do us in. Anything he learns about us, he'll use to our disadvantage … or so the argument ran. Until one day, eons later, it became apparent the whole concept was specious and downright silly. So how's he going to do anything he's not doing now — simply because he learned how much we sold last year and what our profits were? There was an irrevocable rule that held revealing sales volume was taboo and discussions of profitability was an act of heresy if not downright sacrilege.

Competitors were not the only group protected or shielded by this paranoia. A lot of dealers were so goosy they never told their own managers how each was doing. We were in the forefront of providing operating statistics to our managers, thus giving subordinate managers monthly accounts of how each department fared. Not because we were noble and enlightened. It was more likely a gesture of desperation rather than one of altruism because we needed everyone's shoulder to the wheel, and how can a given manager perform at his best if he never knows where he has been, how far along he has come, and

what his pace of progress is? So to help the parts and service guys keep track of where they were and how they were doing, plus indicating what was wrong "where", we built our first budget in 1962 replete with distribution of monthly results. If one wants his managers' shoulders to the wheel (or to the track, as the case may be), he also wants his employees' shoulders there as well and presumably, learning where the company is and what their effort has achieved builds a better team.

So this presumes most employees, aside from their departmental performance, have an interest in how the whole company has fared and at least ought to be able to indicate to a spouse or brag to friends about the size of the operation in which they play a role. They should know, e.g. how many people we have: right now 383; how many stores: five; how much in annual sales: in 1995, $148,800,000. Whether dissemination of corporate statistics proves the point or provides incentive is hard to say. "Management 101" says that each employee is entitled to two fundamental considerations. He must be clear on what his job requires; he needs to know how he is doing. This then tells one and all a bit of how we did last year. And in detail how we did in one department.

The danger in such a display, however, is the appearance of braggadocio, showing off, of strutting about in public with things that should be handled with delicacy. But proceeding nonetheless and taking those risks, let's qualify at once. Though our activity and record are a new high, it is also "relative" and is modest in the larger world of CAT dealers. We are not in the big time. Lest we get too cocky, had better confess our volume was below the average for our Caterpillar peers in the Great Lakes area. But opportunities vary and for a dealership whose 68 counties encompass 4.5 million people we did all right. In our group, however, we are modestly in the middle of the pack. What kept us up to even that pace this year was the record of our machinery sales department (thus, the caption for this article). Doug Clark really had to motivate, threaten, maneuver, and scramble on account the coal business took a dive early on and ended up 41% below the sales budget so painstakingly anticipated last November. And coal sales constitute 45% of our total market (in machinery

Lots of large CAT equipment present at a coal quarry.

or parts or service. When it sneezes, we get pneumonia.) But good news is, we offset coal machinery sales and lowered parts and service volume by record activity in construction and aggregate markets, thanks to an all-out hustle. Which was surprising in retrospect.

The daily transactions sort of go through in the prescribed process and are handled expeditiously, but routinely by Dan Dayton, Doug Clark, and Laurie Halvorson with figures summarized monthly to recap what has happened. Since the reference is to dollar sales, it doesn't provide a total perspective on the picture of activity. Only at year-end when I sit down to add up the number of units we have sold does the scope and degree come into focus. The word "sold" for our purpose means the unit has been invoiced and the title to same has changed hands from ours to "his'n".

Even now I don't believe this. In 1995 the machinery sales department delivered and invoiced 401 new units. Two hundred four were outright sales, 197 sold through rental or lease-purchase options which culminated in 1995. Thirty four of these went to the agricultural market, i.e. were sales of our Challenger line made by Dave Frazee (past Ag salesman). Wow! At the same time we were also selling exactly 304 used units, 213 outright, and the balance through lease or rental options. That means in 1995 we processed 705 units. Good grief, that means 12 machines a week! Plus all the rental units coming in and going out, like 1,500 more "transactions" a year. And we're not talking lawn mower size either. Total machine volume was about $91 million; so the average sale — old and new — was $130,000 per unit.

We have eight men on the traditional sales force, plus Dave Frazee selling ag tractors. From these nine men, and the momentum of half a century in business, the volume and the unit production described is generated. If each salesman was "average" last year, he delivered some 78 units in the course of his territorial peregrinations and billed something like $194,000 worth of machine sales or rentals per week. $834,000 a month! That is some pace. That is $10 million plus per man per year! Our output per salesman is among the top 5% in the country and to get the sort of action we do from eight territorial guys is really a major achievement. Not luck or circumstance or some fortunate aberration. It is due to eight individuals who enjoy the selling mystique and have become thoroughly acquainted with both the territory as well as the customer personnel lodged therein. Five of our

Scrapers being used to prep the ground for building development.

men were selling "other stuff" at earlier periods in their careers and drifted fortuitously toward our operation in search of more opportunity, and what each hoped might be a brighter future.

Backing their effort and day-to-day crusade to convert the "user world" to Caterpillar, the corporation performs its supporting role. We hope through astute and professional management, adequate financing, and mind-boggling inventories, the size of which gives me little twitches from time to time. After all, when I came into the game, the prime source of inventory was the factory, a couple hours away in Peoria and, thus, the need for vast stocks of product was minimal, and the inventory turnover was something like four to five times a year. A change in marketing, namely, the penchant for leasing machines has required acquisition of another whole inventory which supplies customers through the season with 50 different models for a couple weeks' work or for the full season's deployment. Sees, in short, on hand something like 297 new units (meaning units which have never been in the dirt or have been there temporarily and are now back home, still unsold) plus 201 used units or a total inventory of just under 500 tractors, loaders, scrapers, graders, Challengers, trucks, and you name it. Makes for a pretty big parking lot, though a third of these are scattered to the other four stores. Also means an investment of something like $47,000,000 which disturbs the sales managers because they think they are barefoot, i.e. are way under stocked. Ugh! My interpretation! They point out they are responding to customer needs. It is the user who requires this accommodation and to ignore same is to send buyers to the competition when we can't provide, and provide with alacrity. It is the "market's" inventory we are warehousing not the company's. Hmm.

The moral of this essay is not to tell you what a huge dealer we are nor how vast has become our enterprise. All this data is submitted as proof of our commitment to our assignment and the objective of giving the user the best sort of support we can. It isn't always what we want; we are not flawless because we still have people in the system and across the board, daily, we are engaging customers on hundreds of fronts, exposing us to "the law of averages", fatigue, impatience and misunderstanding. Our objective is to be two things...to be three things: competent, professional and successful. We view 1995 as a successful year because we did pretty well what we set out to do. We are girded for the 1996 battle and anticipate some small downturn. Selling machines will again be the lead indicator and continue to arbitrate the future. Machinery delivered today forms the parts and service volume — two, three and four years from now. In our mind all three elements are inextricably linked. Selling evolves from a total corporate support mechanism, the examination of which discloses that in the free enterprise system there is an element of risk required for gain.

Having inventories of $55,000,000 (parts and machines) which were secured partially through bank borrowings for sale to owners or users, contemplates rolling same, and with the profits paying the lenders. If business dries up and no one wants much of what you bought for their benefit, the interest figures don't stop. When you staff with 383 people to do a job one day 300 can perform, there is another major convulsion pending because we have never laid people off. When you have expanded into five locations replete with three mortgages and volume drops, the monthly mortgage payment is as merciless as the IRS. There is a serious cross-cut occurring. Bill Clinton has no rescue programs for business. For the farmer, the minority contractor, the victim of hurricane flood or even snow victims, he has a helping hand. But when we run into trouble, not of our own making, it is our own device with extricates us or it is our own departure for which we prepare. Free enterprise is based on success — not mere effort or even valiant endeavor. In 1995 we succeeded again, profitable for the 48th time in 50 years. 1996 is a new challenge and a new opportunity. We greet it with excitement, confidence, and crossed fingers. ■

Knowing It All

June 1996

It'll be no secret to anyone who has read these quarterly ruminations that most of my success in the tractor business occurred because I happen to have the right name, or more accurately, the right father. Whose long term objective was to build a strong Caterpillar witness in Indiana and at a point in time surrender control to one of his two sons while he gracefully retired into the tranquility of retirement. His longer term objectives <u>were</u> partially met when we succeeded in ultimately establishing a dealership which is the largest in the state, and he <u>does</u> have both a son and a grandson who in sequence became successors and owners of his venture. But the allocated span of years in the business required to get us ready did not come about since his career was nipped just before his sixth anniversary as a CAT dealer. He had to lateral the ball to my brother Dave and me as we charged toward the goal post.

It became obvious at once that a change in managers meant a change in pace and management style with the new guy taking an extended on-the-job-training course in management offered by the market place, Caterpillar, AED, experience, competitors, colleagues brighter than I, and seminars on half a hundred different topics. Which does not seem like a very coherent program for learning the trade of directing others. But given some breaks, enough time, plus a sincere interest in wanting to learn, combined with an effort to keep an open mind, permitted survival for 45 years after my dad hung it up. By now in I'm no longer an apprentice, but an "expert" on managing. Rather I was declared an "expert" recently on two occasions, addressing professional associations, each of whom thought it was rather curious that an old guy as long in the tooth as I, not only was still breathing, but still working. They wondered if there was some trick to remaining relevant in business for 50 years. (I described myself as an "expert" with tongue in cheek, recalling the definition used in the army, namely "some son-of-a-bitch from outta town", the greater the distance the greater the acclaim.) In light of the query as to how one managed change, I had to do some reflecting and after a bit, put down in a single statement personal principles used to manage the tractor works, other people, a vocal competition, a college board, the PEPPER Committee, GIRFCO, and all the rest. An <u>opinion</u> on how one succeeds in business over the long haul, and on occasion, even achieves a modicum of success. Some of which you'll find repetitive, but people forget most of what they read so indulge me, please.

Each of us organizes work in his/her own way instinctively and only when called to explain how, or identify a personal technique, does one finally define his/her own science in art of "management". Mostly, it is evolutionary development which comes to constitute a totality. Meaning, it is rarely deliberately planned or studied—much along the way. It's an inter-connected series of conclusions, premises, personal habits, objective and aspirations, employed when you use your opinions and tactics in dealing with other things and other people. The objective is to supervise, organize, monitor, inspire and unite in order to succeed in the mission which in my case was: Beat the other guy, get the product out, make respectable profits, retain a professional staff, and maintain harmonious relationships with the several constituencies tangential to our business (banker, insurer, auditor, government, etc.). So when someone asked, "How <u>do</u> you manage?", I finally mulled through and accumulated umpteen points. These are not dicta or rules. Let's call them aphorisms—informal statements of principle.

The one conclusion reached immediately as my father left the scene in 1951 was the fact that few of us can manage successfully using someone else's style. The approach to directing others cannot be contrived; it has to be genuine, has to be comfortable, has to fit the situation, has to be authoritative, and has to augment the effort of all others in support of the cause. <u>Managing ought to be viewed as enabling</u>, helping others do their jobs. My dad did that through telling senior managers what to do so was in essence a benevolent autocrat. Being inexperienced (O.K., call it dumb!) I resorted—and am inclined to—collegiality. If he was experienced, opinionated and successful, I was a novice. The advantage to autocracy is few people see your bad calls. Advantage to the collegial approach is arithmetic:

1) There is more wisdom in four heads than in one, and the objective to approaching a sticky wicket is to bring all data available to bear. If my dad had it intuitively, I needed to assemble it.

2) Recourse to delegation. Not being bright

enough to act as our sales manager or treasurer et al (as my dad had done), I found surrogates and decided at once the persons in charge of a department not only ought to know and do the job better than me, but the good ones <u>want</u> a clear shot at running their own show. Moreover, a strong department head will <u>resent</u> someone looking over his shoulder continually, nudging him, kibitzing, and eternally second-guessing. Such activity either drives him elsewhere where he <u>has</u> freedom to do his specialty or else it shrivels up his initiative and discourages his aggressiveness, leaving you with a "yes man" who is of no strategic value.

3) To delegate fully and willingly, one has to have strong, professional people in charge of each operation. And that leads to a ritual overlooked in many companies like ours: careful, planned, and thorough job interviews. This talent does not come with a title, but like anything else has to be learned. To attract good people, one not only has to have a good reputation, but has to be able to identify him/her with the talent when he sees it. This doesn't mean picking him/her with the most charm or winsome personality. It means finding the driver, the organizer, the problem solver, and the winner, personal attractiveness being secondary.

4) In terms of keeping strong people, nothing is more important than fairness, and this is turn requires dispassionate judgment, a very difficult attribute to cultivate or acquire. Our minds are often run on conviction, which translates maybe into prejudice, buttressed by past experience which may or may not be worth a damn. It takes a deliberate effort to listen to someone you don't know or don't like; and takes even more patience to listen to some<u>thing</u> with which you disagree. But we are seeking the truth, and that is rarely found in old prejudices or maybe even in old experiences. If you think this is nonsense, take a look at the former Yugoslavia and note how they are faring as they use prejudice and the experience of the past to resolve their dilemma. <u>Objectivity</u> is the name of the game here and often that is achieved by recourse to activities in other venues with other people where personal status is not that of "manager" and where the logic of a position and the way it is articulated has a lot to do with how well it is accepted. For instance, I have found working with people in the arts particularly "interesting" when it is not out-and-out total frustration. They think about the product (ballet, symphony, opera), and in securing the best, haven't the remotest notion in the world about what a budget is. Achieving "excellence" with the budget you can <u>afford</u> becomes the challenge. When you have brought both sides to achieving that end, you have been through a different experience and you have seen a real triumph. If one gets into Republican politics, he has another mind set to encounter, and if he involves himself with the Presbyterian church, he can look forward to be driven out of his ever-loving skull not by the theologians (which he can handle), but by the do-gooders who want to save the world… and want <u>you</u> to raise the money to do so. Working in this diverse universe of separate causes, one finds different people problems to solve, different thinking, a different role to perform, becoming wiser in the process and more patient with the "lesser breeds, without the law." Getting your own way in these counsels requires real persuasion, cogent articulation of point and principle, sound reasoning. The real secret to successful management in any situation is bringing different, even opposing ideas, into consort behind a given program or movement. When we all vote the same way, it's a slam dunk. Finding progress in divergent opinions and convictions is the real test of the leader. (Bill Clinton and Bob Dole take note, please.)

5) The next tidbit here is the advice to restrain from leaping to conclusions. It is a rare circumstance or problem that does not have two or three or several different sides to it, and my maxim now is to try and get the facts when possible, maybe two or three viewpoints, before dashing in "where angels fear to tread". The objective is to be right, not be quick.

We are best served by listening (carefully) and withholding judgment until the evidence is all in. It is a rare situation that does not automatically suggest its own resolution, once all the data pertaining to it are on the table.

6) Based on aphorism number six, which is never believe <u>anyone</u> about <u>everything</u> <u>all</u> the time; adding we need to be patient with those who shade the truth, because we want them patient with us as we become the hero of our tales…like how far we can drive the golf ball, how much we made last year, how well we know the mayor and congressman what's-his-name.

7) I have also learned that involved in tense situations that there are moments when being right is not key to resolving the issue. There are times when the irritation of the customer or the stance of the IRS is not properly met with my sanctity or infallibility. The tactic might be to finesse, regroup, gain

some time, to let him with the head-of-steam bleed the pressure down. Managing or leading is not about ego. It is about results and in pursuit of that, it is not unusual to get stymied because we have confused form for substance; get focused on the personality or the irritating manner of speech or objectionable personality and react adversely to that.

- Next, when looking for the cause of a particular dislocation or misunderstanding, why not try looking in the mirror first thing and wonder honestly if you might not be discovering at least a part of the problem. Beyond that, do not look for ultimate, absolute perfection in anyone, including yourself. Even Jesus lost his temper.

- Aphorism number ten is to separate the significant from the unimportant, the germane from the peripheral. It is silly to waste sweat and adrenaline on the little stuff when important stuff hangs fire till you get back.

- Moving on: Don't criticize anyone except yourself in front of other people; and don't let a single flaw or an irritating habit discovered in a colleague warp your judgment about his/her full capacity to perform or produce.

- Twelve is to beware of personal friendships developing on the job which override the professional relationship and begin to minimize the requirement for accountability or production.

- "Feeling" is not <u>thinking</u>; logic is superior to emotion, particularly in a crisis. If experience is valuable, recall that it can be a fallible teacher as well, always subject to the test of relevancy.

- The Penultimate acorn is pondering St. Paul's dialectical query, "If the trumpet gives an indistinct sound, who can prepare for battle?" When someone goofs, maybe he didn't hear you; or maybe your instruction wasn't made clear. It's like the old sales caveat: "I don't care what you TOLD him, what did he <u>hear</u>?"

- And last of all, I've learned that most of what happens to us is our own damn fault. And what happens of a screwed-up nature does not decline as you grow older and wiser. I have become increasingly less infallible with the years because along with some wisdom and lots of experience, comes forgetfulness and some obsolete judgment parameters.

I also learned along the way, waxing philosophical about management practice is pretty easy. We "practice" it vicariously on others. Meaning, always seem to know what someone else ought to be doing, better then he/she does. But the proof lies ultimately in the practice. First place to start is at home. And the hardest thing about describing management aphorisms is to follow one's own advice. ■

Are You Experienced?

September 1996

Some wag once observed that "'experience' is the term used to describe our mistakes". Defining it less cynically (without a dictionary), experience is the "recollection of the past as it is utilized and employed in negotiating the present". What guides many of us on our journey whether in the business world, or raising the kids, or investing in the market or cooking a new dish, is our understanding of what might be the right, or wisest option, <u>based</u> on whatever we achieved when we handled this issue before. Meaning, we recall what worked in the past and why; what failed. If someone told us to keep our head still when we are putting and to keep the club head close to the ground to improve our game, we'd stop moving one (head) and raising the other (putter), particularly, if it eliminated three-putt greens.

Of course, life is not a game of golf, and this analogy is thus limited in applicability. But experience generally suggests when we have found a secret for success in a given area, continued success will result <u>if</u> we handle each occasion the same way. <u>Provided there is no element of change</u> involved in the conditions. So once we have the key to a problem, repeated applications of a successful principle will serve us practically forever. It's when the nature or dimension of the problem begins to shift that old solutions might not be adequate. That's how the Japanese, who 30 years ago were no factor at all became our major nemesis. They got here because something changed in the machinery business which we doggedly refused to recognize.

In <u>my</u> book, America got greedy thru the 1960's and 1970's. We had a healthy economy and a strong expansion across all 50 states. In our business, it was pent-up demand in urbanization, infrastructure construction, home building, public and even commercial expansion, mining, logging, etc. In the 1950's we had discovered the shopping mall and the suburbs and with a vengeance began the urban sprawl; likewise did some turnpike construction. In the 1960's and 1970's maintained the pre-fab housing boom, the exodus from the center city, and built an enormous interstate highway system which helped accommodate the rush to the city and from there to suburbia. We weathered some ups and downs, particularly in the late 1970's when a major explosion in the market escalated to induce horrendous inflation.

Everyone appeared so busy trying to out-shuffle the competition and keep pace with the frenetic scramble going on, he lost track of certain perspectives like cost/value relationship, unhealthy debt loads, overall economic stability, and fiscal sanity. Because underneath the bubbling activity a new element called "credit" was created and employed universally. Sales made wholesale across the board on easy terms, thrusting responsibility into the future. Done with too little examination and almost disdain for pricing. During this prolonged, accelerating, and random spree, the unions flexed their muscle each contract time and since activity stayed at a good pace and management was desperate to capture markets, hurriedly signed union contracts, invented a thing called COLA (cost of living adjustment), and cheerfully raised prices <u>letting the consumer</u> <u>pay the bill</u>. We let loose the tiger of inflation and changed the basic economic relationships underneath it all, quoting inflation in Brazil or Albania as proof that it really doesn't make that much difference. In the year 1978, we had at least three Caterpillar price increases; inflation was 13%; interest at 21%. But the tractors sold, so no one worried.

Surreptitiously, we subtly altered conditions and ravaged the purchasing power of the dollar. Economic tranquility became economic turbulence. I bought a house in 1949 adequate to raise four kids and paid $20,000 for it; <u>12 years later</u> we sold it for $20,000. That's how static things were, how stable pricing. But the last buyer I know of paid $85,000, and it is now worth $130,000. It is the same <u>house</u>, improved, etc. But it is not bought with the <u>same</u> dollars. All of which suggests the failure to contain costs, to control inflation, and to concentrate on productivity altered a heretofore controlled or disciplined economic balance. We changed from a restrained pace to a laissez faire policy to "accommodate" the market, but we did not honestly <u>deal</u> with it. We let our skimmer leak, let the devil take the hindermost, and looked up one day after the Interstate was completed to discover a lot of strange names in our industry, moving in big time. The toughest to us was Komatsu, then Kobelco, Hitachi, Volvo, Bomag, Mitsubishi, Fiat, etc. The Japanese came in here with a remarkably good product, priced 30% below us. We can usually get a little premium where the going is tough, but a lot of jobs don't require the same durability needed to load shot rock in a quarry. Just a lot of machines will push dirt, load coal, or dig trenches.

Our experience in marketing, sales coverage, pricing and territorial management, successful over the previous three decades was no longer working ... not in the face of a good product available 25% cheaper. Price competition backed-up down the line till what else "no longer worked" was signing union contracts which added new costs we passed onto the consumer. Suddenly he wouldn't take "the pass". He had another option. Buy something else. What we refused to do as a nation was challenge 25 years of previous experience and create a different strategy in view of the new global aspect now threatening our market. It was the Japanese who made us reconsider and revamp. We, and people building cameras, TV sets, radios, clothing, shoes, tape players, projectors, toys, etc. The Japanese obliged us to trim costs, improve product, Indian wrestle with the unions, add facilities to give better service, and start talking productivity, overhead, and cost control.

If experience is often a great teacher, it is not an infallible one. And her lessons are contingent upon a static condition, not a moving target. The most valuable experience is that exercise which analyzes problems, studies conditions, appraises markets, develops sensitivity to user demands, and ascertains how "what we know" can be applied to new conditions; not how fast we can employ the strategy we used to use. A good deal of what experience has taught me about this business is perfectly useless and totally irrelevant. In the era of "the good old days", the parts business belonged to us because competition was virtually non-existent; machinery terms were 25% down and the balance in 12 months, and buyers made enough profit in those days to meet such conditions readily. Margins were 17-18% on machinery. We measured inventory turn religiously and looked for four to five times a year for new machines. We got most of our machinery from Caterpillar, since they were a half day away and heavily inventoried to

P.E. and Chris MacAllister.

supply dealer needs. Today, we have five people out selling parts and service; are happy to keep a buyer in a three-year installment contract; lucky to make 12% margin; struggle to get one-and-a-half machinery turns; own over $50 million in inventory. To insist on using the wisdom gained the first 25 years in this business as sufficient experience to guide us "forever and ever, amen" is a fatal assumption. Imposing methods and parameters we used to employ would put us out of business in six months. We are not the arbiters or controllers of our own destiny; we are instead the agent that finesses, orchestrates, and monitors those forces as we are propelled into the future.

Experience ought to be a blessing not a curse, but in deploying it, one uses circumspection. I suggested to Chris that managing requires a combination of two elements: judgment and experience. The former, perhaps to evaluate the validity of the latter. The former, also, in the absence of the latter. It is the latter, however, which builds on the past and permits the acquisition of knowledge. It is experience which has gotten us out of the caves and into the ascending sunlight.

Maybe the old acorn about the cat and the stove is a good way to close this corny little homily. It's attributed to Ben Franklin, who once observed that a cat who jumps on a hot stove will quickly decide never to hop on a hot stove again. Chances are also, he will never jump on a cold stove either. He has learned that stoves are the source of heat, uncomfortable heat, and need to be avoided at all costs. But he has learned more from the experience than is there since he also jumped to some conclusions. One being, all stoves are hot. He will never learn that when stoves aren't stoked up for cooking, they are probably no discomfort whatsoever. He will go thru his life using the experience gained in a given situation and never appreciate any benefit he was seeking, when tried to curl up on the top of comfortable stove, assuming there was some benefit. He learned only half the lesson experience was teaching and even the part learned was then misapplied. ■

Appearance vs. Reality

September 1996

I've been learning a lot about "appearances" of late. As a matter of fact, have been looking at literary references which might help me understand same and deal with them. Maybe the quote most appropriate to the subject comes from the New Testament Book of John III and advises, "Judge not according to appearance" which sounds like anything but profound, albeit it is good advice. Epictetus, I'm sure you remember said, "Appearances to the mind are of four kinds. (1) Things either are what they appear; or (2) they neither are NOR appear to be; or (3) they are and do not appear to be; or (4) they are not, and yet appear to be." That must be an old English translation making it very hard to understand. So I'm guessing a bit and figuring the last one is closest to the point for me …"they are not — and yet appear to be," but "judge not according to appearance" also fits this case: the situation which creates convictions about what is, only to discover it is an illusion. I have been learning about what "appears to be" as contrasted with reality the past 12 months because I am the proud owner of a Rolls Royce automobile. It was generously supplied by the company as a reward for my 50 years of service to the noble cause of Caterpillar. What a thrill! A car with an international reputation, one as durable as a D7 bulldozer or as steady as a guy in the dealer ranks for 50 years, an emblem rare in the American landscape, holding its value through the years and as solid as Gibraltar. It would appear that an automobile that cost $167,000 "new" would have no peer in the field of automotive engineering and manufacture. One could assume this is as close as we come to perfection; here is a standard for the world and the ages.

P.E.'s Rolls Royce.

Chris, as many of you recall, is into racing classic cars and has owned Porsches, a McLaren, Cobra, and driven both BMW's and Mercedes, all exotic and again world-class automobiles. He thought the ne plus ultra for a Golden Anniversary would be the epitome in automobile design and, ergo, the Rolls on my Golden Anniversary. I'm not complaining about the car, let's make that clear, but am used to American brands. I had learning to do and some perceptions to adjust to regarding foreign-made vehicles, or at least about foreign-made Rolls Royces. Market value is a surprising case in point. The value of any new product plummets the first six months of ownership, so he ducked that attrition and got me a slightly used one, owned by a doctor who drove it only in good weather, never over 55 MPH, and traded it back at 9,500 miles. So it appears to me, given the Roll's reputation, it's good for another 300,000 or so.

Overwhelmed by a virtual transfiguration into the driving class with kings, ambassadors, Saudi sheiks and rock stars, maybe even professional football players, I treated this new conveyance with some deference. But must confess, secretly at the outset it bothered me a little that I couldn't read some of the dials. I was used to digital figures, large and bold, so to check an outside temperature gauge, for example, or a clock two inches in diameter (with Arabic numbers about the size of the caps on my typewriter) takes some accommodation. Though I can guess by the general position of the hands about how things are, I need glasses for close-up work and so am squinting a lot to see what time it is, or how hot today. But maybe this is the way the Brits do things, so I'll have to join the squinting ranks with my peers.

We do have an automatic transmission with the lever on the right side of the sterling column and a shift pattern legend on the dash that reads "P R N D I L". Very standard (though I never looked up what "I" means) and displayed with black letters on a red-light background. It is especially interesting when the car faces into the sun because the light illuminating the shift positions is dimmer than the sunlight, thus, one cannot see into what position he has "shifted". If he moves it four notches, he is into "drive", but more than once after starting out and getting into a different light perspective, discovers, "Oh, oh!

We are in the unknown "I", and make correction. I notice, too, that the British add some sound effects not standard with most American cars. There was a sort of rasping noise generated while simultaneously braking and turning. Pitched between a low tenor and a high baritone, but about a half note sharp. Didn't sound quite right to me, so ultimately had it checked out, and I was right. It wasn't supposed to squeal when turning. It now squeals every time I apply the brakes, curving or straightaway. But in a car like this, one has to accommodate the eccentricities.

It has the same unusual performance in the cassette tape player. Addicted to "Books On Tape", I use the player continually. In other cars, when turned to "play", the tape starts and the narrative moves on 'til the side is finished. But on the Rolls, during the course of the narration, all of a sudden the tape stops automatically and shifts to the other side as though it has come to the end and is readying to move onto the obverse phase; only to click a second time and bring you back to where you were, only not quite, since there are phrases missing or else wording being replayed. Isn't that unique? Wonder why they do this? And sometimes seven or eight times per side. Maybe it is to insure concentration and keep the driver's mind from wandering away from the text.

Being as how it is a Rolls Royce, not just anyone can work on it and even an oil change is an adventure. The people that ordinarily do this for me were instructed to get in some 20-50 oil and pick up some filters from the dealer so they could give me proper viscosity and filtering. Only to find the service guys couldn't get the oil plug out of the crankcase pan. Steve said, "I've got 'standard' Allen-type wrenches and metric types, but neither one will fit your oil plug. We are stuck 'til we can find a way of draining the oil." Gotta admit a car is pretty special when it eschews common, ordinary wrenches to open its innards and work on its engine. Do you suppose people go around stealing oil from Rolls Royces?

Haven't gotten into the brake fluid part yet so don't know if we can add there or not. But do know I carry around a couple cans of it. This aristocrat won't take any commonplace brake fluid. Has to be special! Probably North Sea oil from British-owned wells. And my relationship with the filling station is improving. This powerful monster gets about 12.5 miles to the gallon — with no wind — and insists on a 93-octane gas. I am a definite factor in the escalation of petrol prices.

I still haven't synchronized all of the action yet. Every so often I hit the turn signal wrong and the wipers and the bright lights come on (if it's after dark). I can't get the wipers off. But if I stop the car, and restart, then it seems to work all right. Oncoming cars remind me of my lights. And we have sun shades with lighted mirrors on the back side in case I need to primp. Very handy! Of course, when driving into the sun, the shades come in very handy indeed. It isn't much trouble repositioning the rear view mirror since every time the shade on my side comes down or goes up, it hits said mirror and gives me a view of the roof rather than the rear window. The other exclusive amenity is a real kicker. It is a small foot rest, triangularly shaped like a big cheese wedge, maybe 12 inches across the seven wide. Really classy! I don't know that anyone has ever used them, but I do know when they are stored in the pockets on the back of each front seat, there is no room for anything else. But, if someday I get a real old codger in there who is used to a little foot rest, I'm equipped to accommodate him/her. Semper paratus, that's Rolls.

It would appear that a car with 25,000 miles on it would not really be requiring a lot of work, and you hope it doesn't because one has to make an appointment with the local dealer, sometimes two weeks in advance. He is extremely knowledgeable, and his guys are very qualified so there is no complaint on that score. But driving out to Zionsville which is 25 miles from the office is a bit of a nuisance. When repairs are needed, the quality of parts is commensurate with the pedigree of this distinguished vehicle. Someone backed into me and put a small pin hole in the trunk and also broke the glass in the right tail light. When I went to buy a new glass, the Service Manager said, "Oh, oh. I don't think you are going to like this. My recollection is this sucker runs something like $618." "For a bloody piece of glass?" (I don't think I was shouting.) "Well, you have to buy the whole assembly, they don't sell just the glass," and he xeroxed the assembly and price out of his book to prove it. It only costs a little more to go first class, right?

It costs, as a matter of fact, just over $500 a month to drive this vehicle (15,000 miles the past year), but that included new rotors on the front brakes and shocks on the back, also a motor tune up to get two of the cylinders back into the game, then some wheel balancing which didn't fix the front end vibration but did tell us the tires were slightly out of round. When the first heat of summer hit, the air-conditioner shot craps so the compressor had to be replaced. So all and all, I am having a real adventure with my Rolls Royce. We are playing: "What's next?" And you haven't heard the best part of it: resale value. My best estimate is that we made a deal for a car with 9,500 miles for about 54% of suggested new list price. Saying, it lost half its value the first 10,000 miles. In the remote chance that we might want to dispose of this little jewel, 15,000 miles later, we can get two-thirds of what we paid for it. In the first 25,000 miles, this hummer has dropped in value 64%, dropped $107,000 in value.

For some reason or other what appeared to be the magic and marvel of Rolls Royce "are not". I was impressed with the legend and a bit stunned by the facts. Maybe sometimes appearances ought to be left unchallenged and the image maintained — though the day we operate on what "appears to be the case" instead of on existing and dramatically different reality, we are in deep trouble. The trick is to get the two worlds in focus — appearance and reality — and see them as the same. ■

It Is Both

December 1996

In the course of contemplating the holiday season, a quasi-philosophical question comes to mind. Is Christmas as we celebrate it in America a calendar date/event, or is it mostly a frame of mind? Before saying "It is both", I begin ruminating about frame-of-mind and "the ghost of Christmas(es) past". Because it has always been a melancholy season for me. What I'm inclined to remember about former holidays is that the world was in better order and less contumacious; our problems seemed soluble or endurable, not insurmountable. Most of all, the "old days" reoccur in a refulgent, ethereal light primarily because we were younger. Poorer, no doubt; less blasé and worldly-wise, but with the dewy-eyed outlook produced by the youthful mind, full of optimism and anticipation. Never mind that it was ignorance as well as innocence that gave us the happy view. Whatever the reason, the impression at Christmas time was "all is right with the world". We fell for the validity of the angel song "peace on earth and good will to men" as though it were a statement of fact rather than an ephemeral sort of aspiration. Which seems to be saying that we rejoiced in Christmas, but wouldn't have been so exuberant had we seen and understood the big picture. ("When ignorance is bliss, tis folly to be wise.") However you cut and stack this, I recall Christmas with great fondness as I remember my childhood and am quietly disappointed that the same joie de vivre, same excitement, and expectancy is now the province of the young. Christmases today don't seem to have much carefree, nonchalant exhilaration.

But maybe in reality, one's <u>attitude</u> about the holiday is the result of one's frame of mind. "Nothing is good or bad but my thinking makes it so". <u>Everyone</u> does not feel melancholy about the season; many greet it with joy and eagerness, even in the riper years. Which returns to the postulation that to a large extent, Christmas is a frame of mind. I recall the 1941 Yuletide, in uniform, on the west coast where the Japanese were about to attack us. No kidding. We actually thought there was an armada on the way. And since the military had

P.E. in Britain, September 1942.

shipped most of its planes to the Pacific theatre that fall, California was virtually defenseless. So the First Fighter Group was dispatched posthaste about the 10th of December (from Selfridge Field, Michigan) to San Diego and then Burbank. Where after our defense was <u>so</u> formidable and air patrols <u>so</u> threatening that the Nipponese totally abandoned their plans to invade from the west, and the nation was saved. The heinous foe spotted our P-38 Squadron's tooling up and down the coast in a menacing formation and wanted no part of an armed encounter with them.

I spent Christmas in the Grant Hotel running air defense simulations all day. Radar was in its infancy, and we were totally oblivious to its value, so on maneuvers we used the early British system, using spotters on the ground calling in flights and heights and numbers, so the controllers could scramble our fighters to the proper coordinates to intercept the intruders. You can snicker now at the value of all that energy expended on Christmas day in 1941, but that is how I "celebrated" the holiday. We did have turkey and dressing, however, for dinner. But I don't recall any carols or tinsel or a fat guy in a red suit. There were no "Ho-Ho-Ho's" December 25, 1941. It was just another day. In my mind, no specific occasion.

And the following year we were stationed in a romantic oasis called "The Garden of Allah", well into the Sahara Desert. (Let me tell you, Allah doesn't know much about horticulture if this was any evidence of his handiwork.) The city was named Biskra, and it was maybe two or three sections of land surrounded by barren waste into which our engineers had dozed out a landing field. During the Christmas holiday, our Commanding General (I think his name was Atkinson) declared we were the "busiest airdrome in the world". As well as the most rudimentary and remote. We were flying bombing missions to attack the ports and depots used by Rommel and his army, using B-17's with P-38 fighter escort, off daily, and in increasing numbers. No one will remember what Christmas was like in the desert. No decorated trees, gifts, midnight worship; no

Yule log, no roasted goose. It was just another day with canned steak and kidney pie for dinner served in a tin mess kit and maybe some rough red wine to wash it down as the celebration vintage. Christmas, de facto, did not exist with us.

The third yuletide was spent in Naples (Italy), marked by a drenching rain, and our squadron ground echelon disembarking from a boat in the harbor. The C.O. said to me "Prune, how's about you getting our gear off this tub while the rest of us move on out for our camp in Foggia. We'll see you in a couple days when all the stuff is in the trucks and on the way." So I spent Christmas day, 1944, unloading a boat in a down pour in Naples harbor, with Vesuvius glowing angrily in the distance. No music, no stockings, no chestnuts on an open fire. Worked till midnight Christmas night and into an army cot in some dormitory, soaking wet. Fa-la-la-la-la-la-la! And a couple of jingle bells.

Given the nature of these circumstances in the military, I'm sure during the three holidays I mentioned, there were a lot of troops trimming trees, whipping up the wassail bowl, holding worship service, doing sing-a-longs, and opening presents from home. The identifying marks of Christmas, the familiar rituals and observances were there. Like counterparts at home, stable army bases must have played the music we use especially for the occasion; produced elements like wreaths, tinsel, decorative angels, crèches, red candles and candy canes, all created for this holiday, all part of its accouterment, all declared in their respective fashion time and again something special was occurring. Which suggests to us the panoply uniquely and specially designed becomes sacramental. It provides physical evidence, produces a change in habit, special rituals all created and employed to interpret a singular event commemorated annually and evolving as "Christ's mass".

It is hard to imagine Christmas itself, devoid of the external mechanisms which herald and mark it. The Presbyterians in their more primitive incarnation a century and a half ago, saw Christmas as the 25th of December and maybe the birth date of the Savior, but thought that any form of outward exuberance or unbridled joy totally inappropriate. And the decorated tree or the garlands, hanging stockings, animal cookies, all smacked of either paganism or popery. They would have nothing to do with it and as a result, never really raised Christmas much higher than the day before and the day after in their blue-nosed observance. So without some of the special signs and symbols,

the holiday falls flat and fails to really blossom. How they viewed it made it ordinary. And how you get any meaning out of the ordinary confuses me. So it is not only how we view it, but how we <u>mark</u> it that makes the occasion special. Because the markings illustrate and identify it, now becoming the signal for us to get our heads in shape. Christmas is still also a frame of mind, and the frame it hopes to induce, is one that <u>makes</u> the day and the spirit different than the rest of the year.

It is not supposed to recall the festivals from which it was derived. This is not the Roman "Saturnalia" or the birth of Mithras, the sun emblem of the Persians, nor is it the winter solstice of the ancient peoples. This was the date established as the birthday of the Christ child since a date was needed to celebrate his advent. It was also important to see Jesus in human form and view him as about as mortal as you and I in order that what followed was not hanky-panky or someone yanking us around. It was a genuine birth (gussied up with some special effects, maybe) of a Jewish child, to a first century A.D. world replete with its problems, pressures and opportunities. It is the life that is important, not the birth date, and it is the life that we commemorate, hopefully, by seeing it as an example that ought to be emulated. At Christmas time, especially, if we can't hold that sort of "goodness" thru the year. The words linked to the season and the birthday are words like "peace", "joy", "fellowship", "love", "caring", "others", "blessed", and manifestations are gifts for others, clothing for the needy children, dinners for the homeless, baskets for the poor and unlucky; togetherness and family for most of us.

Not much of this came out of Mithraism or the winter solstice or the Saturnalia. It came from the mission of Jesus whose influence extended out to impact the morality of the western world like no other force in history and happens to embrace the Christmas event as sort of a reminder to rehearse again what this is really all about.

So I would hold that the day is not as much an annual calendar connotation, as it is a frame of mind. Without the elevated spirit, without some joy, some remembrance, some element of sanctity, it fails to qualify, and in fact, it is the attitude and empathy and spirit itself that constitutes or creates Christmas. It is, indeed, in our hearts, first; our minds, second. Until it appears there and gets us ready, the holiday lacks its dynamic, and in fact, is almost without purpose or legitimacy. It comes and goes without meaning. ∎

1997

Plus Ça Change …

March 1997

The French have a lot of sayings to describe the human pilgrimage through this vale of tears, some fairly esoteric, some enigmatic, some even helpful. This essay is about applying one of them to the tractor business: "Plus ça change et plus c'est la même chose", i.e., "the more things change, the more they remain the same". This is more "enigmatic" than it is helpful, and it bears careful scrutiny before application. It also describes two factors or elements ("change" and "same") which seem hard to reconcile. We are familiar with the former since nothing is more faddish as a topic for discussion and application by sociologists, economists, educators, theologians, and tractor salesmen than the technological whirlwind which swept through America and continues to modify all our systems. The extent and nature of contemporary technology is a marvel to those of my generation who sit back spellbound while those of the current generation take it all for granted, unable to appreciate the almost primitive nature of our operation in the middle of this century.

For example, no one can imagine "accounting", i.e., processing the sale of 636 machines last year, <u>manually</u> on cards and ledgers or try recording manually $45,000,000 in parts transactions. It would take 30 more parts people to manage today's $10,000,000 parts inventory in six stores with a manual system, i.e., records kept on individual part-number cards. We can't imagine adjusting and tracking inventory through each sale with a pencil by changing the item balance on hand each time a part is processed, noting with a red plastic flag when the inventory quantity hits the "reorder" line, i.e., "we need to buy 20 more on Friday with the next stock order".

There is no point in teaching anyone how to run the old system since the entire Caterpillar inventory dynamic for parts is on computer, but it's impossible to appreciate the distance we've come <u>unless</u> one has both vantage points. And because of the progress, there is no way our parts operation "remains the same", French theorists not withstanding. It is vastly different. Like, it is a <u>daily</u> order now instead of weekly: nightly shuttle to six stores; inventories are corrected instantly — by each transaction; invoice, packing slip and bin locations created with the customer order, etc. <u>What does "remain the same," however, is the motivation which induces all the changes.</u> What has driven computerization and instant access to records and their maintenance is the age-old pressure of competition and the race to see who can provide the user the best service. What hasn't changed is the customer's utilization in a seasonal territory, the high initial cost of the machine and the expense incurred when one is down with a broken something-or-other. The phobia about customer service is what drives the change and if it improves considerably, it is because the dealer obligation has "remained the same", i.e., give the owner the quickest part availability in the world of free enterprise capitalism. In pursuit of what is the objective, i.e., competitive edge (making the sale), the framework for <u>change</u> is identified: do things the competitor cannot do. To bring <u>that</u> about requires we institute something new to our list of services. Parts guaranteed within 48 hours; creation of a vast machinery rental fleet for customers who have both the fiscal "shorts" and short term needs for a given loader, dozer or scraper; double-shift service operation — or around-the-clock service in the truck shop. It means broadening the range of product offerings to 170, and it is purchase terms extending from 12 months once

MacAllister service trucks, Plymouth, Indiana, 1951.

to 48 (ugh!) now; it is certified rebuilds; guaranteed maintenance contracts; a big exchange inventory; $80,000 field-service trucks, and on and on.

Saying, we have had to <u>change</u> a lot of the things that "remain the same" in terms of top-notch customer support. Note, too, change costs money as a rule, but money as an investment: to assure continued growth, to meet competition, to outstrip 'em; to do whatever it is faster, better, more expeditious.

We've also encountered a lot of changes in terms of employee relations. One is surely workplace safety; another is merely workplace convenience and quality. We are contracting for a new store in Lafayette, the fourth major building investment in the last four years. Our perks have expanded in terms of personal leave days, creation of a profit share, a 401K, hospitalization insurance, flu shots, uniforms for heavy work, automatic lifting equipment, etc., etc. The general drift in my lifetime has been to doing more and more things for people they used to do themselves, and though there is no point in griping about it, a good many have been mandated as being "essential" (whatever that is), and the cost absorbed by the business owner. To stay competitive in terms of customer accommodation, we likewise need to stay current in terms of employee care and nurture. Our wages have to be decent and conditions of employment better than the average. Because it is only from a good work force that one can provide the service he aspires to provide. One cannot generate a top-notch product with a third-rate staff. We don't want people working for us who don't know their jobs and certainly don't want them if they don't <u>like</u> their jobs.

The element of people vis-à-vis the topic of "change remaining the same" is obviously critical to anyone who expects to succeed. Have <u>people</u> changed that much since "the old days"? The answer, of course, is "yes and no". Mostly "no"! There <u>have</u> been a lot of alterations in the family structure and a declining respect for its traditional role; a loosening of moral conduct and new insouciance. But there has also been a successful move to emancipate women, give a break to blacks and minorities. Noble in concept, incomplete in terms of effectuation; and having its impact on business in America, both good and bad. Capital and labor still have their differences with the unions taking a beating primarily because conditions of working people have improved immeasurably, reaching the objective of the early labor movement. Now unions are about power and economics; workers are almost a sideline. But underneath it all, dealing with the basic component of the individual worker, daily at his job, he differs professionally little from a generation ago. Salesmen seem to stay longer; work smarter, are more independently sufficient. Mechanics have to know infinitely more to gain proficiency. Almost all our people in any category are computer literate. Across the board they work just as long and every bit as hard, have the same range of loyalty to the cause and rate high in support of the company's mission. They understand how sensitive is customer satisfaction to our future and their jobs; meaning, how absolutely essential is good service.

If we can provide the proper leadership, we have the human component to knock the socks off any known competitor. Our challenge is to keep them trained, motivated, properly compensated, and wisely deployed. The issue is not the character of the person and his contribution; it is the issue of how he is lead, directed, and his talent applied.

I could sing the same song about the customers we deal with. Wall Street is not really all Boesky or Milken; S&L's are not all Charles Keating. There might be a lot wrong with American entrepreneurship, but it is still the most productive in the world and the most ingenious. If there is indeed change, it appears in terms of technique and process with respect to our customer base, <u>but</u> it is not a change in character.

Part of the joy in our business is the nature of the vocation itself and the clientele with which it deals. In dealing with people who own a business or are charged to make a profit, we are dealing with a different animal. When one competes to stay afloat, we find a good deal of realism present and a considerable element of judgment. This is not a "snitty" housewife or a dissatisfied school teacher or sales clerk, this is someone battling in the same arena as we are. So we are dealing mostly with maturity and experience. We are also dealing with some big bucks, indicated in a six figure bad debt write-off every year. Not because we got deliberately taken, but free enterprise in a wide, diverse and risky world, where the average life expectancy is seven years. People go belly up in areas where there is not enough action to support all the competitors vying for contracts. They sometimes depart, sticking their creditors. But rarely do we encounter someone out to deliberately give us a hosing. In my half century, I can count on one hand the number of buyers who deliberately conned us. There is weak management, bad weather, a poor collection record, family rifts, poor bidding, inability to grow soundly, etc., on-going, subtly and surreptitiously keeping the best afloat and eliminating the inefficient. But ineptitude and error are far different than cheating or lying.

This annual write-off ritual keeps us from getting dewy eyed, but we are amazed at the amount of trust in this fraternity. We sell $169,000 worth of parts each working <u>day</u>...mostly over the phone on the basis of the owner's integrity and past record. We recently sold the biggest deal to come down the pike in Indiana, and on the basis of the customer's word, committed ourselves to paying for $20,000,000 worth of new equipment from CAT. No attorneys on

Aaron Weinhold, Ag salesman (on right) with customer Glen Apple of Apple Farms, at one of the MacAllister Ag Field Day events.

hand, no long documents, no signatures in blood or personal endorsements. Someone's word. Period. Day after day. As it has been since the day we opened a store. That part of our dealership dynamic has "remain(ed) the same".

So in closing, no matter how things appear, they do <u>not</u> remain the same or we'd still be walking on our knuckles. The trick is in designing and managing change, and it is also determining in that dynamic, what it is we want to change, and which conditions or attitudes or mores we currently employ that ought to remain the same. ■

Why Success?

June 1997

I don't know that being a history major in a liberal arts college was ideal preparation for life in the tractor world. But it was not a total loss. I learned the liberal arts process that taught us how to learn and then once we got the drill, the need to keep learning the rest of our lives. Not only new Caterpillar stuff, but the arts and humanities, current affair, certainly the history of our own era and not only how it impacts affairs in the machinery world, but how past eons continue to influence this people. Part of the liberal arts training also presumes we will search for meanings, evaluate results, study cause and effect, and in examination of our western culture, ponder the nature of our long sojourn here. My conclusion about our record as a species has not been a very happy one. Given the eons of experience and the mountain of mistakes, one wonders why we are not farther along the trail. In wondering "why?" the conclusion (vis-à-vis the human quest) is that our uneven ride results from governmental vehicles which just don't work…in 90% of the cases. A rate of failure which is phenomenal.

Since man organized himself into communities in Cyprus or Turkey some 10,000 years ago; or since the first major civilized experiments along the Euphrates at Uruk 6,000 years ago, political experience in the form of monarchies, tyrannies or military dictatorships have risen brazenly, strutted pompously, then folded limply like my spring daffodils. Whole nations and races have ascended to prominence, flourished and dominated, only to depart one day and vacate the scene with no vestige of their trial remaining. First "Poof"; then gone. History is basically a recounting of mankind's failed movements, its fallen leaders.

The business world furnishes similar parallels. We created about 170,000 new businesses last year in America and by year five, 44% of them will be gone; and by year 20, only 11% will remain. If the entrepreneurial spirit is still alive and well, its sustaining capacity has to be disappointing. Too much like the course of nations. So, given all this, what insight might we gain from past experience, national or business, to find the reasons for such consistent failure? Maybe it's the fact human institutions survive only so long as they are properly directed and administered; maybe when leadership fails, the problems assailing each — unresolved — destroy the enterprise. Civilized people do have to be governed, accommodated, protected, educated, and all the rest, so the query is, "Why haven't we created political institutions that provide for the elements of state (governance, judiciary, education, defense et al) on a permanent basis?" If the answer to that comes out of history, it will come by examining the most successful historic periods or national experiments. Which political or cultural experience came the closest to doing the best job in surviving the longest? Who best negotiated the course between destiny's Scylla and Charybdis? How about Egypt? Rome? Britain? What about China? Switzerland? Who?

Anyone say Venice? That's my nomination: the merchant Queen of the Adriatic which Napoleon tipped over in 1797 (without firing a shot, by the way) after existing, uninterrupted, unconquered, for 1100 years. What's the secret to account for that millennium of success?

One, chief factor might have been her governance vehicle. A participatory sort of republic with a designated voting constituency, electing people to serve in a major council which delineated responsibility to smaller agencies and departments — law, justice, public works, welfare, treasury, etc. All monitored by an executive committee (the Council of Ten) with a chief executive, ceremonial figure called "doge" (leader). Origins of the community — in case you have forgotten — were happenstance, but important to the character of this experiment. After Rome collapsed, the mauled and run-over Romans of northeastern Italy got tired of another barbarian invasion (which always came from the east, rounding the Adriatic and pouring down the boot) and to escape, sought the bleak and soggy sand bars or marshes created by silt from the Po and Adige Rivers. They shivered in the lagoons till they could get their bearings and began to fish, make salt from the sea water, and transport commodities since their watery circumstances demanded everything one did required a boat. Soon they built their own and used them with energy, ingenuity and consummate skill. They became a transporter of goods (the 10th Century American Express), but soon bought commodities to be resold. They developed a brisk traffic along the Northern Adriatic, finding out what was needed in Milan or Verona or Padua and buying it in Dalmatia or Albania for identified markets. Gradually, the scope was broadened and soon covered the Adriatic, then the Aegean, and finally the Mediterranean. In the course of which they also got very rich. Point is, they <u>created</u> an economy <u>without the remotest presence of any natural resources.</u> They built a society and a livelihood on the basis of human effort, organization, risk and ingenuity. The circumstances required they "get with it" and improvise or perish. They opted for the former.

All of which by 800 A.D. had made them a formidable aggregation and secure to a large extent in their canals and man-made islands. Note, this is a merchant people, generating its own capital and creating its own commercial enterprise, wider and wider in scope, organized and standardized on the home front. And pretty well regimented! An example of which was their basic transporting unit: the galley, mass produced by the state in one or two standard configurations with interchangeable parts, conveniently warehoused in Venetian stores in Constantinople, Antwerp, Pireus, Alexandria, Haifa, etc.

It was from a creative, enterprising, successful merchant aristocracy that Venice fashioned her vehicles of state. She identified the leading families in the libre d'oro — Book of Gold — and from this group of maybe 800 successful Venetian households elected the governing organization, as well as the doge, ambassadors, judges, generals, and you name it. They used the track record of mercantile success and, thus, had only winners in their political apparatus. So administration and statecraft were handled by pragmatic businessmen who gave time and talent to the state, but never became professional politicians. She did not "request" public service from successful citizens, but <u>requisitioned it</u>. Leadership was drafted, recruited. To refuse a governmental post meant exile. Result was those who had thrived on Venetian power and hegemony were charged with managing the state, i.e. conveniently constituted its governing mechanisms. Which when done properly, assured their mercantile future as well. To compete politically, militarily and economically, they accumulated a vast information bank, the most thorough and complete records on foreign courts, rulers and societies of any nation in Europe. Both marketing and statecraft were, thus, based on sound data in this process. Woven through all this was a priority consideration, a preeminence given the state itself. After all, the

fortunes of the city and its people rested on the power of Venice <u>not</u> on individual mercantile dynasties.

Isn't there something to be said for using the best people we have in offices of state? We want the best in football or in opera or flying our jet airlines. Why have lesser standards for government service? We noted only the best survive in business, or in the boxing ring or stay the course in our sales force, and only winners get gold medals in the Olympic Games. Why would anyone think he could win or achieve with losers on his staff?

The tractor business as well flourishes in a much healthier fashion when it has professional practitioners in all of its slots and performing respective services with faultless expedition. Incompetence costs us in dollars — and customers — so when we find it existing, we move at once to correct it. And we find it on the basis of criteria established for performance, on rates of achievement or success; on meeting specific objectives. Indicators are pretty arbitrary and if we don't respond, we pay. How sad that government has such fuzzy criteria for its success (i.e. getting elected) and fails to find specific arbiters like balanced budgets, swift justice for the malefactors, established norms for health care costs, a cost effective postal service, a cost benefit ratio of bureaucracy and program. No institution we know fumbles and falters across the board with obvious dereliction, unnoticed or uncorrected. Strangely, governmental imbalances belong to no one. They are "general". Is it possible such nonchalance is <u>not</u> impeding our progress as a nation and is not deleterious to our destiny?

I suggested that early in the history of Venice a matter of ingenuity came into play. In fact, given the marginal circumstances, survival itself would not have been possible without clever thinking and even cleverer management. Building homes, warehouses,

Grand Canal, Venice.

churches, and public buildings on mud foundations was impossible so every edifice in the city was mounted on wooden timbers hammered 10 feet into the earth, then capped with Istrian stone which would withstand the constant attack of salt water. The design for buildings, the creating of an aquatic arterial system, developing a fresh water supply, the hoarding and excavation of sand for islands, the creation of sea walls to protect against erosion, all indicate a part of the challenge faced in the 700 and 800's by this intrepid people. Without ingenuity, creativity and strong organization the community itself would not have risen and certainly without the home base or the headquarters, the empire which followed could never have been possible.

Innovation, the search for newer and better ways of doing things, is certainly what America is all about. The entire revolution in medicine, automation, technology, communication, transportation, computer science, etc., etc. has been primarily created and perfected by American ingenuity. It is a premium in business because it is through better mousetraps that we keep our competitive edge and through constant refinement and improvement that our industrial gi-

Dave and P.E. with a CAT 933.

ant keeps moving. One of the current benefits to government provided by some elements of the private sector is the farming out of public service to private companies. In Indianapolis, our city golf courses are managed by individuals, we have leased garbage pick-up, contracted for management of the sanitary plant, and most recently have hired an English firm to run our airport. What is there about government institutions that prohibits them from generating internally the expertise required to manage the governance function with efficiency? Why does not the institution itself commit to the same sort of demand for efficacy, the same sense of loyalty, the same professional competence it <u>buys</u> from the private sector?

Maybe it is too far a stretch to suggest that Venice became the engine for ingenuity because of the nature of her governing personnel. That she had the internal capacity to meet the foreign threats, the competitive assault from all sides in every decade of every century, the endless maintenance of the governing vehicle, feed and house 100,000 citizens on her islands, build an empire girdling the Adriatic and Aegean, and dominated the area like a colossus for at least 500 years, without a major rival. There was a self-generation to "lead" or to accommodate. And that surely came out of the heart and mind of her leading citizens, maybe letting us conclude that success is most probable when the private and public sector are partners; when the advantages to one are simultaneously the benefit of the other; when objectives are common and the total welfare is the aim of each. Success occurs when we place our best people in public office and when we put a premium on doing rather than dreaming; when we reward ingenuity and creativity and when we find a society where each member pulls on the oars and all are headed in the same direction. When these things occur, when the public interest is the objective of all, <u>then</u> governments will last a millennium or so. ∎

A Winning Partnership: Black Beauty — MacAllister — Caterpillar Home Run

June 1997

On March 3, 1997, the first of approximately 108 Poindexter Transport's tractor-trailer loads of new equipment started arriving at the Black Beauty Farmersburg Coal Mine. That constitutes a sizeable caravan. The cargo also was "sizeable", including the largest Caterpillar machines built to date, at least as far as we are concerned in Indiana. The biggest is a 5,230 front shovel which weighs something like 702,000 pounds and comes broken down into 11 separate trailer loads. Point being, machinery this size is too large to get on anyone's trailer whole and, thus, has to be shipped in pieces to get moved. The other point to this story is the fact that CAT equipment is "componentized" and does disassemble in manageable units so there is virtually no limit to the size of what we can build these days, given the fact they can be readily assembled at destination. Maybe "readily assembled" is oversimplification. When we are manhandling pieces this enormous, out on a field, on the jobsite, it is not like putting together a jigsaw puzzle. It required the work of 18 Washington Service Department mechanics plus two field servicemen from Indianapolis something like 24 hours a day for about four solid weeks to get the job done. That's roughly some 12,600 hours. There were 18 Caterpillar units to "deliver" and every single one of them had to be assembled.

The breakdown is:

(8) 789B Off-Highway Trucks
(3) 5230 Front Shovels
(1) 994 Wheel Loader
(5) D11R Track-Type Tractors
(1) D10R Track-Type Tractor

Poindexter Transport and Crane Service helped us with the off-highway trucks and the track-type tractors; the Johns Mans Company from Haubstadt sent six of their people complete with appropriate lifting cranes to assemble the three front shovels and the 994, while Bob Misner Construction and Welding from Dugger welded the 789B beds together. Which tells you even the beds come in pieces which are assembled and then fastened together with a welding torch. Long hours with an arc completing humongous welds.

This "delivery" exercise is a watershed experience in the history of the company and the fruition of months of painful negotiation with the buyer who was obviously obliged to look at several options. People who read this publication need to know that machinery of this size and this dollar amount automatically means considerable competition. We are not only up against competitive dealers, but likewise their manufacturers as well, who begin salivating furiously when each sees the size of a big coal order like this. We have some real selling to get done before reaching the brass ring and appreciate the fact one more time that there are other people out there selling just as hard as we are, and providing a very decent product. A "watershed experience" because it is the largest deal ever to come down in the State of Indiana. Maybe the biggest one to hit the Northwest Territory since its inception in 1787. We are delighted to complete it and have to congratulate our Sales Manager, Doug Clark, who labored with some diligence over the figures and assurances to the buyer alongside our coal salesman, Tony Reisman, who together with Doug made the pitch to Black Beauty's Purchasing Committee of 10 or 12 people in a protracted late-night session.

Several phone hours and meeting hours were spent with Black Beauty Coal Management Group that included Jim Roberts, Wayne Park, Matt and Clint Ubelhor, and Dan Hermann. Our part of the deal was easier than Black Beauty Coal's. They were trying to buy equipment, sign a coal contract, create mine plans, establish capital budgets, hire employees, and run their business during this extremely hectic negotiation. The Black Beauty Coal team had to be "sleepless" for many weeks.

The package also included a number of guaranteed used pieces supplied by our guys in Washington so the entire delivery included 18 pieces. Beyond that, there are still six D11 carry dozers shipping out this fall and will be put into service by mid-October, Deo volente. ■

Success … or More of the Same?
September 1997

Do you ever get to wondering about our national priorities? About defining problems that most need addressing? And when identified, determining what honestly to <u>do</u> about them; <u>who</u> will do it; <u>when</u>? We engage in a national hand-wringing exercise, orchestrated by media exploration which details what is wrong now and wearies us with a non-stop litany: We have a drug problem that confounds law enforcement and filters into every major community in America, thumbing its nose arrogantly at society. We have admitted defects galore in our educational system, right? Uneven standards and results across the land. We continue to spend more than we take in as a government. We have a flawed policy of assistance to the less fortunate and billions blown on inept addressing or the plight of the poor. We have a federal health care program across the board that is rife with mismanagement and buried in paperwork, costing us four times as much as the nations of Western Europe. We have a Social Security system that is a Rube Goldberg creation, borrowing heavily from the future to support this generation who comes off the most selfish in American history, yet no one in Congress has enough guts to privatize it, overhaul it, and make fiscal sense out of it. We still have price support programs for diary men, tobacco growers (that's a great investment!), farmers in general, sugar cane growers, etc., etc.; when all the while we could be buying elsewhere what each produces cheaper (making needless the subsidy). We have shocking rates of illegitimacy, replete with "fathers anonymous". We have a thing called "AIDS" moving with sinister stealth indiscriminately among our ranks. Although we have tended to curtail pollution to a considerable degree, check the rising traffic on our roads and streets and note how profligately we are burning oil, a limited fossil resource with almost no consideration of what happens when the last barrel is gone. Anyone read articles about the shark becoming rarer and rarer, analogous to the ferocious way we are denuding our seas of fish? We have an internal revenue code no one understands and a jillion feverish agents interpreting it. Etc., ad nauseam.

Point is, we do have plenty of serious problems confronting this people, all of them well rehearsed as though describing and bewailing them were salutary.

But in your mind, what are we really <u>doing</u> about alternate sources of energy, controlling harvest of marine life; or checking the growth of illegitimacy or rounding up nonchalant carefree fathers; or improving academic competence? We play games with the deficits by <u>promising</u> to cut spending — Yeah! — four years from now with the budget balance coming <u>after</u> Clinton's last term when a new administration will inherit his dilatory and procrastinating legacy. I don't sense we get beyond rhetoric when it comes to crime or to drugs, and no speeches I hear begin to deal with the entitlement largess we continue to maintain almost unabated.

It seems ironic to know what is wrong and then spend our waking hours, not in public debate on "how to" make corrections, but rather on extraneous news. Our effort, energy and empathy is poured out elsewhere — on issues which don't mean a bloody thing to the future of this people. We focus on our friend Dan Burton in Congress, heading a Committee on Reform and Oversight, subpoenaing witnesses, and holding hearings about campaign "fund-raising" transgressions. Senator Thompson's doing it in the Senate, something like $8,000,000 or $10,000,000 between them (for starters), all to see "who" got <u>what</u> money from which wrong people in the last federal campaign. (Spending <u>in the search</u> more than the malefactors collected.) (More even than they <u>returned</u>!) Hours of live coverage, eons of staff time invested in discovering how the dollars got there, and whether it was legal or not. While simultaneously, Mr. Starr goes on investigating Bill and Hillary-gate.

What the hell difference does any of this make to the future lot of this people? What existing national nemesis already identified is being resolved? In the litany of the somber, often destructive, and sometimes outrageous conditions ravaging our world, how important is where money came from in the last campaign? Who is surprised at the hustling? This is new? Caesar was buying votes in his race for Roman Consul in 50 B.C., if one thinks campaign shenanigans are a recent invention. Clinton didn't need to cheat to begin with, not as long as the Republicans couldn't get their act or candidate in focus and revved up. It wasn't his innovative financial fund-raising "ingenuity" that won the day; it was the difference in the two candidates as arbitrated by the American voters.

Again, I keep wondering where our collective "head" is at. Establishing what is damaging us in the present even more deleterious in the future, we ought to have public debate on solutions. Instead we spent most of last year glued to the television set watching the O.J. Simpson trial as though <u>this</u> were America's life-determining struggle. I keep thinking of the media paroxysm resulting from the Oklahoma bombing and ensuing trial. No one challenges the pointless and painful nature of the tragedy, but the facts <u>were</u> indeed out and the possible perpetrator convicted. Divert attention from crime and drugs and AIDS to a single, non-correctable incident? Why spill all the ink revisiting an issue with which we are already sated? Is the plight of the postal bomber critical to our future; is the ubiquitous update on the Flight #800 disaster an issue holding America's destiny in the balance? I marvel at how many angles and different spins the media puts on the JonBenet murder; how heated and fractious a Joe Camel cigarette ad becomes; how exhaustively we document sex in the armed forces, and how doggedly we recycle the abortion controversy as though our fate and fortune will rise and fall on right to life resolution.

If we cannot determine what is significant from what is inconsequential or tangential to our current well being, how are we to correct societal ills? In a nation where the will of the people is paramount, are we not entitled to a more substantive diet than TV or *National Enquirer* sensationalism? Until we get serious about solving documented shortcomings through public pressure, there is no way to deal with the major challenges dangling perennially before this nation. One might get the idea that if we spent as much time stewing about education as we did Whitewater, maybe something good would happen; or creating three separate initiatives devoted to the delinquency or illegitimacy or creating a simple tax form as we now spend on investigating questionable campaign contribution, we'd be doing America

— and the next generations of Americans — a far greater favor.

The other skin game we play with national problems is pseudo solving. We have a major budgetary dilemma, of course, spending annually more than we collect and raise both our deficit, thus, automatically our budget every year (to accommodate new interest expense). Everyone knows one day we have to get our act together or all the tax revenue goes for interest on the national debt. At that point all the subsidies and entitlements disappear. This year the Congress dealt boldly and bravely in meeting this evil nemesis head on. We cut substantially the annual deficit and scheduled systematically the ultimate eradication of all future debts five years from now. Huzzah and three cheers to boot!

Only what really happened was the Congress was well on its typical merry way with lots of "sound and fury signifying" again mostly a lot of "nothing" when a windfall in tax revenue came cascading into the coffers and provided a huge splurge of cash. Wow! Instead of using it to trim some sails and simultaneously apply a large chunk to education or infrastructure or research on AIDS or more federal law enforcement along the drug border, we decided to spend it all for current causes in mostly the same old way with the same old annual increases except now the deficit won't enlarge so much because of the extra cash. Congress hasn't really done a bloody thing about correcting our course or their habits or about solving identified problems. The economy, totally apart from legislative action, arbitrated national policy on deficits while our solons continue the very processes which got us in this jam, and they managed, however, to dress it up like an act of statesmanship. Hey guys! Hemingway cautioned us "Never to mistake motion for action." And Emerson observed, "Truth is beautiful, without doubt; but so are lies." Truth is if Washington had seen all this dough coming in, they would have spent it. Irony is, you and I are saved by their ignorance. What a way to run this railroad. ■

Carpe Diem

December 1997

This essay might not be a reflection typical of the holiday season, but the yuletide <u>is</u> upon us and with it comes a mountain of memories. Since most of us are revisiting "Christmas past", it might be appropriate to engage in some further rumination — also about the past, and about "seizing the day", a bit of advice our Roman forbearers handed down. Advice, by the way, without expository elucidation as though the two-word advice is obvious and immortal…if we can figure out "why". What's so great about "seizing the day"?

Maybe what it suggests is that life is transitory; is mostly a series of engagements, opportunities, chances, conditions, threats, events, and options. The way we take advantage of or exploit or utilize the "day" has a lot to do with how we fare as pilgrims on this long journey. It reiterates a little recognized fact: Most of history, personal as well as national, is constituted by how and when we "seize" a given moment.

A recent article illustrates my point. It described how Civic War buffs recreated the Battle of Antietam fought originally on the 17th of September 1862 outside the village (and astride the stream) named Antietam. I relived the battle seven years ago, thanks to the narration of a guide who described how the engagement opened at sunrise with 80,000 Union troops of the ever-cautious George McClellan deployed against 40,000 Confederates. What unfolds as the event is reconstructed for us is not military brilliance, but the utter savagery of the encounter. A crucial part of which took place in a 40-acre cornfield where advancing ranks of Union soldiers opened the engagement, surging forward, only to be driven back by a counterattack, then to regroup and plow forward again, now re-enforced. A see-saw rhythm, a bitterly contested, inconsequential farm field, the visibility "iffy" with the corn still standing. Rank against rank at point-blank range; volley after volley, pouring from each side, on and on, for four or five hours with the dead and wounded heaped upon the field.

Antietam became immortal as a result of that sanguinary struggle because when the day ended (McClellan claimed the victory), a record had been set. More Americans were slaughtered in that cornfield than were ever killed elsewhere in a single engagement; more casualties at Antietam than among all our D-Day forces on the beaches of Normandy.

A visitor now sees only quiet, rolling fields, drowsy in the sun. It's almost impossible to image the melee of writhing bodies; the storm of fire and noise; the convulsion of violence that would create the worst slaughter of American soldiers ever recorded/ endured in a single engagement — in a day, a brief moment in history.

Antietam is not legendary; did not resolve the Civil War. But a battle that was famous and <u>did</u> arbitrate future history was fought in 1066 near the village of Senlac in Southern England when William of Normandy deployed 7,000 troops to contest the crown with Harold Godwinson, the Saxon King. Another battle that wavered to and fro till late in the day when one of William's arrows found the left eye of King Harold. That was "all she wrote" for him. And the Saxon cause; the day was lost - and the Kingdom. In this tragic contest, the English ruler "seized" the <u>wrong</u> day. He had just finished a battle 200 miles to the north where he killed the greatest Norse fighter of the age (Hardrada), also invading England; then hurried back with forced marches to meet the Norman threat. Like a dummy, he also opted for (seized) the day after his arrival to attack William. He should have known his dead-tired forces, marching 430 miles in 30 days were unable to withstand the protracted brunt of heavy combat. Had he waited a day or a week (William is going no where) and re-enforced his army with both fresh fighters and rested soldiers, he could well have

Battle of Antietam; the charge of Iron Brigade near the Dunker Church, September 17, 1862. Chromolithograph by Louis Prang and Company of an original painting by Thure de Thulstrup. *(Source: Wikimedia Commons.)*

changed the outcome. The future of British history would have been dramatically different. William, on the other hand, was luckiest, "seizing" a moment when the Saxon army was otherwise engaged. He landed his troops unopposed. Then got weapons, supplies, horses, and gear off the boats, marched his legion inland and made ready for battle. Had he landed with full Saxon resistance, the whole story might well have had a different ending.

The point at which one commits himself to action is often the point at which history itself turns and redirects. And history's re-directions are, of course, innumerable. Again, the stuff which <u>constitutes</u> history. Like the appointment of Bonaparte to command the army of Italy in 1796; the election of Abraham Lincoln in 1860 with 40% of the vote; Washington's daring attack on Christmas night across the Delaware in 1776; the introduction of Madison's Virginia Plan to the Constitutional Convention in 1787. After each, nothing would be as it had been.

Since this is our Christmas issue, a holiday whose origins are religious, it is not inappropriate to consider the theory of carpe diem as it relates to Christianity. Historians (and gospel writers) quibble about the date of Jesus' birth, ranging from 6-4 B.C.E. to 10 C.E. Those who impute the advent of Jesus and his subsequent ministry to divine initiative can suggest that in this timing, it is God Himself who has "seized the day". Or at least the century. Because there was no other point in the 5000 years of history of the species when Jesus might have appeared, taught, ministered, died, and succeeded in his mission. No period when the message, picked up by the Apostle Paul and revised for articulation to a Graeco-Roman, (Gentile) world, could have been so readily spread and so universally heard and understood. In his proselyting, organizing, doctrinizing fervor, he created an organism called the church (ecclesia) in order to institutionalize the Jesus movement and give it permanent status. In three ensuing centuries, enough of mankind was converted, enough structure installed, enough doctrine enunciated, and leadership developed to survive the maelstrom which the barbarian avalanche would precipitate. There was no other era in human annals when peace prevailed so widely for over three centuries, the world so stitched together with 55,000 miles of paved roads; no time when travel was so easy; no other era linked by a common language, a universal law, one coinage, and religious toleration.

Garden Tomb, Jerusalem.

Paul traveled from Jerusalem to Antioch to Cyprus into Asia Minor across to Greece and back again to Jerusalem, easier than we can do so <u>today</u>. Airplanes are quick and buses convenient, but in terms of crossing borders without shots, visas, passports, luggage search, with no change in language and currency, he had it far easier. So, the church had time to put its roots down and spread its message before the major trouble started. Over 300 years of endeavoring to teach mankind love is more useful in managing the human experiment than power; that peace is more beneficial than war; that God is one, and all men are brothers. An effort, incidentally, that still goes on today, the species being discouragingly obdurate and still eagerly pursuing its ancient trophies: money, power, status.

Seizing the moment also has import to people in the tractor business; (this <u>is</u> a business publication) and not just at Christmas time, but year around. We have something like 485 employees, and my guess is about 35% of them talk to customers regularly, many a dozen times daily. Whether in field service trucks, as Reps or machinery salesmen, as AG guys or people selling stationary engines; influencing <u>truck</u> engine sales, working on the parts counters, office sales people, credit folks, secretaries and receptionists, senior or branch managers, plus several people I have probably overlooked. The folks our team talk to every day are using or needing our products and services. The objective in each encounter ought to be one which makes our dealership more valuable to "users". One that gives more value for the invested dollar and provides solutions to problems when they are most soluble (seizing the moment again).

Success is at maximum level when every one of our contacts is sensitive to the needs and idiosyncrasies of the user and is aware that each encounter presents opportunities for us to be of further use, provide an additional service, solve a problem, make a sale, each seeing the importance of <u>this</u> moment and its opportunities. We must know what is proper, is productive, better than (<u>and before</u>) the owner does. Our success lies in how well we seize the opportunity each encounter provides. We must never view the few minutes we are with a customer/prospect as a "routine call". It is an occasion unique and of itself. It is a moment arranged to make some change.

We need to bring this to a close, referencing again the Christmas event, significant to us <u>not</u> because of what may have happened historically, but what we <u>believe</u> happened. ("Nothing is right or wrong, but my thinking makes it so".) What did the event <u>mean</u> to us, personally as well as corporate? The fact that we can't even pinpoint the date of the first Christmas (it wasn't celebrated officially by the church till the 4th Century) suggests that the <u>con-sequence</u> of the occasion is far more important than the timing. The fact that we need to testify — to celebrate or commemorate — preempts history itself. On a more contemporary note, we view the current holiday in a bit of the same vein. The date is less important than the meaning. And the meaning emphasizes the importance of the family, gathering around the hearth, reaffirming its unity and oneness. Christmas gives rise to sudden and expansive generosity evident at this moment, "seized" inadvertently in response to the gift given us in this free, affluent, exciting, and solid land. A gift we Calvinists call grace. Christmas is also the creation of new memories that will cast a bit of light to flicker in years to come; is a season engulfed in music, and the world decorated as for a festival. A point in time could change the future if we had the will and the memory to make more of life like Christmas. It is a moment seized to "rejoice, give thanks and sing"; a moment different than any day before or after. ■

1998

Either/Or?

March 1998

Indianapolis has been aiming to become the "amateur sports capital of America", and in the course of a 20-year campaign has induced a number of amateur athletic associations to affiliate with our city, i.e., move their headquarters here. Latest example was the NCAA which plans to strike its tent in Kansas and build a new headquarters in Indianapolis. We have successfully hosted the Pan Am Games, Olympic Trials, the Semi-Finals of the National Basketball Playoffs, and did the Final-Four last year, etc. The National Divers are in town, the U.S. Rowing Association, USA Gymnastics, Synchronized Swimmers, Western Tennis Association, USA Track & Field, and the number of athletic <u>events</u> continues to expand in our city. Most recent coup was landing the Championship Playoffs for the World Basketball title in the 2001 Match-Up. Great! When we can successfully compete with other <u>countries</u>, and come out on top, it says that someone is really doing a great job.

But this doesn't mean everyone is pleased. In the case of the 2001 Basketball Playoffs, a friend noted somewhat cynically to me while I was in Florida, "Indianapolis landed some Basketball World Championship game for some far distant date. We have teachers who can't teach; school boards who constantly meddle; parents who don't care, SAT scores in the tank, leaving our educational system a wreck. So what do we do in Indy? We crow about basketball playoffs ... Ugh". Inadvertently, this turned out to be a rather astute observation, far profounder

than the observer expected. It asks, "Which is more important to Indianapolis, our schools or our athletic reputation?" The answer is obvious. Schools are the most important. But the question is specious. It should have been different. Is this world athletic notoriety good for our city? Is it more important than education? Should we stop doing anything else around here till school standards are up? Point is, it doesn't have to be either/or. It can — and should be — <u>both</u>. We <u>should</u> enhance our reputation in amateur sports <u>and</u> improve education simultaneously.

The implication in the rather snide comment was that Indianapolis has its focus wrong and is pursuing the wrong goals. But "Indianapolis" is not one amalgam, it is not a monolith, a single animal which initiates and controls all the activity in town. It is a gallimaufry (a hodgepodge collection), a series of individual efforts with jurisdiction and interest vastly different from one to the other. The point to my friend would be there are two of these distinct and separate emphases here, one does a great job at what it sets out to do, i.e., gather a large representation of amateur athletics in our town. Successful because over the course of 15 years we patiently put together an aggregation of sporting facilities and venues matched very few places in the world. (One reason, by the way, we score so successfully in landing events.) With the IUPUI Campus, Natatorium, Track and Field facilities, the Velodrome, Eagle Creek Park, the Convention Center, Market Square, the RCA Dome et al, we have an array of formidable options hard to beat, seldom equaled. Then beyond that, have built a support group that knows how to market, sell, induce, woo and succeed in more and more athletic happenings occurring here…a fact which brings exposure and economic benefit.

Meanwhile "back at the ranch" we have the other group, the sundry school systems, most of which have been adjudged to the less than average and seem to be improving not at all; complicated by a contumacious school board, unhappy with superintendents and plagued with shifting populations, a teachers union and struggling even with the element of school room student safety. The solution is to make the school groups as competent and well organized as the athletic block. When that occurs, we shall become a pacesetter in education, not "tail-end Charlie". Or said a harsher way, if the people who have succeeded so well in making us truly the "Amateur Athletic Capital" of the nation were put in charge of our school system, my bet is we could chalk up the same won-loss record. They would make changes. They would succeed in providing for our children a Class-A learning experience.

The irony is the School Board and administration are legally constituted in a mandate going back to the Northwest Ordinance. They are created as an official agency for education in a given community, usually run by hired staff, secured by a Board who has jurisdiction for policy. The athletic people are volunteers for the most part, doing what they think is something helpful for youngsters involved in sports while at the same time reflecting prestige to the city.

Ergo, we have the irony of a volunteer gang with superb competence, making an official element of our political system look a lot like bush-leaguers. Amateur athletics' people, this says, have become the professionals (at what they do) while the professionals (administrators, teachers and Board) are the ones who look like amateurs. "It is a puzzlement" as Yul Brenner used to opine.

It is also unnecessary. We have the leadership extant in our community to do about anything we want to do. We just don't always get it in the right places, which is the major travesty of history. I.e., having the capacity to solve one's problems, but never allowing (or generating) the leadership which could fashion the appropriate vehicle to do what is best for the total good in a given situation. This fact is most evident in political situations. Time after time we run into the Saddam Husseins of the world or the Mobutu Sésé Sékos, often with incalculable raw materials, convertible to capital which then could create systems to provide jobs, secure a decent infrastructure, educational systems, medical and research institutes, agricultural self-sufficiency and healthy people. But inevitably we end up giving the power — or allowing the power — to the wrong guy who is totally incompetent or whose objective becomes personal glorification and family aggrandizement while the institution wallows in needless poverty and destitution, robbed of its potential and its hope for the future. Count the historic record of peoples, cultures, even empires, who have risen to hold center stage and create great moments only through bad management and poor judgment collapse, often in a heap, leaving behind no trace of their sojourn here.

We have it a little different in the business world because the control, management, and power to create programs or initiative or to launch marketing efforts and secure professional personnel is not up to an electorate, but to the ownership. The fact that welcomed 1,000,000 new businesses last year indicates how easy it is to move into free enterprise arena. The fact that only 7% of them survive beyond the 20th year, however, tells us how hard it is to stay; because the element of competence is ineluctable in this milieu. There is no way to run the tractor company badly and survive. Generally, then, all institutional existence — whatever its nature — is a perilous thing. Survival is not contingent upon plan or design or aspiration, even on necessity or hard work. It resolves itself around the narrow issue of problem solving. He among us who is able to anticipate and prepare for the next recession, e.g., without damaging the enterprise is the survivor. Or once assailed, he who marshals his best people creates the best strategies, and the required discipline to confront the nemesis is probably the one with the best chance of succeeding. J. Irwin Miller once observed a manager's chief job is "looking for trouble". It takes little skill to direct a "going" concern, propelled by an existing momentum. The real manager is the one who anticipates problems before they get in our face and moves with resolution to find the resolution. Trouble which impairs the cause has to be eliminated; it cannot be endured or accommodated. We don't wait to see whether some benevolent destiny will eliminate the glitch with the passage of time. Anyone waiting for outside forces to automatically "raise his boat" had better be reading the want ads.

Again, the rules in the marketplace demand business succeed. When it does things as badly as the school board, or Fidel Castro, or the Presbyterian church, or the Bob Dole Campaign, each content to idealize a status quo, it misses the point about solving problems to gain success. We can not institutionalize weakness and expect victories. The only place failure persistently occurs is in government. (But we haven't seen the denouement to that story yet.) What can be a greater irony? What we won't tolerate in business, we expect in politics. Yul was right. It is a puzzlement.

If there is going to be a solution to the school system, here or any place, we certainly need to have people in charge committed to doing whatever is necessary — and legal — to make dramatic change. We do know what is wrong. The kids aren't learning. We do know what is right. There are urban schools exactly like ours where the kids are doing great. What is missing is not the technique or the system, what is missing is the popular and political will. If we really want our system better, we need to revert to the model of the athletic caucus…or the business model. We need to put people in charge who can perform, then will do. In Indianapolis, where we are hung with an archaic system, we need to adopt the Chicago model: Give the system to the Mayor and let him appoint a school board, charged with getting us into "All American" status like we are in finance, athletics, cleanliness, and privatization. We have improved the golf course system enormously, by privatizing it: have saved millions annually in our sewer systems by giving management to the water company; have privatized garbage pick-up and the airport, etc. Each is a case — model — for other cities to study. What has it taught us? That where there is incentive and professional excellence, things work better. When failure is not allowed, we are going to have success. But if we accommodate problems and make the system or the vehicle more important than the product, we had better expect deep trouble. ■

What's AED Again?

March 1998

It is a trade association, the "Associated Equipment Distributors", an amalgam of some 1,250 machinery dealers and manufacturers representing our industry. The "industry" being then described as the "construction, mining, logging, and maintenance" markets, but by now has branched out in a dozen ancillary channels (sanitary landfills, power generation, fork lifts, engine power for trucks, industrial plants, snow removal, etc.). *We* have been members since E.W. MacAllister joined in 1942. It is typical of hundreds of kindred organizations that represent the uniquely American spirit. Which is a group of people with a common interest (school, hospital, church, art form, neighborhood stabilization, Red Cross, political party) who get together to express, represent, and enhance their own interests through an official "body".

"Self-serving gang, right? Protecting your own interest which must mean your own profits? At whose expense?"

Not really. AED was founded in 1919 to help a growing technology apply to an exploding economy do a better job of "serving" its own field (the distribution of machinery and its product support component) without going broke in the process. If it succeeded, it strengthened a whole society. By recourse to a broad-based coordination and cooperation effort, we avoided each simultaneously, inventing the same wheel. Why should each of us develop his own sales compensation program, inventory control system, accounting procedure, credit policies and the like? If someone has tried six times before he found a successful way to handle the repair of his used equipment, why should we not learn from his success? Our industry's economic phenomenon is like the nation's: a result of evolution. All started in a primitive fashion and through trial and error, the successful ones just grew.

In 1919 America was beginning the accommodation of a vehicle called the automobile, and the more miles of highways that contraption had to scoot across, the more utilitarian it could become and the more cars could be sold. It converted us to a nation on wheels because our industry moved a step at a time, to cut and fill, make and pour concrete, scalp out drainage, and throw up bridges, et al. that arbitrated the pace of construction and thus, created our national highway system. It was really the application of our machinery providing its constructive capacity that assured the sale of a jillion autos. Also in due time, the location of commercial hubs, the size and configuration of cities, the construction of oil pipelines, the interstate highway network, water and drainage programs, the location of industrial complexes, future sale of houses as we suburbanized, etc. The expansion and growth happened all over the map as the nation itself industrialized, and the corresponding proliferation of dealerships and manufacturers was random and profuse.

Given the unprogrammed nature of this splurge, there was a lot of cutting and fitting, which translates to successes and failures. A patriarch in our fraternity once boasted to me that he had once been a CAT dealer in Michigan. At the point I knew him he was handling an assorted line of miscellaneous products, and when I looked around a year or so later, he was belly up. He left CAT and tried elsewhere. A very bad guess. The dealer in Michigan today is huge.

Success in business is contingent upon success in managing people, inventories, finances, marketing, the manufacturers, the banks; and above all, the customers, while making a little profit at the same time. This means deploying one's resources in pursuit of his opportunity by staying in control and knowing what is happening where. And what to do when (if) it gets out of whack.

One course to follow here is trial and error; the other is using arbitrary norms which experience suggests have been established to assure success. E.g. there is a commonplace formula which says if you pay your mechanics $15 an hour, you have to charge "x" times that much in order to cover

P.E. addressing the Associated Equipment Distributors (AED).

overhead, tooling, re-work, training, management, etc. Plus, a rule that says you have to charge a lesser factor of "x" times for internal work (warranty, used repair, delivery) because you cannot make money by charging yourself. There are norms for machinery profit margins, for parts margins, for costs to run a given department. If these have been established by successful dealers, why should I have to experiment? So the chief benefit of trade organization is to teach and to learn those things which will help individual members succeed.

This gathering of data is a tricky business because we are competing with each other. Who wants to give his good ideas to a competitor, thus providing info to beat your brains out? We do because it is a two-way street. If I am contributing to the pot, others are also. And beyond that, the guy that kills you in the marketplace is not the good dealer. It is the desperate or incompetent bird who runs his business intuitively and thinks (erroneously) he knows what he is doing. In the market dip of 1982-83, a number of competitors hit the wall because they did not have "it" – product, management, staffing or financial reserves.

Meanwhile, as long as the country continues to grow, rebuild subdivisions, resurface and relocate roads, replace bridges, expand ever further into suburbia, restore life to center city, it will continue to need our machinery. Important because when that is of high quality, used with maximum efficiency, with limited downtime, repairs readily achieved – all the trademarks of a top-notch dealer — then the cost for the project is minimized. The builder gets done on time and makes a little profit, and the home buyer benefits. If the cost of construction is raised because of constant machinery breakdowns, long waits for repairs, no recourse to rental units or high charges for dealer service due to his own inadequacies, the pain of that dereliction is suffered all around. Professional performance on our part extends itself not only in suburban development or the resurfacing of highways, but to the cost of mining each ton of coal, hauling out every log from the woods, every semi-load of merchandise moved on our highway, all the material processed in a thousand landfills, every load of stone ripped from a quarry, or a marine boat bringing in shrimp. All have need for competence, strong management, and efficient dealerships to support our product. And, thus, the need to do it the most efficient way. Either through trial and error, recourse to oceans of data, benchmarks, standards or

"know how" irrespective of where it is secured. If we get a lot of this from CAT over the years, we have benefited enormously from AED.

The other area of impact is one of expertise as it is employed to protect or to represent the industry. For example, the IRS has a schedule for depreciating assets and applies this accumulated wisdom in their typically autocratic fashion to our machinery. What is the depreciable life of a D8 tractor? On their charts it is five years. How does the government get this figure? It calls in experts to testify and explain something about the life cycle of a bulldozer. Meaning, we have (fact, I have) testified here representing our industry, submitting data which would give realistic schedules to owners of our machinery.

We get a lot of flack for testifying, however, when lobbying for highway appropriations. It is hard to separate private interests from public welfare, especially when you have a lot of dollars on the line and are commissioned by the stockholders to protect them. One rule of thumb we use here is: "If it (whatever "it" happens to be) is not good for the country as a whole, it is not good for us as an industry." But as often happens, what turns out to be our hot-button item is something most people don't understand or pay much attention to. Ergo, when a strong voice is raised giving direction to a piece of legislation, people wonder what the motive is. For example, there is a major highway bill coming down now in Congress, and we are crowding our legislators to consider the crumbling nature of our infrastructure and make the appropriation as healthy as we can. "Of course, so you can sell some machinery." Maybe. But there's a better reason. After all, the money we are talking about spending is the money collected for this very purpose, i.e. comes almost entirely from gasoline and diesel sales taxes, carefully squirreled away in an account called the Highway Trust Fund. As I write this, there is some $28 billion sitting there, collected from we drivers of highway vehicles and collected to be spent on roads. But for the past 100 years a huge amount has been "sitting there" because that "bank account" is positive cash when we figure our budget imbalances. It offsets $28 billion of spending which happens only because it has been withheld from highway needs.

Is it "selfish vested interest" to say: "Our roads and streets are really getting pretty bad? We have collected money from the motorists and truckers in America to attend to this. Why do we weave through the chuckholes so you can spend some more money on daycare centers or pork barrel projects in Alaska? Why don't you let us spend the money for the purpose YOU had in mind when you set up the system? "The Cheesemakers United in Indiana" or the Future Farmers of America or the ICLU are not going to make a case for fixing our roads or replacing bridges. They have their own fish to fry. It becomes the task of those with particular insight and knowledge of given situations to sound the tocsin and spread the alarm. We see the problem, know how to fix part of it, realize the resources are there, and have

(I think) an obligation to ask for a reasonable program to address the bumpy-street dilemma.

All of which is getting over-long. Please conclude with me that associations such as I have described have more interests in mind than buttering their own bread. The first of these is survival; the second is competent professionalism as the means to the first; and next, as interpreters of that part of the "big picture" which affects that part of the total system about which we have more knowledge than practically anyone else. ∎

Customer Computer Conundrum

June 1998

On the 4th of May we had a brief recognition party in the shop to identify and acknowledge some old-timers who have been with us most of their professional life — 45, 40, 35, 30, 25 years — five guys, 175 years of steady service. Careers for each of them; important careers to us because we succeed by doing class-A work, and we get this from pros, from experienced people. To assure this we try hard to keep good employees and eliminate a bugaboo called "turnover". That's hiring people who don't stay, requiring us to hire all over again. The problem here is obvious: it is in the time (and dollars) lost in training and in getting new folks grooved into the corporate culture, so they understand their job, so they do it well, and appreciate the other elements of a company whose departments and components are interdependent. We have to get along with each other, hopefully, as individuals; certainly as functioning units in a business enterprise which performs a variety of operations. People unfamiliar with our patterns require time to get indoctrinated.

New employees usually bring in a degree of skills, but then they have to learn how to employ them our way which means using our systems. To a large degree this is all trial and error and not too hard a trial, and hopefully, not too much error. They acclimate to our environment by watching their peers who can initiate them informally on the rules of the shop or the office, the paper procedures (inevitable these days), pace of work, source of tooling, supplies, etc. and most important, in performance of the function for which they were hired. I.e., how to take and process a phone parts order, drop the pan on a truck engine, put together a quote on a loader and collect payment on a past due lease deal. Somewhere along the line in any of these there will be an encounter with a computer since everyone but me in this bloody place has to do something, some time which involves the computer. It is amazing how deep is the incursion of this gadget into our systems, how widespread its tentacles; how preoccupied many of our folks become and how enslaved to its screen and keyboard. I'm not knocking it; I'm just surprised how many things are now done with the machine and how much it has taken over our total function. And so along the way, the technology of the dealership has to be learned, and our trainers or peers or managers help inculcate this sophistication into those who need to use it.

You go with the flow in this business, and Caterpillar is hastening us down "the yellow brick (computer) road" as fast as our legs can carry us, hoping that we not only get more efficient, but that in doing so, we widen the gap with competition. The more things we can do faster, better, more accurately, and more economically than brand "X", the better chance we have of beating his brains out before he knows we already signed up the deal. It is pretty awesome, the pace at which all of this is accelerating, and I rejoice with exceeding great joy that our people are becoming so damn smart so fast and furious.

But every so often in our haste for efficiency, I hope we don't forget something. Like say, forget the person. Much of the electronic world is doing that. One example to illustrate what I mean here is a thing called voicemail. Ever try calling your friendly phone company to tell them your own voicemail is not working? What you get to make your point is a voice message telling you several things you can do if you punch the right buttons. After two or three runs at this (probably using the wrong buttons), you decided that the phone people don't have a solution to your problem, so they resort to verbiage, designed to screen and confuse you with arcane instructions in such an overwhelming way that you finally retreat in outrage by banging down the receiver, rejoicing at the efficiency we enjoy since they broke up Maw Bell. Not getting an answer doesn't bug you, what bothers you is that no one cares. No one will listen to your questions. No one will talk to you. Which does not give very high marks to a company spending millions trying to get more customers.

I noticed a very attractive, young, and very confused Oriental lady in the New York airport last year, almost in tears because she could not contact someone — say — in Florence, Italy. And sensing her frustration and dismay decided to come to her rescue, once a Boy Scout I'm always ready for a good deed. Found out where she wanted to call, got the number and using my handy-dandy calling card, thought I could get through for her. I am a college grad, fact, I have three honorary degrees, am a successful businessman, even been to Florence half a dozen times, and on top of that, am a Presbyterian. So I gave it my best shot. You never heard so many instructions, options, obfuscation, and garbled advice about what to do and how to make the call. I tried four times to get through; desperate for someone to come on the line so we could buy their product and complete a transatlantic call. Zilch! At which point USAirways called my flight and saved my reputation. What kind of a system have we instituted when the customer will do anything to make a purchase yet get so confused and confounded there is no possible way he can do so? It is ridiculous. Again, there is no one listening here. They just keep on talking and talking and talking, like the Energizer bunny never telling you the one little secret you need to hear.

So one thing else we have in this incorporation of newer people (and some of the older ones who prove to be slow learners) is to be sure that devices, gadgets, technology, and time-saving equipment are viewed properly. They are to abet and improve the task at hand; they are not an end in themselves, they are in use because of their marvelous sophistication. At this point the old-timers in the ranks need to be sure people recall the initial culture B.C. — "before computers". We don't work in a vacuum or create a product delivered to strangers. We are dealing with people we know personally and consider friends. Person-to-person interface with the customer is critical to the business success. We don't do business via the mail or telegraph or even E-mail. We do it with one of us talking to another so each listens to what the other says. We are not in a closed circuit data, voicemail business. Come to think of it, we are not even in the machinery business. We are in the people business. People who expect us to understand what they want because we understand what they say. Meaning, we really don't sell front end loaders, we sell persons who buy them…if we are clever enough and clear enough and provide both the facility and the benefits they need. There has to be a 'buy" before there is a "sell". And there has to be a convinced, satisfied, trusting person before there is an order. It's hard to think the best way to engender trust, confidence or create value is with pamphlets, voicemail or radio ads. We think the way to do these things is face-to-face where people can ask their questions and can look us in the eye. The customer develops any trust he has in us through experience and benefits he's received, not through a printout. People trust people, they are still skeptical of computers, canned ads, voicemail.

Everyone in our operation does not have direct contact with customers, but the vast majority is involved daily. Meaning, we are different than the people in Peoria who build the tractors or make the parts. They are more oriented to systems, to routines, to systematic repetition of the same task over and over. They are concerned about doing what they do right, but missing in their equation is any personal relationship with the people who sell, or who buy the product they have made. If something goes haywire with it (called warranty), it is the dealer who becomes the surrogate for the builder and has to fix what was screwed up. Not always a happy experience, but guess which one of us is more aware of the owner, of what he does; how he thinks and who he is? Guess who loses the business if it isn't done right? The answer is both of us: the dealer first and then the factory. But we have only one area to proselyte; CAT has the world. We have the greater degree of sensitivity, and it is because we are concerned about the welfare of this bird who bought the unit from us and want to see him succeed more than we are embarrassed about a product that should have given better service. Like my telephone illustration, one could almost make the case that the critical moment between buyer and seller is not at the time of purchase. The real test comes when something goes wrong, and we need help or redress or some fixing done. It is often at that point that the real judgment about the quality or integrity of the vendor becomes apparent. How much genuine honesty is involved in a company that loves you to death when you want to buy something, but won't look you in the eye when you show them where the commodity is flunking the test, is not doing what we both agreed it was supposed to do.

I had a truck salesman one day years ago tell me that if we were in business seriously, there is no way to walk away from trouble. We have to deal with it. Which is why machinery even as clever as computers (who are so clever most of us cannot understand how they operate), why machines will never replace the thinking, problem-solving individual. Machines don't care; my people do. We shall be using technology as much as we can to help solve problems, but machines don't get friendly, sympathetic, interested in what we're doing, and don't really give a damn whether we are successful or not. Ergo, they will never replicate or replace the human component which is the interest of one individual for another, an element so important in our operation. ∎

What's So Great About the Ten Commandments?

June 1998

(Source: Wikimedia Commons.)

I stay perennially confused — and partially amused — about the controversy over the display and exhibition of The Ten Commandments. The degree of heat and ardor generated over this issue baffles me. The question ought not to be about <u>where</u> we mount the Decalogue, but for goodness sake, <u>why</u> we bother in the first place. Don't take me wrong. I happen to be a card-carrying Presbyterian elder and know as much about the Old Testament and ancient Israel as any other tractor salesman in Marion County. Moreover, I'm as conversant with the theology of St. Paul and creation of the Christian church as anyone at your last cocktail party, so this is not cynical deprecation. This is asking seriously: Why do we regard The Ten Commandments as great moral teachings; inspiring milestones instructing the species in decency and righteousness? How can we find the cultic regulation of a nomadic society probably no larger than the city of Kokomo and struggling to survive in the marginal real estate of the Middle East 3000 years ago, remotely relevant in a sedentary and phenomenal nation of 260,000,000 people? Fair scores: we just <u>can't</u>.

The reason the Decalogue is displayed in classrooms, courtrooms, or city-council chambers is totally specious. Nothing more than the momentum of tradition; two millenniums of priests, pastors, and rabbis, assuring us of its eternal wisdom and divine sanction. We are stunned into saying with the multitude "Yea, Lord, Hallelujah!" (How many of us argue with the high priest?) Ever honestly looked at this code dispassionately? Taken a few minutes to assure yourself of their "eternal value"?

Notice the first one. "*Thou shall have no other Gods in front of me*". Does this strike you as a major premise arbitrating your personal conduct? Is it critical in fashioning your ethical or moral precepts? The writer was worried to death about the prevalence and life-giving assurance of Baal worship, about the sacred prostitutes of Astarte or the impressive ceremonies of Dagon, etc. Are <u>we</u> tempted to go around looking for such unlikely deities to put in front of the God we worship? If that was the number one threat to Israel's monolatry in Canaan, it is not the number one problem confounding or confronting our culture or wooing our children into apostasy — where does

one look for other gods if dissatisfied with Yahweh? The temptation to follow other deities is not even a remote prospect. Nor is it even relevant today.

Maybe the next one is more helpful. It forbids us to carve any "*images of anything in the heavens above, the earth beneath or the waters under the earth*". (I thought "under the earth" was a sea of molten lava that pops up from time to time like in Hawaii or Iceland.) At any rate, do you think it is important for people "conceived in liberty and dedicated to the proposition that all men are created equal" to include a provision that it's illegal to be carving images of gods we might be inclined to worship? Is it important that we teach our children "no carving"?

Besides that, if we have already <u>said</u> "*no other gods*" before me, it has eliminated the need to deal with the carved idols of gods we have already forsworn, except, of course, icons representing Yahweh. Maybe that is the secret here: no representations of Jehovah which would, thus, anthropomorphize Him and in so doing imply powers as well as limitation. But left unrepresented, His power and scope become unlimited. Yet, the second command goes on to say that if in the event we happen to make some other images, we "*shall not bow down to them nor serve them*". Don't have any other gods, don't make any images, but then if you do, don't bow down or serve them. I'm sorry. It is hard to consider this convoluted dictum as sublime theological instruction. In 1250 B.C. probably important (if slightly redundant) but in 1998, of absolutely no value.

Third Commandment "*Forbids us to take the Lord's name in vain*". Again, assuming we understand what "in vain" means. Probably swearing, damning, careless and insulting use of the Divine name. One wonders what this has to do in managing our relationship with the wider world and how this makes for a better life. Is it more important than loving one another; than walking the extra mile than tolerating other viewpoints? My hunch is if this one dropped out of sight, the nature of our on-going process would not be adversely impacted one iota.

The fourth Commandment tells us that we ought to "*Remember the Sabbath day, to keep it holy*". We need some help in wondering how it is we <u>keep</u> a day "holy". At my age <u>every</u> day is holy, and every hour is a gift of God. Why should we set a single day apart to keep it holy? Does this mean no driving to church on Sunday, no cooking of meals, no football games? No doctors, pharmacists, policemen, airlines, movies, hotels, telephone operators? How does all this make us a better people? One gets the impression if Moses were writing the Ten Commandments today, he might make some exceptions. Maybe the ancient Hebrew had his reasons. A day of rest, a day of meditation and focus, a day dedicated to God was a good reminder of Divine favor. We don't sense that need. Have we suffered irreparable damage because it has been modified? Beyond that, the mere declaration of a given religious day hardly teaches us how the Lord expects us to get along with each other, work through differences, treat the abused, bring justice to the nations, and find ways to practice peace rather than war.

Number five wants us to "*Honor thy father and thy mother*"; despite the fact there are fathers and mothers out there that don't give a damn about their kids. Again, a reflection of how a patriarchal society was ordered, but works differently in a sedentary, industrial society. Children — especially sons — are no longer the security assurance for aging parents. We have a Social "Security" blanket which "honors gray heads", have retirement homes, 401K and profit-sharing plans as ways of dealing more broadly with the senior citizen group, even those sans children. So we have covered the issue. But isn't it also axiomatic in <u>any</u> society that children have a reverence and respect for parents? Beyond this, if we are trying to find marks that distinguish Judeo-Christian rules for social harmony from, say, Islam; how critical is one that was universal and commonplace long before Moses took his tablets to the mountain top?

So the first five are at best disappointing (to me). They are not immortal, inspiring essentials. Fact is, they aren't even spiritual. And I can't figure out why people want to march and protest or go to war over such narrowly focused, such prosaic statements.

The other five are also prohibitions: against killing, adultery, stealing, false testimony (which is lying) or coveting. Who can argue that these rules are necessary? But don't forget, were also widely adopted and part of man's social contract since he first got up off his knuckles. Does anyone feel that Moses — or the Hebrews — <u>invented</u> these laws? Would it be safe to presume that every civilized society since the days of Uruk (4000 B.C.) or Mohenjo Daro (3500 B.C.) has made killing, stealing, adultery, and false statements all taboo in the judicial codes as fundamental rules, ordering community life? There is nothing distinctly Christian or Jewish about these elements; they are in <u>every</u>body's tradition.

What really made Hebraism different than the cults with which it competed was, first of all, its monolatry (worship one god, forget the rest of 'em); and secondly, the prophetic voices of the 8th Century B.C., which for the first time in history insisted <u>religion become moral</u>. Not ceremonial, sacrificial, sacerdotal, ritualistic, but become ethical. The prophets broke through the monopoly of the inevitable priesthood and finally said, "God is not worshipped with blood offerings, but through the heart and by example. ('I hate, I despise your feasts, I take no delight in your solemn assemblies.') He wants us to care for each other. He wants the widow attended, the orphan nourished, the sick healed, the poor nurtured, the rich generous, the courts fair. Religion is not about me, it is about caring for other people."

What we ought to be extolling, teaching, trumpeting, and mounting on courtroom walls are bits of Israel's great prophets and teachings from "The Sermon on the Mount", the stuff that has re-oriented western society and changed the way we do things. If we wanted ten new commandments, they might be something like:

1. You shall love the Lord thy God with all thy heart, soul, mind, and strength.
2. And you do this because you love your neighbor as yourself.
3. Which means you shall not speak ill of anyone, defame, ridicule, denigrate or demean.
4. You shall respect the opinions of others which differ from your own. The Lord has given few of us the gift of infallibility.
5. You shall treat all persons fairly, justly and honestly.
6. You shall create no systems of class or caste which elevates — or subordinates — one group above — or below — another.
7. All involved in the legal process shall be entitled to an impartial hearing and a fair trial.
8. No one in our midst should be hungry, thirsty, naked or homeless, and you shall give of your substance to assure it doesn't happen.
9. Peace is always better than war just as love is always stronger than raw power. We are seekers and promoters of peace; even in disagreements we deal equanimously with each other.
10. Do unto others what you would have them do unto you. ■

Pots and Kettles

September 1998

Anyone who follows the uncertain, shifting positions of political passion has surely had occasion to say, "Wait a minute! This guy is criticizing his opponents for doing exactly what he did." It's a practice in my day known as "the pot calling the kettle black". We saw this when the Senate rebuffed Clinton's nominee for Ambassador to Mexico whereupon liberal Democrats rended robes and shouted "foul". The Senate was playing politics. It was denying the President his sacred right to appoint officials. But it was really a Democrat "pot" calling the Republican "kettle" black. Because said "kettle" recalled the hearings on Robert Bork and later on Clarence Thomas, both nominated to the Supreme Court and each triggering fierce resistance by the "pot" (who blocked one [Bork] and did their best to kill the other). "We were only raising valid questions and exercising caution on a bad Presidential appointment." The Republicans on the other hand were playing partisan politics. Yeah, sure!

There was some of this pot/kettle dynamic when Clinton went to China in June. The bleeding hearts (pot) advised him to abort the trip; i.e., avoid all contact with China (kettle) because of their human rights transgressions. What the average American, however, knows about Chinese culture, psyche, social structure, and traditions are zilch. We simply don't understand Chinese political expectations, governance apparatus, the real nature of the dissident groups, and what exactly happened at Tiananmen Square. Or let's say we don't know enough to give the Chinese anything but specious political advice.

If I were Jiang Zemin when Clinton started talking to me about human rights, I'd have a retort. "Mr. President, you represent a nation that from 1619 until 1863 bought and sold human beings freely on the open market. Fact, you bred people like animals for sale on the plantations of the south, and you are lecturing me about human rights? Then you transported them into a white culture, but after "freeing" them technically, spent another hundred years keeping them in intellectual, economic, and political servitude. Their "equality" today is more fact than fiction. I don't think your record gives you the right to talk. By the way, do you recall Kent State? Soldiers shooting down students? But it's O.K. to criticize us for using troops in Tiananmen Square."

And then, of course, Clinton (still on a "roll") nudged him about Tibet, the Chinese take-over, and the military occupation of the country. President Zemin could have said, "Bill, old friend, do you know something about how the United States gained dominion over 3,000,000 square miles of the western hemisphere? Did your forbearers buy the land from those who occupied it? Do you remember a thing called 'The Trail of Tears' when the military forcibly removed, physically trekked, 15,000 Cherokee and Creek Indians off their property, killing about 4000 of them in a 117-day walk to Oklahoma so that white settlers could have their land? Not run their nation, appropriate it. At least we have not driven the Tibetans from their homeland."

"Are you familiar with a massacre at Wounded Knee; do you recall what happened to your treaty with the Sioux when white settlers thought they discovered gold in the Dakotas; do you remember Ocala and Osceola; Chief Joseph, Tecumseh and Geronimo? Every time America made a treaty with the Indians — every single time — it sent in soldiers to break it for the sole purpose of stealing their land because 'the only good Indian is a dead one'. The American record is replicated in Pizarro and Cortes as much as Washington and Lincoln. If we were simply following the American model in Tibet, how can you justify in criticizing us?"

I don't know how good Jiang is on American history, but I do know his record in politics is very impressive indeed. Running (as he did) a city like Shanghai with some 15 million people makes running Arkansas with its 2.5 million a cake walk. Which says Jiang understands Chinese politics and is successful under its system. But Bill is undaunted by his lack of knowledge regarding the Orient and has this ebullient, missionary phobia about human rights. He figures everyone ought to be out there voting. He ought to lecture us at home about the value of a republic. Eighty-five percent of the eligible voters stayed at home in our last Indiana primary election. What does this say about the importance of this right Clinton wants everyone to exercise? It says here in Indianapolis it is disdained, meaning it is, "Do as I say, not do as I do". But there is a deeper problem in extending democratic forms to the undemocratized world: Some cultures simply don't want them. Few understand how they work or what sort of maintenance they require.

We "democratized" the 15 "republics" that made up the Soviet Union, and how would you grade their success in handling freedom? "Not very high" is the answer. Freedom is hard to handle. Over a hundred nations since the end of World War I have had a run at it, thinking they can be like America, but one after another, after another, have given up in despair, reverting to one-man (or one-party) rule. Just <u>wanting</u> to be free is not enough. One has to know how to institute free institutions and then make them work. It requires an educated citizenry, one free of tribalism, and generally in agreement on overall objectives. There aren't many places in the world we can find those conditions. Ergo, democracies don't work most places and China might be one of 'em. But I digress. We were discussing pots calling kettles black.

My favorite example in history of this chicanery is the Christian church which with vehemence and loud lamentation rehearses the brutal "persecutions" suffered under the Roman empire. We see this tragedy in movies, on television; find it written up in historic novels, repeated from the pulpit. Images of hundreds herded into the arena with ferocious wild beasts or burned in Nero's gardens, suffering endless agony and wholesale brutalization. All — utter — nonsense! The Christian "pot" calling the Roman "kettle" black. Has it ever occurred to you that the <u>Christian</u> church INVENTED religious persecution? The beef the empire had with the Christians was political. Religion was a function of the state (as it was in ancient Israel, Egypt or Mesopotamia). In Rome you respected Roman traditions, but if you were also into a mystery cult (Isis, Serapis, Mithras, Cybele et al), you got a license from the state to function. Christianity was originally a sect

Roman remnant in Lebanon.

of Judaism since the early group met mostly in the synagogues. Under the early apostles (James, Peter, James and John), you had to be (or become) a Jew before conversion to Christianity; then modified standard Judaism to accept the person and teaching of Jesus, elevated to messiahship and then deified. All O.K. because the Jews were a religio licita, meaning they were chartered by the state (thanks to Gaius Julius Caesar).

But when the Jewish revolt of 68-70 A.D. was put down by Titus, both Jerusalem and the temple destroyed, we suddenly had a new ball game. Judaism was on the ropes, in total disarray, and in a period of reorganization, trying to redefine basic Jewish doctrine, found Christianity unacceptable as an option and rejected it. Christians were no longer welcome within the framework of Judaism and once ejected, were no longer Jews, thus, no longer "legal".

The argument Rome had with the church was hardly about religion or lack of permit; rather it zeroed in on loyalty to the state, a fact usually proven through offerings of incense or oil to the emperor, the central figure of the Roman system. The Christians refused to do so; oblivious to the fact that Caesar was never construed to be a god. Failure to participate meant they refused to "salute the flag" or maybe went so far as to burn the flag, an approach that did not sit well with neighbors. Beyond that, they were a secretive group, who refused to stand for public office or serve in the army; who prayed for the downfall of the empire; devoted allegiance to the sect rather than the community and disparaged Roman society.

Although the Roman state paid little attention to the Christians, tolerating as it did dozens of sects, cults and beliefs, the Christian community viewed Rome as the enemy, The Whore of Babylon (Revelation). While under the safety of the very empire they denigrated, used its network of roads and cities, the existence of a common law, language and coinage, three centuries of universal peace grew mightily. In 311 it gained legal status and by 400 became the official state religion. But its rapid and erratic growth also riddled it with local influence and, thus, into countless theories which we term "heresies". Fact, it was in danger of disintegrating until it was stopped cold in its tracks by the new power of the central Catholic hierarchy, partnered with state. The two dealt decisively with heretics. At the recommendation of Augustine, it redefined its orthodoxy, prescribed its rites, organized, codified its doctrine, and became the Roman Catholic Church of medievalism.

It had a solution for those who did not conform: It asked them to recant and "get with it" and if they did not, it executed them. You believe as we do or you are dead. The church solved the heresy nemesis by stamping it out. In the proscriptions erupting subsequent to the Council of Nicaea in 325, Christians probably killed more fellow Christians in a single generation (Arians who had disagreed on the nature of the person/God Jesus) than all of the Roman persecutions combined. "Tolerate no theological disagreement" became the policy of the papacy.

My point here is that through prior ages, up to and including Rome (republic and empire), no one was ever persecuted, reviled or killed because of his faith. It was the Christian church that handled religious difference through subjugation or with execution. "Faith is a thing which <u>we</u> arbitrate and those who don't conform had better be gone or face the scaffold." This, from the founder who said, "Love your enemies, turn the other cheek." There is no example in history of any institution which for a thousand years persevered in hounding and butchering hundreds of thousands of people because they choose to see God in a different light. The 30 years war (Protestant against Catholic) was more savage than any barbarian incursion as Christians raged back and forth across Central Europe, slaughtering each other in droves all to glorify Christ. Whole provinces in ruin only because one worshipped different than the other. The Ku Klux Klan was more tolerant than the inquisition. Writers, actors, teachers, and preachers who excoriate the persecution of Nero or Diocletian need to look at history's record. The church who condemns intolerance is a pot calling the kettle black.

All of which (again!) ends up more like a history lecture than pursuit of the initial topic which was the hypocrisy lodged in the "pot" who calls the "kettle" black. Although most of us are guilty of doing so. Guilty of the same weakness and recourse to the same obfuscation (confounding or confusing the issue), when to think rationally we ought to recognize how illogical the practice is. Vilifying the other position is not refuting the issue. There is no way two or three wrongs ever get to equal one right. It is generally a mistake to think that <u>we</u> know better how you (the kettle) should be handling your affairs than you do. Said another way, most of us are more adept at advising others about <u>their</u> problems than effective in solving our own. It is a bad tack in persuasion to criticize and close the mind when by finding something good or flattering to say we might better gain the ear or confidence of those we are lecturing. Sitting in judgment is rarely a constructive exercise. It is popular because it seems to elevate our personal wisdom, record, opinion and judgment over someone else, failing to accept the fact we are rarely impartial judges of either our own acuity — wisdom — or motive. ∎

Where Do the Tractors Go?

September 1998

Anyone in business ought to know exactly what his markets are, then how well he penetrates each of 'em. It is not a matter of getting greedy, it is a matter of evaluating one's proficiency. Fair scores, however, if we had our druthers, we'd sell every backhoe, dozer, excavator, off-highway truck, scraper, etc. sold in Indiana because our business is buying and selling machinery. Ironically enough, the objective of free enterprise capitalism is not to share the potential market with others in the field, it is to "get there firstest with the mostest" as old Nathan Bedford Forrest used to say. Get there ahead of competition and have the most attractive product, the most attractive price, and the "mostest" in parts and service support. In short get all the business, except for that going to people who aren't going to make it.

Given the 68 counties we have to cover in Indiana (there are three other CAT dealers on the edges around Chicago, Cincinnati and Louisville) in our counties, figuring out who is in the market for "what" is the job of our territory salesmen. Meaning, most of our sales people live in the part of the state they cover. And since the number of people interested in buying something which costs from $50,000 to $3.2 million per unit is relatively modest (say maybe 1,500-2,000 prospects), it is parceled out to ten guys who then have maybe 150 accounts to contact, accounts who might buy every year (about 10% do) versus some who buy once in a lifetime, or maybe every other year or every five years; or, who don't know, who have no pattern except that of the markets in which they are involved. Point is that we have to know our prospects and how they function, what they operate, and when we might be able to chin with them about replacing or adding to a fleet. In the case of our EMS people, when to repair, overhaul or trade it. Unlike most retail units across this broad and beautiful land, we need to know our customer personally and know a lot about them, what they do, how good they are, and with whom they compete, etc.

Having someone familiar with what is going on in each of the 68 counties helps us track the undulations of the economy and of each specific market. And in looking at the markets, I begin to wonder, first of all, how many there are and then what per-cent of our machine deliveries go into each. By dollar volume. New and used machines. This will be for a given point in time like right now; this year so far, since the percentages shift from year to year. Arbitrarily we establish or designate market categories and come up with eight. Five years ago the biggest market was coal; 45% of our product went into the coal fields. Because coal requires heavy, expensive machinery, works double-shift operations steadily year around, and puts 5,000-6,000 hours on a given unit whereas contractors generally don't get more than 1,500 hours a year on a machine. Digging coal out of the ground means tough going. Lots of rock and shale to cut through, rip up, or dynamite and load; steep grades to negotiate. Coal will be the dominant market serviced by our Washington store, but across the board this year, company-wide, CONSTRUCTION seems to be far and away our biggest opportunity in terms of dollar sales.

As a matter of interest, our consultant on economics and future potential says that we can assume to ride up and down the economic curve on the undulating chart-line of housing starts. When it goes up six months later, we go up, and when it tapers and goes down, we follow inexorably. Well,

Line of excavators at MacAllister.

anyone driving around Marion County (and I mean literally driving around…Southport, Beech Grove, Greenfield, Geist, Fishers, Carmel, etc.) sees tracts of housing clusters exploding. Two-three hundred homes at a pop are not uncommon. And this is not "low income housing", these are big hummers on spacious lawns with community swimming pools, water retention ponds that turn into lakes, recreation centers…the whole nine yards. All this needs grading for proper drainage, requires digging the retention ponds, needs streets, sewer lines, water lines, sometimes sidewalks and landscaping – just coincidentally requiring our type of equipment. Add to those commercial strips which also proliferate when the economy is good and money is cheap and you have a lot of stuff going on which means a lot of contractors working. So construction as a general category is numero uno. This includes the residential and commercial building area, but also means state, county and city road work, bridge repair, widening, black-topping, any water conservation programs, highway or street relocation, and the type of construction that involves roads and streets. (Ditching, grading [in those counties that still have gravel roads], cutting berms, doing field tiling for farmers, fencing, water and sewer maintenance, etc.)

Coal dropped to second place and AGGREGATE production is third. This is the sand and gravel digger plus the people who quarry stone. Sand and gravel are used for concrete, and there is a lot of it in bridges, streets and highways, foundations, in the manufacture of products like building blocks or sewer pipe; gravel or stone is also used for base, i.e. under footings or beneath concrete slabs. A good portion of this stone goes to resurface streets and highways. Asphalt can be mixed with sand then blended with an oil-tar solution, but much of it is composed of fractured stone, which when compacted, knits together the irregular pieces to fit like a jigsaw puzzle. Given the continual resurfacing program necessary in a nation married to the automobile and figuring a surface life of something like ten years, there is a backlog stretching out into the years as long as there are cars manufactured in the current configurations. When they get converted to become something like hover crafts, this will change but until it does, we shall be using asphalt surfaces made from crushed stone year after year. Huzzah for the stone quarries? Because they need tractors to strip the overburden and sometimes to rip the rock, front-loading shovels or rubber-tired loaders to load the

Challenger tractor.

trucks, lots of trucks to carry shot stone to the crushers, motor graders to keep the haul roads in good condition, and rubber-tired loaders on top to load material out of stock piles.

AGRICULTURE might be our next major market. There are now seven different models of Challenger tractors and two sizes (so far) of Lexion combines and something like 3,500 farmers out there large enough to justify one or the other (or both). We'll sell something like 80 tractors to farmers this year, and given the cost of Challengers and combines that's a respectable volume.

At almost the same level in terms of market value is one called OTHER, which is varied and sundry usage. Maybe utilities, the sale of trailers, wrecking or demolition people, an occasional manufacturing plant, orchards, logging, airports, etc.

Stationary ENGINES would be next. This is power not integral to a CAT-made unit, CAT en-

A CAT generator installed at a hospital used for back-up power generation.

gines functioning elsewhere. For starters we have something like 50 rental generator sets clicking off income, but the biggest market is something like $6.5 million worth of CAT engines we sell to stadiums, manufacturing plants, jails, hospitals, schools, fire stations, banks, and you name it, mostly for stand-by power.

The last two categories will be at the tail end, maybe 1% of the volume in each, and these are SANITARY LANDFILL operations and PUBLIC BODY business. Indiana has a policy generally of doing most of its highway work through contract, and thus, it is a rare county that owns its own gravel plant, blacktop plant or its own construction crew.

Having this range of potential customers is a boon and a burden. The burden is getting it all covered, understanding the nature and demands of each, being exposed to a range of competitive product whose strengths and weaknesses we need to know. It thrusts a load on the service people because they have the mechanical nature of each to learn and 50 or 60 different products on which to work and to do rebuilding or repair. All of which adds the same wide

A CAT Telehandler is used to transport rebar for constructing the columns for Lucas Oil Stadium downtown Indianapolis.

span of variation to the number of parts we store and the exchange units we have to inventory and the specialization expertise we have to provide. It keeps our trainers busy, learning new products, and the remodel versions of old. It also leans on our inventory requirements and requires more dollars.

But the boon is obvious. More possible customers. More possible service work, more possible parts sales. The broader the range the better the balance, meaning if construction stops, maybe AG picks up; or if mining eases off, we could get more truck engine business. When building of all sorts tends to slow down to a crawl, then the aspect of maintenance picks up, and some of our new machinery like skid steer loaders or telescopic booms might tend to kick in.

There are two elements to this whole picture which remain personally gratifying. One is the fact that we are in an industry which is essential to the building, expanding, renovating, constructing and reconstructing of society. It is a contributing factor and is a pacemaker for progress. We are a people on wheels only because we have been able to build a network of arteries that permits total flexibility. And the highway system is the end product achieved with our machinery. Ditto housing projects on a mass scale; the proliferation of the shopping center; the universal visit to the regional airport. We are there with our stuff or it happens very slowly, if at all. The other gratifying aspect is the complex nature of the market, the wide range of products, the needs to supply so much different expertise, and the combining challenge it makes for managers. A dynamic that may be vexing, but never gets dull; it can become demanding but is never all done; it challenges and tries us, but gives satisfaction in achievement and is a vocation one can really enjoy. (Especially when we're making money!) ■

Light, Goodness and Joy

December 1998

For many of us Christmas is known as "the season of light". Though, if asked what this means, most of us would start mumbling. One might suggest it compliments another nativity well established in the empire at the time the Christian church was organizing its liturgical calendar. The 25th of December was the birthday of Mithra, a popular deity evolving out of the Near East, deity of a religious sect (Mithraism) especially popular among the Roman troops. Mithra was the Zoroaster's god of light, reminding us it was this prophet (Zoroaster) who declared there are two forces at work in the world: one good, the other evil. (Yahweh <u>had</u> been viewed by the Jews as the source of <u>every</u>thing.) Mithra's imprimatur was the sun, the force under which all things grew and whose radiance made possible the world in which we live. Metaphorically, his light corresponded with goodness, an idea borrowed by the Jews and then the church, each of whom massaged the concept ultimately seeing goodness as the province of God. While the counter-posing influence is evil (Ahriman in Zoroastrianism), who becomes Satan in Christian thought. The season of Mithra's birth was, thus, the birth of light - of goodness. Jesus comes into the world as God incarnate, is born on Mithra's birthday and assumes the same mantle of goodness…and light. Recall St. John: "In him was life and the life was the light of men"… "The true light that enlightens every man was coming into the world."

A corollary and noticeable fact of life at this time of year is the lengthening days…one or two minutes more light each day. So maybe that ancient world, whose forces were shaping the church, wove these two elements in their gospel story. (Not a profound thought but the best answer I could come up with.)

Despite this theory about light and goodness dominating the scene, one has to wonder how pervasive was "the light", how much illumination did it bring, how much joy, how triumphant was good? "Not very" might be the answer. The themes of the Christian church through the succeeding centuries may have talked about "good news" (gospel), but acted in a fashion lacking in joy, buoyancy, optimism, rejoicing in the triumph of God over evil. Its doctrine and official posture started us off by declaring at man's very origin, he screwed up. He disobeyed;

i.e. he obeyed his <u>wife</u>, but disobeyed God. So all the generations of Adam and what's-her-name inherit sin. We are each born already guilty.

The architect of early Christian thought was Augustine who complicated matters by deciding the first sin was really concupiscence (sex), it was not disobedience, thus, reinforcing the fact each child is born sinful, because the act which conceived him was and is, the "original sin". What a dumb way to create a theology! We are in trouble from day one. Not only is the ordeal of life a tough one, we negotiate it "behind the eight ball" with God. But what this does is make religion absolutely essential because there is no hope for us <u>without</u> an off-setting institution that counteracts the malediction the church itself has created. Over time Adam and Eve turn out to be allegory, rather than history, making us realize how outrageous was this guilt complex infused into

Ravenna — last outpost of the Roman Empire.

billions of anxious and frightened people by the institution needed to save them. As late as Luther (a teacher of theology), we are deploring the fact that most souls go to hell where they burn in torment. Martin spent half his early life on his knees trying to be sure he "made the cut" and got at least into purgatory. Isn't it amazing that anyone could get excited about joining a movement such as this, one being created to bring mankind salvation, only then tell him he isn't good enough? How in the world did the church make any converts? Maybe because it was a far different, less educated, more superstitious, browbeaten era. With no other options.

We are simply hard pressed to see much joy, light or hope in the Early, Medieval or Reformation churches. Lots of scrounging and obsession with sin. Ala Jean Calvin, the most gifted theological thinker of his century, who locked people up for dancing, fined them if they didn't come to church, and put them in the stocks for gambling — you can imagine what happened to thieves and prostitutes. Where was the love expressed and extolled in the early prophets, in Jesus, in St. Paul? It is hidden under the autocratic robes of institutional omniscience. The Puritans in New England are a good example of the New World Christianity: a disciplined, educated, aggressive, creative community…booting out anyone who disagreed with them. A community without Christmas joy, by the way, because it was either too pope-ish or too pagan.

It is almost as though the light present in the nativity went out. Goodness sought refuge elsewhere and man continued the long litany of his own unworthiness, depravity and sinfulness. All was lost.

Fortunately, we are less frightened today, less intimidated, better educated, more pragmatic, and have more enlightened leadership. Beyond that, we've broken the clerical monopoly on God, His will, His word. But the church still spends a lot of time obsessed with sin — each Sunday at worship, orally "confessing" to our transgression and human frailty, to our neglect of others, our callousness and selfishness. I have asked our ministers who the heck writes these woeful mea culpas. Frankly, I don't walk around stricken with guilt. I'm not carrying any burden of personal inadequacy and am reluctant to pick up somebody else's. I've not stolen anything, demeaned or degraded, exploited or neglected anyone. And I don't know why I have to sit there abjectly each Sunday and confess to stuff I had no part in doing. The rest of my congregation must be big time sin-

ners. I wish they'd get their act together so our confessional prayers contain a little more optimism.

Maybe the church ought to carry the initial spirit of Christmas light through the rest of its liturgical year. Why not extol the joy in our human experience, the adventure which is life, things we have accomplished, and the neat things we are doing to help each other? Hey, there is a lot of cruelty in the world and a lot of pain in our hometown: crime statistics in every cotton pickin' edition of the paper, horror stories about child abuse, about shootings, drug wars, and the questionable mores of our young people. Fine. This is true. But tell me how this daily recitation ennobles or encourages the human spirit? Why don't we talk more about what we have achieved in terms of caring, progress, humanness, and compassion? There is real evidence that we have made a difference when properly motivated and decently lead. I don't want to live with my head in the sand. But as long as the only emphasis I keep getting is negative, that is exactly where my head is continually lodged.

The philosophers informed us the <u>species</u> has possibility, it is the individual <u>person</u> that gives us the problems. But any way you cut it, I see a lot of good occurring in the last two generations. Take the vexing issue of race, plaguing us as it has for two centuries or more. It's still here, almost universally. But it is certainly not as repressive as half a century ago.

When I drove my parents to Florida in the '50s, there were no motels, so we stayed in hotels in towns…we white people did. I used to wonder where the African American folks stayed when they went south. They couldn't even eat in white restaurants, which seems absolutely outrageous today. It is almost impossible to imagine a Christian society, taking two centuries to deal with something as obvious as this injustice. By now, of course, we have motels at every intersection and <u>integrated</u> from here to Key West.

I was 27 years old before I ever met a Negro (which is what we called them in 1946). Can you imagine living in society today, bouncing around the way I did without ever encountering a person of color? None in school, college, scout troop, church, fraternity, neighborhood; none in my fighter squadron or group; none in my trade association. One reason why it has taken me so long to "come to the party" is this divided culture. So on that very score alone, conditions are vastly different than those in which I was raised. It is hard (but not impossible) to teach an old dog new tricks. (Fact, it is sometimes hard for <u>this</u>

one to remember the <u>old</u> ones.) But when we finally decided segregation was wrong in a rather substantial and protracted paroxysm, we began the change. Not fun, not easy, nor quick, but we did it because it was the right thing to do. Why don't we talk about the steps forward instead of beating ourselves on the back, critical because it is not perfect?

Anyone who has seen "*Saving Private Ryan*" was struck with the realistic depiction of "D-Day" and the ensuing weeks. A sudden realization that war is more terrible than ever dreamed. Not only the wanton slaughter, but its apocalyptic companions: the confusion, pain, random slaughter, the mistakes, the weight and outcome of every encounter contingent upon luck and the judgment of the leaders, being taught on the job. It brought back reflections to this old soldier who remembers on D-Day he was in an Air Corps camp in Foggia, Italy. A fact revealed by our guide in Rome four years ago on the <u>5th</u> of June when she reminded us "50 years ago today Rome was liberated by the allies". (I've told this story before.) When I informed her I was in Italy that day too, her eyes lit up. Then she said, "I will never forget that day". After two years of deprivation, there was rampant starvation in Italy. No jobs, no foodstuffs, towns controlled by German troops, no medical supplies, fuel, nothing. It was <u>bad</u>. Then she saw the American convoy coming into the city and said, "Do you know what the Americans were doing in those big army trucks? They were handing out bread! The Americans were giving us bread! Do you now what that meant to those of us who had nothing in our stomachs for weeks? It meant we were saved. No one who was there will ever forget what the Americans did for us." The convoy was life. It was hope. It was joy.

Not many people think about American policy after WWII, though they identified a thing called "The Marshall Plan". "Didn't it have something to do with the reconstruction of Western Europe?" The same people remember a guy named MacArthur who fought the war in the Pacific, receiving the Japanese surrender on board the U.S.S. Missouri; beyond that, our memory dims, forgetting he created the current Japanese political system. Today, no one is preening about the policy employed after the war with those two powers who had set records in human destruction (both of the body and the spirit), had ruthlessly wrecked and destroyed wherever their armies moved. Today, we recognize Germany and Japan as among the top three industrial powers in the world today <u>only because</u> of our post war attitude and actions, our investment of 13 billion American dollars and the covering security of American troops. Had the Axis Powers won the war there, would have been indemnities totaling hundreds of billions of dollars, occupation troops, drum head courts, political prisons, and all sorts of vehicles to impede and curtail our life as each exacted vengeance. Instead, America went bearing the palm branch.

In the second inaugural address, Lincoln counseled, "With malice to none, with charity for all, let us bind the nation's wounds", a formula America applied to the defeated enemy. A posture mind-boggling to students of European diplomacy; a strategy that has no parallel anywhere I can think of in the history of the species. Why don't we make more movies about our campaign <u>after</u> the war and tell the story of humanness and compassion and unselfish treatment of an enemy rather than retelling again how we out-brutalized him with the very weapons he had chosen to make war on us? Why not "the other cheek" as a successful bit of foreign policy, a recommendation taken right out of the New Testament? It was probably more successful than was the war, in changing the course of history for both Germany and Japan.

Several years ago a Canadian editor wrote an editorial about the USA and said he was tired of people beating on it. He wondered when oppressed people sought freedom, where did they want to go. When there is an earthquake, a tidal wave, a plague, a humongous flood, who is there first with the most food, clothing, medical supplies, and personnel? The Americans! To help! Who else has a Peace Corps? Who gives 145 billion dollars a year of income to support causes they don't <u>have</u> to support, because they are concerned about the general good?

Humanitarian aid arriving at Rinas Airport (Albania) in 1999. NATO soldiers controlled the airport at that time. Taken by Nick Macdonald (nickmacdonald.net).
(Source: Wikimedia Commons.)

Americans! Who is next? Nobody! Who sent sons to Europe twice in 25 years to defined democracy? America. What did they get for it? Satisfaction! We loudly declaim inadequacies in the educational system, inferior to Europe and Japan, yet who wins the Nobel Prizes? We get three-fourths of 'em. We rant and rave about our hedonism and self-centeredness. In the light of human experience, it doesn't look that bad.

Hopefully, the point might poke through in this pompous lucubration. It is pragmatic and realistic to recognize one's weaknesses, his sins and shortcomings. But it's ridiculous to assume that these honestly constitute total character, profile or potential. This is a partial picture. Moreover, it is bad psychology. We are motivated by encouraging words, not nagging, and we are more inclined to strive and succeed when we have a track record of success than when we have a voice saying, "You are too arrogant, you are too aggressive, your approach is wrong, etc. ad nauseam". We are happier with the Hellenic concept of man as a proud being, upright and defiant in the face of adversity, capable of doing great things, eager to be involved and enjoying the battle. We are less than happy when seen as totally sinful beings, "fallen short of the glory of God", people who ought to spend more time on our knees. Weakness in such a recommendation is we can't be of much help to anyone in that position, wrapped further in our own inadequacies. We ought to be busier helping other people, not just at Christmas time, but year round, confident that we have something to offer and glad to be about the Lord's work. We need to remember faith is about light, goodness and joy, but these don't appear automatically. They arrive when you and I introduce them; become their sponsor and practitioner. ■

Hae Victis

December 1998

The aftermath of the recent elections left most Americans a bit weary of both politics and politicians. A lot of us think the process takes far too long and by stretching out campaigns for year and a half (Gore is already running for President, Forbes is making speeches, Quayle has his track shoes on, and my guess is Dick Gephardt is kissing a lot of babies), we have far too much time to talk and end up over-discussing everything, including my "worthy opponent's" myopia and ineptitude. People keep talking when there is nothing left to say. The ubiquity of political posters, newspapers, each day's mail solicitation, the television commercials, lawn signs, and endless pollster reports make us better informed (misinformed) on the whole business than we really want to be. Or maybe we need to be. We could really get all this done…the primary, the campaign and the election…in 90 days and spend our time in other pursuits. But no one seems equipped at this moment to change the protracted and noisy ordeal so we shall put up with it — warts, blemishes and all.

Which is not (after all) national suicide. We Calvinists just have a penchant for making things better. The fact that "it works" may be an accepted premise, but making it work easier, smoother, and more expeditiously ought to be the objective. Striving for improvement is a familiar concept to most of us in business. It is the drive for more efficacy, trying to see both seller and vendor better served, replete with more value delivered, having converted major effort into profits and, thus, to success. The fact that neither elections nor businesses are perfect is what keeps us working. So living with imperfection is an important personal accommodation since it recognizes we live in an imperfect world. Doesn't stop us from striving desperately to win, but teaches us to accept loss with a measure of grace and stoicism. I'm not commending "Learn to Lose" as a fit corporate, personal or political motto. I'm saying that second best *is* one of life's realities. After all, half the people running in the last election got beat.

The genius of the system, however, is that unlike defeated gladiators, the victors do not dispatch the losers to Charon. They try instead to win with élan, composed but not cocky in triumph and enjoy victory without arrogance. After all, the roles are re-versed too often to make all political trips successful. It is the rare politician who has not suffered defeat or the salesman who hasn't lost a sale. Consoled by the fact we probably learn more in defeat than in victory. And there's always next time.

Point here is that in our system there has to be a loser if there is to be a winner. Both are required to complete the equation and eternally have constituted elements of the human dynamic. The way one party deals with the other has a lot to do with the success of our system. Given the extensive political campaigning, the convoluted nature of the interlocking structure, the virulence of the rhetorical, the frequency of contests, we tend to generate considerable heat. To surmount it all with equanimity in the light of how history generally handles the losers is a minor miracle. Meaning, we don't shoot the opposition; don't revolt if we have lost the election, or proscribe all of our enemies and appropriate their property when we are triumphant. We keep them around as part of the dynamic, expecting the same treatment if we lose the next chukker. I contend we have had relatively less turbulence and more sanity in terms of managing our political systems than any other nation in history. (I was thinking of the aristocracy and the clergy when the sans-culotte "won" the French Revolution in 1789; or what happened when the Roundheads "done in" the Cavaliers in the Cromwellian Period; or thinking of Soviet treatment of any party for 40 years; or Saddam Hussein's disposition of dissident political views; or the way Inquisitors handled the Waldensians or Albigensians in 14th Century Europe.) There is an awful lot of mankind's history that doesn't give much slack to the losers. Much of all that is behind us, but there's a bit of Ole Brennus still with us. (Brennus was the Gallic Chieftain who took Rome in the 4th Century B.C. and demanded a ransom equal to the weight of "X" pounds on his scales. When the Romans balanced it out with an equal amount of gold, the Barbarian threw his sword and scabbard on the scale, increasing the weight by that much more at which point the Romans hollered "FOUL". Brennus scowled and said "Hae victis".) (Woe to the conquered! Tough luck!!) I.e., there is a human tendency that wants to be ungracious.

Our American experience in sports or contests

or competitive exercises makes us foremost in probably all of history in the practice of a thing we call sportsmanship, which is the personal attitude that strives for grace in both winning and losing. Brennus was an arrogant winner, but you know how barbaric those bloody Gauls were. Problem in being a team or of choosing sides in business, in elections or in life is the inability some people have to deal dispassionately with losing or with disagreement or with the other side. Getting viscerally and vehemently committed to a given stance can become a blind fixation. At which point, "infallibility" sets in, making me right on this issue, and those who disagree with me wrong. Being right, I have a special status and speak ex cathedra on the topic and those in the opposition are heretics, deserving of punishment. If I cannot respond with logic to their position, then I attack their person, moving the debate out of the realm of the cerebral and into use of any tactic which destroys my opponent. I will see him beaten down one way or another and failing philosophic persuasion, then I shift off the subject and rip up the idiot who is so blind as to disagree with me.

Anyone familiar with the long story of religious wars or with the domination of a theocratic state be it Puritan, Hebrew, Calvinistic, Roman Catholic or Islamic, knows the story of stamping out ideas or convictions by stamping out the person(s) holding same. Each sect has its own lock on Heaven and how to get there. Isn't it ironic that the guy who finally said "Each man is entitled to reach heaven his own way" was not a theologian but Frederick the Great of Prussia? Religious tolerance is not a product of organized religion.

The weakness in fanatics, religious or political fanatics, is the narrowness of their vision. They tend to see the world in terms of their own oxen and instead of considering the long agenda or roster of vexatious issues, fix on one or two items which are rarely representative of the lot, brushing off the rest. Preempting the agenda because of stance on a single item. Hey! The government of the United States will not rise or fall over the painful (and personal) matter of abortion; nor is the business of owning and selling guns gonna make or break this generation nor is prayer in the schools higher in significance than the quality of

James Madison
(Source: Wikimedia Commons.)

education produced in said schools. Which tends to illustrate the point: "Is it more important that my child be given (or denied) the right to school prayer than he is given a respectable education?" There is nothing wrong with convictions, but the mere fact of having them does not make 'em right. Does not provide the only solution nor can it be considered the only viewpoint. Not in a society that sees as much with its "I" as it does with its "eye".

What chills me about the single-issued person is often his supercilious sense of superiority. "I have the one true answer, and there is no room for discussion or consideration of your viewpoint." Supreme Court Justice Roger Taney a century and a half ago declared that Dred Scott, a black slave, was personal property like a team of horses or a new rifle and had to be treated about the same. So much for the eternal value of legal truth. Urban III made Galileo confess the sun revolved around the earth. So much for religious infallibility.

The bottom line on this business (which began about politics and got into "losing" and is now into zealotry) is the fact that in a society such as ours which is diverse in its ethnic make-up, educated in a vastly different way, has uniquely personal family values, and ranges all over the map in terms of religious conviction et al, the one sure thing we can count on is difference. Of opinion, in outlook, fortune, conviction, ability, effort, and you name it. The basic key to survival in such a heterogeneous culture is mutual respect, each for the other and tolerance of our differences, including political opinion. The voters will declare periodically which they think are the right courses (usually what's right for MY interest), but whatever the case, we are committed to going with the popular will, whether we all agree or not. It isn't a matter of consensus. It is a matter of progress. Either we move on and resolve our problems or we don't budge an inch.

I was reminded of the convocation in 1787 at Philadelphia as men sought a way to improve on the Articles of Confederation. The darn things were no longer working, and we had to fashion a new vehicle which would express our sense of national purpose, thus, a political vehicle. In the process (thanks to James Madison), came up with the Virginia Plan which evolved into a

Constitution. It might be the most amazing political document ever written because it was created to fit this people, at both this time, and for a period of growth and expansion in the future. Not an easy assignment and ended without total agreement. Because some thought there were serious defects. "No Bill of Rights here!" for example. Another deplored, "We never dealt with slavery." Both serious omissions. Both proper criticisms. But recall that each was corrected in due course. To have insisted on inclusion <u>from the outset</u> as part of the original document would have doomed the whole endeavor and, thus, any prospect at all of "a more perfect union". Repeat: Had the elimination of slavery been forced as a "make or break" item, there would have been no Constitution. So what we do in terms of human progress, is take what we can get in terms of general support so long as it inches us forward, knowing it is short of the ideal. We have kept the ship afloat and know the journey is a long one. Maybe another time. The system works with temporary aberration and it works even for the losers. Because it is a process which is on-going in its quest for perfection and a ready negotiator of change, reversal, and modification when history requires new accommodation. ■

1999

Vintage P.E.

April 1999

In our peculiar democratic system, identified in America as a "republic", the issue of authority is often obfuscated. It is diffused, confused and imprecise as to source and though a dominant element in our system, often wanders in search of a parent. In this arrangement created by our Constitution, we elect people to sundry bodies in order that they might devise our national agenda and see it executed. Not only national. Each city or county has an elected body (in Indianapolis a <u>City-County</u> Council). The state has a bicameral animal called a General Assembly, with two distinct houses, elected by those eligible citizens who arise out of a general ennui to vote on election days; and of course, we have our National Congress, elected by sending members from each state on a proportionate basis to a plenary body; members to constitute a House of Representatives and a Senate. "Representatives" because they represent us in our sundry locales and represent us to do the business of the nation.

Our democratic tradition, though slow in gaining acceptance, still has a long history. It arose in a Semitic world that had been dominated by three millenniums of autocratic or military rule, interrupted occasionally by tribal-council experiment. Arose abruptly when a new political phenomenon developed in ancient Greece, sometime in the 6th Century B.C. when ancient Attica (i.e. Athens) experimented with a representative system. It was unique and unprecedented because power devolved from the pharaoh, king and emperor — <u>to</u> members of the community. "Representative" because it assembled the <u>entire voting</u> constituency (like a couple times a month): The "voters" being mature, free, property-owning males, which procedure made legislation an ongoing, widely-discussed, consensual process. Attica itself had something like 350,000 inhabitants, probably 90% of whom were females, slaves, youngsters or non-owners of property, so 35,000 men did the legislative work. They formed the administrative bureaucracy which made the city-state function … public works, sanitation, the temples, the military, foreign policy, food supplies, etc. Hard to imagine how a body that large, gathering at the Pynx weekly to debate taxes or reform of the courts or relief for the indigent would work. Can you imagine the cacophony? If only 3,000 or 4,000 showed up, how to manage such a meeting, and the answer is "with great difficulty", this being two eons before Mr. Roberts wrote his "Rules of Order". So for the sake of expediency, despite the fact that this was technically almost a democracy in practice, smaller committees or councils ended up acting for the plenary body and instead of electing archons ("rulers") periodically, in its heyday Athens consistently re-elected Pericles as presiding archon, and thereafter, Pericles ran the state. Ran it superbly well, creating an age so "golden" we look back today in wonder at the great sculptors, the gifted artists, dramatists, the gorgeous temples, agoras, and monuments which flourished under his aegis.

The "Golden Age" ended in a prolonged war with Sparta, after Pericles died and the monarchi-

Parthenon, Athens; circa 460 BC.

cal rule of Sparta proved more expeditious than the cumbersome, deliberating style of Athens. Pure democracies don't work easily in practice because the principle of giving <u>everyone</u> his say is impossible to institutionalize. It is hard to effectuate, delays decisions, changes policy with every season. Moreover, spreading authority over so vast an area has fixed responsibility in no identifiable place. Dumb actions from such a body have no distinct accountability; ergo, blunders abound.

The Romans refined the system in 509 B.C. when Brutus and Collatinus did away with the last of the Etruscan kings and created a republic which was to last until Octavian assumed power in 27 B.C. and brought in the empire. But a similar broad-based involvement and eclecticism was present in the Roman system. In this case, something like 40 or 50 of the great land-owning families in the state supplied the human resource to make the republic work and to thrust Rome from a trading village on the Tiber to the major power, first in Italy and then in inexorable progression, to become ruler of the Mediterranean world … and reaches far beyond. Point here is still <u>representation</u>. In the case of Rome, manifest through a dozen elective offices which candidates gained by campaigns; ditto with election to the Senate and then to the Assembly of Plebes. The principle is to designate through ballot certain people to carry (on our behalf) the responsibility for safety and security of the city, maintenance of the streets and buildings, assurance of fresh water, maintenance of the grain sources, the training of a citizen army, construction of major hard-surfaced highways, managing a system of courts, the national treasury, etc., etc. There were spirited contests for office, and they were rife with mudslinging, vote buying, intimidation, exploitation, malfeasance, and incompetence,

but nonetheless, the strength of the republican system created the legend that was Rome

It is significant to me that a thousand years later when the de' Medicis were opening the eyes of Florence to new horizons in art and architecture, they were collecting manuscripts and providing a library to increase knowledge, doing the first archaeological collecting and a lot of other things; they were examining more than the arts. They gave the same scrutiny to concepts of governance, to drama, to mathematics, to social systems, to mankind and his institutions.

Looking beyond the confining literature of the church, they began to study the ancient classics: Plato and Aristotle, the plays of Aeschylus and Euripides, the architecture of Vitruvius, the histories of Tacitus, Suetonius and Thucydides, the theories of Galen, the thinking of Marcus Aurelius, plus any other of the ancients they could find. In the process reading the history of Greece and Rome, Florence reeducated itself in thinking about political institutions, heroes, legal systems, and economic principles reflected in two high points of Western Civilization. It looked, I repeat, to Greece and Rome and in that study expanded, buttressed, grounded, and shaped the growing movement which unobtrusively became the Italian Renaissance. Mankind changed its thinking not only about art and sculpture, but about man himself and his value, potential, and significance.

The models of representative governance were present in Florence, a rich city, wealthy from wool products and banking. But the council that ran Florence, elected from the guilds and the aristocracy, was really overpowered by the House of de' Medici. Strange, because the leadership of Cosimo and Lorenzo was evident only in the vague title of Gonfalonier — standard bearer … cheerleader — an office with no official power. They dominated the state because of wealth, brilliant political instincts, extensive embellishment of Florence, source of the greatest painting and sculptor apprentices in the world, and through adroit use of both financial power and political connections. Republican forms of governance were not popular in the 15th and 16th Centuries, not with so many counts, barons, landgraves, kings, emperors, and military dictators around. Meaning, the issue of serious representative government was absent from the scene, and the de' Medici brilliance, glittering for two generations died with Lorenzo in 1492. But abstract familiarity with modes of Greece and Rome resurrected and restudied in Florence, remained. Representative models pop up here and there — Switzerland, Iceland — but do not take the world by storm.

Until revived in our day and until the Constitutional Convention of 1787 created a new document, especially fashioned for this people — sensitive to its common law, its background, its experiments with colonial systems, and its allegiance to a given colony. But combined with the fact that none would survive without a strong federal alliance. It is representative in form and the slickest working plan for a republic ever conceived, either in theory or in practice. Some give credit to the Presbyterians for the model. Because John Knox created the kirk in Scotland without funding from the state, sans pastors nominated and paid by the government. Each individual parish was responsible for building its own edifice, recruiting and maintaining its own congregation, electing and paying its own staff, managing its own program and budget. The governance, a product of Jean Calvin in Switzerland, had created two ecclesiastical bodies: the "session" for legislative, judicial, and administrative jurisdiction; and a "deaconate" to care for the poor, prepare the communion, etc. Two bodies <u>elected</u> by the members of the church to serve limited terms, rotating off in a systematic fashion and bringing in newer ones. This was in principle an upper and a lower house; it was an enterprise shaped by elected members of the congregation who managed and controlled the destiny of its mission, interpreting Presbyterian polity by hiring a pastor to serve at the will of the congregation. I'm not going to push this too far, but the dominant persuasion of the Convention members was of the reform tradition, Puritan, Presbyterian, Congregational. (Madison incidentally was a graduate of Princeton.)

The theory is still the same when applied to government: Elect people who will assure the proper course of action for the rest of us, meaning decide on how much money we are to spend each year, how it is raised, manage the relationships between the states, create a monetary system, provide for the defense, handle relations with foreign powers, etc. The first obligation of said persons is to get acquainted with the responsibilities implicit in "representing" us and then to act in the best interest of the state … "We, the people." They do this by becoming smarter than the rest of us about all the affairs which inhibit or accelerate or resolve the problems of society. They are supposed to know more about the impact of NAFTA than the average cheese-maker and un-

Loggia de Lanzi; Florence, Italy.

derstand what economic impacts can be expected, in which sectors, from an increase — or a decrease — in taxes, how far we get into education, how much military we want, who votes, etc. "Representing" us does not mean, "Do what we want done"; it means, "Do what is right". We don't <u>want</u> speed limits, don't <u>want</u> to pay the taxes we do; would abolish the IRS, have misgivings about EPA and OSHA. But if we <u>NEED</u> them all to serve the general good, someone must assure we have them.

A leadership distinction, incidentally, which is falling by the wayside in an age when solons want to feel the public pulse before they act. Ergo, the ubiquity and sacro-sanctity of polls. Before we decide to limit welfare payments or raise the minimum wage or vote on GATT, let's take a poll and see how it will affect us. "Us" not being Americans, "us" being office holders who fear that acting counter to popular opinion is damaging to the reputation and jeopardizing <u>my</u> seat. Campaigns are geared around popular hot-button items, rather than major issues; stances taken on the basis of where the head of the average voter is "at", not what makes the most sense. Reminds one of the old doggerel about Robespierre, seen scurrying along the Champs Élysées. "What's the hurry, monsieur?" "I must 'hurry' and catch up to my followers. I am their leader." Governance by polling is the wrong way to govern. Mr. Burke had it right. He once observed: "Your (elected) representative owes you not only his industry, but his judgment as well; <u>he is betraying (instead of serving you) if he sacrifices it to your opinion</u>." Don't do what I want, do what is right.

The Hellenic experiment with a form of purer democracy proved totally inadequate to govern a state when you had thousands of people involved. The chief reason being interest in issues was sporadic, opinions were based too often on parochial interest, knowledge about a good many things was beyond the competence of most people; few of us care about trivia or mundane things, despite the fact they have to be dealt with and you can take it from there. My point is that large bodies don't have the integrity or wisdom or altruism to deal consistently with the total good. If that happens to be a reasonably accurate assumption, to ignore the phenomenon which <u>elects</u> people to act on our behalf, then do polling (which reverts to bringing large numbers of naïve people <u>into</u> the decision-making process we tried to limit) is to "wire around" the safe guards. It's to brush off knowledge, experience, pragmatism, and research. Why train and create experts in contemporary issues, provide staffing and research only to set that wisdom aside in deference to a poll opinion derived from people who have only the most cursory knowledge and who are biased with inevitable prejudice? "It is a puzzlement."

Despite the ancient aphorism, "Vox populi" is <u>not</u> "vox Dei". ("The voice of the people" is not "the voice of God.") To keep faith with the principles in a republic, those we elect ought to learn issues and options, assess value and damage, craft legislation which provides resolution and stay focused on what is fairest, most efficacious, decisive, and best serves the purpose of the governmental jurisdiction — city, state, nation. If recourse to popular opinion becomes the procedure of choice, we can dispense with elected bodies and run affairs with a series of referendums. Any elected member of our plenary bodies who is too timid or too lazy to decide what is right and most appropriate, and has to ask us what he/she should do, has no business serving in office. ■

Generation Investing

June 1999

All of us tend to look back at the past and remember yesterdays in an exercise that could serve a useful and sometimes even therapeutic purpose. Because a review of the past reminds us again who we are and where we've been. Beyond that, revisiting family hearth, our education, theological progress, favorite music, friends, broken hearts, great teachers, and career, all help define how we developed our outlook and character, created our psyche, caused us to be what we are. Certainly, we are a product of our genes, but aren't we also fashioned through our encounter with the world and its institutions? Moreover, as the shadows lengthen, former times often seem more pleasant or just more comfortable than the current hassle, and retrospection becomes a refuge. The inclination is to move back in the mind's eye, spend more time living "back there" than doing battle with the prickly options confronting us today. There is a lot of value in those previous years and a debt owed for the nurture, insight, experience and lessons imparted in our journey so far. Especially, if we are happy with where we are and what we've become.

But we are <u>living</u> in the present and that means automatically thinking about tomorrow. Periodically, I ask my patient and ever-loving wife if she'd like to view the future in a smaller nest, one without steps to the basement, and maybe one with a big lake out in the front yard. (We currently have four empty bedrooms, two unused baths, an oversized lawn avec beaucoup grass plus a jillion trees and a helluva lot of leaves to rake every fall.) It doesn't take her long to answer. About as long as it takes to say "No." I.e., not very long. And we close this conversation till next year. She usually gives a reason. "I have too much invested in this home to leave it." Like <u>designing</u> the structure, supervising its construction, determining the color scheme, buying the furniture, picking out curtains and drapes, etc., plus nurturing four kids for whom we really built the place. The landscaping is hers, the plants flowering every summer; the patio, the furniture, the grill, fountain … all stuff she selected and secured. Our home is her talisman, it carries her imprimatur. Which implies for most of us the past is special <u>because</u> that is where we have spent our life; because we have a good deal "invested in it".

Downtown Indianapolis, Indiana.

Someone was carping to me recently about Indianapolis and its "Hoosier ways" (meaning "redneck", I suppose) — the disappointing school system, random unplanned urban sprawl, the caliber of the arts, the basketball craze, "500" phobia, etc. But "picking on" Indy around me is touching a raw nerve. I remember what this city was like when I moved here half a century ago and will be quick to point out a lot has <u>changed</u>. I'm proud of where we are and what we have done across the board. We haven't got it all done, but the fact that we are <u>not</u> Vienna doesn't bother me. The glass is half-full, not half-empty. But most of all, like a lot of others "I have too much of myself invested" in Indianapolis to be knocking it. Trying to prop up opera, a theatre, the Symphony, 12 years on a seminary board, a genera-

Football fans enjoy attending the Indianapolis Colts games.

tion running a tractor business, 17 years on CIB, a rescue effort with the fumbling Presbyterian church; a forlorn salvage operation for the Republican cause, etc. To ignore or gainsay all we have changed and achieved is pointlessly cynical. Besides, even our failures have value. Most people here don't <u>want</u> to be in Vienna in the first place. They merely want what we have — to be better. In the process those who have invested, working at the picture/problem the past generation have not only shaped Indy, but at the same time Indy shaped most of us. We have gained thru the involvement, and in the process created a human infrastructure designed to confront given problems and resolve them rather than accommodate same. Or complain about same. We have developed the team work and synergism to induce United Airlines here; buy the Pacers and keep them here; build the Dome and get the Colts; land the NCAA Headquarters; house the Hudson Institute; build a zoo; support a downtown mall; expand the airport, etc., etc. The change in 50 years is not axiomatic or mere evolution. It is progress resulting from good leadership, hard effort and broad support evolving from civic pride and <u>deliberately executed</u> to make this a better city.

This sort of reminiscing and recollecting might be a kind of palliation, which separates us generation-ally. Meaning, once into the twilight it is more fun looking back than looking forward. My generation is into recalling "the good ole days." We "own" the past because there is a lot more <u>of it</u>: we are unsure of the future. A sure way to grow old quickly, however, is forget where we <u>are</u>, look mainly backward and sigh deeply. Nothing wrong with that if you have no place to go. But if part of your life lies ahead, you are surely more curious about the unexplored, i.e. about the future. In business, we do have a "place to go" and to get there need people looking <u>ahead</u>, preparing for the journey. Chief reason we have a lot of younger people working for us is not merely because they don't have much past upon which to reflect, and they not only dominate the present but own the long future stretching out ahead. As they confront it, let's remind them of the Indianapolis model. Directing, shaping and engineering what lies ahead automatically arbitrate the degree of success. The future will depend on how it is managed. If the nature or form or status of an ongoing company is a "given" like the gene structure, what happens each day in the tractor works is the result of how we utilize that gene structure. Employees

have a vested interest in this enterprise which is their vocational choice, and our presumption is by their performance they are taking steps towards insuring it is a sound future. Their job satisfaction and ultimate degree of success lay not in how strong the market is, but how diligently they perform personally and operate as a team.

And the team is built through coordinating effort and thru daily activities. It does not require reflection on the past like what a great year it was in 1997 and 1996. Or remembering 1986 and our first major coal leases or the elation with a new facility on 30th Street (1966). All totally superfluous to those who were not around in those "good ole days". There are no shared memories for folks hired the last 12 years, folks who missed the new building and big coal leases. So we are linked as much by the prospects of the future as we are by memories of the past. We are not locked in time; recollection reminds us we are on a moving stream. It is to note the distance covered that we look back.

But what many of us have "invested" of our lives here is still critical in terms of today's operation. An investment that made this the largest dealership in the state — because of a superior product line, strong key managers, good sales and marketing, heavy investment in facilities, and unparalleled service. The corporate name is (hopefully) a respectable one, tested now for 54 years. The foundations laid in the past now serve as a benchmark to measure the quality and proficiency of the current effort. So there are inherent standards here and a set of criteria, successful enough in terms of its success, to re-employ and

Chris and P.E. MacAllister wearing their Scottish attire for the MacAllister 60th Anniversary Party.

to keep on using. Ergo in that fashion, a bit of the past is thus still relevant. The journey from 1945 to 1999 was not one of long pastorale tranquility and idyllic insouciance. It is rather marked with trial and, of course, some error; plenty of challenge (like being every competitor's chief target); lots of risk and enormous change.

The secret to success in any venture (my generation or Chris') is finding problems before they damage too much and getting them resolved. Alertness to threats <u>and</u> awareness of opportunities are as critical to the survival of the next generation as it was to mine. The need for intelligence, some daring (I wish you could see the size of our inventory!); high competence across the board and mutual intra-company support are all elements daily in need of reinforcement. Today's market leaves no room for snoozers.

And always important whether in my watch or the next is liking what we are doing. It is great to work at something one enjoys and from which he takes pride. This is a fascinating vocation, merciless

for the haphazard, rewarding for the proficient, still expanding, capital intensive, and requiring extensive interpersonal relationships. So love of the game is part of the contract today as it was when E. W. MacAllister signed his contract with Cat 54 years ago and thought he had reached nirvana. His love for this business and its people was enormous. It was critical to his success and will be an integral part of our solution to the conundrum of the future.

It is from that respect for the craft, joy in excelling therein, threat of punishment for failure, meeting the continual challenge of the marketplace that makes this today's adventure. To make it a success, however, we need to find people willing to <u>invest</u> their working time with us and opt for a full-time career. Our hope would be that as we succeed, each employee shares in that success, content he/she has become a factor in perpetuating an enterprise now into its 54th year. One whose product is respected and whose effort contributes to the onward progress of the species. ∎

The System Needs Help

September 1999

Congress has been stewing and mumbling about the budgetary surplus and how it might be approached. I've got an answer for them, recalling "that government governs best, which governs least". Ergo, the best strategy: do nothing. Let the surplus (if real) keep accruing until we have eliminated our national debt. As it goes down, so does cost to service it. Now, this is neither professional nor profound advice nor does it come from one experience in those precincts which echo with trillion dollar rhetoric. It's just conditioning. Most Americans in my generation are bothered by indebtedness; they want to see bills paid as quickly as is possible. There has been scattered conversation about using a bit of the surplus for such purposes, but as I write this, nothing definitive is coming down and chances are the amount applied to reduce what we owe, is minimal.

Did you notice the whole issue seems to have caught our legislators by surprise? It is pretty apparent (given the record of the past 40 years), that had this windfall been suspected or anticipated, it never would have occurred. "Expenses rise to meet anticipated income" is a general aphorism or maxim applicable to American congresses, which is not meant to ridicule or to impugn. It reflects a fact of life when needs are many in the land, and government becomes an agency responsible for resolution of all of our societal problems. This wet-nursing and hovering about arises when we are convinced the individual is no longer capable of managing his own affairs; or when disparity of effort, luck, or birth sees uneven distribution of wealth. Meaning, needs or discrepancies which traditionally have been personal responsibility (or maybe that of the city and state) have become federal concern and, thus, the range and scope of opportunities to intervene (I almost said "meddle") is virtually endless.

But getting onto the point of this essay (diatribe?), two issues targeted for redress in the current discussion are Social Security and Medicare. The President wants to save them. I wish the President had said he wanted to <u>fix</u> them. To clean them up, pare them down, cut the fat and fluff out of them. Why not eliminate the waste first and see what Medicare <u>really</u> costs, not merely what we pay? Again, selling tractors is a far cry from the health care or insurance field, but elements like efficiency, management, fair pricing, cost-benefit ratio et al are applicable across the board. My conclusion is that as long as Medicare is construed to be a blank check, there is no way in the world to curtail spending. We shall never have enough money to pay what patients <u>want</u> covered <u>and</u> what doctors want <u>recovered</u>. At my house we've just been thru a pretty heavy siege of illness; and several years back (at different times) I monitored and managed the final weeks of two parents, both ending up in hospitals. Meaning, I have a nodding acquaintance with what goes on. Not an expert, I have been an observer. My conclusion from cursory inspection is categorical: There appears to be one helluva lot of waste in the system.

Part of our recent experience involved some intravenous feeding of nutrients to get my wife's weight up, a process that took about a month and involved manual procedures and medical housekeeping. We did most of this at home so I got the instructions on how to connect and disconnect the tubing to the one liter bag of solution; learned how to swab and sterilize injection ports, how to inject vitamin supplements into the solution, how to affix and prime the pump, how to disconnect and then de-coagulate, etc. Point is, there were a dozen different medical gadgets from syringes to valves to tubing to connections, etc. All came in ten-day supply parcels. None could ever be reused. There is no such thing as recycling in medicine. The only thing recycled is the patient. A visiting nurse periodically stopped to check in, see what was left of the gadgetry, and ordered what would be needed for the next ten days. When we finished the treatment (three days before the final ten-day period), there was an inventory of unused material. But not three days' worth. I had among other things in surplus, <u>17</u> syringes which I wanted to return for credit. "We don't take anything back. Standard procedure. Government orders." There must have been $300 worth of stuff there, <u>all unused, packaged in plastic and sanitized</u>. "Don't worry, the insurance will take care of it." That's not the point. The point is a mistake on the part of the agency in their calculations and this needless stuff, which, thus, pointlessly raised the cost of the treatment. The health care people had a mark-up in all the goodies we didn't need, and they got paid by the insurance company. "Corporate policy" or "government policy" is a dodge. What do you suppose a customer would say to us if he needed four pistons for his engine and we shipped him six ... and told him it was company policy? He'd think we were crazy. And he wouldn't pay his bill.

Which brings up another item. A major leakage in this whole bloody system (excuse the inadvertent and very gauche pun) is the paperwork. Have you ever had experience with doctors and hospitals followed for months on end by one piece of paper after another, each with arithmetic factoring all over it that says "This Is Not A Bill"? The paperwork in handling today's medical phenomenon has got to cost as much as the doctor ... in many cases.

And doctors cost money. We are still getting invoices, sorting out "who pays for what" (we have three levels of insurance coverage), and the latest batch had a list of hospital calls. This is the doctor visiting — to see how you are doing. Five minutes. $70.00 a pop! Then a different doctor, time after time, cut-rate price $45.00 a pop. "How do you feel today? Does this hurt when I touch it? Is the incision healing? That's nice. We'll see you again tomorrow." Five minutes. $70.00! What the guy is checking is the effect and impact <u>of his work</u>, in this case a procedure and (second doctor) a small incision. In the tractor business, we repair the transmission on a loader and check it all before it leaves the shop. If we sent someone out next day to see how it was running and whether what we did was right, or if <u>we</u> followed with a bill, the owner would scream bloody murder. Of if there was a glitch in the job and we had to go back and tighten something up, there is no way we can charge because we did not do something right.

But in the medical world, no one screams bloody murder because we <u>don't get a bill</u> from the doctor. It goes to the insurance company. "They" have to see if the charge is legit, and "they" send the check. It is a different processing operation. Important, because we overlook something in

the process. We fail to note whose money "they" are spending. Where does the insurance company get its money? In our case it is American Medical Security and it gets about $123,430 <u>a month</u> from <u>us</u> to pay for medical expenses incurred by employees and their families. What happens is we deduct $37,430 from our monthly checks to cover the family, add to it $86,000 paid by the company to cover each employee and use these dollars to pay <u>our</u> expenses. The insurance company is not "they". It is <u>we</u>, those insured, who have sent the money to be used in an emergency. If payments come from Medicare, guess who supplied that money? Those insured and rest of us. It is our money the doctor wants. Where do we get the idea there is a limitless third-party source paying the bills?

I saw this attitude when my mother "passed" (at age 95, by the way, and ready to try something else) after two or three weeks in the hospital. Issue of "who pays" popped up three months later while doing the probate work on her will and needed to get all the bills paid. I called the hospital for an invoice or a billing or something so I knew where we were. "She won't owe anything. Medicare will take care of it." "How can you be sure?", I wondered. "They always do." Three months later, still no accounting, repetition of the bureaucratic snarl this has become, at which point I got fairly hostile and said I wanted a bill, damn it. "O.K., O.K., we'll get it out", which indeed they finally did. But notice the fact that "Why sweat, the government will pay for it." Which means no matter what billing they sent to Medicare, someone would have written a check for the amount requested. (I think $13,000.) Then it struck me that maybe one group in our society <u>has</u> the proverbial "license to steal". No one checks their work. No one knows in advance what they are going to charge. No one has any idea whether all the stuff on that long itemized invoice was really provided, was necessary, or it slipped in from another patient; or maybe the doctor didn't make all those visits; or maybe some figures got transposed. Can you imagine paying $13,000 without any critical scrutiny of the service or material supplied? We don't pay for stuff around here until someone OKs the bill and says, "It is what I ordered. It is the price quoted. It belongs in this expense account." Get it? Accountability. There is none I can see in the medical industry. I'm not saying there is a deliberate conspiracy to rob the public. I'm saying people make mistakes in factoring, adding, entering in a computer. I'm saying he who does the collecting, ought not to be he who decides how much we ought to spend.

Again, don't get me wrong. I have nothing against doctors and hospitals, and my experience with those encountered in the past several years is long on bedside manner, marginal on clerical help and procedures, leisurely in terms of pace, but from doctors and nurses, infinite patience, solicitude, kindness, giving every evidence of caring and concern. But it makes no sense to put even a legion of angels into a hospital environment with the understanding they can charge whatever they want. "You may discuss the malady with your patient, the medication and the prognosis, but for God's sake, <u>don't</u> tell him what you are charging for this procedure or what the follow-up costs will be. We don't want to worry him about it; their insurance companies will send the check." How's come we have a society which provides an endless array of benefits, opportunities, options, commodities, and ways to spend money, but we single out one of them that never tells us what it costs to secure? Everything else we buy has a price on it and often we decide the tag is too stiff so we take a rain check. Because <u>we</u> are going to get an invoice and <u>we</u> are going to have to pay.

What would happen if the money our company spends in insurance premiums were co-mingled with the family coverage each employee supplies and put into an employee's bank account? Then each time he had an insurance claim, <u>he</u> had to pay the bill from his designated account. My hunch is, if it were <u>his</u> dollars he was spending, he'd wonder about costs, about visits, about why visit, about those separate items on the bill he never authorized. And I bet, too, that until there are a lot more questions asked about "Why did you spend this money on this stuff?", we are gonna have a "blank check" strategy for health care.

What is wrong with a new era of "full disclosure"? When someone calls in here with a long list of parts, he is entitled to ask us what they are going to cost and if he wants to wait a few minutes, we can tell him what they cost. Or if someone decides he wants a CAT engine in his semi overhauled and wants to know what it costs, we give him the package price depending on the hours run, condition it's in and what we know from the past it costs to bring it back to A-1 condition. He gets a quote. It's printed out; we can slide it across the desk and show him what we do and what it costs. Why can't doctors do that? And then explain that this will also include a minimum of seven hospital visits at $70 a pop (providing they take no longer than five minutes), and we have this medication to take and this price for taking out stitches, etc. In short, why can't doctors and hospitals function like the rest of us? Because the insurance company pays the bills. They don't have to account for actions or charges. There is no buyer resistance.

My point will be that if the doctor told us what he was charging for each visit <u>while we were there</u>; or reported on what treatments were going to cost, he'd get paid just as readily as he does now. But after he heard, "You said <u>how much</u>! My God, man, where is your mask and gun?", it might begin to have an effect. Very few of us are self-correcting and self-disciplining. In the free enterprise system, there are choices to make between which brand we buy, and this "comparison pricing" is the very dynamic which has demanded we find more efficiency, demanded we cut waste and cost, and has held our inflationary rate to an astounding minimum. Except in guess what field? And have you noticed, there is no price comparing, no shopping around, and there is no revelation of costs to the buyer. AND there is the insurance company who is gonna absorb the cost anyway, which puts medical care in a world (Utopia) of its own. It is the pressure of competition that holds things in check in almost everything we buy. We probably are never going to introduce that into medicine, but maybe we can require a patient's OK on doctor bills before insurance companies pay. Meaning, the bill goes to the patient so he at least sees in clear, bold and frightening precision what it is he has incurred in terms of expense for his visit to the medic. My hunch is there'd be more shopping and change of source. There might be some price-cutting and cost-cutting as well. One thing is sure in all of this: There'll be no fixing of anything until the buyer gets into the act and exercises the same options here he has in buying groceries or loaders or automobiles. ■

Taxes Tax Us

September 1999

There is a great deal of rhetoric about taxes these days and as typical, when there is so much "sound and fury", there is usually an equal amount of misunderstanding and nonsense intermingled. My pet peeve arises from the refrain of Richard Gephardt, the Minority Leader in the United States House of Representatives, who secretly wants to be President. Who builds his case monotonously upon the topic of rich versus poor, agitating a sort of class warfare thereby hoping to pick up support? His theme is the rich in America not only get all of the breaks, they do so at the expense of the poor. Moreover, the rich-poor gap is widening, not narrowing. ("O Tempore, O Mores" as Cicero used to declaim.) He reads about corporate bonuses and stock options which can get very big indeed. Never in our history have major company executives been rewarded so handsomely and never has Big Business accumulated so much wealth. Bill Gates, right now, is larger than the Gross National Product of 36 of the 70 major <u>nations</u> listed in my *American Almanac*. On a good day, he is reputedly worth a hundred billion plus dollars. I say "Huzzah for Bill Gates". He vindicates the system and proves that creative ingenuity, good business judgment, a certain ruthlessness, a modicum of luck, and endless days of incessant labor permits one to realize the American dream … in spades. Horatio Alger, step aside for the new champ!

What Bill Gates or Steve Hilbert is worth — or makes annually — is not the criterion, however. Meaning, it is fallacious to compare the average worker's salary in 1950 with that made by Charles Wilson or Henry Ford III and <u>now</u> examine the difference between today's average worker and Michael Eisner or Sidney Taurel (of Eli Lilly) or Brett Fauvre or Cal Ripken or Tom Hanks. The comparisons ought to be the compensation paid a given worker <u>vis-à-vis what it costs to live</u> in American today versus what it was 10 years ago or 40 years old, or you name it. Is his purchasing power, in other words, greater or lesser than it used to be? What the upper 5% of America makes is irrelevant in this circumstance.

A recent book entitled "*Myths of the Rich*" by Michael Cox and Richard Alm deals with that issue as they discuss this whole topic. (I bring them in here to lend authenticity to my argument since theirs is a study, not an old tractor guy's opinion and bias.) First step is an examination of American life in general. We <u>all</u> enjoy bigger homes, safer cars, dramatically improved health care, abundant and affordable food, easier access to higher education, and retirement security unknown when I got my first paycheck in 1936. Talk all you want about the good old days, because good as they may appear, they can't hold a candle to these good old days.

To get specific, comparisons are made thru the unit of the hourly wage rate. What could one buy <u>then</u>, compared with rates now, is the sort of standard I think objective. Let's try the cost of housing, for example. Since size varies, we resort to a common increment — the cost per square foot. Forty years ago it was 6½ hours worth of labor to pay for one square foot of housing. Your house is 1000 square feet, that's 6500 hours of labor — 37 months. Today, a square foot amounts to 5½ hours — 30 months. What's that? 15% difference! Meaning, purchasing power is 15% greater today than in 1950's in the field of housing. If you wanted an air-conditioner (get this), it took you 40 hours to pay for a 1000 BTU unit. Guess what it is today? <u>Four hours</u>. One week versus one morning. In the '50s (note the date changes) a cheeseburger cost half an hour's wage; today, three minutes. A gallon of milk takes less than <u>half</u> as many "work hours" as it did then.

The rich might be getting richer, but the poor are buying more in the marketplace with less effort than they ever have.

Using dollars is another yardstick, provided they are adjusted to account for inflation. In 1936 I could buy six gallons of gas for a dollar to fill up my old Dodge, meaning, gas sold for about 16¢ a gallon. Today, it's maybe $1.20. But the dollar has shrunk in value. To reproduce 1936 purchasing power, multiply by 10; so what my 16¢ bought in 1963, takes $1.60 today. Viola! Despite the ranting and raving, the bloody stuff is still cheaper in weighted dollars today than it was in the recession ($1.20 being less than $1.60). So the rich may be getting richer, but the "un-rich" are buying more for the same effort. Which translates to a higher standard of living than anything considered in the past decade or generation.

The other theme of my friend Dick Gephardt is still reverberating because the resolution of the budget package and proposed tax cut are not determined. His wailing against the Congressional bill was, "Cutting taxes is another way to take care of the fat cats; it's a gimmick to give the richest people the biggest break." His mathematics are flawless. If you give the person making $200,000 a year a 2% tax cut and the guy making $40,000 a 6% cut in his taxes, who gets the break? The wealthy taxpayer because he gets a $4,000 break while the other bird gets a $2,400 break. We are helping the rich taxpayer reduce the rates, despite making his percentage reduction 66% greater (dollar-wise). Talking about reducing rates, do you realize that if we did just that, 48 million people get no break at all? Reason: They don't pay taxes to start with. Rates going up or down won't affect them.

This (like the tax code) gets very complicated, so let me regroup. Two hundred seventy million of us in America, right? Converts to 122,000,000 tax returns (in 1998). These productive citizens report a total gross income of five trillion dollars — $5,000,000,000,000. But we don't pay tax on gross income; we have deductions. Each person in the family reduces income by $1,500; interest expense comes off, contributions are deducted, depreciation (if that is applicable), medical expenses, local taxes, etc., etc., all depending on how busy or how creative you are. These come off the top and what is left is $3.4 trillion of taxable income. The taxes on that last year (if you have stayed with me) were $737 billion. If your slide rule is working, that's an average tax rate of about 21%. And the contributions to this pot are more cockeyed than airline fares.

For starters, 1% of the taxpayers may have earned 16% of all the income identified above, but they had to pay 32% of all the taxes! One percent of you paid almost one-third of all of the taxes for 270,000,000 Americans. The 8% of you who made over $100,000 last year paid 62% of all the income tax. On the other end, 70 million taxpayers produce only 4% of all income tax collections. If you aren't dizzy from the figures, 42% of you pay 96% of the income tax revenue. Gephardt thinks this is lopsided in favor of the rich, who aren't carrying enough of the burden. He thinks 5% of us who pay over

half the taxes or the 8% who pay two-thirds are getting a ride.

If we are dependent so desperately and so inequitably on a small fraction of our people, we have to find them as involved proportionately in the tax cut as they are in the tax contribution. It just works that way, Dick.

Said another way and putting the situation in context, all this was triggered because we have apparently collected more revenue than we need to run the government and projections indicate that might well be the situation in the future. If we want to correct this "imbalance", i.e. equalize income and outgo, we can do two things (NOT raise the latter to meet the former, please, but): (1) Annually return the surplus to taxpayers, or (2) reduce the amount we collect. If we decided on a rebate, where would we return the money? Give every taxpayer a check for $1,289.00? Or would we return it in proportion to the way we received it? If we did the latter, who would get the most money do you suppose? Right, the people who paid the most taxes. One percent would get a third of the money returned, the next 5% would get the next third returned and shaking on down, 58% would end up sharing 4% of the rebate. I don't think Dick Gephardt wants to do it that way. He wants it split up so a lot of what you and I paid in goes back to people who paid little or no tax, so they end up with a tax dividend rather than a tax payment. That is the way he'd see that richer Americans paid their "fair" share.

If we don't go this way, we end up reducing the intake and that comes in the form of a tax cut. How much can you reduce the revenue stream if you are dealing with the rate of people who only contribute 4% of the total? Mathematically, you aren't making much headway. Fact is, mathematically, you probably can't get there doing that. You need to go where the dollars are and that is the odious class of people whose revenue contributions support the federal government. I don't know how you can deal with tax cuts without giving the "rich" a break, since that is where the money is and the only place a cut would affect the numbers.

Someday I'm going to try and figure out why we consider this a relatively "fair" system of taxation. I know it is cheaper than Europe, but I also know there is an amazing amount of private, institutional, religious, civic and artistic contributions here that supply amenities and opportunities people in Europe pay the government to provide. So our involvement in support of this society is surely not restricted to our tax burden. Somehow we have to account for all of the "donated" or recruited or volunteered effort supplied, including another $140 billion given away to worthy causes in addition to the tax bite.

Sometime, too, I'm gonna have to wonder why I should pay more taxes than the family across the street. The answer is: "Because you make more money". What's fair about that? When I go to Milwaukee, the airline doesn't differentiate my ticket price based on my income; if I go to a Colts game, they charge me the same price as the people next to me; if I buy a movie ticket or load up on groceries or fill up with gas, we all pay the same rate. The city doesn't charge me more taxes per square foot for my house than people down the street.

The system is set up this way because it is easier to raise the amount we need and can be done without provoking a revolution. If we had to pay the same amount per person across the board, no doubt it would weigh far more heavily on most families than it does now, but it could have a positive effect. There might be so much hue and cry about how monies are spent we might get Congress to get the budget down to a reasonable size and minimize the frivolous spending. But by now this looks like the writer is drifting out into left field and since we are beginning to speculate, it must mean we've said what we had to say and ought to move on to something else. ■

Christmas Stories

December 1999

The Christmas holiday has become universal in the western world. Though in the process, said "world" has so adopted or adapted it that one might see more of the secular than the religious. Unless he looks very close indeed. And if he examines this closely, over the years finds that the whole business has shifted its ground considerably from the magic it had when I was young. I don't know that this is altogether bad, but I do see a different "take" on the event; meaning, in the process of looking at the scriptural material out of which the holiday evolved, sees it all with a new (i.e. different) light. As a youngster, I learned both Christmas stories verbatim and could recite them at the drop of a hat. Fact, with a little tinkering, can still do so. As a youngster, I was excited about the shepherds, and thought it great that angel chorus not only sang, but gave directions as well. Took for granted the birth occurred after an 80-mile burro ride initiated by a census the emperor had ordered. More glamorous were the wise men who found the infant by following a star and more somber the narrative when we learned of Herod's order to kill all the young children, precipitating a flight into Egypt. So the action, the color, the characters, the wonder, and romance all overlaid the vignette and gave it uniqueness and a marvel that is rare in New Testament literature.

The holiday (no matter how secular) is still represented with the same images … the crèche, the gifts, the special music, the iconography of the Virgin, floating seraphim, but advancing years and closer scrutiny of the two accounts lead us to a raft of puzzling questions heretofore ignored. Why is the dating 15 years different from one story to the next? Is it shepherds or wise men (neither story mentions both)? There is no record of a census in Judea during the reign of Augustus. Why run someone all the way down to Bethlehem because an ancestor a thousand years before lived there? Just to count or tax him? Who says "the city of David" was Bethlehem? Historically, his city was Jerusalem. Do we dash off in a hurry to Egypt or do we wait eight days and go to the temple to be circumcised? As a youngster, the stories to me were familiar, poignant, shrouded in wonder and charm. But "when I became a man" and "put away childish things", discovered all these "idiosyncrasies" in the text and the conflicting detail.

Which over time gives one pause to think.

What happens in the process is reason kicks in, some of the magic departs, and I am left to sort this out. If I love the story of Christmas as a youngster, riper now in years, I need to ponder the meaning of the story. I know what it says but what is the point? For starters, the gospel accounts dealt mostly with the life, teaching, times and mission of Jesus whose humanity is affirmed up front through the Christmas story. Having achieved that, then we try to express what it was he came to do, or to be, or to teach or to change. Caught up in a theology which is pretty hard to digest, the writer's motive was not biography, it was the "good news", and the device used was biographical narrative. The message contained is delivered in the narrative and to get hung up on historiography or geography or even timing is to miss the point. The writer couldn't care less about season or locus or visitors, he wanted us to mark this life as something startlingly different and the impact of it, watershed in terms of its evolving results.

The ensuing story also recounted what things were changed and how Jewish theology was to be recast. Jewish people don't happen to accept his version and a lot of Christians won't have much more regard for my take on this whole business either. But this lack of consensus becomes one of the lessons represented in the whole phenomenon. We don't have to agree on everything to be "followers" or "disciples". Theology has to be personal; it cannot be programmed or pressed on us, not if we are all given intelligence with which to perceive and interpret such things.

That we have a variety of opinions about both the Christmas story and the subsequent results is not surprising. A variety of opinions is typical in Judaism and was endemic in the church from the 1st Century on. "Rejoice!", I say. "Don't despair." Paul advised us to "think upon these things" and if he was serious, our thinking will be conditioned by our training, culture, education, teachings, personal character, and intellect, i.e., we will come out at different points along the way if indeed this is a universal subject. If it is not bound by sect or region or ancestry, it will spread wide enough to envelop and accommodate all mankind.

The cast of characters in the tale sort of represents variety … shepherds, wise men (magi are sages, not kings), old timers in the temple, Joseph's family upset with Mary's "condition", "Herod the King", "the chief priests", and "the scribes of the people". Then note, too, the geography, the distances … all the way from Iran, yet; from Galilee, to Egypt. So, looking at the range of personalities in this drama and the distance traveled, one sees the elements of human kind to which it had connections. The broad involvement might lead us to believe this is a faith that travels. Note its subsequent course. Across the Mediterranean in the initial century, then two centuries later, it conquered the empire. It is, also, a faith that travels in time. The fact that it has changed for me from my first experience till the current status indicates it has two distinct and different values. It continues to appeal to different ages. Because like Judaism, it has the capacity to flex and to direct across the ages.

When our forefathers wrote the Constitution, they were aware of a nation newly-born and one which would expand enormously, so they were wise enough in their document to permit emendation. They wanted a document equipped for the future while managing the present. A faith, to be eternal, needs the same properties. The Constitution had to be modified as "we the people" required and almost immediately wanted ten amendments, now called "The Bill of Rights". New states were added, a cabinet evolved, franchise was expanded, slavery abolished, etc. It is significant that any governance vehicle take into account its charge to order affairs in a fashion which is pertinent to the times, not using an apparatus instituted to govern 210 years ago. Laws have to be written to deal with today's problem; they are not a revered souvenir of the past, inviolable, and irrefragable.

The same (I repeat) has to be true of theology. Although Judaism tends to look back to Moses and respect his edicts, some contemporary Jewish people think it not irreverent to eat shrimp cocktail and ham sandwiches. Meaning, why should a desert manifesto for a semi-nomadic agglomeration of tribes be helpful or sacred today? Because it is 3200 years old. The question ought to be, "Is it relevant?" Does it help us in ordering a just and equitable society? In applying this to the Christmas story and the subsequent account of how the church was established, that which is still applicable needs to be preserved, but that which is more appropriate to 110 A.D. ought to be parked along side the road … e.g., denying women any leadership roles, acceptance of slavery ("Slaves, obey your masters"); Jesus' obsession with the wickedness of the rich, Christians maintaining, limiting, owning any access to God, etc. At which point the Christmas story reappears, especially if we are looking to find (or impute) meanings.

One starts by noting the whole event occurred in a rural, bucolic, ordinary setting. If this is a Messiah being born, it's a new version completely because this one would spend his time with the farmers and fishermen, the tradesmen and housewives, an occasional carpenter, and even a tax collector. So he was not an ambassador to the powerful, the ecclesiastical hierarchy, to the mighty. His concern and mission was where he thought the heart of God would be, with the needy, the humble, the unimportant, and the mass of humanity — the less attractive and probably most numerous.

THE VISIT OF THE WISE-MEN

Photographic reproduction of Birth of Jesus with visiting Magi. *(Source: Wikimedia Commons.)*

The other implied meaning was emphasized as the later mission took shape and unfolded, opened up discipleship. We are not going to restrict this to a small minority: "You only have I known out of all the nations in the world", i.e. restricted to the ritually pure. Most of the above-mentioned fisher folk and small sharecroppers would have been ritually impure a dozen ways and thus eschewed, avoided by priest and scribe. They were not kosher enough for God. But they would soon be welcomed in a new fellowship for those outside the law.

The Wise Men seem to

prove a Gentile interest … can we say involvement … in the young child and what he represented? These are Zoroastrian seers visiting the manger so the child <u>has</u> import and relationships beyond his own race. Ironic that foreign sages pay respects to a family the local Jewish people refused bed or board.

What I'm doing in this rambling monologue is a bit of "isogesis" … reading <u>into</u> the text what I want to see there. You can make your own interpretation or leave it less complex and be content with the imperfect history. The final "reading in" was done by St. Paul who saw in the Jesus event a mystery called the incarnation, too esoteric for me to dwell on long. Except to say it sort of tails off into theological speculation and wanders into highly ethereal conjecture. Paul thought it fit his theology, so congratulations to you, St. Paul! Great work! Except I can't quite figure out how it works <u>today</u>. The incarnation is the theoretical presence of God in the persona of Jesus and, thus, the Divine essence merged with the physical at that moment in time. Makes more sense to me, considering what Christmas is all about if the incarnation still occurs and the Divine presence <u>invests us</u>, to enhance the spirit, make sacred the mission, inspire, and ennoble the faithful. In the outpouring of gifts, in the sudden joy of the family hearth, in the reliving of the manger event, let's hope <u>we</u> are incarnated … inspired, excited, motivated … to recreate the old magic in Christmas, and for a few moments refresh the occasion with a rejuvenation of the spiri-

tual instead of the secular, just to see how it all feels.

Whatever meaning you read into the story, be reminded that it motivates us to a new feeling about our fellowman, our families, neighbors, colleagues at work or in the school only insofar as someone acts in response to the implied message. Whatever inspiration is there becomes honestly manifest when we decide we must do something as a result. We do a lot of giving at this time of year and that is part of it. When we are helping, encouraging, listening, accommodating, and succoring, we give evidence that the age old re-visitation of the Christmas "miracle" is still powerful enough to create a few moments of joy each year, and a realization that the core focus is not about my tree and the loot anticipated, but what we might do for someone else. ∎

Fie On the Airlines

December 1999

There is a new outrage in the media about airlines, their poor service, lack of understanding, and general ineptitude. We are even proposing federal legislation to force action in the air-travel industry which will protect passengers and require airline people to be more civil, more accurate, more accommodating, and to provide more services. As someone who has been on an airplane about once a week for the past 25 years, flying mostly in the eastern half of the country, and doing 80% of his travel on one or two airlines, maybe my experience is not typical or my action, one of proper dissatisfaction. But my exposure is genuine and prolonged. There is no argument about the fact that service on the airlines has been less reliable than formerly; there is more inclination to screw up flights; there are delays and more counter congestion. But I think there is a reason for the change.

What contributes to the problem is an industry currently (if I recall the figures correctly) negotiating 200,000 landings and take-offs a day in America. You cannot look at the azure sky on a clear afternoon and not see half a dozen vapor trails streaking randomly across "the vault of heaven". Most of the flights I'm on are jam-packed with people, and in the first ten days of this month I have flown in from Rome, been up and back to Milwaukee, and then over to Boston and back. Not without some exasperating delays. The worse coming out of Philadelphia for Indianapolis on the last weary leg of the Rome trip where, first off, we had to wait in order to find a docking gate coming in; then spent nearly two hours beyond departure time getting out. Exasperating! Except we couldn't get a gate because we were half an hour early and

thus, out of the planned docking schedule and had to fit back into sync. We couldn't get out because of a string of bad thundershowers between us and home. Exasperating, but though we moan, "When you have time to spare, go by air"; I don't know what the airlines can do when schedules they set have been breached, or when weather moves in which makes flying uncomfortable if not unsafe. We can bitch and need to blame someone, but fair scores, this is delay; but it is not mismanagement or dereliction.

The real point to the problem I think is that the airlines have been too successful and the economy is too strong. The expansion of air service has made more and more cities available and thus, added more and more flights, and the economy sees more and more passengers. The expansion of airlines themselves providing thousands of airplanes and millions of options have made air travel the accepted mode. In that process, we have had to cram an exponential increase of activity in the same physical airport space we used 25 years ago. Point being, our airports have often been revamped, but still were built to accommodate a far less congested and less employed mode of transport that turns out to be the case. More planes and travel mean more traffic in and around airports and thus, more traffic jams and with more usage, more wear, and technically, more exposure to failure. No one planned for this sort of travel pattern. We planned for a much more modest one and are "making do" by over-crowding what we have. In the midst of all this, have to point out, too, that though there has been a mishap this year, in 1998 there wasn't one single fatality caused by commercial airlines in the U.S. Incredible achievement! And makes one wonder if the sort of caution, precaution, restrictions, and limits imposed might likewise impede the normal operation of our air industry, causing some of the waiting and delay.

I know pretty much what the problems are, but when I get my belly full, I can react. I don't have to fly. I can drive. Or in rare cases, take a train or a bus. Air travel is an option, not a necessity. And if it has some glitches, we use commercial airlines because they permit us to do a heck of a lot of things we would not otherwise even attempt. If it wastes time and delays us, my point will be, it saves us more time than is lost to screw-ups. And the thought of suggesting that the airlines are so badly managed the United States Congress can teach it new lessons in efficiency chills the blood. Don't forget — Congress is the organization that brought us the income tax system and tax laws that are so intricate, four different IRS agents figuring the same return get four different answers. This is the genius, also, that invented and runs the United States Postal System; the aggregation of men and women who fail with resolute consistency to build a federal budget on time year after year. Personally, I would sooner have the Boy Scouts giving instructions to the airlines than looking for more federal legislation.

But beyond that, the irony to me is: climbing on the airline industry. The congestion and time delays, the mishandling and mismanagement of air travel are not America's biggest traveling problem. Anyone been out on the highway recently? If I fly to Milwaukee or Boston, it is sporadic. But I have to drive each and every cotton pickin' day to work. Or get to church on Sunday or the doctor's office or the market or the barber, crawl in my car and take

off. We have to use our city streets and highways in moving through life's routines. Anyone notice what has happened to traffic in town (my town or yours or Rome or Boston or Cairo or Istanbul) the past 25 years? If we need to take some action about inefficient travel or want to deal with frustration or traffic management, how's about having Congress do something about a situation that is strangling American cities and wasting millions of hours of time and dollars because of lousy planning for surface traffic arteries. We shrug this off as though nothing can be done about it. We adjust to it and wait in line for the next light to change and then change again. We think we have no other choice. I'm saying that a similar phenomenon is occurring in the air traffic industry, but there we are hollering for redress. The one problem outside our window, we have to "get used to". We have to endure. We can't find someone to blame. And we have every expectation that it will do nothing but get worse.

It is a puzzlement! ■

Time, You Old Gypsy Man

December 1999

Time, you old gypsy man
Will you not stay,
Put up your caravan,
Just for one day?
　　　　　　　– Ralph Hodgson

Since this is an essay on changing centuries and thus about "time", the poem of Hodgson came to mind. He says time marches on inexorably … and by now is moving us to a new age. We are moving from one millennium to another and shift our counting of years from the 19's to using 20's. We do not, of course, start the new century or the new millennium January 1, 2000. It still belongs to the old century/millennium. (If I owed you $2,000 and paid you $1,999 instead, you'd say, "You're short. I need one more.") Though it is obvious we are technically a year away, everyone is getting charged up to celebrate as though it were a new century. (A friend, last January, made reservations to spend December 31, 1999 in Hawaii and had trouble getting reservations on both planes and in hotels. Lots of "plan ahead" going on.)

The topic of time and timing got me wondering how and when we developed our current dating patterns. When did our ancestors create a calendar and mark the seasons? Fact, how would they ascertain the number of days in a year? Answer is: "They started very early and understood universally. Without any crossword puzzles, television sets, or radio, men studied the stars, the cycles of the moon, and the shifting pattern and timing of the sun." Alexander Marshack theorizes that a notched bone found near the origins of the Nile in Central Africa might be the first calendar. It seems to mark the phases of the moon and is dated about 6500 B.C. A general consensus affirms we have been working with one sort of calendar or other since 3000 B.C. (That's BCE to contemporary daters.) But again, "How would they find a procedure to measure the year?"

One way is to locate a bit of level ground, then plant an upright stick in the middle of it. Start one morning in early summer and put a small stone at the tip of the shadow cast by the stick. Come back in an hour and put another stone where the shadow tip is now.

As the sun moves across the sky at appointed

intervals, put down another dozen stones. At day's end, we note our stones form a large arc. One end stone marked the morning shadow and the other the last before dark. Next day, going thru the same motions, we note that the arc has moved slightly, the new curve a bit away from the first. And the third day and thirteenth and twenty-third days will see successive arcs, all moving away from the first one until a given point, like June 21st. Then we shall see the arcs start creeping back, retreating, moving beyond our starting point and finally maxing out (on December 21st). Then again, the arc reverses direction. By now the place is cluttered with small stones, and if the kids haven't kicked them out of place or made Pokemon images of them, we will see the pattern. If we notched a stick marking each twilight, we discover it has taken 187 days to reach from one extreme to the other. It will take 365 days for the arc suddenly to reappear exactly where the first one was laid out. To reach this point, we've cut 365 notches.

The Egyptians had a less complex process for counting the days in the year. They noted somewhere around 4235 B.C. that a stellar phenomenon was being repeated and a physical change also reoccurring. Like the Nile was beginning its annual flooding; simultaneous with the Dog Star (Canis Major) also called Sirius rising at early dawn right next to the

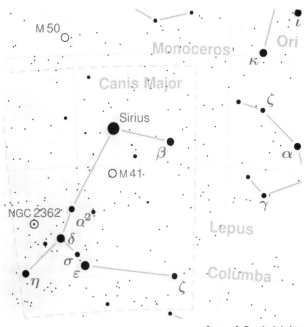

Star of Canis Major
(Source: Wikimedia Commons.)

Roman Forum.

sun. It was unmistakable, and it happened once each 365 days, so counting the days between each rising of the Nile and each re-appearance of Sirius gave them a measurable handle for marking the seasons.

The Mesopotamians used the moon instead of the sun to count, the moon cycles being 29 ½ days which they rounded off to 30. Twelve months of 30 days gave them 360 days, and each day was divided into 12 periods of two hours each (do not ask me what the clock looked like or how they kept hours). But note the sexagesimal system, in use among us today. Twelve months, 24 hour days, 360° circles, 60 minutes per hour, 60 seconds per minute. But 360 days is not a full year. Aha! Let's add an extra month (30 days) each seven or eight years and pick up the difference. Truth is, the actual span of our year, 365.242199 days does not lend itself neat segmentation, so we have to diddle with it. Like say, add a day each four years.

All of this deals with years and months but hardly centuries. Like in what Egyptian year did Menes unite upper and lower Egypt? What year did Joseph come to work for Potiphar? What year did Moses lead his people out of captivity? That is a different story and not clearly told. Ancient peoples often tracked by the reference to the regnal year of kings or monarchs. I have a small cuneiform tablet from ancient Babylon with some writing on one side. It is dated in such and such month in the umpteenth year of "Sin-iddinam, King of Larsa." An archaeologist friend translates it to read, "February, 1865 B.C." The time established by the scribe or the king refers to a given year of his reign. My friend translated that regnal date to our record keeping of the total historical sequence, thus providing a relative timing, unknown to ancient peoples.

The Greeks kept time by the Olympiads; the

Romans being pragmatic used a long span system. Their calendar was a modification of Macedonian and Mesopotamian formulae, re-jiggered by Aristarchus in 239 B.C. It had 365 days per year, then added an extra day every fourth year. But this was superimposed on a more systematic record which dated events "*ab urbe condita*", from the founding of the city", i.e. from 753 B.C. They sort of screwed up when they revised their calendar in 153 B.C., changing the beginning of the year from March back to January. Which explains why some months are mislabeled, September, October, November and December, are no longer seventh, eighth, ninth and tenth months as the Latin terms imply. Rome also relied on a lunar cycle with all the inherent problems that entail until Caesar's time. He's the one who in 46 B.C. decided to adjust and correct tracking days according to Aristarchus. Beyond that, we got the Mediterranean world in sync with the Roman (the Julian) calendar. Which tells us obliquely that each area of the world had its own way of measuring time, so figuring out what June 21st in your calendar would be in mine was a nightmare. After G.J. Caesar, however, the civilized world fell in step with the Julian system and so did we.

Incidentally as an aside to break up this protracted monologue, the word "calendar" comes from the Latin calends which was the first day of the month. "Kalends" because that is when you paid the interest on your debts. The payment was entered in a "kalendrium", an account book, ergo, "calends" graduates to calendar. (Tho by now I'm beating this into the ground.)

But coming to where I wanted to be. How did we get from AUC (*ab urbe condita*) into the A.D.'s and B.C.'s? We got there thru the work of a Scythian monk named Dionysius Exiguus (Little Dennis) who was instructed in 523 to "implement rules from the Nicene Council", which I think had to do with preparing the calculations for dating Easter. At any rate, his overall plan sort of put all of history into perspective by designating world events "before" or "after" a given point in time. The dividing point (the world being pretty Christian and the Pope being his boss), the benchmark was the birth of Jesus. A date, by the way, undefined in the scriptures and ascribed to two different periods: before the death of Herod the Great (4 B.C.) and "when Quirinus was governor of Syria" (10 A.D.), the month itself also being up for grabs. (December 25th arrived as the day in the 4th Century.)

Little Dennis began with the system in place at that time, one used by the church, dating historical events "from the first year of the reign of Diocletian", i.e. 283 A.D. Don't ask me why. The emperor had been a persecutor of the Christians, so using his coronation as a starting point is very strange indeed. But since Diocletian had been as systematic and organized in terms of managing the empire as anyone before him, there may have been a reason to use his era as the starting block. In tracing this back, Dennis dated Jesus' birth as occurring 753 years after the founding of Rome. Then took it forward from there and put everything in his new system, X years after the birth of Jesus and X years before. Must have been a major piece of research and cataloging to bring the whole Christian world's dating system up from 240 after Diocletian to 525 *anno Domini* (the year of our Lord), then to take it all back in systematic and relative fashion. Can you imagine factoring all that with Roman Numerals? Wow! But he got it done. With one problem. He missed the birthday of Jesus (don't ask me how or where) by four years. Thus, Jesus is born "four years before Christ".

The mystery and the miracle lay in lining up people and events from several different national sources and getting them into a common sequence.

We'd have a list of pharaohs prepared by Manetho, find the Greek Olympiad, record the Hebrew king chronicles out of the Old Testament (" ... in the 18th year of King Jeroboam ... Abijam began to reign ... he reigned for three years ... in the twentieth year of the reign of King Jeroboam, Asa began to reign ... "). We'd add the consular terms of the Romans plus *ab urbe condita*; the Assyrian king lists and ditto with the Persians, Seleucids, and who knows who else. This laid out each nation's timeline; then transposed each different record to a common calendar or analog in its relative B.C. or A.D. position. When finished, we can tell who in Assyria or Egypt or Rome was a contemporary of Josiah, who "was 8 years old when he began to reign and he reigned 31 years in Jerusalem", i.e. the period 640-609 B.C.

How Dennis did it amazes me. What a major contribution he made to historians, politicians, biographers and chroniclers. An item we take for granted, unaware of the confusion and ambiguity relative to these matters in the ancient world. As we begin the new century or new millennium, we ought to make January 1, 2000 Dennis Exiguus Day and raise a glass in his honor. After all, he's the one who determined when a millennium begins and ends. ■

P.E. Reminisces About the Millennium

December 1999

We might be over doing this business of changing centuries, moving into a new millennium, but it is, after all, a very unique experience. Think back on the number of people in history who have lived thru that moment when we move from one epoch into another. To determine just how many we'd have to know "the number of people" who <u>existed</u> since the first humanoids moved out of Africa a million years ago to populate the rest of the globe. Anyone want to guess how many individuals have walked the same earth as we, since the beginning of the entire experiment? We are about six billion strong now in the world today. Only estimates I have seen of cumulative population (and this was years ago) was something like 5,000,000,000 persons. If we have more than that many alive today, and if we then double the figure of the two just to be safe, we are looking at something like 20,000,000,000 Homo sapiens existing in the total human experience.

Which comes up to the astounding fact that 30% of all the people whoever lived are alive today. Americans make up 4.3% of today's population. So if my math is correct, it says that 1.3% of the total all-time human population are living Americans. Something like 72 persons have come and gone for each one of us alive today in the United States of America.

We begin by saying this is a rare sort of experience, i.e. very few of that 20,000,000,000 were ever around to watch one millennium end and a second begin. When this happened last time (999 A.D.), our guess is that there were maybe 280,000,000 folks inhabiting the planet. But we doubt seriously they had a huge celebration to commemorate this rare historic quirk. To begin with, about a quarter of the population was Chinese, living during the Song Dynasty, and of course, using their own calendar. One year would have ended and another began. No big deal. Islam, stretching from northern Spain, across North Africa, all of Arabia, across the Tigris-Euphrates water course, then down into India, stretching into Southeast Asia; Islam constituted another 21% of our population, but geared to its own calendar. It was the year 391 to Mohammedans and the peoples whom they ruled in their vast and fragmented hegemony. In the new world, the Mayan culture, by 999

A.D. was past its prime and marked the period as 10.8.12.5.0., a designation as esoteric and enigmatic as are the Mayan people to me. In much of Europe, the coming date was designed briefly as "M", which I think is the Latin symbol for 1000. If we are still using Latin a lot, that makes sense.

And since most of us have our ethnic origins in Europe, we'd be more likely to wonder how our forbearers greeted this special moment in time. And the answer is "with varying degrees of interest", ranging from the fanatical to the "ho hum". The brightest guy in Europe might have been Pope Sylvester II from Aurillac in Aquitaine (France) and though he was aware of the loonier fringe being obsessed with the apocalypse, he was a scholar, thinker, astute politician, pragmatist, and must have read Augustine who advised against taking the prophecy in the Book of Revelation too seriously. He (neither Sylvester nor Augustine) believed that at the stroke of midnight, when the thousand years since the birth of Jesus had arrived, the Lord was coming back with his angels to assemble mankind for the final judgment. There would literally be hell to pay when he got here because those among the populace who thought much about Catholic theology were convinced that "many were called but few were chosen", and most mortals were so sin-ridden and defective they would spend long stints in purgatory or go straight to hell because of their wickedness. The return of Jesus was not necessarily a great moment of rejoicing. And we have accounts of Rome being thronged, crowded with pilgrims; many now clad in sack cloth, penitent, and worried to death about the final trumpet. The Pope

Built to last for generations.

sort of pooh-poohed the whole business as gently and as theologically as he could, but then most people were not in Rome hearing the Pope or aware of what he was saying or thinking.

Europe was not a happy place at the end of 999. The Viking raids continued to plague many parts of the Atlantic Coast. Britain was limited to a modest section of the Midlands with all the rest in foreign hands, be they Scots, Irish, Welsh, Saxon, Jute or Norman. The national states of Europe had not as yet evolved except for a tiny sprout. In France, the start was clear, but meager. After the long and often dubious reign of the Carolingian kings (Charlemagne's successors), the Frankish barons, along with Gerbert of Aurillac (soon to be Pope), engineered the overturn of the reigning dynasty when the crown prince died in a horse-riding accident. Before his supporters could find a successor, Hugh Capet was crowned king and began the Capetian Dynasty which would create and rule France thru the line of Valois or Bourbon till the fall of Louis XVI in the French revolution (circa 1800).

Point here is, that England, France, Italy, Germany, the Lowlands, Central and East Central Europe into the Balkans were still in the mode we know as feudalism. This is a collection and connection of dukes, margraves, archbishops, counts, barons, earls, electors, and you name it, all owning lands, forts and castles; functioning as small political entities within a larger domain run by a king or margrave, a prince or an emperor. This was not an age gifted with much sensible organization, and very few of these birds got so strong they provided a lot of security or continuity. Not enough to become ecstatic as we celebrated the first New Year's Eve of a new millennium. Supporting all the clanking of armor and the clatter of mounted horsemen was an economy for the most part agrarian. And the lot of "the common man" who constituted it was dismal indeed. It is depressing even to imagine the daily grind of the peasant from one generation to the next, unworried about whether the apocalypse was about to occur or not. He was worried about where his next meal was coming from and how he would make it through another winter which was about to descend. Living in a crude hut, probably made of sod, white washed, a thatched roof, a hearth of flat stones on the dirt floor where a fire would provide a bit of warmth and cook the food, one day was just like the next to him. Whether the King was Louis V (just done in by a reckless horse) or Hugh Capet, it

made no difference to him. The rules of his servitude were the same from one earl or knight or king to the next, and from one generation to the next. He tilled his small farm and paid a third of his crop to the landlord plus an occasional assessment from time to time. He probably slept in the same bed his grandfather had used and probably dressed in his cloak as well; and maybe wore his father's shoes. To provide warmth and safety, his animals … any pigs or cows or horses he might have, along with dog and cat … slept in the hut with him. It was, thus, one BIG happy (?) family. Odds are the hundreds of thousands of peasants in Europe, slogging along day after day, wouldn't have the equipment to tell what day of the week it was and, thus, totally oblivious to December 31, 999 A.D. They were geared to the seasons, not the days, and their connection with Mother Church who could have enlightened them was a bit remote to say the least. If we are all worried about how 2000 is going to affect our society on account of Y2K, our progenitors were spared that anxiety.

If you come to the idea that life on a farm in France, Belgium, Germany or England was almost unbearable, you get the picture of what it was like ten centuries ago. The world, their grim outlook, the abysmal ignorance and poverty, the depravity and spirit of hopelessness would be all but impossible for us to honestly understand.

But all the world was not like Europe in 999 A.D. If in our century, the west has sort of run the show and given to mankind most of its technology, medicine, agronomy, science, political models, leadership, Levis, tennis shoes, movie stars, jazz, and beatniks; that was not the case a thousand years ago. Islam was the bright star then. Preeminent among European cities was Cordova. Right, a little town in Spain. On December 31, 999 A.D., it was a city of 450,000 people (some sources say maybe 250,000); it was part of the Mohammedan empire and perhaps the largest city in the world. The Caliph of the province was Almonzor who appears to have provided a good deal of the city's wealth thru extensive military campaigns. But though a bit long in the tooth, he was able to see the 11th Century arrive and, thus, the second millennium. Juxtaposed with the hard, grimy, and dreary fortunes of the people in Western Europe, Cordova was an amazing spectacle. The land is sunny, of course, the countryside rich. The population at that time was polyglot: Arabs, Jews, Berbers, Blacks, Christians, and native Spanish stock, probably still of Visigothic origins. The city was clean, paved streets, lighted streets, fresh water, 700 mosques, 3,000 public baths, sewers, grand villas along the Guadalquivir River, and countless libraries — the big one possessing 400,000 volumes. (This is before printing; must be hand-written manuscripts.)

Cordova is, of course, hooked by culture, religion, and politics to the Islamic empire which stretches halfway around the globe. What evolved was a vast mercantile enterprise which linked up India, China and Southeast Asia to the rest of the world, providing relatively safe caravan travel, extensive merchant-marine activity, building a world economy out of produce arriving from the Indian Ocean. Given safety and order in much of the Middle East, given wealth, thriving economies, and huge appetites, the Orient blossomed with an outpouring of goods and commodities. Silk, tea, spices, pepper, nutmeg, incense, jewels, gold, ivory, exotic fruits and vegetables, the game of chess; we think the concept of zero; the first oranges and coffee, paper, spaghetti, gun powder … though this might be after 1000 A.D. Point is, that the interchange of goods and ideas brings benefits on an exponential scale and raises the standard of living to a degree which makes Western Europe look like what it still is, barbaric.

The greatest of Jewish scholars in the Medieval Period was perhaps Miamonides, a product of Spain, but of Arabic training. The brightest guy in the world in 1000 A.D. was probably ibn-Sina, called Avicenna by the west, he is described as "a Renaissance man while Europe was still stuck in the dark ages". A bachelor who liked his toddy from time to time, Avicenna wrote the classic works on medicine and philosophy for the Arabic (and through borrowing) for the Western World. Fact, his text on medicine was used by Europe as the gospel till the 17th Century. He was 20 years old in 1000 A.D. and had "completed all of the science". He was an attractive prize for a rich court and traveled extensively, lectured, taught, and wrote over 100 books. One of his interests was "squaring" (reconciling) Greek philosophy with Christian theology, harmonizing religion and science. His fame here was such that Thomas Aquinas read him eagerly as he wrestled with the same issues.

The Mohammedan rulers across this expanse of empire had trouble getting along with each other, and there were inevitable and persistent tussles, but nonetheless there existed a large repository of learning, culture, replete with magnificent buildings, improvements in agriculture, in medicine, the sciences, in mathematics, and technology. With commerce and freedom to trade and travel comes the interchange of ideas. All this linked up to the Arabic expansion (and thus inadvertently to Europe), the largest country in the world in 999: China. Ruled by the Song Dynasty, it is likewise an amazing "piece of work". I don't know about you, but my liberal arts education taught me nothing at all about its history. All I learned is that Marco Polo traveled there, and that at some time, China invented gunpowder. That's about it. I should have learned that at the beginning of the second millennium of the Christian era the Song Dynasty in China was a land of 80,000,000 people. Its trademark was "orderly and virtuous governance", maintained by a bureaucracy of some 20,000 civil servants called mandarins. Officials who bore the responsibility for governing the world's largest empire and selected for intelligence, moral integrity, and discipline. They were carefully and skillfully trained and were monitors as well as practitioners of Confucian teachings. Under their direction, the nation achieved a prominence and stability rarely seen in any annals. Resulting, again, in brisk economy and considerable ingenuity. The Song production of iron in this era was considerable, <u>seven centuries later</u> Britain was producing only half the annual Song quota. The first printed books were made here; explosives arrive; so did the mariners compass; and four-decked sailing vessels to carry 1000 men were built. The capital city of Kaifeng housed 500,000 inhabitants, the second largest city in the world (or by some accounts the <u>first</u>). The quality of the government was such that for the

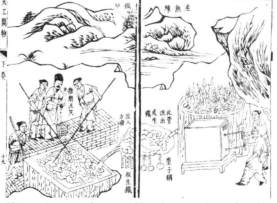

Chinese iron workers smelting iron ore to make pig iron and wrought iron. The left half of the illustration shows the puddling process, while the right half displays men operating a blast furnace. This illustration is an original from the Tiangong Kaiwu encyclopedia printed in 1637, written by the Ming Dynasty encyclopedist Song Yingxing (1587-1666).
(Source: Wikmedia Commons.)

next four centuries, China lead the world in technological development, commerce, and industry. They should have told me more about this remarkable people in grade school.

The other bright light, moving back toward the west, would be the greatest power in Christendom at that time: Byzantium. In 999 the Byzantine Empire was riding high, having regained much ground lost to the Turks. It controlled all of Asia Minor and the eastern shore of Greece — the brightest, most sophisticated, and most impressive of the European states. It sat astride much of the trade coming out of the east and for centuries earned both income and profit from wise management of same. A nation of 20,000,000 in 999 A.D., its history looks a bit like a roller coaster. The city was founded by Byzas (a Hellene from Megra) in 658 B.C., enlarged and fortified by Rome and made capital of his empire by Constantine about 320 A.D. The city and its culture were under steady pressure from Islam, but it would be another 4½ centuries before the Ottomans would finally breach the walls and convert it to an Ottoman capital. Though, as we look at the year 1000, all seems well and surely a big celebration was held in St. Sophia, the enormous oriental basilica built by Justinian four centuries before.

There is a limit to a reader's patience and, thus, to the number of geographic locations we can include in a single editorial, even if it only happens once every thousand years. The melancholy aspect to this situation is the retrospection involved as it is superimposed upon subsequent events. The history of Europe, of Byzantium, Cordova, Western Europe, and China has filtered thru the shades from time to time. It is a jumbled and unhappy tale. Western Europe, the clown and derelict of 999 A.D., turns out to be the hero. Looking at the map today, Cordova is a mere tourist attraction. It has no role in shaping great events and is no longer a model of culture, city planning, heterogeneity, and splendor. Islam itself although still powerful remains so <u>only</u> because of a thing called "oil", little of its power is due to Arabic ingenuity, organization, political or mercantile acumen. Without oil, the Arabic world would slip into third-class experiments. China's story has been a long, see-saw, and dismal one, and for the first time in a century, there seems to be signs of progress, movement, and change.

The bottom line on all of this is recognizing our inability as a species to govern our affairs or to keep things balanced and in good order. Churchill observed in one of his writings that when the Roman legions left Britain in the last of the Fourth Century, they took with them some of Rome's distinguishing characteristics, like running water and planned sewers, which promptly disappeared from England <u>till the Victorian age</u>. The question is, why cannot a people maintain its level of achievement? Why is there so much back-sliding? Is it not sad to see citizens in a given city whether Cordova or Samarkand, or Kaifeng or Baghdad worse off today at the end of a millennium than they were at its start? Why do we allow the jamming and glutting of peoples and traffic; the overloaded drainage and sanitary systems; the tasteless water and the industrial smog? Who is in charge of our cultures? Who is managing our systems? Is it destiny? Given pressures at a given time in a given place? Do peoples despise their own traditions so much that they resign from protecting same? Maybe the effort to maintain the glory is too great and rather than exert ourselves, we'll let it slide and hope someone else can see to its preservation.

The great enemy of a given people or region or system for most of our millennium has been violent attack by a foreign oppressor. Or it has been, in an equal number of instance, the ineptness and incompetence of our leaders. Rarely could a given village or city do much about assault by a superior force when well planned and led. But surely if the only problem is one which we create, harbor and tolerate, there is other recourse than nonchalance and indolence. As we watch the century and the millennium slide away (really over the course of the next 12 months), we need be mindful of this disgraceful history which is our record as a people. We ought not let the next generation be denied the privilege and achievement we have garnered for it. Let it not be said that our grandchildren are less well off, more poorly housed, tended, educated, and governed than are we, but just the opposite. That we have brought them this far, and we are not going to give an inch to fate, destiny, the Democrats or the Nine Gods. History, from now on, shall not repeat itself. ■

2000

In The Loop

March 2000

A lot of us are scrambling to stay in the loop on technological advances, particularly in the area of communication, that being an area pullulating with new ideas, gadgets, and modifications; wonderful efficiency, marvelous accommodation, endless variety, and great expediency. I'm way behind in the search and scrambling to convert in order to communicate with the contemporary world, but as I stumble along, hope I'm not rationalizing when I wonder <u>if efficacy and speed</u> ought be the ultimate objectives. My good friend Martin Yager brought current technology to my attention. (Martin is our Sales Rep in Fort Wayne, holding the northeast frontier for us.)

He is resistant to Voicemail. (Here is a <u>real</u> throwback, right? A Neanderthal!) When people call the Fort Wayne store (he maintains), they <u>want</u> something. They expect — fact, have a right — to talk to a live, thinking, upright creature with a cheery human voice. <u>Not</u> an automated Voicemail system with 12 options, none of which pertain to the reason for the call. Someone who seeks our services and has the right to a hearing. Ergo, he will hear a live voice on our end of the line or won't find us home. If this seems a trifle primitive, this <u>is</u> the way it was eight years ago and had been since Mr. Bell invented the telephone. What would have happened if he dialed his assistant on that historic first call and said, "Mr. Watson, come here, I want you", and what he got was: "Your call is very important to us. But all

our lines are busy. When the first line is open, we'll get back. We estimate, given the current backlog, it will be 46 minutes. But please hold on; your call is important to us." (In the background you hear a muffled but protracted chuckle.) The person who responded doesn't know you from Adam's off ox, so how the hell could he/she "care" one way or another? At which point we have neither speed nor efficacy, but instead a new element: caller irritation.

Fair scores, we've all had some success with the automation and been able to find the answer to our question. But there are other times when it gets maddening. Why is it that people who write the instructions think all the idiom, terminology, and arcane techno-talk are familiar to the world? Why, in the phone system isn't there a panic button that gives you a live voice saying, "We are sorry our system is so bloody confusing. What may I do to expedite your call?" No way. Unable to negotiate the multiple choice options, we often hang up, ticked off, and wonder about a society growing increasingly hostile to people.

Of course, there's a reason for eliminating the human element. It's the drive in American business to keep down costs and provide better service. To lower costs we cut something out (like a telephone rescue operator) even though this "economy" damages the end product. Nonetheless, business continues to scramble, honestly trying to do it all better, faster, cheaper. The resort to <u>systems</u>

Presentation of MacAllister 40-year Service Award to Mike Toffolo (on right).

is a way to reduce people (and commensurate costs like health insurance, unemployment premiums, profit share or 401K contributions, Social Security contributions, vacation pay, etc. ad nauseam). Working counter to our efforts is the rising cost of a professional workforce. There are not a lot of good people <u>looking</u> for jobs (unemployment around here is about 3%); ergo, talented practioners command handsome salaries and we need their skills. So if cost-conscious on one hand, there is wage-<u>increase</u> pressure on the other with<u>out</u> proportionate rise in the charge for our services.

Another offset (the squeeze) is out-sourcing — buying the commodity elsewhere. From whence do most of our fresh-cut flowers come; most of our melons, berries and bananas; most of our radios, shirts, TVs, and Nikes? They come from abroad. Isn't this cutting out a ton of American jobs? Right, hundreds of thousands. But why? Because foreign flowers and fruits and shirts and portable radios are infinitely cheaper than those "grown" locally. Would the housewife agree to a 40% increase in the cost of all these things in order to bolster the American worker's status? Hah! You can bet me! The objective of the market is to provide the best product at the cheapest price and essential in that dynamic is locating the cheapest labor costs, often half of the total price of a commodity. In an oblique fashion, this might be a <u>good</u> thing for the average American <u>not</u> involved in the flower or fruit or Nike business. Because as it contains prices, it holds a tight rein on inflation, which if unchecked, not only raises hob with American households, but with America's business enterprise across the board. Raising the selling price of our produce can put us <u>out</u> of world competition. Then sales drop, profits plummet, eliminating not only salary increases, but salaries themselves. Count the loss of tax revenue as other (cheaper) producers move into our markets. Then plants close, even tractor dealers, grocers, and florists go belly-up in the dénouement. Bill Clinton himself couldn't talk us out of this one. Point being, the unremitting challenge to contain costs is real. It hangs like the sword of ole "what's his name" over not just we in

the business world, but all of us.

So America has held inflation to a minimum by building more cars and pouring more steel with a smaller workforce. Simultaneously, eking out a profit (smaller this year than last). Because we have ferreted out waste, instituted every economy we can employ, and resorted to much technology. But we are on a treadmill and sustaining a precarious balance, losing one element (the customer, product line, the bank, staff, inventory, right price etc.) in the teetering interlocked and over-balanced agglomeration jeopardizes the entire structure. This is all free enterprise, and it is the adventure upon which we have embarked. No complaints, but this is not a cake walk.

I was around in the old days when our buyers made money and viewed our accommodation as integral to their success. Now there are times when they see us as part of their cost structure (food chain) and wonder how <u>we</u> can participate in <u>their</u> cost reduction program. Which makes for a merry scene as you can well imagine. And which may account for the rental rage now waxing fiercely across the land. But I'm deviating from my point, which is recourse to economies depending on current technology, economies that eliminate people.

The major revolution effecting people is extensive use of computers, capable of producing more transactions than clerks can process manually; recording more data, accumulating, analyzing, tabulating same, while also performing actions (like automatically ordering parts) "than was ever dreamed of, Horatio" in the old days. All of which reveals the secret: increasing productivity from both person and machine. It's impossible to crank out today's parts, service jobs, invoices, deliver 600 new machines a year, process a couple thousand rental transactions the old way. Not without a 30% increase in people. Non-revenue producing people. We could not survive today at this level <u>without</u> doubling and tripling our output per person. So why not rejoice, why not look ahead and around you instead of dreaming about what used to be? And the answer is nostalgia for the missing component: the interaction between <u>people</u>. Probably less in my business than most others I know, at

Chris Nold, MacAllister PSSR, with a customer.

least till the Internet takes over and purchases are made by people <u>we</u> don't know, from sources <u>they</u> don't know.

My father would go nuts in this situation. If he couldn't interact daily with his own workforce, chat with the factory, and had to sell machines without the discussion with the buyer, he'd feel cheated. He wasn't a very sophisticated manager of systems, but he was a superb "relater". His element was not yards per hour, but the human family. His success came not because he was the owner, but from his skill in the human encounter. In his day, had no peer. (Once told me he had sold over 30 stationary gravel processing plants, while with Drott tractor, more than anyone else in the entire Midwest.) He would hardly enjoy doing business the way it is carried on now. He was not, alas, an apostle of change. Why change that which made you a success?

We aren't going back to his style because it doesn't work that way anymore. But apprenticed in the early days, I note the depersonalizing aspect of business today. On the big scene we (America) are doing lots of marketing <u>without</u> sales persons. Try magazines which come to my house by the gross; check the Internet. And we have shifted the servicing aspect as much as possible to the owner. If you don't believe me, try to get someone from the phone company to come out and check what you think is a malfunctioning system. Their Voicemail solution is to tell you where to go to buy another phone. Throw this one away. My complaining is not going to change anything because a new generation is rapidly maturing who thinks the phone company was always this way and that service in general is supposed to be performed through voice instructions which you, the owner, then carry out, thank you very much. In other words, the benchmarks that evaluate or rate transactions are changing, and the one I had in mind is obsolete. Doesn't say it isn't gonna work this way; just says relationships between persons are minimized, and the concern about the buyer is dissolving like Frosty, the Snow Man. If big enough, we don't <u>have</u> to care about the buyer. Caveat emptor.

I sat through a seminar recently on service operations for construction machinery dealers. Conducted by a consultant who had never run a service department, but who was long on data, surveys statistics assimilated, and vicarious experience in other dealers' shops. One theme was the need to raise service rates. Said if raised 'em $5.00 an hour tomorrow, the customer would never notice. When he is down and panic stricken, he wants action and won't quibble. Despite the advice, we are <u>not</u> raising our service rates $5.00 an hour whether anyone notices or not. Because <u>we</u> sure as hell shall "notice". The rate ought not be determined on what people "notice", but on the basis of what services we deliver. There is a fair charge, and it is based upon our costs and what the traditional margin of profit should be, not on how much one can get by with. Here is a guy who having no direct contact with owners views the customer as lambs ready for shearing. Caveat emptor. A very unhealthy attitude.

In our world it is hard to be effective through mass marketing. We don't have a commodity that puts everyone into a single category; we can't service all the same way. When you get enormously big (G.E., Westinghouse, Motorola) and become a nonentity, that is what happens. But given the fact that each of us is different, whether in operating style, economic, well (or ill) being, degree of intelligence, standards for performance, or you name it, "one size" can not "fit all". Our commodity has to be tailored to the conditions which makes each different than the other. And it takes <u>people</u> to make that distinction, which is why in the tractor works we need to know as much about our owners and prospects as we can. More of them exist at this juncture than any <u>one</u> of us can know. But we have enough people in the field everyday who <u>do</u> know what makes a given owner tick: field servicemen, 16-18 salesmen, parts and service reps, and specialty guys in asphalt paving, agriculture, coal, and small machine usage. Their assignment is to see each transaction as a special opportunity to relate to an owner (or prospect) and figure out how it is we might help him. Because if we are not interested in him or his situation and how that is best handled, we aren't going to be of much benefit. When we are no longer an asset in his equation, we have lost track of our function and reason for being. ■

Reflections

June 2000

I just discovered the late great war (World War II) could still be teaching us lessons. Or maybe the instructions not clear 58 years ago, only come into focus now because I read *"The Borrowed Years"* by Richard M. Ketchum, a profile of *America* in 1938-1941. An era, by the way, I recall with great nostalgia because I was "there". Sixty years ago about now I graduated from college, couldn't find a job (17% unemployment) so joined the U.S. Army Corps and became an Armament Officer in a P-38 Fighter Squadron … all during those "borrowed years". The book is a trip down memory lane <u>and</u> a rehearsal of America's attitude, economy, political leaning, military status et al at a given timeframe in history. The climax to the story came on December 7, 1941 when the Japanese attacked Pearl Harbor and as the author reviews the pertinent detail, brings about some startling insights.

One lesson being the calamity which results from adopting policies derived from ill-chosen, but passionately-cherished convictions. (Of which we had many and sundry in those days.) Foremost among same was the conviction that Europe was a separate world, enmeshed again in another catastrophic paroxysm that could somehow be contained,

P.E. during WWII.

i.e. none of it would spill out to bother us — 3,000 miles away. Fact, America was so self-sufficient we had no need for relating to events going on "over there" since "they" were "always battling about something anyway". Even the plight of thousands of Jews fleeing Hitler's jurisdiction was <u>their</u> problem so we turned them away from <u>our ports</u> when they sought sanctuary. The source of this attitude was a handful of statesmen persuading us to ignore what was in reality a struggle for the very survival of western civilization and forcing a "spectator role" on America.

Their persevering recalcitrance resulted in a lack of military preparedness which proved to be an unmitigated disaster. Their reasoning was hard to figure. We had passed a Selective Service Act in September of 1940 requiring 16,000,000 young men to register for military service as a way to bring our Army up to some strength. (It was about the size of Romania's.) As the term limit was about to expire, the President fought an uphill battle against diehard isolationists to have Congress renew it. Hitler had already overrun Austria, annexed Czechoslovakia, conquered Norway, and decisively defeated the French and British armies. All Europe was controlled by the Axis Powers. Mussolini had taken Ethiopia and Japan had occupied Manchuria and was on the way to conquering China. Yet, we don't need a standing army or military conscription? Give me a break! Only after protean efforts did Roosevelt and Sam Rayburn get the extension extended, squeaking through the Senate with 45 votes (there were 20 abstentions) and the House by one, lonely, single, solitary "Aye".

It is mind-boggling to contemplate a nation which created the revolution in technology, industry, medicine, communication, arts, transportation, and political innovation warped by such parochialism and myopia. But this goofy idea that we are a people apart from the world — and be better off — was a dominant theme. We recited a mantra originated by William Borah, George Norris, Father Coughlin, Robert Taft, Gerald Nye, and John L. Lewis, repeating again and again: "A plague on both your houses; our interests and obligation lie exclusively within this nation."

The point in his rambling peroration is simple. Our perceptions on (or about) a given topic lead to conclusions about same, and on the basis of what we know (or think we know) we reach given positions <u>and from these</u> determine to take — or withhold — certain actions. However, in the course of gathering data, the sources we select are often those bending the same direction we are bent; the material we read is often chosen <u>because</u> we agree with the writers. We <u>resist</u> looking at opinions that are contradictory to our own. In this unbalanced process, the truth escapes. Caterpillar had a slogan that makes better sense: "Intelligent people, reasonably informed, seldom disagree." If we received accurate information, we arrive at the same conclusion. When info varies, our opinions vary; when our intelligence, perception, and objectivity range, we come to different conclusions.

The Pearl Harbor story is a classic example of opinionated people in high positions requiring conformance to their assumptions on the basis of authority, or position, but rarely on the basis of objective evidence, truth or empirical example. Instead there were gut feelings, emotional reactions, and partisan pride involved; sanity or common sense both totally absent. And so might it be with all governments either occasionally or consistently and so might it be with other institutions, yea, even some Caterpillar dealers. But the costs as reflected in this story are incredible.

The tragedy came through interconnected gaffs, misconception, and blunders careful judgment would have avoided. The Japanese had tipped their hand as to their intentions several times. But people observing the evidence were smarter than God Himself and knew how irrelevant such data was when contrasted to their own fixed opinions. In January of 1941 a Peruvian envoy had informed a friend in the U.S. Embassy of a war plan drawn up by Admiral Yamamoto to attack Pearl Harbor. Message went up to Admiral Stark whose Naval Intelligence said, "Ridiculous. There's no such plan in the offing." The Army looked it over and declared the Peruvian tip a phony.

We had broken the Japanese secret code some years before and knew what they were communicating. Japanese spies in Honolulu for long months sent reports on ship identities and movements, on docking positions and repairs, counted airplanes and loci; gave info on weather, repairs, and naval traffic. We intercepted all these, sent same to Intelligence where they were examined, pondered on…and filed. Enigmatic, but not serious stuff. Despite other

signs and omens, a popular conception existed that no matter how tough the Japanese war machine, Pearl Harbor was "the most impregnable fortress in the world". Admiral Kimmel claimed "an attack upon Pearl would be suicide". Even the Japanese knew <u>that</u>. Yet in the war games of 1936, a Naval exercise carried out a surprise raid on Pearl by sailing in from the north at night to release aircraft at dawn and "attack" the harbor. General Martin and Admiral Bellinger were commissioned to find a defense against such an unlikely prospect and came up with an air surveillance plan, i.e. patrol 360° around the islands using 150 B17's and other supportive aircraft. But in the fall of '41, only 109 B17's existed <u>in the</u> world. <u>No surveillance</u>. Nonetheless, General Marshall assured Roosevelt in '41: "With adequate air defense enemy carriers, naval escorts, and transports will begin to come under air attack at a distance of 750 miles. This attack will increase in intensity until within 200 miles of the objective when the enemy will be subject to attack by all types of bombardment closely supported by our most modern pursuit." Humph!

As Japan continued military expansion and saber rattling, and as the outlook for peace diminished, Admiral Stark got nervous. On November 24th he sent out a memo, suggesting "a surprise aggressive movement in any direction" might occur. Could be — but never against Pearl Harbor! On the 27th, he stepped it up to a "war warning" against "an amphibious expedition" though he never mentioned the target.

We had spent nine months negotiating with Japan to no avail and suddenly two things happened. On November 1, 1941 they changed their codes and call signs. We scrambled to unravel the new encrypting; then December 1st they changed them <u>again</u>, a real sign something is awry. Next, the Japanese ended negotiations in such a bellicose manner, the President said: "This means war."

In late November we discovered several huge Japanese convoys leaving home waters, but going where? Maybe the Kra Peninsula, the Dutch East Indies or Singapore. On December 4th Frank Knox (Secretary of the Navy) said, "We are very close to war. War may begin in the Pacific any moment. But I want you to know no matter what happens, the U.S. Navy is ready. Whatever happens the Navy is not going to be caught napping." Yeah, sure! On December 3rd the Japanese Consular and Diplomatic Corps were ordered to destroy all documents, files and papers. American Forces continued perfunctory routines.

At 6:40 AM December 7th Lt. Outerbridge on the Destroyer Ward, cruising the outer harbor at Pearl sighted and sunk a Japanese sub. Then within 15 minutes picked up and likewise destroyed a second one, reporting at once: "Attacked, fired on, depth bombed, and sunk submarine operating in defenses sea area." The message was sent to the duty officer, to Admiral Bloch, to Kimmel who opined he'd come down when he shaved and dressed. By now it is 7:40 AM, 15 minutes before the first Japanese planes arrived.

Don't forget, the Nips had maps of the harbor and knew where planes were parked, where every single boat was moored, and where the batteries protecting Pearl were located. Once the attack was under way, the Oklahoma prepared to do battle. Lt. Ingram suddenly discovered he could not open fire because (get this) the firing pins had been <u>removed</u> from the big guns and were being polished up for an inspection. Beyond that, all the ammo was down below so the magazines could be painted. On the Cruiser Phoenix, the crews had to hammer off the locks on the ammunition boxes, then had to take down the awnings covering the guns, only to learn that the anti-aircraft fuses were set for peace time to prevent them from exploding too close to the ship. Useless.

You know the rest of the story. Ten battleships sunk or badly damaged; 10 other vessels (cruisers, destroyers et al) ditto; 188 planes destroyed, 159 damaged; 2403 men killed; 1200+ wounded in 1 hour and 40 minutes. Because opinion setters and those in command totally misjudged the situation and sent a misleading message down the ranks: The conviction that Pearl Harbor was impregnable, the most unassailable fortress in the world; that no one can possibly bring an armada of 30 great ships, a flotilla 50 miles in diameter, across 4,000 miles of open sea, afloat for 12 days and not be spotted. Yeah, right. They can do it if the radar you were issued months ago is inoperable because the Commanding General

Pearl Harbor attack on Dec. 7, 1941. Photo taken from a Japanese plane during the torpedo attack on ships moored on both sides of Ford Island.
(Source: Wikimedia Commons)

thinks it is ineffective gadgetry. Despite its proven value in the battle of Britain.

America's top leadership in "*The Borrowed Years*" used thought processes which fell into a given pattern, but <u>excluded</u> the consideration of certain questions. Minds were blocked, then locked. The <u>right</u> questions were never asked. With a given supposition that Pearl Harbor can never be attacked, all considerations of a defensive nature were thus irrelevant. So when General Short got Stark's "War Alert", he knew what the threat had to be. Since it cannot be an attack on Pearl Harbor, it has to be sabotage. So it was sabotage he protected against. "They aren't gonna get our planes, since I'm ordering all the ammunition removed and no refueling. To make guard duty easier, park the planes as closely together as possible. So they can't sabotage our troops, I'm taking back all their live ammunition. They might want to sabotage our big guns so I'm taking all that ammo as well and locking it in safe places five miles away." (Brilliant, General, just brilliant!)

All actions taken on the basis of a presumption about what a given threat <u>might</u> be, sizing up the threat wrong, lead to action diametrically opposite to what they should have been. By now making the point clear.

Many of us have trouble hearing Bill Clinton because of how we view what this bird <u>is</u>, so our antipathy to the person blots out the message, even when he is right. Mere prejudice here might not be damaging to me in the tractor business, but the same intransigence applied to a diminishing market, with rising interest costs can be very painful indeed. Business decisions need to be made on the basis of dispassionate judgment not on intuition or gut reaction. Lessons from a past experience need to be relevant to this situation and not randomly applied now because they worked once. Conviction alone has nothing to recommend if it's mistakenly held. John Brown had an answer to solving the slave question. Passionate, well meaning, but totally wrong headed blundering. The truth is more easily arrived at when all options are explored and in pursuit of a course, I have found that by thorough analysis of all the options, one survives. The process of elimination proves the way to go.

This experience reiterated the need to listen to what people say since most of us learn more from listening than talking. No pertinent questions ought to be disparaged, disregarded or discouraged. The longer an option is held these days, the more it needs to be examined for pertinence. Conditions in America and the world have changed dramatically since "*The Borrowed Years*". The only caveat about that prospect being the fact that human nature hasn't changed all that much. ■

Rumination on "The Fourth"

June 2000

There is a vignette about George Washington, encountering a burying party outside Valley Forge in the bitter winter of 1777-78 and stopping briefly to converse with his men. Trying to sympathize with them, suggested he understood the situation; he explained it had been a very hard, miserable time. That like them, he was anxious and disappointed and looking down the pike he could see very little change in their fortunes, meaning, more starvation rations, more bitter cold with miserable inadequate clothing, more battles, more blood, and more bodies shoveled underground as far as he could see. Although the war was essential to the future of this people and although the courage of the troops was unparalleled, the price being paid was inordinate. He ended up saying, "This liberty will look pretty cheap, when no one dies to gain it".

As we commemorate the 224th Anniversary of the famous "Declaration" and reflect on Washington's observation, wonder if he was right. If faced with the same sort of challenge today and confronted with consequences which thrust us into the unaccustomed misery of drenching winter rains, erratic rations, bivouacs in the mud, long marches and bloody fighting, how many troops could <u>we</u> keep in the field defending that liberty those minutemen militia purchased for us? When I visit in Egypt or Greece or Italy, think cynically of a situation where given nations exist as objects of veneration to millions of foreigners <u>on the basis</u> of what men had created 2000-3000 years ago; we holding contemporary natives in low esteem for letting the ancient past mark their moment of glory in the sun as they coast yet on the legacy of heroes dead for millenniums. Bringing us to the question, are we different? Yes.

Using the same visiting-tourist comparison, no one coming to visit here (stopping first at Disney World) can suggest that America is past her prime, a spectator to history,

not when all the world apes our lifestyle, tries to emulate our governance, seeks the same open and mobile society, the same standard of living, and makes our dollar the world's currency. We <u>are</u> the major influence across the board in this age. Which really begs the initial question.

The guys at Valley Forge and Saratoga, at Guilford Courthouse and finally Yorktown gave us the option of creating our own systems, refashioning the way men govern themselves and live together as social creatures. So fortunately we have shifted the focus to what we have done with the opportunity that colonial generation provided. I.e., we have capitalized; have done well with what they bought for us. It does not say, given the similar trial which they were endured, we would automatically shiver and bleed, ache and march; yes, even die with the same courage and selflessness. To most of us, this liberty does look pretty easy, and there is no way we can imagine the enormity of the cost. But fair scores, there is nothing about us that shapes or conditions us to put ourselves in those circumstances of 1776, 1777, and 1778. So the question remains unanswered.

But note, please, that as heirs to your colonial victory we have blundered and stumbled and continue experimenting, but you can take pride, George, in the fact that, thanks to your Army's sacrifice, we have created an experiment that has no parallel in the annals of the species and provided conditions which have given more benefits, privileges and opportunities than any Utopia ever dreamed of. In that sense, we have kept the faith and can say to the ghost of the Continental Army and its leaders "What you have handed to us we have cherished, capitalized upon, and exploited. We have been responsible stewards of your legacy and deployed the liberty you gained to enrich this people immeasurably and provide a beacon to the entire world." ■

Painting of George Washington by Charles Willson Peale (1741–1827).
(Source: Wikimedia Commons.)

Enigmatic … Jerusalem

September 2000

As the Jews and Arabs scuffle over their respective futures and deal with repatriation, return of the land, resettlement, reparations, and governance, they likewise glance sideways at another issue, one identified as "Jerusalem". Who owns it, runs it, claims it, and who lives in what parts of it? Of course, each side says it is his capital; each thinks he should own and run the city. Hmmm! I have usually pooh-poohed the idea of an Arab Jerusalem, conditioned for years by my Biblical grounding which declared the site is sacred to the Jews. No other city in the world is as linked to a given people or destiny as Jerusalem is linked to the House of Israel. I've been re-enforced in this conclusion by examination of the Arab claim. Which I think reads very much like a fairy tale. Well then, do you believe Mohammed, on one of his venturesome journeys, was hoisted up bodily (avec his horse Baraq) and transported miraculously to the City of Jerusalem? And from Mount Zion he was thence whisked away into heaven? There he saw the seven levels of paradise, after which he was re-whisked back to the holy city and finally home to Mecca for breakfast. Giving the Muslims a "bill of sale" or a title to Jerusalem on the basis of this slightly outlandish claim seems a bit far-fetched to me. Arab proprietorship got realistic, however, when backed by the prophet's armies, by physical occupation of the city, the erection of dedicatory mosques, and the failure of any Christian power to resist Bedouin conquest. I don't know how many followers of the prophet accept this "magic journey" legend, but in terms of intelligent people working their way through some pretty basic and fundamental issues, this rationale for ownership struck me as being a little far-fetched. Historically, Mohammed may have visited the city while working the caravan business with his uncle, or for his wife Kadijah, and thus, was acquainted with its history. We know he leaned heavily on both Jewish and Christian sources for his theology, and he had several Hebrew heroes among his pantheon of saints. But I think we have to find better proof than this. Moreover, in the sundry and subsequent annals of Islam — be they written by Umayyad, Abbasid, Seljuk, Mameluk or Ottoman hand, each with a peculiar period of glory, power, pantheon of scientists, scholars, warriors, and theologians lasting some 1,360 years — none ever put its headquarters in Jerusalem. Repeat: It was never the Arabic or Mohammedan political or military center. But the city itself? The venerable walls and crenellations, the winding narrow streets in the old city, the minarets and markets? This is a Mid-Eastern pattern. It's built the way Arabs built the cities in the Middle East. The Dome of the Rock and Al-Aqsa Mosque are prototypical Arabic architecture; the existing walls were erected by Suleiman the Magnificent; the souk or bazaar is typically Arabic. It's an Arab town, populated mostly by Arabs since the 7th Century.

Now, how about Jewish claims to the city? Alas, too much like Islam. Meaning, mostly legend, folk tale, tradition, association, poetry and prophecy, all familiar to Christians, conditioned to believe that Jerusalem was once the abode of God. The heartbeat of Hebrew (or Jewish) culture from time immemorial, but only because Jewish writers said so. Menachem Begin called the land "Judea and Samaria"; said God gave it to the Hebrews as a patrimony. (A cynic could point out wryly that Yahweh also lost patience with the line of Jacob, cancelled the covenant, and gave the land to the Chaldeans first, then to Cyrus.) The sagas of the Jews, the Biblical tradition, and the perpetually nourished aspect of hope which have inspired them for two millennium's ("next year in Jerusalem") are what infer Jewish ownership of the city.

With respect to realistic Hebrew occupancy, it does start pretty early. Jerusalem was taken by David's mercenaries about 992 to become his personal administrative center, replete with a palace, tabernacle, barracks for his troops, a harem, plus a big treasury. David's estate became nationalized under Solomon, working toward nationhood, but even that lasted less than a century. Seventy-five percent of the Hebrews (ten of the twelve tribes) broke away in 922 and set up their own state (called "Israel"), leaving Jerusalem the capital of "Judah", a small entity no larger than Marion and Johnson Counties with a population maybe one-tenth of ours while the 75% of Hebrew citizens who had rebelled made Samaria their capital. At least they did for the two centuries they enjoyed autonomy. Judah was conquered in 586 B.C. and did not regain the land 'til the Maccabean revolution, circa 165 B.C., when it again became the center of Jewish political and religious authority. But they blew this in a family row about 63 B.C. and found themselves "annexed" by Rome. So fair scores, although Hebrew "occupation" of the city goes back to the early 10th Century B.C. (3,000 years ago), Jerusalem has been the capital of a viable Hebrew/Jewish nation for only 100 out of the last 2,500 years. Until in 1948 when (Phoenix-like) it arose from the ashes of a bitter war. Vivid in writings as Yahweh's gift (part of the covenant promise), it remains the land most sacred in all the universe to the Jews. But though marked and sanctified by the heroic presence of a legendary past, it has little claim on the basis of possession or occupation. Do the reported and rehearsed promises of the Hebrew God constitute a title anyone can take to the bank as collateral?

But wait, there is another element in this picture, watching with interest and if not Indian wrestling for control of the sacred city, still wanting to protect its turf. It is the third faith, Christianity, which could enter a claim as good as the other two. Its founder was gibbeted there in the most dramatic execution in history, and his legacy and magic carried on through the subsequent generations to create an institution which dominated the Western World for nearly a millennium. The martyrdom of Jesus sanctifies Jerusalem and so do his tomb, the route (Hmmm!) to Golgotha, point of his betrayal, place of judgment, scourging, site of his Last Supper, etc., all sacred ground to the church which preserved not only his message but his memory. Getting to the point, Constantine became a Christian in something like 324 A.D. and made Christianity the official religion of the empire, and of course, Rome governed Jerusalem. Ergo, its status as the official religion, reaffirmed in the Byzantine incarnation would make the city's faith Christianity. Not Judaism, Zoroastrianism, Manicheism, Mithraism or Islam

(which isn't here yet), it is Christianity. Granted, that only lasted for 300 years, but it was the faith of the city 'til 638 A.D. Why did it change to Islam then? Because the Arabs conquered it and the conqueror calls the shots on how and whom the state worships. Jerusalem became a Mohammedan city. But note, this is not a decision arrived at by referendums, plebiscites or meddling peacemakers. Nor did it become an Islamic center because of any miraculous horse ride. The city had no option. There was some religious tolerance, but all the power was with the Arab conqueror. And no one argued with it. So when it shifted from Christian to Muslim, it did so through conquest. That was so unequivocal a tactic and strategy; it dominated the destiny of the city for the next 1,280 years (minus a century under Crusader rule).

How's come that sort of arbitration which gave it to the Arabs then is not valid today? I mean the Muslim world rejected the United Nation's division of the land into two parts, Israel and Palestine, back in 1948 and decided they would make it all Arab. They vowed to drive the Jews into the sea. Had they really defeated the Jews, what sort of discussions do you think would be going on today? Do you see Yasser Arafat, Dictator of a Greater Palestine, sitting down to discuss how much land goes to the Jews and who is gonna manage Jerusalem? Had the Arabs won the 1948 war, there'd have been no Israel. So, having lost the war not once but three times, how's come we have to argue with anyone about who owns and runs the ancient city? The Jews conquered it in 1967 like the Arabs did in 638.

Of course, that kind of argument isn't going very far, partly because a great portion of the world's oil lies in the control of our friendly Arabic colleagues (none of whom wanted any part of Clinton's July tête tête). If the Jews get a little truculent from time to time, it's because they are only going to lose the

Jerusalem in the early 20th century. *(Source: Wikimedia Commons.)*

war one time. There is no regrouping for them. But in order to go "the extra mile" and if the Christians are not going to enter the list to claim their pound of flesh, where do we go from here? We continue to negotiate. The imprecise and nebulous titles to the land being of little real value, we are dealing with pressures, political fracture and disunity in both camps, emotional fixations building for generations, and a striking paucity of reason in the whole business. Can you see what is missing in this scenario? Control? Authority? It is a circumstance created by forces and prejudices most of us in America cannot appreciate: action and reaction often dictated by pot luck. There is no plan or program to impose, and there is no authority figure calling the shots. It is like raising a family with four children and letting the kids do what they want. Bedlam. If they ate when and what they wanted, attended school when and if they wanted, dressed and behaved without parental guidance, developed their own sanitary habits, ignored the rights and property of others, we'd have hell on our hands. Worse than a nut farm. Families require rules, patterns of behavior, examples, conformity, and a lot of things all imposed by the parents. What is missing in the Middle East picture is the "parental control", a boss; what is rampant is unilateral national obsession.

The Old Testament creation story begins by Elohim shaping order out of chaos, designing our galaxy with its intricate, incomprehensible rhythm and interlocking unity. Chaos, even political chaos, is a throwback; it's an aberration within the design of a functioning universe. (Alexander Pope reminded us that, "Order is heaven's first law"; ergo, orderly systems are the divine plan.) But unhappily, even natural order is not ideal and must accommodate hurricanes, forest fires, volcanoes, droughts, typhoons, and floods. All transitory in nature and rarely lasting half a century like Arab-Jewish antipathy and conflict erupted amid our contemporary Mid-East condition.

Maybe to take the onus or the responsibility off the two fighters in the ring, we call a timeout, tell them the match is forfeited, and the world is tired of this fruitless and unwinable contest. "So no one can blame you for what happened, Yasser or Ehud, we are taking over. Here is the way it is going to be …." Maybe the next President does this, finds the solution which is maybe the terms Ehud Barak was considering: a piece of Jerusalem goes to the Arabs, maybe it is the eastern quarter including the two mosques and the rest goes to Israel. Maybe it is all run by an international commission except the holy institutions. Each side can make it his capital, own property, do business, pay taxes, travel freely, and control his own religious affairs. But governance and security are under the United Nations, or some international control. I think someone has to find the right course and get tough. Do something. If it turns out wrong, then adjust it. But to leave this time bomb undiffused is courting catastrophe.

If there is a conclusion to this monologue, it will be duo. First: waiting around for either side to reach an agreement upon its terms for settlement is "whistling Dixie". There will be no national consensus in Israel or Palestine and to hold off until we reach internal agreement is to wait forever. It is the wrong way to start. Take a reasonable position; then build the consensus. Second is like unto the first: if either side thinks it is going to get what it wants, what it's "entitled" to, what is "right" (according to our own legends) or what we can prove in court belongs to us, we'll be waiting 'til we hear Gabriel's trumpet. Any settlement proposed will leave both sides figuring they got rooked. Each is entitled to his opinion, but the security of the area and the settlement of this dilemma supersede local opinions on the validity of partisan claims. ■

Christmas

December 2000

Christmas time, the Yuletide season, is not particularly significant in the Islamic world and is probably not a major feature in the celebratory agenda of the Orient either, but in our so-called "western culture" there are few occasions more universal. It is the biggest day we have, augmented by the biggest shopping splurge of the year. Without stopping long to analyze it, research on the handy, dandy computer gave me an indication as to why this might be the case. Why is it such a blowout and so widely celebrated? Because it is the oldest of religious events. It's the earliest of cultural commemorations, and has some sort of replication or existence in practically every, single age and area from which we have records. Fact, it is as commonplace as the seasons because it is derived from nature's rhythms.

The Babylonians in 2000 B.C. sort of set the pace when they identified and marked the shortest day of the year. Because <u>after</u> December 21st each day would commence to get longer and mankind would have one to two minutes of additional daylight. Reason: the great god Marduk was "renewing the world" for another year. He fought a mortal duel annually with the monster of chaos to assure order in the world and after his successful struggle we would be secure for another 12 months. Huzzah! The citizens rejoiced in their god's triumph and expressed their jubilation through religious processionals, feasting, carnivals, house-to-house visitation, singing, lamps, and merriment. Went on for 12 days and was called (as I'm sure you remember) Zagmuk. The Persians noted the solstice as well and adopted the same rituals, but called the festival Sacaea and added the novel gimmick of trading stations…the slaves became the masters, the workers became the bosses.

The Egyptians, a thousand miles away, also recognized the advent of winter by making whoopee for 12 days, analogous with the 12 months in their calendar year. It was also the birthday of the God Horus, and he liked a good party. The Greeks in their turn had a festival in support of Kronos who would battle Zeus and the Titans. The longer winter nights in Hellas brought not only fear of the dark, but likelihood of "monsters" called kallikantzaroi. Kept underground during the year, these demons escaped during the 12-day Christmas period to roam the earth. Mostly, what they did was practical joking — souring the milk, snarling the horse's tail, peeing on the hearth fire, etc. To scare them off, the Greeks burned a bright log (or else old shoes, whose smell repelled the monsters).

The Romans were not to be left behind and called this winter celebration the Saturnalia, after Saturn, the god of seeds and seedtime. It started same week as the solstice and lasted till the 1st of January. It included masquerades, huge meals, home visitation, the exchange of gifts, literally "decking the halls" (with garlands of laurel and trees lighted with small oil lamps). Grudges were forgotten (supposedly); schools, business and courts closed, and apparently life came to a standstill till the celebration was over.

Later on, folded in with the Roman holidays, but zeroing in on the <u>25th</u> of December (there is some jiggling of calendars here) was natis solis invicti, the birth of the unconquerable sun. This god was called Mithra and his birthday happened to fall on December 25th (made official in a proclamation issued by the Emperor Aurelian circa 270 A.D.). Made doubly significant because the same emperor made Mithraism the official state religion of the empire. But Constantine 50 years later had a different idea. He kept the same date, but made <u>Christianity</u> the religion of the empire since he was using every device he could find to bring a sense of unity to the empire, ergo, the merging, blending, uniting of the old religion's trappings with the festivals and ritual of the new. It was easier for the pagan element to digest Christianity if we could celebrate in the same way. Incidentally, it was Constantine as well who made "the venerable day of the sun", a day of rest moving the early Christian Sabbath from Saturday to "<u>Sunday</u>". Finally, Christmas became liturgically

'Twas the night before Christmas…

correct when the Roman pontiff, one Julius I, chose December 25th as the official birthday of Jesus and, thus, from 350 A.D. onward we had it endorsed by both state and church.

There is a lot of merging, borrowing, adopting, and replication in this story as it moves through the ages and regions. But it starts from Day One with the fact that gods or <u>The</u> God controlled the pulsation of nature and rather than being capricious was irrefragably inexorable in his consistency; a fact we made certain through our offerings and our chanting, our sacrifices and ceremonies since every time we do these things on the winter solstice, the days start getting longer again. The Christian church (when it got the mass fairly well structured) had a special holiday mass, Cristes maesse, soon "Christmas", and said church continued to add other contemporary understandings and components during the Medieval centuries as it finished converting Western Europe, bumping eternally into a lot of other celebrating ceremonies and special days.

We noted the reference to "12 days", a basic unit of the sexagesimal system created in ancient Babylon and sort of carried on through in this theme. The church found it in pagan cultures like in Norway

Rear view of Notre Dame.

where part of the solstice was celebrated by bringing a huge Yule log into the fireplace and setting it afire (a background light and a back<u>side</u> warmer) as we feasted and made merry. The log hauled in burned about 12 days. Cattle were often slaughtered at this time of the year to avoid feeding them all winter, and so for a few weeks we have a surfeit of meat, ergo, the feasting. We used the 12-days motif, again, counting 12 days after December 25th and end up with Epiphany, January 6th, the day the wise men arrived in Bethlehem bearing gifts to the Christ child.

We got St. Nicholas from a 4th Century church bishop who lived in Smyrna (Modern Turkey) and noted for his generosity to children. Since gift-giving was part of early pagan festivals, we attribute to this venerable character the novelty of delivering gifts by galloping on horseback over the roofs and dropping candy down the chimney into wooden shoes the kids placed before the fireplace. St. Nicholas became Sinterklaas to the Dutch, and from the Dutch in Early America evolved to Santa Claus. The Christmas tree might come from the "paradise tree", another medieval institution celebrating the advent of Adam and Eve, the tree decorated with, what else? Apples. The Germans in the Reformation Period added fruits, nuts, painted egg shells, cookies, candles and candy, etc. Of course, they brought this to the new world and were already commonplace in the early 1800's among the Pennsylvania Germans. (My German grandmother decorated <u>her</u> tree with lighted candles, cookies, popcorn, strings of candy et al.)

There is surely a point in any given essay when one comes to the "So what?" part. Like, "If there is a <u>point</u> here, what is it?" Given the age and diversity of the Christmas holiday, one point is already noted: The occasion or the commemoration if not as old as man himself, is at least as old as civilization. It is triggered by natural phenomenon and was noted and feted generally in all cultures. Note, too, it is religious; is related to a "divine" source, an acknowledgement of the supernatural. We recognize there is a higher power in control of nature so the solstice is a divine mark, symbol of an orderly universe.

Recall as well a way to observe this day or period is not with solitary fasting, but with communal singing or chanting; eating; with jubilation. It becomes a period of gladness, marked by gatherings, feasting, drinking, dancing, and other expressions of joy. In many instances it involves giving presents, which is a common gesture, but one unusual since it brings happiness to someone else. Note as well, the event was often coincident with a given birth — Saturn, Mithra, Horus. And, of course, Jesus. The common spirit of exaltation or celebration linked the god in the process as though he were the sponsor of happiness and wellbeing — at least for the moment. But after the party was over, all of the gods save one, turned respective backs on the human condition and returned to their cavorting, scheming, seduction, trickery, and badgering we poor mortals. Only one left a "presence" and his "presents" lingered to mark, not merely each year, but each day of each year. The gifts which he introduced were not wrapped in gold and scarlet paper, but rather psychic or spiritual in nature, evident in attitude and demeanor, in gentleness and warmth which, when embraced, remain year round as though all the year were like the Christmas season. The gifts were optional to use or to ignore. A grace extended which had value only when in use; when we respond. So from that standpoint, there is nothing seasonal about them.

Christmas occurs to highlight, to shine the beam on, and to remind us once again that this charm and mystery exist.

Note, too, that in the western world a dozen prior expressions are subsumed into the Christian pattern or else have fallen by the wayside. In the process what was previously religious has become so inculcated in our culture it is part of our secular calendar. In this long evolution, we depict as well the impact which this faith had not only on a given holiday (holy-day) but on the entire texture of our American life. Our regard for the dignity of the person; tolerance of differing points of view; concern for the less fortunate; status of women; equality before the courts; high regard for fairness and outrage at injustice; wide scope of freedoms et al do not derive from any other source, creed, system or society than the Christian faith (whose spiritual and ethical wellspring is Judaism). All of which have been woven into the fabric of this society converting subtle <u>religious</u> tenets to elements of culture. If not totally fait accompli, at least we have sketched out the principles of how we ought to

function and articulate the ground rules for the game of life.

It is impossible for us to understand how ancient peoples linked together "the gods" and the celebrations. They were sort of divine birthday parties; or they were annual seasonal commemorations or they were efforts to engage a whole people in a common event. But whatever logic or tradition or practice was applied, the holiday became a metaphor. The <u>celebrations</u> became acts of worship; the giving of gifts expressed the largess of the god; feasting on a sacrificial animal was dining with the god to whom it had been given. What happens over time is we remember to do the shopping for presents, and we decorate the home, and we eventually bring in a Christmas tree, but all these have become ends in themselves. They become completely independent of any religious connections. Today, people who are not Christians enthusiastically make merry on "Cristes maesse", but independent of any religious connections. I would hold in Christianity we find more tie-in than was present in the ancient cults out of which it evolved… because the Christian church still plays a role in the nativity event through its members. We are publicly and annually reminded (in case we have forgotten) exactly what it is we <u>are</u> celebrating. Insofar as it is possible the biblical themes and characters present in the first Christmas are present among us in town squares and church lawns and household rooftops. In store windows, in cards, television programs, news articles, and you name it, we relive the story of Jesus' birth and in that fashion keep refreshed in terms of how this all started and what it is we are remembering. Moreover, the faith that inspired this "metaphor" is still alive and kicking, still nourishing our hope, repeating its message, and rehearsing a tale and a mystery it has propounded for 1700 years. As it does so, continues to see Christmas joy in the faith, fellowship, a sense of exuberance, seasonal music, the centrality of the family, and hopefully sustaining courage for the days which lie ahead.

Have a rich and Happy Christmas! And note, too, the days <u>are</u> getting a little longer. ■

2001

See Things As They Are …

March 2001

The economy (local, national and even international) is getting a lot more attention than it used to. One reason, of course, is the change in ground rules forced upon us by the tremendous competitive pressures, which though rarely examined, are the driving element that restrains inflation, holds prices down, spawns technology, but does so only through an incessant search for more efficiency. This can lead to curtailed overtime, layoffs, consolidations, mechanization — which replaces people with systems, one odious example being the ubiquitous Voicemail with its nonchalant dispassion and irrelevance when you try to get some information about a bill you don't understand from the telephone company. Instead you get seven options, none of which is pertinent to your problem. The device, however, will remain because it cuts "people" costs and cutting costs is a key to survival. In free enterprise capitalism there has always been a keen awareness of competition because that is what puts the loser out of business.

So we are on a perennial search for economies, short cuts, and superior products to make us unique and providers of more value. Since the economy undulates, there's a "boom"/recession rhythm which both strengthens and deludes us, making life tricky. Strong economies create overconfidence which leads to plant expansion, larger inventories, and ebullient marketing. But then in corrective periods or crowded markets or a sharp curtailment in spending, the policies that work great in the boom are the very tactics that lead to our undoing. I've noted before that the major competitors standing toe-to-toe with me back in the '60s and '70s have for the most part vacated the scene — involuntarily - because conditions re-

quiring dramatically new styles appeared and the awareness that there were too many people producing too much for the market to absorb; i.e. were building machinery faster than it could be used. The system is self-correcting. When there is a surfeit of businesses in a given sector, the market itself winnows out the weakest arbitrarily by eliminating its profits and sends each to a silent, unheralded retirement or to the bankruptcy court. The survivors move cautiously on in conformance with their seasonal routines. Patterns of past success in a previous cycle — this tells us — will be no assurance of success in a new and different circumstance.

And in our system, anyone who <u>wants to</u> can start a business. But only the very lucky or the professionally skilled will stay the course. We have a sort of economic promiscuity about start-up that lacks both criteria and discipline, and the result is wholesale failure under heavy going because most are badly managed. Meaning, they fail because they are under-capitalized; because the product is marginal, marketing inadequate, servicing bad; some are victims of catastrophes, i.e. floods, droughts, etc. or escalated interest rates, strikes, labor shortages, etc. Point is, <u>managing</u> is a lot harder than <u>entering</u> a business, and once in action, every day, every month, the challenge to keep it all in synch, all producing and consistently profitable is irreversibly ineluctable. Result is few people in business succeed; none by resting on the oars or drifting with the current. There needs to be continual movement, tinkering, readjustment, change. We see the response to competitive pressure in airline consolidations; watch all the local banks get gobbled up; noted a decade ago the departure of the local grocery, the friendly meat market, the home delivery of milk and bread, the retirement of the friendly pharmacist, desperation of downtown merchants and the incursion of national chains. The message is clear. The buyer wants cheaper prices and he gets them by the sacrifice of service. He saves a buck but ends up with Voicemail rather than a sympathetic person. He gets a better interest rate, but has to provide identity to cash a check in a bank branch he has used for 30 years.

Dealing with a cagey buyer, competition, a supplier cutting back, an uneasy Dow Jones, please conclude free enterprise is a risk perpetually threatened from several vantage points, leaning heavily upon its owner's leadership or its hired manager's skill and subject to a lot of outside influences which impact disastrously, sometimes favorably. Like many human institutions, the skill with which the manager employs in solving problems, managing people, providing services, and realistically managing his organization to function within the business environment existing now determines whether the enterprise — not survives — but succeeds. Implicit in all this is the dynamic of the challenge, the trial of arms aura, the pitting of one group against another, the contest to see who can survive. We are on this course for two reasons. If you have the right mettle, this is the adventure of the 21st Century; it is still about seeing how tough I am and how well I can deliver.

Secondly, if we plan right, organize, market and manage well, we can also get rich; we can build a major institution that makes a difference in the lives of its people and its community. (Did someone say Eli Lilly and Company? Fabulous place to work, major contribution to the world of pharmacy, medicine, and personal health [insulin and Prozac]; model corporate civic leader.) So the challenge is both to the ego and maybe to the greed. The dynamic is thoroughly typical of the American experiment ever since Massachusetts' Bay Colony or that of Jamestown or Penn's experiment in Pennsylvania.

MacAllister's CAT Rental Store, Indianapolis.

It's a test and an experiment; its proof positive of human ingenuity and the creative capacity of the given Homo sapien to do something significant.

My guess is that the headlines about Chrysler's merger with Daimler Benz, about Olds going out of GM's model line, about Lowe's Movie chain being sold to Onex, about Cummins Engine cutting payrolls, about Bill Gates' problems, and the dive in Cisco and Lucent and AOL and Amazon.com, and most of the other stocks I own, is not a period of unusual unrest. It is a cross-section of what has been occurring since time immemorial, on a more modest or unobtrusive scale. Now there are more chips in the game and far more people playing since far more Americans than ever own stock. Moreover, the allure of technology and its revolution in the way we do or see or find or buy things has added a new dimension. The nature of the animal itself, its uniqueness and the fact that few of us understand how it works (even as we take off our E-mail) simply makes it more notorious ... more famous or fabulous or more newsworthy. The ferment which is the current economic scene, the worry about recession, and the adjustment locally in businesses we know who are taking some dramatic actions to correct and become more seaworthy, tends to give the whole picture a slant. Maybe even a bias.

Anyone who reads this publication knows by now the last person he would ask for advice about the stock market is this writer. But anyone involved in a capital-intensive business who is not checking the wind direction and velocity or watching for signs of impending "weather" is derelict in his duty. Figuring out where we are going in the next year or two is critical since plans for staffing, inventorying, credit lines, marketing, and you name it are not sudden reactions to a situation we just discovered. They are part of the plan to keep the company successful (i.e. profitable) by anticipating the needs and preparing accordingly. In the midst of this checking-for-signs et al and the appraisal of economic health, the total environment in which business operates is of some interest. I think it is good to know that as we do battle with whatever demons lay athwart the path, we take stock occasionally and note we are part of an economic system which is the most efficient in the world. Although it is hard to make comparisons with the "slave labor" of Africa or parts of Southeast Asia, etc., when compared with the western world and its systems, let us observe that none work at their respective jobs harder than we do. Fact, we are working longer hours than we did in the '80s — by 208 hours per year (about 10%). Fact, we work the equivalent of eight weeks longer per year than the average western European. This is not just the guys on the assembly line, it is from top down: owners, managers, supervisors, and employees. Thanks in part to the pager, the cell phone, the fax, and laptop. Maybe part of this is due to the fact that more people enjoy their jobs, and this might be due to the fact that we have fewer and fewer blue-collar type positions. At the turn of the century, 70% of America was oriented to agricultural or manual/service labor. Today, it's down to about 15%.

Speaking of salaries, reminds me of the mantra recited by Dick Gephardt and Tom Daschle. It's the fact that the rich get richer and the poor are stuck with the tab as a result. Overlooked is the fact that we are providing 3,000,000 new jobs each year in the United States of America; that the 20th Century created far and away the largest middle class ever seen in this nation or in history. That if the rich are sometimes getting obscenely rich, they are realizing a dream most Americans harbor, i.e. everyone wished he/she was a millionaire. But the political comparisons are badly skewed. The ratio ought not be what the worker at Microsoft gets versus what Gates is paid, it ought to examine what the worker earns today vis-à-vis what it <u>costs</u> to live and support a family: as compared to the same cost a decade earlier. Gephardt has his own comparison. He looks at someone who makes $10,000 a year compared with one who makes $100,000 a year. The former gets a 100% increase in his pay ($10,000) and moves to $20,000 a year, and latter gets only a 15% increase in pay ($15,000) and makes $115,000; and this is unfair. It has penalized the common man. The rich guy got $5,000 more ($10,000 versus $15,000). It makes little difference that the <u>percent of increase</u> happens to be 100% to 15%, happens to be six times greater for the little guy. What's that old adage about figures lie and liars figure? They do here.

Lost in all this gloom is the fact that any American today who is halfway qualified <u>has</u> a job if he wants one. We've held the unemployment rate around 4% for a long time (compared to France at 12%). Some people aren't working at what they'd like to be doing, but I wonder how much of that is different than it was a century ago. Of still further interest is the number of Americans invested in the stock market these days (60,000,000) and the number who participate in 401K's and in profit sharing

plans, added to their Social Security. It is hard to think of any generation in history who has prepared as well for retirement as this one. All the products of the economic engine drive our systems and pull along a good deal of the rest of the world in its wake. If you don't believe that, ask the Japanese what currency they use to buy their oil. The secret is (I think) free enterprise capitalism, probably getting freer under the current administration than it has been for a while. The reason the German worker costs so much to support and the reason the French worker worries about keeping his job is the strong intrusion of socialist economies into the life of the nation. The concept that says we shall take care of everyone irrespective of what he produces and we do so with taxes, which has to discourage large and serious reinvestment in speculative ventures and which fights the introduction of Wal-Mart into the retail scene because they are such tough marketers and provide so much more value than the local shops. The objective of socialist economies is to redistribute the wealth and in the process stifles creativity and enterprise. Wealth is easier to distribute when it is created in abundance, and taxing systems are more productive when they allow decent rewards for those whose business initiative creates payrolls. Profits and the taxes are derived from both, i.e. the generation of capital through free enterprise business endeavor.

Business, like life, or like politics or like a lot of other things hinges on solving problems. We are trying to be aware of those which threaten us in Indiana and particularly those hammering the tractor business. We have had 55 years to learn how to do so and hope the process of finding given threats and then dealing with them will stand us in good stead as we cope and change and refit to endure the shifts and see change which lies ahead. First of all, being sure of what the change <u>is</u>; then how it will impact our customer base and what we need to do as we react. I don't think this is a question of survival (I mean for us), I think it is a matter of <u>how</u> we shall do it and what it will take to stay profitable and then how long the pressure will last before we can look for a period of normalcy. Or maybe even figure <u>this</u> is normalcy, now how do we change? But the picture is not altogether clear, too much Greenspan. At the moment, we have too many signals, too many forecasters, too much guessing, and too much pessimism. I still like Marcus Aurelius: "See things as they are, and deal with them as they deserve." That ought to be Chris' motto for the next year or two. ∎

Remembering Becky

March 2001

On the 8th of January, Becky MacAllister passed away, a victim of congestive heart failure and sundry other maladies which had plagued her for the last 25 years. She had reached her 80th birthday on Christmas Day, and we celebrated same traditionally with all the family together in our Briar Patch home, participating in the sharing of gifts, champagne toasts, Christmas board, and the joy of family together once again for the holiday — for one last Christmas holiday. But by the day after New Year's she became restive and uneasy. Next morning she was obviously unwell, so I summoned the nurse, then the doctor, and then the ambulance. The staff at St. Vincent's told me at once it was congestive heart failure, and the situation was serious indeed. So during the next week in intensive care, the entire family was instantly gathered to extend love and support, taking turns around the clock in a vigil at her bedside, until our long partnership — 56 plus years — was over.

It had all begun when she met an Air Corps Captain on a blind date sometime in the fall of 1944 while he was stationed at MacDill Field in Tampa, Florida, and she was Supervisor of Surgery in Mound Park Hospital, St. Petersburg. One thing led to another and on the 17th of May, 1945, we were married immediately prior to my journey north for a discharge from a military base in Northern Illinois. After which we settled down in Indianapolis where I went to work for MacAllister Machinery Co., Inc. Becky was thus the daughter-in-law of the company's first President, wife of the second, and mother to the third.

Although a stockholder and a corporate wife, she found her career most fulfilled as a housewife and mother of four children. Raised in Georgia and nurse's-trained in Florida, she dutifully became a Hoosier, a Presbyterian, and a Republican as well as trusted aide-de-camp to a husband whose sundry activities and peregrinations tested her patience, stamina, and disposition. The fact that he did so many things and tried so many more was due in large part to her loyalty, understanding and ministration. She had a myriad of interests, one surely being travel, usually with me, but also count four different junkets to Europe with her grandsons and others with friends plus several with my mother. (We counted up to 40–45 overseas trips.)

P.E. and Becky MacAllister

Becky was an energetic, active, almost insatiable shopper, single-handedly supporting half a dozen mail order catalogue systems when not on the road in Oriental bazaars, Arabic souks or European shopping malls. (We average 20-30 catalogues a week — three to five boxes.) She was a fantastic housekeeper, a string saver, a generous giver, an omnivorous reader, proud grandparent, loyal cheering section, a great leaf raker, and a tender of shrubs, plants and flowers. She was intellectually curious, loved music, was a fine seamstress, a super mom, and "suffered fools badly".

Our final chapter together began on May 21st when out of the blue, she suffered a serious stroke while eating Chinese food after a Sunday afternoon movie. St. Vincent's Hospital, the therapy center, and finally the Forum Healthcare Center all did what they could to bring her back around, but she never regained use of her right side, suffered considerable discomfort, was depressed, disappointed, and finally weary of the massive medications and the "burden" she had become. Although I spent the first three hours of every day with her, it may have provided some comfort, but was of little tangible benefit in terms of the healing process. Saying we gave it our best shot, used all the advantages of modern medicine and technical science, but the physical frame at her age, debilitated by the long lung disease, an attack of cancer, and finally the stroke, combined to bring her life to a close. She left behind three children, five grandchildren, a discomfited husband, an empty space in our lives, and a thousand, thousand memories to mark her sojourn here. The recollection of who she was and what she gave continues to both sadden and console us as her family now moves on to live out lives enhanced by her influence and ennobled by her memory. ∎

Is The Lord "My Shepherd"?

June 2001

If we think a bit analytically about much of life, we conclude the world seems to work on two separate levels. Although seemingly coincident, a given <u>perception</u> about an occasion or an incident or historic occurrence or even Biblical assertion may fail to coincide with the <u>truth</u> of the matter. Assumptions aren't automatically truths, and mere repetition does not enhance accuracy. For example, there is a much-quoted Biblical aphorism that declares, "Money is the root of all evil." The quoter rarely realizes that the <u>real</u> text reads, "<u>The love of money</u> is the root of all evil." It was not the wealth of the rich young ruler Jesus saw as the weakness, it was his preoccupation and obsession with same. Or try, "The Lord is my shepherd, I shall not want … my cup runneth over … surely goodness and mercy shall follow me all the days of my life …", the beloved 23rd Psalm, an idyllic version of the Lord's care and nurture. Anyone who assumes this an eternal verity and waits for the Lord to bring contentment and success is in for a long wait. It doesn't happen that way, and it's a delusion to anticipate it will.

More to the point, the Chinese recently took advantage of an incident involving two airplanes and demonstrated the distance between perception and truth. The United States had a 35-year-old, prop-driven box flying over international waters, set on automatic-pilot yet and tooling along routinely to check on activity in a land generally enigmatic and a bit baffling to understand. The Chinese story adds a dimension that creates a new assumption. They say our clumsy vehicle, in their backyard, made a fierce and predatory attack, deliberately tearing up one of their fighter jets, and sending it into the briny deep. We say, truth of the matter is simple. A tub as big and clumsy as ours, with nowhere near jet speed, can never "take on" a modern jet fighter much less one with a military-pilot trained in evasive action. The reality here and the Chinese perception simply don't intersect anywhere along the line.

A classic favorite historic perception deals with the Fall of the Bastille in 1789, a trigger point in the French Revolution and the very origin of French "Independence Day," July 14th. The Bastille was a glowering stone edifice in the middle of Paris replete with appropriate dungeons and cells and all of the dank conditions — real and imagined — typical of such institutions in that period. It was notorious as a symbol of the decadent, frivolous, spend-thrift monarchy because it was here that political prisoners, critical of the inequities and unfairness of the regime, were held. And, to further the point, <u>with no</u> due process, no habeas corpus, often no trial, no accountability for arrests or appeal from the incarceration. So come the Revolution, it had to go. And thus it did; in a bloodbath that slaughtered the guards and released all the prisoners — all seven of them. Not hordes of defenseless victims, but a measly handful who came blinking into the light of day. This blow for freedom and righting of ancient wrongs suddenly had the strange light of truth cast on it. To make matters worse, none of the inmates was a victim of royal vengeance or tyranny. Four were deadbeat forgers; one was crazy; one a spy; and one an assassin. Any connection between the evils of the crown, the injustice represented in the system and this act of violence as a rectifying agent to redress ancient wrongs is at best ridiculous. Truth of the matter is, the storming of the Bastille was absolutely pointless and fruitless; nonetheless, this moment is memorialized in French history as some sacred epiphany.

To examine this comparison between what is perceived and what is the truth with more relevance, there is a terrific article in the latest "*Indiana Policy Review*" that picks up a series of favorite mantras of the liberal left (or of the average newspaper editor) pertinent to our day and time. These are common perceptions quickly juxtaposed with the truth. Dick Gephardt, for example, has (oft and monotonously)

"La prise de la Bastille" by Charles Thévenin (1764–1838)
(Source: Wikimedia Commons.)

repeated his perception that the rich are getting richer and the poor, poorer, i.e. the gulf is ever-widening. Truth of the matter is that today in America, the richest 5% of you harvest 19% of the nation's total income. Is that bad? Not as bad as 1930s when that top 5% generated <u>30%</u> of the total. Is this getting richer? Hardly! In every year since 1913 when we began to keep records, the top 5% got <u>more</u> of the total take than they did last year. With respect for the poor, who keep getting poorer despite the fact that Jesus thought would "always be with us", America has made a pretty good stab at minimizing it, if not eliminating it. There is the old element of vantage point: What makes for poverty? Last data I have says in the United States, poverty is income of $7,750 per year in a one-family household. From the international perspective, our perception of poverty is a joke. $7,750 turns out to be higher than the <u>average per capita</u> income in all the nations of the Third World, and our "poor" also earn (or receive) more income than the average worker in Greece, Saudi Arabia, Brazil, South Africa, Venezuela et al. Fact, our "poor" are "poor" comparatively, and we sympathize with them, yet rejoice in the fact that even among this group, 92% own colored television sets.

The poor get special attention from legislators because they are a body of votes. If we can give them the proper perception about our concern for their condition, we might be able to gain their ballot support and, thus, we extend the continual "class warfare" (instead of "welfare") which goes on. As the rich get richer, they do so at the expense of the poor who are getting poorer, according to Tom Daschle. And since he is going to rescue them from the rich, they might indicate their approbation at the ballot box. He is fighting their battle to stop getting poorer. He doesn't know this (or, come to think of it he probably already does), but the poor are getting <u>richer</u>, not in leaps and bounds, but in the previous decade, their spendable income rose by 6%; it did <u>not</u> fall. Maybe we could equalize this a bit by taking every penny of spendable income earned by America's millionaires and that might give the rest of us a break. Alas — not much. Truth is, if we took <u>all</u> they earned next year, that's only 4% of all taxable income (only enough to run the government for six whole weeks). Maybe not "a drop", but surely a "spoonful in the bucket".

I've always had a "thing" about taxes and wonder why I am taxed more than the guy down the street. The answer, of course, is that I earn more. I

have more income to tax than he does. The fact that I work and he doesn't, is superfluous. That I have worked for 56 years — invested, borrowed, hired, managed, and risked — has no bearing on the issue. I don't pollute more, take up more space, generate more garbage, require more police and fire protection, make more noise, need more room on the highway; it is simply because I earn more. Makes me wonder why the newspaper doesn't cost more, since I have more money to pay for it; why there isn't a different scale of prices for groceries, toothpaste, movie tickets, gasoline, hair cuts, and books at Barnes and Noble since the basic understanding of taxation is "from each according to his ability". The issue of taxes (back to the topic) is also subject to common and popular perception. Not that people who <u>make</u> more should pay more, but the perceptions that rich people don't pay taxes and certainly not their share. It is repetitive to point out that 1% of American taxpayers do pay — not 1% — <u>but 30%</u> of all the revenue generated by the income tax. How about the bottom 50% of American wage earners and their fair share? Turnouts, this group pays 5.2%. Is this a great country or what?

We read frequently of business consolidation and downsizing and plants closing leading us to <u>perceive</u> that a heck of a lot of Americans lost their jobs last year. And we all know some of them and grant to them, it is a major economic as well as psychological shock. How much is "a heck of a lot"? Truth in the story turns out to be three out of every hundred employed workers lost their jobs last year. Three percent were adversely affected.

If there is one topic more misunderstood than the rich-poor fable, it has got to be Social Security. First being the notion that Social Security is there to provide a retirement income for senior citizens. It started really as a supplement to the retired citizen augmenting what he had saved and the kids gave him. It grew in proportion because people are happier studying perceptions than facts. And it is numero uno on the list of discussions year after year because it is always running out of money. And it is running out of money because it is now supposed to supply full retirement needs and the mathematics leave it nowhere near self-funded. They are not returning to us what we put in. My check each month is $2,320. What in the world is going on here? And I never filed for Social Security. When I hit 70, the money just started coming in. I've been in the system since 1936, but long years back, I collected all I put in and zillions more. Which accounts for the problem. We weren't supposed to collect enough for a complete retirement program; it was to be a little kicker. Given the new understanding and practice today, Americans take out of Social Security all they have put in and then collect another cool <u>quarter of a million dollars</u>. My cynical guess is that if people over 70 are exempt from voting or denied voting rights, the hue and cry over "saving Social Security" would quiet down to a faint echo. Where the votes are, that is where a legislator's heart lies.

Truth and perception applied in the tractor business need to be reasonably harmonious. Perception is not random or casual conjecture with no penalty for careless postulation. If we sail merrily along assuming our service is great, but in reality it turns out to be "found wanting", we begin losing customers whose "perception" turns into fact. When they stop buying, we encounter an unpleasant, deleterious truth. Their judgment (not ours) determines how good we are and sees them leaving — or coming back. If we happen to think our product better than the competitors and over-sell and over-promise, we suffer a serious credibility — and sales — backlash.

If we think our sales force is great when it is honestly mediocre, the marketplace will note the truth, and we begin losing ground — rapidly. Equally critical in capital intensive business and more chimerical is perception about the strength of the economy. We have to plan ahead and estimate business six months to a year out. If we think it's gonna be super, but it turns sour instead, we suffer the consequences because we end up with too much staff, too much equipment, needlessly high interest bills, too many vehicles. The balance between perception and reality as they play out in the business world is a significant equation. Our perception had better be more than visceral reaction. It needs input from our consultant, from Alan Greenspan, intelligence from our customers and salesmen. It needs to be good as we can make it or the enterprise suffers. For most of us in business, it is more than a dialectical exercise or random gossip. Forecasting and business planning — the perceptions — are key to our profitability and the arbitrary <u>truth</u> of this year's profitability becomes the yardstick by which the dealership is measured. We have to achieve what we conceive. ∎

Dealing with Difference

June 2001

In mid-May an article appeared in the local paper about a judge in Illinois who handed down a ruling prohibiting the graduating students from including prayer in their high school graduating exercises. A suit had been brought by a student (whom we'll call Mary Jane) and pursued by attorneys of the ever vigilant Civil Liberties Union, leading to the "no prayer" ruling. This action struck me like a hammer. The issue, of course, is separation of church and state, something battered around over-much. In this instance, it looked to me like we are reaching way out to try and construct a case, using a marginal technicality to flex some muscles and to create a cause celebre where none, in all honesty, need exist. Article noted the school has included prayer in its graduation exercises for 80 years, and it was part of this year's program because the students who ran the graduation and did the praying naturally included it. The officials noted prayer was not something suggested by the school board or the administration ("the state"), so it was not official fiat, it was mere tolerance of an existing tradition.

Mary Jane didn't care about traditions. She testified that she had heard prayers at previous exercises and, "She was opposed to anyone praying on her behalf. She was pleased by the ruling", is the way the article read. The ACLU had its reading. To them it was "a great civics lesson" — the students learned that they can exercise their rights in a thoughtful, considerate and mature fashion. If this is "considerate", there is something wrong with my thinking. It would appear that including prayer in graduation ceremonies as informal protocol continued because the majority of the youngsters accepted, tolerated or even appreciated it. A fact of life Mary Jane failed to consider — or worse, considered and decided to arbitrarily change. The real civics lesson here is that one malcontent can get her way legally with proper representation and deny to the vast majority a prerogative we assume they enjoyed and expected. One has to wonder why we need to stretch so hard engaging our court and legal system in an occasion as specious as this: Someone prays for me — once a year — and I want it stopped. I'm trying to figure out how Mary Jane is damaged or harmed or even impacted through generic prayer, offered for a school. Wow! Does it seem contradictory to note the United States House and Senate have official Chaplains; City Council and Township board meetings begin with prayer, and all of our coins and paper money carry the slogan "In God We Trust"? Contrary to what she thinks, Mary Jane needs all the prayers she can get. Someone who chortles at imposing her opinion on others just to be mean is the very sort of person that really tests the faith. Not hers…ours.

I have been a member of the Civil Liberties Union for several years because I felt it shielded many from the tyranny exercised by the majority who, if unchallenged, could run rough shod over the wishes of the few or the helpless or the inexpert. Here is a case where it has become a tyranny of the minority, forcing its will upon the majority when there is no major threat to the community evident anywhere on the landscape. What have we achieved in this encounter to protect someone, defend someone, enable or ennoble someone? It is very hard to see how my prayers for another person can be upsetting, damaging, insulting or in any way demeaning to a given individual. Mary Jane says her "rights as an individual" were "upheld". Her rights here appear to be the rights to deny to the rest of her class a tradition long-established and faithfully observed.

Thomas Sowell had an editorial six months ago that depicted this side of our human nature in a most dramatic way. It came through "an old story about two Russian peasants, Boris and Ivan". Both struggled on marginal farms to put food on the table, fought the earth grimly for a livelihood. Their drudgery through the years was unremitting, and the only difference between them was Ivan owned a goat. A little edge here! One night a fairy godmother appeared to Boris, explained her unlimited powers and promised to help. Like, she agreed to give him one wish. He could have anything in the world he wanted. Boris thought painfully for a full minute and then said, "I want that Ivan's goat should die."

One would think we have enough trouble handling our own affairs and solving our own problems without spending time to see what damage we can inflict on others.

Dealing with lack of reason, specious judgment, or merely with disagreement is something the business world has on its plate much of the time. The way we handle it measures our success. An example which comes into play regularly occurs in machinery transactions and pivots around trade-ins. What are they worth; a dynamic putting people on two sides, this time one buying and one selling. A customer owns an old bulldozer for which he paid "x" dollars and now he wants to trade it off. In his mind there is a proportionate "used" value, a percent of the initial price that ought to be considered. Beyond that, he looks at replacement costs and in view of that comes up with a figure for his unit. A $100,000 machine ten years old ought to be worth $50,000 — if it is in decent shape. But the buyer (our salesman) knows that irrespective of what the owner thinks, the market pricing for that machine won't reach $40,000. Our guy has his price because we've "been there, done that". We are in the business of selling used machines, and in the case of Caterpillar units, are probably determining the market value. Because of other units sold for specific dollar amounts, we have positive evidence of the value. We are not guessing. The customer is dead wrong — to us.

But to hope his machine falls off a trailer or blows an engine as a way of dealing with the value disparity is leaving the issue unresolved. In order to "do business", one of us has to back down or come around or both of us have to do some moving. The discipline of the sales dynamic does not leave us unchallenged, and there is no court to which we might appeal for adjudication. We have to finesse the pricing conundrum, always wary of winning the argument but losing the sale.

Selling is a transaction in which we need two winners, not a winner and a loser. Each needs to be happy with the fact that his lot has improved and the experience has benefited both parties. So given no option, our tactic is to bring reason and evidence to the table. We want truth to decide the issue, and who can reject the validity of truth? We have to convince the buyer it is not our opinion we are providing but documented history. Moreover, our value is a professional one, the figure an insurance company would use if the machine were stolen or fell off a cliff; ours, the figure a court would use if the owner were

A CAT 345B excavator is used for road work along an interstate ramp.

involved in a partnership dissolution or a divorce settlement. If rejected, we suggest an auction will resolve the issue, aware there is no guarantee of getting half of what we have offered. A second tactic is shift the discussion to the value of a new unit — its productivity, durability, lower operating cost, ease of operation, and higher trade-in value. Age has made his unit obsolete which is the reason for our lower value and if he wants to realize the value he had in mind next time he trades, his value will be closer if he upgrades, gets modern. It moves up and down, but any commodity is really worth what someone else is willing to pay for it. Our experience tells us where that is. His book value, avarice, personal attachment or gamesmanship is real in his own eyes, but is not the universal standard.

He can reject our pricing and win the argument by going elsewhere to buy a competitive product and like Mary Jane, prove the validity of his stance. And though we grant here, "the customer is always right", it's a Pyrrhic victory. He will never get the product service anywhere we supply; there is a huge difference in trade-in values when he disposes of a competitive machine (versus what ours bring) (check the Blue Book records); he'll wait weeks for parts when ours are across the counter or overnight. The win, like Mary Jane's, is really an empty one and if it makes him happy, he's really proved nothing. ■

P.E. on Napoleon

September 2001

In the past year I have read five books on Napoleon (of the 100,000 that exist), amazed that three were contemporary, meaning 181 years after he "checked it in" at St. Helena, authors are still reanalyzing his history and impact. The conclusion reached from my new erudition is that Bonaparte was the most gifted and the most fascinating figure in western history since Charlemagne…or maybe since Gaius Julius Caesar. Well, he's close anyway. Lord Acton said, "The most entirely known as well as the ablest of historic men." Durant said, "We've not found in history another soul who burned so intensely and so long." Stendhal thought him, "The greatest man the world has seen since Caesar." So I thought a little review of his record might teach us what leadership is all about.

Bonaparte was born August 15, 1769 in Corsica of influential parentage, at least "influential" enough to get him into French schools, including the École Militaire in Paris where he graduated in 1785 as a Lieutenant in the artillery. After a slow start, he broke out of the pack when assigned to the Army of Italy, which ultimately embroiled him in a siege at Toulon where Royalist insurrectionists in 1793 had invited the British fleet into occupy the city. The hastily-gathered French republican forces were unable to pry them out, though Captain Bonaparte couldn't figure out why. The French troops were strung around the U-shaped harbor, their seven or eight cannons moved erratically and fruitlessly. Bonaparte suggested they mount cannons on a promontory called Cape Aiguilllette which controlled the forts and harbor. The diddling commander "didn't have the guns; a British stronghold protected the Cape; an assault would be too dangerous," etc., ad nauseam. When a new commander appeared, he liked the Captain's plan and told him to proceed. So Napoleon scrounged 100 cannons from up and down the French coast, bombarded the protecting fortress before taking it; then brought in cannons galore to the Cape and began shelling the British fleet in the harbor. It raised anchor at once and immediately lit out for the sea. The siege of Toulon was over.

He was an instant hero and made a General. Now fast forward to 1795 (age 26) when he was idling in Paris as the Estates General convened. The Paris crowd, dissatisfied with the assembly's record and whipped to the edge of rebellion by Royalist agitators, was growing larger each day and dangerously more truculent. Feckless politicians (again) formed no strategy to resist until someone said, "Where is the 'hero of Toulon', this bird, Bonaparte? Let's get him." They did. He took one look at the mobs, evermore brazen and on the move down several streets, and determined at once what to do. "Do we have any cannons?" There were 60 on the Plain DeSablon so he dispatched Marat at full gallop to bring them back; then he ordered a couple of guns facing down each of a dozen streets, loaded with grape shot and aimed at the advancing mobs. He asked the crowd to disperse, to retire, to disband or he would be forced to fire. They called his bluff and stormed forward. He ordered "Fire!", and in ten seconds the riot in Paris was over. Again, he was a national hero.

Now they sent him off to command the Army of Italy, 50,000 men on the French-Italian border down at the base of the Alps, which got him out of the way and into an impossible assignment. At the first muster only 38,000 men showed; the others were ill, AWOL or recalcitrant. Those who did "fall in" were badly clothed, hungry, unequipped, and unpaid for months. He issued government purchase orders and in a week's time had food, ammunition, weapons, uniforms, and horses. Then prepared to attack the armies ranged against him. From April 11th to May 10th he moved with unprecedented daring and alacrity, fought 12 battles; and on May 11th entered Milan victorious. By November he was north of Venice, and February 2nd the entire Austrian Army surrendered to protect Vienna. The French were ecstatic; the Austro-Hungarian

Napoleon
(Source: Wikimedia Commons.)

empire in shock; Europe stunned. The world had changed.

We are not going to spend the little space allotted me reviewing military campaigns, but hope to illustrate why he was a terrific leader. In these three instances…Toulon, Paris, and the Italian frontier… we learn the first lesson. He looked at a situation about which others wrung hands and knew at once what to do — and how. This did not come from 20 years experience. It came from a gifted, analytical mind equipped to solve problems — common sense, combined with conviction and resolution. Armies have to have decent shoes if they are to march; they have to be fed, paid and properly armed if they are to fight. He not only saw all this — he acted to fix it — with dispatch. "His first rule in case of unforeseen emergencies was to attend to them immediately." But despite this sense of urgency, he was also a meticulous planner and thought through consequences of perceived action. "When I plan a battle, no man is more pusillanimous than I am. I magnify to myself all the evils possible under the circumstances." But life's end is action, not about planning-to-act or contemplating what to do. And this requires having the courage of one's convictions; it's taking a chance through deliberate effort rather than making no mistake by resort to immobility, afraid to risk less we lose. Maybe acuity is <u>not</u> something we can learn, but <u>intelligence</u> has always been my top criterion for leadership. Goethe thought Napoleon's mind "the greatest the world has ever produced." But he who knows and is too timid to act has not helped us. Erring is forgiven; stupid is forever. Napoleon's "take" on this was succinct: "Everything is in the execution."

Another gift was "human relations skills" (as we call it today). His soldiers not only supported, they idolized him. Mostly because he was there, present, visible in action. "At Toulon Napoleon lived with his men, ate and drank with them, trained them, swore with them, praised and chastised them; he listened to them and when the going got tough, he led them." While in the field,

"He was everywhere — ordering, praising, encouraging, scolding, dictating new orders, munching a piece of bread and cheese bummed from a Private, never far from the battle or from the officers and the men." Another said, "Probably no commander in history has ever paid so much attention to the individual soldier's clothing and equipment, indeed to his well-being." Wellington said of him: "The moral effect of his presence is worth 40,000 men." Read in all of this that he was a "hands on" guy. He knew what was going on with all of his units — all the time; knew strengths and weakness; saw the position and disposition of the enemy; knew the capacity and prowess of troops and leaders.

"During the Ulm Campaign, not only did he pre-plan corps marches in minute and accurate detail, he followed their movement; daily issuing new orders; daily shifting divisions from one corps to another; daily prodding, inspecting, complimenting, and scolding all ranks from Marshals to Privates…an awesome performance in total contradiction to the traditional command procedures. His leadership in this campaign has few if any parallels. From October 8th when heavy rains and an occasional snow began falling to the surrender of Ulm (eight days later), <u>Napoleon had not once removed his boots</u>." Here's someone who loved his work! It's an example of personal commitment to the task at hand, making quick decisions, staying hourly abreast of the flexing situation, indefatigable in performance of duty. The sort of intensity and involvement we like to see in others, but probably don't demonstrate ourselves. Here is a leader who is "with the guys" through thick and thin, enduring what and where they are as part of the total French effort in which all share and in which each has his role. A leader doing the tough stuff instead of delegating, making decisions based on personal knowledge of the circumstance.

He was likewise effusive and generous in praise, quick to reward, and acknowledge performance. After Austerlitz, for example, he gave three months pay as a bonus to any man wounded.

Paul Delaroche: *Bonaparte franchissant les Alpes*, Paris 1848 Paris, Musée du Louvre H.: 2,89 m; L.: 2,22 m. *(Source: Wikimedia Commons.)*

The wives of the dead received lifetime pensions. He adopted the kids of those killed and educated them. His Marshals, Generals, and Colonels split up a $5,000,000 bonus for the victory. He issued press releases in all campaigns, praising groups or regiments or often individuals which demonstrated particular bravery. Heroes of battles were loaded with honors, passed out in the form of engraved muskets, swords, commendations, trumpets, ramrods, etc. as mementos of their valor in specific battles. He also created a "Legion of Honor" which at his death counted 48,000 persons; 11,000 of whom were civilians who had given exceptional service to the state.

Those who worked closest to him — his secretaries, personal valets, butlers, aides — all gave him high marks for not only ability, but the respect they were shown and the treatment they received. A good model here for those of us who have to get things done through people. The more the people respect or like you, the better will be their effort, the more pleasing the result, and the better the manager looks. Combined with the fact that as Consul or Emperor or Chief of State, he was an indefatigable worker. Got to his desk about 7:00 AM and expected his secretary to be ready to go. He was capable of dictating to four separate scribes at one time on four different topics. "He crowded a century of events into 20 years because he compressed a week into a day." His career was made more effective because of his prodigious memory and vast knowledge. He asked thousands of questions, read hundreds of books, studied maps, visited farms and factories, read countless reports, and processed facts and learning like a computer. Daily, he scanned the countless dispatches from subordinates; he required the updates, assessments, data, recommendations, objectives, calculable results. Durant says, "He was probably the best informed ruler in history and as a result, the ablest."

He optimized the potential in given opportunities. First off, he was a product of "the revolution" which had overthrown the monarchy, disbanded the church and put government, theology, legal systems, economics, and society in general back "to square one". The old rules were gone and his opportunity came because the revolutionary governments had lost credibility, were inept, inefficient, grossly mismanaged, and shockingly corrupt. Here was a moment to make monumental change which others were incapable of effectuating. Within the first three years of his Consulship, he was a whirlwind. He scrapped the confusing, overlapping and contradic-

tory crazy quilt of French law rife with 1000 arcane feudal penalties and restrictions, varying from province to province (un-codified and presided over by venal judges) and overhauled it; worked with the best legal minds he could summon to create a new civil law code — now. Pulling them together, he involved the parliament, and they met incessantly for four months; 100 meetings, half of which were moderated by the First Consul, who was forever simplifying language, keeping them at the table extra hours, and working often deep into the night till the product was finished. The "Code Napoléon" was clear, fair, simple, and applicable to all citizens. It fulfilled promises the revolution had made to the citizenry: equality, religious tolerance, property rights, a new system of courts, the abolition of feudalism, the right to due process, etc. The same legal principles were imposed in the territories he conquered or "managed" (some 88,000,000 people). The Code still presides in France and its principles are "apparent in the law of all European countries".

He created a new school system with new teachers and new studies; overhauled the tax system; reorganized the administration of the national and the provincial governments; rebuilt the canal and transportation systems; created the Bank of France; established a bimetallic money system; abolished serfdom; provided universal male suffrage in his subdued empire; provided each subordinated state with a parliamentary system, a bill of rights, free public schools, a new court system and legal code. He likewise reformed the army and its administration; subsidized the arts, science, technology, medicine; created industries; assured the rights of 500,000 farmers to new lands appropriated from the church or the crown.

Between 1801 and 1802, "No leader in history has ever worked harder on behalf of his country." The point here is "carpe diem" … seize the day. The moment for change and improvement was ripe, and he "seized" it with gusto. Succeeding to a large extent because, "My motto has always been: A career open to all talents without distinction of birth." The exceptions to this would be his family who for the most part had few of his leadership qualities. The army might best represent the "open career" concept. Only one of his 15 Marshals came from nobility and one or two from the upper classes. The others were mostly ordinary men who had risen through the ranks by virtue of outstanding performance to become extraordinary commanders. Murat was sort of an ass on the ground, but in the saddle he was a calvary leader without peer; Davoust, Lannes, Des Saix, Marmount, Berthier, MacDonald, Soult, Massena were all Marshals of consummate skill and prodigious achievement. Michael Ney, "the bravest of the brave" (he had four horses shot from under him at Waterloo), was a legend in his own lifetime, a tribute to his courage and leadership in battle. So Napoleon attracted the ablest men whether military <u>or</u> civilian, and the result was that he provided for the French the most efficient, streamlined, effective government they ever had. In the principalities he controlled the Papal States, the Cisalpine Republic, Belgium, Milan, Naples, Poland, 20 others…the same orderly accountable government. "The most compact government with the most rapid circulation and the most energetic movement which ever existed." Prime Minister Canning said, "I am not a panegyrist of Bonaparte, but I cannot close my eyes to the superiority of his talents, the dazzling ascendancy of his genius." Metternich (certainly no bosom buddy): "What at first struck me most was the remarkable perspicuity and grand simplicity of his mind and its processes."

Part of his secret along with selecting talented people was the clarity of his instructions, maybe derived from military experience wherein success lies in the coordinated effort of countless elements harmonized by orders issued to constitute an indestructible whole. Regiments, corps, divisions, batteries, cavalry; advancing, retreating, flanking and charging, all dependent upon precise instructions. Bonaparte claims he won 40 battles (fought 50), and no two were alike. The ability to plan brilliantly is pointless unless the forces are brought to bear in perfect sequence and in numerical strength to execute, and this occurs when commanders understand and follow their orders. His dispatches to his commanders were clear, detailed and thorough. In the departure for his unfortunate campaign to Egypt, someone noted, e.g., that he personally wrote the orders for loading each ship with <u>which</u> companies, <u>which</u> cannons in <u>which</u>

positions and in <u>what</u> order. When he moved three armies from the Atlantic Coast to Eastern Germany in 1805, he personally spent the night with maps, aides and candles moving each group (each day) in a fashion where they would not be occupying or living off the same area, yet were within summoning distance if the need for consolidation was necessary. Reasonable expectations, feasible demands, and clear instructions are a natural trait in any good manager.

So with respect to leadership and management, what has all this rambling said?

1. Take time to see the problem clearly. Deal with it quickly, but with circumspection based on personal conviction. Don't allow a committee to talk you out of the right course. Bold action is often the best action — where there are no "guts", there is no glory.
2. But plan thoroughly and accurately. Assure yourself of professional support. We can't produce a first-class product with third-rate employees. A team spirit replete with total support from the troops is essential.
3. It is re-enforced through clear, reasonable assignments, and reaffirmed through rewards commensurate with the service.
4. The good leader knows the drill, what's happening in his operation because he usually has a role in fashioning it. One cannot bluff successfully very long.
5. Understand the probable threats and anticipate how to handle them.
6. Lead by example; know and work seriously at the job. Continue to understand what's happening in your "world".
7. Seize whatever opportunities you find open. Lead on a broad scale not a narrow specialty. Be a teacher, innovator, motivator, executor, monitor, architect, model.

Having achieved all this, you won't be immortal, but you will leave your mark and more important, you will succeed. ■

Beyond the Frills ... The Magnificent Character

December 2001

Is Christmas an ecumenical holiday? It is religious in <u>origin</u> if we think back carefully, though it is also buried in glitz, commercialism and the loot under the tree, all overwhelming the manger and the Christ child. But before we do too much tsk-tsking as we recall our own childhood, need to wonder if what has happened is a good or a bad thing. Let's concede the event itself has captured society and if we have bent the mode of celebration a bit out of shape need to recall it is still about family, about giving gifts, about wondrous music, midnight church services and ultimately somewhere, the babe of Bethlehem surfaces. Christianity has surreptitiously imposed an event upon society. Might even say that Christianity has "converted" said society and even retained certain theological fragments (just identified). In this country we might use "ecumenical" because just about everyone takes the day off without necessarily changing his personal theology or beliefs. "Loaning" our holiday to others (at least in the Protestant church) should be construed as a magnanimous gesture. It's a good sign that folks in America can all participate.

But it was not always thus. My Scottish ancestors would have frowned on such attention. They had little time for Christmas, considering it too "pope-ish" or else too pagan in its symbols. Probably got this from old John Calvin, who despite his brilliance, was somewhat of a blue nose — one of these birds, long on man's sin and weakness, was short on man's glory and strength. There has always been an element in the church that feels anything which is joyous or brings happiness is automatically a tool of the

devil. Gotta be some "better" with the "bitter" in my book. And what we wonder about at Christmas time is whether or not the holiday really belongs "to the world". The Gospel accounts, particularly John (who omits the nativity) is obsessed with Christology and adamant that there is only one safe route to the hereafter and that is through the Christian church. "I am the way, the truth and the light". "No one gets to the father except through me" and paraphrasing that a dozen times in the New Testament. The rest of mankind is out in the cold. Fact, that really puts Abraham, Moses, Elijah and good king Josiah out of luck. Or maybe there were some special privileges granted, but the prospect of a billion people living and dying long before Abraham got here, all consigned to the abyss, sounds like a pretty bum deal. I mean what is the point in creating the Homo sapien if his only destiny is oblivion? (In the Old Testament, it was a modification: "You <u>only</u> have I known out of all the nations in the earth" ... "<u>You</u> are to me, a nations of priests, a holy people" and that means no Canaanites, Philistines or Moabites need apply. We are not enrolling non-qualified applicants.) It is hard to think highly of a creator who designs and produces the species only to sort out a handful for salvation and ships the rest off to roast a hell fire, "seven times hotter; hotter than it oughter be".

What I'm moving around <u>to</u> is a general appreciation of a given Christian holiday being stretched to invite others into the same spirit...the spirit of peace, of sharing, song, joy, friendship, gift giving, music, wonder. I think this "general appreciation" occurs because some Jewish neighbors send me holiday greetings; my good friend Shu Irani (a Zoroastrian) is first to get his Christmas cards mailed; Bahia colleagues in the past also joined in the season, and I'm sure if I ran into K.P. Singh (a Sikh) on Christmas day he would wish me "Merry Christmas" (Christ mass). Jesus is one of the prophets of Islam so I'm sure many Muslims would not be inimical to fellowship at Christmas time. But note: None of this ecumenicity was extant when I was a kid. Jews, Catholics and blacks lived on the other side of town and didn't get invited to Christmas Eve services. The church in those days was as sinful as the rest of us, having a lock on God's favor and owned the rules

The Saints are watching you!

for access to "dem golden slippers and dem golden streets". Moreover, they weren't passing keys around. The Bible gets very clear more than once about who goes on to the next world under divine auspices.

So what I'm wondering as we examine the season upcoming if a conversion hasn't taken place in my lifetime. Because as a kid, all of us viewed the nativity as a historic event. Joseph actually packed his pregnant wife on a burro and traipsed 80 miles south through the hills and the rains so he could register at Bethlehem because some ancestor a thousand years earlier happened to live there. The child was born the very night he arrived, fact, born in a grotto or a barn because the village was crowded with other "registerees". An angel chorus celebrated the event with four-part harmony in the starry heavens and curious shepherds ambled by to wish the couple luck. Or maybe it was three wise men who came and brought presents, after which they turned around and went back home to Iran. In the ensuing days, the child was named Joshua/Jeshua (Latinized to Jesus) and was taken to the temple to have his foreskin removed. (Ouch!) Or else maybe he went to Egypt because King Herod (in the last year of his life) saw a threat in the youngster and ordered all male children killed. Later the story opines that Joseph really lived in Bethlehem, but after the big events of the nativity and the threat of Herod, he, Mary and the youngster went north "to a city named Nazareth" where Joseph opened up a carpenter's shop. Or maybe they just came back from Egypt when it was safe and returned back home to open up the store for the post-Christmas specials.

We all <u>know</u> the story but never tumbled to all the inconsistencies, contradictions and inanity. (Moving to a new locus remote from all one's wealth in order to be taxed? Come on! Augustus was smarter than this! Beyond this, we find no tax or census in 4 B.C.) When I was a kid, no one challenged the Bible whether it made sense or not, whether we were "digging" what the writer was driving at or not. We read the written word and accepted it. <u>These</u> days it makes more sense to see the Christmas vignette as a story that will introduce us to the miraculous character of this child in preparation for what we are going to say later about his ministry. To try and prove the narrative is to challenge our credulity. But if indeed it is illustrative, it is fulfilling prophecy (hmmm!), and then it has a point besides inerrancy. This day and age many scholars see the nativity event as a metaphor. It is an illustration which is quasi-divine

(but isn't all of life a bit like that?), charming, idyllic, homespun and tender. But viewed as a figure of speech — metaphor - it also takes on a universality. The story has the ingredients that make it appropriate for practically any culture or at least make it plausible to virtually any people. And attractive to them. It is an experience (child birth) with which all the world is familiar. It is transferable across virtually all borders.

There is a school of thought that says religion is losing its impact or its effect in America. Its day of strong influence and considerable moral power is gone. Insofar as the church <u>has</u> fashioned individual conduct, sexual morality, business practice, open housing and hiring, standards of decency and integrity, it is a great thing to have going for you. Here is one who thinks the mores of America are indeed a product of the Protestant culture. It has shaped our outlook, living style, manners, education systems, type of governance, and you name it ever since Governor Winthrop and the Puritan Colony in Massachusetts. But there is also a flip side, like viewing Christmas as too "pope-ish", the inexcusable Christian vendetta against the Jews for nearly two millenniums; current violence against abortion clinics; our tolerance of slavery for two centuries and often a general monopoly on the divine will as viewed by <u>our</u> sect. But let's face it, the church is composed of sinners who are all too human. Though, if it has brought about the emancipation of women, more education, free flow of information, representative government and a new stature for the individual, we have to interpret this to be a good sign. We have changed our conduct; we are more tolerant; we are less prejudiced. If we have even changed enough to let some other groups under the tent and share our holiday, then so much the better I say.

The church and its theology must be relevant to the conditions of the day or it has no use for us. Teaching 18th Century ethics to a 21th Century society is not going to work. This could be heresy to a lot of folks, but it is not all that outlandish. A conservative educator-pastor named Barclay has written wisely and extensively on understanding scriptures, a verse by verse labor and says: "The Christian can refuse to grow up in knowledge. He can be guilty of what someone called the culpable incapacity resulting from the neglect of opportunity". There are people who keep on saying that what was good enough for their fathers is good enough for them. "There are Christians in whose faith there has been <u>no devel-</u>

opment for 30 or 40 or 50 years…who have deliberately refused to try and understand the advances that Biblical scholarship and theological thought have made… remaining content with the religious development of a child." He goes on to wonder how we'd like a physician who said what he learned as a student 50 years ago was good enough for him. Now he is gonna use that knowledge on you. (I'm out of here, man!) Barclay implies an awful lot of individual initiative if he expects each of us to maintain some sort of program to stay updated on translations, archaeological finds, new theories, and think for ourselves rather than wait for someone else to tell us what to believe. The idea that each of us personally ought to explore these things is a bold one but to him, absolutely unelectable. We don't get to heaven on the basis of what the preacher thinks. And if we can assume genuine understanding comes from genuine and reasonable (albeit occasional) study, we are in essence loosening the grip a bit.

What is wrong then with granting some slack for differing opinions since as we approach any theological question, we are going to come up with answers based upon our differences as persons: background, experience, degree of education, type of education, mentors, etc.? And from there it is only a slight jog to a piece I read recently in the biography of Buddha. The writer comments that between the 8th and the 4th Centuries B.C. something happened that set religion on its ear and in nation after nation, people began to discover a personal faith, learned each individual was important and rejected the tyranny — the long, <u>long</u> tyranny of priest and king. It was the age of Confucius, Zoroaster, the prophets Amos, Hosea, Isaiah; Ikhnaton, Buddha, Thales and Socrates. Each had revelations; were great teachers and organized new understandings of our role in life. And if indeed, "Religions are many, God is one, all men are brothers (and all women sisters)", we have only the issue of interpreting the God to a given culture. Having Amos write to the Chinese would have been an exercise in futility since the traditions, institutions and history were so different; the teaching would "not translate". Buddha could not have dealt with the free-wheeling, hard-drinking society of Persia and begun to have the impact that Zoroaster did. So it says that there are several different ways of delivering the message, and it is contingent upon a given mind set, existing institutions, past history, the folklore and legend of each specific race since much theology is in parable, allegory, Midrash.

Ironically, one would think religion ought to be the agent which opens hearts and links mankind together, not establish shibboleths and keep us divided. This proprietary business about <u>my</u> way being the only way needs to seriously be challenged. Rather than making rules to disqualify folks, we ought to keep Christmas in mind and find ways of joining up and seeing our destiny as a species a common challenge, which requires we understand each other, work together and jointly celebrate the opportunity … like we do at Christmas time. ■

CHAPTER 17

2002

Confidence in Your Style

March 2002

Many of us are looking at the future with mixed emotions. "It" is coming, meaning "it" is <u>out</u> there (whatever "it" is). And depending on just how it assails or assuages or confronts us, we need a strategy to capitalize on it; maybe we tack into the wind; maybe coast with the current. There is nothing new in this dynamic which has always kept us alert and made the chase interesting. Of note because business management has a lot riding on its ability to forecast, i.e. foresee what is "out there". We can better accommodate the threats that impinge it if we spot them in advance, i.e. have a program to employ appropriate to the condition. If interest rates climb back up to 9%, it means either accept less profitability, cut expenses or increase margins. When national rental houses go broke, move into the vacuum created and secure their customers. There is action-and-counter-action, just like in certain laws of physics. One prompts or triggers the other. OK. But who can forecast the future that well or with consistency? No one! We assume past experience lets us get halfway home, then we recourse consultants, rely on customer input, tea leaves, economists' predictions and a dart board. Beyond that, there is a second option. Have an organization so professional and accomplished it is able to meet any threat head on and convert it to opportunity.

The point here is that the future by its nature is vague and imprecise. Corporations operate in the "now", intent on maximizing profits in whatever climate there is. Hopefully, we are geared so each part of the company has the ability to respond independently and automatically to outside impacts ... a Pavlovian reflex. To assure success in the new condition or circumstance or situation, we have to catch the signal

and change. The capacity to move and to change and to succeed no matter what the climate is basic to the fundamental success of any organization. Know what action to take when a new condition — good or bad — arises, respond now without a lot of dithering around.

I was trying to find an example where sheer professional competence provided an example of invincibility, you won't be surprised if I drift back into history for a near perfect instrument which survived endless buffeting and challenge only to triumph in every instance. (It is a sad fact that I learned "history" long before "business" and find its illustrations more dramatic.) The model that popped up came out of the Aegean world in the 4th Century before Christ in the form of Phillip II of Macedonia replete with a new tactical weapon called the phalanx. His was a professional army, balanced with whatever auxiliary components (hoplites, archers, light and heavy cavalry) enhanced its versatility and effectiveness; arranged in positions or battle order to give it maximal capability. Then it trained ceaselessly, all winter long, drilling maneuvers and formations, spreading and marching in open ranks, recoiling in close order, shield-to-shield for attack. Masses of men and horses shifting quickly in coordinated fashion hither and thither, duplicating combat situations. Drilled so it responded automatically and accurately, gaining a confidence that made it formidable.

Then it was tested in one military campaign after another, the last against the combined city states of Greece, the ultimate battle fought at Charonea. Alexander was part of the command in this engagement, 17 years old, he lead the left flank of heavy cavalry which broke the Theban lines and decided the encounter. He came to his charge well equipped, having gained remarkable skill with weapons and the art of hand to hand combat. Like Richard I of England (The Lion Heart), he was a classic warrior, a formidable opponent and a rage on the field, usually leading the charge in person.

When his father died in 336, the scattered, accumulated provinces broke into revolt. His 20 year old son wasted no time in assuming both the throne and command of the army. Then set out on a campaign to restore the kingdom and punish the rebels, taking his army through the Balkans, ranging north to throw a bridge across the Danube and pursuing the enemy into what is modern Romania. An amazing exercise successfully carried out. After putting things back in place at home, he reassembled an army of some 35,000 men and prepared to complete his father's plan of uniting the Greek power to drive the Persians out of Asia Minor. In 334, he crossed the Hellespont and began his march toward the Persian capital only to be met by the forces of the western Persian satrap at the Granicus River just a few miles inland. He spread out his line of battle this time with heavy cavalry on the right and once again, led the charge into the Persian flank. Before the foe could say "Alcibiades", he had punctured the lines and sent the enemy reeling from the field. Then to protect his flanks, he swept south through Syria and Palestine to land in Egypt where the priests surrendered to him without firing a shot and even proclaimed him a god. Back north to upper Syria, he brought his forces into action first at Issus and then a year later at Arbela. In each instance, though considerably outnumbered, he out fought the Persians and inherited their empire.

In the next 13 years he did this 50 times or more — <u>because of the military instrument</u> his father had fashioned, trained and honed. The Macedonian phalanx was a body composed of squadrons of syntagma, each with 16 rows of men across the front and 16 rows deep, a square 100 x 100 feet — 256 footmen armed with shield, swords, breastplates, helmets and greaves, and a <u>16-18 foot spear</u> (Wow!) called a sarissa,

The Winged Victory of Samothrace; a second century BC (220-190 BC) marble sculpture of the Greek goddess Nike (Victory), located at Louvre, Paris.

barbed on both ends (in case it broke in the middle). Twenty or thirty in formation presented a front bristling with steel heads, five lines of sharp points, one arrayed behind the other 24 inches between each rank. How in the world could anyone get through it? The opposing enemy soldiers might beat down one spear but behind it four more aimed at him and on both sides the same thorny thicket. This was scary? And the momentum from the mass, pushed forward inexorably by the rear ranks with their sarissas raised in the air out of range (for the moment) provided a force impossible to withstand.

This was more than just a conquest; this was a revolution which over a decade introduced the secrets of the "Greek Way" to all elements of the Fertile Crescent and to great portions of the orient; lead by a student of Aristotle, bringing cartographers, biologists, agronomists, botanists, philosophers, geographers, seers, doctors, engineers and historians. A wave that subdued but then reorganized, setting up governmental units, communications, building new cities, dredging harbors, intermarrying with the natives, introducing new crops and new technology. Also new architecture, mode of dress, abstract thinking, drama, games, and a new concept of both man and the gods which would change the ancient world. But only after battles had subdued all who resisted — hundreds of thousands of Asiatics on the fields of Arbela, other unnumbered thousands in fortified cities, in mountain strongholds, in the midst of a burning desert, locked in the snows of the Khyber Pass, and thousands upon thousands more on the plains of India. On the phalanxes went <u>without ever losing a battle</u>. Because here was a military instrument unique and hard for the enemy to handle.

But having the instrument is not enough. One must know how to deploy it skillfully and utilize the potential of which it is capable. If part of this was in training, surely a lot was in leadership. In Alexander they had a vigorous and gifted commandeer. Not only was he a superb fighter, he was present on the field in the biggest melee, a psychological fact which was enormous. Beyond that, was a born tactician, invariably took the offensive to do the battle his way, had an intuitive sense for the right strategy. He used newer weapons like the catapult, was brilliant at improvisation and lead troops always confident of victory. Beyond that, if his army was thoroughly professional, his generals were masters of the craft. Parmenion, Ptolemy, Seleucus, Cleitus, Lysima-Chus and Nicanor in battle after battle managed their sundry cohorts with increasing effectiveness and the élan of indestructibility. So time after time, in one challenge after another (including the armed elephants of Porus), he inevitably triumphed. Set up in any part of the world, they knew in advance they were going to destroy their opposition. Never a doubt and never a failure. In this business, there was no finer aggregation in the world.

Although he must have had some sort of intelligence corps, Alexander relied less on long-term planning than he did on superior efficiency in the art of inflicting casualties. His recourse and his success came from utilizing the most efficient apparatus of his time to shape his destiny and in the process, changed forever the western world. I'm trying to see why much of this pattern does not apply to the Indiana Caterpillar dealer who, goodness knows, has a lot of competition plotting his downfall, testing him every month of every year, in a free enterprise war of competition. We are better served when we can dump inventory we don't need and should not be financing; and are equally well served when we can load up just before a boom hits so we don't lose sales. We are more successful when we avoid sales to deadbeats, no matter how big the number is, and continue to be patient with good customers who run into temporary trouble and need some extension. We are better served when we "lock in" money when the interest rates are low than when we ride the curve soaring upwards. It pays us to know a lot about proposed housing starts and state highway construction programs since this means lots of earth-moving of one sort or another, and we can get owners to do some planning with us about machinery needs. All of which says we keep the crystal ball as clear as we can and hope we are reading it right.

But underneath that, we know bloody well the signals get mixed and conditions both unheralded and unexpected can land on us abruptly. Trying to raise our competence, we went through the service operation last year and examined the number of employees we had; marked those who lacked either the desire or the skills to fit in our future and reassigned or sent into new careers 30 people. (We have 294 in said Service Department as of now.) Then business turned out better than we expected. When the coal mines went crazy last winter (natural gas got pretty expensive), we had a severe load thrust upon our Service Department which sent the guys, especially Washington, into overdrive despite the diminution in manpower and with appreciably <u>fewer hands</u>, we increased volume by 24%! They jumped on the chance and just found a way to meet enormously larger demands. We've gone into the rental business because that is the way the industry is drifting and added three more locations (lease payments), 50 more people, and $17 million in new inventory <u>without</u> increasing total nose count or increasing our borrowings. We have finessed the increased strain and funded it not with borrowings but with profits.

The objective again is to build a professional staff so judicious, experienced and so mutually supportive that anything threatening in the economy, from the competition, in the hiccupping of Caterpillar can be met readily and without convulsion. The objective is to be able to handle all of the problems endemic in dealer operations and assume they are part of the contract; that part of our obligation as owners and managers and supervisors and employees is to solve problems no matter what they are, when said problems end up in our portion of the battle field. That a dislocation in Washington or in the Engine Power Division or in the sale of skid steers is not "his" baby or "their" tough luck, but is something affecting all of us and deserving of help from the entire organization. "No man is an island", and no department a solo act. We are interconnected. It is the mutual support provided each department that makes execution easy. It is 56 years of successful operation that distinguishes us in the field and makes for a can-do spirit, for high morale. It is the gradual recruiting over the years of outstanding managers that gives us a technical and professional advantage not granted those who economize on managerial salaries. It is the endurance and surmounting of endless cycles, rising and falling markets, new products and new competition, that gives us the savvy to encounter difficulties albeit like those we've solved in the past. It is confidence in our own style that goes head to head with national rental chains and pushes them into bankruptcy courts. It is the confidence of veterans bent on a defined mission, working in close order drill that gives us the edge, the competitor his challenge, and the customer professional benefits, better products, service and cheaper costs. ■

Optional Time

June 2002

Ever stop to think hard about an element called "time"? Like hours and days and years and centuries? The part it plays in our lives is not always sort of detached and "out there". If you are an "hourly clerical employee", time is pretty significant because it establishes and tallies your daily application to the job. And on that basis, determines what you will be paid. Note, it's not what you have <u>achieved</u> but the hours you have worked. (Our naïve assumption is that each employee works at an optimum rate of capacity, so time imputes performance.) Our sales people earn differently, partly by virtue of a salary (which presumes they will work 2080 hours a year) and partly on the basis of production. They are given commissions on dollar sales which means a good deal of the compensation depends not on time spent, but on productivity. How much did they sell and at what profit level? Shop and field mechanics are in a comparable situation. Their effort is also related to volume of work completed — achievement — on given repair jobs performed for a paying customer whether owner-user or else the company itself in warranty, preparation and delivery, repair of our used machinery, etc. Also considered in this element of compensation is the <u>nature</u> of the job or the department in which each performs and the special skills or degree of import to the enterprise which is then reflected in the compensation level. Telling us different sorts of time invested provide different levels of returns to the employee as each contributes in his job.

Repeating: Time is the component of livelihood. We exchange our expertise for the dollars, thus, providing for our day-to-day living.

Expanding on that theme, let's move to "the big picture". Historically speaking, our current generational use of time is different than the past. Not just work time, but daily or yearly time. Noting for starters that the 20-25% hours spent today in the "salt

mine" or at the bench, typewriter, computer or on the road amounts to but a single element of total allotted us. We spend another third resting, but the remainder is optional. Hearth and family, recreation, travel, hobby, home maintenance, etc., all discretional. How <u>different</u> this distribution is from previous generations, who for 5000-6000 years slogged away their hours in drudgery. For ages immemorable, the waking hours — not a mere 25% — were committed to livelihood. The better part of each life — like 65% — was invested in the production or acquisition of food; the remainder invested in keeping living accommodations habitable, protection and rest.

Those in my generation can recall in early childhood, a vestige of this very same pattern. A century ago we were an agrarian society. If indeed producing and securing food was the prime focus of the species, we had a break (we on these shores) because the climate was temperate and the soil fertile <u>if</u> we could get it cleared adequately to put in vegetables, then grains, then orchards, then fodder for livestock, etc. Saying our investment of hours in farming was enormously more productive than any gang who preceded us. As early as the American Revolution, the 13 colonies (roughshod and primitive as they were) produced the highest standard of living in the world. We had enough land so each family owned a piece and could take care of itself. Ninety percent lived on farms and had chickens and eggs, had cows, thus milk — and thus butter and cheese, a vegetable garden, then wheat for bread; pigs, cattle or maybe sheep; apples, cherries, berries, etc.

My grandfather is a model of that society. He was about 90% independent for his food supply. Did his own butchering, smoking hams and bacon; stocked the root cellar in the fall with cabbage, beets, carrots, apples, potatoes, onions, pickles, sauerkraut, turnips, dried apples, dried corn; churned his own

RoGator spraying beans.

butter, made his own maple syrup; in fact had built his own house and barns (with a pitch-in from all the neighbors). He raised 12 children and was considered prosperous and modern (when he got the first running water, the first electricity, the first huge Ford lugged tractor, bought the first Model T).

So he, like traditional farm families, ate well and thrived, mostly because food was never a major problem. But note, it exacted a price. It required <u>full-time</u> commitment. Labor was almost all manual — or equine (horse-powered), needing six or seven people on the job daily to keep it all going. The work week was probably 80 hours because technology was rudimentary. Plowing with a single bottom plow took a guy forever to get finished with a 20-acre plot; hand-scything and drying hay, pitching on wagons, moving to the barn, then hoisting into the loft, and spreading was arduous and sweaty (been there, done that). Planting potatoes one hill at a time or cabbage or tomatoes by hand took long hours. Cooking a meal meant lighting a wood fire to heat the stove before we could prepare anything. Average farm wife spent five hours a day in preparation of food and clean up — just for breakfast and dinner. Laundry meant hauling in water to heat after which we dump in the dirty clothes and scrub by hand (with soap my grandmother made), hung out to dry; iron with a manual iron that is heated on the stove, an all-day Monday ordeal. To maintain the basic lifestyle on the farm demanded 90% of the waking hours available.

Mostly because farming technology was crude, sources of power clumsy, and the size or nature of the tool limited usage, thus, curtailed the degree of productivity. A single bottom, moldboard plow pulled by two horses turned a furrow at ½ mile per hour; took all day to plow 10 acres. Check that with today's technology wherein a seven-bottom plow at 6 MPH does the job in one-tenth the time.

The ratio of the tools technology and the powering capacity limited man's achievement across the board. Potters worked by hand, a single piece at a time; women spun thread from wool or cotton, a single strand at a time and put it into the loom to make cloth with a shuttle, one pop after another;

grandmaw knitted mittens and gloves and sweaters with two needles and though she went lickety-split, it was also one stitch at a time. Carpenters felled trees with axes and saws, cut to lumber by hand and then fashioned tables or chairs or cabinets with hand tools and great patience…though did kick in with a lathe early on. All this until the late 18th Century when the industrial revolution began setting in, and we began to spin thread on machines, weave cloth with automatic looms, invented power saws run by steam and belting. By the turn of the century (1900), we were recoursing engines and that marvelous, inexhaustible power replaced animal muscle (and there was no manure to clean up). The remarkable thing about the industrial revolution was not slave labor, bad lighting, and employing 10-year-old kids for piddling wages. The remarkable thing was cutting down the time it took to make a bolt of cloth, plow a field, thresh a stack of wheat sheaves, saw and fashion lumber, fertilize a field or bale 20 acres of hay.

The offshoots of that, naturally, were an escalation in productivity and the development of surpluses, thus, exportable commodities. But it also had significant side benefits. It provided better wool or furni-

This is how the term "Horsepower" derived. One scraper and team could move 10 cubic yards of earth 500 feet in one day. (*Source: CAT World Magazine, 1966.*)

ture or apples or bacon that the landowner produced and at a cheaper cost. It also provided a raft of things the farmer couldn't hand-make, enriching his lifestyle which simultaneously gave him hours of time each day to use as he pleased. Buying is quicker than making. If the landowners and aristocrats of old did a lot of loafing and hunting and traveling, soon everyone had a chance — had the time — to explore new areas of human endeavor. The hours saved were used to enjoy social gatherings, travel, study, reading, watching and learning. My guess would be that half the time a given dairy or corn farmer spent in earning his living in 1902 is now free for him, thanks to new technology. So a new question gradually surfaced: "What do I do with 30-40 hours a week I no longer spend walking behind the plow, pitching hay with a fork, butchering hogs?"

Well, how about expanding my horizon? How about taking up golf, meeting more people, reading more books, traveling, playing the piano, visiting a museum, collecting stamps? There's time now for the symphony, aerobics or jogging, working on a political campaign, joining birdwatchers, movies and crossword puzzles. Course, we can't eliminate radio and TV time, newspaper and magazine reading, lectures and operas, shopping malls and Colts games. Point here is that as available time expanded, Americans created an endless roster of opportunities, enjoying a larger slice of life and broadening skills, interest, minds and communities.

Well, it's a bit like handing us another life with our own dance card. It has made us the best informed people in history. We spend more time in school, have a smaller student-to-teacher ratio, go for longer periods. (My mother and father each had eight years of formal schooling — <u>one</u> teacher. My kids and I have each had 16 years.) We introduce kids to lots of options besides hoeing, milking and planting; try Little League baseball, scouting, soccer, Disney World, hockey, summer camp, the whole universe of computer travel and exploration. We all have infinitely more knowledge than did our forbearers and are better acquainted with the world, hopefully, making us more sophisticated, broadminded and tolerant than was the case when I was a kid. We take two-three-four week vacations, something my grandfather never considered. We join endless associations (hardly possible in an agrarian society with farms spread out all over and travel arduous) like St. Margaret's Guild, Rotary and Kiwanis, the Sierra Club or the National Rifle Association. We participate in blood drives, Run for Hunger, Habitat for Humanity, political campaigns, bird watching, early morning jogs, Pacer games and the Indy 500. We have time to read two or three magazines a week, novels in bed before sleep, enjoy movies couple times a month, a concert or an opera now and might bowl regularly, shoot skeet, haunt the shopping malls, and eat out with some regularity.

The journey of life (all this says) is infinitely richer than it was for previous generations because we are able to cram more living in each hour or each day than our forbearers ever dreamed of. Measured in terms of these experiences, we "live" five times as long as my grandfather did. We experience 500% more "living" than he did. Optional time is a relatively new commodity; the range of institutions and organizations seeking involvement is almost a nuisance. And the ability to do more things has exploded our world and our knowledge of the world. E.g.,

the Hubble Space Telescope is so complex we cannot begin to understand or explain it, much less the ability to send it off out into space, get it positioned, control all of its processes from earth, directing it to show us what happened in our universe five billion years ago, and then <u>overhaul it</u> out there in remote space. Indicates the degree of distance we've come when putting a man on the moon to my grandfather would have been totally insane. We have not only "<u>dreamed</u> the impossible dream", we are living the impossible dream.

Being capable of more, knowing more, living more, thinking more or engaging more, are we as <u>productive</u> relatively with our time (given this leverage) as was my grandfather was with his? If indeed we measure his "efficiency" in terms of milk and butter and corn and potatoes and the lifestyle of his family, we need a different yardstick for this generation. Devoting a life to raising a family and making a productive farm was "the name of the game" for him because the conditions required it. The measure today ought to be not only what different things are we doing with our allotted time, but how much of it (no longer needed for my family or my farming enterprise) am I investing in making my community better or alleviating the lot of someone less fortunate, or doing chores from which others benefit? Life in our generation provided different opportunities, and it ought to have different perspectives.

Having been free from drudgery which occupied our waking hours, aren't we obliged to reciprocate for that break by dedicating part of those hours-days granted us to some humane gesture, some noble enterprise, some effort that lets us participate in making our world or family or environment or political party less introspective, more altruistic and ecumenical? That free time (so long in coming) needs to be <u>used</u>. Not frittered or idled. After all, the agrarian style, family center, did give way to an urban setting which says "community". We become part of a neighborhood, live amid clusters of people involved in group enterprise activity and orientation. The objective is to make our group best of the lot. More productive, civic minded, altruistic; finding thusly the optimum use of the "extra life" conditions so fortuitously provided us.

At which point I've shifted to preaching, which puts me out of my league. Better knock this off and get back to selling some tractors. ∎

On Corporate Responsibility

June 2002

I usually start the day by waking up to NPR (National Public Radio) which brings me the good news of the world as I prepare for battle against whatever Philistines might lurk in the path ahead. Though, of course, what I usually hear is not <u>good</u> news at all, but who shot up what school ground last night, how many more suicide bombings we had in the West Bank yesterday or how much the market fell. The ancient Greek used hard luck stories better than we. They invented drama and made it as much a part of their life as our newscasts. But used it for teaching, venerating and entertaining. Subject matter was rehearsal of historic or mythological tragedies in a literary style that marks them as immortal. The subtle rationale behind same was an element of catharsis. Drama reminded the Greeks how their heroes faced death, assassination, betrayal, triumph and incestuous love. Living vicariously through the exploits of Menelaus, Electra, Medea, Oedipus, Helen and Clytemnestra, they also suffered, wept, rejoiced, and agonized. The audience empathized with them as they fought through the vicissitudes of the heroic life, joined in the protean drama which broadened the scope of man's knowledge, and taught how their greatest figures endured failure, disappointment and tragedy. They got to realize that pain and failure were a part of life, and it was better lived with a noble spirit and a personal courage than cowering in the dirt helplessly. Their way of accommodating bad luck, tragedy, divine blessing, and the pain of divine anger seems a lot nobler to me than me getting my "tempering" through repetitive reports of gloom and doom through the media (different than Medea). Which (we all know) emphasizes the bad stuff and ignores totally the triumph of the spirit in acts of generosity. But, alas, what sells to the general public is gory or dramatic or violent material.

The morning news report that triggered this outburst was a hassle between the Hershey Candy Company and its union, undergoing a labor negotiation which had just broke down when the corporation offer was rejected. The reason: Hershey did not offer enough increase in remuneration. Not based on industry norms but based on their earnings, strong balance sheet, brisk business, and a load of cash. The union spokesman said the company really didn't "care about <u>anything</u> but the bottom line and they

were like most corporate America who has the same obsession — protecting the profits". I thought that was a rather curious statement. What else should corporate America think about? Well, there's the environment, safety, toxic residues from a given process, fair hiring practices, internal protection against gender bias and harassment, and several other things, including competition. All of which, by the way, are defined by laws and ordinances or Supreme Court decisions spelling out what the ground rules are for conducting business in the United States of America. So a business enterprise has the obligation to obey the law, to pay its taxes but beyond that, if it <u>doesn't</u> make money, the purpose of the founders, owners or managers has been thwarted. Its purpose for being is foiled. It has <u>failed</u> if it is not profitable. Why is that strange to everyone?

I've been down this trail before and people think it's pretty harsh and narrow thinking. But the obligation of a business … of corporate America … is not hospitalization, pension programs, support for the arts, giving to the United Way, supporting political candidates, daycare facilities, Little League teams or involvement in Boy Scouting. Corporate America happens to make most of these things possible, along with support of Symphony, the Art Museum, the Hudson Institute, etc. (ad infinitum by the way), but not because it is their duty or obligation. It happens because <u>their management</u> feels an obligation to support the society in which it functions. It is not a legal requirement. It is not one of the provisions demanded by the state. It is a voluntary gesture of generosity and civic pride determined by those who run

P.E. MacAllister (center) presenting the 2002 MacAwards at the Indianapolis Opera.

1953 Neuerburg Field; Playground for Little League Baseball at 10th & Emerson, Indianapolis. Eleven different contractors contributed machinery; organized by MacAllister.

the operation. It is, thus, personal judgment that supports beyond the mandated requirement and makes for good relations and good corporate policy.

Course, it is pretty hard to give to anything at all if there is no profit from which to do it. Will Durant once wisely observed that: "Money is the root of all civilization." Until there are excess resources beyond those necessary to sustain life and provide security and take care of the gods, there will be no temples, no public buildings, no religious rituals, no drama, no art, sculpture or literature. My guess is if we see three profitless years for all of corporate America, we shall see the demise of most symphonies, opera companies, ballet groups, theatres, professional basketball, pro football and baseball teams dejectedly walking off the court, field or diamond.

Because I have been richly blessed, I'm inclined to generosity. I was thinking of Al Gore and the revelation that his gifts to charities had amounted to $1,500 in a given fiscal year. That is what I call tight. I do that much a week. Point here is, Gore is quick to knock corporate greed but not to demonstrate personal generosity. So I am not knocking worthy causes or institutions invented to provide society some medical attention, educational experience, artistic performance, recreational enjoyment, etc., etc. I'm saying that we are structured as organizations to do a specific thing. In business, it is to provide a product or a service and by doing so, make a profit for the investor. That is why he invested the money. It is not to provide personal leave days for employees, drug and dental care, uniforms weekly, medical insurance, and a vehicle to drive if their job requires it. Profit (with us) is a budget item just like interest ex-

pense, vacation and holiday pay, and season ticket to Colts, Pacers and Indians. But unless we "serve our purpose", the rest has to go.

The Indianapolis Colts are in town so Irsay can make money. He came here from Baltimore because we assured him of better profits than he was enjoying there. The Colts "make more money" when they play better and are real competitors. Anyone think part of their contract is helping Big Brothers or the YMCA? No one pays a bit of attention to what they supply the community. Pacers ditto, and two guys on the Pacer payroll take home more money than 500 of us at MacAllister Machinery combined. Anyone griping about the lack of participation in support to Butler or IUPUI or Meals on Wheels or Second Helpings? No one expects this from them, despite the fact they too are "corporate America". As an aside, I do not see big union support for noble causes. Their names are absent from major donor lists. How's come?

Oh well, I have let the steam out by now. We shall continue to give 2% of our pretax profit to charities, still level Little League diamonds, send 5th graders to visit Washington, DC; support ballet, two art museums, dig church basements, help the Symphony, Opera, Progress House, Scouting, Parks Foundation, etc., etc. because we live here. The better we can make this community, the more enjoyable, the richer, more diverse and pleasant it becomes — from this we all benefit. But it is civic pride that motivates it, not mandate or ordinance. The owners here feel we have done well, and it is "pay back" time. Every year, for a long time to a lot of causes. ■

My Rules for Giving

August 2002

If you're like I am, you are also continually amazed at the range of opportunities existing for us to give money to noble causes. You are also astounded, irked, offended, and boggled by the persistence of solicitors. They multiply like fruit flies, and they have access to more phone numbers than the FBI. Or access to more addresses than the post office. By Wednesday of this week, for example, I had invitations to play in not one, but four separate golf outings raising money for some notable endeavor or other, and thought this was coming on a little strong. But was not altogether flabbergasted because the mail daily contains "Please Send Check" appeals.

On the other side, I have been known personally to participate (and instigate) similar "opportunities" (i.e. the very process I now excoriate). Confess to mailing out more than one "Please Send Check" appeal. Because behind it lays one of the most exuberant phenomenon mankind has ever produced. It is the American volunteer experiment, a vast enterprise that on a thousand occasions has seen problems that need attention (hospitals, colleges, blood banks, Red Cross, symphony, rotary et al) followed by citizens who organize efforts which will respond and make something good happen. It has produced a culture that has no parallel in terms of the options provided: for education, amusement, information, enjoyment, relaxation, assistance, community gathering, and you name it. We have a whole random, private, infrastructure larger by far than the vehicles of governance, businesses, services or the rest of life's apparatus, far more varied, richer, looser, more spontaneous and therapeutic (in a hectic, pell-mell society).

But alas, we also have a lot of schemers taking advantage of the acceptability of this whole universe and using same for self-aggrandizement or personal gain. Who don't mind calling at dinner time or on Sunday afternoons, don't bat an eye at loading the mails with crap; or badgering us anyway they can for causes of truly nebulous and questionable value. The solicitation of funds, along with the good which

parts of the process provides, has become a nuisance as well. This is a two-edged sword, almost like a law of physics which says for every decent and productive enterprise there is a counterproductive, Ponzi scheme or rip-off.

Conclusion, of course, is the range of opportunities combined with the ubiquity of fundraising which has made the process of volunteer giving pretty commonplace. So we are "chunking in" to the church, the United Way, arts organizations, supporting the Smithsonian, political campaigns, the old alma mater, opera ad infinitum (and ad nauseam). Giving, in our culture, is not something strange, and my guess is it's done on a far broader scale, more often and to more organizations than would be the case anywhere else in the world. It is part of the American mystique granted the amounts and nature of causes that varies with the individual. Given the inevitability of "the touch", the request or appeal, it finally occurred to me that one can't automatically get high marks for just giving. What we ought to measure is <u>sensible</u>, prudent, and careful giving. There is a stewardship element involved here. I happen to have lucked out and made a little money in my lifetime (very <u>long</u> lifetime). (Gives me an edge on people who die at mere 80.) I figure what has been sent my way is something I am charged to manage. In essence I become a steward of the funds in my possession. Money sends no message; does no good until one spends it. But the spending of same ought to be more disciplined or programmed or thought through than my erratic, spontaneous writing of checks. It would seem that given the limitless causes seeking support, we often do some foolish giving, i.e. sending money to people who don't deserve or don't spend well or want too much or don't really need it. When we make out a check to a marginal cause, we automatically deprive a worthy and valuable institution of support it could have had instead. We have overlooked doing some good or providing some help by sending money to the wrong organization.

Question in my house is how to bring some sanity, judgment, joy and system to the process. It is not "good giving" when done willy-nilly, spontaneously, gut-reacted. In my case there is no set of rules, no standards to apply; there is no governing criteria to which I can resort. Giving (in my case) is not planned, even from one day to the next, and this cannot be the best development of one's resources. Even though we don't know what is coming up next, there ought to be a standard sort, a process of justification, a qualifier, a test which each cause has to pass. There probably ought to be a cumulative, annual total in mind as well … percent of income, flat dollar amount. There also needs to be a firm, but polite way developed to resist even the cleverest of suitors when the cause does not pass muster.

So I'm making some "mid-year resolutions" to do this better from now on. If I keep my level where it is and develop some ground rules, I can say to the next visitor appealing to me for a check, "I'm sorry sir, my policy is to add no new giving to the list since I am "maxed" out to the extent I feel generous and fiscally sane. I have been tithing for years and have done more than my share; though your program is commendable, it needs be sustained by those who ought to give more and not added on those of us who are already way over the average." All this is easier to <u>say</u> than to do. I'm a sucker for a soft sell; it's worth a try, right? So here are some guidelines to think about… at least as I see it:

- I don't contribute to organizations I do not know, whose leadership is totally unfamiliar to me and whose efficacy I cannot affirm.
- I don't give to people who cannot present sound reasons why I ought to consider their cause. Too many people think that because they troop out to your office, identify the cause and give you a pledge card, you ought to reach for your checkbook. We should give just because they are there — Wrong!
- I'm not gonna consider a gift which has not been specific in terms of dollar amount.
- I don't like causes away from my community unless I have a personal involvement in them. We have a lot here that still needs doing.
- Never consider organizations raising money for veteran's organizations, police, sheriff or fireman. They surely have worthy causes that need support, but I wouldn't think of asking cops to support our Dealer Foundation or PAC. That's for equipment people.
- Do not give to someone who is being paid a commission on what he has solicited. ∎

Why Not Goodwill Toward Men?

December 2002

We usually devote a page of the December issue to "Christmas", putting it in the form of a philosophic or quasi-theological rumination. Annually wondering how many different lessons one can extract from the Christmas story. I've been at my typewriter 18 times in this exercise, but fortified with tendency to forget what I said a mere four or five issues ago and counting on readers to have the same careless memories; so I just skate along like each effort is all brand new. (Every so often, one <u>is</u>.)

It is hard to think of a Yuletide in recent memory, however, more in <u>need</u> of the Christmas message than this one. A time more desperate for "peace on earth" and "goodwill to men" or walking the extra mile and turning the other cheek. Given the maniacal eye-for-eye, tooth-for-tooth, bomb-for-bomb mentality in the very land of the nativity itself, the cynics among us wonder how much progress we have made since King Herod ordered all male babies killed. Haven't come a very long way, have we?

As backdrop or context for this pessimism, we've had the bombings in Bali, the sniper killings around Washington, fighting in Kashmir, Chechnya terrorists, 44 million children starving around the world, the explosion of AIDS in Africa and the mountain of human pain that implies. Plus the condition of our own 401K's, lest we think all discomfiture is remote. It's really hard to say "God bless you merry, gentlemen" with much enthusiasm. But, alas, this is too much like the local media, i.e. sorting out the grim and ghastly stuff for publication and downplaying or ignoring anything which is encouraging or ennobling or selfless.

Let's move on and suggest the gospel story might be locked in place by both the Matthew and Luke accounts, but its application or meaning depends to a large degree on the world to which it is applied. During a "golden age", the <u>meaning</u> is less profound: existing order, tranquility and contentment need little ministration. What can one do to enhance an already satisfied constituency? If there is little

need, the message is superfluous. But when peril mounts or crises arise or sadness and despair stalk the land, the prospect of hope, any harbinger of better times becomes infinitely more precious. The Jewish world of 4 B.C. was an unhappy one. Israel was subservient to Rome, fragmented with violent theological controversy, structured by caste with the masses exploited and longing for redress. So an angel chorus and the "miraculous" birth held promise of a newer, brighter age (like the lamb lying down with the lion), a period of justice, personal happiness, a chicken in every pot, if the prophets were right. In short, the Christmas story implied the imminence of a major sea change, a dramatic turn of events and long awaited reforms reordering human society. If not next week, surely within our lifetime. And such promises brought hope, shimmering and radiant; brought smiles and good feelings. With that hope, an element of joy. Or so it would appear to the writers of the story.

Returning to the present, 2006 years later, and pursuing the Christmas theme, let me shift to a convenient musical analogy. I had occasion this fall to interview Patrick Summers, in town to conduct the Indianapolis Symphony (before moving on to New York where he was conducting *"Lucia"* at The Met). A prodigy from Indiana University, currently resident conductor for Houston Opera and guest conduct for San Francisco, he has traveled the world interpreting the great masters. Much in demand, he is a gifted musician and a mesmerizing conductor, a real "comer" in the classical music world, a meteor. From him I learned some things I'd never thought about. Now don't forget I'm an old E-flat clarinet player who started in the 4th grade and played in band or orchestra all the way through college. That means I read a heck of a lot of notes, thousands upon thousands of 'em; got acquainted with some fabulous music, became addicted to the classics.

There were just two reasons I didn't become a professional musician: I didn't have any talent; I played the notes rather than the

Conductor, Patrick Summers.
Photo by Christian Steiner.

music. Fact, I never did much <u>more</u> than read the notes so my playing was automatic, mechanical and perfunctory. There was nothing of "me" in the product (which may be just as well). Musical scores are very precise, clearly defined, and each note requires a different fingering. They also have the composer's instructions in terms of the tempo, the phrasing, degree of volume, etc. It's all marked. (Usually in Italian and why they haven't changed to English so "pianissimo" becomes softly; or "lento", "leisurely"; "fff" becomes "I mean <u>really</u> loud", I'll never understand.) I thought my job was to follow the score. In the process I learned Mozart wrote different material than John Phillip Sousa; that Rossini's overtures were a far cry from Stephen Foster, so composers rearrange notes and rebalance instrumental combinations and alter tempo to produce different products. That's no big deal. But zeroing in on a <u>given work</u>, Patrick tells me that Andre Previn will conduct *"Lucia"* differently than he would and Levine will surely texture it different than either one. Beyond that, within the orchestra, the solo oboe parts (e.g.) played by one musician will come out quite different than the same notes, in the same passage when played by another oboe guy. So the combination of given <u>musicians</u> in an orchestra and the insight or interpretation of the music by the <u>conductor</u> combine to make *"Lucia"* different when directed by different maestros. Same notes, same markings and tempo, same scores yet never the identical sound, or impact or impression. And each probably very moving and very well done. There's more than one way or two or three to play a musical composition.

What this infers is that each element (musician or conductor) is putting a piece of himself into the composition. Whatever his conditioning is, his understanding of melody and rhythm, he is now applying that to the passages and makes each a product not only of the composer, but the performer as well. (Not always good. I don't much care for rock singers at Colts' games who waver all over the scale trying to find the notes of *"The Star Spangled Banner"* since I don't think random improvisation adds much to the mood or the melody. Though fair scores, the oboe player did not <u>change</u> the notes in *"Lucia"*, he changed the

embouchure or the tonguing or the tonality. He gave the notes life, made them part of something bigger, infused impact.)

Luke and Matthew wrote the words and music to the Christmas story. They gave us the themes and the cast of characters, they endowed it with mystery and wonder, they inserted the aura, reflected Hebrew expectation, and a hint of promise but left the interpretation to us — to succeeding generations. It is, after all, a score, a blueprint, a written narrative which has meaning or impact only when and if someone works it into action. It needs effectuation before it can become real. Until someone "plays" it, there is only the vision or idea or the promise — a silent score. When we pick up the oboe or the clarinet to play our part and look at the music, we have to figure out what the writers (composers) had in mind and how they wanted us to interpret each passage. At which point we have to do some transposition. Knowing what we do about our cosmic system, the sudden appearance of a great blazing star strikes us as highly unlikely. There aren't a lot of Magi around anymore and the prospect of three travelers moving out of Iran these days to visit Israel seems a bit far fetched. We don't run people around to count them when a census occurs so the trip to Bethlehem has to be really pianissimo. How do you feel about a 35-voice angel choir, floating 50 feet over the highway singing praises to God? Really haven't seen (or heard) one since 4 B.C. All of which says there are elements to the story (notes in the score) we have to consider realistically if this is to make sense in 2002. We are reading the score differently than Matthew or Luke.

So after subtracting these elements, what is left? Or said another way, taking out the fluttery stuff, removing the magic and supernatural and the wizardry, <u>is</u> there anything remaining for us personally to interpret? Of course there is. The babe in the manger. The centerpiece. The one real, honest to goodness, historic element in the tale. (Now I'm dealing with this story in <u>my</u> fashion. You'll have to figure out how it is you want to consider it.) The part we can accept as "gospel" is not the supporting cast, the stage, set; or celestial music. What lives on into the world of reality and transcends the elapse of centuries is the child. Because of what He did, taught, proclaimed and interpreted when He grew older. Providing perennial evidence of that the original event which with a little modification has had an impact in each age since. And because of it, the world has changed. Which is why the Christmas event happened in the first place.

Where is all this going? Well for starters (as I come to the <u>end</u>), note that the cast of characters in the original story were basically spectators. The angels, shepherds, Magi, neighbors, innkeeper even Joseph and Mary are dwarfed by the event and seem to just "be there". The story of the ensuing and subsequent ministry, however, is just the opposite. This was not a teacher or rabbi that held classes in the temple portico, here was someone out in the hustings. Here was a life of action, healing, feeding, succoring, comforting. Demonstrating what he thought religion was all about. It may exist to instruct, but only as a step toward deliberate involvement. So for a change theology is no longer passive, it is proved in action. People have to vindicate the faith not by prayers, but by manners, interaction, deeds, acts of kindness, patience, helping. We have to find — make — roles for ourselves in the 21st Century Christmas story. And what we <u>do</u> will give it meaning or substance or vitality. We impart our own spin, our unique stamp or imprimatur, a little like the oboe player. And like he/she, we do it with others. The Judeo Christian faith is about community, ecclesia (Greek for church), about a gathering of the faithful, hopefully, gathered for mission. But a ministry within our range of control. We can stew about Bali, Chechnya and Kashmir, but what can we do about them? Zilch! We have clout in our own community, family, businesses, school districts where there is enough work to keep us occupied. If we want to engage, let's focus close up on issues we know and understand. And this Christmas let's find someone outside the family who needs help and let's give him/her/them a hand. Let's do something nice for someone else as our way of celebrating.

And for the larger world, the message has to do with living as community and learning how to react when we can't have our own way. Christmas is about how we treat others and when we get to a point where <u>that</u> becomes paramount and when we understand what is driving the other guy — the competition, the Arab terrorist, the Israelis, the pro-life and pro-choice types — maybe we can figure out how to get along with each; <u>short of</u> eye-for-eye, tooth-for-tooth, and the winner takes the prize, the defeated are out of the play. There isn't a lot of patience in this world, forgiveness, tolerance or second chances. Instead there's a surfeit of egoism, tribalism, one-upsmanship, vengeance and pride — all standing in the way of "community". But despite all this, we might find some consolation in two facts: First, we do know what is wrong and what should be done. The pathway is clear. We are simply loath to act to get involved. But the Gulf War and the Balkans intervention suggest we do have limits and when really shoved (for the first time in history), we do not let thugs and tyrants run over innocent people at random without corrective response. Secondly, the world is not as bitter and hateful all over as it used to be. There are hundreds of millions living in peace, enjoying increased standards of living (China, India), beneficiaries of new medicine and technology. There are infinitely more democracies around than a generation ago and many tyrannies have vanished. More than ever, ironically enough the Christmas theme might still be employed; it ought to say, "Let there be peace on earth, and let it <u>begin</u> with me." ■

Let there be peace on earth...

It's All About Style

December 2002

Most Americans are involved in one (or several) "organization" like — say — a church, a school, a business, a college board, arts, scouting or you name it. There are so darn many groups around, contributing enormously to this society it is hard <u>not</u> to become involved and play a role. As we become part of the mission or the product, we automatically monitor the ongoing operation; note success or failure; provide service, advice, funding, etc. Not unlike involvement in a tractor company where 550 participants are doing 100 <u>different</u> jobs, serving 3500 customers, supplying a formidable product line, carried out by all sorts of people who like you are concerned with keeping it all together, headed the same way and planning for success. Focus here is not necessarily on success or failure, however, but rather finding the secret that keeps an organization together, keeps it moving, and makes it a winner. Whether business, a Brownie troop, the Red Cross, a college or a Little League team, there are two determinative components at work. One is institutional STRUCTURE and the other is LEADERSHIP. How effective each is and how well they unite to operate provide keys to survival and success.

Philosophically, we wonder here which is the most important: the leader or the structure. Which comes first? Examples of the dynamic produced by the two are what history is all about, and when they combined effectively, created the first civilization in the Fertile Crescent around 3200 B.C. (probably in a community called Uruk). Archaeologists have excavated a remarkable city, containing major structures; a written language, thus, accumulation of knowledge; a developed theology, vast irrigation systems, implying engineering plus land ownership with deeds and surveys, etc. Requiring rules, thus, a law code. The organization — structure — produced surplus food and wool which segue into trade, exchanging our commodities for things we don't have (wood, metal, stone, etc.) and inadvertent exploration of other cultures. The pattern established, however, was one of "undulation" — the creation of city states, enormous progress, only to collapse and unravel followed by a period of desuetude. When adversity sweeps in, the people scoot back to the villages and farms, seeking both security and sustenance.

If history itself is made and written in the cities (like Uruk), <u>nations</u> are invariably based on agriculture so <u>the farm</u> is the society's foundation. But for power and progress we need the concentration of mind and muscle. One does not build a ziggurat or 30-foot city walls with farm hands. The question is: Why the failure? What causes success? Which of my two elements, structure or leadership, is most responsible for this undulation?

I'll bet this is a toss up that can be answered both ways. First off, people don't gather to do something without being called to do so. They convene for action when a leader appears to summon them and often structure itself is secondary. Proven in dynamic leaders who change the world by their own endeavor, like the Mongolian tornado, Genghis Khan. Rolling out of Asia in the late 12th Century, he directed his horde westward about anywhere he wanted to go. Two hundred thousand armed and mounted men sweeping all before it and sucking into its wake a second horde of mercenaries and freebooters. If a part of the Khan's vehicle, survived his death in Russia, all other evidence of the horde in the west vanished like the late spring snow. The shattering success of this invincible force reposed in a single figure: Temujin — Genghis Khan — the creative, directing, motivating, governing element that marked the Mongol presence and terror. A century later, déjà vu in the form of Tamerlane, who himself replicated an even earlier predecessor, Attila the Hun; each a whirlwind riding out of the east to ravage Europe, indestructible and totally devastating. Both of these versions of the apocalypse threatened and triumphed, <u>only so long as the leader survived</u>. But at the death of each (Attila and Tamerlane), the apparition vanished totally, leaving little behind except countless graves and empty cities. Personal success here through the leader, but temporary, because there is no enduring impact.

Zigzagging back earlier in history, the legendary Babylonian Empire, so hated by the Jews as a model of depravity was a relatively brief experiment. Despite the fabulous nature of the capital city itself, the Empire lasted only through Nabopalassar and Nebuchadnezzar, maybe 50 or 60 years. The <u>shortest</u> great empire on record, one still incredible in its impact was the political hegemony of Alexander of Macedon which lasted less than a dozen years before the Diadochi took it apart to rule as five <u>separate</u>

pieces. So the point is leaders change (make) history single-handedly controlling, altering, impacting society.

Illustrations of the imprint provided by structure as the arbiter of history might be as profuse if not as glamorous. First example is Egypt where the established system decreed Pharaoh owned all the land and made distribution to the priests and to his nobility; who in turn passed it on down to tenants with commensurate responsibilities and obligations to the donor. Our structure here is an absolute monarch considered divine, ruling as a God, controlling virtually all of life. It's supported by the rhythmic regularity of the Nile whose inundation arbitrarily established the cycle of food production and the national agenda. No one had to wonder about how government would function or who would be calling the shots or what sort of system we are going to employ. So rigid and intractable, the mediocre nature — or name — of a given pharaoh made no difference. In this system the leader existed but the pharaonic model was one wherein the vehicle usually subordinated the leader.

Another example of structure was that created by Octavian, the grand nephew and heir of Gaius Julius Caesar. His finessing of Roman affairs subsequent to the death of Caesar resulted in maybe the most remarkable period in history (my judgment). Sparring with Mark Antony, Octavian succeeded in gaining control of Rome after Cleopatra and Antony lost the battle at Actium, becoming the "first man in Rome" which meant first man in the Western world. Called "Augustus", he ended a century of savage civil war and used his power to create "the Roman Empire". The brilliant structure of his governing apparatus would last 500 years (though the last century saw considerable sputtering and stumbling). His requirement for competence in his governors, proconsuls, ethnarchs and whatever plus his scrutiny of performance provided decent governance. The very composition of the empire was strong enough to withstand the aberrations of a nut like Caligula, the monomania and cruelty of Nero or losers like Domitian and Commodus. Saying even with lousy emperors, the system itself remained, and in the provinces moved on course inexorably.

Most unique model of a superb structure carrying the state was in Venice. Which began as a refuge from the barbarian incursions and ended building a city in the lagoons. By 700 A.D. they had developed a basic political and economic style which would car-

ry on till Napoleon's day, a system which permitted Venice to own the Mediterranean basin for five or six centuries. This was the best example of human ingenuity I know of in creating a formidable, economic power, and political vehicle out of sheer human ingenuity, organization and effort. There was no raw material, no agrarian base, and no natural resources to develop. Everything "Venetian" had to be created, including its gross domestic product. The hard and exacting process produced a society of clever, capable, self-sufficient merchants whose leadership talents were requisitioned by the state and whose governmental vehicle was so carefully contrived, dynastic ambitions were automatically thwarted. The state was run by a senate of sorts with power devolved to a smaller council, all lead by a doge (leader) who was elected in such a convoluted, four-step fashion, no one could rig the system. The doge was the figurehead "authority of the state", a ceremonial functionary and convener, but the merchant oligarchy held the power.

The departments, whether Navy, Commerce, Foreign Affairs, Justice or Relief of the Poor, were directed by appointees from the merchant aristocracy, i.e. the 800 families listed in the Book of Gold (Libre d'Oro). We have practical men with a vested interest managing our affairs. To have the "best and brightest" controlling national and local affairs is something we ought to study more carefully in this country. The point again is that the internal structure of the republic in terms of its departments, laws, traditions, elective and selective processes were so interlinked, perfected and effectuated that governance was automatic. Marvelous operation, totally without sentiment or romance, but as pragmatic as any ever created.

It might be a mistake to separate so decisively leadership from structure, and I do so only to emphasize the advantages of each. Maybe the conclusion is that a happy combination between leadership and structure is best. Like that which appeared in 1066 when William conquered England. The invasion from Normandy was his venture, his investment, his strategy, and his risk. Having won the battle, there was no question about who was in control, William owned England (sort of like the Pharaoh). He gave the church 25% of the land; he took 20% himself; 27% went to ten Norman nobles who had supplied much of the manpower, and the last 27% to 160 knights who had helped win the kingdom. The peasantry became serfs, tenant farmers, reporting to the knights, the barons or the church. The king assessed his barons and knights for money to run the state, and they in turn assessed their subordinate landowners, farmers, cities, and institutions to pony up. There is no parliament to fool with; the king calls the shots and runs the show. But "the show" ultimately evolves to a parliamentary democracy as political evolution occurs over the centuries. Wherein the roles are reversed and kings become subordinate to structure, but both remain as elements of control.

But the Norman-British pattern was unique; in the rest of Europe, the story was different. Decentralized monarchies did not succeed until the dozens of dukes, margraves, seigneurs, counts, archbishops, princes, viscounts and what have you surrendered their provincial authority to the crown. In Italy that did not occur till Garibaldi (19th Century), in Germany, simultaneously under Bismarck eight centuries after William. France had a long, painful, internal battle bringing Anjou, Maine, Burgundy, Aquataine, Normandy, Brittany, Languedoc, and a dozen others to heel. Spain and the Balkans ditto. Not so in Britain. William settled all that in one fell swoop. His leadership and structure functions were found in harmony and illustrate the point: When mutually supportive, they provide optimal success.

This topic ought to be of interest to both those of us in business and we who are Americans. The Founding Fathers spent a good deal of time talking about the balance of powers between the structure and the leader, i.e. the Constitution/Legislature and the President. What's the best design for each to function? In the process, how do we create a synergism which would strengthen and make more efficacious the republic? The Articles of Confederation had bungled our fortunes, raising questions about the effectiveness of squabbling legislatures juxtaposed with the enormous political stature of George Washington — the strong man on a white horse. Was he not a better option? Maybe. But, only for the time. For the long haul, they put our money on a clever, relatively simple structure which declared we were a system of laws, not of men. Our governance vehicles will arbitrate the division of power. It does some changing, but no one wonders how it is constituted or how it works. What's amazing is how we gain our power and prestige with such

remarkable mediocrity in the White House. Most of our Presidents have been decent men, but rarely a genius or even a cum laude type, much less Phi Beta Kappa quality among them. Structure is king here.

Caterpillar dealers contribute some insights on this topic. Our company began as a monarchy, resting almost entirely on the ability of one person, E.W. MacAllister ... ole Mac. It struck me as strange (I was its Secretary from day one) that despite all the initial state filings and organizational documents, we never once (then or later) held a stockholder meeting or a board meeting. My father was the Board and since his record of success was proven, his style seemed the one to continue. It had, of course, secured the CAT contract. But it was adequate for him — and for that moment. Underneath he was also dealing with a "structure": the vast Caterpillar system including the manufacturing component plus a market product and a large body of owners. A condition or circumstance which was moving, unobtrusively changing. So our style, effective in a given era, was tested by the long haul. The weakness in "leader models" is reliance on a single person who can be considered successful only if he finds a worthy successor. When Ole Mac slipped out in 1951, his successor reverted almost entirely to structure. With the charismatic figure gone, the next guy didn't want to make decisions for the Sales Manager, the Service or Parts guys. That is why they were there. He also lacked the competence and will to retain the "strong leader" model. Good thing. Anyone who tries to manhandle a dealership these days with its divergent product line, involvement in the rental business, recourse to computerization (I can see my dad opening a computer every morning, Uhuh!), ten physical locations, the staff a 1000% larger, etc. would either go out of his mind in a month, leave two-thirds of what he has to do undone, or capitulate to using staff and structure. In our case, the reversion to structure has saved the bacon. But the lesson now is that this modus operandi is the vehicle of the leader to enhance corporate competence, vigor, stability and market share. Organizations can function with either model dominant, but the optimum success comes when each is the product and agent of the other in pursuit of the common objective. ∎

E.W. and P.E. MacAllister signing
CAT contract on June 2, 1945.

2003

An Inquiring Mind Learns

March 2003

My friends know I belong to a group of 20-25 men who breakfast together on Wednesday mornings (at 6:45 AM!) to do a little Biblical "research". This is <u>not</u> a series of testimonials or "conversion" experiences. There is no "speaking in tongues". This is a study group, committing us to modest research with an operational pattern that functions on a rotating basis so one at a time each of us becomes a "teacher". The underlying premise is that everyone ought to be his own theologian (to a degree and within bounds). But to do that, we need to know both scriptural content and how it might be interpreted. So our fellowship is a process which acquaints us with both the Bible and the resultant Christian theology.

The logistical approach is simple. We select a given "book" in the Bible, like say I Corinthians, written (or dictated) by Paul of Tarsus in about 51 A.D., then list the 15 chapters in Corinthians beside a corresponding calendar date. Each of us then signs on for a specific chapter. Plus one: an "introduction". Which puts the whole book into context, noting the historic, theological, geographic and literary circumstances appurtenant thereto. Why was it written; when; by whom; to do what; how much "diddling" has been done with the text; what sort of bias or tilt it might have? Etc. The next week we take chapter one and the assignee exegetes the text, then onto number two and so on. Each leader has to research his chapter and figure out what is going on here.

Which means recourse to available study material. For my turn, I use *The Anchor Edition Series;* a series by Robert Barclay (a bit conservative for my taste but a great scholar); the early *Interpreters Bible Commentary* and now the updated, *New Revised Interpreters Bible*. Each of these examines every sentence of the scriptural text and tells us what we need to know about the original languages and translating problems, pertinent biographic data about the characters; explains any peculiar customs of the times; notes the writers' sources for references, Jewish law or similar beliefs in other cultures, etc.

Reason again is to learn not only what the words say <u>but what they mean</u>. How much sense do they make (or why they don't make any sense); how well the original language translates into English; what element of truth is evident; what's this got to do with an existing historical situation, etc. If the Bible (as we Presbyterian believe) is "the infallible witness to the truth", why don't I find out for myself what it says and why not get help from authorities to see it more clearly? Why read it year after year rarely clear on what it was written to teach or impart?

Land hallowed by Hebrew history.

In this exercise our amateur research makes the story real, teaches stuff we didn't know, and moves us out of the fluttery mythological milieu to a rational and historic appreciation. One becomes not only familiar, but downright <u>friendly</u> with a text, formerly austere, mysterious and sacrosanct.

The reason for this long prolegomena is to provide illustration for the key premise in this essay. By now, 40 years after starting, we have been <u>through</u> much of it sundry times and funny things happen, a fact I first noticed in restudying Genesis (for the third time). I was surprised to be learning as much the second time as I did the first. Then — mirabile dictu — learning as much the <u>third</u> round as I did from the second. Why have I been so slow out of the blocks; why didn't I pick this up or did I "pick it up" and promptly forget it? Besides there is a lot of material in Genesis, like <u>50</u> chapters. But it finally occurred to me that each time I review the work, <u>it's from a broader base of insight than I had before.</u> The exercise has taught me more about the world of the patriarchs, about the Bronze Age of Canaan, about the other cultures Abraham encountered, all making me wiser than I was first go-around. Moreover, I have <u>seen</u> the land. <u>Been</u> to Shechem, Bethel, Shiloh, Beersheba, the Judean Hills, plain of Jezreel, Jordan Valley. Beyond that, now have contemporary source books, both more numerous and graphically depictive; seen television documentaries and National Geographic productions dealing more frequently and dispassionately with biblical material. If it started as a whimsical fantasy beginning in the Garden of Eden, the setting has become by now a real life society whose nature and culture we have reconstituted, proven through cities excavated and inscriptions translated, tombs explored, wall paintings interpreted. So I'm concluding: The more complete one's understanding of a given subject, the more readily and broadly he can assimilate new knowledge in the same or similar field.

A quick illustration: The second time we went through Genesis, I encountered a couple of surprises: Sarah was not Abraham's

only wife; Ishmael and Isaac were not his only sons. Late in life he married a woman named Keturah (Chapter 25) and had six more sons — Zimran, Jokshan, Medan, <u>Midian</u>, Ishbak, and Shuah, all facts of life to which I finally tumbled, though this second marriage is largely ignored; the additional family members unheralded. A year later when our study moved to the Book of Exodus, we rehearsed the saga of the Hebrews in captivity. Moses fled Egypt to avoid a homicide charge and ended up in the Sinai Peninsula, bunking with a prosperous rancher named Jethro, who the text identifies as a Midianite. Say again!! "Midianite!" Hey! Do you suppose this is a tribe created by one of Abraham's sons? The children of Israel in Egypt have totally forgotten who their God is (Abraham called him "El"); they no longer practice circumcision; the whole patriarchal emphasis and the worship of a single God is lost. Till suddenly Jethro, <u>the Midianite</u>, introduces Moses to his own God who is named Yahweh. If Israel lost track of its faith after Joseph, another line from the patriarchal seed retained it so it could reappear 400 years later and continue the story of developing monotheism.

My point again is that if I missed these little nuggets the first time around, more evidence in the memory bank made it possible to connect links in the story. First pass left them languishing unidentified. Only when I knew more did a light bulb go on.

Minerva (Athena) —
Goddess of Wisdom and War.

Expanding knowledge provides a broader base to learn things impossible to grasp before, thus, adding to the mental repository and providing greater illumination. I wonder if mathematics is another way of illustrating this point. I marvel at guys like Steven Hawking or Einstein or Newton or Galileo whose use of physics and mathematics led to unlocking the secrets of our universe. But I'll bet they all started the same way: learning how to add and subtract, then how to multiply and divide. Then to do square roots and move onto algebra, probably geometry to calculus and who knows where. I'll bet none of them started with logarithms as the first step. Each one built his knowledge and his proficiency a level and a stage at a time, negotiating each of these steps necessary before one could advance to the next. Again, it's the accumulation of experience or wisdom that gives us the capacity to do more and better things.

What this says to me is that experience is valuable not merely because it adds to our knowledge but also because it expands our capability to both understand and <u>do</u> more than was possible had we not become wiser.

My battle with the computer provides further illumination in the exploration of this topic. (It also provides for novices an ample amount of frustration and wasted time.) But to utilize the amazing capacity of the laptop and visit the endless wonder "out there", the system requires one start in the elementary stages of operation and progress slowly, learning one phase or technique before he graduates to another. As he progresses, the flood of data or information or resource comes pouring in. And his options for more enlightenment multiply. The frustrating point to we who are still struggling is fact that certain learned skills are required before the world of information at our fingertips, mind-boggling in its scope, is accessible to us. One might note the vast array of knowledge awaiting him, but knows as well he will be limited in accessing it, whatever variety it might be, until he has gained enough wisdom, proficiency, and knowledge to insure the unlocking technique is acquired before he begins the search. The conclusion (again) seems to be that the addition of wisdom is contingent upon existing knowledge and that given the mental capacity to learn, the more one is at the task, the more likely he is to expand this acuity in an exponential fashion. It takes learning to learn more, and the more learned one is, the more limitless is the potential to expand his knowledge.

It needs to be said that these observations or impressions are not applicable to everyone. All societies have both people inclined to watch, and others who choose to <u>do</u>. They have those who lead and those who follow. In our circumstance where education is universal, the general conviction ought to be that learning does not stop with graduation, but that it is life-long. The phenomenon of acquiring new wisdom from an expanded base applies to those accustomed to thinking, to reflection and retrospection; to those interested in solving problems and gaining a wider vision of the entire world in which they live. We have to possess a certain self-motivation; we have to "want to" if we are to grow cerebrally. If indeed we do

just that, my premise about learning from an ever-expanding base is a given; it is automatic, endemic.

"O.K.", you are saying, "But what has all this to do with the tractor business?" I hope a lot. Because I hope behind said tractor business there is a considerable degree of intellect at work, buttressed by the past experience, wisdom accumulated through two previous generations. This should give us an edge on both the current marketplace and that which is to come in the next phase. We easily get caught up on the emphasis given coverage or service or product and market differentiation; on the chores required to keep 550 people diligently and <u>intelligently</u> at their assigned task, developing a synergism that helps equate to success. Our day-to-week-to-month cycles focus on such tangible and measurable factors as dollar sales, units delivered, size of bank loan, return on paid assets, profit before taxes, etc. In short, on the functions involved in the dealership. Said focus is what provides the individuals at their respective tasks with measurable objectives and guidelines that indicate success or failure and to what degree. But in terms of creating the processes and setting the budgets, the game plan and the strategy for the fiscal periods, there has to be a large measure of figuring, planning, sorting, projecting and harmonizing so that the entire workforce is looking at the same targets and judging by the same standards and marching to the same drumbeat. If the overall objectives for 2003 are determined by Doug and his team and then fine-tuned by Chris, the plan has to be adopted and supported across the board. It has to be the plan of each one and the directions or implicit orders for each.

But note that we <u>plan</u> before we <u>do</u>. The validity and accuracy of the cerebral exercise maximizes the potential of the whole team. The estimation of economic climate, inventory and staff needs, effort required to sell 600 units, market coverage consistency, competitive strengths and weaknesses, all have to be managed if the plan is to succeed. This is not an ad hoc spasm or acting extempore <u>on the spot</u>. It is deploying all our resources to get as close to total excellence as we can.

Each year (often each season) has its own threats, opportunities, challenges. Part of which are foreseen and built into the agenda, part of which are off the wall and need quick and lively administration or strategy. The "wisdom" which we have accumulated from past experience ought to equip us for meeting any given threat or seizing any given opportunity.

We ought to be getting better at marketing and managing with each passing cycle and have to view each marked phase as one which teaches something new and permits us to do better. It will if we keep thinking and learning, understand cause and effect. Encourage our people so seeing each assignment as a craft that can be done better as an axiomatic habit.

And trying to-get-better-at-what-we-do is something we never stop "doing". Because if we get to be the smartest dealer around, maybe we also get to be the most successful. And once getting there, the annual challenge is to stay here … and to distance our self even more from Number Two. ■

In Memoriam: William F. Diehl
(November 28, 1918 – February 13, 2003)
March 2003

Bill Diehl and I had certain similarities in our sundry careers. Both of us went to college during the depression; both spent time in the military, he in the infantry as a tank destroyer and I in the Air Corps. Both became officers: One a First Lieutenant, the other a Captain. Each of us joined the construction machinery industry, he working for Iowa Manufacturing Company; I working for a dealer who represented Bill's product. We were three months apart in age; we came together because in Wisconsin my father had been a terrific salesman of gravel plants and had taken the Iowa account when he got the CAT franchise in Indiana. Turned out we did <u>not</u> have a lot of rock-crushing business in Indiana and when a prospect did appear, no one was smart enough — or became smart enough — to really do a selling job or design an installation. Ergo, call Bill, our Iowa Sales Rep, who impressed us with his poise, knowledge, sales ability, and his success with the prospective buyer. In 1948 we suspected he was unhappy with the endless days on the road and ambiguity about his future. Sensing this, my dad invited him to come to work for us. Thanksgiving of 1948 he had dinner with us and signed on as an Engine Salesman and doubled as well in crushing/screening equipment to begin what would be his life's career.

One brief insight into his character occurred when a year later I sold a new replacement engine to the Chrysler foundry for one of their cranes. Only to find our service manager couldn't shake someone loose to install it. So Bill volunteered to do it. Next day we are over there, the two of us, jacking a CAT D8800 around in the crane with a crow bar, aligning flywheel and coupling, assuring the mounting and anchoring same to the floor till mirabile dictu, we started it up, and the darn thing worked.

Bill didn't feel like waiting around till a serviceman who might not know any more than he became available, he just said, "Let's do it" (though like Bill Clinton, I had no idea of what "it" was). Bill had supreme confidence that what he didn't know, he'd sure figure it out. A measure of mechanical knowledge involved here; a lot of confidence, a no-nonsense determination to get the customer going as quickly as possible and if we can't achieve this the routine way, we'll find another way. Bill didn't lack for guts, but

he never let his confidence exceed his level of professional competence.

As I was ruminating last week about our 28 years together in the Caterpillar business, remembering the first time we played golf at Sun Blest out on North Allisonville Road. Our first, of a couple <u>hundred</u> golf games. The starting hole was along the road and a short par four. So I hit a decent drive, then hit the green and knocked in the putt for a bird. Bill was likewise on in two <u>and</u> down in three. He did that a lot. I did it twice a season. And I remember first birdie since it corresponded to the last game we ever played. Out at Crooked Stick, well after he had retired and into the period when he was becoming less and less active, had virtually given up the game and he wanted us to try 9 holes — again. He began tiring at seven holes. Said only one more. The 8th is a short, treacherous par three. I had some difficulty finally getting to the green and probably double-bogied it. Bill Diehl hit his drive on. Then knocked in the putt. He ended our golf exercise as he had begun: birdie/birdie. And I got to thinking that was the way he functioned as a Sales Manager and Vice President. He didn't strive for pars, the sort of score the rest of us want. Bill was a <u>birdie</u> shooter. He was determined to excel; he wanted to win.

Wanting to win is essential in any manager but though many <u>start</u> that way and are aimed in the right direction, it takes more than desire to succeed. It takes competence, it takes preparation; it

William Diehl

takes perseverance, acuity, energy, and a lot of self confidence. In other words, it takes a lot of different things to become a finished, a practiced and successful professional. In this case, a Sales Manager. Bill had acquired them all…without any managerial training or formal indoctrination. A good deal was learned through his natural athletic prowess and experience. Meaning, he <u>understood</u> the game he was playing, whether on the baseball diamond, basketball court, bowling alley, the bridge table or the football field. He conditioned himself to achieve and used that same dynamic in his professional career. Anything he got into, he wanted to master and the scrap books Mary kept of his sports career testified abundantly to his success. (He was an all-American at Iowa, captain of the team; most valuable player; basketball scholarship but played baseball instead. Scratch handicap on the golf course. 6'4" — he was a "piece of work".

When I took over in 1951, my first appointment was Bill as Sales Manager. Because he was a very bright guy, loved and excelled in the selling game, because the salesmen respected him enormously, because he was level-headed, fair and judicious; because the rest of the company admired him. He was not an emotional or visceral thinker. He was a pragmatist when it came to budget building, threats from competition, programs from Caterpillar, alibis from salesmen or impractical ideas from me. There will be no wishful thinking, no dissimulation. He did not make a lot of mistakes. His ability was recognized by Caterpillar and for 25 years, Bill Diehl was the dominant figure in the eyes of Caterpillar for our dealership. Why not? The cutting edge of our operation — like any distributor — is selling the product. Only

Bill Diehl and P.E. with D8 Ripper; 1959.

from that flow the parts, service and rental business.

During Bill's career, Indiana built its toll road and hard on the heels of that, our interstate highway system, 1100 miles of it in Indiana. Those were rollicking times. Competition exploded, contractors waxed blustery and arrogant; there were a jillion things going on over a broad front so it was a phase of intense activity, sort of crammed together. If it was a period of exuberance, it was also a sort of a knockdown, drag-out exercise, one so exhausting when it ended, virtually every major competitor we had hit the wall. And the manufacturers they represented were likewise soon bought out or subsumed. During it all, we had the right guy smack in the middle of the whole fracas. Someone (first of all) who was never intimidated by tough, smart-ass major contractors from out of state who enjoyed beating up on our competitors. They never backed Willie down. And beyond that, he was a salesman who knew when to "walk" on a deal. When it gets too lean, you <u>want</u> your competitor to have the sale. It was great to have a guy who could talk to the earthmover and sell him a package, but also someone who understood the land-clearing contractor, the paver, the bridge builder, the aggregate people, and is able to deal with each on his own level and in his own language. Mostly, we had a guy who could sell CAT benefits to overcome the inevitable lower price of the competitor, no mean challenge then or now. In Willie we also had someone who was absolutely honest, was loyal to the company, could work with our subordinate departments, and had not only terrific rapport with CAT but superb relations with our neighboring dealers from who we often borrowed or traded for the machines we needed. Add to that the fact he was a hard worker, loved his job. 7:15 every morning — including Saturdays. In 1966 he accounted for 155 units sold, ordered, processed and invoiced by Bill and one office guy. 3000 new units delivered during his career.

It is hard to overestimate his importance to our company. If he had dropped the ball in the '60s, and I had been required to pick it up, Chris would be doing something else today, believe me. Bill was the best friend I had in this industry and one of the best friends I had ever. He was not only kind to me when I was right, he was still supportive when I was wrong. I leaned on him for advice, borrowed heavily from his confidence, and appreciated his partnership. Despite numerous chances to join other dealers, larger and more challenging than ours, he rejected the offers and stayed in Indianapolis.

He was a very tough competitor and played the game, whatever it was, to win. So one of his hardest trials was playing gin with my mother. Bill would stop by occasionally and mix Hilda a scotch. After which she expected to play gin … a half cent a point. From the get-go, it was no contest because Willie had played hundreds of hours of gin (a lot of them with or against me), and my mother could barely shuffle the cards. But appreciating <u>her</u> joy in winning and since he was keeping score, he made sure part of the time, he had to pay up. That had to go down against the grain, but he was really kinder inside and gentler than was often evident on the surface.

Watching him the last ten years has been a lesson for all of us. Here is this guy who was the epitome of physical excellence and a model of intellectual sophistication, gradually immobilized and imprisoned in a straight jacket, not of his own choosing but of his own stricken physiology; slowly battling the advance of MS which robbed him inexorably of his ability to function and participate. Complicated by the loss of Mary almost five years ago and, finally, virtually immobile in a retirement home. He'd tell us what had happened to him now, but never complained, never criticized, never bitched, never ever whined. He spent some tough times overseas in '44 and '45, and I recall one incident where he and his driver were sitting on a ridge in a jeep checking out the kraut activity. There was sporadic gun fire and a sudden whoosh very close by. He turned to see his friend had been decapitated by an artillery shell. Bang! and Van was dead. Meaning, he got in some spots that required enormous courage during those long bloody months in trading fire with the Germans. But he was never more courageous than the last years of his life. Sucking up and enduring, aching, frustrated, ill and unhappy, but gutting it out. What a rare guy!

Ernest Henly has some words that to me describe Bill's stoicism:

Out of the night that covers me,
Black as a pit from pole to pole.
I thank whatever Gods may be
For my unconquerable soul.
In the fell clutch of circumstance
I have not winced nor cried aloud
Under the bludgeoning of chance,
My head is bloody but unbowed.
Beyond this place of wrath and tears
Looms but the horror of the shade
And yet the menace of the years,
Finds and shall find me unafraid.
It matters not how straight the gate
How charge with punishment the scroll
I am the master of my fate,
I am the captain of my soul.

Another English poet told us not to never "send to know for whom the bell tolls". When a great friend and colleague like Bill goes, the bell of mourning tolls for us. <u>My</u> world and memory of the tractor years will not be the same with him gone. He was a fabulous guy, a superb operator, and close, dear friend. Our only consolation is knowing his travailed has at last ended. May he rest in peace. ■

Unfair and Un-American: Why?

June 2003

The topic of tax cuts is monotonously prevalent in our American political conversations and has the disadvantage of being monotonously repetitive as well. The arguments — pro and con — are what they were since the republic was founded, and each cycle sees a reiteration of the same objections or support, using the same clichés that bored us last time around. "Last time around", the rational for proposing a cut was probably "it stimulates the economy." The objection was also familiar: a retort from Daschle and Gephardt, "It's a tax break for the rich!" Those with the most wealth benefit the most. Then the rebuttal: the dollar difference here is <u>arithmetic</u>, not deliberately selective. Tax cuts apply most to those who pay the most taxes. 1% of you-all pay 28% of all income tax; 5% contribute 58% of the tax revenue. A cynic (a <u>wealthy</u> cynic) wonders if taxes on wealth are fair. Is it fair to charge him more because he breathes more oxygen, needs more snow removal or uses the roads more than the next guy, has more fires or pollutes the environment more?

But taxes are not the issue here, rather it is the style and nature of public debate, taxation being a single example of that ongoing interchange. "Any broad tax cut is a break for the rich" is not a reasoned conclusion. It's a reaction and one that carries an inference of unfairness. Unfair <u>and</u> un-American. Why? Why isn't a tax break for <u>anyone</u> a good idea? Should we hate the rich who save more money even though it costs me nothing? To indicate the bias about cutting taxes, the people who deplore easing off on the rich would <u>applaud</u> long and chortle mightily, rejoicing in any tax break for the lower brackets. It <u>is</u> O.K. to provide a special benefit to a given citizen category, but not to all citizens. Hmmm.

We have two sides here because <u>my opinion</u> determines what a <u>fair</u> tax is. There is no universal fairness definition. A sales tax might come close because it's one rate for everyone. Taxes on cigarettes, booze and gasoline are not fair. They only apply to smokers, drinkers or drivers. Which extracts revenue from certain people for the benefit of all. How about property taxes? Well, they hammer me unmercifully while allowing a huge real estate agent or insurance company down the street (with same profits but no inventories) to pay a pittance. Inheritance taxes hit some not others; then change rates with estate size. Americans also pay different taxes and different rates from one state to the next. Anyone who thinks taxing, as we do it, is fair and equitable hasn't examined the whole range of diversity; or been in the ring with the regional IRS agent.

Point being, this is very complex and like most serious political concerns is enormously and deceptively complicated. In approaching it we have a tendency to create a premise in our own minds on how good or bad an issue is and on that basis construct a rationale. If our viewpoint is erroneous, you can imagine how faulty our conclusion is. So national debate usually gets localized and personalized and is delivered primarily from the perspective of a given vantage point, not eternal verity.

Most arguments about policy depend on "Whose ox is being gored?" How it squares with my financial well being, viewpoint, tradition or circumstance. Then, the way I present my case moves into style, language, approach. By shouting "Tax break for the rich!" I not only defined the issue but imply a given perspective. Which includes a judgment, i.e. it is wrong to give a tax break to the rich? Wealthy are now a separate group of Americans, deserving of different treatment. And the rich are different <u>because</u> the "differer" implies it, and they are <u>supposed</u> to pay more than me.

The rhetorical mode divides us into sides: the wealthy who are unworthy of a break; the unwealthy who deserve a better break. This tactic also shifts the level of argument from logic or from fiscal reasoning to a hypothetical circumstance, concluded on the basis of opinions, viewpoints, conjecture and

Statue of Liberty.

supposition; a process that can see objectivity (fairness) depart; with reason, logic and openness often following along as well.

The list of issues Americans discuss and upon which they disagree is legion: the whole Social Security business (increasing cost/fiscally frail future), abortion, ethnic rights, gun control, foreign policy and America's role in the world, healthcare costs, education, NAFTA, the environment, crime, drugs, church-state stuff, etc. Part of a diverse and colorful assortment, the discourse on which generates occasional rancor. But not to worry. This is not a bad sign. Fact, disagreeing openly and amicably is a symbol of a strong republic. Governance is after all the provenience "of the people", not the property of a special class, and one way of having our voice heard is through public debate on issues. Which takes the form of cocktail conversations, letters to the editors, guest appearances on news shows, involvement in political campaigns, joining organizations with special interests and projects, table talk at business lunches, etc. Our government would lose contact with the constituency did we desist in, or deny, public debate and freedom of expression. So the process is good but can be damaged by a prejudicial posture on the basis of a simple newspaper editorial or an opinion trumpeted by the Jane Fonda – Barbra Streisand types. With no effort to look at the "big picture" or checkout both sides, we "surface-think" a subject and disregard its complexities. Discussion or protest or rally or the argument itself can make us better acquainted with nationally-important topics and in rare cases, maybe help influence action. We are after all a "government of the people, by the people and for the people".

The admonition here will not be "Love one another" or "Please, don't rock the boat"; it will be "Look before you leap" or "Please, engage mind before putting mouth in gear". It encourages the elevation, nature and texture of the debate, pleads for recourse to facts, cautions against snap judgment. We need more sentience in America and less sentiment. To all of which you say wisely, "Good Luck". The strength of the system depends on personal opinion and free speech. Which dynamic keeps us in the system and when strongly supported, can shape public policy. These freedoms of action and expression ought to be wisely practiced since they are basic to both the operation _and_ perpetuation of our republic. Will Durant opined our 228-year-old experiment is a legacy from the ancient Athenians who fashioned the most remarkable political experiment in history. Its success probably due to the development of abstract thinking, the democratic elective process, free speech, trial by jury, etc. — all representative and citizen-engaging. But alas, the record proves democracies espousing freedom are not automatically sagacious or even right. Fact, the Golden Age of Athens was also inadvertently deceptive, managed not by the Athenian gerousia (council), but really directed by Pericles who was elected chief archon year after year, thus, evolved into a benevolent (if voluntary) dictatorship.

The representative process is unique, but is only as efficient and equitable as we make it. Despite its novelty and promise, the Athenian system failed because you couldn't do business with a voting assembly of 5000-plus men milling around the Pnyx every ten days. Open discussion by all eligible citizens of all pertinent topics does not guarantee success. But it does guarantee an exposé or an airing and displays the sundry sides of many topics though it works only when wisdom, intelligence, patience and pragmatism lead to the proper action. A prospect best assured by open analysis of major issues.

In a relatively pure democracy, or its evolutionary model, which is our republic including modified prototypes like trade associations, Kiwanis Clubs, colleges, churches, and a thousand other voluntary organizations, problems are solved by examining all possible options for solution (public debate). In this exercise ultimately — and usually — through process of elimination, one proposal proves the best way to go. But getting there is complicated. As we deal with abortion or healthcare, education or tax rates, military spending or unemployment, not only do judgment and reason kick in, but partisan politics and vested self-interest interject themselves as well. How this effects <u>me</u> or my group overrides a lot of clear thinking. And, what is best for "me or my group" may not necessarily be what is best for the republic. So getting oneself into an objective frame of mind is easier said than done. Finding a way of considering the "republic" rather than my party or my city or my white-Anglo-Saxon predilection is a tough row.

Fact, it won't be achieved by shallow thinkers or by those who are so infallible they won't countenance any counsel (may-be-wrong-but-never-in-doubt types). Once committed to a certain stance, we have our reputation on the line and to grant we have erred means we must confess to culpability and reverse our thinking. Not easy for large egos (like mine) but

P.E. in 1962 when crew cuts were in vogue.

then finding the "easy" way is not the objective. It is finding the right way. So over the course of time, a couple of rules have helped me edge closer to the large-picture overview. First, one rule for finding the truth is to stay concentrated on the issue. It is common practice when we are losing the argument to shift the focus and attack the character (intelligence, wisdom, motives and prejudice) of the opposition. We abandon the debate and the subject to disparage those who disagree. Not helpful.

A second bit of advice is don't merely listen, but honestly <u>hear</u>; try to comprehend (like it or not) what the other guy is saying. We know he is a bleeding heart liberal, has a diamond in his nose, and needs a haircut but that has nothing to do with what is coming out of his head via his mouth. Voltaire once said, "What you <u>are</u> speaks so loudly I cannot hear what YOU are saying", and in the process makes my point. Voltaire expected people to listen to (or to read) him. Why not extend the same courtesy to others, instead of leaping to conclusions about what their appearance said?

It is also good to examine one's own fallibility, check the personal batting average occasionally. How often am I right and is that often enough? On long trips, I have been lost enough times to know my convictions about the right street or highway is kind of a joke. No one has picked more political losers than yours truly. I've been wrong a long time. I thought in the '60s friends marching in Selma or Montgomery, Alabama for civil rights were butting into someone else's business. Leave the south alone. Wow! Bottom

line is, I'm right about 60% of the time, but I am just as vehement the 40% I'm wrong. Each of us is fallible and prone to error. Passionate conviction is no evidence of validity.

People who disagree might in the process teach me something. The fact that they challenge my reasoning makes me think seriously and examine the wisdom of my position. I often learn more from those in the opposition camp than the choir to whom I've been preaching all these years. I tend to read authors with whom I agree, associate with people, join movements, build relationships, and carry ongoing interchanges with people on my own team. Which is often recycling ideas rather than discovering new material. I need some Democrat friends to keep me honest politically.

Moreover, the <u>articulation</u> of a given position or conviction helps straighten out the kinks. I have maintained we do not understand what we believe theologically until we have to explain our faith to someone else, and in the narration of ideas or concepts, only vaguely formed and generally assumed, we have to get precise; in that process we finally know what we believe. In emoting about the mistake in declaring war on Iraq, e.g., we can get all lathered up, but in verbalizing and stating our rationale for objecting, we not only have to get specific but let others take apart our argument and either correct it, demolish it or re-enforce it. Discussion helps both sides.

In concluding, I think wrapping one's self in a given position, oblivious and impervious to outside argument or pertinent data and feeding only on personal prejudice, we preempt the aspect of human community and destroy any prospect of the harmony which must exist if we are to get along on this planet. Partisan politics, religious extremism, ethnic arrogance, rehearsal of ancient grievances and tribalism in all its forms have plagued man since he got up off his knuckles. Knowing what the problem is and understanding society itself depends upon the surrender of certain human tendencies as a given in exchange for communal benefits; the success of any political enterprise depends upon the degree to which its citizenry injects tolerance, reason, openness, and commitment to the "greater good". ■

How to Move an Interstate

September 2003

Had a chance a week ago to visit the huge construction job on I-70 south of the airport which has been a beehive of activity all year — with the biggest spread of machinery we've seen around here in a long time. Turns out this is a seven-project program preparing the way for — and including — the new airport facility. All the churning around reminded me of the old interstate days. This takes place as we build a new terminal, a picture of which by the way appeared in the Indianapolis Star so we know its design and the proposed cost (just under a billion). It's to be built midfield and that new locus means we have to find a new way of getting to it <u>while</u> we keep the old way open and interstate traffic moving on I-70. The current entrance is from the east, off I-465 and proximate to I-70 but since this will no longer work, we are moving the front gate to the southside with another gate to the west. (It is hard to describe this verbally; we need to have that picture "which tells a thousand words"). But to get the entrances relocated, we need more space than exists. So we have to move I-70, 300-600 feet <u>south</u> of its current location. This has triggered the huge piles of dirt and all the machinery scurrying back and forth.

There are a number of contractors on the project working mostly under the "prime" who is Walsh Construction, out of Chicago. If the name rings a bell, it's because they were also the contractors on the recent "Hyperfix". Then, a year or so <u>earlier</u>, did the major renovations and re-ramping of I-465 on the east side which sort of screwed up traffic for me coming to work each day. They have successfully bid three of the first seven airport contracts awarded, including those which entail moving I-70 south; plus the construction of two humongous (I think the man said 2500 feet) overpasses; the road work on the west side and beyond that, relocating of at least two water courses.

At which point a slight excursus: I never saw a man-made river before. The riverbed actually designed and laid out in the construction trailer, alongside the prints for the cuts and fills and accesses and structures in the highway relocation. The striking feature of the river is the wiggle pattern. It looks like a connected series of "esses" with virtually no straight stretch of any sort. If I were laying out a new water course, I'd minimize the number of yards of dirt to move, or feet of bank to rip-rap, or square footage of wetland in the overflow and anything else. But, aha! I have forgotten the erosion factor created by a straight flow of water, building up speed as it hurries on, eating away the bank at a fierce rate and cutting gouges all over the place. O.K., so environmental accommodation costs money, but provides aesthetic beauty and for the long pull, avoids the future damage of erosion. To assure the integrity of the stream and the limitation of where the water is going to be flowing, they have actually manufactured a way to slow speed and prevent erosion. I have a hard time finding a name for the protective agent because I never saw one before. The area in which the new river is to flow was heavily wooded, and that is now gone. So we uprooted a jillion trees, 12-20" in diameter and cut them off maybe four feet above the root level, but have saved the stump plus the huge root system. Then we sharpen these tree stumps and drive them in the bank of the stream, roots facing outward. The dozens of root plugs act as a buffer for the current and at the same time, provide a network of protection for small aquatic species of all sorts to live and grow within the snarl of roots. Then hand pick a lot of <u>selected</u> stones and rocks for the river to provide the right sort of under-base which will generate the proper sort of turbulent action to keep the water aerated. I mean, it's the most sophisticated stream east of the Mississippi.

The span of the whole relocation project — beginning to end — is something like four miles. Beyond the I-70 section south of town is another component we can't see very well, bringing in the

CAT motorgrader smoothing dirt for a ramp along I-70.

traffic from the west to the second entrance. What provides specific access to the field itself (and, thus, the terminal) are two great swooping, overhead ramps taking the traffic up and over, depositing same inside the airport fence and on into the field for union with the terminal. The amount of cut and fill on this job was 3,000,000 yards; a stockpile with 700,000 cubic yards displaced to be relocated where needed; 75 pieces of equipment on the job; pile drivers hammering in steel uprights for the bridging; tractor/scrapers moving fill dirt 17,000 yards to the west; compactors finishing the compaction on the fills; off highway trucks, dozens of hydraulic excavators, motor graders, new (to me) units with a pull tractor and <u>three</u> connected scrapers in the rear; dozers leveling and cutting, guided to accuracy by global-positioning gadgetry on their blades to find the right level; huge troglodytes scarifying lime into certain areas to deal with moisture. In short a hundred different processes going on simultaneously over a four-mile stretch and active in three or four levels. All ongoing since January. I can't imagine,

given the winter we had, these people out there daily slogging away and pilling up the yardage and laying in the pipe and getting piles in for overpasses, etc. But it gives evidence of considerable skill, tremendous coordination, huge investments in time and material, endless planning, and checking the maintenance of a jillion pieces of machinery; the sequential completion of different elements to allow a cut and fit procedure. Being sure the "cut" is accomplished before the "fit" is attempted. It is a complex project and keeping it all together is a real challenge. Tim Johnson is the Project Manager, a Purdue grad (we are proud to say), and a native of Lake County. He suggested something of the scope of our new airport project and also indicated to me what "the big leagues" are all about. Completion date estimated to be November — for <u>this</u> section. By which time the terminal will be under construction with all the traffic and confusion and activity that will entail. Indianapolis keeps moving forward. ■

What Was Really in the Box?

September 2003

We probably get into religious issues more often than is prudent in this publication but feel when said discussion becomes current news, it becomes legitimate as a discussion topic. New stuff keeps happening in the religious field like it does in pharmaceuticals or tractor design or video games, and it's good to stay current. For instance, late last summer a discovery titillated the Judeo-Christian world and its appearance in the *New York Times, U.S. News, Time Magazine, The Wall Street Journal*, etc. made it a "current event" more than a mere religious commentary. The subject was a stone box discovered in the hands of a Jerusalem contractor named Oded Golan who is reported to have the largest private collection of historical artifacts in Israel. It was probably unearthed by a pilferer from who-knows-where in the area around Jerusalem, sold to a dealer, who in turn sold it to the current owner. Since it seemed to have little unique about it, he put it away in storage.

Then one night an expert named Andre Lemaire met Mr. Golan at a social event and while chinning about collecting or archaeology, Golan wondered if Lemaire would look at photographs he had of inscriptions found on articles in his collection. One turned out to be a photograph of the writing on this peculiar box which is in truth an ossuary — a container to collect bones. The inscription was easy to read: *"Ya'akov bar Yosef akhui di Yeshua"* which means "Jacob (or James), son of Joseph, brother of Jesus". We all know that Jesus was attributed to be the son of Joseph; we also know that one of his four brothers was named James. Although never a disciple he did become the leader of the early (probably the first) Christian parish in Jerusalem.

When news of this translation reached the media, everybody said, "WOW!" Then wondered, "Could this be possible?" There were a lot of Josephs in Jerusalem in 50 A.D. and plenty of Jacobs, then a fair amount of Joshuas, but then how many would form the same relationship pattern? Well the best guess is that perhaps 20 out of a Jerusalem population estimated to be 80,000. There was no doubt this was indeed an ossuary, a stone box weighing about 45 pounds, 23 inches long, maybe 7 inches wide, and 9 inches deep. And it could have been the repository for the bones of James, the brother of Jesus. If so, it's the first piece of physical evidence connecting us to the historical Jesus. And that's great news.

But there are some curious conditions involved here. Where was the box found? The dealer who sold it said it came from Silwan, a settlement adjacent to the old walled city of Jerusalem just south and east of the temple mount. What's the box for? To collect the bones of the deceased and then replant them in the tomb of his family. Which gets us into a very unusual practice. The Jews rarely believed in life after death, except as a place called Sheol, a dark nether world into which <u>all</u> souls departed. So why save the bones? Because in the First Century before and after Christ (roughly 20 B.C. – 70 A.D.), a new theory arose among the Pharisees evolving out of some Old Testament or Talmudic commentary. It involved a prophesy predicting "the great day of the Lord" which saw the end of this world and the inauguration of a new age. A judgment occurred and the righteous would be blessed and the wicked condemned to eternal fire. On that day as the Messiah returned with legions of angels, the dead would arise from their burial places and their reconstituted bodies would meet the Messiah in the air.

Ergo, certain Pharisees took special care of their bones to be sure they would be all together when the trumpet sounded and "they were called up yonder". We have the written instructions in a will: "My son, bury me first in a grave. In the course of time, collect my bones and put them in an ossuary …" Which would have then been placed in a family tomb, usually cut into the rock on a mountain side. All of which indicates the purpose of the box. Incidentally, we've

Two ossuaries near Naqsh-e Rostam, Fars, Iran.
Photo by Arash Zeini. *(Source: Wikimedia Commons.)*

recovered lots of these boxes from the First Century A.D.; 897 of them registered, 233 with inscriptions.

I noted earlier some curious conditions and one has to do with the inscription. Is it legit or is it a forgery? We have to get by the question: "How can somebody have a priceless article from the First Century A.D. belonging to he, who is the brother of Jesus, stashed in a store house?" And then someone serendipitously happens to read it? Come on! Ignorance of its original location, the mystery about its discoverer, and even the anonymity of seller compounds the mystery. Arabs made a fortune for centuries selling Christian tourists, crusaders, churches, monarchs, soldiers, etc. pieces of the true cross, slivers from the crown of thorns, fabric from the seamless gown, knucklebones from John the Baptist, or a tassel from Salome's shawl (used in her famous dance), or stains of Mary's milk, or a cane used by Peter's mother, etc. ad nauseam. This business of making sacred objects is among the oldest con games in the world so eyebrows are justifiably raised.

From the get-go, experts have been skeptical. The archaeologists quoted say, "The box is legitimate. But there has been some tinkering." The writing is the "enigma". Because it was written by two different hands, two styles (like part is printed, some part is cursive). One letter is backward. And there appears to be a glitch in word-forms. We have an ancient container and a tantalizing mystery.

I saw it in Toronto with thousands of people, ooohing and aaahing; wondering was this indeed the ossuary which held the bones of James, who had lived in the same household as Jesus, probably helped him in the carpenter's shop, had breakfast with him each morning, and remembered the day he left home in 27 A.D. to go off preaching? Few people doubt the historicity of Jesus but positive, tangible evidence does not exist. So this is the sort of hypothesis, submitting physical support a lot of folks want to believe.

During the discussion (which is still ongoing), a couple of my more erudite archaeological friends said, "Tsk, tsk. It is a forgery." The box? "No, the box is real; the writing is not legit." A month ago a panel of Jewish scholars in Jerusalem got out their chemical sets and began examining the patina, the incising and the script. "A fake!" they said. The "aging" of the stone took place by rubbing some sort colored lime across it, and the nature of the writing appeared as though a modern scholar tried to emulate ancient modes (and failed). In the mind of these 12 experts,

the inscription failed to pass the test. No question. But all are not convinced.

All of this makes us reflect on the whole subject of religion, and in my case the proof offered by the scriptures as the basic historic fundamentals to support the Judeo-Christian faith. Fashioned from the warp and woof of Middle Eastern cultures (which we have no trouble proving), then gestating for centuries to take form and shape in the three to five centuries before and after Jesus. After which it is locked in place, doctrinized, dogmatized, expounded in hundreds of thousands of interpretative books replete with expository sermons, essays and exegesis proclaiming the divine truth; all delivered to us as "gospel". Fifty generations of the faithful have wrestled with it, examined, testified and accepted it. Only in the last century to be put to a different sort of chemical test, one of scientific and historic scrutiny which sees point after point sort of washed away and declared "phony". Mostly by archaeologists and historians. So we are asked to reexamine the integrity of many claims and contentions (i.e. the covenant which saw Yahweh giving land to the Jews as a perpetual inheritance) and see if we are reading them right.

Then, end up in the same situation as those who examined the ossuary. The historic origins of both Israel and Christianity are facts hardly debated any more. Like the box, each is solid; is legit; both happened; both are alive and well. But how they happened and the way writers or scribes understood or told the story, or more specifically demonstrated the meaning or the lessons or the teaching is what becomes suspect. Allegory or metaphor is too often construed as fact; vignettes illustrating the power of the God sometimes get over exuberant since the genuine power of said God is impossible to properly portray to finite minds. We do the best we can to illustrate or demonstrate; and in that process expose ourselves to misstatement if the reader fails to understand our figure or analogy. The consolation to us ought to be the very fact of examination, discussion, argument and accounting, all of which explore and expand the topic. All of which lead us more quickly and more closely to the truth than the old way which was an edict, proclaimed by a Mullah, Shaman or High Priest telling us what it is we shall believe...and don't ask questions. We don't care whether you understand or not. Interpretation of things theological is our role not yours. ■

Religion is Personal

December 2003

Since this is a Christmas editorial and since Christmas has its origins in the Biblical stories of the nativity, it is surely not inappropriate to include some scriptural or theological rumination. Starting with a passage from the creation story in the first chapter in the Bible where Verse 20 tells us that, "God created man in his own image and in the image of God he created him." This venerable theory is fundamental to Judaism, probably Islam, and long accepted in Christianity. I don't propose to dispute that verity, but I've developed a strikingly similar, maybe heretical, counter proposition. It concludes that the opposite is also true. It is after all <u>man</u> who created the gods. They came to be — and are defined through — a human intellectual exercise. Deity — whether singular, triune or multiple — is not a solid object like an oak, a new born child or a Caterpillar tractor. It is a mental concept, a perception or supposition held by humans and since it exists, no other place, God indeed is the creation of man.

And has been so from the earliest times, reminding us of both the diversity and commonality in religion. Egypt (2500 B.C.) gave us amazing and startling variation in all sorts of strange animal gods. A cow figure for Hathor; an ibis for Toth; Anubis is a jackal; the cat was Sekmet; add the beetle and the cobra, the sun god Ra and the moon goddess Isis, etc. Egypt's definition of said divine forms arrived early and differed in characteristics as seen across the ages from the uncomplicated Great Spirit of the American Indian (1000 A.D.) to sophisticated Bronze Age Mesopotamian (3000 B.C.) which produced (reputedly) 700 divine, semi-divine, and quasi-divine beings. India sort of went wild with fierce critters like Kali and Vishnu while the Greeks and Romans fashioned their gods like mortals with the same passions and weaknesses; Norse gods glorified battle, were overly fond of mead and not much more complex than the race which created them. The gods of the Celts arrived out of Europe's forest lore; add the scowling dei-

When chapels were more ornate.

ties of Japan and China, the primitive-tribal figurines of Sub-Saharan Africa, and the awkward stone faces on Easter Island. This variety produced unique patterns peculiar to a given race because, again, it is men who describe for us the nature of the gods.

Why did they appear at all? To explain why "things" happen and herein lies the commonality.

Everyone in 3000 B.C. was frightened by great slashes of lightening, shuddered with the deafening roar of thunder; wondered why a nine year old child died; what caused this wound to become inflamed and puss-laden? Why do the days change in length and temperature? What causes earthquakes or blizzards? <u>We</u> know the answers to all of these; <u>they</u> had to guess and ascribed most of the unknown, often unseen, rhythms and patterns to other worldly forces in the form of gods, spirits, numen, sprites, dryads, ogres, demons, and you name it. They fashioned personalities to differentiate each, and then had to figure out how we negotiate with them and find a measure of peace and contentment as mortals. Along the line ancient man made a big mistake. He allowed a group to arise, specialized in explaining nature's forces: "priests" — the oldest, most exploitative element in history. Moreover, when linked with "the state", we have a force to cow mankind and keep him subservient.

If there was diverse interpretation of the gods, the functions and mysteries they accounted for were common as explained by the priesthood who introduced us to the sundry deities, provided names, defined powers and character, but also recited demands. They told us what the gods required to assure personal safety and well-being. The tool used to gain acceptance and assure obeisance was not knowledge or logic. It was fear. When this handy and convenient condition existed, it was a "no brainer" for the state (the king, tyrant, monarch) to use it in maintaining order among his people through laws, imposed as the will of the gods. Woe to he who disobeys.

Over time as mankind produced larger populations replete

with great cities, extensive cultivation, deeds and contracts, commerce, trade, agriculture and manufacturing, we needed rules to keep it all together, i.e. to interconnect in an orderly fashion. Voila! Laws occur; instructions are issued for personal or corporate conduct with religion (fear) as a partner in this process rather than a by-product of it. Looking across the spectrum of humanity in 1200 B.C., the beginning of the Iron Age, there were dozens of the peoples in the Fertile Crescent who had achieved a high degree of culture, a complex theology, a bustling civilization, each with its own political, territorial and theological uniqueness. They have left us records of their gods and cults. Yahweh was God of the Hebrews, controlled Judah and Samaria. Chemosh ruled Moab; Hadad protected Syria; Dagon, Philistia; Baal Melcart, the Tyrians; Marduk, the Babylonians; Molech, the Phoenicians; Ahura Mazda, the Persians, and you know the Greek and Roman pantheon, etc., ad nauseam.

What is surprising in this primitive, often destructive era is another common feature: a general tolerance, a laissez-faire attitude about religion. "You worship your gods <u>there</u>; mine are different; I'll do the same here." I can find only one period of religious intolerance (Antiochus Epiphanes) in the ancient world aside from Israel where the Jews systemized religious <u>intolerance</u>. Moses, Joshua and the prophets had this obsession about drifting over to see what Milcom, Asherah and El were doing. Elijah had such a fixation about the Tyrian Baal he butchered 400 priests with his own hand to remove the temptation … and the competition.

In Israel, as in Rome, Athens, Babylon or Nineveh et al, the cult itself was a vehicle and appendage of the state. It was handmaiden to the ruler. We are surprised to learn religion had little to do with morality. There was no implied ethical instruction, no inspirational teaching. There were ceremonies and processionals, shrines and sacrifice, tithes and curses, blood offerings and always constant fear of the malevolent erratic nature of the gods, who had no respect or regard for man and who beat on him for 4500 years.

With that verbose background, we might look at the religious patchwork in the world <u>today</u>. The picture is one which ought to make us cringe. Bronze and Iron Age man left the matter of faith up to the individual and as long as the citizen obeyed the law and did not desecrate the national gods, he could care less. We've changed that situation in this educated, sophisticated, enlightened society of today where Catholic fights Protestant in Northern Ireland, where Israel and Palestine are at each other's throats in an endless orgy of bombing and artillery attacks; the long war in the Sudan pits Muslim against Christian, a slaughter 20 years old. Saddam Hussein (and some of his successors today) made Shiite Muslims "fair game", killing countless thousands of them for one reason: They were not Sunni. El Qaeda and millions of Muslims in the world today want Sharia, holy law, to replace secular law and, thus, a national religion <u>intolerant</u> of nonbelievers. Hindu and Muslim are still assassinating each other in India and Pakistan only because each has a different religious faith. It is not a good scene, sports fans. It is a disgrace.

In this season of "peace and goodwill to men", I have an adage, ironically enough, may be more pertinent to the spirit of the season than traditional Biblical sources: "Religions are many; God is one; all men are brothers." Born a Christian, baptized in German by an Evangelical Lutheran preacher, raised ultimately as Presbyterian, I happen to have certain convictions about the creation and the creator, suggesting as well what's expected from by me, defining the conduct I ought to be demonstrating. It arises out of my own conditioning, background, education, rumination and study, and is a continually developing thing. Because of my "conditioning, background, education, rumination and study", it is both a personal modification and interpretation of Christianity. To some extent, I am still "creating" my own version of God. Religion is not corporate, national, tribal or cultural. It is personal. One has to know what he believes about the divine power in order to understand how he relates to it or fits with it; and then what this obligates him to be or do in his society. I can't "wear them golden slippers" because of what you or my parents believed.

Now, taking all this prolegomena into account, a bit of dialectical speculation, "Which of the gods (Pantheons) in the ancient world had it right? Which gave us the best answer, identified the creator of the universe, the wellspring of fertility in field and vineyard, maker of man and animal? If you come up with Elohim (1750 B.C.) or with Yahweh (1250 B.C.), the early God of the Hebrews, then who was the creator and true god 1,000 years <u>before</u> either arrived on the scene? (Ur of the Chaldees was bustling with activity 1200 years before Abraham was born.) The New Testament which is remarkable as both a work and theory declares my question is heresy. It is fairly narrow-minded about all this, fact, it is apodictic. Christianity insists that unless one is a <u>Christian</u>, he has no promise in the eternal plan. ("No one comes to the father except through me", Jesus declares…or rather, <u>John</u> has Jesus declare… "He who does not believe (in Jesus) is condemned…" "He who believes in the Son has eternal life, he who does not obey the son shall not see life, but the wrath of God rests on him", etc., etc., a dozen different places.) Scripture does not dwell long on this issue, but makes it clear enough that those who reject Jesus are damned, a place Jesus referenced as "eternal fire".

But Christianity is not unique with respect to possession of the true faith. My guess is the Jews think Adonai or Elohim (Yahweh) is the sole and supreme god of the universe, of time and eternity. Islam says that may be true, but since the penultimate prophet died (Jesus, by the way), a new revelation has given by a deity called Allah who changed the rules for salvation, making the dictates of Mohammed the rules for life, and his god is the supreme lord of history. I don't know a lot about Buddhism but, generally speaking, their concept is that life recycles itself until one reaches a state of perfection, making him one with the universal logos and is instructed in that process through the teaching of Siddhartha, the Buddha. My friend Shu Irani believes that the one great god is Ahura Mazda, as did his ancestors in ancient Persia 2600 years ago. Bahaullah taught his Bahia people a sort of universal amalgam of collected religious wisdom as their singular, peculiar and struggling faith. About Confucius and Lao-tze, I can not expound.

But which of the existing world faiths has it right? Which has the correct answer? Which has found the truth?

Scientific knowledge of the cosmos blew all of early man's theory of gods and creation out of the water and makes his convictions look pretty silly. It is hard in any age to understand the infinite with finite minds, to understand that which is non-understandable. Moreover, it makes one uneasy to have so much "contemporary religious" foundations laid in the Bronze or Iron Age and find them still determining contemporary theology. A fact of life theologians today might ponder when they make categorical claims about issues we can only postulate. Maybe one reason I'm hooked on Christianity is the fact that though begun eons ago, it is one religious phenomenon (Judaism is another) that reinterprets its doctrine to fit the age. It is "a faith that travels".

But since the questions, "Who started all this? Why? What are we doing here?" haven't changed, maybe there are answers — lessons — from the an-

cient world which might be instructive and should not be discarded. Fact, maybe Christmas is an example of same. If its theological basis is somewhat sub rosa, the spirit nonetheless survives. And retains a certain vitality and appeal. The season is rich in familiar symbols and images; it is focused around the family hearth. The theme from Luke and Matthew (75 A.D.) depicts a human phenomenon familiar to all peoples, a birth story rich in local color so superbly told that the literary style alone has assured a sense of perpetuity. The charm and warmth are human rather than theological attractions, inescapable at this time of the year. Significant to us because we have read the last chapter. It's the story of one whose life created the largest of contemporary faiths and popular because of what it promises or teaches. It harks to the prophets of ancient Israel and recasts the source of morality and ethical conduct found there (Amos, Hosea, Isaiah, Micah). It praises selfless living and declares those most in want or in need ought to be the center of human concern. Religion is about helping each other. It says that love is a greater force than power and claims (thanks to St. Paul) that there are no "untouchables" in the Christian community. Righteousness has replaced ritual; that we reach discipleship through our minds, demonstrate it through our actions. It says the human spirit is more important than the state; that God (whatever its form or locus) is patient and forgiving, not vengeful and vindictive, disdaining man and disliking him. That this God hates conflict and rejects war as a human option despite its prevalence. Though the instructions to "love one another" or "walk the extra mile" are more often than not ignored, there is never a point so far down the road the human soul cannot get back, cannot be "redeemed".

Bottom line in this essay is that through the long search to identify the creative force, for many of us this makes more sense than the hundreds of options tried through the ages. Not flawless or perfect, but one without peer in how it speaks to the human condition. None I know promulgate rules for behavior as decent, as wise and as solicitous as those found in the New Testament. And I guess if we didn't need <u>people</u> to represent it, this creed or cult or faith would look all the better. It is not the message or the instructions that are lacking, it is obedience and conforming that makes it look bad. At least it would appear to one with my condition, background, education, rumination and study. You'll have your own take on this.

Have a Merry Christmas! ■

We Farmers Have a Hard Row

December 2003

Those of us who do gardens each year realize we are dealing with elements of nature which are almost primordial. Fact, they are much older than the humanoid species and replicate the miracle of growth and reproduction in place long before Adam appeared. Eons later (like 2003 A.D.), they still demonstrate the same creative rhythm which makes life possible. We farmers don't ruminate long on these esoteric things; however, we merely demonstrate the wonder through our annual planting rituals. And we "wonder" each year, too, how faithful to the process will our seed remain. Every spring a set of enigmas: What sort of weather? What sort of germination? What sort of pests? What kind of luck? The final grade for this year was maybe a C to C+. Cold, wet spring with lots of rain (10 inches ahead of normal Labor Day), and temperatures generally 5-15 degrees below average with almost no warm, humid nights. Two-thirds of the corn I planted never germinated. But what did take root produced the best ever. Eighty percent of my potato seeds never sprouted; zucchini which ordinarily comes on so fast I can't keep 'em picked, appeared timidly one at a time, and the summer squash, ordinarily "a piece of cake" to grow, finally, with noticeable anguish gave me its first miserable fruit in September. But I had the best onion crop and best strawberries ever. Tomatoes were fair; eggplant so-so; no cukes but good peppers. And a bumper, I mean, "five star" weed crop. All in all, after being at this for 15 years, begin to realize what the professional Indiana farmer is up against. He's in a perennial crap shoot; I'm in for some good outdoor exercise, watching the age-old magic of growth and some fresh produce.

But the gardening "open" here is just an analogy to the machinery business where effort and action and aspiration can also end in results which may not be rewarding. Like my planting, effort can fall afoul of forces beyond our control. We go through the "cultivation" endeavor across the spectrum of our sundry dealer specialties, but effort or energy alone do not guarantee results. Our "harvest" (read "sales") depend on strength of the market, work-backlog of the buyers, weather conditions, quality of given product, competence of our people, nature and craftiness of competition, and how the buyer views us. Outside economic and psychological factors inter-

vene. When contractors or miners get jittery about the economy or about terrorism, a stock market drop or imminent war, confidence is stifled and a sort of desuetude is induced. Sagging economic indices cast a pall and like my potatoes, result in marginal, almost imperceptible sales. So through long experience, we farmers and machinery people make plans, knowing things might not happen as we had contemplated.

That's a long introit to a conclusion that reports the tractor business (like my garden) has been a disappointment, not only this year but four years running. If business generally is marginal in America, deliveries of our product lines have been sliding since 1999. We got spoiled early in the '90s with sales up year after year only to hit a swale, which is just plain hard going. Born out by monitoring reported manufacturer deliveries. There is an accepted statistical indicator out there so we know where things are happening; which models are sagging or holding; what markets are softening.

The record in Indiana is both clear and complex. We are dealing with over 400 different models in six branches and seven rental outlets. We accumulate and analyze the delivery data to see the picture, since one cannot manage wisely what he cannot measure accurately. We have to find out specifically where we are weak; who is giving us a problem and determine why we come up short. Is it product inferiority? Over-pricing; asleep on the deal? Poor customer relations, fewer people are buying; coverage or what? We track all deliveries in our territory by category; then our ratio to that total. One can't fine-tune his business with estimated guesses; we have to know what is happening and how we fit in with "what's happen-

Challenger combine at work.

ing". Ergo, our phobia about deliveries and how we stack up in the total matrix.

The major point was a declining and disappointing market. In our territory, 2983 units were delivered in 1999. This means everyone's dozers, scrapers, backhoes, trailers, excavators, rollers, skid steers, pavers, loaders, combines, et al. 2983 units in our 68 of the 92 counties in Indiana. The following year, that number dropped to 2763 units, and if you have your slide rule out, computed the decline to be 7.3%. Year three, it eased on down another 10%, and the following year (2002) it went to 2493 which is another 10% drop. Indiana delivered 846 <u>fewer</u> units in 2002 than it did in 1999. That's a decline of 29.4%. In terms of dollar sales, the total volume for 1999, all products, was $225,439,000 and in 2002, $149,151,596. $76,000,000 less dollars delivered: 33.8%.

Selling in a shrinking market gets tough for we sellers, but constitutes a break for buyers. Because operators desperate to generate income, cut prices and make screwy deals. So we have to meet price or duck out. I learned very early in the game one can't generate profitability on small losses. Or better yet, one might learn more on how to compete. Much of the business is new to us. But most of the same business fundamentals exist: provide an excellent machine at a fair price and exceed customer expectations. So in tough years, though we fight the good fight, we can miss our budget. But don't necessarily come up "barefoot". We just aren't as profitable as we ought to be or need to be or hope to be, and try to figure out why. In both the backhoe loader or skid steer markets, we began with zero share of the business. So the first measure is "progress". After year one, how much did we increase our percent of the total? Though a modest dollar item, this is a <u>huge</u> unit market, and John Deere and J.I. Case were flooding the land with loaders 20 years before CAT ever considered the idea. Same story with skid steer loaders where Bobcat has done a fabulous job for years. So the objective is to wedge our way in and be realistic about our success. We aren't going to hit 50% in three years.

A disappointing garden crop this year has not ruined my life, though it impaired my reputation as a backyard farmer. But even that was not without satisfaction. I had modest luck and engineered more by heavy fertilization, more diligent insecticide application, hands-and-knees weeding. There <u>was</u> improvement in the results. The belabored point to this diatribe is being able to do things which alter given trends. In the machinery business we have taken cor-

Ag salesmen: David Wilson, Brian Gum, Aaron Weinhold, Al Gaff, Dave Hayse, Adam Zeller (and a few others not pictured.)

rective action to counter the disappointing economy. Our product line has expanded, so we find new customers and markets. By now the number of models a single salesman has to learn is beyond a "point of no return", so we lessen his load by reverting to the "specialty" route. We gave the Ag line to a separate sales force; another group sells only small machinery; one does only paving products, and there is a team for the coal mines.

Beyond that (as the economy was faltering), we generated a new revenue stream from a rental segment which this year will be close to $35,000,000. We have in that process opened seven new, geographic locations. Internally, we have improved the professional competence of our people through weeding, training and motivating so their sensitivity to customer needs has no parallel in the marketplace. Final effort to newer efficiency is recourse to the Six Sigma process with nine teams looking for ways to cut waste, improve margins, and reduce costs.

It takes more skill to manage in tougher times, and often we learn more in adverse conditions than easy going. Objective is to keep the operation mechanism adjusted to the given circumstance, not functioning to handle the past. We are far better at what we do today than we were a decade ago. So leaner markets don't mean we stop trying or throw up our hands. It says this is the only business we know, and we have to figure out how to make it profitable and what we must do to insure the livelihood of 557 families depending on us for a paycheck. Because one day the slide will stop, the economy will turn around (we think we see it happening now), and demand will increase. When that day arrives, we intend to jump on it like a duck on a June bug and make up for the meager crop the last four years. ■

2004

We Need More of Thales

April 2004

"A new GOP plan to expand health insurance will go nowhere in Congress this year. Democrats will thwart Republican efforts to pass tax credits to help the uninsured buy their own health coverage. Democrats want the government to do more and in any event are loathed to hand Bush a plum legislative win in an election year."

The afore-stated quote appeared in a recent issue of *Kiplinger's Weekly Newsletter*, and I read it without too much shock or surprise since the observation seemed fairly typical of American politics. Then stopped to consider the full impact and meaning of the statement and was struck with what this casual opinion was telling us. Then wondered why anyone who deemed this posture as fairly normal for Congressional attitude and conduct wasn't instantly and absolutely outraged. It infers rather cynically that the American governance at the federal level consists primarily of partisan strategy. The political objective is not efficacious direction of national affairs, but first and foremost, the triumph of a partisan conviction which in this case might well impede or prevent legitimate legislation <u>because</u> it would enhance the opposition's stature. (My party's interest is preeminent to the public weal.) The double-whammy — again — is (1) that we consider this normal and (2) in acceding dutifully we tolerate (accept?) a philosophy or tactic which can be detrimental to the interest of 280 million Americans. Why in the world should either party's agenda be allowed to preempt legislation beneficial to the nation?

This plays out in another level when we view the Presidential battles to get Federal Court judges con-

firmed. People old enough to remember the nomination of Judge Robert Bork to the Supreme Court bench find a reprise of the same dynamic. Despite the fact he was reputedly one of the outstanding judges in America, his appointment was successfully blocked for reasons that had nothing to do with his technical or professional competence. He was denied the bench because he disagreed on certain issues, which were supported by the Democrat party. It wasn't ability, wisdom, his record or judicial qualification at stake, it was his difference on social issues that the Kennedy-Biden-Sharpton-Jesse Jackson people espoused and aimed to protect. On the flip side of this judge issue, Ruth Bader Ginsburg and Thurgood Marshall, i.e. judges who agree with the liberals on abortion, education, oil drilling, the environment, Fidel Castro, and gun control pass the litmus test and qualify for the Supreme Court.

When using qualifications other than judicial competence, we tend to reduce the impartiality of the court, the final arbiter — the avatar — of the American political system. And let's confess this policy is not the practice of only one party. It is evident and operative in both.

But this skewing and compromise goes on from there and impacts society randomly because people appear to react — or to act — to sundry sorts of stimuli. One is maybe visceral; one cultural; another from fear, maybe one from ambition. Hopefully, <u>most</u> are cerebral, involving a mental exercise called deductive reasoning. Although commonplace, it's also complicated, sorting through sundry facts, one leading to the next, on a sequence in search of an answer to a given question or quandary. This was a process probably absent early in the ancient world where the priest told humankind what the gods want revealed, and you can bet that was very little. A 7th Century (B.C.) Greek named Thales suggested there were other ways. Following the record of Babylonian astral charts, he discovered that solar and lunar eclipses had appeared with certain regularity. Using the pattern established, he predicted one. In short, he concluded eclipses were not an aberration but a systematic, cosmic pattern. There was no magic involved. His point — and process — would prove we could find the truth through accumulating data, which as individual elements are not surprising but when combined, leads to broader conclusions. Sort of like a golf swing: The right combination of stance, grip, take-away, turn, weight shift, position of hands, speed of club head, all combine to create a 260 yard drive. (I get about half of them right and can't hit it over 180…with a tail wind.)

Or maybe we'd get closer if we suggested it's sort of like working on a problem in geometry or algebra, employing certain given facts, which when properly assembled, lead to an inevitable, irreversible conclusion. Pythagoras demonstrated the process to prove the square on the hypotenuse of a right triangle is equal to a sum of the squares of the other two sides. (I have never found an application for that particular theory anywhere in the tractor business and end up saying, "So what?" Yet this is a famous and an oft-quoted verity.) Even if he never uses it, one can reach a conclusion by recursing a series of "proofs", a series of "givens" and accepted truths. Subsequent generations called Thales' process "reasoning" or abstract thinking, a phenomenon that dramatically changed the course of western history.

Geometry and, hopefully, inductive and deductive thinking find the solution by using established principles or facts. If followed faithfully, the result is an element called "truth". Political "thinking" (if we can use the term loosely) as evidenced in this campaign year poses as being thoughtful and hopes to be compelling, but it is "reverse-action" reasoning. It generally <u>begins</u> with a premise or a conclusion (which we call in the tractor business a SWAG

Thales, one of the Seven Sages of Greece. Born 624-625 BC. Many regarded him as the first philosopher in Greek tradition. He attempted to explain natural phenomena without referencing mythology.
(Source: Wikimedia Commons.)

"Simple Wild Ass Guess") and then lines up a series of postulations or assumptions which are meant to support our position. We start, not end, with the conclusion, and that is very fast thinking. Fact, it's a short cut, but fair scores, no way we can see this as "reasoning" or "logic". It is oratory, bluster, demagoguery, and downright nonsense. But its direct impact for the moment is minimal because a lot of it is currently aimed at wooing voter support and establishing party preference. But whenever truth becomes a stranger, dissimulation, the order of the day, we are deluded into expectations that never materialize and the republic suffers. But for the moment we are selecting candidates. The next stage in the process, i.e. legislation or governance is where the rubber meets the road. As long as we recognize our political operation for what it is, sort of a national sideshow, no-holds-barred, rhetorical wrestling match, we can survive. But whenever phony logic is substituted for statecraft as it too often is, we fall short of what we might become and the whole protracted ritual becomes an end in itself.

I don't say that the business world is a model to represent the validity of sound and honest reasoning because the instant I do, someone will say, "You mean like Enron? Or IPALCO or Conseco?", which looks like it blows me out of the water. But in actuality proves the point. When <u>we</u> use guises and sham instead of the truth, we can expect reality to ultimately triumph because there is an irrefutable law in place, governing business. Principles which are irrefragable, i.e. if one spends consistently more money than he generates, he goes broke. Poor service, a faulty product, inadequate marketing all spell disaster and failure. Badly trained employees destroy prospects for repeat business. In the arena in which we and our customers function, there is not a lot of room for fuzzy thinking, and one can rarely disguise weak management through rhetoric or declamation. Business is about <u>doing</u>, not promising. It is about results, not plans.

So there <u>are</u> elements in our society that are graded and held to account. We happen to grade students, but strangely enough never grade teachers. We don't grade pastors, attorneys, dentists, cops, housewives or weather forecasters. We do grade football coaches, football players, fact, most athletes; we grade our salesmen, auditors, car leasers, insurance companies, etc. On a larger scale society grades <u>all</u> businesses. Tests differ, but the bottom line is the same: performance — whether in terms of wins, pricing, sales, earned-run average, yards gained. In my case, profits or value delivered for price charged or service quality. This persistent demand for accountability I think has a direct impact on the thinking process involved because if we "call" it wrong, misunderstand, forecast badly, don't recognize threats, we pay dearly. Survival depends on how well we produce just like Peyton Manning's job depends on how well he performs. This is not merely about survival, it is about succeeding. And most success depends upon the intellectual capacity of those managing the enterprise. It gets down to how well we think. That deals directly with how well we are able to interconnect, interface and interact with the wider world. We are, after all, a sort of microcosm within a larger universe, and all of life depends on successfully accommodating the impinging forces…of which we are a part by the way. In some areas one can "get by" playing fast and loose; in other cases, considerable discipline, circumspection, organization, and planning are involved. Knowing the demands of the free enterprise world, we are conscious of competition, of manufacturer relations, interest rates, consumer needs, the value of technical competence, interdepartmental coordination, the absolute necessity of a strong marketing arm, and a lot of things. All requiring careful analysis, strong direction, continual initiative, alertness, and good communication. In short this is not something that runs itself, like Danny Burton's political campaigns or like a dentist coming to work each day with a schedule of patients lined up or a teacher with the same classroom and the same textbooks again this year. There are situations where the nature of the vocation all but arbitrates how it is handled. One does not need a consultant or a focus group to figure out what to do next in most situations, but the element of reasoning is pertinent to all of us.

A timely exercise in citizen thinking — reasoning, rationalizing, etc. — occurs this year across the nation and at several levels during our quadrennial elective process. (Rome elected all offices <u>annually</u>! Can you imagine this sitcom being perennial?) The choices made determine, to some extent, the direction we take as a county, state or nation. A cynical observation would content that despite the determinative nature of the process, the degree of inductive or deductive thinking is minimal. For starters, about half of us won't even get to the polls. Which makes "reasoning" irrelevant. Then we who do, usually vote on the basis of party, war record, ethnic nature or the sex or campaign promise of given candidates. We select those with whom we agree and beg the key question: Which of these is the brightest, the most selfless, and the most practical person for making laws required by the nation? If we do a lot of studying when handling our own investment portfolio, we become almost whimsical when selecting our legislators and chief officials and mirabile dictu, we get by with it. So in a roundabout way, minimizing political mediocrity in the form of run-of-the-mill candidates could be checkmated by an alert electorate. If indeed voters became less parochial, more discriminating, more judicious and applied more reason, we could elevate the level of administrative service delivered by electing people with brains, altruism and good judgment. But when we voters prove no more objective and open-minded than the NRA or the Teachers Union, bent in serving MY interests first, we tolerate, in fact <u>elect</u>, men and women to office already programmed for disappointing performance. All of which proves the prescience of Jefferson's comment about the weaknesses in a democracy. We "get the sort of government we deserve". We cannot provide Class A governance with a C- constituency.

So all in all, we are, thus, not as good as it could be. But for some reason remain the best system ever promulgated and effectuated <u>because</u> of the work from those who stay involved.

Is this a great country, or what? ∎

Prodigals

April 2004

The Bible is full of illustrations and anecdotes depicting human habit and behavior — good, bad and indifferent behavior. The illustrations are diverse in nature and cover so many human situations they seem miraculously relevant. All are not easy to understand, are not pleasant and uplifting; all do not have happy endings, making them typical of the human experience. One of the most ancient, well known of the lot is the story of a certain "Prodigal Son". The metaphor itself is surely familiar and the illustration and its terminology have become commonplace in western literature. The story was told as part of Jesus' teaching ministry and is drawn from Near Eastern wisdom literature, perhaps rehearsed in several surroundings. The characters, then, are Mid-Easterners and if remote in time, manners and distance, prove eternal in terms of conduct and deportment.

A wealthy farmer/landowner has two sons: One of whom is a wastrel, the other hard working and reliable. The former cons his father for a share — "my share" — of the inheritance. (This would probably be one-third the estate, the other two-thirds going to the older brother, who is the "good guy" in the story). Taking his appreciable stake, the younger brother — the loser — sets off for the big city and blows his entire fortune on reckless, loose, and dissolute living. Finally broke, he ends up in virtual servitude, working out in the boonies for a hog farmer and eating no better than the hogs. He is clothed in rags, starving, and totally destitute. Beyond that, probably living daily without hope and plagued with regret over his silly actions. Finally, tired of the whole business, he hitches up his jeans (girds his loins) and decides to eat some crow, i.e. to go back home. It is either <u>that</u> or slowly starve to death and so the crow, though hard to digest, is the better option. With his tail between his legs and with a heavy heart — but with some tenuous optimism about the future — he goes back to the old homestead.

When his father sees him coming up the trail, he erupts in joy, probably the largest charge of real happiness he's experienced since the renegade left home. Fact, he's so elated he decides to have a huge come-as-you-are party and invites the entire neighborhood in. His cooks butcher a fat lamb and prepare a humongous meal. All are delighted for the old man

and come in throngs, rejoicing with him and making the blast, the biggest social event in years. The center of attention, of course, is the reformed younger son, now cleaned up and shaved; new sandals, rich robes, a gold ring on his finger, and probably a new red turban. Having partied considerably himself in his former life, he enjoys a good hoedown, and this is his "piece of cake". He has got to be astonished at the lack of rancor, lectures, penalty or punishment, and very grateful.

But alas, not everyone is happy with his homecoming. The older son has been sort of shunted aside in all this welcome activity. He learns about the "return of the native", sees the ebullient outpouring of affection the old man is lavishing on this bum who took off and disgraced the family and notes with surprise a host of people living it up in celebration. No one ever killed a sheep in his honor. When he gets to the party after working all day at the chores of the ranch, he wonders: "What gives? Why all this to-do?" He points out to the old man that while the reprobate son has been frittering away a sizeable fortune in doing nothing but pleasing himself; <u>he</u> (senior son) has been back at the ranch, doggedly working his buns off day after day to get the crops out and the harvest in, keeping the fences mended, the cattle branded, and the sheep sheared. He's never missed a lick, made the old man millions, and what has <u>he</u> gotten as appreciation for his loyalty, efforts, respect, performance and hard work? Zilch! No one ever so much as bought his lunch or a cold beer at the end of a hard, hot day. Yet this stumblebum who is everything a father abhors, now sits in the seat of honor and adulation, while meritorious service is ignored. It is taken for granted while a party is given in honor of he who has disgraced the family. If Yul Brenner were still around, he would say, "This is a puzzlement!" He might even say, "This sucks."

I'm having trouble getting the real message here, but the one that strikes <u>me</u> might not be the one the teller intended. The old man said: "Your brother, who was lost and gone from us, is back and has repented. He is no longer in a far country, wasting his talents and estranged, so our worries about his situation are gone. He's home! Hallelujah! Beyond that, surely you know I appreciate all your work, your faithfulness, and your filial obedience. Your brother got his piece, but more important, everything <u>else</u> I have goes to you. It is yours." (Well, old man, what other options do you have? The tax collector or the youngest son? You chose a course that is the lesser of two evils. Is it indeed a great gesture of compassion? What you gave the younger one was not only money but also your affection, attention, empathy and compassion.) The party here tells the world how you regard him — and inadvertently what you think of me.

The first phase of the story deals with the weakness of the younger son and his foolish dissipation of an inheritance. It describes the results of his pleasure-seeking predilection and the cost of his carelessness and irresponsibility. One could say, "Well, why be surprised? What else do we expect from young folks with a pocket full of cash and little experience in the hard, cruel world?" And could also wonder why the old man, who must have known his son was not yet dry behind the ears, nonetheless handed him the means to his own ruin. Had he <u>not</u> given the share of the estate early, the kid would doubtless have avoided all the trouble. But the story doesn't end there; the downfall and degradation are not the whole message. They are the condition or situation <u>out of which</u> a sort of moral might be fashioned. One point here might be the fact that junior did not stay a swine herder, living in filth. He swallowed his pride, admitted his mistakes, went back to make amends for the grief and trouble he had caused and found some use for his life. There is hope for me. We see then an element of redemption here, and the point might be made that rather than being totally lost, underneath it all, the kid had a semblance of moral strength that overcame his weakness and he did indeed have the personal courage or gumption to rise above a blunder that might have been his permanent undoing. He did rectify a circumstance he had created. A corollary message might be: There is more proof of courage in defeat than in victory. That the strength of his character, slight as it may have been, was revealed not in the taverns and dance halls of "a far country" but at the depths of his misery and despair. That his real character was ultimately proven, not when he left home but when he looked at his conditions at the very bottom of the ladder and said, "Hey! I'm smarter and stronger than the rest of these yokels. I'm getting out of here."

And you can take it from there. But the plight of the older brother has always interested me. He has a very good point. One a lot of our company employees could be making. "I do my job day in and

Israel farm country.

day out, fact, do stuff beyond what I'm supposed to do, but whoever says 'Thanks', or 'Nice work, appreciate what you did' or 'You really handled that problem very well.'" Management around here takes good performance for granted. It is a norm not an exception. We all learned in school or maybe in the military or some similar place, the people the teacher or the C.O. knows first, identifies at once, are the screw-ups or troublemakers. It is the bad apples the leader knows while the rest of the class or the company could be reasonably effective but likewise virtually anonymous. We get too busy at the top, obsessed and preoccupied with our own dragons and demons to spend a lot of time wondering how the rest of the gang is doing. Despite the fact that <u>what</u> they are doing at the grassroots level is what sustains the succeeding levels all the way up through the top layer. We tend to be long and precise about expectations and very short on "attaboys".

The other point, key to the story and repeated in other Biblical parallels is an emphasis or focus on "the aberrant one". Like the parable of a woman who had ten coins and noticed one day, there were only nine. Ouch! So she set about scouring the whole house to find the one lost coin. The other nine sat on the bureau, virtually ignored, taken for granted, deserving of no attention. Though nine times the value of the one, who cares? Because, of course, they were not lost, not in jeopardy, out of our possession. Same lesson in the story of the lost sheep. Ninety-nine in the fold, but where is number 100? Where is that last miscreant? "We got one missing, guys. We have to get out and find him." So half a dozen shepherds pen up the 99 and all go chasing after one, measly, cotton pickin' stray. The lesson is obvious. What we seek for is that which is lost, not that which is still around, still inventory. What we are dealing with is the one that got outside the pen (or purse).

The missing unit becomes a problem because it is missing, and because it is, commands our attention. The parallel to the tractor works might not be that hard to illustrate. It is not that we are losing machines, though that would make the point pretty quickly. If someone steals a loader from the backyard, we do not call the cops to watch the other 400 pieces still there; we want them to find he who drove off with our property. Fortunately, this is a weak sort of analogy because we do not have a lot of bulldozers stolen. But we do have a host of other problems in need of policing. And the point is that we don't stew about markets in which we have high penetration and are waxing the competition. Rather Doug, Dave and Dan study hard on those areas in which our share is minimal and ought to be larger. We don't fuss long each month over a thousand customers who pay their parts or rental invoices, but we do take notice — and action — on the small, minority group that fails to respond and owes us money. Turns out those "troubles" or "problems" to a large extent soak up most of the time for a good many managers. Partly because that is a manager's job: Looking for troubles — with the intent in mind to get them fixed. But fair scores, part of a manager's job is saying, "Well done"; "Good work"; "Keep it up." If he doesn't, he is really uninspiring and unappreciative.

If our company functions like the normal successful CAT dealership, we adhere to the rules or parameters or norms or budgetary figures which indicate at once what the level of performance should be. We are structured to function in order to produce according to an agreed-upon plan or formula. The day-to-day task of — say — the parts manager is not to rejoice in the sales figures for the past several years and boast about increases or the number of line items we deliver. It is to find those elements in the operations statement not up to standard <u>now</u> and find out why. What percent of our parts ordered by customers do we fill out of our inventory? What is the inventory turn? How big is our annual parts return? Why do we pay so much in emergency order charges? (Stuff out of the depot cost us 5%.) So across the board it is the single issues, out of whack, that tell us where our time should be spent. The more we get corrected, the better we perform, the happier our customers are, the prouder our employees become, and the more profits the dealership accrue to expand its service. It is attention to one element at a time…one lost coin or a single sheep…that brings us closer to excellence.

The mistake is not rejoicing in the return of the weaker son but rather according credit and gratitude to the steadfast son. Fixing the problem ought not preclude the recognition of loyal service, which after all is the standard set by loyal employees to whom the sluggards or misfits or slackers are compared. We ought to be inviting the neighbors over and giving the seat of honor to he/she most responsible for our continuing success. ■

Export and Import of Jobs

July 2004

Most of us remember a character named Ross Perot who fought NAFTA with some vehemence and made it his issue when he ran for the Presidency in 1992. Fact, created such a racket, he probably assured the election of Bill Clinton. Perot's fixation was patriotic enough since it assumed the North American Free Trade Agreement (which took down tariff barriers between the nations of the Western Hemisphere) would work adversely for Americans. Business would seek cheaper labor and find it in Mexico, therefore, would begin to build future manufacturing plants south of the border. That meant <u>business</u> might thrive, but <u>workers</u> would suffer job loss. His phrase described the new reaction: "That great sucking sound you hear will be from jobs siphoned out of America and gushing into Mexico". (It is obvious I lost track of the quotation but have its essence reasonably accurate.) Bill Clinton took our minds off "where jobs were going", and his escapades made Perot's predication almost irrelevant for a time.

Then Ole Ross dropped from view a couple years ago and resurfaced on my screen along with his dire prognostications just recently when shopping (with my bride) for a new London Fog raincoat. We found an awful lot of "possibles" but nothing exactly like what she had in mind. (My secret guess is she enjoys the shopping more than she does the buying, but that is my problem, not yours, and hardly germane to the issue at hand. Which are foreign exports, jobs gone elsewhere.) The coat rack at Sak's, Ayres, Penney's, Nordstrom's, Burdines and Sam's sure looked like Perot might have had something approaching an uncanny prescience. I went through labels and could not believe what I saw. The United Nations. Belarus was making coats; Bangladesh, Slovakia, Russia (can you imagine that!), Laos, China, Poland, Bulgaria, at least a dozen foreign manufacturers. Know who was missing? The United States. We never found a single one on the racks in store after store that came from America. It was absolutely astounding. Perot's suspicions came back to mind. "Newsflash! U.S. loses 2,000,000 jobs in 2003."

Conjecture about exactly where those jobs are going, however, is not all that precise. Fact, it's downright confusing. As proven in this week's *Kiplinger* bulletin that noted we shall <u>add</u> 2,000,000 jobs

in America this year (2004). But the unemployment rate will stay at 5.6%. We add 2,000,000 jobs; why doesn't the employment rate go down to 5%? Because the population grows and so does the number of people entering the job market…in excess of those leaving. This is a complicated picture, sports fans.

Now Kerry is waving a Perot-type flag at every conceivable moment because when he gets in, Americans who <u>want</u> good high-paying jobs once again will certainly get them. (Although I have a hard time figuring out how the government is going to hire that many people. Though since it is Kerry, maybe that is what he had in mind. Ordinarily, it is not the government who does most of America's hiring or job creation. The private sector is what provides most employment … large, medium and small-sized BUSINESSES are the employers, not the Federal government, Senator Kerry. Nor will jobs arise out of the phoenix of campaign oratory.) But the candidate has highlighted a significant issue: "How many jobs did go (do go) to Mexico?" The question proved specious. The first thing I learned was that the jobs which <u>did</u> go to Mexico because of proximately and cheap labor, moved from there to China, Belarus, Armenia et al, places where the labor is cheaper than even Mexico. A jillion service-type jobs in the computer industry or a given computer process have gone to India, thanks to the marvel of modern communication and the miracle of cell phones, voice and data transmission, etc. So it's not unusual for someone seeking information about a given charge on a credit card to be clearing it up with an operator in Calcutta. Wendell Wilkie should

P.E. in front of the Indianapolis corporate offices, 2004.

see the way we do commerce these days. He sort of predicted this would come as he talked in the early 40's about our living in "one world". Our interdependence now is vast and keeps growing with each passing month.

The Forrester survey tells me that job loss is indeed for real, that we have shrunk the payrolls at least for the moment. Between July of 2000 and October of 2003, a total of 2,700,000 jobs were lost. But only (get this) 300,000 were lost to "outsourcing". A little over 10% of them went to Mexico, then to China, Pakistan and Indonesia. Where did the rest go? It went the way of the elevator operator who used to take us to our floor in office buildings, hotels and hospitals. Meaning, he got "obsoleted" by technology, surrendered to a new elevator with a series of punch buttons. It went the way of the old McCormick reaper and the threshing machine now preempted by the Caterpillar Claas Combine, which shucks more corn in a week than a reaper/thresher would process all season. Across the board in manufacturing, technology is the culprit. Two-thirds of a given product's manufactured cost is its labor component. So in a $90,000 CAT loader, $30,000 is for steel, $60,000 the assembly line people. Robotics, computerized milling, boring, punching, stamping machines have replaced factory laborers by the thousands. Our technology has minimized the need for people. Call the telephone company with a problem some day and see if it's possible to locate a real live person there.

The forces at work here are the result of intense competition, scrambling ever to do it quicker, better and in larger volumes with fewer people. The result is an endless productivity drive, ongoing, since the Great War. So we are building the same number of loaders as before but now with fewer people because we have computerized robot-operated machines that never tire or need coffee — or potty — breaks. Each time we improve our productivity 1%, we lose 1,300,000 jobs. The last 10 years we have improved productivity 5%, each and every year. We have whacked out 6,000,000 jobs, part of them come from our loader assembly line. Awesome! Making a much larger sucking sound than Perot ever thought about. But it's not NAFTA who is the villain. It is progress. Anyone who looks at his five year old computer today is looking at a virtual collector's item, a museum piece. We keep changing for faster operation, larger storage, more functions, and clearer visuals incessantly, and in the process not only do more things,

but make obsolescence routine.

And this shift is a major factor in minimizing the work force. Retailers (like us) move the sales volume of 1999 with (alas) 35% fewer people. Home Depot, for example, installed self-checkout computers in half its 1700 stores. A thousand cashiers went to the sales floor. Southwest Airlines increased its air fleet from 375 to 388 planes yet their payroll shrunk by 1000 workers. Think of the purchases made for hotel rooms or drugs or books or cruises or garden seeds, etc. today on the computer versus zilch in 1990, and you'll see again what this technology has done to buying habits. All of which adversely effect the people who used to sell or process. Mexico has nothing to do with this phenomenon.

The job market and our unemployment figures are easy to recite but very hard to understand. To give us the big picture, America has 138,000,000 workers employed today, and in a normal year 18,700,000 of them will lose their jobs. (Wow!) But even more people will get new jobs (released employees in new slots and people coming in the job market). In a decade 302 million jobs were lost, but 327 million new jobs were added. The mantra about losing high-paying jobs and replacing it with one at McDonald's is another piece of bad conjecture. The CATO Institute tells us that, "Management and professional specialty (high-paying) jobs have grown rapidly in the recent era of globalization." Fact, they have grown 80% in the decade ended in '02. Have gone from 23% to 31% of the total employment. The big hit has been manufacturing, an employment decline of 11% from 1995 to 2002 (but miracle of miracles, China has dropped 15%). Maybe the best way to summarize and represent this whole dynamic is to look at agriculture. In 1870, 47% of America's total employment was involved in farming, stock raising, orchards, etc. Today, it is 1.7%. We are producing for 150% more people and delivering so much we cannot begin to sell it all, with 5% of what we employed a century and a third ago.

What we tend to overlook is the opposite of the "sucking sound". Let's call it the "puffing sound" — the number of jobs which are coming into this country, backed by foreign capital and owned by non-American people. I recall the Governor's campaign 16 years ago when Evan Bayh was running against John Mutz and the flack he was sending up about Indiana giving tax breaks to support the installation of a Japanese Isuzu auto plant in Lafayette. It amounted to high treason. Surely the Senator knows world trade is a two-way street; that it can work to our advantage. So just as we are investing overseas in business and industry, the opposite is true. Note the huge Toyota plant down in Princeton, Indiana we fought like heck <u>to get here</u>. Remember Daimler Benz buying Chrysler? BMW has a huge plant in Spartanburg, South Carolina; India's Essel Porpack, Taiwan's Teco Electric, and Enmark's Wind Systems have all built plants on these shores in the past 18 months. In our industry Daimler owns Freightline; Volvo owns White Motors and has just bought Mack Trucking. Most of our competitors in the machinery business Komatsu, Kobelco, Hitachi, Volvo, Bomag, O & K, Allis Chalmers, Samsung, Euclid, Daewoo, Liebher, Hyundai, Hamm, Wirtgen et al are all foreign in ownership. Some manufactured here; meaning, more jobs for Americans but beyond that, thousands more Americans have been hired at the distribution level, selling and servicing foreign labeled products. Think of a hundred different models of foreign cars in showrooms across the United States and the salesmen and service people who support them. Again, untold thousands of jobs, all directly dependent upon foreign business enterprise. Jobs from non-U.S. companies in the United States grew by 4.7 million between 1997 and 2001. It is hard to think there is not some advantage in the NAFTA principle.

By now these figures are making even me dizzy, but one last point. Why are almost all our raincoats made overseas? Because we can have them made to our standards at a cheaper cost elsewhere. If this gets a little tough and unsettling for the textile workers, what about considering the other party in the equation. What about the enormous savings <u>to the purchaser</u>? The one who gets the break is he or she who buys the raincoat. The way to keep inflation down is to hold prices down and to get that done, we have to find the lowest-cost producer. They are "lower" elsewhere because wages are considerably less since living costs are much cheaper in Kazakhstan or Vietnam. Moreover, production in Slovakia probably does not have other charges adding to the cost of production. Like social security for workers, unemployment compensation premiums, profit sharing or 401-K, uniform expense, and no $2.00 to $3.00 per hour for health care insurance. Far-Eastern employers are probably not bothered with the cost of accommodating OSHA, equal opportunity hiring, EPA, safety standards, clean air act, etc. The price of gasoline in this country and the cost of liquor have exploded over the years, <u>not</u> because of the higher material and labor costs. They are off the chart because government at sundry levels has stuck on taxes to each product. Meaning, the cost of doing business in America is more than material and labor. It is increased by additional burdens imposed by society or government. The degree of difference between those remote and less sensitive parts of the world <u>and</u> the United States of America is hard to measure from a desk in Indianapolis, but it has got to be considerable. Our health care cost alone probably exceeds the hourly — or daily — wages paid in most of the Third World.

If this is more confusing than illumining, maybe I've made the point. Global economics with record levels of commodities, volumes, transactions, etc. is very difficult to interpret and very easy to misunderstand. Rare is the person who knows, rarer he who understands and legions are those who pop off about it, telling us what they think might be a version of one part to the story. A good place for the old motto: caveat emptor. ■

Quid Pro Quo

July 2004

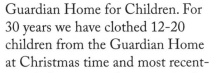

It is certainly not proper to boast about how generous one is or chortle about how much he does for a community, but it is important for our employees to know that the company (and the MacAllisters) has always felt grateful for our good luck in Indiana. The economy here, the nature of our buyers, the workers we are able to recruit and train, the political environment in which we function, have all combined to make our 63 years here most rewarding. My father moved to Indiana in the late summer of 1941 with $20,000 to take over an Allis Chalmers dealership and was successful enough in his marketing skill the next four years to awaken the interest of Caterpillar who in June of 1945 gave him the Caterpillar account. Three generations down we are still at the task and look back with some satisfaction. Management acumen might have played a role in all this, but the Hoosier environment also has a lot to do with success or failure. In our case it has provided us a good marketplace, great customers buying the finest equipment, banks willing to underwrite expansion, all allowing us "to increase and multiply". The original $20,000 has then "multiplied" exponentially, suggesting a modicum of progress.

So a part of our corporate philosophy says we ought to respond to our good luck by giving back to the community which has nourished us so graciously. That means the support of those causes which embellish and ennoble our area. That "support" comes about mostly in the form of cash donations. Last year between us (the company and the writer), we gave something like $700,000 to 83 different "do-good type" organizations. Beyond that, over the course of time we have dug scores of church basements, graded and finished numerous Little League ball diamonds, put machinery in church, campus and youth organization site developments; contributed mightily to schools, golf course renovation and local clubs; the writer serves on a dozen boards and works as he can in the political apparatus of Marion County. All because we have an obligation to the system which has given us such good fortune and continues to support our enterprise.

Two of the typical "opportunities" we have represented recently popped up. One is the local Guardian Home for Children. For 30 years we have clothed 12-20 children from the Guardian Home at Christmas time and most recently discovered they needed some tote bags to provide youngsters being sent elsewhere a way of carrying their meager belongings to the next stop along life's way. My daughter sent me a note and asked if this was something we might look into, and Viola! our parts people ordered and supplied 100 tote bags for these unfortunate kids. Mike Henshilwood, our general factotum, saw to their delivery.

The second organization is Boy Scouting and a little different story: Can we borrow a dozer or a loader till we build Camp Buffalo near Liberty, Indiana? The rental for the equipment amounted to something like $4,200 but having been a Boy Scout, know there is no worthier organization in the world, and we were happy to "loan" it.

And along with these, 42 other organizations received grants from the company last year. Our policy was a fixed percent of gross profits. All because we feel the world around us is, to a large degree, not what we <u>want</u> it to be but what we are able to conceive and then financially support. It takes dollars as well as instruments and players to keep a symphony; takes paintings, sculptures, buildings as well as dollars to provide an art museum; we need sets, costumes, directors, actors, <u>and dollars</u> to be a theatre. And you can run this same string with the Seminary, archaeology, the United Way, Garfield Park, ballet, opera, theatre, Junior Achievement, YMCA, Heritage House, Choice, ad infinitum. So our community is reliant on volunteer giving to maintain a myriad of worthy causes whose end product results in the ethos which is Indianapolis. We aren't key to any of them nor are we unique in town, but we do remember the long climb up and the success we've had in Indiana. We want <u>it</u> to do as well as <u>we</u> have, and the only way to see that accomplished is to assure the continuation of those causes and organizations that make us better, make society more wholesome, and make our citizens wiser and more tolerant. Not a big deal, but we think it essential — mandatory — to prove our appreciation through continual investment in our community. ■

Fort Wayne Branch

July 2004

This is the first of several installments which hopes to deal with our physical facilities through write-ups on one given store at a time, describing the history of each as well as its current status. We have a lot of locations at this point in time (I count six branches and six separate rental stores) and the character or nature of each is different. Beyond that, "the character and nature" of most are a mystery to our own people who rarely get a chance to see the company outside their own work cubicle. So we start the series with Fort Wayne, the earliest of our outposts.

If the dealership was "born" June 2, 1945, the provisions in the contract with CAT for this territory required we subsume the other CAT dealer existing in our territory. This was an "Ag dealer" of long standing, respected and well managed. The first crawler tractors were designed for farm work and first sales were to western farmers. It was natural to develop a dealer network geared to the farm, and soon agricultural dealers popped up all across the land. Over time, however, with the explosion of the road system in America and its heavy earthmoving component augmented by the Second World War, a myriad of new opportunities were produced. If CAT had set up a raft of smaller farm-oriented dealerships, it recognized both the decline of agriculture and the hurrying ascendancy of industrial, mining, construction, aggregate, utility and logging usage. We needed to change the dealer orientations and configuration. So we bid a fond farewell to the Ag branch, it having served its purpose, and in our part of Indiana the end came when E.W. bought out Mr. Cockrell in November of

Fort Wayne Pearl Street Building.

1945. Incidentally, he was delighted to sell since he had no continuity plans. We took over his location at 247 Pearl Street in Fort Wayne — with an accompanying service operation a couple doors down the street.

The folks at Fort Wayne are currently working out of a service operation that is pretty rudimentary, built as it was in 1947 but bad as it might be, it's still a far cry from the original shop with its dim lighting, rough floors, layers of oil and grease, its chain-link hoists and flimsy work bench. But buildings were hard to come by immediately after the war and dollars were short. Underneath all of this, too, is a subtle conviction that buildings don't make you money. It is the expertise and function going on <u>in</u> a building that generates business and profits. We immediately enlarged the work force at Fort Wayne to anticipate contractor, aggregate, paver, municipal, etc. needs and cranked off.

My brother got back from the service in the early months of 1946 and reported to Fort Wayne for duty. In two years he was running the branch and building a new shop out on Coliseum Boulevard. Followed up a couple years later (1951) by adding on the parts department and the office area onto the first structure, completing what has been in essence the Fort Wayne prime product operation. The truck engine building, far more modern and efficient than the other, came on board in 1979.

The Fort Wayne area had spawned a number of major contractors (J.C. O'Conner, John Dehner, Dan Weikel, Meitz, Spears and Dehner, Grace

Remodeled Fort Wayne Branch, 1953.

Construction, Moellering Construction) who competed for state highway works and became successful in the toll road period (1950's) and segueing then into the interstate highway construction boom. Point being, it was the second largest collection of major contractors in the state (after Indianapolis) and our second largest opportunity in terms of total customers, most of whom were grading strip malls and housing projects, owning three or four small dozers. The community itself has a character of its own and through the course of time has bent us to fit the conditions and culture of the area. Of course, our major competitors discovered the same potential we did, and all put stores there: Indiana Equipment Company, Stockberger Machinery, Reid Holcomb, Flesch Miller ... all of whom — like Mr. Cockrell — have departed the scene and left a new generation of competitors to vex us with <u>their</u> lines and <u>their</u> marketing endeavors.

We survived the winnowing because of the CAT product line and our ability to flex in providing different products to new markets while at the same time, nurturing the old. We survive as well because we have been able to attract and retain unusually committed employees. Ruth Booker in her day was a parts expeditor nonpareil and ran the store for us wisely and well; Paul Fuhrman (still on the payroll) is a living legend. A cadre of skilled mechanics under Dick Hagen's leadership served our customers

inordinately well, setting new standards for customer support. Two years ago the Fort Wayne "customer satisfaction score" was the highest in North America. (Or so said CAT when looking at their customer survey data.) Current operating group is 75 strong, 37 mechanics, 7 parts people, 6 guys in the field selling. The overall Manager is Dennis Fawcett, who is capable enough to oversee this operation and manage as well our South Bend store. Dennis has been with us 20 years, worked in both the northwest and the northeast areas and knows the drill exceptionally well. John Smith is the Parts Manager; Mike Piqune is Foreman of the prime product shop, and Tim Doehrman runs the truck engine operation, currently working two shifts.

Dennis Fawcett, Manager Fort Wayne and South Bend Branches

The rental store is across the driveway on the other side (to the west) and has its own crew, buildings, inventory, problems and opportunities. Incidentally, though the ground is only rented there, we do have just about nine acres involved in both areas. ■

Newly completed Fort Wayne Branch, 2006.

MacAllister's new Fort Wayne Rental Store

If At First You Don't Succeed

September 2004

Off and on during the course of a year Americans pause to experience some historic flashbacks. They stop to remember what happened, on say — December 7th or maybe June 6th or July 4th — and expand to the reviewing or re-living the original event. We took note on D-Day this year of President Bush's visit to Normandy, subtly reminding our European "allies" they'd all be speaking German today if America had not invaded Normandy on June 6, 1944 to overpower the Wehrmacht. (An action France observed by the way, sitting in the bleachers.) Since I was remotely connected to December 7th and June 6th (being "in the military and all" at the time), have some personal flashbacks.

Not by landing on Omaha Beach in 1944, but by a previous invasion on November 8, 1942 in an exercise called "Torch". The objective was to wrest North Africa from the Vichy French and the Nazis, broadening our ability to hammer the enemy from air and sea. Ruminating on that invasion concluded that American "military strategy" was somewhat of an enigma, and "strategy" is too kind a term. A goodly part of the African invasion spearhead was composed of Air Force troops. We could hardly do an "about face" or a "forward march", much less attack a machinegun emplacement. Any Germans observing our incursion were doubtless convulsed with laughter. But the impracticability not withstanding, like a good soldier, I scrambled down the netting into a LCT (Landing Craft Troops) that sped toward the beach and dumped us unceremoniously into the water where we waded to shore like conquering heroes. Thus, we "took" (well, we "occupied") our objective, Arzew, a suburb west of Oran.

This wasn't funny at the time because there was intermittent gunfire all around us and a great aimless, milling of troops. No one knew the posture of the French Foreign Legion; we were vague about the strength of the German opposition or what the local populations thought about all this. Had anyone of them been seriously provoked by this unseemly intrusion, we could have been in deep trouble. This motley collection of Americans, tumbling pell-mell onto the beach, sopping wet, thoroughly

confused, was obviously no threat to anyone. But reassuringly <u>behind us</u> on the boat were both infantry and armored corps, far better trained for invading — and fighting — then we. What kind of strategy — I ask — leaves tanks and half-tracks on the boat and unloads harmless Air Corps guys who weren't mad at anyone?

So we slogged up the hill, moving aimlessly inland with the gunfire un-abating and ended up in a vineyard for the night. The next day got strafed twice by Spitfires (which had landed before we secured the airdrome) prior to marching off for our appointed airdrome, Tafaroui. And a scene cluttered and disheveled with the wreckage left by the previous occupiers. Two nights later we moved to LaSenia where our planes had now landed. Only to reload and take off for Nouvion, a French pilot-training school, deeper into Algeria: Thanksgiving there and three dozen or so missions before packing up for Maison Blanche, the airport for Algiers. Two weeks later (December 18th), we are off again, into the middle of the desert to an oasis called Biskra. We sent planes up daily, escorting bombers to hit enemy targets till early February 1943 when we moved again to an airstrip, the most desolate outpost imaginable, Ain M'Lila. On February 15th we moved to Chateau Dhun and finally stayed long enough to send laundry out and actually get it back. That was seven separate bases, seven separate pack-up-and-move-then-unpack cycles in 14 weeks.

Pondering the <u>strategic consequences</u> of this peregrination proved fruitless. I concluded we were doing "on-the-job warfare". The higher-ups were on a trial-and-error course and after guessing wrong, we had to correct by moving to a new location. Was all this muddling around in reality a strategic plan to judiciously position our attack and escort aircraft

Operation Torch - North Africa November 8, 1942.
(Source: Wikimedia Commons.)

for the air war against the Nazis? I doubt it. Official reports will describe what happened, but we will <u>not</u> find a scheme that pre-arranged or planned or programmed this random, helter-skelter pattern of movement.

Anyone who has examined the war strategy in Europe will find a similar pattern; i.e. plans and execution, which are not synonymous. E.g, on D-Day the rough channel seas made thousands of G.I.'s seasick, left them wading, stumbling, crawling onto a beach "prepped" by the enemy for our arrival with deadly, decimating, and abusive firepower. The Air Force that <u>should</u> have knocked out much of the German artillery was absent because of the "socked in" weather. The Navy, commissioned to blast the beaches in advance and pocket it with shell holes (to protect our troops from machinegun fire), laid their barrage inland from the beach, providing no protection. Rangers commissioned to scale a 100-foot cliff at Pointe la Hoc and wipe out a German cannon emplacement found no pill box there and when they moved inland to locate it, discovered the gun abandoned. The 101st Airborne's pre-dawn drop scattered men miles from each other and the targets.

This story of the whole war is replete with plans gone astray (or as Bobbie Burns put it "gang aft agley"), providing the theme of this rambling essay. It was not necessarily the planning that tipped the scale on D-Day, or in North Africa, at Guadalcanal or Iwo Jima; it was a hundred actions fashioned quickly under fire, which found the solution to unpredicted situations, locating the gun emplacements, bulldozing the protective hedgerows, annihilating Japanese defenses cave by cave, that won the war. The guys doing the winning were not those who did the planning. The best strategies were often those created on the spot in a given situation and shaped by men already in action. What won the war for us was our enormous logistical superiority, and equally important was the capability of the American fighting man accustomed to thinking for himself when abruptly thrust upon his own ingenuity. The sergeants, corporals and foot soldiers won the war. The generals got the press and wrote the reports.

This is not meant to give our military a bad name. The existence of foolish orders is part of war's great schematic and a key element in the conduct and outcome of the war. But with a telling difference in how the two sides reacted when things didn't go according to plan. The Japanese soldier in a major snafu circumstance had no idea how to correct the foul-up. He followed bad orders, even in impossible situations and died by the thousands as a result. The Germans were seriously impeded by the ridiculously ironclad orders of their Fuehrer whose dumb schemes, like invading Russia and fighting on two fronts, were cut in stone. Hitler's ego about his tactical brilliance 500 miles away was absolutely intractable. Given bad planning, he complicated it by making corrective action tantamount to treason.

Von Paulus lost a whole German army because he could not revise silly plans, which might have rescued his troops. Telling us in an oblique fashion that plans are no more than <u>theories</u>. They often work and are ways which engaged us in action but when they don't work, need to be altered in view of accurate intelligence which commends a different pattern. The point is not to follow orders blindly. The point of action is to fix what's wrong, to move toward resolution.

The current situation in Iraq makes the point in spades. We went in with a certain plan in mind, which partially succeeded, brilliantly. But part of it failed. Since we could not gain access from Turkey to launch a second offensive from the north, we missed a chance of destroying the Iraqi military that had plenty of time to melt into the landscape and take with it all the weaponry and explosives we now discover are readily used against us. Beyond that, we miscalculated plans for the peacetime management of the nation, leaving us scrambling frantically to find a fix for it. The incursion of El Quaida troops, filtering in piecemeal from the Arabic world, are obstructing and destroying everything we are trying to put in place, creating a problem as wide as the country and impossible to anticipate. The jury is out as of now on taking proper corrective action but is again a classic example of planning for results that never occur, ending up with a mess that needs sorting out to bring order.

It is amazing how this phenomenon is repeated all across the human experience. I think at once of the Colts games and their "game plan", which often doesn't work since at half-time, we are two touchdowns behind. At which point the coach has to scrap his initial program and design a new one; or else change his lineup so different guys can effectuate the strategy he had in mind. Familiar dynamic: Analyze the challenge posed by the opposition and then instantly create a design, which will allow us to triumph and succeed in our endeavor. Political campaigns are almost always part of the same pattern, starting off with given issues, a design to carry the message, a thousand personal appearances and continuous polling. The fury of the contest proceeds, the pure-in-heart who wanted to take the high road finds his lead slipping under the opposition's on-slaught. It's time to reject the carefully-planned campaign and get down and dirty, give the crowd what it wants, i.e. personal attacks, mud and scandal.

Hey! Even marriages resort to regroup-and-fix tactics, requiring changes in habits, schedules, diets and leisure; the Protestant church in America is looking anxiously at its agenda, wondering "wot hoppen?", scrambling frantically to find ways of luring sinners into the church and soliciting their membership and support. Let's scrap the robes and look casual. Forget organ and let's try some guitars; engage more youth in jeans and running shoes; alter the music so it is more "modern", and can't we shorten the service by 10 minutes?

The business landscape is littered with evidence of this same tug of war and the results of what happens when we cannot repair fast enough or well enough. Fact, nothing better represents this age-old contest to succeed in the presence of threat or competition or opposition or "the dark side", than selling Caterpillars. Because we are in an arena like Rome's gladiators. Winning is the only option. To lose means death. The free enterprise system takes no prisoners or tolerates no failures. So the art of flex, or of thrust-and-parry, of experimentation, trial-and-error, modify and adapt, are more at home in the business world than in almost any other institution. The human personal comfort in fixed patterns; homely routines, familiar places and people are an inclination or attribute of nature. But fixed patterns can be suicide in capitalism where one <u>wants</u> a stable workforce, a commodity he knows and understands, loves a steady, strong consistent market, but <u>survives</u> only as well as he navigates the turbulent waters of consumer fickleness and international competition. There is an axiom used by the people in liberal arts that tell us "learning is lifelong"; it should not cease with graduation. An aphorism that is ineluctable in the business world where the quest for dominance is eternal and the vehicles for achieving it are under constant readjustment. I keep telling our guys this may be a taxing and frustrating vocation (especially now that we can't get machines, find enough good mechanics, have to redo the entire computer system again, move more steadily into rental, take on newer lines to sell). It is a demanding business, but there are two things you will find: It never gets boring; there is always something else to fix or change or modify. Business pulsates; it moves; it has a life of its own and as we direct it, we enable it to flourish and thrive, or when negligent or dilatory, watch it shrivel and die.

The current economy is a good example of modifying plans. After four years of declining sales we should have looked for a recovery. To have it rebound was not a major shock but see it explode, not only here in Indiana but worldwide was a bit mind-boggling. So exuberant was the recovery that even Caterpillar could not keep manufacturing apace, and now we have irate customers wondering why they can't get delivery. A situation we hadn't planned on dealing with a year ago but now have to accommodate. By getting special attention from the factory, borrowing machines from other dealers, renting, loaning equipment, and finding other options. Something that has its disappointing moments, but reminds us once again of an important verity: We are not in complete control of our destiny. The bottom line to success, again, is ingenuity, professional knowledge, recourse to other angles, and working successfully through the problem. This is what managing is all about. Managers solve problems; all problems not just the easy ones. The impossible just takes a little longer.

If a good many of our market undulations or requirements are discernable and allow us time to predict what might be happening, it is wise to build the annual business plan, defining staff size, inventories, marketing campaigns, re-enforcement in weak areas, special CAT programs, etc. But along with that a considerable amount of our opportunity or threat pops up unbeknownst to anyone and has to be dealt with. We think the dealer with the best record at fixing problems, the longest track record…the widest experience plus the cleverest and most acute labor force will better modify corporate resources and strategy to deal with a given nemesis than those who have to wonder what was wrong and how to get it fixed. "Experientia doucet", I learned in Latin. "Experience teaches" but along with experience, one needs intellectual or innovative or creative thinking to negotiate something new in the pathway, or something old — with a newer twist. Reason is management's chief asset, experience its handmaiden. At least this is how we see it in the tractor works. ∎

Remember Miletus?

December 2004

I journeyed to London in October to hear a colleague deliver "The Schweich Lectures" to the British Royal Academy…and to revisit the city. I never heard of Mr. Schweich before and though the lectures were outstanding, the British Royal Academy took second place to London itself. I had been there during the war but never in and about the districts and boroughs on foot, in cabs or with a guide. A remarkable and historic place, it was founded by the Romans and operational as a port, cultural center and seat of governance for both a nation and an empire. The archaeological orientation of the lectures focused on the Iron Age Philistines, a scourge of the Mediterranean in 1200 B.C. and a formidable force in ancient Canaan as the Old Testament recounts. If Celts, Romans, Saxons, Danes and Normans exerted their influence from London for 2000 years, the Philistines were not so lucky. They faded from power after two or three generations; winked out completely after four centuries. As did the Hebrews who subdued them, the Assyrians who subdued the Hebrews, the Chaldeans who overturned the Assyrians and the Persians "did in" Babylon, Alexander, Persia; Rome did in everybody, and the pattern goes on ad infinitum.

Why can't more cities be like London and stay the course for a couple of millenniums? As one whose reading often rummages around the ancient world, the topic has a certain tantalizing interest.

Namely, how does a people assure its continuity? The story of Damascus, Cairo, even Paris or Rome can also provide evidence that success for centuries does happen, but why is most of history the record

An odeon. Every notable city had a theatre.

of Nineveh, Thebes, Karnak, Babylon, Ashkelon, Hattusalis, Persepolis, and more "infinitums"? Each "king of the hill" for a moment and then sliding into oblivion. My favorite loser among these "gone but not forgotten" victims is the colony of Miletus, located on the west coast of modern Turkey.

Titillated with its greatness among the twelve cities in the Ionian League, I made a pilgrimage there ten years ago. It was colonial wealth after all that really financed the age of Hellenic glory. Only 10% of Greece is arable (as you know) and though the land is spectacular and the climate invigorating, colonies were necessary to absorb the expanding Greek population and provide the necessary foodstuffs to feed Hellas plus supply the timber, furs, metals, gold, cloth, etc. required to build and burnish an empire.

Miletus was located where the Meander River meets the sea, providing an excellent harbor, favoring sea trade. Achieving economic success, it wisely sponsored experimentation in scholarship and the arts, developing the first Greek science and philosophy. This was the home of Thales, first among "The Seven Wise Men of Greece", a brilliant innovator who dabbled with Egyptian geometry and Babylonian astrology. Fact, he created new geometric theories, which required a sort of sophistry that perfected "deductive" thinking. A process that improved intellectual examination, leading both to philosophy and science. It was Thales — of Miletus — who invented abstract thinking, i.e. the art of reasoning, a fact I rehearsed in an earlier issue. Thales' mind and process are illustrated in homely illustrations. To determine the height of an Egyptian pyramid, he measured the length of its shadow when his own equaled his exact height. A cerebral exercise with no supernatural power involved.

His student Anaximander refined philosophic speculation, declared the earth a sphere in the center of the universe (this is 580 B.C.!); constructed a sundial showing the movement of the planets and marked the succession of solstices, equinoxes and seasons. A later member of the same school, Hecataeus, invented geography as a science and drew the first world map. A student named Anaximines continued the trend, defining the importance of air (in Greek, pneuma), as in spirit or breath; or as in "god". A later native was Hippodamus, the chap who developed the rectangular grid pattern for cities, evident in the layout of Miletus itself.

This combination and synergism produced an intellectual explosion that spread to the Greek world and through Alexander, to all of the Middle East; subsumed by Rome, it passed down to us, doing for the intellectual, scientific, artistic, political, economic et al world what computers have done for us. Space travel, telecommunication, high-altitude bombing, heat-seeking rockets and remote sensing, endless business transactions, all possible only because of the computer. Revolutionizing accounting, movies, communication, medicine; even trouble shooting and repair on Caterpillar tractors; practically everything… that is what I imagine taking place in the Aegean basin in the follow-up phase as philosophy and logic were perfected in Athens under Socrates, Plato, Aristotle et al. This altered the way Greeks thought about the universe, about society, about man and his uniqueness, about the emptiness of their gods, about political systems, about truth, duty and honor, etc. It made possible the founding of science that Aristotle would define and advance. There has been no more "impactful" age in Western history than this one, and its birthplace was Miletus.

All this came flooding into mind while standing in what had been the home of Thales, Hecataeus, Anaximander and Hippodamus, transforming it to sacred ground. But this random rumination was now shaped by the disheveled wreckage, which is today's <u>reality</u>. If once the greatest in the Greek world, it's empty of life now, an endless clutter of disconnected stones with skeletal remnants indicating this might be the temple to Athena; here, maybe the Nymphaeum, and that might have been the vaulted Roman baths; and over there a large piece of an amphitheatre or an Odeum. The agora (70 acres) was the largest in the Greek world as befits a city, which had planted 90 colonies from Egypt to the inner edge of the Black Sea. The chief export was wool woven into cloth and exchanged for timber, metals, flax, foodstuffs, gold, etc. Trading required accounting and correspondence, so we aren't surprised the Greek alphabet employed <u>here</u> became the script adopted by the rest of the Hellenic world. So I considered this city to have had enormous impact in characterizing the Greek culture, passed onto Rome and then the western worlds. Yet here it lies, long abandoned, desolate, forsaken and in ruins. The world owes it a better fortune.

Great thinkers gain immortality, too.

History might tell us <u>what</u> happened. It is up to us to determine WHY it happened.

Well, for starters, the affluence and easy wealth induced internal lassitude (as it often does), harboring indolence and decay. Epicureanism became fashionable; patriotism passé. It became a doggerel that "<u>once</u> the Milesians were brave"; add bitter class strife, the rich against the poor and extensive bloodshed. So the city's energies were wasted in internecine warfare, sapping the state through pointless controversy.

Next, political decisions impinged. When Croesus (next door) annexed the other Greek cities, the Milesians wisely made a pact with him and rode out the storm. Then when Cyrus (the Persian) moved west to overwhelm Lydia (546 B.C.), it absorbed all the city-states in Anatolia; Miletus, again, cleverly cut a deal. But dumb Aristagoras parked reason in the outhouse and organized a large-scale revolt against Persia, which Darius crushed by destroying the city. It recovered slowly after its defeat; Alexander and his successors (320 B.C.) gave new life. Rome's emperors endowed her with new splendor, but the old impact never returned.

Underneath a third fatal element was at work: Mother Nature. Once a bustling seaport; today, the city is several kilometers inland from the coast. The silt brought down from the hills by the Meander moved the sea away; the Milesians failed to dredge the harbors or move west by extending the city. Access to maritime trade on which the whole operation had depended, vanished. Our livelihood and raison d'etre are gone. Declining through the Ottoman Period, it closed shop in the early 1600's.

The query posed at the outset was, how's come London survived and Miletus failed? One reason will be geography. An island citadel has its protection to a small degree (as Napoleon and Hitler learned), whereas Miletus laid in the path of a series of back and forth conquerors. Location, location, location. But the major reason is that some cities solve their problems and others don't. Society is perpetually renewing itself; change is not just a factor in our time but has been perennially at work. Each generation is called upon to prove itself. The mere glory of the Victorian empire did not assure ongoing success or retention of empire. There is no way of remaining triumphant on the basis of past achievement — unless one is satisfied to be a destination for tourists, interested in your past (like Athens, Karnak or Florence) but oblivious to contemporary contribution. We have a maxim in the free enterprise quoted here many times: Only the successful remain. When we can't compete, we are history. And no ruins are left to mark our sojourn here.

The nature of political systems plays a role in this game as well. British society is composed of merged cultures and a political system which awards to the successful, huge benefits, but the uncertainty required individual participation and figuring out how to stay on top, it evolved to a participatory governance, maintained by strong leaders working to protect what each has, while protecting the system. This is not a placid, inert, immobile society. The lot in repressive societies…like that of Persia, Assyria or Egypt … is one of obedience where I greet the ruler groveling on my stomach. States that penalize individuality and discourage improvement; also restrict or prohibit the change needed to stay relevant. If enterprise and reason were present 2600 years ago in Miletus, they were dead as a doornail under the Persians, then the Diadochi; certainly under the Byzantine control and ditto for the Turks. Rational thinking is of little benefit if it is discouraged and leads to heresy, treason, and insubordination.

It requires little deductive reasoning to find the causes for failure in the history of Miletus. It was not due to a tidal wave or a volcano but rather an internal collapse. A gradual implosion. We did not solve the problems which assailed us; failed in political adroitness; neglected to retain the access to the sea upon which depended on our livelihood. The challenge that earlier had sharpened our wits and stimulated our patriotism paled, changing our attitude about life and glory and success. When the will dies, so does the enterprise.

People in the tractor business rejoice in the contributions made in Miletus 2600 years ago and genuflect before the altar of Thales, reason being a tool used extensively by those who hope not to merely succeed, but to excel. Fact to augment that process, we now employ a new $1,000,000 computer system to help us think faster, execute more quickly and more accurately, and bring every conceivable ounce of talent we can to the task at hand. We have tried to make problems a <u>benefit</u> since they tell us where to fix the system and beyond that, if <u>we</u> learn to solve problems our competitors are <u>unable</u> to resolve, we make more deals. We haven't been models in terms of broad employee participation, but realizing the need for that input, have a dozen Six Sigma teams now, studying our records in warranty or lost sales or flat-rate pricing or management of core inventory, etc. that use the input of people working in these areas because they understand each situation best and have long had ideas about how to make it better. The thrust is to do less top-down thinking and more from the bottom-up. We are applying the "Thalean" process of study, examination of data and applying the art of reason to the new insights to gain more efficiency, better service and more profits.

But unlike Miletus, we have no intention of leaving our problems unsolved. We hope that success is gained from new efficacy and confidence; that one does not rise to a given point of achievement, and then figure the assignment is complete and our work is done. Though we are 60 years old, never find the daily charge boring or repetitive or dreary. The nature of the unsolved problems and the examination of unexplored opportunities are precisely what continue to make this sort of endeavor the adventure of our age. We are to a degree, the arbiter of our own destiny. We get hammered by outside forces and elements we can't control, but generally speaking, our success is directly contingent upon how well we cultivate our market and succeeds in capturing more of it through simultaneously solving problems which arise daily in the course of our endeavor. ■

2005

Politics — Nothing New

March 2005

The 2004 political campaign is fading from memory but what we remember of it did little to improve our opinion of the American political system. It was a deluge of commercials, charges and countercharges, allegations and inferences gushing with such force the presence or relevance of <u>issues</u> drifted into the murky background. The blatantly biased opinions had us cringing. Bush is a cowboy who shoots from the hip. Fact, his sequence is "ready, fire, aim". He rides roughshod over reason, evidence, protocol and world opinion. His "Lone Ranger" approach has insulted our allies and antagonized much of the world, Great Britain excepted. Kerry on the other hand was seen as a flip-flopper, "for it" today and "agin" it tomorrow. He never sponsored a single piece of major legislation in 20 years; decried jobs going overseas, while his wife's company exported them to dozens of <u>foreign</u> countries. His war record depicted acts of cowardice, and his own troops said he was unfit for command, etc., etc. Many of us were left wondering what was clarified as a result of all this "sound and fury", which we thought did indeed "signify nothing" (to quote King Macbeth).

But, fair scores; this is not something new in American politics. It was here from the get-go. Our very earliest experiment in the 18th Century was equally fierce and maybe even more vituperative. Then or now, what occurs is fairly commonplace in a free society where difference in opinion is integral to our system, provoking or triggering exchange or viewpoint. A dynamic familiar in personal affairs; in theological, business or family situations so we have all "been there; done that". As a nation, we've had protracted arguments on civil rights, abortion, same-sex marriage, size of government, foreign policy, e.g. Israel, Palestine, NAFTA, taxes and a dozen others. In Indiana it's about daylight savings time. When the debate continues for years and the discussion has not brought consensus, in frustration we move to the next stage. We challenge the credibility of the opposition; fact, challenge his integrity, logic, motive, even character, hoping to gain some points that way. Illogically! The personal attack to ruin the opponent's reputation is not a way of dealing with an issue. It has left topical discussion completely aside and become totally extraneous. Demeaning the opponent does not have us win. Because if we did, the opponent would change his mind.

Philosophically speaking, divergence of opinion can be a good — and even a desirable — thing. The introduction of a new perspective can change minds, add a new dimension and a different logic. Dispassionate minds generally look at all aspects of a given situation. But alas, most of us are so obsessed with our point prevailing, we are categorically unwilling to consider another viewpoint. Even when listening might teach us something. I have said before that I learn more about a given topic from the opponent than I do from hearing my own side, "preaching to the choir", already knowing what is about to be said. Bottom line: Too much of our thinking is visceral rather than logical. The objective ought to be the best course, not <u>my</u> course simply because I have my pride and conviction staked on it.

I learned something about political arguments in the early days of the republic from a number of recent biographies, which have redefined our founding fathers in a wonderful fashion. The latest is a bio of Washington; two years back one appeared on

Franklin; simultaneous with a terrific recounting of the John Adams story; there's one on Jefferson and a fantastic 731 pages now on Alexander Hamilton. Studying these demigods in new and remarkable detail has been both enlightening and occasionally disillusioning. We discover despite their uniqueness they had the same frailties and weakness "that flesh is heir to", and the very process of creating a nation naturally brought strong differences to light. Differences about the size of government, about its representative structure, foreign policy, the post office, slavery, taxes, states rights, Indians, and you name it. The differences arose over geography like north versus south. Arose over "cast" with a pseudo-aristocracy on one hand and frontier farmer on the other. There were economic interests to protect like great plantations and frontier farmers; there were whaling, small manufacturers and merchant traders; add Quaker, Anglican, Puritan and Catholic colonies plus a dozen tiers in between, each protective of its own right and privilege. Add to this degrees of education, knowledge of the world, influence of the culture in which one is raised, and we create this melting pot which became America, acknowledging differences as part of the system.

Resolving these sundry interests at colonial level was far simpler than resolution at the <u>federal</u> stage when we suddenly have all 13 colonies in play. The Constitutional Convention had worked a miracle in

Alexander Hamilton portrait by John Trumbull, 1806
(Source: Wikimedia Commons.)

negotiating, compromising and crafting a structure that would both unite colonial entities into a whole and simultaneously provide for a century and a half of expansion and enlargement. But once "the several" had become "one", a variety of opinions arose about how we function, and in the post-Convention years the governmental <u>plan</u> had to become governmental action. In that process, inadvertently, differences of opinion on several major issues created a coalescing around political positions. These quickly evolved into rudimentary political parties, and they arose over the issue of federal versus state power and jurisdiction, then how we handle the several colonial and the <u>national</u> war debt ($25 and $54 million, respectively); create a monetary system; set foreign policy with respect to the war in Europe (France versus Great Britain); taxing (meaning revenue sources); the creation of the banking system; how about a standing Army and Navy? Etc.

The articulator of the policy for one side was Alexander Hamilton, perhaps the most gifted of the founding fathers, aide-de-camp to Washington, war veteran and first Secretary of the Treasury. He was the major force in pressing for a strong federal state and for a strong Presidency. He favored consolidation of total war debt into one and in paying it off. A New Yorker, he felt the nation needed a strong economic base and was, thus, the champion of the manufacturer, the trader, ship captain, and the merchant; and since we had origins from British exploration and colonization, we used English common law, the same language and had stronger ties of kingship; he favored the British against the French. His opponents were sundry but lead by Jefferson and Madison (both scions of the southern aristocracy and cultured gentlemen). (Hamilton began working at age 12 and was a self-made, self-educated man.) Jefferson had avoided military service, served as French Ambassador (during the war and after), and excused the French revolution since "the tree of liberty had to be watered from time to time with the blood of tyrants". He was opposed to consolidating the debt package; resisted Hamilton's proposals for a National Bank; strongly protected states rights since Virginia (the largest and richest of the 13) had been used to considerable latitude in conducting its affairs; was edgy about too strong a President and was obsessed with what he saw as a drift towards monarchy.

Both Hamilton and Jefferson held positions in Washington's cabinet, the former in Treasury and the latter as Secretary of State. Since Washington dominated the affairs of the nation, his word or will amounted to national policy. Having spent four years during the war on his staff, Hamilton knew how the President's mind worked, which was most frequently on the side of federal position, thus, favored Hamilton's viewpoint. So besides an in-the-cabinet battle for the favor of the President, the two parties engaged others in support of their respective positions and carried on the war in the legislature, argued and debated in the taverns, pressed their claims and declared the calumny of the other in pamphlets, and took the campaign to the newspapers. America had an astounding number of these (some writers say 10,000) and given a literate public, the discussion of important matters (local and national) found their way with some regularity in the media.

Jefferson took a step beyond and created his own newspaper, *The National Gazette,* to carry his party line, hiring Phillip Freneau as its editor. (Freneau was a poet whose work I recall from high school.) But hired officially in Jefferson's Department of State as a translator, like translating French. Hamilton noted that Freneau was barely literate in French, a lousy translator, and since Jefferson spoke the language fluently, what was his job? Frankly, it was to cut up Hamilton and refute the federal position on issues. Before the days of liable suits, an unbridled press got vituperative indeed and one could say (write) practically anything he wanted about an opponent. So accounts were short on fact and long on opinion; scurrilous, inaccurate and without qualm or principle. Freneau demonstrated these characteristics and unable to attack Washington directly (a virtual God in his lifetime), Jefferson, Madison and Freneau used the *National Gazette* obliquely to rally support for viewpoints often contrary to that of the very administration Jefferson served.

Jefferson had an insatiable appetite for political discussion, copying down bits and pieces of gossip on small slips of paper, which he one day edited and produced as his *"Anas"*. Only problem with Jefferson's notes was the fact that he copied down everything he heard, anywhere he heard it: fabricated stories, second-hand

National Gazette newspaper
(Source: Wikimedia Commons.)

gossip, rumors, casual critical comments, hearsay, etc. to which he added his own interpretation and bias. In this opus Hamilton becomes the melodramatic villain of the first administration. No fewer than 45 entries describe the horror story of Hamilton's evil influence. Again, instead of dealing with the weakness or danger in (e.g.) combining the national debt and working out a payment plan, he attacked <u>the architect</u> of the plan. Instead of providing a rationale for our support of the new French republic, fresh from its blood bath and guillotining, he finds new evidence of Hamilton's peculation. Instead of cogent argument against the creation of a currency and banking system or post office, he finds new treason in his opponent's motives. Hamilton was an "anglophile, a royalist demon", the cat's paw of a cabal to destroy the constitution and install a monarchy. He not only wanted a monarchy but one "bottomed in corruption".

Madison chipped in with his two cents as well, writing for the *Gazette* and saying his opponent was "a corrupt influence", and he was putting private interests ahead of public good. He was coddling speculators, inflating the national debt, scheming to bring an aristocracy to America. He was counseling "a corrupt squadron of voters in Congress" to vote his measures, because they owned bank stock or government paper.

Between the two, they resorted to the House of Representatives, hoping to have Hamilton disgraced and to do so, drew up <u>nine</u> censure resolutions against Hamilton, which they had William Branch Giles (a member of the House) introduce late in the session, too late to allow rebuttal. These declared that the Secretary of the Treasury was guilty of being "indecorous in dealings with Congress" (whatever the heck that means), improper in mixing foreign and domestic loans, guilty of "maladministration" in the duties of his office; secretly scheming for a monarchy, using financial policy to enrich his friends, etc. Giles was rocked back on his heels when every single one of his charges was soundly defeated seriatim in a vote by the House. Having failed in the Congress,

Madison and Jefferson appealed to Washington, accusing Hamilton's Treasury Department of threatening "to devour the government". All of the country's problems rose from a single source: Hamilton's system, which was luring citizens into financial gambling. (Maybe because he proposed a universal money system for the nation and the establishment of a national bank that was funded by investors who bought shares.)

Hamilton spent much of his time in government countering Jefferson, Freneau and Madison with his own articles, essays and rebuttals. He declared Jefferson was "a man of profound ambition and violent passions". He leads a cabal trying to win the power in the next election. He is an out-and-out hypocrite. His despotism is disguised cleverly in republic clothing, but underneath he is ferociously politically ambitious. He made reference more than once to the fact Jefferson was a libertine and made illusions to his affair with Sally Hemings. He was "an intriguing incendiary, the aspiring, turbulent competitor".

Hamilton carried the day on most issues through his affiliation with Washington, shaping a good many of the institutions conceived by the founders while simultaneously helping to create the necessary structure needed in a given administration as it goes about the task of governance. The endless challenge posed by his opposition surprisingly had a salutary effect. It forced Hamilton to defend his ideas, numerous and sundry as they were and because of an opposition to clarify publicly his stance, to defend it, provide rationale for its existence and interpret its importance. Although the discussion was carried on in a cheap and nasty fashion, it did get done what free governments hope to do: require the justification of policies, prove they were sound, engaging the public in debate, and thoroughly examining each item before effectuation. You can tell in all of this that I am a Hamiltonian and contend history has dismissed charges of Jefferson, Madison, sometimes Monroe and John Adams, of an ongoing plot to bring in a monarchy — their most repetitive theme and constant fear. They proved not only to be warning of nonsense, but ridiculous nonsense. History also proves the currency system was sound, and today the dollar is the world exchange instrument; the combining of the war debt and a sinking fund to pay it off was right; the decimal system for our money was a good idea; the creation of a national bank was wise, and the credit policies allowed by it provide the currency to underwrite the expansion of America, commercially and agriculturally as well.

The value in the era of Hamilton and Jefferson was in examining federal policy by opposing it; looking at options, discussing it publicly so the voters were aware of the issues and then deal with the who, how and where of implementation. Its shame was retort to personal attacks, misrepresentation, allowing personality conflict to override dispassionate exchange, and dislike or disagreement of a person resulting in rejection of sound policy. This having been part of our political process from the start, my guess is it will not change. As a matter of fact, by now we take all to be part of the political dynamic and integral to the system with respect to which, I complain with Cicero, "Oh tempore, o mores!" And get on about my business. ∎

A Reflection

March 2005

We have pretty well recovered from the shock of the tsunami, which devastated a good piece of Southeast Asia and have had a chance to digest the enormity of that calamity. Life hurries on and the unfortunate people impacted by the disaster are reorganizing to rebuild and recuperate while we continue attending our affairs as well. But before the image has gone allow me a moment of retrospection.

When first accounts of the news came pouring in through every conceivable media outlet, I was amazed at the reaction of the world. On-the-scene descriptions of what was occurring and measuring the widespread destruction triggered an instantaneous reaction from countless sources. Almost universally, the response became a single question: "How can we help? The tragedy became <u>everyone's</u> loss. Reflecting John Donne's opinion that we are so much a part of mankind that what happens to one happens to us all.

I was absolutely astounded at how quickly aid and money, promises and volunteers came hurrying to the rescue, irrespective of nationality, ethnic constituency, religious affiliation, previous history or political structure. There was one single overpowering objective, and that was to bring relief. It was to succor those in distress.

It was a remarkable demonstration indicating how our world today (underneath its tribal posture) feels about "other folks". When the conditions became dire and most extreme, differences seem to dissolve and reappear as, "How can I do something to help you-all?" Amazing because in my mind, this never could have happened a hundred years ago. I don't think our forbearers in the British Empire (upon which "the sun never set") would have begun to emulate this sort of empathy. I don't see Germans or French or Japanese or Chinese of previous eras responding in the slightest fashion to a catastrophe of this magnitude. It would not have happened in the Roman Empire, during the hegemony of Ancient Greece, the high-water mark of Arabic conquest, in the Holy Roman Empire or even the medieval church. So how's come it appears so readily and so spontaneously in our age?

Well, one reason might be the power of TV and "on the spot" depiction of the scope and nature of the tragedy, capturing the pain and sadness not through quoted statistics, but seeing human beings stretched out in hospitals or makeshift morgues or huddled for shelter or sorting through the ruins for what is left of their life.

Another factor surely must be the growing awareness and understanding of each other on this globe, thanks again to our media, to our affluence, to unprecedented international travel. A general knowledge about other parts of the world make us suspect everyone subscribes to *National Geographic*. So that awareness produces a common denominator, indicating human traits, trials and travail are very much the same everywhere.

I'd like to think a final element here might be the influence of the Judeo-Christian ethic. Doesn't mean that we are more pious than before or that we are a purer, more saintly generation of people, but does mean we have gone back to the Old Testament

Photos for a promotional effort "Dynamite Deal" in the '90s

or the Sermon on the Mount, churchgoer or not, and understand that a lot of life, or character, or theology centers upon how we treat those in need. Christianity is about helping the "least of these". The prophet Amos in 750 B.C. was the first to bring this to our attention. He declared the Hebrew's religion had a new focus: nurture of the poor, the widow and orphan, the destitute and those up against it. He told us to spend our time and resource (coins not having been invented yet) in helping the unfortunate. That theme — concern for the "least among us" — has been transferred from the church and leaked into our society, effecting business hiring practices, seating at Colts games, welfare budgets, wage and benefit rates, hospital care, hunger (food stamps), the legal systems, and is manifest in a hundred volunteer organizations like the Red Cross, CARE, Christian Children's Fund, Doctors Without Borders, the Peace Corps, Opportunity International. This concern or commitment is part of the contemporary culture and is espoused by atheists and agnostics as well as mainstream America; the source of benevolent practice being less important than the objective itself. It is there. We think more about other people than we used to and to see that as a universal trait, even though maybe just a blip on the screen is a good sign. It says there is hope down the pike.

But the "blip (of altruism) on the screen" after careful inspection did not appear worldwide. We know the nations most severely impacted by this torrential washout were non-Christian. Indonesia with 200,000,000 people is the largest Islamic nation in the world and the population of Sri Lanka and India must be Buddhist or Hindu.

Yet the religious motivation of the larger world, I repeat, is best described as "Judeo Christian", i.e.

moving to help persons in trouble, ignoring their religious affiliation but assuming human beings who require our assistance deserve our attention. A slight theological distinction appears in the list of donors who came up with $6 billion worth of aid, food, medicine, services, water, you name it (*The Economist* of February 5th). We note the largest donor was Germany. The second largest was Australia, and the third (at just under one billion) was the United States. These three then provided half the total. The list included only the top 13 nations and shows China and Japan contributing around $400,000 and $550,000, respectively. These are industrial powers who I described as "other than Christian" but again shared a portion of the financial responsibility. Confounding to us — and disappointing to me is support from Islam. There is only one Arabic country listed, and that is Kuwait. If the rest are there, the contributions are too modest to make the chart. And it is ironic indeed that Saudi Arabia, the Emirates, Turkey and Iran (all Islamic nations) appeared to have considerably less concern about the countless thousands of Indonesians — fellow Muslims — in distress than did we in the United States, the Orient and Europe. This might look like a bit of "sitting in judgment", but I think it is worthy of note. What one holds as theological premise or conviction becomes evident in resultant actions. I wonder what this tells me about Mohammed's expectations of his people with respect to how they treat one another, and do they indeed have any responsibility at all for the lot and the misfortune of other Muslims suddenly in great distress? Then, how do they feel about others, not of the same faith? Just thought I'd ask.   ■

Lessons Learned on Turning 60

June 2005

This issue of *MacToday* is roughly coincident with our Company's 60th Birthday. It was on June 2, 1945 that my father signed the contract with CAT to become their dealer. It took another three weeks to clean up some odds and ends, complete the purchase of some real estate and make the move to 2118 North Gale. As one looks back six decades, he automatically notes how much since the world has changed. Our "world" of machinery distribution and the world of communication, of pharmacology and medicine, of science, travel, international relations, healthcare, cities, our concept of the cosmos, etc., etc. Significant because <u>change</u> is nature's testing and sorting mechanism, a theory probably propounded by Charles Darwin. It tries our traditions, technique and culture, modifying them to fit the age. In this exercise all do not survive, so there is a process of replacement; of new companies for old; new threats and conditions, new nations, systems; a jillion products depart the scene, an equal number arrive. Sixty years is long enough to test the validity, relevance and efficacy of given entities, retaining those of substance and value while sifting out those who can't qualify, can't manage, can't justify their existence or in many cases, can't compete.

To say we have survived that long as a company says something about both the product we sell, the continuing need for same, the success of the manufacturer, and maybe even the resilience and skill of the dealer. We don't spend a lot of time in business planning for events 40 or 60 years out, but rather assume that if we manage the moment well — this day, this year — we have done the job and that in so doing again and again, acquire the competence to develop a style and a structure adequate for the long pull. So the trial and error of the distribution dynamic produces an endless series of both challenges and opportunities, which when properly handled become the blueprint or template for conduct of the enterprise. When adequately done, leads us with increasing confidence into negotiating the seldom-predictable future. Much comes with time and through experience, and little of this is unique to the tractor business; meaning ongoing trial is common from one institution or organization, or even situation to the next. The basic, the fundamental secret to success and survival is not all that complicated. It is anticipating and solving inherent problems; eliminating or finessing those forces which impair or impede the process, while moving resolutely toward a predetermined objective.

I have a penchant for illustrating postulations with historic vignettes which might reiterate the point. So seeking a prototype of a model manager, encountering problems and getting them solved to drive forward, my recourse (again) is Napoleon Bonaparte. They keep writing more books about him, so I keep reading same. A recent one (proof text of my point) is *"The Apogee of the Empire"*, which rehearses the 1809 "Danube Campaign", culminating in the Battle of Wagram. After reading this story another time was struck with the clear way it illustrates how successful managers operate; how leaders function.

Although one of the most gifted men in history, Bonaparte was not without enormous ego and having triumphed time after time, thought himself invincible, an error in judgment he discovered by invading Spain ... and proved conclusively when he attacked Russia. But before that roof fell in, there was Wagram. Which played its role in history in the spring of 1809 when the Austro-Hungarian Empire, seeing Napoleon mired in Spain, thought it an ideal time to whack him along side the head and free Europe from his control. In early April Archduke Karl broke the peace by crossing the Inn River with some 300,000 troops and attacked the French in Bohemia. He met with instant success in three or four encounters due to the bungling of Berthier (French's top commander there). But Bonaparte had

sensed earlier the change in the air, had hurried back from Spain and went into action by calling up the 1809 recruits, ordering quantities of supplies and munitions, spreading out his maps to locate the recent actions in Central Europe. It was mid-April before he could get to Bohemia where Prince Karl for the moment was resting on his laurels.

Napoléon at Wagram, 1809.
Painting by Horace Vernet (1789-1863).
(Source: Wikimedia Commons)

The Emperor immediately reorganized his army, brought in reinforcements, and in battles at Ratisbon, Eckmuhl and Abensberg turned the situation around as he had so many times before. By May he had pummeled Karl decisively, occupied Vienna, and was positioned south of the Danube, across from the Austrian army. Although outnumbered two to one, he decided to attack and drove a major offensive across the river at the Austrian center. But he had overlooked another enemy: the Danube, now in full flood. The bridges had been destroyed but temporary pontoon planking had been laid by French engineers, enabling troops to cross. Supplying them the next three days, however, was a nightmare. Because the Austrians sent great logs, fire rafts, huge obstacles down the current, punching gaping holes in the makeshift roadway. Suddenly no supplies, ammo or reinforcements. Although the battles fought at Aspern and Essling were encouraging despite the huge Austrian superiority, lack of steady reinforcements and supplies required the French to pull back.

Between the armies in midstream lay the island of Lobau, maybe four square miles, which the Emperor sent Massena to fortify. Having "blown" the first phase through his misreading the river <u>and</u> the caliber of Prince Karl's generalship, Napoleon sat down and went to work with an intensity that marked his style. It involved examining <u>every</u> detail of <u>every</u> facet of the situation at hand and contemplated the problems to come. To consider the next attack, he had to first defeat the river. It was done by summoning a gunboat flotilla to protect his engineers who drove huge pilings up stream, replete with a connecting barrier to stop floating logs. Next, he ordered a number of portable bridges, positioned at different points on the river and constructed in sections so when hooked together, the current swung them into place on the other shore where they were

anchored. He brought a sawmill onto the island, built a network of roads, set up a bakery, forges; he scrounged the countryside to round up 500 cannons, sent agents out to secure 30,000 horses for his cavalry. The army was reorganized into brigades, divisions and corps; dummy attacks were made on the Austrian flank to the west of Lobau; the area heavily fortified and bridged as though that is where his attack would be mounted, i.e. toward Aspern and Essling. In planning the next offensive he consulted with his marshals; wrote out clear, detailed assignments for each, fixing the size of their command; the nature of the reserves; the units and commanders on either side in the line; the time of attacks; and the military objective of each.

Bonaparte thought through every conceivable contingency, moved his headquarters to Lobau and personally spent each day inspecting, changing and modifying. The key was coordinate attacks, well supported and supplied with all the needed cannon, cavalry, ammunition, bridging and reinforcements.

The battle started on July 5th with a pseudo attack on the west while secretly during the night bridges went up to the north and to the east with troops pouring across to assigned positions. Massena was on the extreme left, Macdonald and Oudinot in the center, Davoust with the III Corps on the right, using Wagram as his objective. Although these marshals were among the best in the business, this was not the army Napoleon had brought to Austerlitz, Jena, and Friedland four years earlier. Part of the veterans were bogged down in Spain, many had been lost in action, a lot were Saxons, Bavarians, Germans or greener, less experienced recruits; a fact the Emperor had to take into account in his formations. The Austrians were superbly equipped and lead by the best commander they had ever put against Napoleon. The battle itself was the biggest land engagement ever fought so far in the continent of Europe. It involved 320,000 men (some say 200,000 Austrian; 160,000 French: <u>360,000</u> men) and raged for two days, along a five-mile front. Napoleon's complex strategy structured across the extended line worked. When Davoust finally drove the Austrians out of Wagram and Macdonald punched a hole in the enemy center, the opposing line broke, reeling in retreat. The strategy of the Emperor, the heroic performance of Oudinot, of Davoust and Macdonald, Eugene and Massena carried the day.

All were the result of Napoleon's extensive preparations, his analysis of the field problems, anticipation of enemy reaction, the balance and interlocking of forces, and the heroism of the French Calvary. And, of course, during the battle, the Emperor's continuing re-deployment of his forces as conditions changed and new opportunities appeared. A solid plan; <u>professional</u> execution. A taxing, exhausting affair during which he probably hadn't slept more than two hours in the last 48. There were miscalculations, bad intelligence and less experienced forces, but the management of his resource and the soundness of his battlefield strategy won the day. And the war. A key element, of course, was the leader. A hands-on commander, fully in charge of every component, properly assessing what it was his guys could do, clearly outlining the assignment, knowing who among them was best equipped to lead, how they mutually supported the effort, and what corrections to make along the way when "Plan A" did not work.

In re-reading this author's interpretation of the account, a dozen parallels to business management popped out. Axioms or verities also true in most of life. Like rule one. Almost elementary: We ought to anticipate problems and resolve them before they occur. It's cheaper and quicker than allowing a preventable miscarriage to happen, then expending the time and effort to undo the damage. In the course of that exercise, we ought to find <u>the</u> situation most critical or most deleterious to the cause and fix it first. There's no point in planning a battle if we have an unreliable bridge to cross. It implies as well that we need a crystal clear plan of what we intend to do; where are we going? What does it take to succeed here? And everyone involved needs to understand his responsibility and how each interlinks and supports the other. Beyond that we have to provide professional leadership at each level: platoon, company, regiment, brigade, battalion, division and corps. Because the success of each element is contingent

Equipment at Fort Wayne branch, 1950.

upon success of others engaged in the same fight. It is unlikely one section can collapse or fall and the rest survive.

We need to appreciate that nothing exists exactly as we conceive it to be. We make plans <u>assuming</u> such and such is the case, realizing that when the firing begins and when we confront our assignment, it will be a different sort of animal than we anticipated. But recall at once our job is to succeed. If that requires a change to our plans to meet the new — the real — contingency, let's adapt. The plan was one way to do it. But is only a device, not an end in itself. Completing a plan is fruitless unless we achieve the anticipated result. Add to these, the need for absolute commitment to the cause and loyalty to its leadership. Bonaparte had an almost hypnotic effect on his troops. Wellington said that "his presence on the field of battle was worth 40,000 men" because his guys got that fired up. Under his gaze, they would attempt … and often achieve … anything. The old "get one for the Gipper" attitude adds a special thrust; delivers extra all-out efforts because the troops want to succeed. Our own professional example helps. It is proven if we have reasonable expectations from our troops — and ourselves. Pragmatism ought to be the grounding of both planning and execution.

There is a harsher lesson here as well. In the midst of the second day's battle fury, Macdonald was commissioned to drive straight into the Austrian center drawing Austrian reinforcements from their left where Davoust was about to land the knockout punch. Except when Macdonald was fully extended, his supporting commander Bernadotte with two Saxon divisions decided to <u>retreat</u> from the field, leaving a gap in the lines and Macdonald's left totally exposed. Bonaparte watching the action, hurried Lauriston and hundred cannon to plug the hole till reserves could arrive. Then accidentally encountered Bernadotte who had almost ruined the day. The Emperor stripped him of his Marshal's rank, sent him off the field, and out of the army in disgrace. Not a new lesson. When we have a loser in the lines, act decisively. Get rid of him. Someone who lets the team or the army down, who fails because of his lack of skill or courage is no asset. He needs to go.

All of which came to mind as I finished *"The Apogee of the Empire"*. But it doesn't imply that we have done the same, i.e. reached our high-water mark. It reminds us instead that the tractor business like life itself is a constantly pulsating, flexing and moving organism like the ebb and flow of the Danube campaign. Directing its course requires constant, hands-on attention. One does not manage well for 60 years and then assume a pattern is set that will automatically direct the company henceforth. No sweat. Each timeframe brings its own assaults as well as its opportunities. These can be understood only from <u>that</u> given perspective, which often requires new, not old, strategies in response. Intellectual alertness is an element essential each waking hour.

So the conclusion (after 60 years) might be that having learned how problems are solved, new laurels gained, other products and markets successfully negotiated, the professional recourse to alertness and ingenuity, and the patterns and agents of the past, when professionally employed, will help us manage the future. Maybe with even more success. ■

60th Anniversary Celebration!

June 25, 2005

at

The Murat Temple

510 North New Jersey St., Downtown Indianapolis

Cocktails at 5:30 pm, Dinner at 6:15 pm, followed by a program

Appropriate dress will be suits or sport jackets for the men;
cocktail dresses or pant suits for ladies;
hotel accomodations will be provided free for those who need some.

Please join us for this once in a decade celebration!

Formal invitation to follow in the mail

Then and Now

September 2005

We have announced, proclaimed and declared this is our 60th Anniversary. So, having established that fact, presume it appropriate to <u>reflect</u> on the past 60 years and comment on some changes in the machinery world (in fact, maybe changes in the <u>entire world</u>). Let's confess, however, that these are personal recollections of 1945 or '46 and, thus, are probably selective; sort of smoothed out by time and by now have taken on a different meaning than was perceived when they occurred. So what I recall is not pure history as much as it is what I remember or construe the history to be.

The altered conditions from the previous era loomed large when I filled up at the gas pump this morning and saw Premium at $3.21 a gallon. One of the first "differences" anyone notices is the cost of living in America today compared to what it was in 1945. At the bottom of the depression, regular gas was five gallons for a dollar — 16.5¢ a gallon; while in 1945, it was 25¢ a gallon. Let's go on from there. I remember getting a Coke for 5¢ or a Hershey bar, a package of gum, a double-dip ice cream cone for the same price and remember it for a good reason: Because the cost of these commodities were identical from 1925 <u>to</u> 1945. How unique: <u>A period</u> in our experience when prices were static for a generation; a time when there was no inflation at work. I can't explain what factors existed in the economy then, or in the mentality of the American citizen, the nature of competition or governmental fiscal policy that held things steady anymore than I can explain <u>now</u> why prices have to go up annually, pushing salaries to meet the new costs and why we are better off because we have one chasing the other in an irreversible, endless pattern.

Watching the Colts start out their season reminds one of another cost: contemporary salaries paid to athletes. When Peyton throws an interception or Tarik misses a block or James fumbles on the one yard line, we cringe at such blunders, given the outrageous sums paid for these guys, whether playing badly or well. A lot more than Caterpillar Tractor presidents or dealer principals. Athletes a couple generations ago got similar notoriety when Babe Ruth made $80,000 a year. Outrageous! Made more than President Hoover. (When reminded of this, the Babe is reported to have said, "But I had a better year than he did.") Before go-

ing much further, we need to confess that inflation has distorted our dollar's value. There's a vast difference in what it buys today versus what it bought in Hoover's day or in 1945. $80,000 then equals approximately $1,000,000 today. So to find out what it takes in today's dollars to equal the <u>purchasing power</u> of a dollar in 1945, multiply by 12.5%. An equalizing factor called the "Consumer Price Index". It tracks the purchasing capacity of a dollar as related to a given point, an arithmetic multiplier which gives us an apples-to-apples comparison.

But it's tricky to depict properly the reality or accuracy in the "now" and "then" equation because of unaccounted peripheral factors. They called Yankee Stadium "The house that Ruth built" because people loved to watch the Bambino play. Moreover, his unorthodox, extracurricular activities and his nonchalance about personal discipline made it most remarkable that a guy with such poor conditioning and so un-athletic in build, could hit the ball so far and so often. Point being that Ruth brought in the fans, and the fans brought profit to the owners of the team and the stadium — a fact of life which exists today with athletes. But our comparison falls short here because Peyton Manning and Edgerrin James not only bring in the crowds to watch the action, they add enormous, additional revenue because of a medium called television, unknown in Babe's day (or in 1945). The revenue produced by televising professional football is enormous. It's a huge financial kicker to each team, particularly when said team is leading the league, playing heads-up football, and gets into the playoffs.

But let's look at more mundane costs. Like food, for example. Hamburger in 1945 went for 27¢ a pound (that becomes $2.16 today); porterhouse steak for 40¢ (now $5.00 a pound); eggs were 31¢ a dozen ($3.88 a dozen in today's money) and tells us the course is uneven. Indian River grapefruit (which we still buy) was 6.5¢ each; coffee for 36¢ a pound; Kellogg Corn Flakes 12¢ for an 18 ounce box; oranges 20¢ a dozen ($2.40 in today's theocratic terms versus the actual market price of $6.00); Campbell's Tomato Soup 9¢ a can; Pepsi was 23¢ for six, <u>12 ounce</u> bottles (2¼ quarts!). Buying lunch at the drugstore counter was 15-25¢, and you could buy a full course meal at most restaurants for 25-40¢. In clothing items, a pair of boys shoes went for $4-5.00; a man's suit for

$22.50; denim overhauls for $1.57; women's skirts $3.00 each; dresses from $7-18.00; handbags from $2-8.00; women's coats from $20-35.00; men's shirts 99¢. Toilet paper was 5-10¢ a roll; razor blades a quarter for 18 of them; a bar of soap was 5¢; a permanent wave $5.00. Incidentally, at this time the minimum wage was 55¢ an hour. The average salary for college faculty (Montana State College) was $280 a month which comes to $3,360 per year. Clerks and janitors made about half that, i.e. 80¢ an hour.

Bringing relevance and accuracy into this thing, is moving me rapidly over my head because maybe my means of comparison is wrong. I talked earlier about Babe Ruth and his salary, relating it to equivalent dollars today and used the traditional Consumer Price Index formula. But there are other ways of comparing values, then and now. One is the <u>relative cost of unskilled labor</u> in America, applying <u>that</u> percentile to our calculation. If it took 27¢ to buy a pound of hamburger in 1945, what percent was that of low salaried, unskilled labor wages then? What percent of his income does that take now? The answer is it

takes a smaller percentage. He works less time to buy a pound of hamburger. The income of an average unskilled laborer in 1945 is <u>42 times higher</u> in 2005 versus 12.5% used in the Consumer Price Index. We read about the disparity in compensation, i.e. what chief executives are paid today vis-à-vis salary of the average worker, so looking at the record of unskilled help, it is good to note that a considerable improvement has occurred here — if we compare unskilled wages with that made by skilled workers. If we apply this percentile to Babe Ruth's $80,000 per year salary, we get a new figure, 42% greater, i.e. $3,400,000.

If I haven't lost you yet, there is another relative comparison: its salary or compensation as it relates to the Gross-Domestic-Product per-capita. This attributes to the individual <u>his</u> share, i.e. individual portion in the total output of all goods and services produced in America which, of course, has exploded, thanks not so much to a harder working labor force but to the introduction of endless mechanical and computerized technologies which allows doing more things, faster.

This factor is eighty times greater now than then, so Babe Ruth's salary becomes $6,430,000. And at this point it is getting too complex for me to handle.

In this long litany of increases, some stand out as remarkable. How about the increase in a pack of cigarettes? I worked in a drugstore while going to high school and sold two packs of Luckies for a quarter (13¢ a single pack). Today, a pack is about $3.00. 220%! It should be $1.62 (and maybe is if we knock off all the taxes). A major shock to me is going to the movies: $8.00 for a ticket to see "*The Penguins*" and $4.50 for a small-sized box of popcorn — $12.50. Sixty years ago the movie was a double-feature and cost a quarter; the popcorn, a dime — 35¢ versus $12.50 (should be $4.37). (Ugh!!) Or try the cost of hair cuts: 35¢ in 1945 versus hair styling today at $20. Surely by now someone is going to ask: What about the price of Caterpillar tractors? Good question. This is also a bit tricky to measure because we end up comparing apples to oranges because in 1945 a D6 CAT tractor and cable-controlled dozer (the apple) weighed 21,000 pounds; was rated at 75 drawbar/horsepower and sold for around $7200. Today's <u>D4 bulldozer</u> (the orange) weighs 23,427 pounds; has 78 horsepower and sells for about $90,000. That just happens to be a price spread of 12.5%, the exact pace of

MacAllister's first actual contract.

the Consumer Price Index. Note a <u>D4</u> now equals the old D6, and that isn't where the story ends. A pack of cigarettes looks and tastes the same in 2005 as it did in 1945; the barber uses the exact same tools, takes the same time, applies the same technique he did <u>60 years ago</u>; movies and popcorn are clones of 1945. <u>In no case has any value been added for the astronomical price increase.</u> This is not true with our tractors. It is not the same-ole, same-ole. For one thing, CAT has expanded its dozer line from five units to nine, but more important the machines themselves have changed as much as cameras or telephones.

The old D6 was started manually through the use of a "pony motor" (a time-consuming nuisance), and most of the dozers were cable-operated, using a modified winch on the back of the tractor with cables strung up front to a control pulley and thence to the dozer for raising and lowering. Downward pressure was the weight of the blade and no more. No one <u>builds</u> cable-controlled dozers anymore, <u>any</u>where, not even in Lower Slobovia and, of course, all machinery is electric start today … crack the throttle and press a button. Shifting then was done manually with clutches and a shift lever; turning accomplished by pulling levers to disengage power plus application of brakes. The operator was busy all the time. Today, transmissions shift automatically; steering is finger-tip action, and the dozer is raised, lowered <u>or tilted</u> (new) with a flick of the wrist. Machines are now equipped with rollover protective cabs (thanks to OSHA); are sound suppressed and air-conditioned. Engines used to be effective up to 5000 hours before rebuilding, and the track might last for 3000 hours. Today, we look for 10,000 hours of engine life, and the latest in track design is aimed to give service for 5000 hours. Engines do perform more efficiently, burn less fuel, thanks to EPA and emission controls. When considering "added value", estimate the savings here in repair costs and in length of machine life. Big bucks! Half the number of replacement or rebuilds.

Machines today have been designed to facilitate all routine maintenance through redesign, providing readily accessible grease fittings, oil and fuel filters, so less time is required to perform daily/weekly checks. Tractors are also more "componentized", meaning when repaired they come apart in sections, a given unit coming out without taking half the tractor apart to get to it. With this we have troubleshooting computers which indicate what is going bad and where. Meaning, diagnoses of a problem is infinitely easier than listening to the sound, watching the smoke or

Bulldozer of our times.

taking something apart to inspect it. So when it comes to repairing machines today, our systems are infinitely more responsive. A tough breakdown then meant calling from a pay phone or the customer's instrument and if a complex problem, it took consultation to solve it. Usually a trip back to the shop and research of technical records of maybe a contact with CAT in Peoria. Today, the same problem is researched right now by the serviceman on site, using his computer which gives him access to all CAT's data. Viola! He solves the problem at once, has parts shipped on the shuttle, and the machine is in operation next day.

Machine <u>productivity</u> is also enhanced with computers as well, employing a screen that can be set to indicate for the dozer operator where he needs to cut, how much and where he needs to fill. Think of the time such technology saves and the efficiency now available to the operator who has the guesswork eliminated. The technological system involved works not only in dozing but in scraper or motor grader work as well, and the process is defined as "AccuGrade". It is use of instruments, beams and global positioning that almost takes the operators out of the picture as unit responds automatically to grade huge areas to within millimeters of the exact level the engineers want. A science that adds exponentially to the area (in square feet or in cubic yards) that a single operator can reconfigure as compared to the old way of sight estimate, leveling and filling with dozens of grade stakes to suggest grade levels.

In summary, let's suggest the old D6 of 1945 was the finest unit in its class with a record for the most available working time and, thus, the greatest productivity, augmented by long machine life. The current D4 <u>matches</u> the old D6 since it costs exactly the same in weighted dollars, yet readily doubles the production of the old one because of easier handling, better operator comfort (i.e. equipped with enclosed cabs and lights, has longer daily and seasonal possibility), and the technology of AccuGrade. Beyond that it costs probably 40% less to maintain through easier adjustments, less down time for rebuilding and longer life in undercarriage life, engines and components. By generating more production and lower maintenance costs it adds more earnings to the owner.

The story of improved performance, greater productivity at less cost sounds a bit fantastic but is the pattern typical of business in America which has continually, through ongoing innovation, increased our productivity immeasurably. And that in turn has been the chief factor in keeping inflation down and costs at a minimum. At first glance, the savings an owner gains through increased productivity and techniques to improve efficiency, combined with appreciably lower operating costs should net him a sizeable return; and he ought to really be getting rich. And he would be, except for that thing in the marketplace called "competition". What happens is the owner ends up passing along his increased capacity, lower costs and larger profits to the consumer, the person buying his services. So in order to underbid his competitor, he gives part of the new margin gain to the buyer of his service and probably ends up with the margin he had 20 years ago. The search for ever-improved operating machinery or techniques continues on in the next phase, building upon what has been achieved in the past. To stay static is to fall behind. The nature of our industry, whether in manufacturing or distribution is such that the search never ends. When Chris celebrates his 60th year, he'll be able to point back in time as I am doing and tell a similar story. Is this a great system, or what!! ∎

Whatever Happened to … Ole Bob Poorman?

September 2005

Well to find out I called Bob, had lunch with him one sunny Friday in August and we teed it up for 18 holes. On the first tee he wanted to know, "How much are we playing for?", demonstrating at once that his competitive spirit had not abated with the encroaching inevitability of age. So we agreed on "a dollar, three ways" and that was it. Bob was always competitive and that is not a bad characteristic to have in any employee, especially one in sales … or in sales management because Bob served us in both capacities. Wanting to win is what produces the best performance we are capable of delivering.

Bob was raised in Peoria, Illinois, where his father worked for the Caterpillar Tractor Company. The family moved to West Virginia in 1927 when his father joined the CAT dealer as a mechanic and demonstrator-operator. Bob spent his school years (K-12) in West Virginia and three years with the 4th Marine Division in the Pacific Theatre during WWII. The family moved to Cincinnati in 1946. His dad worked for the CAT dealer there. Bob was not only acquainted with his dad's profession, but was fascinated by it.

As a young man, he began doing some brokering of used machinery … an occasional crane or a dozer, slipping into the industry gradually and getting some experience under his belt. In looking at the history, it is hard to find many instances where our salesmen or even sales managers started life with our particular profession as their objective and moved steadily on course to pursue it. Most "gravitated" into it after trying their hand in other jobs or opportunities. Bob knew the vocation he wanted to pursue and began

early, simply to "do it". We learned about him and his activities from a CAT Rep, covering both Ohio and Indiana. He suggested young Poorman might be worth looking into. In the fall of 1952 Bob came over for an interview, and Bill Diehl hired him December 1st. Bob stayed with us the next 30 years. He was a stockholder and served on the Board of Directors for a year after his departure in October 1982.

His career marks what I called "the halcyon days" of the industry. The "good ole days" though in reality, one is existentially living in "the good ole days" since they become that only when we are <u>reliving</u> them in retrospect and have had time to burnish them a bit. I said good ole days because the industry was healthy and beyond that, was busy. We were finishing up a spate of toll-road building and were entering the period of the interstate system when Indiana would put down some 1100 miles of brand new divided, double-lane paved highways. This not only nourished the road contractors but all the affiliated industries, like sand and gravel, fencing, land clearing, asphalt, trucking, bonding and you name it. It was an age filled with action, with lots of competition and a certain vibrancy. Bob put his toe into the water officially with us to play a role in the ensuing drama and assumed a territory in the Terre Haute area; ultimately ending up in 1958 with the Indianapolis territory. We had an appreciable turnover of sales people in the earlier days, mostly because we hadn't thoroughly examined or prescreened them and because few of them knew the drill or the industry as well as Bob did. Nor did they have the patience and professional approach he used.

Bob Poorman (left) with Pete Nold in 1968

Bob Poorman, 2005

He knew his customers well, was a hard worker, strong in product knowledge, kept extensive and accurate customer history records, and approached the assignment as a true professional. Selling was not just something to do; it was indeed a virtual science with Bob and he treated it with respect, practiced it superbly. We could tell "the keepers" in the sales force by their "closure" attitude and record. When Bill Diehl wondered if he should help a given salesman in closing a sale, two or three of the guys invariably said, "No thanks. I can handle this myself." Bob was always capable of making his own deals. This trait was not surprising since it showed up in his Personalysis File (a test we gave our sales and management people). The "tester" noted among other things that Bob would: "Count on personal strength and self-confidence to lead others; be decisive in style; make practical decisions to secure measurable results; work energetically; would stay in command and focus energy for purpose."

In 1965 Bill made Bob the Assistant Sales Manager, hoping he could teach our territory people something about not only selling, but about territorial and customer management; about files and product knowledge. They also might learn something about work habits. Bob was usually in the office at 7:15 AM, including Saturday. His contact with the salesmen was such that he knew weekly what was going on in all of the 13 territories. He did much of the trade-in pricing, financing package and market strategy, having "been there, done that". So it was natural when Bill decided to retire in 1978 that Bob should succeed to his role and did indeed become our General Sales Manager. Recalling that era, we were all better acquainted with each other personally than seems the case today. Of course,

we were much smaller (our total sales in say, 1975, were $17,000,000; our sales last MONTH were $31,000,000). With fewer people in "the family" we lunched together daily, had a bowling team, had softball games, played some golf, occasional poker or gin game and some bridge. There was a social aspect more extensively interwoven into the business relationship than is the case now so we noted the same competitive spirit in Bob whether on the diamond, on the tee, at the bridge table or on a deal.

Speaking of that, Bob said one of his hobbies today is bridge: plays three times a week, occasional round of golf but not a lot. Two years ago (age 80) he finally had to give up softball. He and Caye raised five children; three girls and two boys, all of whom live in the metropolitan area and all well established in personal careers. There are seven grandchildren and two great grandchildren. Bob and Caye were — and are — devoted Roman Catholics and begin each day by attending Mass at Our Lady of Mount Carmel Catholic Church. They spend a lot of time on their home turf in Village Farms, putting in the flower garden, tending a rock garden and fish pond, and enjoying the family and good friendships. For a guy who has two artificial hips and a factory-made knee, Bob played a good round of golf and though he beat me the front nine, I won the back nine and beat him by two strokes for the total and a dollar. Here's a guy who is still spry, alert, competitive, attentive, and has moved gracefully into the evening of the golden years. We remember him because he made a contribution to this company, finding and strengthening customer clients and demonstrating essential qualities of professional salesmanship as employed in the Caterpillar Family. ∎

A Tale of Rome and Nazareth

December 2005

This is a history lesson (again) combined with a Christmas commentary…it being the 2005 Yuletide season. The history theme is that of Rome into whose empire Jeshua of Nazareth was born, probably in the 31st year of Augustus Caesar reign (which Dionysius Exiguus would compute to be 4 B.C.). This comes to mind because of a recent TV series called "*Rome*", an earthy, occasionally bloody, often vulgar story of the last days of the Roman republic, focused on the career of Julius Caesar. It weaved in the roles of Pompey, Brutus, Octavian and Antony and provided the most realistic interpretation of republican Rome I have ever seen.

The subtle theme below the radar screen is a scrambling to reconstruct the Roman governing apparatus; the element of unmanaged change thrust relentlessly upon a system which ruled the affairs of men and nations. The reason for the civil wars, which wracked Rome for nearly a century, was unprogrammed, unassimilated growth from a farmer's market to a respectable city to the Italian peninsula, then mastering the Mediterranean world. The political vehicle which successfully directed affairs of a village or a bustling town of 50,000 was hopelessly mismatched when applied to 50,000,000 diverse people across a million square miles of land and water.

Rome's system was a republic much like our own with officers elected annually for a one-year term. These managed the sundry departments of city and state like public buildings, welfare, utilities, the militia, courts, religious rites, etc. Training for office was pretty much "on the job" with an acolyte ascending from praetor, to aedile, to questor, to consul, learning the ropes along the way. But collecting the garbage for 5,000 or even 50,000 persons was a "no-brainer" when compared to the same function now needed for half a million. Think of the freshwater requirements (400 gallons a day per person); recruiting and training the army; building hundreds of miles of roads, operating the public baths; distributing grain to the poor; imagine the uncontrolled tenement development; public health and sanitation; traffic jams. It got pretty loosey-goosey. So while Caesar as Consul was figuring out how to import more grain, how to pay for it, building more market stalls in his new forum, installing a common-world calendar, seeing to the water supply and fire protection, he had

a year to get it done and then he was out.

Legislation was processed through two governing bodies, a senate and the assembly of plebes, who gave authority and funding for all proposed programs. The process was like our own, snarled in the bitter partisan politics, impeded by budget battles, protracted debates; side-tracked in appointment blockage, vetoes and continual assaults on those in government. So the solution to "one year and out" for ambitious men (consuls) was to extend their term of office by becoming a senate-appointed "dictator". That is how Marius and Sulla in their respective days (80, 70 B.C.) and Pompey and Caesar in theirs short-circuited the system as a way of dealing with the growing city, growing problems and growing needs. Final resolution came in 31 B.C. when Octavian was anointed Imperator (Emperor) and given supreme authority <u>for life</u>. He cleverly institutionalized his office and though annual, local elections continued, The Empire was governed by he who is the "Caesar". Old patriots like Cicero, Cato and Brutus et al fought this consolidation to the last ditch, defending a system hallowed in tradition but creaking badly and so archaic it fostered corruption, inadequacy, rigged elections, and civil wars with no fix in sight. It's commonplace to note wisely "the fall of the Roman Empire", but dishonest to ignore it was also the most practical government in the ancient world and functioned fairly well for a good 360 years. (Roman <u>history</u> extended from 753 B.C. to 476 A.D.)

It was in the 15th year of the reign of Tiberius Caesar (Emperor number two) that Jeshua of Nazareth came to his unfortunate and untimely end.

Stage of Theatre in Libya.

A monastery cloister.

(Dionysius Exiguus would make that 29 A.D.) Jesus had a strangely unique role which I think has certain parallels with the Roman story just rehearsed. Because what Christmas celebrates is the birth of he, who would become the "Caesar" (changer, reorganizer) not of politics but of western religion. He converted Judaism for his followers from a single sect to a faith with universal appeal and defined a lifestyle which prescribed a mode of living and code of conduct that allowed society to function like none other before it. One could conclude, like Caesar, Jesus provided a watershed moment, to a degree we dated time as "Before" or "After" Christ. Converts in the early church were all Jews and what they established from his teaching was a sect of Judaism, competing with Pharisaism and Sadduceeism, with the Zealots or the Ebionites or Essenes. The Christians distinguished themselves by proclaiming their rabbi had been the predicted Messiah and the practitioner of a new covenant.

What I think Jesus did was rehearse and rephrase the exhortation of Israel's 8th and 7th Century prophets, who for the first time in history saw religion, not as ceremonial pageantry and endless ritual but rather focused on what we call the "social gospel": ministry to those in need. It declared God was served when man was responsible for fellow man. He wanted the great mass of humanity — the exploited, the bruised, the maltreated and the impoverished protected and served. Amos had said that God was tired of all the busyness and wanted His people to worship him by being kind to each other, particularly to those needing a hand-up or a handout. Jesus then proceeded to demonstrate what this meant by walking the roads and villages, healing, teaching, consoling and encouraging. Christian

theology taught mercy, forgiveness, kindness, tolerance, and it eschewed any more burning meat on the altar, buckets of blood and the rigid orthodoxy of the temple. It focused on the uniqueness and value of the person. This new sect caught on and expanded in the 2nd and 3rd Centuries, becoming ultimately a force more powerful than the empire: changing societies, the nature of God, changing men and women.

In this convoluted analogy, I have interlinked Caesar and Augustus in the Roman story. The former being the architect of a reconstruction movement responding to the enormous demands placed upon the state by the growing empire but then giving to Octavian (Augustus), the credit for a genius amazing enough to <u>create</u> the vehicle for implementation: the Roman Empire. It was a governing vehicle which would run the world reasonably well for a long time. Note: All of Caesar's work would have been lost without the skill and pragmatism of Augustus.

If one is to examine the Jesus story, he finds the same model. Jesus' teachings would have vanished within a generation <u>had it not been</u> for the interpretive role of Saul of Tarsus. It was Paul who not only translated but <u>transposed</u> the life and mission of Jesus to the western world. A task impossible for a Peter or a John or a James who were barely literate, were fairly parochial, and raised in a bush-league fragment of greater Syria called Galilee. It is Paul who made Jesus the Messiah, made him a god, wrote the doctrine of the church, suborned the law to the gospel and gave the life of Jesus an enduring quality. A bit like Octavian instituting the reforms and modifications envisioned by Caesar. Each was a force which radically effected western society and introduced a new modus operandi that altered lives and changed forever the world into which each was born.

The impact of Rome on its world was incalculable. Its 55,000 miles of hard-surface roads made travel easy and hooked the empire together. Add a common coinage, a common language (really Koine Greek), one major set of laws, the same calendar from London to Persepolis, an unparalleled period of peace enduring from one generation to the next. Roman military camps are today flourishing cities, and the presence of the legions protected the local populace from robbers, so Paul of Tarsus could travel from Jerusalem through Syria and Phoenicia, half dozen provinces of Asia Minor, sidestepping into Macedon, then to Greece, ending up in Rome without a passport, without tetanus or cholera shots, with no need for an interpreter; nor periodic searches at security points in major terminals. Try making that trip today and see how laborious we have made it. This was the product of Rome's wars and Caesar's politics, recast by Octavian in a new mode of governance which still required local citizens to assume responsibility for their own drinking water, public baths, theatres, forums and fire department by using the Roman governance pattern in Alexandria, London, Leptis Magna and Vienna, but all under the aegis — a scrutiny — of the empire.

Christmas is a great time to recall the impact of Jesus and Paul on the western world, concluding it has been even more impressive. It gave the western world a religion that was independent of the state or the ruler, based on ideas and conduct rather than ancient ritual; preached piety and generosity, and ruled much of Europe through a common creed and rule for life. Jesus created a religion which Protestantism saw freeing the individual from the ever-present priesthood that had linked with the crown to keep humanity groveling on its knees since the dawn of time. Here was a faith which emphasized the equality of man (at least in the church), shared resource, saw peace as preferable to war, and viewed a divine being as one who was not disdainful of man but was available to care for and help him. As a little kicker, this faith added the promise of a glorious afterlife. Just think! A new place where there is no slavery, no plagues, no hunger, illness or pain. Wow!! The church was built around the person, not the tribe; it wanted voluntary enlistments, not people driven by fear into its fellowship. And Paul expanded the arms of Jesus' God so they reached out to embrace all mankind: a casteless society, each person of equal value in the eyes of the creator.

My guess is not very many people ever think of Jesus as a "cutting edge figure", a revolutionary, responding to a given historical circumstance and deciding to change the theological outlook of the Jews. When this appeal failed to catch on, Paul took the message to the wider world. So between the two, Jesus and Paul, they exploded the long legacy of Judaism, repackaged it for the universe of 40 A.D. and sent their vision to the "uttermost parts of the earth". In my analogy, both the Caesar/Augustus "combine" and the Jesus/Paul hook up brought a plan that reordered their respective worlds and provided a new vehicle to deal with the mired-down and out-model ineffectiveness of the old. Each happened at a point in time and in a given age, spoke to

Sea of Galilee.

specific peoples and institutions.

And in each case, success resulted for an appreciable period of time. But the lesson underneath these two stories should be apparent: No part of life is permanent. Like our own personal experience we begin as nurslings, move to childhood, puberty, youth, adulthood; each has its own distinct phase, governed by personal character, circumstance, experience and dozens of conditions, always ushering us into another phase needing new rules. Can we suppose nations are similar in nature? We know what served us well in 400 A.D. as church structure, doctrine, mission, opportunity and role was up for grabs in the Renaissance, was further challenged by the Enlightenment and worked over again in the Industrial age. What Jesus taught was revolutionary — then. But now is different. We would have trouble with the relevance of his ideas on the role of women, racial issues, the Jewish take on homosexuality, ethnicity and manners today. What could he possibly say about stem cell research, organ transplants, teen pregnancy, AIDs, drug addition? Not much because these were missing in his society.

A good deal of what goes on in our life is not covered in the Bible, telling me that it was written for a given time and set of conditions, some of which are maybe eternal but some never mentioned. The practice of stretching 1st century A.D. teachings to govern 21st Century challenges does not always work. But some of the blueprint is still there, guiding us into making our own decisions in a pattern consistent with the past. We do those things which help the other person, and we want him given a fair shake. A familiar theme this time of the year when giving for most of us has become a greater joy than receiving. So maybe in view of the need for contemporary morality to govern contemporary society, looking at the Christmas spirit might give us a leg up. We can dissolve the Christmas myth and legend without throwing out the holiday if we retain the spirit of "Peace on earth, goodwill to men". The message of the 8th Century prophets and the First Century Jesus still have relevance for us and still contain the key ingredient in any covenant we design for the new phase in a more challenging, complicated, deadly and struggling world. But before it can do any good, the social gospel, "the other guy first mentality" has to be adopted by us all. I guess maybe starting with me.

Merry Christmas! ■

2006

Maximum Effort

April 2006

People in the tractor business don't spend a lot of time studying history — unless it is a history of our past experience; or the contemporary history of successful dealers. Chris studies the record of Baldrige or Six Sigma; Dave Baldwin skews sideways to check writers like Peter Drucker or Edward Demming and columnists in *Forbes* or *Wall Street Journal*. Reason for doing so is to find ideas or concepts that might improve our own operations, and the current generation of managers in America skips history, focusing instead on wisdom gleaned from contemporary sources. But we in the old school find current theory a little prosaic, lacking in excitement or a spirit of adventure. Past history does have examples in the long human experiment that might cast light on today's problems; because there are certain timeless verities or principles which continue to instruct us. These might include leadership or importance of teamwork; the value of integrity; creative ingenuity; maximum use of existing resources; might deal with loyalty, and how it contributes to our success. The last of these — loyalty — is the focus of this essay. The conclusion being when we can assemble and retain a strong, professional workforce, dedicating careers to us, we probably have what it takes to produce unusual business results. We need serious and steady commitments from our people from top to bottom if we are to provide superior benefit to the customer. If we are to be unique as a company, we start by being unique as individuals.

The examples of all-out effort in support of the institution or the cause are commonplace in history: The Minutemen at Concorde in April of 1775, Pickett's charge at Gettysburg, the devotion represented in the lives of Mother Teresa, Father Damien or St. Francis of Assisi. There was the famous Light

Brigade at Balaclava; the Alamo and the old guard at Waterloo, but the example which has always struck me most dramatically occurred in the 5th Century B.C. when Xerxes, King of Persia and ruler of half the world, decided to conquer the other half and in 480 B.C. took an army, 150,000-strong into Greece. They crossed the Hellespont on a bridge of boats in August, moving inexorably westward through Thrace and Macedon, then south into the hills of Thessaly and aimed towards Athens, the leader of the 30 Aegean city-states.

Scrambling to assemble the forces of the Greek city-states took time and then assembling a navy which could meet the vast armada of Xerxes had everyone on the move. To engage these barbarians (anyone who was <u>not</u> a Greek was a "barbarian" in those days), Leonidas was dispatched with 10,000 Spartans to stall the Persian attack. These, the finest soldiers in the world, now marched northward till they found a place in the Persian route where mountains crowd close in to meet the sea, creating a very narrow pass. The constrictive space scrunched down to two meters wide, making a broad thrust or flanking movement impossible. The site was called Thermopylae, the Hot Springs, and here the Spartan army took its position, barring the way. Given the uneven odds and the narrow area of the encounter, Leonidas sent back all but 300 men, and it was they who the Persians encountered when they reached the Hot Springs.

This confrontation on September 17, 18 and 19 has always been uniquely heroic to me. Protean in scope, rich in violent and bloody action, it was a model of courage and patriotism. Descriptions of the Persian host that day are recast in my mind's eye. Rank on rank of assorted colors with armor glittering in the sun, strung out for miles back along the mountain road, the military contingents from thirty nations, assembled to blot out the Greek experiment and convert the land to a Persian satrapy. Stalling this enormous avalanche was a handful of Spartans, combing their long hair in preparation for death, armed and ready, determined to uphold the honor of Sparta. The Persian machine had been invincible, lead by a crack corps known as "The Immortals", the king's most experienced, professional soldiers; never defeated.

If results heretofore had always been inevitable, this attack on the Spartans proved to be a big surprise. The arrow barrage failed, limited by the space and thwarted further by the heavy armor of the Spartans. Then the attacking corps of spearmen was met by a solid wall of experienced hoplites who failed to collapse in terror, but instead met the thrust with a savage obduracy that stacked the roadway with Persian slain. The attacking vanguard regrouped continually, only to suffer one costly rebuff after another. Time and again they dragged back scores of dead and wounded. Hour after hour in the hot sun through the long day, the carnage went on; to be repeated again a second day as the battered and wounded Spartan contingent continued the savage duel — fighting the invaders to a standstill. Then a traitor named Ephialtes "ratted out" on the Greeks and showed the Persians a way <u>around</u> the mountain to allow an attack from the rear. When that became obvious, Leonidas formed ranks again with what was left of his heroic band and fought the foe on two fronts until every Spartan had been slaughtered.

If you visit the area today though, the terrain has changed dramatically (the sea is now miles away). The site is marked with a twice-life-size statue of a Spartan warrior, gird for battle and beneath it a quote Leonidas might have made: "Stranger (passerby), tell the Lacedaemonians, we lie here in obedience to their orders". This suicidal stand of the small band epitomizes "all out effort", doing the very best soldiers could do in fulfilling their role. It did not mean winning the battle. It meant completing the assignment. It meant stalling the incursion to buy some time; doing everything humanly possible to carry out orders. The illustration points not to the result, but the unequivocal nature of <u>the effort</u>.

But beyond that, reasons for giving up life itself and any prospect it holds, was for a cause that was <u>corporate</u> rather than personal. The individual Spartan soldier had little to gain from the contest whether victorious or defeated, yet each went without equivocation into the jaws of death. Honor was more important than life; glory the ultimate achievement of a warrior.

Sparta was a harsh, militaristic society with males beginning at an early age to revere the state as much as the family and trained incessantly in the rigors of camp life and in the art of combat. So frequent was the occasion for battle and the possibility of death, the son was told to come back from the campaign "with your shield — or on it". No shield meant the soldier had thrown it away (being clumsy and heavy) and had fled the battle. Such survival was utter and total disgrace, far worse than death. Better to have the corpse brought back by his comrades (using the shield as a stretcher) for burial. This was not the sort of society most of us would enjoy, but it does suggest why the Spartan was the finest soldier in the world and why they got the post at Thermopylae.

Fortunately our society is far less bellicose, less domineering and demanding, focused not on survival but on family life and vocation, on the amenities offered in a republic such as this and in the multitude of opportunities and promises our system provides. Ironically enough we have a good deal more to protect and preserve, even die for — if it came to that, but our culture does not require this type of sacrifice except on very rare occasions. The underlying theme here is <u>commitment</u> to a cause and what it takes to induce or instill it. If Sparta forced it down one's throat, that is <u>not</u> the case here. There has to be something at stake in order for the average American to "give his all". We are competitive, however, in different ways; most of them peaceful. In our society early training of the young likewise generates both the selection of a cause, participation in same and generates the same element of partisanship, of loyalty, support and effort to sustain or triumph extant in my earlier illustration. We team up our youngsters to participate in competitive sports, Little League being a good example. One joins a group, practices and competes to see which team is best, and in that process how each player contributes to the outcome. We have this same pattern in terms of professional sports. Indianapolis "went ape" this past football season when the Colts almost made it to the Super Bowl as week after week they won their games. We were part of those victories and took vicarious pride in the record of OUR team. The same dynamic occurs in our political system, an ongoing contest played out on a dozen levels during campaigns and between; each supporting certain strategies or priorities or policies for our governance in city, county, state and federal levels. Again, we buy in; we get involved; we contribute money and have meetings; we argue with friends, write letters and bone up on issues hoping that our options, first of all, are right; and second, that they prevail in becoming policy or law.

The other form of competition in which I am most interested, of course, is the machinery business and, again, a do-or-die-competitive struggle. Chris could play in 15 Little League games and lose each one, but come back again next season and start over with 15 more ahead. That is not true in the business world. Losing (years without profits) is not merely painful, it is fatal. Success for us is measured in terms of those profit dollars (which is the way business "keeps score") plus in terms of relative position with competitors (i.e. market share). Success for us depends on the nature and quality of what we sell; how skillful we are in getting the product out, and even more important, how diligent we are in backing it up with parts and service support. The location and size of the dealership have a lot to do with success; add the local economy, interest rates; and more important

than anything else, both the character of the leadership and the professional performance of the corporate team.

The element we characterized as loyalty, or commitment or "buy in", is not something that can be "ordered". We can't issue a directive saying, "From now on all employees shall give all-out support to the company". It has to be induced, earned, wooed or promoted. I have said a hundred times that the importance of the individual employee is paramount because each day several hundred of them are not John Doe or Mary Smith, they are <u>the entire company</u>. The fortunes of 640 people who work in the ranks are impacted by the way a given person at a given instant handles the problem a customer brings to his/her desk. So if we have the product, have the parts and service facilities, have a strong economy in a fruitful territory and have hammered our competition, it all amounts to naught if we take customers for granted; fail to live up to our promises; don't know our job and refuse to learn it; can't provide the data or parts or solution an owner is seeking. Our daily routines boil down to our people talking to customers or prospects and only when that has been done <u>successfully</u>, can we expect an order for anything.

Aerial view of Indianapolis branch, 1955.

In many systems today and in most systems through the course of the years, there were not a lot of choices. The Spartan youth went off to a "day school" like Hitler's kids did, where the state took over his training. In tribal societies or in most of Islam, kids (especially girls) don't decide what they are going to do, they are told by their fathers what has been selected for them. In much of the world, though freedom of choice is there, it is long on "freedom" with virtually no "choice", i.e. no economic infrastructure; no Little League; no "want-ad" section. To have both careers and free choice in a capitalistic society is a brand new ballgame, despite the fact we take it for granted as being "normal" or "typical". What this means then is that we who hire, have to make our jobs so attractive employees want to stay. We need to provide decent salaries, modern accommodations, chance for promotion; work which is interesting; a staff which is collegial and mutually supportive. In short, the initiative is up to management. The degree of corresponding support from our people is voluntary, and the quality of that effort defines and arbitrates the corporate character in a dynamic where each makes it his own. We have to earn the loyalty and respect of our people and know the more they like working for us, the more effective their performance will be. Which is kind of a funny way to put this because it says the degree of commitment we get from people, is up to us rather than to them.

One does not use hypnotism, hallucinogenic drugs and extravagant promises to secure loyalty. He secures it by what he is (or in this case "what we are"). Don't tell them; show them. In pursuing this line of reason we look for what attributes or characteristics will most impress professional people and merit their loyalty. Since this is a corporate effort, its status in the industry ought to say something. We feel being the largest and the oldest tells a story; proves a point. We are on top of the heap in our arena for a reason. Ours is a business essential to the economic life of the state (and, of course, the nation) with a lifestyle structured around the mobility of the automobile and the airplane, supported by the shopping mall and the business enterprise scattered randomly around the community. It is diverse in operation and interesting to manage. Maybe sitting behind a computer all day working with figures is not very exciting, but Cindy Wallpe and Ken Wilde have been doing it for 30 years now and seem perfectly content. Moreover, we are a "people business" that happens to deal in machinery, meaning there are lots of interaction, both internally with each other and externally with our marketplace. We who are gregarious find this more attractive than working in a brokerage or an insurance office where figures dominate the activity. We treat people with respect and have an interest in their wellbeing, thus, the profit sharing, hospitalization, flu shots; nagging for better health (and a foe against smoking). We are an active part of our community, contributing and involved personally in symphony, opera, theatre, the Arts Center, two art museums, politics, theology, Scottish festivals, Little League, Parks Foundation, Historical Society, charter schools, archaeology, etc., etc., etc. In short we hope that those in our community react favorably when an employee says, "MacAllister is my employer".

We don't do it all right; everyone is not ecstatic with his/her job; making the business attractive, efficient and profitable is a perennial struggle and efforts to induce loyalty and commitment are never ended. I don't know how we are marked by results, but give us "A" in terms of effort. ∎

Indianapolis truck shop mechanic group: Max Bliss, Mike Bodwell, Jeff Monesmith, Steve Ray, Bruce Princell, Tom Trahin.

Areté

June 2006

A perennial topic among many citizens these days is the subject of education, which usually means public school education — K thru 12. It monopolizes our attention from one decade to the next, primarily because the problems we saw twenty years ago still exist today and may have even gotten worse; reminding us of Mark Twain's comment about the weather: "Everyone <u>talks</u> about the weather but no one seems to do anything about it." I need to point out to Mr. Taiwn that "the weather" is a condition arising from forces beyond our control; the school system is a product which we have created carefully and deliberately, and continue to direct on a daily basis. So discussion about the school system makes more sense than talking about the weather because we can do <u>nothing</u> with hurricanes except buckle up and endure them. We can do <u>considerable</u> about improving education if we have the right ideas and the skill — plus the courage — to get them implemented. Ergo, the travesty is not the system itself, but rather it is knowing something is seriously imperfect and failing to correct it.

Educating has been a concern of folks in our western culture for a long time. Four centuries before Christ, men in Athens were pondering and examining this same topic. In his "*Politics*", Aristotle states categorically that "…there should be legislation about education and that it should be conducted on a public system". A surprising statement; all Athenian kids go to school, mandated by ordnance of the City Council? Wow! But he ponders next… "What constitutes education and what is the proper way to educate?" There are differing opinions. One says we need to teach virtue; another feels we must deal with issue of the intellect or maybe to shape character. And even then there was ambiguity about teaching virtue because "…all men do not honor the same virtue so that they naturally hold different opinions in regard to <u>training</u> in virtue". Beyond that he wonders "whether pupils should practice pursuits that are practically useful".

The Greek concept of education, called "paideia" was the transmission and the acquisition of "areté"… "excellence". Early on, it meant military skills, excellence as a warrior. Then along with the physical drills we added philosophic exploration, studying Homer and the Greek heroes of the Trojan War;

reading Sophocles and Aeschylus. Learning how heroes strive and how they endure adversity. Over time academic themes shifted to adding dialectics and rhetoric to the curriculum as a basis for more broadly equipping the citizen soldier to become a leader in politics and business as well as in war. We also added mathematics (remember the Pythagorean Theorem and ole Euclid?), so that by the end of the 3rd Century are able to condition young men intellectually for service in the military but also in the city assembly and with some knowledge of philosophy and the arts as well. Instruction could include a form of argument called sophistry, which is love of ideas for the very sake of process; reasoning and rhetoric become ends in themselves. Overall, there's a subtle objective: equip citizens for rational political discourse, understanding problems and issues so they might respond in the legislature by enacting policies most advantageous to the state.

Late in the Middle Ages (1200 A.D.) as Europe was emerging from the Dark Age, learning reappeared through the university systems. A remnant of the old Hellenic curriculum was retained but modified by Thomas Aquinas so logic and mathematics replaced rhetoric and dialectics. Philosophy, the arts and theology emerged but now became preparatory courses for advanced study in law, priestly functions, medicine, architecture, etc. The system and themes passed with time to England, appearing in both Oxford and Cambridge; then in due course migrated to America with the Massachusetts Puritans (1630) who as good Calvinists likewise wrestled with the educational option and curriculum. Here

Decorative frieze — Greek temple.

was a closed society with an austere and common style of life that needed both a learned clergy and literate citizens to function effectively in this godly community. The colony wanted wise, firm leadership which is rarely autochthonous and should not be randomly surrendered to cobblers, mechanics, brewers, and tailors. The destiny of the state ought to be determined by educated men, reflecting a good deal of the Aristotelian principle. We must still teach how to reason clearly, to articulate ideas, and now be conversant with the moral teachings of the Bible. In this fashion the state carefully trained ministers, its political and business leaders, whose continual growth and development would enhance the efficacy of both the church and the colony. The new curriculum included Latin and Greek, logic, rhetoric and philosophy so it reflected the concept of general literacy and learning mandated by Athens and Aquinas.

Education in these three examples both shaped the individual person <u>and</u> equipped him for an active role in society, enabling him to act as mayor, lead an army, serve in the courts; write sound legislation. He was trained in critical thinking (logic) which taught him how to solve problems, to determine right from wrong, to understand existing systems, but always with one eye cocked to see that he served the cause of the state as well as himself. But let's confess this education through the ages was both rare and eclectic. It was training a ruling class elite. We are suspicious of the common man, obsessed with personal aggrandizement and oblivious to the welfare of the state. We want men of wisdom and sound judgment, trained to serve the common good running affairs for us.

This reflection on education and its role in our culture is of special interest to one like myself, involved in the affairs of a liberal arts college which like academics from time immemorial, continually examine and modify their raison d'etre. And discover principles today which were common with Aristotle and Jonathan Edwards. We have the same purpose, i.e. teaching the

student critical thinking and broadening the mind with the arts and history to enhance the character and equip each for leadership in our society. But beyond that there is a growing awareness in that particular education which Aristotle described as being "practically useful"; i.e. how do I employ this education in the work-a-day world? The average parent sending kids off to college hopes that learning takes place and the youngster gets a certain polish; learns to live and work with others, but that he/she likewise develops the vocational skill to assure a livelihood. Meaning, we are equipped to teach school or practice law; become a nurse; pursue a career in accounting or computers. With the understanding that education provides a grounding in the arts and sciences, but that learning itself goes on indefinitely. The "post-graduation school" is really society (or life) itself. We continue the search for knowledge so education may be an end in itself, but its practical non-business deployment satisfies the Hellenic model of wider service to the community through work in the United Way, politics, the arts, the church, travel and you name it (i.e. the state). It is making something good happen; it is leading, participating, continuing to grow beyond the vocational expertise through engagement in the countless organizations that make our society so dynamic and so fascinating. And institutions never considered — or covered — by Aristotle or Aquinas and providing for participation across the spectrum of society, engaging all classes.

Formal schooling is not the only way to educate. A good many generations of humans have been "schooled" at home. Farmers in my grandfather's generation learned their trade from parents, watching how and what they did with respect to the multitude of chores and functions around a farm. A hundred years ago Indiana farmers resisted schools because they needed the kids home at plowing, seeding, cultivating and at harvest time. For centuries prior to ours, coppersmiths, jewelers, weavers, carpenters, painters, stone masons learned through internships in the guilds and were interns, apprentices, journeymen and masters. That is the same style of learning today for many housewives who learn at mother's elbow. A great model because it combines learning and doing; the real way to gain any proficiency. One can read manuals about rebuilding a diesel engine, but that is a far cry from taking one apart, replacing the worn parts and then reassembling it. I have read a dozen manuals on assembling Christmas toys and never, ever ended up with the gadget working — or without parts left over. Same is true with computers. The way to success is at the keyboard, hitting the buttons, manipulating the mouse, learning the icons and swearing a lot. The objective of learning is execution, which reflects both the theoretical and the practical ala Aristotle.

The application of all this to the business world is fairly transparent. We assume every employee has some degree of "education". Our objective is to marry that which has been learned to the specific requirements implicit in a certain job. Given the capability, our system can teach required skills and improve proficiency which has to be truly professional. The objective again is areté, achieving excellence which seems a bit grandiose when considering a warehouse man, steam cleaner, truck driver and master mechanic. But we figure the better each is at his job, the quicker he gets it done. Beyond that, as a company we are interdependent. We cannot succeed totally unless each component successfully does its job. All departmental services or functions ought to be delivered as if each were the only service we supply. Getting to this status means continual learning is mandated because no matter how good someone is when signing on, he/she has to understand what his/her job is and how it relates to the department and the company (the "whole"). Then each has to keep learning. Our five Six Sigma teams are created solely for that: Learning to do "it" better. We know this is an era of rapid and dramatic change with a continuing stream of adoption, upgrading, modification, something-different flowing along; all of it aimed at improved performance achieved more economically. Unless we have people able and eager to learn, we get locked in place while the world around us moves on over the next hill.

Quality of staff is always a "work in process" and it starts with hiring. (A fair amount of which I've done in my day; not all of it good because no one taught me how important was this exercise.) Matching the talent and potential with the job is not a slam dunk. It's a "fit" we have to orchestrate care-

fully. It's crucial in every department and with every manager. Bad calls are expensive. Most of us should take a leaf out of Chris' book because he is a top notch recruiter. His examination and analysis of candidates is most thorough; including exhaustive character and background data, long personal interviews, psychological testing with all senior staff, and extensive reference checks, all employed to deliver superior results through superior people. Part of the training is knowledge of job function, corporate systems, importance of the customer, working with others, positive attitude.

I don't know that Aristotle or Aquinas would think teaching and training people in the machinery business has much relevance to the educational theories they propounded and the curriculum they espoused. But this is a far different age. And there is some commonality. One being the ongoing quest for competence in each of the countless functions we have to master and employ. Our areté is not in dialectical rhetoric or theory but in the hard-nosed reality of the given job where its integrity is measured and tested on a continuing basis, dovetailing with twenty other practitioners of a like number of different skills. Our learning is proven in practice, not existing as mere theory. Excellence exists at the job station as well as in the grove of academe. Our success in each or any process lies in the critical thinking capacity of the employee who routinely discovers problems and automatically begins at once to correct them. We likewise have a high reliance upon the individual person as an independent and willing recruit, ready to perform his duty, not to the state, but to the enterprise which during his working hours is the company. The world in which we operate encourages diversity, centered first in the vocational task and unavoidably involved in the exploding world which is the computer, and a virtual universe which "blows" potential for learning exponentially into a proportion that would both astound and confound Aristotle. Beyond that is the economic imperative in the free enterprise system that refuses to tolerate failure so success is the only option. That pressure does not leave learning, improving, understanding, resolving all mere options. They exist as necessities. It is our own internal initiative and the competitive pressure that moves us into newer products, systems, structures and locations, and the realization there is no way of staying ahead of the pack if we do not learn, do not practice, do not perform, ahead of the pack. ■

Every Summer …

September 2006

Every summer we pause at each of our eleven locations and hold a brief recognition ceremony, handing out "awards" to people who have service anniversaries with the company. Beginning at five years we move in increments of five to all who have completed 10, 15, 20 years, etc.. Highest this year was 35. (Highest last year was 60.) The photos and write-ups of this exercise are included in this publication. But more important than the 2006 ceremonies is the motive for doing them. It's to recognize and thank people who have served us well and to indicate the high value we place on tenure. We are a better organization when we can hire good people, train them well, fit them into the corporate culture and continue to engage them over the years. The more any of us knows about a given topic or craft or vocation, the easier it is to learn more. Tenure thus means a longer learning and broader curve, giving one a decided edge on an apprentice or on the average worker. It is experienced employees who ultimately determine the degree of professionalism we exhibit, and the retention of that high degree of personal competence is what keeps us ahead of the pack, which curve is not a condition of happenstance, not automatic or axiomatic. It is programmed. Because we think getting to the top is one thing. Staying there is something totally different. A corporation, theoretically, has a life that is perpetual. It is limitless. To last longer than a generation, surely special attention has to be paid to maintaining high degrees of performance. It is, in fact then, a life or death imperative.

Most of our processes are repetitive, as I expect are most of yours. Given that fact, the drill itself can well become tedious. We perform the given exercise readily and do it automatically, almost mechanically, assuming it is adequate and will carry us along with minimal effort. And sometimes it does. But if we really know society is constantly, unobtrusively in flux, unless we too are shifting and altering course, we are not dealing realistically with circumstance. A rowboat moves forward when it is paddled. The faster we row, the swifter the speed. When we ease up and cradle the oars, the boat still continues its forward movement but at an ever-decreasing rate until finally it comes to a halt and we are dead in the water. Taking for granted given processes or routines simply "because each has always worked and there is no reason to worry about it working now" may be comfortable; but it may also be merely coasting; still moving imperceptibly, slowing down.

The critical nature of maintenance is evident all around us, dramatically manifest in arts organizations. I was involved early on in getting an opera company going in Indianapolis and lucked out time-wise because there was a lot of CETA funding available (federal dollars) the first two years; beyond that we lived next door to the finest opera teaching campus in America. By merging the two elements into one product, we moved in three years out of an auditorium on a college campus into the Murat Theatre, that's from 300 seats to 2200. Lots of work; lots of auditions; lots of artistic temperament and plenty of trial and error. At the end of the third season, we sold out performances of "Aida" to standing-room-only houses. Then after chortling happily and reading the reviews, it was necessary to start all over, back to work again, identifying opera for the next season, lining up singers, rehearsal space, renting costumes and sets, and most of all scrounging perpetually for dollars. Building a company was a lot of fun. Maintaining it proved perennial pain. The patron saint of arts (to me) is Sisyphus, the character in Dante's *"Inferno"* who spent his life in hell rolling a huge stone up to the top of a steep hill only to see it slip when he got it to the top ledge and roll back down where he had to begin his grinding, exhausting ordeal all over again — through eternity.

In most human institutions there are often two sets of talent involved. First one builds the company…the opera company or the tractor company; but then secondly, one has to maintain it. My father had the gift for building. It consisted of horse sense, total integrity, the right product line, an inimitable style of salesmanship. People bought Caterpillar tractors because first off they "bought" ole Mac. His character was every bit as sterling as the machinery he sold. Doing business with him was easy. He was a "hands on" manager and ran the company mostly with personal magnetism, which you can do with 12-15 people; maybe with 35 or 40. But there is a "span of control" issue here that ultimately requires more sophistication and shared authority.

Of course, my father created the company, using what skills he had learned and speaking to an age that understood and appreciated what he had to offer. He exemplifies one of the two components involved in a successful undertaking, that of leadership. He set the tone for the company, gave it a sense of his style; it reflected his mores and ran it profitably. He could rightly consider himself reasonably successful. After six years he abruptly left and it was up to us to maintain it. A chore handed to me, who had no past record or fixed patterns for managing. Beyond that with 75 employees (now 640) one does not manage with personality or charisma. He does so with structure which sees personalities diminish and manifest themselves in systems which appear in the form of an internal frame that allows each part to interrelate with the whole but also to function autonomously. For example, our parts department is a separate operation in terms of its manager, its space, training, function, crew, marketing, relationship with CAT and the customer. So distinct that a given customer's contact with our parts people might go on daily, never knowing or caring who our sales manager or our president is. They don't need to. The parts department operates independently. It is hooked together internally through our eleven parts outlets, runs its own shuttle service, has its own salesmen, stocks the department and <u>processes 796 orders a day</u>!

If my dad could decide how many dollars to spend on parts, collect some past due accounts, make sales calls on customers or give direction to the service manager, that "hands on" style is inadequate today … given those 640 people and our eleven different locations. So to keep the oars stroking and the boat moving forward, we do it with systems, with procedures, with rules, job descriptions, departmental objectives and budgets, all of course requiring special people to both direct and execute.

This analogy of "leader and system", of "creating and maintaining" has wide application, extending across the board and extant through the centuries. You won't be surprised if I apply it to history. Looking for the best example, I ended up immediately with Rome. In 753 B.C. it was a small farmers market on the Tiber at the base of seven unimpressive hills. Ruled by seven kings the first 2½ centuries, a population growing larger and more confident, kicked out the last king in 509 B.C. because he was a tyrant and decided to run the show themselves — a totally wild and inconceivable notion that day and age. What they did was create a thing called a re-

public, managed by "we, the people" (which was really the aristocratic class, a large landed segment of some 36 clans or families). We shall select from our own membership several officials who will each be given responsibility for a part of our system. Thus, aedile, praetor, questor, consul plus tribunes and religious appointees were elected for one-year terms and charged with the water supply, the maintenance of roads and public buildings, the feeding of the poor, the temples and religious ceremonies, the courts and justice system, etc. In short, we are taking charge of our own destiny. We can make Rome a "shining city on a hill" or shantytown, but our fortune and future are lodged in our own hands, not those of some outside monarch or tyrant. "We, the people" can create the sort of society we want. Expanding through Italy about 250 B.C., it finally managed the entire peninsula. Then fought the Carthaginians and ended up with Sicily, Spain and Egypt. By the time of Christ, under the Emperor Augustus, they managed the entire Mediterranean world.

The reference to ancient Rome is generally derogatory, i.e. pointing to "the fall of Rome" apparently ignorant of the fact that from its start in 753 B.C. till its fall in 476 A.D. we encompass 1229 years. A long time in action before falling, right?

It was remarkable experiment because like our age, it has to deal with continuing change, demanding the ability to negotiate and respond. The vehicle that ran a small city-state and then a peninsula was one thing; running provinces totaling 30 million, something else, and then to have an empire

P.E. congratulates Doug Clark, VP of Operations, for 30 years of service at the 2009 employee awards.

of 50 or 60 separate peoples, tribes, countries, and 60,000,000 souls, required a major effort. To accommodate changes they endured considerable bloodshed, a great deal of milling around, a series of generals, plus a century of civil war. But at the end of all that (31 B.C.), "king of the hill" Octavian (called Augustus and the first emperor) reorganized the state. He emphasized competence in administration, dumped bloodlines and social position for leadership. When the governor or prefect or tribune or procurator was inept, he sacked him. He reorganized the Mediterranean world, and the chain of command from his palace down the line was one of defined responsibility. It ended up, again back in the provinces or the major cities with a familiar pattern, i.e. local officials standing for public office as they always had. This lodged the day-to-day governance functions with the citizenry and always where the given need existed. The value in this lay in the autonomy of the local element, yet connected to the central system. Proven when totally incompetent, emperors arrived. Fact it got so bad in one year we had four of them (68 A.D. if you are checking up on me).

But if the central power was confused and imprecise, the governor in Dalmatia or the prefect in Cyrene or the procurator of Galilee continued to check the brigands and raiders, maintain the roads, preserved the courts, assured the water supply, collected the taxes and held the annual civic elections. The lifestyle in Leptis Magna or Vienna or Lyons did not collapse because of clowns like Nero or Caligula or Elagabalus. The <u>structure</u> was reliable and responsible; the markets remained open; the vessels still loaded and unloaded cargo; the crops were still being harvested and a measure of peace maintained. It was surely the leader Augustus who created the system and he did so only because he was "the last man standing" and had the clout to do what he wanted. But what permitted the empire to endure was the apparatus he created; the structure the world employed.

But for the long pull the two elements have to work in consort. Someone at the top has to fix what is wrong, keep the sundry parts together, solve problems rather than evade them. Meaning, even the best designs need improving and their relevance needs attention and the performance continually monitored. Lacking that, the pieces of Augustus' empire began to implode and in area after area there was no leader to repair the local structure, now under threat of foreign invasion. The absence of that element of local participation created gaps in the system and weakened the structure. If citizens in a given community did not feel responsible enough to serve in those offices which characterized their society, they deserved what ensued: implosion, invasion, fragmentation and decline. The leaders no longer repairing the vehicle the ponderous mechanism, a piece at a time, ultimately coasted to a dead halt.

The system which we employ has some structural similarities to the one just described and learned the lesson. We have been overly attentive to the leadership element as preeminent in assuring the strengthen and efficacy of the operating structure. Required by size and demand to employ others to do the functions, the compatibility between department head or manager and his given area of responsibility is paramount. Each has to do his job as good as the owner would do it if he had the time and talent. Getting each employee to carry out his assignment as if <u>he</u> owned the company is the objective. Instilling that attitude is the charge of the owner-managers. But we are aware of the facts that "buy in" or all out support cannot be forced. The employee must <u>want</u> to be a part of the team. The degree of success in enlisting support determines the degree the corporation succeeds in its mission. Those who do not want to play the game need to find something else to do. There is no room in our ranks for nonchalance, recalcitrance or disinterest. ■

Reprinted from "Go Time" December 1977

December 2006

I read somewhere recently that light is a wave and if projected through a hole into a dark room which contained air as pure and undefiled as Jimmy Carter's version of himself, you'd see nothing. That light itself is not, "physic-ally" speaking, that bright. What happens is the waves hit a jillion small particles of dust, lint and moisture flying around the air and when reflected off these becomes the light we see. Astronauts floating around in outer, cleaner space don't find the brightness of our day, but a purple dimness, a sort of a dark blue twilight. What causes light from the sun or from a bulb are the rays striking something, like all this stuff suspended in air or earth and clouds, trees or houses, cars and pavement. Only then, when an object thus obstructs the ray does it become light. Now that isn't very scientific, friends, because no one is dumber in physics than I, which is why the whole idea of light being dark struck me.

"Sound" is similar in its technical construction. When a tree falls in the forest (old acorn) and there is nothing living around to hear it, is there noise? Unheard noise? The answer is, "Nope, no noise. What is produced are sound waves or vibrations of sorts, dashing through the air to finally run out of steam. If those vibrations do not strike a tympanic membrane, or a hearing device, they do not become sound — because sound is a result of hearing." Now that isn't very profound either, because if you are dumb in physics, you are equally dumb about light and sound.

What's that got to do with Christmas? Well, what is Christmas? Is it an event that shines by its own "light" or is it "noise" without an ear? Or is Christmas like both my light beam and sound waves, something which needs a translator or an agent to capture and reflect it? This little essay says the latter. The Christmas story itself is eternal, charming and attractive, but flunking the critical tests as narrative. Studying the books of Matthew and Luke (where the nativity originated) gives us all sorts of problems. The dates do not agree. One says, "In the days of Herod the King" and the other says, "When Quirinus was Governor of Syria". We know when one died (4 B.C.) and the other started as governor (6 A.D.) so there is at least a ten year spread — could be thirty. Both locate the scene in Bethlehem because Joseph "was of the house and lineage of David". Then each recites a genealogy to prove it with names of forbearers inconsistent and then… so what? Joseph is <u>not</u> the father. One has only wise men, the other angels and shepherds "in the field … by night". (Night pasturing in winter was not practiced in Judea.) Joseph is down there, 75 miles from Nazareth for a census. Why didn't they count him back where he lived? It's Bethlehem, we said, because of King David. But good grief! The king had been dead a thousand years! Are we chasing people all over Palestine to find the site of antecedents who lived ten centuries earlier? No one can trace his pedigree that far! So you get the picture about Matthew and Luke providing clear, consensual history. They don't.

Know why? They were not concerned with history. They were concerned with what the Christmas story meant. Why did it happen? What does it say to us? The historic incident in itself, without an interpretative agent is like sound waves without a membrane or light waves with no physical elements to reflect them — proof of nothing.

The story was written in retrospect some 80 years later, i.e. 80-100 A.D., viewing that life long after it was over, imposing the nativity event upon

P.E. in his favorite hat!

the whole narrative (a technique called "redaction"). The message in the wise men, to a church then spreading rapidly, was the universality of a gospel which attracted all persons, even astrologers from far-off Persia. The angel chorus brought the whole of creation, even the peasants, into the "happening" Christians called "an incarnation" because it was so universal all mankind was included and so wondrous stars participated and the heavens rejoiced. The shepherds liked simplicity; the basic earthliness of what will be a momentous revolution proved God's power so strong that the lowliest elements qualify in His redemption. The Christmas story is a seedbed out of which the rest of the life might grow and provided a basis for the evolution of the unique biography which was recorded in the four gospels.

Christmas proves the impact of that one life still extending like waves or beams into our day, reappearing and reaffirming resoundingly each year about now. Hopefully with more than office parties, lighted trees and shopping sprees — which are indeed related but only emblematic like Matthew's history. Because the message of Jesus resonates the meaning of that ancient nativity as they sense the waves radiating from so long ago. Distilled from His ministry is the fact that love cannot exist in a vacuum or an empty room. It is a product demonstrated in the lives of persons as they share it, scatter it about, use it in human conditions, and reflect in the process the source, which is the teacher Jesus. Also implicit in this new awareness is the concept of equality of persons, the element of human dignity, the value of human life not exhibited in a series of vibrations, but demonstrated in how we react, converse with, talk about, work with; how we interface one with another.

The concept of hope for a better world arrived in the nativity but is a mere abstraction unless a transmitting agent carries it forward, active in countering evil, subduing animosity, conquering despair. You remember the other themes as the ministry developed and the mission took shape — repentance, friendship, compassion, the second miles, purity, peace and all the rest designed not as theories but rules for living. They are traits that illumine human society, and like these waves of light, must be bouncing off us and our interface or no one knows they are here. Without us, they are as incomplete as sound waves, never heard — thus never "sound". Peace, love, hope and dignity are not "Christian" if not used.

Christmas is to reflect the life heralded by the light of a star and the sound of angel choirs. It is not for itself, but what it gives forth from those of us who are in this day, the reflective agents of that same wonder. ■

2007

About Heroes

April 2007

If my competitors (or the IRS) ever marooned me on a remote, tropical island and allowed some reading material, I would take along "*The Boy Scouts Handbook*" and Will Durant's "*History of Western Civilization*". The former could instruct me on how to make a fire, catch fish, crack coconuts, trap and skin animals, and make hula skirts. The latter would rehearse the long story of how civilization developed and "what" cultures were achieved, only to be destroyed by "which" group of outlanders, who in turn fell afoul of a stronger gang ad infinitum. Left to shift for myself I'd be determining my own destiny, instructed by one of Mr. Durant's conclusions: "The initiative hero is the most formative force in history." A given person on a deserted island, or a legendary character surfacing in ancient Mesopotamia, exploits existing opportunities, creates a surge of movement and organizes forces to establish and manage his society. It is bright men and women who characterize or color or shape the overlapping episodes which constitute the chronicle of the species. We know further that if this is indeed the causative effect in history, it is also the major weakness. Because after a Solomon in Israel, we ended up with a Rehoboam; after Nebuchadnezzar we got a Nabonidus; after Tiberius, there was Caligula. Finding the "initiative hero" is one thing; sustaining what he built is an entirely different story because genuine heroes rarely come back to back, much less three or four in a row.

Durant's "*History*" also revealed that what constitutes "hero category" can be ephemeral as well as concrete. Fame acquired in a given period can fade over time. Historians have proven to be prejudicial, even inaccurate in depicting "heroic" images, often to be corrected by future generations. (Procopius and Suetonius come to mind.) Pierre Salinger and an assassin's bullets made John Kennedy immortal; subsequent writers join to create the "Camelot" theme. But more realistic editors find Kennedy's legislative record in Congress was virtually zilch, his personal character flawed and his foreign policy flimsy; forgetting he got us involved in Vietnam and remained uninvolved in the "Bay of Pigs" fiasco. On the flip

Bartolomeo Colleoni Italiani Condotiere 1470
by Verocchio.

side, Harry Truman was always a haberdashery sales-man to me. Today, he is construed to have been a pretty fair President. Mao Tse-tung was a formi-dable power, altering our policy in both Korea and Vietnam, and a major nemesis. In retrospect we learn despite his formidable potential he was one of most inept and incapable leaders of all time. Henry comes off as a rollicking "good ole boy", when in reality he was gifted, but vicious, unappreciative, cruel and evil.

"A Team of Rivals" tells the story of a hero whose growth continues even in our time. It rehearses how Abraham Lincoln's Presidency and pursuit of the war elevated him to protean status. Three of the men in his cabinet had run against him for the presidency in 1860, each thinking himself far better qualified than the frontier lawyer whose weaknesses they criti-cized in the campaign, depicting Abe as an uncul-tured country clod, crude in dress, naïve in outlook. But once in his cabinet and watching Lincoln oper-ate, each changed his perspective till it became one of admiration and deep respect. The country bump-kin himself never changed. But every one of the five or six men in his team, who judged him, altered their opinions and stood in awe of him. "Nothing is 'right' or 'wrong', but my thinking makes it so." Elected with only 40% of the votes, Lincoln emerged over time to become one of America's greatest heroes.

Fame then is real, manufactured and presumed; can be mis-assigned, falsely depicted, transitory, or slow to arrive. Maybe it is impossible to appreciate the greatness of a person until his <u>current</u> efforts are tested and proven in time. Could anyone dream in 1920 when Henry Ford mass-produced his Model "T", he not only simultaneously restructured the style of some manufacturing but also foreordained the na-ture of American cities? (Meaning sprawled out rath-er than stacked together like Europe.) Could anyone imagine the enormous impact on our society follow-ing Edison's introduction of the electric light bulb? Did anyone in December of 1903 realize that the crazy Wright Brothers down there in Kitty Hawk, North Carolina had designed a machine whose on-going development would one day put a man on the moon and loft vehicles into outer space, sending us x-ray pictures of the "Big Bang"?

One of the "evaluators" or cross-checkers" of <u>ancient</u> history is the science of archaeology. It is designed to reconstruct the past, scrutinize the old tales, legends and accounts and judge how those he-roes withstand the test of reality. We know almost all peoples create anecdotal vignettes, tribal stories

or historical accounts to pass on down through the eons. Fact, it is from such material the Christian Bible evolved, was revised, retailored and refined into the remarkable product we have today. So now to have scholars tampering with long-accepted, "di-vinely inspired" material which is a tricky business and best treated with the utmost delicacy. How do we handle ancient records now proven metaphoric or political or blatantly prejudicial? How do we accept long-held tales of biblical sages and seers, proph-ets, kings and heroes which prove empty or merely mythical? What happens is: "Trouble in River City". But we press on because core to the issue is search for the truth. And "the truth" is that many folks are beginning to find different insights, new reasons and messages in the Bible. It is not a sacred tome, invio-late and inerrant, personally dictated by Yahweh to certain holy men committed to memory (before we had writing). Rather it is a collection of incidents, character studies, poetry, history, wisdom, parables and instructions collected out of existing cultures over a thousand years to recount the pedigree of a people we call the Hebrews (and then later on, a sect we call "the Christians"). We really ought to be a bit suspect when a proud people deals with its own great leaders; extols their successes, exaggerates their contributions and legacy. We know now the Bible is indeed <u>about</u> history, that much of it is historic; but it is not (nor was it meant to be) an authentic history book. Nor is it very helpful in science, geog-raphy, physics, astronomy or religious tolerance. Its purpose is <u>theological</u>. It is a textbook about God and his people, how the two relate and respond. But corresponding to our central theme, it is an account created around the work of individual "initiative he-roes". All ordained divinely and telling the story in terms of their contributions. Scrutiny of the heroes and their work is really important because of what it means; what it produces; <u>what it teaches</u>.

To misread or misinterpret is to avoid or ignore the truth; or to wonder if one man's truth is another's fable. It has become increasingly difficult for me to be instructed in my theology and deportment by 1st and 2nd Century A.D. logic or mores or standards. I do not feel comfortable with an age that accepted slavery, believed in witches, subordinated women and intolerance with others, instructing me in morality. I don't propose to throw the baby out with the bath-water but to determine for myself how I approach and utilize "the faith of my fathers" in 21st Century terms. I accept its validity but not in the 4th Century terms Jerome used when he compiled the first bible. Revelation did not stop with St. Paul or Jerome.

So reconsidering and reappraising historic — and Biblical — figures is a proper and interesting exercise. But let's follow the advice of Marcus Aurelius and "See things as they are and deal with them as they deserve", even though this might well deny some hero status to former "great" men.

History — and Bibles, Korans, Avestas, Bahgavad Gitas et al — are written by people as interpretation of what they think might have happened. In the process there is a certain implication or judgment included since the writer can hardly write a totally objective account, using as he does his own personal norms and standards to reach an opinion. So fame is determined by others, it is not self-implementing. We get a taste of both, the making and breaking of heroes, in our own time by watching TV talk shows where accounts of the war, global warming, the economy, the budget and everything else in the list is subject to several different renderings. People are divided in their opinions because each incident or individual or bill is seen in reference to a given person's perspective. The right choice or course or action is rarely unanimous because judgment standards vary. We live in a world of practicality and technology, jettisoning romance and sentimentality, cutting today's heroes from a different cloth. The crusades are over; the age of discovery ended; most empires have imploded; the frontier is gone. But there does exist today an element yet of the "daring-do" that still requires extraordinary efforts; produces great success and abysmal failure. It develops leaders, tests and tries them as they spearhead change and movement. To me business itself is the adventure of the 21st Century: Here the initiative hero is providing leadership <u>and</u> rewards; recruiting and deploying people; doing battle with competition. Success or failure still rests on the abilities of the directing hero; all follow an ancient pattern. Also like momentous battles, is governed by the qualification contained in the motto of my old Fighter Group: "Aut Vincere Aut More" — "Either Conquer or Die". Succeed or depart. Deliver profit or go broke. In the business, fame and fortune cannot be contrived or falsely depicted. It is impossible to pose as something you are not; a fact of life Enron, Conseco and others ignored. The idea of success is not rhetorical or presumed; it is determined by certain immutable criteria like acceptable product, strong marketing, total employee support, and above all else, profitability consistently.

1966 AED Group: *(back row)* Dick Schumacher, P.E., D.W., Woddie Haseman, *(front row)* Becky, E.W. and Hilda.

We report and are evaluated on statistical data not opinions or conjecture. We cannot have a salesman who "<u>appears</u>" or (even "<u>endeavors</u>") to serve us and the customer but does not perform. Reputation is not built on someone else's interpretation of what one is or what he achieves. Success is absolutely ineluctable; it is measurable and is measured; it's proven in orders and margins and profits with vast and non-negotiable areas between what is <u>promised</u> and what is <u>delivered</u>. There is no way to bluff through a failure, and no way to stay a course which lacks success.

Then like empires or dynasties there are the two inevitable challenges: the need to maintain a successful operation and keep order and dominance by driving back the barbarian hordes or checking the avaricious nobles or the over-ambitious captains; which translates to the requirement for adequate <u>daily</u> sales volumes and expense control, meeting changing demand, accommodating higher interest rates, the sale and service of newer products and meeting incessant competition deal-after-deal, day-after-day, year-in and year-out … forever. There is an hourly payroll to meet every two weeks and salaried payroll every month with no skips or delays. This means staying the post year around, responding to needs and demands. Beyond that is the preparation of back to back leadership. It is, first off, training the next "hero" to avoid the Rehoboams and Caligulas so readily available, assuring steady management from one generation to the next and to the next. In a family-owned business that can get pretty tricky. But there is rarely success in any institution without a strong figure at the top: the quarterback, the correcter-of-course, the pacesetter, the weeder-out of incompetents.

Succession is not a single function; it is one

extending through the chain of command. <u>Each manager</u> preparing his successor so that we maintain high quality performance through high quality people and finding a topnotch general manager or sales manager or treasurer or service manager is not a casual exercise. Because when you operate (as I think we do) with the highest caliber professionals in the area at each management level, the bar is set so high it is all but impossible to improve; ergo, mere replication is a challenge. So keeping it all in order today while planning for the <u>next</u> phase is an ongoing component in the game. Success or failure depends on how well we deal with people and assure their performance; how wisely we select geographic locations; the size and number of outlets; depends on proper inventorying, which means enormous bank lines and cash flow; add to that processing thousands of documents each month; selling over 350 models of machinery; setting up and managing ten rental stores besides six branches; wondering whether we have too many people and where they are; too much inventory; how we share workload and function scattered across the state; all parts of the demand imposed by our business. Charlemagne's empire wasn't

this complicated and beyond that, he never dealt with the IRS, labor unions, hospitalization insurance, 401K's or sales tax, unemployment tax, internal revenue tax, OSHA, ERISA or Caterpillar. But the point to all this since Charlemagne has converted the Saxons, checked to the invading Lombards, beaten the Saracens back into Spain and created an empire, he has had his day in the sun. These heroic factors have no relevance to our charge. But if one wants parallel risks, a sense of adventure, personal responsibility in working with a horde of people, the challenges of all the outside forces and the threat of ignominious failure or appreciable success, get into business. It is an operation where all the problems are never solved, have every issue put to rest, competition vanish, Caterpillar is happy, and customers are making no demands. The very fact that everyday problems have to be dealt with; each day offers new ideas to make the operation better and where results are commensurate with the human effort deployed. All this I say is as close as we shall get to the real adventure in this our time. ■

A Personal Reflection "Go Colts! Go Indy!"

April 2007

I had the occasion to attend the Super Bowl Game in Miami this year and watched the Indianapolis Colts <u>out</u>play and <u>out</u>score the Chicago Bears in what was truly a memorable occasion. The crowd was some 72,000 plus milling about and like ourselves trying to figure out where to go. Miami could learn something about crowd management and appropriate signage from us since there was considerable ambiguity about where we were, where our parking slot was, which gate we should be using, how to find seats, etc. Getting there two hours before game-time was of no particular advantage. Getting out after the game was, thus, equally frustrating. At any rate in due course we negotiated the security checkpoints, found our seats and settled in for the big event…prepared to endure the inclemency. The day had been sullen with <u>periods</u> of showers, then clouds, then clearing, ending with a no-let-up rain from the kickoff <u>through</u> the awards ceremonies, half-hour after the final whistle. It was "memorable" because it was my first Pro Bowl; because it proved to be the only Super Bowl Game played in the rain; and first time ever a kickoff was returned for a touchdown. After 17 seconds we were down 7-0. Not a memorable start!

We all had rain gear but the continued pelting finally soaked through everything. <u>Tuesday</u> morning I noticed the bills in my wallet were still wet, and the gloves in my raincoat pocket soaked. It was never a torrent, but it was steady as clockwork, incessant, continuous.

But it was memorable beyond these reasons for those of us involved in the days before the stadium and the Colts. We were remembering Mayor Bill Hudnut's decision to <u>build</u> a stadium. The Colts not only came <u>during</u> his tenure but came <u>because</u> of his tenure. Back in the late '70s and early '80s there was widely-accepted speculation afloat that professional football leagues were considering expansion. Bob Welch, of late-lamented memory, was the first to run up a flag which asked in essence, "Why not Indy? Why don't we try to get a team?" Building on his

enthusiasm we began to look at the chances and decided if we were really serious, surely we would need a place for a professional football team to play. And that didn't mean Victory Field. It meant a new stadium…team or not. After the discussion percolated for a spell, the Mayor agreed we would give it a shot and asked the members of the Capital Improvements Board to undertake the assignment. Other cities would have probably <u>appointed</u> a new group called "The Football Stadium Commission", requiring a new director, new staff, new offices, new bonding authority and all the rest. The existing CIB had been created (1965) to provide "capital improvements" for Marion County which really meant, "Build a convention center", a chore we had undertaken in 1970 and completed by Race Day in 1972. Convention business had picked up over the years, thanks to our marketing, location and the skillful management of Dean Phillips, to the point we needed to expand. Or continue losing business. The solution was to build the stadium in conjunction with a convention center expansion so our stadium serves several purposes and has other usages.

Fortunately, there was available land contiguous to the Center, which we proceeded to acquire while the architects began planning the structure to fit said property. Simultaneously, we studied options

P.E. MacAllister (at podium), president of the Capitol Improvement Board welcomes the Colts in 1984 to Indianapolis with Mayor Bill Hudnut and Bob Irsay (seated front row).

Celebrating the Indianapolis Colts Super Bowl win in Tampa, January 2007.

for financing the project. Dave Frick was the Deputy Mayor in those days and did most of the heavy lifting with respect to financial feasibility and then later on (and more important) carrying out the very long, complex negotiations with the owner of a team interested in moving to Indianapolis. Turned out the "talk" about league expansion never got beyond "talk" for the next ten or twelve years, and we could very well have had egg on a lot of faces, had that been our only recourse. But Destiny, Providence or the Nine Gods smiled on us in the form of a team from Baltimore whose owner was unhappy there and considering a move. Not a move to Indianapolis. A move to anywhere he thought the team might be appreciated; and had a modern facility with better attendance. In the course of his peregrinations, he was invited to take a look at our Dome, now about finished (1983) and he liked it. Though he continued to equivocate, Dave finally had a prepared, tentative agreement we could both live with.

When the State of Maryland passed legislation which put the Colts into a category of assets the state (or city) could redeem under "eminent domain" proceedings, the plot really thickened. Then when the City of Baltimore decided the Colts were going to stay there, like it or not, by passing ordnance giving the city the right to take them over, Bob Irsay called and said he was ready to move. Now! Tonight! We were primed to accommodate him, and Johnny B. Smith had a dozen of his Aero Mayflower moving vans converge upon the Colts' locker rooms and equipment stores so by nightfall, in the light of the television cameras, the country watched the Colts move to a new location ... in time for the 1984 season.

So having been on the CIB in those days and recalling the selection of an architect, finding a construction manager, watching the bids come in, seeing the footings go down and steel and concrete go up, watching while the roof inflated, sorting through what we should name the structure, remembering the arrival of the Colts and the opening ceremonies, all precursors, slowly, painfully, building toward February 4, 2007. All the circumstances and issues pertinent to both the Dome and the Colts seemed to complete the chapter started 25 years ago. During this period, Indianapolis achieved All American status through its renovated (and still-being-renovated) downtown, the re-creation of the near North Side, our professional basketball and hockey teams as well as AAA baseball; our incredible art museums, Zoo and Canal; the monuments and parks, the diverse and excellence of its performing arts community, and now a World Champion Football Team. My role in all of this had been miniscule indeed when compared to $30,000,000 the Lilly and Krannert Foundations supplied, but the point will be that Indianapolis is an All American City because literally hundreds of citizens lent their time and talent to join in making it that, propelled by strong political leadership and a liaison formed between the public and the private sectors. The synergism developed permits us to do practically anything we want to do.

We determined in 1982 that the benefits of a major league football team would add to the prestige and stature of Indianapolis and had the hands and heads ready to make that happen. These efforts were demonstrated across the land the first Sunday in February when the Colts won the Super Bowl Game, and Peyton Manning received the Most Valuable Player Award. Unidentified in the hoopla, the press, parade and rally were countless number of the rest of our citizens who can take justifiable pride in their efforts at making the Colts an Indianapolis product. Peyton Manning said the victory in Miami was a team victory. Every player contributed and that sense of unity in a joint undertaking proved world class; made it a success. I see that as a metaphor for this community which becomes a product of whatever we aspire it to be. We may have a lot of work to do, but the Colts demonstrated again the secret: Sound game plan, dedication, all-out effort, utility of action, perseverance and absolute commitment to the cause.

Go Colts!

Go Indy! ■

The Jackal, Kando and Mar Samuel

June 2007

Perhaps the most intriguing archaeological event of the last half century has been the discovery of the Dead Sea Scrolls. Reports are about <u>when</u> they were found and where, and about how they got to market and through whom, are not very consistent. The predominant opinion accredits members of the Bedouin Ta'amireh tribe with making the discovery. Accustomed to foraging for ancient artifacts in Jordan and Southern Israel, they hit the mother lode by finding the first seven scrolls and late in 1947 brought them to market. The "finder" was Muhammed edh-Dhib (The Jackal or The Wolf), who reports he tumbled to their location when he threw a rock at some errant sheep he was trying to corral and missing the flock, the stone flew into a cave. Instead of a "thud" echoing back, he heard a clinking sound and clambered up into the declivity to see what caused the peculiar noise. The rugged cave was cluttered with trash, shattered jars, shards, bat guano, cloth and 9 (or 10 or was it 40?) unbroken jars…the source of the "clink". Inside two smaller jars, carefully sealed, were three rolls of parchment with writing on them. Somewhere else in the same cave (defined as Cave 1), four additional scrolls were produced. In subsequent forays, The Jackal and his friends ransacked the site to collect other pieces of parchment and sold them separately.

How long The Jackal left the scrolls hanging in a bag on a tent pole we do not know (one account said 38 years!). Most theories say a year or two at most, but we know for sure that ultimately the Bedouin brought four of the seven scrolls to Bethlehem (their market town) to visit with a cobbler or maker of shoes, one Khalil Iskander Shanin, nicknamed "Kando". He happened also to run a small antiquities business on the side and, thus, was not ignorant of desert finds. As their agent, Kando paid them 5 dinar ($14) for the scrolls (or was it $64.80?) and promised to pay in addition a third (or was it two-thirds?) of what they brought on the market. The other three scrolls ended up with Faidi Salahi, another dealer, who took them to Jerusalem and met with Eleazer Sukinek, a professor of archaeology at Hebrew University. The scholar instantly saw the value and legitimacy; examined the parchments, borrowed 1,500 pounds and bought them. They are on display today in an Israeli museum. It took longer for the other four to reach the public. Kando seems to have had a connection with the Syrian Orthodox Church and used that relationship to intercede with the Patriarch of the cathedral, one Athanasius Yeshue Samuel (Mar Samuel), who had contacts with the wider world. He could also read Hebrew and might be able to determine what the scrolls really were.

In the course of trying to determine the origin, subject matter, authorship and age, the cleric was abetted by fellow monk named Butros Sowmy, who took the liberty of passing them under the nose of John Trever, Interim Director of the America Schools of Oriental Research in Jerusalem. Trever quickly realized he was looking at the Hebrew Old Testament Book of Isaiah, another work which would be called "The Manual of Discipline", and a third which proved to be a commentary (Pesher) on the Old Testament Book of Habakkuk. All were in the linguistic style and script character of the Qumran period (200 B.C.-68 A.D.) and unprecedented in terms of importance. Woweeeee! Trever gained Mar Samuel's permission to photograph the scrolls before they got away. And our chapter ends with the Patriarch buying these scrolls from Kando for $97.20. Then he had to get them to a collector so he could make "a killing".

Except selling them proved enormously difficult. This was all happening (1947-48) as the United Nations was creating the states of Israel and Palestine out of the old British Mandate. You may recall the

Dead Sea scrolls shown in Amman Archeology Museum.
(Source: Wikimedia Commons.)

Arabs rejected any proposition that gave Jews possession of Arab land, much less 8,000 square miles of it. So in late November of 1947, six armies attacked Israel with the intention of destroying the would-be nation and driving the Jews into the sea. But that is definitely <u>not</u> what happened. The 40-year migration struggle of getting the Jews into Israel produced an unremitting skirmish with the British who forcibly resisted the flood of immigrants. The Jews responded with counteracting force, which lead to the creation of at least two very well organized, modestly equipped, underground military units. These now lead the national conscripted militia which met the Arabs' attack on all fronts. By April 1984 after savage fighting the Jews had won the so-called War for Independence, expanded the borders of Israel, and militarily confirmed the legitimacy of the original state.

All this conflict complicated marketing artifacts. Beyond that, international law was an impediment. Anything of an antique nature found in Israel, Jordan or Palestine (in any nation) is the product <u>of</u> the state, not a given finder. The scrolls technically "belonged" to the State of Jordon, who claimed jurisdiction over the Dead Sea territory, where the scrolls were discovered. When the United Nations drew its boundaries, the scroll site shifted to the new State of Palestine. So bottom line is the scrolls had technically been stolen (rather than found) and could result in a legal action by Jordan or by Palestine, demanding return to the nation of origin. This fact (i.e., buying stolen property) may have had some impact on their marketability, and failing in Israel, Mar Samuel brought them to the United States. Scholars here were equally reluctant to buy tainted merchandise. And remember, too, that we had pictures of the documents and could study the content. There was no compelling reason to possess the original scrolls.

The story ends in 1954 when Mar Samuel put an ad in the *Wall Street Journal* asking $1,000,000 for the find. No takers appeared with cash in hand. But Yagel Yadin (Israel war hero, scholar and archaeologist), lecturing in the United States at the time, saw the ad and began negotiating to buy same. He ended up paying $250,000 for the four scrolls (thanks to money from Mr. Gottesman). They were sent in due course to the Shrine of the Book in Jerusalem to join the first three already on display.

Mar Samuel learned something about marketing in his long effort to sell the scrolls. He discovered that his <u>perceived</u> value did not equate to the customers' estimate of "<u>received</u>" value. What <u>was</u> the right price for the scrolls? Was it $14 or $97.20 or $250,000 (the three prices realized during the different stages of the scrolls' odyssey)? Today, my guess is that you probably could not buy them for less than $50,000,000. A curbstone expert would say, "Commodity is worth whatever someone will pay for it." That doesn't help much when four different levels establish four different prices from $14 to $50,000,000. The fact that Muhammed edh-Dhib would take $14 for his find did not establish the true value. His price was nothing more than a personal opinion. He had no particular use for what he found; he did not know what it was; or any idea what its value <u>could</u> be to he who understood it. Kando and the Patriarch were wiser but still far from accurate in their appraisal of its value. One could suggest instead that there is in the ideal world an arbitrary fair price. That objectivity, knowledge of the market place and altruism combine to form "true" standard that places a definitive value on things; on goods and services.

In the real world to establish a given "value", it helps to have a record of experience, i.e. comparative examples or illustrations to corroborate the price. The price of gasoline changes daily but reappears from station to station at remarkably similar levels. A good deal of the groping and fumbling took place in the scroll story because it was such an unprecedented find, one whose impact would not be instantly recognized…and in a market lacking comparative sales data. It was not on EBay. So we stumble around trying to figure out who is likely to want this and what is he willing to pay. We are mostly motivated here by: "How much do I get?"

The seven scrolls out of Cave 1 would probably suffer a similar fate today if they secretly came out of a cave on an Indian reservation or from a sleepy farm in Owen County, Indiana. Because, again, people in the local community would have a hard time pricing same since no sales pattern exists. Before we create one, have to understand what we have. Trouble here is that the value of the scrolls lies not in their physical product, but in the remarkable insight they reveal about the world of Jesus' day. The greater scroll collection provides evidence of Jewish thinking and discussion about things theological, a topic about which there has been mostly assumption or conjecture. We are surprised — and astounded — at the variety and abundance of theories at play in both Christian and Jewish communities. We no longer guess how the Essenes differed from traditional Jews; the documents tell us. Unaware of how people viewed or regarded Jewish scriptures or even what they included, we now have ample evidence of the hermeneutics which exegeted the orthodox theology. Had The Jackal read the materials he would have found them far too esoteric to appreciate. He'd have been happier with a gold bracelet from the same period or a handful of silver coins. Antique objects can have two values. One is venerability, the rarity or uniqueness: a collector's item; second, the intrinsic value as precious metals. Meaning, "X" dollars an ounce. (Today, gold is $647 an ounce.) Telling us there is value in the "thing" and value in its meaning; whether buying either (or both) the sale occurs only when both buyer and seller concur. And my guess is that he who buys for the historic value would pay more than he who transacts in precious metals. But what would The Jackal do with an eight ounce gold bracelet? His perception of value would be cash in hand. Gold is universally accepted; is easy to weigh, easy to melt.

In our world pricing is more finite and less ephemeral. It is established by what innumerable <u>other</u> people are paying so continuing transactions at the same market value constitutes verification. History takes out the dickering or the guess work. Partly because the rationale for a given price is accepted; we understand it is based on cost to produce. Whether it is a pair of shoes, or a can of peas, or a pound of hamburger or a skid steer loader. The seller <u>purchased</u> the raw material for the product, paid the production costs, the packaging, freight, storage, overhead and marketing. He invested his own money getting it here. Then, we recognize he needs a margin of profit to stay in business. So his price is based on definable costs. None of this was applicable to the Isaiah Scroll or the Commentary on Habakkuk. Throwing stones at goats is hardly much of an investment. Any money realized is all profit. On what factors then, was the price based? Not on the investment of cash or on the value established through repetitive experience, but on what the buyer would pay. The seller was interested in his gain, <u>not</u> in the value he provided because he hadn't a clue as to what he was selling.

In our world other elements are sold besides physical things. They are cerebral or intellectual commodities or may be physical effort. The former commodity is given knowledge or expertise provided by the professions…a doctor, a teacher, consultant or an attorney. The second but similar category is purchased services that involve <u>doing</u> something to cre-

Berns Construction Co. with their CAT equipment in the '50s.

ate the product. This is not so much what we <u>know</u> but what we <u>do</u>: a masseuse or a barber, a carpenter or a professional football player, an opera singer or a pastor.

A third area (more familiar to us) and is the one already referenced: a physical item which has basic costs to recover; this is the most arbitrary of the lot and has the least wiggle room. A toaster, a pair of shoes, a D8 bulldozer, a new TV or a Big Mac from McDonalds is securing something composed of fix costs. All need to be recovered. The perceived value of these items is based upon customer's need or desire for same. And he understands specific, justifiable elements have to be conceded in the sale price when he buys.

I don't care much for this comparison, but we are a little like The Jackal and Kando in the fact that we are also sellers of a commodity. But unique among the "physical items" identified above. The only commodity listed above which generates the income to amortize its cost is the D8 dozer. Which is why our selling philosophy also is vastly different from Mar Samuel's. Though we exist to make profits we have a more responsible way of determining: "What's in it for me?" For starters we are <u>not</u> in the business of selling iron. We are making possible a <u>livelihood</u>. We sell productivity, benefits, profitability. "You aren't buying a bulldozer or a loader; you are buying a unit which will move-or load-more material — for less cost — than anything else in sight. Your own economic interest requires you to examine carefully our proposal." Next, we know our users personally and how they operate; we are not usually dealing with strangers. Beyond that, we are committed to helping owners succeed. That might be pseudo-altruistic, but we don't fare well with buyers who go broke. We want them profitable — and back to buy more. <u>Our</u> own vested interest suggests we are better served when the buyer is more effective than his competitor and our machinery makes him so. Further, we do not sell machinery the buyer doesn't need. Our assignment in helping someone scope a job is to determine how much he can do with what he owns.

Last off, we survive on repeat business and have to deliver measurable value to every customer to be sure he comes back. Hitting a home run on a big deal through overpricing does not serve the long term interest of the company. It's not fair; it is bad policy and reflects adversely on salesman and company. To damage a reputation merely for one shot at big bucks is destroying our major asset — corporate integrity.

The world of Mar Samuel and edh-Dhib is marked by another difference. Aside from motivation, there is a world of difference in degree of marketing competence. Trying to sell something for the sole purpose of making a quick buck does not require much experience. The lack of which is precisely why they fared so badly. To take $14 (or was it $64.80, or was it $97. 20, and finally $250,000) when its value was in the multi-millions indicates too much avarice or too little patience. Mostly it proves all of the sellers involved were out of their depth. Conversely, in our area and age of marketing, we not only know the value of our product, we set it so it moves; we know who the buyers are; what their professional capability is; how the machine will be used; all coincident to a productive investment on which the owner makes a return. Not once, but time and time again as he moves from job to job. Beyond that we continue annually to examine customer satisfaction with company and product so we might move and flex as the economy, interest rates, product lines, competition and customers themselves change and progress. We are not interested in a one-shot sale. We want long-term relationships, and so the favorable opinion of the buyer is the ultimate objective to our own success. Sustained success is impossible with unhappy or distrustful buyers. But then The Jackal was really a shepherd; he was not in business, and though I haven't cut him much slack, he was the single element that promoted and provoked a flurry of searching that would lead to what Albright called "The most remarkable manuscript discovery of modern times." What has since been recovered, translated, distributed and analyzed has been of more benefit to biblical scholars than anyone can possibly measure. We ought to regret that The Jackal was not better rewarded for what we learned from his random foray, rather than for the messy and random way his discovery was ultimately treated. ■

The Indianapolis Store

June 2007

We have done a series on each of the five branches and have again been reminded we never covered "The Mother Store" so this article on Indianapolis will complete the series.

Maybe some of you do not know that 30th Street was not our original location. When E.W. MacAllister signed the contract with Caterpillar in June of 1945, he was succeeding a dealer already established. More specifically, was replacing Jack B. Haile Machinery Company located at 2118 North Gale Street in an area called Brightwood (it's dramatically changed today since I-70 went right through the north edge of our property and chopped the neighborhood in two). We located there for a couple of reasons. First off, it was on a railroad spur and a good deal of our machinery in those days came in by rail. Secondly, Jack Haile had gotten the franchise during the war when building sites were hard to come by and the shortages of everything made constructing a new facility totally impossible. He was lucky to find a place (1) zoned for business and (2) large enough to accommodate big machines. The original builder (in 1928) had designed it for a lumber warehouse which was <u>his</u> business. So in 1945 it was only 17 years later, meaning that it was not that old; in fact, we would use it for 21 years, so this building accommodated a lot of action.

It was an uncomplicated layout — a large 'L' shaped structure with the office area and the parts department in one leg and the service department in the other. My recollection is we had maybe 19,000 square feet under roof; ultimately augmented by a sheet-metal storage area maybe 30 x 100 feet, parallel with the shop extension so the configuration from the air might resemble a segregated "U" shape. My father had run an Allis Chalmers dealership during the war in an old truck garage, once owned by a bakery with a square footage probably no more than a third the Gale Street building, so this was a major move up. Point again, with the war against Japan still on, all sorts of shortages and restrictions continued to exist. The economy had exploded with the war effort, putting to use almost every site we had, creating a building shortage. The options were few or none. But on the bright side, CAT customers knew the location; the building was adequate to our needs and we had to buy the existing parts inventory and shop equipment which was then conveniently left in place. Beyond that, paying for the parts, making a deal for the office equipment, plus buying Haile's receivables, left no room for the additional debt a new building would impose.

Besides that, I maintain we <u>do not</u> make any money on buildings. We make it on the services and products we provide, and these require a centering cluster to accommodate the people and the function. Excited about being the new CAT dealer, we were content with an edifice vastly larger than the old MacAllister Tractor Company had used and were busy combining what of Haile's staff we kept, along with the dozen people E.W. moved into the new set-up where we would continue to function until 1966. As an aside, there are a couple impacts or reactions evoked by a given building. One hopes to connote utility; another considers the location; and a third would simply be physical "presence". Character! To a degree, a building somehow demonstrates or represents the sort of organization it houses or maintains and CAT dealers have generally been the "primus inter pares" (first among equals), leaders or pacesetters for the industry. Given the sizes of the product line are also usually the largest dealers. Our building on Gale (after we got our feet on the ground and began rolling) worked okay. We got the job done. Sales grew. The line expanded. Through the years, we had to negotiate the situation of E.W.'s departure (in 1951), then the restructuring of management after he left and then provide some more expansions (like into Plymouth, Bedford, South Bend, all branches on the fringes) as the economy flexed. We also had to

View of Gale Street building showing railroad access, 1945.

jack-up our net worth. Despite the adequacy of our Gale Street home, the time came to look more like a leader and deal with the "image thing"; i.e., build newer, more attractive and more adequate quarters.

In 1956 the Board authorized the "… purchase of ground on 30th Street, east of Highway 100". The property was 13-plus acres of a 40-acre parcel (the agent thought we should own the whole plot, but our treasurer was groaning and weeping at the expenditure of all this money, $20,000 … $1,600 per acre). (We just bought the land across the street for $59,507 an acre). And at the same time the Board authorized $40,000 to put up a building which would house our used equipment repair facility (which is still there, converted to our undercarriage and welding shop).

By moving the rebuilding of used machinery (which employed eight mechanics) out of the Gale Street operation, we loosened up the scrunched conditions there and also gained considerable area, not only for parking new and used machinery but rental as well. Rocking along with the two sites we got a little fat on our bones, and in 1964 we began the conversations with CAT about a new facility. Given the ongoing growth and expansion of some 95 dealers in the United States, CAT had long become specialized in "specking" dealer facilities and was most helpful to us. We hired a local, contract manager (Geupel-Demars), who was also the architect and took him to Peoria as we began the process. We need to determine, for example, what size the shop doors should be? What is the most practical configuration inside the shop? How thick do we want the floor slab? What traffic patterns work best? How to position the sundry operating departments? How do we handle pressure cleaning or painting, etc.? We broke ground

P.E. and Chris at the ground breaking for the Indianapolis corporate offices.

in mid-1965 and in the spring of 1966 moved into 7515 East 30th Street. The cost was half a million dollars, and our building was 40,000 square feet. 1966 turned out to be one of the best years we ever had, due to the general economy and the reputation the company had established so it was a good time to be building, expanding and moving. Bottom line: The design proved very efficient, and the location adjoining the interstate worked well for us.

CAT not only helps us design buildings, it gooses us to <u>build</u> more buildings. In the late '70s we discovered a truck engine market had expanded to a point that needed special servicing. Supplying CAT Power aside from that in CAT machines was most evident in the truck engine market where countless

Corporate Offices — 7515 East 30th Street, Indianapolis.

thousands of semis across the land, powered by more and more CAT diesels, required more attention. Ours has not been a state noted for huge opportunity in the field of stand-alone engine power, meaning we have no marine market whatsoever, no oil drilling to speak of, not a lot of cranes, draglines or compressors needing big power units. Yet every dealer has a special "engine" section to cultivate whatever power market there is. In fact, CAT has maintained a separate division which directs <u>its</u> engine business, i.e., units going to other than to CAT products. One example of this engine market would be supplying electric generators powered with CAT engines. We have a jillion of these in the state to provide alternate or emergency power for banks, supermarkets, hospitals, convention centers, office buildings, schools and jails, etc. Likewise, a couple dozen trailers parked in our backyard fitted out with generators, serving as portable, rental power. Circuses, outdoor concerts in the park, carnivals, trade shows, summer festivals, reunions, street fairs and you name it. Generally speaking, little of this market is readily understood by the average tractor salesman who has 300 other products to sell and can't become as informed as he who devotes full-time nurturing the engine market. So to maximize the opportunity, we created a separate entity for all aspects of engine power and created the Engine Power Division.

To make it really work, this group needed its own facility and so in 1978 we built a truck engine shop at Fort Wayne, and in 1980 created the Engine Power building at 7575 East 30th Street, better to accommodate and promote our total engine business. This divorced the management and operation completely from the prime product manager and hired an expert to direct the experiment. His name was Jim Bernhardt, a former engine rep for CAT in this territory, and today still our Engine Power Manager. He volunteered not only to handle the sale of en-

gines but to take over the new building and all its operation: truck parts, service, rental, EOM accounts, traditional market and TEP accounts. We were the first dealer I know of to peel out engine power and put it in a separate facility where Jim warehoused parts, managed a crew of mechanics, rented generator sets, sold engines to local manufacturers when he could, managed a sales force for standby power for any large building, hired a crew to influence the sale of truck engines so local dealers would specify CAT power in their Mack or Peterbilt or Kenworth semis. The building, once again, made a statement. It said we were serious about this phase of our business and if we put a real professional in charge, we could boost our own sales and develop another respectable stream of income. So the building went up; Jim came on stream; we added another structure in the back couple years later to accommodate a dynamometer, and Engine Power has been onward and upward since then.

The last building on the premises was created to put us in the machine shop business which is a good-news, bad-news story. Attempting to diversify, we decided some of the work farmed out (re-boring blocks, grinding crankshafts, etc.) we could do ourselves and for others. We found a manager, bought some tooling and had reasonable success, which lead to more tooling (all that stuff is huge) and more business and the need for more room. So we built a new shop next to the old rebuild facility to accommodate all the big tools and inventory, only to outgrow that in two years. Next step was to locate off the premises on 35 acres of land west of Shadeland on 34th Street, then put up a building and continue the machining work. All came to a halt when the manager left us, whereupon his assistant agreed to buy the business and the company departed the scene. The first structure, 3,000 square feet on 30th Street, available when we moved the machine shop, now accommodates the used machinery repair operation, sort of bringing us around full circle.

Aside from discussion of buildings, the 30th Street operation serves as company headquarters and locus of top management. First off, under Chris and Doug Clark; then Sales of Prime Product under Dan Dayton and Dave Clark; the computer group under Garry Buechler; Human Resources (Betty Blunk); Ag, Parts, Promotion Service and Treasury Departments are all on 30th Street. Alas, however, all our Indianapolis people are <u>not</u> here since we have outgrown our physical space. 26 folks in Accounting,

MacAllister Engine Power offices, Indianapolis.

Credit and Warranty work are housed on Franklin Road just a half mile from here. The cramped conditions here make obvious the reason Chris bought the land across the street after looking fruitlessly the last four years for property on the edge of town. To find it so close is the best of luck. But don't anyone start packing. We won't be moving soon.

In the 40 years we have been here, Caterpillar has imposed newer and more extensive demands upon its dealers as the line changes and expands. Although we have the capacity to extend this building in any direction, that would not retrieve lost efficiency. Designed and built to accommodate the requirement of a different age, now with far more products to sell, our storage and parking area for machinery is too small. We have added four branch locations since 1966, allowing them to carry inventories once parked here; our space requirements still remain unmet. Shop doors, once standard, did not envision the enormous machinery CAT builds these days and some won't go through the door without disassembly. We have virtually no front display area; our parking provisions for employees is minimal; our office space for clerical and supervisor people is woefully inadequate and has a "provisional" or "temporary" look to it. There is no room for visitors to wait; no extra space for salesmen to close deals. Although we seemed to have stayed the pace and marched in step bravely into the future, in terms of the overall operation our building remains what it <u>was</u> and by now is "weighed in the balance and found wanting".

As the central office, we naturally have the largest staff. The breakdown looks like this:

Accounting and Credit	21
Administration	4
Ag	10
Engine Power	68
Human Resources	10
Information Services	11
Parts	27
Sales	33
Service	86
Warranty	5

If you added this column, you should have come up with 275 people. As this goes to press, we show a total payroll at 13 stores of 720 people. That suggests 26% of our employees work at, or out of, the Indianapolis 30th Street location. So it has served us well.

As an aside, when contemplating the acquisition of the 69 acres across the street, we needed to be clear that it could be zoned for business and during that process notice goes out to the area that we have applied for a business permit. A hearing is provided for neighbors to voice objections and complaints. The impression received from the neighbors was generally quite surprising. The big customer semis going in and out here and our machinery trucked in and out to rental jobs have not discombobulated them a bit. They were most laudatory in terms of our deportment as neighbors, remarking on the neat condition of the premises and the lack of any disturbance or nuisance so if <u>some</u> business enterprise is to use the property, they were glad to see that we would be the operators of same. Our objective is to keep it that way. ∎

Air Travel and Trial

September 2007

Everyone who flies very much has his/her own "airplane story". Or has his/her stories by now. I'll bet mine set a record for repetitive bungling and because so, it becomes the center theme for this particular editorial. It all started on the 27th of June when Fran and I began a trip to Dubrovnik (that's in Croatia in the event you think I have misspelled something) to examine the Dalmatian Coast. Flight schedule was not needlessly complex in terms of arrangements. Fly from Indianapolis at 6:00 PM on "Huckleberry Airlines" to Philadelphia and arrive at 7:45 PM. Then we catch another "Huckleberry" flight for London at 9:00 which arrives at 9:10 AM on the 28th. We move next to British Airlines for the final leg to Dubrovnik, departing at 12:00 o'clock and landing 2½ hours later. Between take-off time in Indianapolis and arrival time in Croatia, 22 hours by the clocks if we ignore the different time zones.

Turned out that the schedule had no particular relevance to reality almost from the get-go. Because "Huckleberry Airlines" called us about 4:00 PM on the 27th saying the plane we were taking to Philadelphia would be 75 minutes late getting to Indianapolis. And with this forewarning, we checked in at the desk and said to the lady printing boarding passes and issuing baggage checks, "We were wondering how you-all are going to work out our scheduling problem?" My arithmetic said that we landed in Philadelphia 15 minutes after our next flight had left. We are too late to wave good bye, much less catch the connection. The lady to whom I am speaking says to me, "How do you know the Indianapolis plane is late coming in? No one told me this." I thought her computer screen might help and sure enough the data there corroborated my contention. It wouldn't work. "So, how do we readjust our schedule; what do we do now to effectuate Plan B?" She didn't have a clue. Beyond that, she couldn't care less. But recommended we go to the gate where the people checking us on the flight would find a solution. Now, this is an agent whose job is making flight arrangements, who takes (has taken) your money for the flight we booked. But being incapable of helping she sends us to Step II and behold! the young lady to whom she had committed is of even less help. She came up with: "Waiting till the next day and use the same connection. But wait a minute! That won't work be-cause the London flight you are catching is already booked". No room in the inn. "Okay, given that, what alternate airlines can we recourse?" None! This was not her problem.

We decided to go, hoping our plane to London would be as screwed up as the one we're now awaiting…or brighter people could provide another option. Our craft for Philadelphia showed up 75 minutes late, then killed another 40 minutes in adding ballast because the weight was wrong. Finally off to Philadelphia; we landed, sweating out the connection only to sit on the ramp for an hour and 20 minutes before getting to our gate. Great way to start a European trip

It is now pushing Midnight; our flight — very late — is long gone so "What now?" This is the query for several hundred passengers in the same or similar circumstances. Most airlines in this situation have someone helping you find an alternate route on theirs or another airline; and they say, "Come back in the morning. But here's a hotel reservation voucher and one for some food. We'll see you in the AM." But we are not flying with your average airline. We are flying "Huckleberry Airlines" who has no one within miles the least bit interested in re-booking anyone; or finding us lodging; who feels obliged for a meal or two until we can rectify the situation. No one to tell you where to go or what to do. No one is responsible for getting you to the destination even though

P.E. and his adorable wife, Fran.

they took your money to do so. At one o'clock in the morning we are sent down to a given terminal and a given desk half a mile away only to learn that the re-booking line is over <u>there</u> and indeed, the line "over there" has a hundred people standing in it. But if you are going <u>overseas</u>, someone tells us, you go to the International Terminal…that's another half mile away. "Oh, yes, it is open all night". We are now walking to the said terminal and find out from the cleaning people they are not open (stupid!) and won't be back till 4:30 AM.

So at 2:00 in the morning I decided to try the Marriott connected to the airport and get us a room till it be morning except the hotel is sold out, and people are sleeping in the halls and corridors. Then checking a dozen hotels listed in the area we find everyone sold out. "Maybe in Jersey or in Delaware." Sure! Like which one? Where? No one knew anything and no one had the least interest in our plight. So back to the terminal and more inquiries, finally ending up at a block-long counter which is the Huckleberry Airlines station where four people are behind the desk re-routing weary and despondent passengers. There were 51 people in front of me when I got in line and one hour and 40 minutes later, I'm finally at the desk where someone spends 35 minutes telling me it is hard to resolve this, and his "solution" is to put us on the same flight we had on the 27th to Dubrovnik, but since it is sold out for the 28th, it is pot luck…Stand-By. I request he tell British Air what has happened so they hold us a spot on the same flight. It is now close to 5:00 in the morning.

The only break in this sad experience was the concierge at the Marriott who suddenly took pity on us. People were checking out, so surreptitiously he slid us into a room about 7:30 AM where we finally got some sleep. Wondering when we awoke at 4:40 PM what our stand-by luck would be with this wonderful air carrier. Without dragging out the story, we did indeed get seated in Business Class and breathed a sign of relief. Only to jack around with servicing, then repairing, then delaying some more and finally loading; again, about three hours late. Late enough, of course, to miss the flight on British Air but fortunate enough to find a lady at their counter who knew exactly what to do: exchange our tickets for a pair on Croatia Airlines which finally got us to our destination — seven hours after our initial schedule. (Instead of 22 hours using two clocks it was 48 hours; we are 31 hours late.) Only to find our baggage did not make the trip despite the efforts of the

lady at the London desk. (The bags would catch up with us <u>four days later</u>.)

Going back home we were doing fine to start with because we were flying Croatia Air but returned to the world of bunglers when we checked in at the Huckleberry counter. "The plane is here; it'll load in two hours, why not go to the Club Room (where there is free 'spirits')?" We did as directed. At loading time we are called to the desk and advised that a couple lights are out in the cabin of our plane; namely, the ones lighting the "Exit" signs (flashlight bulbs). Now dig this: "Since the lights are out over rows one and two, no one can sit in those rows." We were booked in row two. "So, sorry, except we are scrambling to see if there isn't room back in steerage where we can put you." And after two hours they found two seats for us. We were off. But by now our connection in Philadelphia is in jeopardy since we are over two hours late. But Huckleberry's consistency helped. The Indianapolis connection was also an hour and a half late so we made the flight. Finally home safe and sound. <u>This</u> bungle worked to our advantage.

Between the four flights on Huckleberry Airlines, we had 8 hours delay time, i.e. late departures or arrivals. I wonder if this shouldn't be submitted to Guinness. In our official complaint to the airline about getting "hosed", we paid for a hotel room in Dubrovnik we never used — $700; paid for a hotel room in Philadelphia we should not have needed — $300; plus miscellaneous meals, buying some shirts and accessories and medications — $350, necessitated because luggage hadn't arrived. Add to this the difference in what we bought and what was later provided: the Business Class seat was about $800 <u>more</u> than coach on the return trip so we got rooked out of $1600 in just that screw-up. To satisfy us, the Huckleberry Management agreed to give us a couple $400 <u>flight coupons</u> to travel anywhere we wanted on their carriers. They even bungled the settlement.

Now what is the point in this lugubrious story? It is the fact that Huckleberry Airlines is very badly managed. They have been desperate for passengers these last five years; now they have a given economic situation which suddenly sees millions of people traveling. Booming business hides a lot of blundering, so they get by with it. I was stunned with their people who didn't know and hadn't learned. Not knowing is bad enough but not caring one iota is unforgivable. I wanted to punch them out except whoever they had behind the desk was simply evidence of a major personnel failure. The people I dealt with so fruitlessly did not change when they got the assignment to ticket passengers. They were dumb when hired AND NO ONE TAUGHT THEM WHAT A CUSTOMER IS AND "WHY SERVING HIM IS IMPORTANT TO OUR FUTURE AND YOUR JOB". In the scramble to cut costs and compete, emphasis is on stringency so training and checking and teaching and screening have gone by the board. Repeat: They can give lousy service and survive…for now. But they would be well served to look at the automobile industry and see what complacency about bad product and poor service and non-competitive quality can lead to.

Aside from that, their systems are geared to handle people under normal conditions and when business balloons with inordinate, overwhelming volume to contend with, no one has been taught to move at a different pace or changing to a different style. They can handle the routine; they fail utterly when a bonanza inundates them. There was no fallback or emergency plan to compensate for storms which screw up the schedules of unanticipated hordes of people simultaneously deciding to take vacations; despite the fact this occurs with some regularity. The test for most of us is not how we react or respond when we are doing the familiar thing, but how we react when threatened by circumstances, new conditions or new opportunities we never planned for.

The way to succeed in businesses is mostly pleasing the customer and providing a good product. Nothing mysterious about that! Serving the customer is what you want in business to do, and that means day after day, not most of the time. The bane for many of us is budgeting and staffing for an estimate volume of business and then watching it sag to the floor and fall short (with a lot of people standing around with nothing to do) <u>or</u> to see us overwhelmed with volume, particularly in the service operation where half our people work. When it explodes in our face, we have several options: one is extensive overtime; another is move into double shifts; the third is moving repairs within our system. If one store is inundated and another is marginal, we can relocate the load internally between us and take advantage of all our mechanical skills. In a pinch we can give the owner a rental option or loan him a machine. So he can keep working. Another device is "anticipatory planning", meaning encourage the customer to "repair before failure". I.e., schedule maintenance and rebuild, don't wait for a machine to shoot crap on the job site. Last off is to set a date when we can accommodate the customer.

All of this will not always bridge the gap, but it does respond in a fashion that helps many folks; it is flexing with the pressure and the demand; it does indicate we're busting our "tocus" to <u>do something</u> for the guy whose machine is down. Anyone in business knows there are conditions we cannot control impacting our ability to respond. When that occurs, the issue is not of performance but of attitude. The one unforgivable transgression is to shrug one's shoulders and say, "We're busy. No way can we get to you." I.e., to act like we don't care. There is a way to decline empathetically and with some panache.

Bright people respond naturally and logically; the shoe clerks collapse under the strain. A hundred good flights on Huckleberry Airlines is now history to us, and the record in mind is that of the most recent experience which we shall do our best to avoid ever experiencing again. ■

Few Things I Have Discovered ...

September 2007

In my 63rd year here at the tractor works and reflecting philosophically upon the long trail traveled so far, I am not persuaded my experience has given me rights to deliver pearls of wisdom but do figure I have learned lessons that might be passed along. So with no other ado, here is a bit of what I have concluded:

- It is wiser to think rationally than to react viscerally. Logic is usually superior to emotion especially in a crisis or a tense situation when overwrought feelings want to dominate the situation.
- It is not wise to let a given flaw in a colleague's personality warp your judgment about his overall potential or capacity to contribute. None of us is perfect. Some weaknesses like dishonesty and peculation cannot be tolerated. But those weaknesses which do not affect the person's performance ought to be accommodated or "wired around".
- Everyone has a tendency to shade bad news and to exaggerate the good news.
- Do not expect perfection from anyone, including yourself.
- You don't have to like people to work with them. A guy who is doing a good job qualifies for the team on the basis of performance not my personal opinion.
- Do not believe anyone <u>all</u> the time.
- It is a mistake to let personal friendships impact a business relationship. In a company where our employees are also social friends, the line between business and friendship has to be kept clear. Because I like someone does

not mean I have to overlook faulty performance in the job.

- People do not judge their own operation or performance with the same candor or exactness they apply to others. We are usually the heroes of our own stories.
- It often takes me a long time to make a decision about hard issues, but I've discovered by carefully examining all the options, <u>one</u> usually surfaces as the most logical — and acceptable — course.
- It is a rare person who gets himself up to be what he <u>says</u> he is (or wants to be).
- In our work situation, it is fine for me to feel good about what is happening, but it is more important that <u>our subordinates</u> feel good about what is happening to them.
- It is easier to hate or dislike something than to understand it.
- We see things not as <u>they</u> are, but as we are.
- Too many people want the rewards, but are not willing to pay the price to get them.
- Getting things done is not the same as doing things.
- Experience is not what happens to a man, but what he <u>does</u> with what happens to him. It's a gift for dealing with "the accidents of existence".
- Fundamental maxim in human relations: I don't care what you <u>told</u> him, what did he hear?
- The art of seeing what should have been done after it occurs is called "Tail-Gunner Management". It's the perspective of the gunner in the tail end of a B-17 bomber who was well aware of where we had <u>been</u>, but oblivious to where we were going. Called the art of "hindsight".
- Managing is often the art of asking the right questions.
- A problem properly diagnosed is a problem half solved.
- All men are born unfree and unequal. Each is subject to conditions imposed by heredity, physical and intellectual stature, family training, education, experience, culture and geographic location.

- Freedom and equality are sworn enemies; those at the bottom of the human system want equality and those at the top want freedom … freedom to work, create, develop.
- The initiative hero is the formative force in history. Great periods or eras will have at the core an individual who was the architect: Moses, Alexander, Caesar, Augustus, Charlemagne, etc.
- Most governments ... and institutions ... are managed by oligarchies.
- It is unnatural for the majority to rule.
- Civilization is not inherited; it is learned and earned in each generation.
- If you think education is expensive, try ignorance.
- School ought to prepare us not merely for business but for life.
- There is a difference between the brain and the mind.
- Business is a good game. Lots of competition and minimum of rules. You keep score with money.
- Our problem in selling today is due to the fact that the buyer has learned better how to buy than the salesman has learned to sell.

- After all is said and done, more is usually said, than is ever done.
- Trust in Allah — but tie your camel.
- Truth is beautiful, to be sure…but so are lies.
- "Forgive your enemies, but never forget their names." — John Fitzgerald Kennedy
- Never mistake motion for action.
- Sinners can be forgiven; stupid is forever.
- The great end of life is not knowledge but action.
- Confidence is the feeling you have before you understand the situation.
- The punishment wise men suffer from indifference to public affairs is to be ruled by unwise men.
- Your representative owes you not only his industry but his judgment as well; he <u>betrays</u> instead of serving you if he sacrifices it to <u>your</u> opinion." — Burke
- "Each man fancies that no harm comes from his neglect and so by the same notion being entertained by each separately, the common cause, imperceptibly decays." — Pericles. ■

Bah Humbug!

December 2007

This issue usually includes a "Christmasy" type editorial which means the scrivener is obliged to come up with a new insight or Yuletide message not withstanding the fact he has editorialized the Christmas event for the 22nd time already. Though, fair scores, the scene keeps changing and shifting. The conditions which prompted an editorial in 1985 are vastly different than those we experience today. Juxtaposed with the central themes of Christmas which are relatively constant from the 4th Century (when it was first observed) down to our time. The message, the stories and the accounts are summarized in the New Testament and despite some epigraphic diddling, read today the way they did to Charlemagne. (Excuse me: "in Charlemagne's time". Charlemagne couldn't read.) The Advent hymns we Presbyterian use also rephrase, expand and harmonize the themes which depict the mood. So this year we sing "*Joy to the World*" once again.

Despite the fact that we still have a savage war going on in far-off Iraq which has cost us 3,660 lives, 38,451 causalities, spent $1.4 trillion, destroyed hundreds of thousands of homes, shops, terminals, plants, schools and probably 60,000 Iraqi people. Not much "joy" in that "world". A conflict induced by fanatical Islam which outraged Americans on September 11, 2001 and brought to the front the nature of a radical ideology, stunning us with all its terror and mindless destruction of bystanders…with promises to go on dynamiting forever.

Carolers will also again regale us with "*God Rest You Merry, Gentlemen*", too, though it is hard to get very "merry" about gas prices. They were $3.29 a gallon this morning for the middle octane which I use. And Kiplinger's saying $200 a barrel is not an impossibility. (As a kid in college, I bought six gallons for a dollar.) Try switching your attention to the stock market whose track on the chart looks like an EKG. By now a thousand points below where it was three months ago (or was when I wrote this). And no idea where it is going next. Do we buy — or bail out? Real estate agents are not very "merry" either, with the housing market in the tank and sloshing around down there for a year now. Replete with repossessions and a jillion bad loans; and no important change in sight till the beginning of 2009. 2008 looks a bit bleak for many of us; CAT is predicting a decline in domestic sales, and a lot of dealers are expecting 5-10% decline in volume. So we'll see shortly how good we are as managers. Anyone can guide an upswing. The test of leadership comes with a decline in sales and intensified competition wherein dumb competitors screw up the market with dizzy discounting.

Another familiar hymn encourages "Good Christian Men (to) Rejoice" except if you are here in Marion County where we are headquartered and note so far 140 people have been murdered. Rejoice? Jails are overcrowded so we release criminals early and the interminable delays from crime to judgment prove justice very slow indeed. Education is another disappointing story, starting with a 13% school dropout rate due often to kids who can't wait till they are 16 so they can bail out and roam the streets. Add to all this 2,500 homeless people in town who spend a cold Christmas huddled under bridges or in abandoned houses, alone, depressed and destitute. The local litany would add the shock of recent property tax bills, so egregious that a lot of folks are forced to sell their homes because they can no longer pay the 35-100% increase in taxes. This dreary recitation calls to mind the reaction of Ole Scrooge who deplored the whole depressing scene with two words: Bah Humbug!

But wait a second here. Let's confess this is only one side of the Christmas picture. It hardly represents the complete character of human activity. We can find a reason to "Deck the Halls with Bows of Holly" by looking from another vantage point. It would acknowledge the "goodwill to men" scenario represented a lot of places across the land including our own community. Good news stories of good people in a hundred guises like the folks at Old Bethel Church, a congregation over on 21st and Franklin Road with 900 members who for 24 years have run a food pantry for those down on their luck or who can't find a room for the night or gas money to make a job appointment or cash to pay utility bills. A handful of people, 15 or 20 who week-in and week-out pick up the food from wholesalers or canners or "Gleaners" or distributors or major grocers; who sort and display it on racks; man the two stations where those in need appear three or four times a week. Old Bethel is a temporary refuge provided for those in the middle of a personal storm; last year 10,663 households were served (31,782 persons); Christmases provided for 315 families. Annual <u>payroll</u> expense: $0.00. No hullabaloo, no publicity, no professional staff, just people who retain and demonstrate the Christmas spirit … all year.

Operating in support of Old Bethel is another organization, one <u>securing</u> the food which helps supply outlets like Old Bethel, Loaves and Fishes, food pantries, soup kitchens, homeless shelters, churches, etc. It is Gleaners Food Bank. It has contacts with suppliers, retailers, processors, distributors and manufacturers for disposing of excess inventory; cans labeled wrong, cases dented or damaged, cancelled orders, simply gifts of excess beyond needs. The work of folks like this continues under the radar screen because the condition of hunger is not one we discuss frequently in our cocktail conversation or chitchat around the dinner table. There are something like 750,000 Hoosiers living in poverty. 80,000 of them are under 18 years of age. Meeting this need has not necessarily been the result of major governmental intercession but rather from the private sector wherein caring and sensitive folks have taken the initiative to do something — beyond talking — about the dilemma. Gleaners is a major player and dispenses food to accommodate 210,000 people annually, supplying 400 different agents of distribution (like Old Bethel). 515 volunteers; 15,000,000 pounds of food a year valued at $21,000,000; the contribution of 17,000 individuals and corporations like ConAgra, Kroger, Macy's, Wal-Mart, Guidant, Power & Light Company, Finish Line, United Way, etc. etc. 140,000 Hoosiers <u>each day</u> do not go hungry because of Gleaners' charity.

Second Helpings is another unobtrusive Good Samaritan in our community, serving something like 50,000 meals a month. This is food already prepared but not used or needed (we Americans throw away about 27% of our prepared meals). In 1998 a trio of local chefs, familiar with the waste on one hand and the irony of local citizens malnourished on the other, decided to take some action. So they created a rescue vehicle. A given banquet might prepare 30 or 40 servings <u>beyond</u> what is needed or a buffet line for 200 people might have only 130

show up; conventions, holiday gatherings, weddings, fundraising dinner programs, sporting or entertainment events, all with food left over. This becomes the supply source for Second Helpings. Again, a volunteer effort which salvages 100,000 pounds of food a month, formerly dumped, now becomes a godsend to countless hungry people here in Marion County.

On a larger scale is the Salvation Army preaching — and demonstrating — the gospel in over 100 countries and in 160 languages for the past 127 years. It began as an evangelical group to bring Christianity to the un-churched and since then has broadened its agenda to providing disaster-relief service, running daycare centers, summer camps, medical facilities, shelters for battered women; does substance abuse training, family and career counseling, AIDS education and who knows what else. Structured like the Army, it has 3,500 offices worldwide, 60,000 employees, 113,000 soldiers, 430,000 adherents and more than 3,500,000 volunteers. How does one count or measure the number of lives salvaged, trained, instructed, ministered to and set aright? Their Christmas-time Santas with the donation kettle and the bell ringers are evidence again of volunteers, helping raise money to abet the unfortunate. And they want us to note: 83¢ of every dollar raised is spent in direct support of some luckless soul.

The United Way is another "mission" more broadly based and involved; the fundraiser for an endless number of noble causes in our community. The initial "mission was to improve lives by mobilizing the caring power of communities." It was created in Denver, Colorado in 1887 by three religious leaders: a Roman Catholic, a Protestant and a Jewish Rabbi and raised $71,000 to sustain local causes. By 1949 there were 1,000 communities established as United Way organizations. In 1974 the first billion dollar record was set nationally in fundraising and by 2002 it had cracked the $4 billion mark.

When a hurricane ravaged Florida in 2004 or the tsunami hit Indonesia or Katrina hit New Orleans, the United Way through its international chapters focused effort and resources to the partner member on site and was able to pour in all sorts of help including manpower.

Another local service is Wheeler Mission; founded in 1893 with strong religious orientation and motivation, spearheaded by William V. Wheeler who orchestrated its period of growth and progress. Wheeler was a hardware salesman so came from the ranks of business (which might account for his success) and matched his devotion with his enterprise. Wheeler Mission relies heavily on volunteers in rescuing men who are currently (or permanently) "on their uppers" and without either bed or board. We have often seen them on North Delaware Street, lined up outside at meal time waiting for a free lunch and when necessary, a bed for the evening.

There is a limit to how much "goodness and mercy" you can absorb in one article but the list is legion. Some are highlighted to make my point… but there are hundreds more. Boy Scouts and Girl Scouts, Big Brother and Big Sister, Progress House (for recovering alcoholics), Damien Center (AIDS), Habitat for Humanity, Catholic Charities, Red Cross, Noble of Indiana (disabled folks), Special Olympics (sports for mentally-impaired children), YMCA, Julian Center (domestic violence), Janus Development Center, Indianapolis Senior Center, Heritage Place, Humane Society, Fairbanks (alcoholism), Church Federation of Greater Indianapolis, etc. etc.

Recount as well the "walks" or "runs" or cycling, banquets, silent auctions, golf tourneys, bazaars, musical performances et al established to cure cerebral palsy, multiple sclerosis, heart problems, fading vision, AIDS, cystic fibrosis, Lou Gehrig's Disease, tuberculosis, Downs Syndrome, addiction. Not only are governments and universities and hospitals at work here with state and federal dollars, but the private sector as well voluntarily pitches in to see if they can't be of some assistance. Best example is Rotary International who has inoculated over 2,000,000,000 people against polio the last 30 years and has virtually knocked it out of existence. Not the U.N. or NATO but a private group of caring people in cities across the world, united in a common cause and making the decisive difference in eradicating this disease.

Living in a city which has been taught philanthropy by Eli Lilly and the Lilly Endowment, we assume all these causes and rallies and continual scrounging for funds to make a difference in lives less fortunate is normal. It is the "golden mean"; it is just something people do. Wrong! Just something

the American people do. Some of us. In most of the world, the state or province is the prime mover in issues of health and poverty and personal potential. We have the same thing going on with our own government, but have augmented its programs with a broader, more effective, more efficient private support system constructed to minister "to the least of these". Important…because hunger and disease and abuse are local. The noble causes abounding here are almost a nuisance since they are so insistent and so ubiquitous they lead us to assume volunteerism is commonplace. How long and how widespread do you suppose this all-out, on-going phenomenon has been a common concern with the same wide involvement in the lives of the less fortunate? If you said "since time immemorial", that is the wrong answer. The world has been mostly a story of Darfur, of The Congo, Afghanistan, Israel/Palestine, Chechnya, Somalia, and Zimbabwe, played over and over through the generations.

I don't think our sort of generosity has parallels anywhere, and my personal conviction implies we have derived it from a theological underpinning found in Judeo-Christian teachings. But given said teachings, they also existed in the Middle Ages during the Reformation and Enlightenment. Difference is the presence or absence of a vehicle for implementation. For millenniums the existing political systems running Western society had the motivating initiative coming from top down…from monarch/emperor/czar through layers of nobility to the artisans, to freedman and down to the mass of peasants. Said orders by the way inevitably supported the existing structure, the status quo, and resisted sharing or change. The point being there was no implementing agency in the picture so any prospect of being "doers of the word, not hearers only" was impossible. The existing system was constructed without need for broad support. It did not involve or presume or anticipate sharing which eliminated as well the element of responsibility. If there is no ownership, there is likewise no reason to buy in. The hierarchical nature of the Roman Catholic Church hobbled the intent of its founder through endless rules and prohibitions, leaving little freedom of either thought or action. There was no role to play aside from obedience and obeisance. The system, like the monarchy discouraged participation or voluntary enterprise.

But when a new nation was created on these shores, albeit with considerable fumbling and pain, it also based its moral code on the Judeo-Christian dicta. But its political vehicle was one that required, <u>demanded</u> the participation of its citizens to make it function. We had to vote, serve in public office, obey the laws, and we also had to find our own vocation, determine our own schooling and handle our own problems. The freedom to act without the restraint of the crown or the church allowed the growth of personal careers and adventures and development. Citizenship involved responsibility (taxes, military service, agencies of government), and so this theory of participation and the indoctrination into self-sufficiency created a culture of involvement. The outgrowth of that, is development of a lot of parallel subsidiary agencies like local militia, the protestant church, the private college, the Masonic Order, etc., i.e. agencies in which groups of people with sundry interests unite in order to simply do things which improve the local environment. In this dynamic one has a way to engage and contribute. He has a place to volunteer his/her service, give his money, and use his influence to add amenities to his community; make something good happen. It was one thing to talk about Sermon on the Mount and being committed to serving "the least of these" when you are a 12th Century share-cropping farmer in Burgundy, but it's another when you are a farmer today in Marion County. The former had no place to plug in. No place to go in order to serve or join his talents

with others to start a new school. The latter has a hundred options every week to contribute whether effort — or dollars in conjunction with others and makes the world a tad brighter. The enforced sharing of the government load in the republic also implies a sense of responsibility and since our society spawns agencies beyond those of the government, the contribution of time to the school board or the opera company is equally important in terms of shaping our civic psyche and as we volunteer, we enhance and ennoble the community, which in essence is advancing the theological "kingship".

"Bah Humbug" yourself Mr. Scrooge. And by the way, Merry Christmas, too! You can spend the holiday deploring the grubbiness of the world but I and mine will be reflecting on the impact emanating down through the years from "The Prince of Peace" and "rejoice with exceeding great joy" at the change made in the world since your day; grateful for a society that produces more good people than ever before who generate more kindness, consideration and fair play than the species has ever seen. It isn't perfect, but we are still a project in process.

In closing, Ebenezer, why don't you try having a genuine MERRY Christmas this year instead of a grumpy one and while you're at it, have a really HAPPY New Year! ∎

About Healthcare …
The Good, The Bad & The Ugly

December 2007

We are never too weary to talk — or complain — about the nation's healthcare conundrum. Based upon what we read or what we hear, we make judgments about how good or how bad it is, then often begin wringing our hands. Except I stop and point to the healthcare arrangement when I first came to work for MacAllister Machinery Company. The paperwork was minimal and the system simple and direct. When my wife went to the hospital to have our first child in 1946, said hospital sent me a bill and I sent them a check. I went to a dentist upon moving to Indianapolis after my military career. He looked into my row of "pearly whites" and said, "Tsk, tsk tsk. Your dentist may have been thorough but he really wasn't up to par professionally. You probably ought to have an overhaul, and I estimate the entire redo job will cost $1,200. We can do this over the period of a year if you'd like to stretch out the payments." We did the work; he sent me the bills; I wrote the checks. That was the healthcare system in place when I started to work. He who incurred the expense paid the tab. Healthcare was really <u>my</u> responsibility, and I managed (or mismanaged it) like the rest of America.

All this is now irrelevant, however, since a new responsibility for citizen is assumed by the state which made the options available to some, become the <u>rights</u> of all and citizen health is a Federal obligation replete with the endless bureaucracy endemic therein. And by now the extension to include dentist and druggist and tests and therapy and surgery is so complicated we have trouble keeping up with who pays what. I have three layers of coverage which start with the corporate carrier (being still employed), and each coverage itemizes the amount of dollars allowed for its given layer of coverage and will pay for "X" dollars for each procedure or malady. Reams of paper follow each medical incident, continuing sometimes for two years but mailing me endless statements stamped "This is not a bill"; each replete with a long range of arithmetic calculations. Ultimately, one day, announcing jubilantly that we have figured out "You owe this, case closed". I'm guessing at least half the medical expense is not "medical", it is clerical. It is paperwork.

There is a lot in this which is confusing based on what we understand, and there is no rationale for what the practitioner actually charged. Often it turns out to be more than the company chart allows. Along with our own experience in this area there is continual comment about how well or how badly we are served here. Maybe a bit of that confusion or ambiguity will change if I can provide some new insight or information, which appears to give us yet a modified take on the dilemma. It is extracted from the National Center for Policy Analysis and tells us for starters that despite Hillary's ranting, the <u>proportion</u> of Americans lacking health coverage has not changed appreciably in the last ten years. If there are more uninsured, it is due to more people (note the above said "the <u>percentage</u> of people not covered", not the number of people). There is the obvious increase in (1) the population, (2) immigration, and (3) individual choice. What was that last? Choice? People choose <u>not</u> to take the coverage? Yes, exactly. The 2006 census data tells us that 84% of U.S. residents have some sort of private insurance or are enrolled in government programs. (That's 250 million of us.) But there are 14,000,000 folks qualified for government programs but <u>who never enrolled in them.</u>

Beyond that, 18,000,000 people live in households with annual incomes above $50,000 who have never contracted for insurance coverage. The assumption being with this kind of income we can probably afford to buy our own insurance. People could have it, but opt not to take it. In case you haven't added this up, that's 32,000,000 people who could have government or personal insurance but do not cooperate and secure it. 68% of the "uncovered" fall in this category, and it is hard to waste much sympathy on them, being as how they deliberately forgo coverage. Add this all together and it says if these people would get with it and sign on for the coverage, 94% of Americans would be taken care of. We are down to 6% not having coverage. A far cry from what popular opinion has concluded.

Political alarmists claim there are 47,000,000 people without coverage but neglect to tell us that aside from the above data just recited, the statistic is a moving one. Many are not covered because they are in between jobs or not yet renewed. Maybe they have a fatal illness or some other reason which puts them on the "uninsured list". The Congressional Budget Office estimates 21-31,000,000 might be uninsured, which is well under the 47 number Hillary uses. But get this: The report goes on to say that less than half this gang will be uninsured a year from now. Beyond that over a quarter of the uninsured are foreign-born residents. Finally about 19,000 of you-all are age 18 to 34 and have a conviction of personal indestructibility. You just won't get sick; won't need operations; won't incur expenses, so why spend money for insurance? (First 30 years I worked here I lost two days when I dropped a piece — a heavy piece — of iron on my toes and was out. Other folks my age likewise went for years without seeing a doctor or emergency ward.)

Underneath all these figures there is another subtle factor in play. People don't want to pay insurance premiums because they know that free healthcare is available once they get sick. Federal law forbids hospital emergency rooms from turning away critical care patients whether they have insurance or not. Records indicate this type of patient costs between $1,000 and $1,500 a person. Why sign up for insurance when you can get it free from the emergency room?

This is a major problem for all of us in America because costs have steadily risen two or three times the rate of inflation, and there is no end in sight. We have reported before that the average cost for us to cover each employee is about $6,000 a year — total premiums: $4,259,000 annually and going up. We complain about property taxes going out of sight and recently reached a point where a carefully-budgeted family suddenly was hit with another $8,000 tax increase, which was never anticipated and finds it now impossible to live in "this ole house". The taxes have blown the budget apart, and the additional money is just not there. Apply that example to hospitalization insurance. We can also get to a point where — say

$9 million — for insurance premiums right off the bottom line makes one wonder if the risk and effort in running this business is worth it. Because the money has to come from profits and that is money we don't see, so now must borrow to build a new building or renovate old ones or pay employees better salaries.

I'm half persuaded that the entire structure of our medical approach incorporates a flaw in principle: furtive pricing. None of us would pretend to buy a new car or a dining room suite or a new television without knowing what it is going to cost us. Yet we go into the doctor with a problem and haven't a clue as to what his bill is going to be. But worse than that, we never see what he has charged us. At least I don't. They don't consult with us about charges; they send the bill onto the insurance carrier where it is paid, though the insurance carrier knows nothing about the circumstances of our encounter with the medical people. No doctor says, "This is going to cost $850." If he did, we still don't really have much option or worry much because the "insurance covers it". If we were buying this like we would a computer, we'd say, "Wow! Thank you but let me do a little shopping on this. Maybe I can get it cheaper." Or if the system just sent a copy of the bill to us when they filed a claim and we found out what it was, we might have some phone calls going back and asking him how he could justify charging $850 for taking two little spots off my cheek. A little comparing of costs for similar procedures would ultimately lead to changing doctors. It does not work to our advantage when our specialist will now take no more patients because he is loaded. Competition tends to control pricing when there is none; what sets the limits or indicates "tilt"? Most of us who purchase things for the tractor works understand what the cost is and before any invoice is paid, we concur (1) it is what was ordered, (2) got value received, (3) the price is as was quoted. Why not use this system with medical bills? With such a loose system in place, with no competition, are you telling me all the possible economies are realized? When he who is charging has no one checking his work or challenging his bill?

Writing this during the season of "Joy to the World", it is not fitting to leave such a depressing and critical article without some sort of redemptive close. Our medical system has to be renegotiated because one day we reach the point of diminishing returns. But moving on, the systems and the costs and the coverage or lack thereof is only one side of the story. The other side is that considered by a guy who has just seen his 89th summer and enjoyed it immensely. (I was able to get my golf game back into the '90s about half the time.)

The conversation level in my group of "The Venerable Ones" is not very exhilarating. It is medical in nature and chats about my operation, medications, recent emergencies or who had a stroke last week and whose knee had to be replaced. Physical deterioration leads to more sedentary pursuits, and retirement changes the priorities from the vocation and involvement in a busy, productive world to a more contemplative stage. But the point is that most of the people in my group would not <u>be here</u> today were it not for medical science. The number of heart attacks and valve replacements is legion; the treatment for arthritis, back problems, macular degeneration, osteoporosis, allergies — all endless. Cocktail conversations are medical "show and tell sessions". Include in this the shots, pills and doses which constitute the science of pharmacology. Living on into the twilight years is really pointless if one is physically miserable all the time. The reason we get to this

MacAllister Girls Christmas Party, 1954.

age and continue to knock around is due to the doctor fixing us up from time to time, replacing some worn parts, doing some tune-ups, modifying the horsepower, and add the pharmacist who allows us the joy we experience and encourages us to stay active. I think of the diabetic patients and the godsend insulin is. The high blood pressure types and the benefits of Coumadin; the cholesterol problems corrected with Lipitor; the simple aspirin tablet and its blood-thinning capacity to minimize strokes; the common antihistamines that allow us to function when we get our annual common cold. My drug is Synthroid since my thyroid does not kick out enough juice, and without it life is one of lassitude, sleepiness, inertia. So one little yellow pill a day provides what nature ran out of and lets me go charging into the windmills like I were Don Quixote … which makes all the difference in the world to me.

Whatever is wrong with our system and its practicing professionals, the years of life it gives us and the ability to correct what is wrong takes much of the pain, discomfiture, misery out of day-to-day living and is an inestimable gift, provided by the fraternity we support through the current healthcare system. Christmas is indeed a joyous one for most of us, not only because of our family round the tree and the groaning board and gift transfer but because we are healthy enough to enjoy same and appreciate the benefits of life in this society, a joy not possible when we are ailing or hurting. ∎

2008

Concerto

Securing, Recruiting, Engaging ... Hiring

Losing & Losers

The Economy

Ideas

Peace and Reconciliation

Concerto

March 2008

Peter Ilyich Tchaikovsky wrote the first of his three piano concerti in the fall of 1874 with a draft of the final score finished just before Christmas. A complex person, sensitive, highly introverted as well as enormously gifted, he decided to run his new opus by a friend and fellow composer/ musician, Nikolai Rubenstein, so on Christmas Eve he invited Nickie over to audition the new work. There's a lot of action in this piece, making it the most difficult as well as the most popular of his three concerti. Most of us know one of the themes, the passage converted to a ballad called "*Tonight We Love*". Another part of this music was chosen by Orson Wells for his Mercury Theatre Radio Program and the concerto was selected by Van Cliburn when he won his first International Tchaikovsky Competition in 1958. (His recording of same sold a million copies.) So Peter Ilyich played the first movement for Rubenstein; then pushed back the piano bench, wiped his brow and waited for some reaction. Tchaikovsky reported: "I heard not a sound, not a remark. Oh, for one word; for friendly attack, but for God's sake why not one word of sympathy! If you only knew how disappointing, how unbearable it is when a man offers his friend a dish of his work and the other remains silent."

Rubenstein might better have left it that way, but instead finally unloaded. The composition he said was: "Worthless, impossible to play; the themes have been used before; there are only two or three pages that can be salvaged, and the rest must be thrown away. It is vulgar, bad, hackneyed and clumsy." He then proceeded to play a ridiculous caricature of what he had just heard. The composer was naturally stunned and so bitterly disappointed, he fled the room ... but saying as he left, "I will not change a

single note." Then he proceeded to have another nervous breakdown.

Tchaikovsky dedicated this opus to Hans Von Bulow who was delighted with the music and brought it to America in October of 1879. He immediately arranged for its world premier in Boston where it received rave reviews. Fact, the orchestra had to <u>replay</u> the final movement to please an ecstatic crowd. (As a bit of trivia, the conductor's telegram to the composer announcing success and expressing congratulations is reputed to have been the first cable sent between Boston and Moscow.) Given the ultimate popularity of the work, it is obvious Rubenstein was dead wrong; made a very bad call and appeared so flawed in his judgment we wonder why Peter Ilyich regarded him so highly.

Any of us participating in activities involving several people is familiar with practice of submitting plans to others for reaction. It's a normal exercise employed widely in democratic societies. There are occasional heroes who seem to know instinctively what to do without endorsement, but none I know, whether Caesar, Alexander, Moses, Napoleon or the prophet Elijah

Peter Ilyich Tchaikovsky, 1888
(Source: Wikimedia Commons.)

could boast a record of absolute infallibility. Being right most of the time is possible; being right <u>all</u> the time is illusory. So the reason for outside input is to improve the product. And this decision-making-in-consultation-with-others probably starts early in life when our mother tells us to put on a jacket before we go outside or to eat our carrots or to share our toys. Through this period of learning and discovering how to participate, we become equipped to lead, i.e. to make something happen or help get something done. It becomes natural to ask others for advice or input, so that the final product might be the combination of several ideas. But in recourse for advice, there is need to control the input because part of it will come from the inevitable Rubenstein or from one whose power of persuasion or rhetorical talent disguises weak thinking or bad logic. A contemporary ritual in politics is the use of pollsters to determine action, transforming us so we "<u>lead</u> by following". The consultant determines the opinion of the masses; then relays that result to his client, who adopts same as <u>his</u> position. Pseudo leadership…ensconcing oneself within the framework of an already existing conviction. We have surrendered or modified our own conviction.

If Tchaikovsky's approach of asking a colleague for an opinion is something we all do regularly, his chagrin when encountering disapproval, lack of appreciation or understanding is likewise familiar to each of us. Not merely the rejection but the disparagement or exaggerated criticisms of an idea <u>we</u> viewed with great pride. When this happens, the average spirit recoils and withdraws. Exactly like Tchaikovsky did. I don't have to look far for a personal example of "Been there and done that". I remember an illustration from college where my "Rubenstein" proved to be the freshman football coach; encountered when I decided to go out for football. I had played 6,000 hours of sand-lot "touch" football and could catch a pass better than anyone in Southern Wisconsin. Beyond that could throw one with some accuracy 50 yards (and this was the old pudgy football, the one we were still drop-kicking for extra points). Plus I could out-run 20 out of the 22 guys on the field. At 5'9½", boasting 155 pounds of sinew and muscle and with some optimism, I tried out for the freshman team, despite the fact most of the guys competing were there on football scholarships. I, like Tchaikovsky, needed validation and though comfortable with my ability was somewhat naïve, self-conscious and highly introverted. When

checking in the first day, they gave me this arm full of gear to put on. Hmmm! I had to watch the other guys dress to see where to put what pads; then figure out how to walk in shoes two sizes larger than my own. But I was eager enough and went through the routine drill, scrimmaging and daily practice. The third week we were assigned to go up against the varsity and the coach put me on the left end to see what I could do. Guess where the first play went? Right… around my side! So I watched the ball carrier with two "lumazons" in front of him come pounding my way; moved out to keep the play inside; got through both blockers and tackled the ball carrier. I knew I'd been hit but pleased to stop the play. The retort from the freshman coach was a little surprising. He yelled out, "I thought I sent someone in to play left end! Where the hell is he? Are you sleeping? Can't you find the ball carrier? Etc. etc. The runner had picked up about four yards, and the coach is all over my case about not sacking him in the backfield.

No one inspires me by explaining to the world how inadequate I am, how defective or incompetent my effort. The Lombardi style of management by browbeating and sarcasm never motivated me very much. On the contrary, it destroys any real interest in responding to what I considered Neanderthal conduct. As it turned out, that tackle resolved my career gracefully since one of the blockers cracked three of my ribs in the mêlée, and I retired to intramural football where a couple weeks later ran the fraternity team. Got to thinking years later, our varsity went 9-and-0 that season. The guy I tackled would be an honorable-mention All American as a junior (for smaller schools). I kept wondering what my one play said for an offense which lets some huckleberry so green who doesn't know how to put on his uniform, break through the blockers and tackle their star half back. I wondered why someone was not "on" the blockers or the runner because neither could handle a rookie as inadequate as the coach characterized me to be.

I didn't suffer any nervous breakdowns over all this, but there was no way I could drum up any excitement about freshman football, given the hard-ass nature of such a coach. He wasn't interested in teaching me anything; he was interested in being a tough guy, and to my mind there were already enough of his kind in the world to last us forever. When a given management style destroys initiative, demoralizes, stifles desire and allows no slack, it is hard to see it producing superior results. Most of us want to find an environment where he is part of the team, can grow, learn and perfect whatever the art or science is. The college did not suffer because of my experience, but it didn't gain much either; and proved that most football players are made of sterner stuff. But in terms of my rebuff, it left a bitter taste and made me conclude that "tough guy" leadership works with certain people; that I wasn't one of them. But the lesson gained was invaluable. Because in due course my style would be in finding a way to induce "buy in", cooperation, joy in the enterprise and prospect for growth…if I ever got to be the "coach" directing a team.

The nature of given counsel or advice is not always insulting or deprecating. And, fair scores, the "professional", more accustomed to hard knocks and rebuff, takes all this as part of the drill. He assumes: If you honestly want an opinion of your effort, it is wise to <u>expect</u> disagreement or lack of concurrence. If you are seriously looking for ways to make it better, don't have a mind closed to suggestion because someone disagrees with you. If the objective is a successful project, the viewpoint of others as you proceed is critical and if your advisors spot the weakness before it gets to market, you are better served; though your pride of ownership might be compromised a bit.

The message here to the critic (and we all play that role too), analyzing a given set of plans is that his way of delivering useful advice especially if it is contrary to the author's material, is to do so as an <u>ally</u> not a foe. The counsel has to help, rather than damage, the plan or product. Rubenstein's strident and needlessly offensive criticism so offended the composer that his mind dealt with the insult rather than any constructive insight; reminding us that we need to be dealing with substance, not personality. We stay "professional", making dispassionate judgments about the product or project.

When I ran the tractor company, there were four of us who worked closely together in directing the operation. We had the Product Support component, one for Sales, and the other for Accounting, Credit, Finance; plus one on top (me) doing the orchestration. The model applies today in principle since the functions are the same, though we have added Engine Power, Ag and Rental, etc. Recourse to frequent meetings (monthly) helps us stay together on the same page and beyond that to make decisions with joint input. Each brings a special insight and competence so when Jay Swearingen is describing his rental plans or Jim Bernhardt his engine program, we have given expertise in each field none of the rest of us can supply. It adds considerably to the balance and the validity of how each area participates in the company. Awareness of each department allows decisions considering all the major factors at play. The weakness might be the fact that we see the landscape from different vantage points. Each department fixed on his own responsibility, scrambling "to be sure I have enough inventory in <u>my</u> area to protect our sales target since that is my job and it is what the company expects of me". Departmental priorities and requirements are essential but enhancing one at the expense of another is not what we had in mind. Providing fair support to reach in view of the total result across the board is the challenge. If everyone is satisfied and has the budget he wants, we are doing something wrong. How to apportion or invest most wisely is the objective, providing what each <u>needs</u> rather than wants; thus, the ritual of monthly meetings plus individual departmental meetings between interrelated departments (since all are interrelated one way or another). The trick again is to make the right call, and we cannot do that by having a consultant poll the managers.

I was largely a "consensual" manager, usually giving department managers what they wanted, meaning taking a lot of advice. Then one day, age 50, discovered that my own conclusion or understanding was every bit as good as the advice I was given. Partly because our managers in that era were basically technical specialists (like in Service or Parts or Engine); they served as managers de jure rather than de facto. A great field mechanic, 20 years later becomes a service manager, but doesn't <u>manage</u> a heck of a lot aside from fixing machines.

The dynamic of seeking consensus or new input can introduce bad ideas, so how does one know which of several options is the right one when they appear to be 180 degrees apart? Posited a different way, with a dozen major departments, 705 people, 14 locations, how does the company determine where to buy more inventory, add another facility, hire more staff? It does so in a traditional fashion: Each of the sundry aspects represented through a given manager outlines his proposal; what it will cost; what it will generate in terms of revenue and profit. The function of the President at this point (and at innumerable points along the road) is to fix reasonable limits to our total indebtedness; evaluate propositions which

Chris MacAllister.

help advance the mission; assess the economic climate to determine profitability; assure ourselves this is compatible with Caterpillar and evaluate the ability of the department to execute its agenda. Impacting all of this is the experience of the players (particularly Chris who has been top dog for 17 years) and our ability to execute the contemplated program. It sounds cumbersome and theoretical but my axiom is that when all of the evidence is in, when every factor and facet of the project is on the table, we are lead to only one conclusion. If soundly researched and authentically documented, the answer appears. That is most clearly seen by someone who has an equal interest in all departments, who has the total operation continually in view and is driven by the results produced through the combined efforts of every segment of the operation rather than a given component. Since the failure of any specific area reflects on the bottom line and since the bottom line is what the larger world looks at, the results — good or bad — are <u>corporate</u> results, compiled by the stores and departments and entities of the company itself. The record to date attests considerable efficiency and success, but every month is a new challenge and every year different than the one before it. We look forward to this year and know the going will be a lot tougher. But one gains the most experience when he is most challenged. ■

Securing, Recruiting, Engaging … Hiring

March 2008

There is an axiomatic exercise in government agencies, in science, the not-for-profit sector, education, manufacturing, the military, agriculture, fact in <u>any</u> organization requiring peculiar expertise that is too often taken for granted. It's called "Hiring". Inevitable, commonplace, familiar; it's an experience we have all shared. I was hired by my father through a venerable tradition called "nepotism". Probably because I had a college education, five years in the Air Corps as an officer, directing 40 or 50 men; but most probably because I <u>needed</u> a job. Part of my qualification was inadvertent. When we went to Peoria in June of 1945 to sign the contract, my father wanted CAT to know that there was a conceivable "succession" possible. That he had two sons, both educated and each with some "job" (as well as military) experience and, thus, if things went well, there was a continuity prospect which might secure the dealership for two generations. (Turned out to be three generations and still counting.) (The previous dealer had lasted <u>less than a year</u> — demonstrating to us the weakness of poor selection and inadequate scrutiny.)

The given understanding was simple: I would perform the role assigned and do so as well as anyone else. Through strategic rotation, would thus learn the business so if some day the owner "wanted out", he had prepared for continuing management in the form of a successor. I spent six years learning the parts business, the service operation, advertising and promotion and even knew something about operating in a sales territory but have no recollection whatsoever of anyone ever mentioning the fine art of interviewing and hiring. It was a "given"; it was innate. We can all do it. So what is the problem? Well too much turnover; too many unproductive people we have to get rid of. That's the problem. Everyone <u>cannot</u> learn any job you give him/her and do it well. And most managers could not hire effectively. And since we profess to be a "people business" rather than a machinery business, it should have been obvious that finding the best people to fit each specific assignment was the only way to become the best dealers. The CAT brand carried a lot of freight for us in attracting people, but even then, not everyone who wanted to work for a CAT dealer was automatically equipped to do so. We "got by", but "getting by" is a lot different than excelling.

First time I heard this topic discussed was in work with AED. Both Bud Hermann (who ran the operation) and Ted Cohn (a frequent program consultant) recognized its importance. Bud showed me his interview questions particularly those used after dealing with technical knowledge and reverting to temperament, character, talents, hobbies, convictions, taste, morality, etc. The fact that he prepared carefully enough to write a page of questions was a good model. Cohn talked about what the given position <u>needed</u> in terms of professional skills and administrative ability and then how to interview to see if the given applicant was going to fit. I got serious about the subject after sitting in on an interview with one of our managers because I wanted to see what the prospect had to offer. I was stunned by the interview. My guy talked 80% of the time. He was selling the candidate on the company rather than exploring the nature and character of the applicant. This should not have been a surprise because when we promote someone to "Manager" or "Supervisor" or "Foreman", we <u>assume</u> each has all the skills required. We never thought to coach or teach interviewing and hiring. No one stopped to explain this was an exploratory

interchange to appraise someone's ability, personality, potential, strengths, experience, congeniality, characteristics, etc., which does <u>not</u> surface without some digging.

That casual, carefree era has not only gone, its style is totally inadequate today. Our approach to this critical function now is vastly different. Does not say it's easier; fact, it's harder since the responsibility for recruitment is scattered through several department levels and at a dozen locations. It is lodged primarily with major managers. And how they assure some professionalism might be interesting to note because success here will be reflected in the end result of our <u>combined</u> effort, i.e. the <u>individual</u> contributions of 704 people.

The nature of the conditions in 1945 were such that about anyone who wanted a job <u>had</u> one and the scarcity of manpower put "availability" above "talent" or experience, assuming what we had to do was something anyone could learn. My father had operated under that assumption and was enormously successful. But a business with 15 employees operating with fairly familiar routines, working under the stricture of WWII conditions, was not a major management challenge. It does not compare with selling 300 CAT models, an endless array of attachments and ancillary equipment, running six branches and 14 rental operations, and monitoring an inventory of 5000-6000 pieces.

The regime of finding good people and replacing marginal ones stays the same; but is now large enough in scope for us to rely on outside expertise. The source our top managers now employ in securing managerial talent is a professor from the University of North Carolina named Dr. Gerald Bell. He runs a leadership institute and counsels hundreds of managers each year on how to improve management and operational skills. He starts the hiring course by referring to something we already know: The rationale for careful hiring is obvious. Turnover of personnel is deleterious to the corporate efficiency; impugns our reputation; adversely impacts others in the company; impairs our efficiency; loses business; damages the luckless employee who has wasted time and reputation because <u>we</u> did not properly evaluate his ability to do the job. We have long ago stopped putting the blame for mismatches and poor performance on the individual concerned but suggest those of us who signed him/her "on" are the guilty culprits. We are the ones who gave someone an assignment beyond his/her capacity to perform.

So in the exercise of recruiting people for "Team MacAllister", especially for positions of leadership, Bell says we have to look for folks with certain core competencies: entrepreneurship, competitive nature, productive ability, stability, team builders and naturally creative. The interview and hiring ritual is not solo; it's a <u>team</u> effort, usually overseen by the HR Director and includes the given department manager, a subordinate and a peer manager. Preparation in advance has to determine and define a specific number of things we want said hiree to achieve the first year on board. Then what are the action steps; what are the obstacles? We need to be assured of commitment, of technical and personality skills appropriate to the assignment. The character and ability have to match the challenge and opportunity of the position so knowing as we do (or at least part of the team does) the demands of the position, we have to find that person who <u>wants</u> to do it and who has the persona and competence to get it done. We learn about said person through the interview process, and the rule is to have him/her talking 80% of the time while we use the other 20% (the exact reverse of the policy I saw employed by our managers).

What is the interviewing supposed to uncover? A sense of commitment, a strong work ethic, enjoyment in the given position or profession. We need to find other projects, activities or organizations in which our candidate is involved. We look for achievers; surely we need a "technical match" (a librarian would not qualify as a parts manager despite the fact <u>both</u> deal with rows of stuff, stacked in racks and hourly in-an-out activity). Personally, I always looked for a measure of intelligence and for leadership roles in high school or college; or in the Chamber of Commerce, or the church, or Kiwanis, etc. Find out what the interviewee likes about the proposed position and things he/she is edgy about. And finally, we need to see some references, both those the <u>candidate</u> provides and several he does not necessarily know about.

This ritual takes several weeks and three or four sessions with different elements of the team involved in different levels. And when it comes to a close and we have agreed that so-and-so would make a great team member, there is one last exercise: the psychological test. Back as far as my day we have used an industrial psychologist in town to help us understand the psyche and mental as well as emotional make-up of those who constitute the management team. The test is three-four hours and is invaluable in establishing the character and capacity of a person, a part he himself does not even recognize. Having worked with us for a generation and knowing our managers well, this consultant is virtually flawless in finding the right fit for us. If she says "Go", we are in; if she says "No", we think long and hard about rejecting her recommendation. Experience has proven she is "righter" than we are.

This is not, repeat, <u>not</u> an exciting part of any business and maybe the one done most poorly, only because we trust our personal judgment; because we are poorly prepared; because we don't think it is all that essential. Hey! We're doing just fine right now the way it is, thank you! Improving our market share in a given product from 10% to 20% takes a certain special initiative. Getting it up to 30% requires twice as much horsepower. To get it up to 40% is a major

challenge and then to move it to 42% requires inordinate effort. So when one has a workforce rated maybe 85%, to get it to 90% efficient is a major challenge and then to get from there to 91% or 92% requires concentrated, deliberate and exhaustive dedication; broad involvement. So being relatively good to start with makes getting "very good" and then "superior" humongous challenges. But if we are to move ourselves in a special category of "superior competence", we do it only with extra special people and we get these only through deliberate, careful, professional and thorough recruitment and hiring practices; which by the way, never ends. The pressure and search for excellence is continual, and we think the one way of meeting it, beyond product line, location and financial capability, is securing the finest people available to us in the Indiana market. ■

Losing and Losers

June 2008

We have to be amazed at the quality and frequency of current authors who are recounting earlier American history using the facility of research to produce oceans of detail, much of it heretofore ignored. One aspect new to this generation is the frankness and honesty employed as we strip away the gloss and legend to disclose foibles and weaknesses; a candor and almost brazenness Pastor Weems never dared employ as he idolized George Washington in his quaint but memorable apotheosis. Like the story of George throwing a dollar across the Rappahannock and another where he chopped down the cherry tree only to confess his mischief because "Father, I cannot tell a lie". The pastor ignored the General's bad teeth and eternal trouble getting plates, his owning 200 slaves, and his capacity when enraged to swear like the proverbial trooper. Military historians are equally honest about his expertise on the battlefield where he falls short of Napoleon or Caesar. But fair scores, he was a genius at working with what he had at hand; an expert in the art of retreat, which may have been more important than tactical brilliance

in fighting the ranging imprecision which was our war for independence. His misfortunes are key to this essay — because Washington became a lesson in learning from losing.

If hostilities in our war for independence commenced at Concord and Lexington in April of 1775, they began before we had an official Continental Congress, thus, before we had a national army. Those troops fighting:

> *"By the rude bridge that arched the flood,*
> *Their flag in April breeze unfurled."*

They were indeed "embattled farmers", i.e., local militia, organized primarily to protect the settlement against Indian attacks. Each colony had its own defense units; "drilled" and deployed them; kept powder and lead in a common arsenal; had muskets for those who didn't own one. We saw this pattern in our Civil War wherein local citizens like Eli Lilly could raise, equip and command his own Indiana gun battery, enrolled it in the Union Army to serve where appointed to do so. Today, our Indiana militia, i.e. the National Guard, has a regiment serving in Iraq.

The Revolutionary War moved from Lexington to Boston with the British provoking the next battle at Breeds Hill (i.e. Bunker Hill) where they won the day but were amazed at the resolution of the Americans and the major losses inflicted on His Majesty's troops. We hurried to form our Continental Congress which created a "Continental Army", i.e. "federal" troops in support of the colonies wherever required; to be augmented with the local militias. The principle was sound but weaknesses abounded: the lack of training, the paucity of weapons, the scarcity of good officers, and six-month or one-year <u>enlistment</u> periods. Result was random term expiration. At one point 6,000 ended their enlistment and after pleading, cajoling and bribing, only 3,500 signed back on; the other 2,500 went home. So how many men we shall have for a given campaign was always iffy and imprecise. Then committing to battle was another challenge. Time after time, when the first volley was fired, hundreds turned and ran away. Or just the sight of a great line of red coats with fixed bayonets moving inexorable toward us was enough to trigger a wholesale scramble for the woods. Washington's challenge, given these conditions was enormous, almost impossible.

"Porthole" portrait of George Washington, 1825-1860, Cincinnati Art Museum by Rembrandt Peale.
(Source: Wikimedia Commons.)

After driving the enemy out of Boston Harbor, thanks to Knox and his caravan of cannons from Fort Ticonderoga, the Brits moved on New York where they invested the city. Washington decided to push them out, but General Howe had other plans in mind. One was ending the war by a massive strike with the largest expeditionary force in British history — 32,000 men, many landing in New York. On August 22nd Howe moved 15,000 men ashore on the Brooklyn Peninsula and struck in three columns to attack the American forces. The 9,000 Colonials gave way almost across the entire front; some men running like rabbits for cover.

The coordinated attacks from professional troops were impossible to withstand; we were both outclassed and outnumbered. That night Washington secretly left Long Island and moved across the channel to Manhattan in a masterful exercise that saved every soldier and piece of equipment. The Brits delayed and muddled giving Washington time to regroup, but on September 15th Howe attacked at Kips Bay blowing apart the American defenses, scattering the Militia troops. Washington then fell back to Harlem Heights and another defeat. Then to White Plains. The enemy followed and reported the Militia "fled in confusion, without more than random scattering fire ... MacDonald's brigade never came up ... three Delaware companies retired in disorder". Finally holed up in Fort Washington, the Colonials were again attacked and "soon as the rebels saw us, they ran away". Meaning, we had to evacuate again; this time traveling west through New Jersey, heading for Valley Forge. During which trek 2,000 more Militia men checked out to go home; ending up with a mere 3,000 men — tired, depressed and disheartened. The early chapters were not propitious.

Washington saved the cause on Christmas night by defeating the Hessians at Trenton and then attacking Princeton after which he settled in at Valley Forge, Pennsylvania for the winter of 1776-1777. The following year he attacked again at Brandywine and got clobbered; then suffered another loss at Germantown. The following year saw the largest major battle in the north, fought at Monmouth not far from Philadelphia and though not a complete loss, was no better than a draw. Meanwhile, the record in the south was not much better, beginning in late 1778 with the loss of Savannah to the British. The following spring the enemy besieged and took Charlestown. The next engagement was at Camden where again the Americans were routed; to be slightly redeemed at Kings Mountain when they defeated a force of a thousand Royalists; then followed a victory at Cowpens only to be clobbered later at Guilford Courthouse.

Of the ten battles fought down south, we lost seven. Time after time the Continentals and our Militia were out-generaled and out-fought, but it's important to note they invariably retired from the field in some order and were re-grooved to fight another time. Washington's personal determination, his obsession about continuing the struggle is a perfect example of absolute commitment to a cause. Despite the lack of support in the Congress, the wishy-washy nature of many regiments, the lack of supplies, absence of pay and overwhelming numerical odds, his dogged almost-obsessive determination held the army together and drove it in pursuit of our liberty. He has to be far and away the single reason the war was prosecuted at all; and secondly, that it continued doggedly until he got a break. In due time experience conditioned his troops; Von Steuben created military discipline; commanders became more effective; we got help from France and his colleagues, infected with his loyalty and dedication would ultimately triumph. This is a story where the perennial loser, <u>wins</u>.

People don't write a lot of essays about losers, despite the fact that all of us end up in that category one time or another. The fact that they occur is inevitable. But how they are negotiated becomes the determining factor. How the loser treats the occasion is what's important. Washington's eye was not simply on the battle, it was on the war he was charged to fight. A battle lost was not the final arbiter, not a termination because he refused to regard it as such. In fact losing became a lesson. What did we do wrong? Was the strategy bad? Was the implementing agent defective? Have we underestimated the enemy? From Monmouth he learned that complex battle plans employing four-coordinated commands, all on unfamiliar terrain, presented problems too formidable to manage. Theory did not fit reality and so he failed from improper knowledge and inadequate preparation. We learned, too, troops in battle the third time are more savvy and confident than those enduring the first encounter, so understanding the attitude and courage of the men has a lot to do with what we can achieve. Beyond that, is our plan achievable or is it blue sky impracticality? How good is our leadership and is that a problem? (Washington sacked his two top-ranking generals, Lee and Gates, and changed his results.)

One example of learning from past losses was displayed at Cowpens where Morgan had a large body of militia (unsteady) troops, along with the Continental Army. He selected his battlefield with his back to the river; then put his militia in the front ranks and said "Fire two rounds, then retreat through the lines of Colonial Army and reform <u>back</u> of them and reload. And by the way, any man who breaks ranks and runs gets shot by sharp shooters." The militia duly fired the two-rounds and retreated. As they moved back, the Red Coats interpreted it as a rout and came barreling forward, only to be met with a mass volley from the long line of regulars plus an enveloping action on each flank. The British were trapped, badly mauled and lost the encounter, thanks to Morgan's tactics, which made it impossible for militia to desert.

In letters to his family and his friends about conditions, Washington complained about the lack of food, men without shoes, disease, demoralization, paucity of medicines and supplies but never let on to his troops that he was down in the mouth. And he never held back, waiting for things to get better. He was content to do the best he could with the resources at hand...to play the hand he was dealt rather than speculate as to what might occur if he had 10,000 more experienced men, fully armed and perfectly lead. He accommodated the defections, the disappearing militia, the ragged nature of his army, the limited cavalry and numerical inferiority and used them the best he could, deploying, leading and inspiring what was there. He taught us that more can be learned from mistakes...often...than is learned in victory.

When we are doing something wrong, we often don't know it is wrong until it brings bad results. When we lose a big deal in the tractor company, we don't shrug it off and go on about our business. We asked, "Hey! What happened? Why did we get beat?" Because if we find out where the glitch is, we know what to do next time around. A way to spot weaknesses in the sales force is through losses, not victories. In looking at market share or delivery records in each of our umpteen salesmen, it is easy to spot who is below the average. Improvement usually comes from change, and change occurs because we have found something that isn't working. So what happens is that each loss requires corrective action and in the process, if we can save our troops, step by step, we ratchet up and improve the operation and the results.

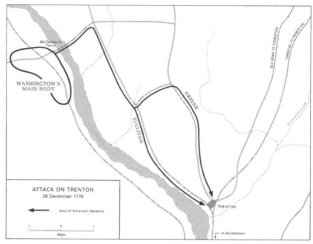

Battle of Trenton: The plan of attack under Washington. General John Sullivan was to advance from the south, and cut off the Hessian escape, while Greene was to surround the other side of the Hessians. Author: Center of Military History. *(Source: Wikimedia Commons.)*

Losing is not fatal or necessarily a disgrace. Half the college football teams on any given Saturday lose their games. Fifty percent of all our candidates running this fall will get beaten. In most circumstances it is endemic to the process but is likewise one phase in said process. The objective is the long-term triumph, convinced that given another chance we have learned enough to deliver a better product and keep improving till we become the winner.

The changing geography of the battlefields, the differing commanders and the unpredictable nature of his forces required Washington to constantly adapt and readjust, accommodating ever new conditions. Each occasion presented a new opportunity to deploy his forces and each likewise contained the prospect of defeat. Today, we harp on the prevalence of change and the ever-shifting world in which we function, an environment which has become a moving kaleidoscope, so we, too, confront the same nemesis (or opportunity). And we treat it that same way. It is part of the given circumstance into which our vocation has thrust us. We assume uneven conditions are "normal" and even essential if there is to be progress. The issue is not that they are there; the issue is how we deal with them. We start by dividing them into two categories: those which are predictable and those outside our control. For example, we can count on seasonal differences in our business. In winter contractors cannot profitably move a lot of dirt or pour a lot of concrete, ergo volume declines. We can see sales rising and fading in synch with the housing market. When housing starts to increase, within six months our business expands; when sales sag or goes over the cliff, we likewise feel a sharp drop in deliveries.

But we cannot <u>predict</u> the cost of borrowed money or the price of gasoline or a factory strike, a hurricane or a failing corn crop. Point is in either event, as a new threat approaches, we do some scrambling. It is "planned" when we see it coming; but reactionary when it is unforeseen. The latter, of course, is the real challenge. But like Washington, each phase (glitch) is temporary. There isn't much that's permanent in our business cycles. So we need to balance the crisis response of the moment to any impact it may have long term. Rather than slashing the work force in a slump or closing stores, we might better eat some losses instead because in six months, we'll need the resource we are jettisoning now. Beyond that, we hand off to individual managers the responsibility of reacting, each in his/her area to meet what is a local, or market, or seasonal slack-off. There may be a general order to curtail, but it is to be applied in each case as the situation requires. The coal market has not been all that great but that is almost irrelevant to the rental people, <u>who in the same area</u> are opening a new store. On close scrutiny, all problems are local. They need to be dealt with from the standpoint of what is best or most appropriate for a given, specific situation; what is best for the long pull. One solution may not fit all. Washington had Morgan at Cowpens who saw the advantage of the ground, knew how to make the Militia fight, did accumulate a respectable cavalry force, and had a plan that best used each of these given factors, endemic to his particular situation. But alas, Washington could not trust Lee or Gates to design a given strategy for the next encounter, when he knew both fled from battlefields. If we are commissioned to lead, we need to do it right.

The key in the crisis is the leader and he/she is there to act, not hypothecate or temporize. The condition might call for retrenchment or easing off and if that is the right course, it vindicates the judgment of the leader. It is then not really failure but success.

■

The Economy

June 2008

Given our degree of affluence and our success in the employment of media technology, we might be the best informed people in the history of the human race. But given the proliferation of material coming over, through, in and "as a result of" said media, we might also be the most confounded or confused generation of hominoids ever. What is passed along to us as information or news often carries a bias. My theory is that no one can avoid reporting without also interpreting. His adjectives, adverbs, his nouns and punctuation and his language itself all speak to us as well, in a subliminal fashion so that surreptitiously, unwittingly, inadvertently we color what it is we report. Beyond that, is another component. News is programmed for us, whether in the paper, a weekly magazine, radio or endless, round-the-clock television news, which requires "X" volume of content because deadlines for reporting are established. They are provided whether there is any news or not. We have to go on the air and talk. Report! Comment! The appetite for news is so pressing and essential that we often rush too quickly to get something on or over or in the media obsessed more with timing than with accuracy. Buried as well in this surfeit of material will be a lot of items that editors or journalists have <u>concluded</u> or assumed, given the circumstances. Unemployment claims go up because hundreds have lost jobs. We note simultaneously more stuff carrying the "Made in China" sticker than carrying the "Made in USA" label. This appears to mean that a lot of companies have laid off employees. Hook that up to the "China" label, and the conclusion is the reason for the lay-offs is the fact China is making and selling stuff Americans used to make or sell.

Indiana has long been a major player in the automobile market, at one time having more models built there than anywhere else in the world. Thus, the 500 Track, a remnant of that era when we tested cars on the oval. As the center of production shifted to Michigan, we did not abandon the market but instead transformed our emphasis into supplying Detroit with auto parts. The foreign makers of automobiles know America is the greatest market in the world so gravitated here both with manufacture and distribution tipping GM, Ford and Chrysler out of first, second and third place into some subordinate

standing. Honda, Toyota, Daimler Benz et al have out-produced and our-marketed us in this arena America once owned. So Detroit hit the skids and with lower demand, more stringency, more competition and a lot fewer jobs, we have been hammered severely as a manufacturing economy.

Add to that the decline in our heaviest manufacturing component, steel. Once boasting the greatest production in the world, the steel mills have lost 200,000 jobs the last decade or so, as other nations with cheaper labor and less environmental restriction have quietly moved into our market and either produced their own or bought American's output, a further inroad into our manufacturing base. All of this...and more...add up to a decline in our Gross Domestic Product, a decline in our economy which needs a 2.5-3% annual growth to keep up with inflation and stay steady.

- The housing market is in the tank.
- The dollar has lost its purchasing power.
- We have an enormous trade imbalance.
- The Fed intervenes by cutting interest rates to bolster the sagging economy.
- Unemployment is at 5.1%. Tsk, tsk, tsk.

All of this gloom and doom seems reason a plenty for depression and declining optimism. But hey! Are we reading the picture fairly? Are we seeing a true picture or a series of assumptions about how lousy the economy is and how high unemployment is and generally how perilous the time? Let's look at the "flip" side of this picture.

I have used a personal illustration a hundred times to deal with unemployment. When I graduated from college in 1940, the unemployment rate in America had <u>dropped</u> 15 points. It had gone from 32% at the nadir to 17% in June of 1940 when I started job hunting. Today's 5.1% is hardly a calamitous condition, threatening the nation's survival. Not in terms of my perspective. Of course, the reason for unemployment is because we have exported all our good jobs to China. A little extreme! First off, it's not a bad thing for the consumer. American companies move abroad because they can make things cheaper and may be make them better than we do here. Why does it make any difference <u>where</u> a car is made if it has superior trade-in value, top reliability, all the latest in technology, a very reasonable price and good service capacity from the dealer? <u>Where</u> it is made is totally irrelevant. The same holds true of shirts, golf clubs, raincoats, toasters, flashlights, Christmas tree ornaments. After all, the existing companies who make these products are survivors who in previous generations drove <u>other</u> makers of the same commodity out of business because of superior value, marketing and product. Guess what happened to the corner grocer, drugstore, gas station and restaurant? Gobbled up or driven from business by Kroger, CVS, Esso, McDonalds. The same process goes inexorably in capitalism, only this time it is a foreign nation that produces the product rather than the takeover successor in a competitive shoot-out. And who benefits from this? You and me because to put everything back in the corner grocery or dry goods store would probably double the cost of commodities we have farmed out for others to make. The single reason for containing inflation is this ability to hold the line on prices, which takes help from cheaper labor.

The decline in manufacturing jobs is indeed a verity. But why? Export? Not really! In 1982 the U.S. steel industry produced 75,000,000 tons of steel and employed 289,000 steel workers. Today, that labor force is down to 74,000 employees, but what do you suppose steel production is? 102,000,000 tons! (These figures are a couple years out of date or they would be greater.) We produce 25% <u>more</u> steel with 74% fewer people. Sounds impossible! You know the reason: technology.

We talk about exporting jobs; do we ever talk about <u>importing</u> jobs? Foreign companies who come here and hire American employees? Our Indiana Governor has been marketing Indiana to the rest of the world as a good place to do business because he is concerned about our economy and employment. In the past three years foreign companies have invested $12.3 billion in Indiana and brought about 11,500 new jobs. Last year 54% of the new jobs created in Indiana came via foreign investors. 92,000 Hoosiers get their paychecks from foreign-owned operations. I wonder if Japan and Germany are complaining about exporting jobs to America. Incidentally, the foremost foreign investor here is Britain; the second Japan; the third is Germany. In all, 16 different foreign companies have put operations in Indiana. The biggest segment for investment?

Automobiles; the second, electronics and business equipment. Now, add to this whole foreign group, subsidiary supplies. Honda and Toyota want

all its manifolds, batteries, gauges, windshield wipers, etc., etc. to come from locations within a hundred miles of the assembly operation. Indiana has indeed lost manufacturing jobs. Fact, we are down 9% since 1991 but have the highest percent of manufacturing jobs of any state in America. And by the way, let's note Brazil, Japan and China, respectively, have lost 22%, 16%, 15% of their manufacturing jobs.

Another fact about locating overseas is the issue of geography. The second largest market for Caterpillar equipment since 1950 has been Japan. Doesn't it make a lot of sense, given that potential, to put a manufacturing plant <u>in</u> the Orient, maybe even Japan? Save the enormous shipping and transport costs. So to capitalize, CAT did indeed put one in Akashi as a way of retaining a large share of the Far Eastern market and given the rise of China and the awakening in India, can a shareholder say CAT made a bad decision if it wants to remain a world leader? For 30 years South America has been a major opportunity for construction and mining machinery. So CAT built a huge plant in Sao Paulo, Brazil to assure its dominant position in the Latin American market. A stronger Caterpillar worldwide means a stronger Caterpillar in America. Traditionally, about half CAT's sales were overseas. Last year it was 60%. Doesn't one go where his market is?

This piece is getting too many figures in it, driving the reader to distraction, i.e. making it difficult to keep track of what the point is…but one more paragraph or two in the emerging potential and threat from China. We think it is growing annually by leaps and bounds in expanding Gross Domestic Product. The growth figure given per year is 10% versus what we did which was maybe 2½% last year here; let's say

Caterpillar manufacturing plant in Peoria, IL.

3% in a normal year. The conclusion reached is that they are racing by us. The 10% growth is on a gross total of $2.5 trillion a year, coming out to $250 billion a year. Huzzah!! Our growth, let's say at a measly 3% is on $14 trillion a year or $420 billion. Who has the better growth?

Our papers are full of stories entitled "What's Wrong with America Today?", and we know the record on crime, the environment, education, urban sprawl and a spirited (I almost said "vicious") political battle being waged daily. So let's compare problems. China has a few of its own. 400,000 people a year die from air pollution. 85% of the water is too polluted to use. Inflation is running at 7% a year; 60% of the home heating is supplied by coal or wood. There are 200,000,000 "surplus workers" in the central and western provinces, and there are 125,000,000 more men than women in the population. Oh yes, last year 87,000 political protests. There is no doubt about the amazing progress made by China the past ten years, especially when compared to the previous 20. But let's see the whole picture in making our judgment. All is not peaches and cream in the land of Kublai Khan and Mao Tse-tung. Meanwhile, back at the ranch in Indianapolis we are not as happy as we were last year either, and a good deal of the reason is fiscal or economic. But while we are in a serious struggle to keep up the rate of tractor deliveries, we need to also realize that in the larger picture, we are still in the catbird's seat here in America and especially so in Indiana. The national economy about which we are stewing happens to be the largest in the world and equals annually that of Japan, Germany, China and Britain <u>combined</u>. Our major challenge is to preserve and improve what we have, and on that score it is hard to find any other repository of innovation, experimentation, technical brilliance, available capital and free market environment that matches our own.

So forward Indiana and onward America! ■

Ideas

September 2008

I read an observation 40 years ago I have never forgotten. It declared: "Money does not solve problems." Oh? You sure?

Problems are solved by ideas the writer contends. But confesses that often said ideas require money to implement. Spending big bucks cannot make a bad idea, good. Recent Democrat primary campaign for the White House had some spending/result illustrations. A relatively inexperienced Senator set records for raising — spending — dollars. Obama may well burn up in excess of $400,000,000 trying to win the Presidency. The sums he has generated are remarkable, and he buried one of the toughest, canniest and most unscrupulous polls in the country. So who says money doesn't do it? Well, the dollars were surely part of it, but there were also public dissatisfaction with the President, a quivering economy, the Iraqi war; there was timing; a roller coaster stock market, outrageous gas prices, you name it. Beyond that, I say his win came not because of the dollars but because he was superbly managed. The way he has "plugged into" the proletariat, persuaded the young, wooed the ethnic groups, unions, the unemployed, the dissatisfied has been phenomenal. What the money bought was brilliant speeches; on the right topics; strong position on hot button issues; the attractive theme of hope; good staging. The ideas behind his ads, news releases, fundraising teams, sound bites, endorsements et al have been carefully and cleverly selected and employed. This may be a mass movement, but it is triggered by the skill with which the candidate has been positioned and presented. Hillary was "out thought" and defeated by a better and more ingenious, more effective campaigner. She was defeated by the ideas that were exploited by the big bucks.

Our Mayor's race in Indianapolis last November speaks more to the point. The Democrat incumbent was completing two terms and running for a third. He was attractive,

popular, and supported by a strong machine so far ahead in the polls, the Republicans couldn't find a contender. Till out of the blue, an Ex-Marine Lieutenant Colonel, who never held public office and with no record in the party, decided he would run. We said "Good luck; we'll see you around" and worked on the council races where we had a chance. The Colonel raised $200,000 for his campaign, competing with $2.2 million raised by the incumbent mayor. The Colonel won the race. Money did not assure results. The results were determined by dissatisfaction. Due in part to a wild increase in personal property tax bills (mine went up 35%; many up 50%; some doubled which outraged citizens). Add to this a continuing incidence of murders in the county, the real estate disaster and record levels of chuck holes. Neither taxes nor crime is the fault of a single mayor, but the angry electorate demanded a scapegoat.

An unpredictable occurrence or discovery often alters the course of events, usually as the result of an idea. In 1775 the discovery was "taxation without representation" … in 1860 it was "interposition" … in 1920 "voting rights for women" … in 1960 "about civil rights". The same principle has prevailed since the dawn of history. A critical need for recording business and temple transactions led to the invention of writing; a way to communicate abstractly, to disperse, to record and accumulate knowledge; in short, to create civilization. Eons later writing facilitated literacy by the invention of movable type; Gutenberg's printing press disseminated ideas in profusion and with alacrity. Other major ideas were the wheel; coins to replace barter; the domestication of animals, spinning and weaving; the boat then better boats; the bow and arrow; the gods; law codes; irrigation; Caterpillar tractors. A bad invention was warfare, but it became the universal, the chief agent bringing dramatic change…for better or for worse. Most impactful user of warfare was probably Alexander of Macedon, relevant in this essay because his armies became the agent for scattering new Greek ideas across the Fertile Crescent. These imparted the Greek gifts of abstract thinking, i.e. reasoning; elevated the status of man, emphasizing his value and importance while snickering at the gods. Hellas brought as well democratic forms, drama, classic temple architecture, freedom of speech, light and airy garments and sun-drenched homes. The Greek culture altered thinking so dramatically there was no way the dark Semitic tradition would ever erase the influence or renew the authority of the inimical and forever angry gods.

Greek phalanx.
(Source: Wikimedia Commons.)

Alexander had the money but success lay in his own brilliance in deploying an army which had conquered all of Greece by virtue of a new military configuration called the phalanx. It was an ingenious instrument that organized and deployed weaponry to make it virtually indestructible. The building block was a syntagma, i.e., 16 rows of hoplites (soldiers) with 16 men in each row…256 warriors armed with an 18 foot spear called a sarissa. These were thrust forward by the first five rows creating a front like a porcupine. Sixteen spear points out front in full length; then 16 lines of points set out 13 feet; the third line at maybe 10, and the next lines seven and three feet. Put a 20 syntagma together and you have a brigade; 5120 men with five lines of 1600 spears stretched for a quarter mile across the front and 11 rows of reserves. Now add certain skirmishers, cavalry and archers, then drill them incessantly so they click like a machine. Take this disciplined formation against the unwieldy mass Persians, relying on thousands of archers, commanded in a dozen languages, assuming intimidation would frighten the enemy. But battle-season warriors don't panic easily and at Arbela and Issus the superiority of the Macedonian instrument overcame the countless hordes of armed opponents. The vehicle was so well trained, organized and deployed that Alexander never lost a battle, and he fought a jillion of them. For the next couple generations this military formation — this invincible vehicle — was used by the professional soldiers who fought the wars of the Diadochi and maintained the Seleucid and Ptolemy Dynasties in the catbird seat.

If you are Roman in 275 B.C, how do you contend against an "unattackable" military nemesis?

With a better idea! Which Pyhhrus discovered to his chagrin. One of the greatest of tacticians in history, this Greek king took his phalanxes against the Romans in the Third Century as the Latins were expanding south in Italy, bumping into the Greek colonies, established before Rome was a city. No one ever heard of Amaelius and Trinicius, but they ought to be more highly touted since these are the Roman Generals who found a way to defeat the vaunted phalanx. They did not go at it with volumes of arrows followed by massive hordes of manpower. They did it by looking for weaknesses in the structure. Ideas …not muscle!

They forced the battle action off the flat plains and onto hilly or uneven ground where the solid lines of the phalanx could not be maintained. Breaks or disjointing occurred when there was rough, hilly country eliminating the ability to hold a quarter mile, spear wall symmetrically intact. The Roman challenging formation was one of flexibility. The base unit was a platoon of ten men called a contubernium; ten of these composed a century (100). Two centuries were a maniple … 200 men; three maniples was a cohort. Ten cohorts formed a legion … roughly 6,000, etc. Each level had a commander which allowed it to deploy and functioned unilaterally as well as in synch with a larger body. So the mobility afforded by this breakout composition would allow immediate dispatch of three cohorts in attacking a break in the line of the syntagma which could quickly be exploited by piecemeal re-enforcement. If the Greek commanders could not respond quickly with an unwieldy dispatch of syntagmas, the impregnability was gone. Pyhhrus technically won two major engagements and lost the third but his losses were so considerable (more men than the losers), he finally abandoned the effort. His name became synonyms for costly victories. He was the last I know of to employ the phalanx as a battle formation.

We are familiar with "segregated units" in the Presbyterian church, a school system, governance components from township to federal levels and stretch out to include Caterpillar dealers. Subordinate elements in these configurations are essential since they are readily manageable — easy to correct, to reinforce, to expand. Our corporate breakout is by product category … Agriculture, Mining, Power Systems, Paving, Construction, etc.; further segregated by geographic branch location to coordinate localized function. Within these identities the workforce itself splits into technical specialists like archers, cavalry, infantry only with us they are parts types, servicemen, rental reps, salesmen, clerks, etc. And leadership assigned across the board like the Roman army, each element … legatus, centurion, optio, cornacularis … becomes leadman, supervisor, assistant manager, manager, Chris. In this illustration, below the surface the same are two existential elements: money and ideas come into play. We operate in an assigned environment (territory) where we fight the battle for Caterpillar. Owners create appropriate structure and apportion the resources (money), then deploy staff (ideas).

These may exist in a great many organizations, success being contingent on the capability of staff, quality of product, the capital to meet payroll, buildings, pay for product. Markets like armies move and alter, expand and contract, so we need to flex with the time and the market; each breakout unit responding as it senses the need. Merely "being there" is not what makes the difference. Getting results, selling the product, growing volume and profit is the plan. Caterpillar cancelled one dealer in 1944 and appointed another. Nine months later in June of 1945 they gave the franchise to my dad, who would operate in the same market with same competition, selling the same product line. We succeeded where two former distributors had failed. The criterion, of course, was leadership, not dollars. It is the repetitive motif of excellence displayed at each level and in each component that separates the professionals from the amateurs. It is how one uses ideas to meet the challenge, serve the customer. It's burying competition that distinguishes the winner from the wannabees. It is how best to conjoin the two components: dollars and ideas.

We exist in a culture which is moving. Reminding us of Eratosthenes who noted once that "we cannot step twice in the same stream". The current brings a continual volume of water, differing in each vertical inch from the previous, which I make analogous to the world in which we (tractor people) live. A moving current of change! From ten products in the line to 300; into the truck engine business for 45 years and then out; 15 years scurrying to break into the Ag business, then CAT ducks out. Perennial "leasers", we are suddenly thrust into the rent-to-rent market. Built the business on bulldozers, then look around to see it is now backhoe loaders, skid steers, hydraulic excavators, pavers and trucks. But in each new phase or product we had to elbow someone else out of the way to get in. Case and Deere owned the backhoe loader business and did not want us around. But we grunted and ground our way in so last year we were a larger player than either of them. These two giants also owned the farm market, and it is into their arena once again we made our foray, knowing no farmers and nothing about growing corn. This year our sales will be $35-40,000,000. Rental is a similar story only better. Up against a number of national rent houses like Hertz and Nations Rents and United et al, we opened a small store and made it work. Today, we have 10 rental locations, only because we took market from someone else to a point where we are a major factor — over a hundred million in rent-to-rent business this year.

None of this happens simply because we are a CAT dealer or because we are well financed or because this is an automatic pattern within our industry. Au contraire! It is not a "cake walk; it does occur because we had the capital available (money), but we succeeded only because we have greater innovation, a belief in our abilities, determination and better people. The key is wisdom and strategy, not the fact we have dollars available and in place. ■

Peace and Reconciliation

December 2008

We toured Central Europe in October to visit Napoleonic battlefields and in the course of traveling from Wagram to Leipzig (one a major "win" and the second a calamitous loss) had a chance to visit the city of Dresden. The guide took us on "the tour" through this most charming city and along the way stopped to comment on the Frauenkirche, a historic church, destroyed like most of the city in the British raids March 13 and 14, 1945. Strangely enough the building initially survived the bombardment, but two days <u>later</u>, proximate fires still burning in the city, ignited the roof which quickly burned and "did in" the basilica. Then long decades passed under Russian domination before the people of Dresden could turn attention to rebuilding their city and its venerable structures. But once they got going, found themselves abetted in the cause by a number of international groups organized to raise funds for Dresden's reconstruction. Among the buildings being resurrected was the Frauenkirche, just about finished after 10 years of effort, but still lacking two major components: the altar and a large golden cross. But not to worry, because citizens in far-off Bath (Britain), remembering Hitler's destruction of Coventry's 500-year old cathedral, were particularly sensitive to Dresden's tragic fate. They raised the funds to build an altar, fashioned as a replica of the old one and sent it as a gift to the citizens of Dresden.

But that's not all because the Brits followed with a second gift; one containing a large, 24-karat gilded gold tower <u>with cross</u> to finish the project. This was fabricated by Frank Smith...*whose son had flown a Lancaster bomber on the March 13th raid.* And now here's a gift supplying the sacred symbol of Christianity to the people of Dresden, provided by a man whose son had been a factor in the city's destruction. This is a neat story of one people who suffered enormously the reckless devastation of the Nazis, only to

extend the hand of kindness and compassion to an enemy counterpart because they understood thoroughly the scope of the Dresden tragedy. An inscription on the cross-and-turret declares it is a "symbol of peace and reconciliation".

We have to be struck with these acts of kindness and good-for-evil, for this humane and distinguishing decency. The element of expiation or penance evident here seemed highly religious and particularly moving. Reminding us that like these two gestures, the Christmas season and its spirit, transcend nationality, language, political difference, class and culture, inviting us to rejoice and demonstrate the generosity latent in the human spirit.

There was another lesson down the road.

Further in our peregrination was "Luther country", including Wartburg Castle, a massive and formidable stronghold, anchored high above the surrounding village and wooded countryside. Incidentally, the Frauenkirche just referenced was Lutheran in character with a huge statue of the Reformer standing solid in front of the entrance. That same Luther was able to complete his "reforming" <u>only</u> because of the courage and generosity of his sovereign, Frederick The Wise, Elector of the Holy Roman Empire and Ruler of Saxony. Luther (as I'm sure you remember) was an Augustinian monk, secured by Frederick to teach in his new university in Wittenberg. While immersing himself in wisdom, both biblical and theological, Luther began having serious questions about parts of the Roman Catholic doctrine or policy which had much to do with papal and "counciliar" directives but had little derivation in scriptural sources. Sent by the Elector on a mission to Rome, he was further repulsed by the avarice, hedonism and worldliness of the Roman clergy and returned, convinced that "something was rotten in the state of Denmark" (or more accurately

Luther's Door, Wittenberg

"in the city of Rome"). Then began compiling the areas of disagreement he found in contemporary practices, theology, authority or dicta he found "unbiblical". Ninety-five in number, they were assembled on a large sheet of parchment and posted on the public "bulletin board", i.e. the door of Wittenberg cathedral as an invitation to discuss or defend same. The date was October 31, 1517.

Since a lot of people were secretly wondering about the same things as Martin, by publicly identifying the problem areas, he triggered two reactions: One was an inadvertent challenge to the church, a "throwing down of the gauntlet" to justify itself; and secondly, an automatic linkage of the opposition defined now by issues in support of Luther's complaint. His motive was discussion, not revolt but nonetheless sides began forming up. The printing press made distribution of the material almost at once, thus, expanding the area of support and publicizing the topics. The Roman Church naturally looked on this upstart monk with disapprobation and called him persistently to recant his heresy. The struggle increased in tempo, moving to a council at Worms (1521) where Luther stood before the powers of both the Holy Roman Emperor (Charles V) and the Pope. After three days of debate and with no recanting on Luther's part, the council ended and the conveners went their separate ways. But Luther was a marked man, excommunicated by the Pope on one hand and marked for death by the Emperor on the other. During the scurry to depart Worms, Luther was abducted by his patron, Frederick, and secretly moved to Wartburg Castle where he spent the next 10 months incognito. Growing a beard he assumed the name "Junker (Squire) George", and while there translated the New Testament from Latin into German so thousands of his countrymen could now read the scriptures. So popular was the book and so dynamic the language that it had a lot to do with the formation of the modern German tongue.

When the furor died down and the church and state went off to meet other problems, Luther slipped back to Wittenberg and to the safety of his elector where he finished out his career as a teacher, preacher, theologian and a prolific pamphleteer, writing one tract after another (94 in all) as he defined his view of the Christian faith and how it should be practiced. (He also translated the Old Testament into German.) His central Christian thesis was taken from St. Paul declaring that we are not "saved" by what we do but by God's lavish grace freely ex-

tended to all, which made fasting, confession, sacred relics and indulgences all superfluous. He modified worship, wrote rules of conduct, liturgies, and even hymns; instructed, demonstrated and virtually created Lutheranism. His church had no pope; two sacraments rather than seven; no holy orders, confessions, fasting; no papal infallibility; no galaxy of male and female saints or celibate clergy, etc. His faith, his "priesthood of believers", swept through Germany and other parts of Europe, reducing the power of the papacy. Luther's break manifested itself in dozens of denominations and is still splitting away in our time with sundry groups interpreting scripture a different way and finding new missions and expressions.

The unique element in this story is the fact that Luther's prince, Frederick the Wise, never converted to Lutheranism; he protected Luther, employed him, let him teach and preach but remained a loyal Roman Catholic. Here was a ruler who saw injustice and exploitation unchallenged; papal profligacy unchecked; the sale of church offices; universal sexual misconduct; endless grubbing for money. He also saw one of his citizens threatened, truth suppressed, greed victorious, justice denied. Here was a church badly in need of reform, but failing to act. Frederick supported a heretic because he thought the heretic had "certain unalienable rights". He gave sanctuary to the enemy because he thought it was the Christian thing — the right thing — to do. Again, here is someone rising above caste and station and reaching out to help someone in need with no thought of reward. Frederick accorded Luther a sense of value and respect which the Roman Church denied. (Lest you think me over-harsh on said Catholic church, a wave of reform triggered by Ignatius of Loyola swept Catholicism shortly after Luther's rebellion, thus, responding to 95 thesis. The subsequent Roman Church was markedly different, cleansed from the papacy down to the remotest parish, abolishing simony, indulgences, mistresses, a dissolute papacy and Vatican military exploits.)

I have a penchant (probably learned from the clergy) of reading into situations the messages I want to find there. (Pastors read into a scriptural passage what they want to find. A practice called isogesis. It is a commonplace among fishermen, mediocre golfers, stock brokers and politicians.) The message read into my two Germanic illustrations is that decency, compassion and goodness are both individual and collective attributes (ala Frederick and the city of Bath). They are universal, therapeutic and consoling. They distinguish the species as indeed the highest order in the creation and on occasion demonstrate a kindness that is "a little lower than that of the angels". I had never heard of the "Dresden Trust" or "Friends of Dresden" but after the unspeakable brutality the Nazis thrust on Europe the 15 years they were in power, to have British citizens, pounded nightly by German raids on their helpless cities, form committees to help rebuild <u>any</u> German city is a remarkable gesture. To spend $210,000,000 restoring a German landmark like the Frauenkirche is a significant testimony to the capacity for good in the species. The capacity to forgive and to move on as though it didn't happen is not commonplace. Leaving the rehearsal of "what had been" and pushing forward to find good things we can do <u>now</u> is a commendable trait. What a marked departure from the human process that nurtures hatred until it is institutionalized, then passes it on from one generation to the next so evil continues to wax in the world eternally. This is still happening in tribal Africa, in the Balkans, in parts of Islam, Chechnya and Sri Lanka, etc. "Moving forward" is the better option; is the only practical hope. What is past has already been lived and cannot be redone. Omar Khayyam put it more eloquently:

"The moving finger writes, and having writ moves on; Nor all your piety nor wit can lure it back to cancel half a line; Or all your tears wash out a word of it".

Maybe it is easier for the ensuing generation, only vicariously experiencing a fire bombing, to avoid adopting or inculcating the initial bitterness held by those who were victims of same. Without vivid personal exposure to the carnage, perhaps one's passion is less inflamed, making it easier to say sententiously life goes on. But "therein lies the rub" as old Hamlet observed. We are indeed consigned to "play the hand we are dealt" but expect some to play it well and others to play it badly. And some sit on the sidelines like he who is "dummy" in bridge. Marcus Aurelius said it another way, "I shall see things as they are and deal with them as they deserve."

Both the citizens of Bath, those of the Frauenkirche Parish as well as Frederick the Wise, opted to not only be players in the game but to raise the engagement pattern to new levels of character and quality. Each had the ability to ignore a "go-with-the-crowd"; i.e. rehearsing the injustice as though it were a mantra and instead seek to do something both noble and unique. In the Elector's case, something courageous and forthright...focusing not on personal credit or glory but rather supporting a policy which was distinctive; "things that are just, are pure" and "of good report". Being selfless sort of fits in with Christmas-type editorials, heralding a season when all of us can join company with the above and think of ways in which each can make this a better, happier, more enjoyable or bounteous holiday for those around us. Better for others in need of sharing our joy or security and confidence. Hoping we can prove that the season is more about relationships than packages, more about peace in the world than about power or about sharing rather than possessing. ∎

CHAPTER 24

2009

A Cultural Contrast

Remember Ole Maimonides

Assumptions

A Cultural Contrast

April 2009

On June 5, 1967 the tenuous peace in Palestine was shattered when the Israel Air Force (threatened by an ominous and preponderant buildup of Egyptian strength across the western border) struck preemptively and with vehemence. For three hours they hammered Egyptian military targets and airfields, destroying 300 of Egypt's 450 aircraft and leaving the Egyptian war machine seriously impaired. Simultaneously, Israel's ground forces drove into the Sinai to attack the Egyptian positions, strongly fortified on three sides by minefields with the fourth side protected by an insurmountable sand bank. Which the attacking tank armada skillfully made "surmountable", breaking through the defenseless flank whose weaponry were all pointed the wrong way and headed for the Suez Canal while Jewish infantry moved in to consolidate the gains. The reports from the disheveled Egyptian commanders foolishly omitted the carnage in the air and suggested victory on the ground, so when the invading tank corps reached the next positions, the defenders were caught totally off guard. A shift occurred when Egypt recaptured Jiradi Pass in bitter, hand-to-hand fighting, but Israel countered by frontal assault with simultaneous flank attacks the defending army could not withstand. By the 8th of June, Israel was at the Suez Canal and concentrating on the main Egyptian

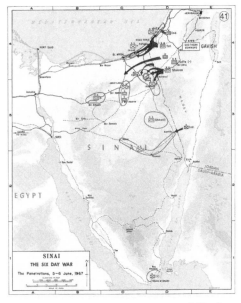

1967 Six Day War — Conquest of Sinai, June 5-6 *(Source: Wikimedia Commons.)*

force now enveloped in the Sinai while the Israel Air Force was wrecking havoc at will. The next day the Egyptians sued for peace.

The so-called Six Day War began with preponderant Arab strength, including attacks by Syria, Jordan and Egypt, committing up to 215,000 ground troops, 1770 tanks and 586 aircraft while the Israeli force consisted of 120,000 infantry, 1150 tanks and a mere 207 aircraft. What in the world went wrong?

Whatever it was, a reprise of the same scenario occurred October 6, 1973 when a devastating storm of fire and steel poured into (and over) the undermanned Israeli positions holding the east bank of the Suez Canal. The source was 1850 Egyptian artillery pieces, 1000 anti-tank weapons pouring 10,500 shells on the defenders, further enhanced by sorties from 250 aircraft who extended the devastation deeper into the Sinai. Behind this precursor was an advancing column of 100,000 field troops, supported by 1600 tanks, artillery and banks of rocket projectiles. (More surface to air missiles than were contained "in the entire United States arsenal".) Add to this avalanche, a separate thrust of 60,000 Syrian troops, 1440 tanks and 600 artillery pieces, attacking north on the Golan Heights. The Jews opposed on the south with a mere 18,000 men and 300 tanks. Conclude: The Israelis had trouble, big time! The Egyptian strategy was carefully planned and meticulously carried out, committed to avenge the disgraceful beating in the 1967 War and aimed now at smashing Israel into very small pieces. 80,000 troops attacked over 12 temporary bridges across the Suez Canal behind furious artillery barrages, replete with a fire-and-advance pattern that moved inexorably forward.

Three hundred Israeli tanks responded at 2:30 when Colonel Reshev counterattacked and got badly clobbered. At twilight two new tank brigades joined battle with equal lack of success, and by nightfall only 100 of the original tanks were left. Next day two more Israeli tank divisions <u>did</u> appear and in disjointed frontal attacks, again, got their comeuppance. Finally wising up, the Israelis changed tactics and began calling in their own artillery whose heavy and accurate barrages halted the pace of battle. Next, they sent tanks in, not frontally, but against the flanks and in the process disrupted the order of battle, compromising the entire offensive. Which means Egyptian commanders now had to modify their strategy to accommodate a new configuration. Beyond that, the defeat of Syria up north required continual pressure in the south, which Egypt supplied by committing its reserve of 800 new tanks. But now launched without a script or a cohesive plan, leaving to field commanders the options for battle.

But the fortunes of war were changing. Two hundred eighty-six of these reserve tanks were destroyed at once to Israel's loss of 46 (40 of which were back in battle the next day). This reverse further undermined the Egyptian strategy since the front was now askew and committing the reserves had left the Canal unprotected. Finding a gap between Egyptian forces, both Sharon and Colonel Adan drove their tank divisions west through the breach, crossed the Canal, cut the Egyptian supply line and positioned menacing assault threat in the rear. In the skies the Israel Air Force shot down 152 enemy fighters and harassed the tank forces with fire and bombs. Bottled up and being shot to pieces, the Egyptian Army was saved when the great powers organized a ceasefire and the Yom Kippur War was over. 505,000 Arab troops were beaten by 310,000 Israelis, despite the fact Arab tank superiority was 2-1; artillery dominance was almost 4-1. This was David and Goliath all over again and military students wondered "wot hoppen" and then "why".

The analysts have some unusual comments about Arabic armies in their war against the Jews. Beginning with the military leadership that was the product of Gamal Abdel Nasser, a Colonel in the Egyptian Army and architect of the coup détat which had successfully overthrown the monarchy and created a theocratic republic. When Nasser became the President of Egypt, the officers who helped in the revolt were given control of the military. But political allies do not assure tactical ability or skill in battle. Apply that principle up and down the ranks: We are long on political loyalty but woefully lacking in combat sagacity. Beyond that, the indifferent relationship between the sundry military services failed to assure cooperation between amour, infantry, artillery and air force so essential in combat. The "whole" needs to be greater than the sum of the parts, but here was only as strong as its weakest link. What dominated was rigid centralized command, which meant eternally sending requests up the line for directions. "The enemy is attacking, what do I do now?"

Beyond that, though they had superior weaponry, the technical (operational) skill of the average soldier was disappointing. Arab tankers were poor marksmen; Egyptian pilots in Soviet MiGs had the best aircraft but could not outsmart or outfly the Israelis; artillery was superior but not wisely commanded nor was the marksmanship acceptable. Moreover, equipment was poorly maintained so availability was low with planes and tanks in the shops waiting for repairs.

Behind all this was a subtle cultural influence arising from a strongly patriarchal society where one is told what to do. Individual initiative is less prized than we would find in Indiana, subordinate to family or tribal loyalty. This attitude hinders mixing random elements of the population so any sort of "bonding" or new loyalties, typical in our army, are rare. One driving motivator in the heat of battle is the commitment of the soldier who fights to <u>protect his buddies</u>. Lacking collegiality changes the attitude and effectiveness. Another curious element is Arabic pride; the need to avoid insult or shame, evident here when we get badly mauled but report "the engagement was a standoff and our soldiers fought bravely", providing a false circumstance for the commanders to deal with. In the 1967 War, the Egyptian Air Force was rubbed out by 11:00 AM, a fact command headquarters <u>did not learn</u> till 4:00 in the afternoon. This strange fear of defeat makes directing large, extended forces very difficult since accurate intelligence data is compromised or absent.

And last but not least was the inability of the individual sergeant or lieutenant or corporal to make decisions for his unit when there was no existing plan. Once the timetable got delayed and the action converted to a new exigency, commanders did not know to respond. Sharon said: "Egyptian soldiers are very good. They are simple and ignorant but strong and disciplined; and their officers are sh_t. They can fight only according to what was planned." The <u>conditions</u> themselves would tell the average American G.I. what needs to be done. Hell! He is right there and can see what he is up against or what opportunities he has to act, a capacity not evident in the Egyptian ranks.

I have suggested before that societies, institutions, organizations, even nations require two fundamental elements. One is structure, and the other is leadership. The Arab wars are classic examples of providing the structure in terms of a military organization and the 1973 War, enhanced with extensive, detailed and rehearsed plan of attack. A massive buildup of power overwhelmed all before it, supported with all the complex and extensive materiel of modern warfare…but lacking a commensurate governing, correcting leadership. And surely critical components of leadership are ingenuity, analysis, response, direction; the capacity to make change when needed. <u>Before</u> needed if possible. It is pointless to set up any enterprise in our society, like say a Caterpillar dealership and expect to run it totally on prearranged plans or policies or departmental objectives or budgets. Because within said plans or objectives or purposes are elements of competition or the customer or the factory, each operating on <u>its</u> own priorities and needs but <u>differ</u> and may be conflicting with mine. It is by responding to resistance or pressures or unforeseen circumstances that we get anything done. The capacity and ability to solve problems is exactly why we are here. When we remove that human capability (think "voicemail" for example), we cut out costs, deliver a cheaper product, may expedite the interchange, but too often we shift the need for ingenuity and "fixing" back to the purchaser. The "emptor" is then

rightly entitled to "<u>caveating</u>". No system is all inclusive, covers every problem. No machine or device functions like a thinking human brain; none is able to "track" second by second with unfolding shifts in the narrated problem. Only thing "chancy" about the human brain is deploying one incapable of solving the problem, but energetic enough to try any way and, thus, muck up the works.

I would suggest that most systems, families, churches, certainly dealerships, <u>create</u> operating procedures that allow – in fact <u>assume</u> – people working within them can make decisions and order the nature and direction of the action. Fact, they ought to be designed as that vehicle which <u>facilitates</u> the reaction of the human component. One would guess that having a bright person out where the action is and the problems occur is the ideal way to structure any efficient operation. We send 120 field servicemen out every day and have 186 more working in shops, each continually making decisions about where malfunctions or wear exist, how bad they are and what it takes to fix them. If our salesmen working with a customer can't figure how to make each sale beneficial to both parties, he doesn't understand his role. If one has to stand over tank commanders and draw pictures as to what needs to be done to a busted-up vehicle, because the driver doesn't know, then no wonder they are left in the field, inert and impotent. The lesson, of course, is that success lies with he who has the most intelligent and capable personnel, not simply he with the best utensils. The <u>pilot</u> is what makes the airplane effective, not some amour plate or degree of maneuverability!

To some extent, the capitalistic system in terms of a free enterprise republic is a training camp for honing human leadership skills because everyone who works for us is required to make judgments day-after-day and hour-after-hour; the effectiveness of which separates us from the Arabs. Systems like our government or the school room or the volunteer organization or the tractor works succeed in direct relation to

MacAllister Field Service at a quarry.

those in charge of directing and implementing them. Competition, whether in sports, politics or industry, keeps continual pressure to excel and to perfect, and in that process drives forward our continuing assurance of change in this technological age. The "change" meaning "facility" or "improvement" or "economy" or "production". Our own U.S. history has trudged along pretty happily through three and half centuries. When I appeared on the scene in 1918, half our population was located on America's farms, so in my lifetime we have seen the broadest, most complex, most dramatic change in the style of life ever invented by the species. We can wonder if it was <u>not</u> accelerated by three things. One was universal education, broad communication and the transformation which terminated our "patriarchal" period with white males dominating society and kids doing what they were told without questioning. We got sophisticated. We discovered that "father does <u>not</u> always know best", unless he is flexing with the change in the world around him, which a lot of fathers resist doing.

This is getting far too long but in parting, let's examine a final structure/leadership example impacting all of us: the body politic. Isn't it ironic that we provide the most unique governing system in the world, one "deriving just powers from the consent of the governed" and find ourselves awash today in problems so protean in range and size we are baffled by how to solve them? We are given a vehicle that equips us to manage human affairs in the fairest, most practical, effective, flexible and responsive way ever devised, and what do we do it? We recruit Arabic practitioners in to manage it; folks whose current approval rating is probably the worst of any institution functioning in the world today. 17% of the American people graded performance of our Congress "favorably". I'll bet Hamas has a better record than that. It is not the apparatus or the system that is at fault, it is legislators who are managing our affairs…who don't work to coordinate between the services (parties), substitute partisan loyalty for judgment (patriarchal obedience) and prove competence in pork barrel entitlements as demonstrative of leadership (leaving damaged tanks unrepaired). When one examines the 44 Presidents we have elected to highest office and examine character, capability and effectiveness in leading the nation, it almost appears as though we are afraid of strong men and women and want people of mediocre ability. (Think Peirce, Fillmore, Grant, Johnson, Hayes, Garfield, Taylor, Tyler, Harrison, Buchanan, Harding, Van Buren.) The survival of our experiment is due to more responsive action by state and city where leadership relates between parties but where problems have to be solved (garbage, snow removal, street maintenance, etc.). It isn't that this experiment is a large floperoo, it is rather considering what we have achieved in results compared to what we <u>might</u> have established with consistently good leadership directing our governance vehicles that becomes disappointing.

The bright side to our picture is living in a society whose endless interlocking political, religious, artistic and economic institutions provide and require enormous input from the human component. This gives any of us who wants to participate, multiple opportunities to make something good happen. Rotating governance refreshes the leadership, thus, the end product so the ethos or psyche of the community becomes a product of what "we, the people" make it. Our choice of leadership, or <u>performance</u> as leaders, arbitrates the nature of American society. ∎

Remember Ole Maimonides?

July 2009

Historians fix the timing for "The Middle Ages" from the collapse of the Roman Empire (technically 476 A.D.) till the end of the Italian Renaissance. (Lorenzo de Medici died in the same year Cristóbal Colón landed on St. Salvador.) A 1000 years of grim times, rightly termed "The Dark Ages". The feudal system resisted progress, ergo, Europe stayed locked in place for generations with brute force as the operative agent. Illiteracy was universal; diseases rampant; justice — if it existed — was local; warfare was intermittent; prejudice and barbarism governed conduct. Any glimmer of light that flickered from time to time came unsteadily from the Roman Church but also radiated sporadically from the Arabic world, largely through Spain while under Muslim control. This means philosophy, Roman engineering and Greek drama were transmitted by the Arabs; medicine, agriculture, the arts, horticulture, science, Cicero and Seneca, commerce and mathematics, Augustine and Boethius, were all salvaged by Islamic scholars. The role of Spain and Islam might be represented by noting that halfway through this depressing era (December 31, 1000 A.D.), the most outstanding city in Europe — maybe the world — was Cordova. Prospering under the rule of Moorish sultans, it was a model of enlightenment, heterogeneity, economic prosperity and advanced city planning. Included in that remarkable society was the assumption Muslims, Christians and Jews would get along amicably through mutual respect. Not all the time and not totally, but in comparison to the lot of Jews and Arabs in Britain, France or Germany, Cordova was Eden.

Scholarship flourishes better in stable, urban conditions than in the trackless forest of Germania, rebellions in the Byzantine Empire or the unstable chaos that was Europe, so it is no coincidence that the best minds develop and exert influence where tranquility and safety exist and knowledge is respected; its pursuit encouraged. No surprise then to find (after this lengthy prolegomenon) that out of the Jewish community of Cordova there appeared one "Maimonides" — Moses ben Maimon — (1135-1204) who would become the superior intellect of the age. He was an acknowledged student of the classics; a savant, philosopher and theologian; a merchant, writer, astronomer, mathematician, legalist, pharma-cist, and likewise physician to Salah ad-Din, the great Kurdish Sultan. Fluent in several languages, he was universally acknowledged as spokesman and leader of the Jews worldwide.

Since Maimonides' father was a judge and a learned man, he had his son carefully schooled, starting in Cordova. But in 1448 the Almohades conquered the area and made conversion to Islam <u>mandatory</u>, sending most Jews scurrying into exile; many to Fez in Morocco. It was in the local university there Maimonides gained most of his secular knowledge. A recognized prodigy, he wrote his first work at age 13 (a treatise on technical terms used in logic and metaphysics). Next, an essay on the calendar. Then at age 31, a landmark commentary on the Mishnah (repetition), a large compilation of Jewish oral law. Of major significance because his reorganization brought new clarity, wisdom and order to the rambling body of Jewish material, randomly produced over the eons. His restructuring and editing brought such coherence, it is the form in use today as "canonical authority and the most widely accepted codification of Talmudic Law". He is deemed one of "the foremost rabbinical arbiters and philosophers in all of Jewish history". Next, his "*13 Principles of Faith*" became part of the orthodox liturgy and are currently recited in Hebrew synagogues today. His "*Guide for the Perplexed*", harmonizing philosophy and religion influenced Albert the Great, Duns Scotus and Thomas Aquinas; was translated from Arabic to Hebrew, Latin and other European languages and "exerted a marked influence on the history of religious thought". His "Mishne Torah" (Torah revised), written in lucid Hebrew, provides again a brilliant, systemization of Jewish law and doctrine.

A respectful student of sacred writings, Maimonides was in practice "an intellectual". His faith, like his medicine or mathematics or astronomy, was understood on the basis of

Moses Maimonides,
portrait, 19th century
(Source: Wikimedia Commons.)

intense investigation, a search for proof, for facts. A phenomenon in a world where demons existed; vampires stalked victims; witches were burned; the devil was after my soul. His theology was a struggle <u>to understand</u> what it was he believed — or should believe — about justice, medications, Mosaic Law, the movement of the celestial bodies, authority of scripture, about God. In his world, the supreme expert on things biblical was <u>the scholar</u>, not the patriarch of the family, not the traditional sage or local prophet. Enlightened intellectuals became (in his mind) the arbiters of the faith. Which tells you how he would feel about Jerry Falwell or even Billy Graham or a hundred other TV evangelists whose recourse is having "faith in the faith"; and assuming the bible is as reliable as the calendar. Though it really proves to be baffling and confounding, contradictory, vague, inaccurate, platitudinous. (Simultaneously granting its beauty, wisdom, inspiring passages, promise and superb language.) Because it is perplexing at times, a good deal of Jewish sacred writings dealt not with only what was written, but what was <u>meant</u>. Filling in gaps. What does it mean to "keep the Sabbath holy"? Defining when "the Sabbath" begins and ends by the way. What makes something "holy"?

People in the tractor business probably ought to leave theological exegesis alone and attend to things they understand. And people who attempt to craft essays for corporate publications probably ought to get on with why they are writing a given piece and not take his readers tracking through North Africa in 1188 A.D. In that year Maimonides was in his prime, living just outside Cairo; and in that year Richard, the Lion-Hearted became King of Britain, Normandy and Aquitaine. Maybe the points to this article are illustrated through an analogy on these two men. Richard was a man of action, thriving on war, living in the saddle, and forever battering on someone's shield with a broad sword. Foremost European warrior of his day, leader in the Third Crusade, Conqueror of Cyprus, he was also one of the most inept monarchs to sit on the British throne. Richard died a warrior's death: from an infectious wound caused by a crossbow shaft lodged in his shoulder while besieging a Norman castle in 1199. Incidentally, it is rumored that earlier while besieging Acre in the Third Crusade, Maimonides had been called as a physician to attend and prescribe for Richard. Probably under the auspices of Salah addin, who would ultimately drive the Crusaders from the Holy Land. The irony in this discussion is the fact that almost everyone who reads this publication will know the immortal Richard, the Lion-Hearted; thank you, Sir Walter Scott and Hollywood producers. But very few of us can explain how England fared during his reign; describe his style of governing or why he is so universally famed. At the same time not one in 50 of us has ever heard of Maimonides, whose power of intellect had a major impact on Judaism, on religious thought, on pharmacy, medicine, and was of such import it has transcended history; became history. A modernist in a medieval world; one whose wisdom resonated through the eons.

We don't spend much time reading about Maimonides in the tractor world nor do we condition ourselves in philosophy, logic, mathematics and science the way my hero did … as though learning just for itself was a worthwhile endeavor. Our talismans here tend to be steel behemoths with buckets or blades or beds and tires ten feet tall. A vast array of assorted machines built to change the landscape of America and connect in ways not apparent to the realm of the sophist or the scholar. But if we are not inclined to abstraction or pedantry or the manipulation of thoughts, theories or ideas, it doesn't say we eschew things conceptual or hypothetical. Au contraire! It is a huge mistake to assume the only profound thinking these days occurs in the laboratory, the classrooms at MIT or the lectures at Princeton Seminary. Or that all brilliance, acuity and high IQ's are reserved for the sciences and humanities. An awful lot of substantive thinking goes on in the business world and, by the way, is proven more readily in terms of its validly than is the case in academe. Bill Gates was not just a tinkering inventor nor were Henry Ford and Thomas Alva Edison mere dilettantes. They were creators of new systems, new technologies and leading a virtual revolution, which took exhaustive forethought, experiment, planning and organization. Exactly like Darwin, Copernicus, Newton and Einstein.

A common mistake in the business world is to assume that bold and vigorous action is the key to success, using Richard, the Lion as the model. Labor omnia vincit! Power wins! When in fact the biggest mistake business people can make is plunging ahead with a new product or a new plant lacking adequate study, data, consideration and thought — ignoring Maimonides' recourse to proof, track record, evidence. Energy released without direction and balance is as good a course as any to suicide. A fellow dealer we heard of out west was slow in succumbing to Caterpillar's constant urging he get in the rental business. When he at long last acceded, used "a Richard, the Lion-Hearted approach": quick action. He bought five existing "mom and pop" rental stores. Viola! Just like that he was a factor in rent-to-rent business. But alas, not much of a factor. Not as long as he loses money. The objective of the investment — profits — eludes him. Ready! Fire! Aim! Only made three errors: wrong inventory, poor marketing, irresolute management.

Our government resorts to the same recourse. We see a huge problem, intricate and devastating (like the one we are in now), and the instantaneous response is to buy our way out. Money to is the resolution. Really weird because we don't know what caused this implosion or how it is best fixed. The money is supposed to have some magic power but, alas, money does <u>not</u> solve problems. <u>Ideas</u> provide solutions; give us new footing; lead to progress. <u>Thinking</u> resolves hang-ups and maladjustment, versus action for action's sake. So we believe there is little success in our business without planning, evaluating, executing, earning.

When Jay Swearingen opens a new rental store, he starts with a market survey of the proposed location and gets data on new commercial construction; the number of existing businesses; number of our customers close by; the locus and nature of the competition. When all this looks promising, finds the right location and cost to rent it; size of required inventory; nature of staff, and stacks these costs up against assumed revenue. It's Maimonides' investigation and search for the facts; get all the data impacting the proposal to see in advance what the results will be. Ready! Aim! Fire! There are immutable laws

governing the business community just as there is a cosmic rhythm in the progression of the seasons or phases of the moon, movement of the tides. Understanding them and working in conjunction with the flow is critical to success. It is fruitless to proceed without understanding the rules existing in the market place.

All of which has moved us toward the close of this discourse. The major contribution of my 12th Century Jewish hero was revising, editing and updating Jewish theological material. Both clarifying and modernizing it; keeping it relevant. Remembering Eratosthenes' observation that "One cannot step twice into the same stream." Meaning, each age has unique circumstances which ought to be considered as we determine our conduct, practice and responsibility. We must adapt style and practice that fit this day's pace, irrespective of how great it was 50 years ago. We'd like to think that like Maimonides we are not simply negotiating or finessing it but like he, become the agent of change itself. We expect a flow of innovation and response to new demands. Hope our people — especially managers — keep thinking about how to broaden our value to the owner, user and customer. We have to find new ways to vindicate and justify our role. And we do that <u>only</u> if we have people ruminating daily about how to do it better. I have used Chris Novotney as an example before; our salesman in Terre Haute who twenty years ago wanted a "presence" there. "Let me get an abandoned filling station where we can put in a couple of backhoes and maybe a small dozer. Just to see what happens." Today, Terre Haute is a full fledged branch, 16,800 square feet of building, seven acres of property, and 42 people working full time doing a bang-up job. As you read this, we are opening a new rental operation in Columbus, Indiana. Because Jay has discovered untapped potential there; found a market, ergo, future sales and the right number of surrounding communities to support the investment. The 12th time in ten

Terre Haute Rental store.

Columbus Rental store.

years we have had him respond when and where opportunity exits.

Another "value" was invented in our parts operation. <u>We</u> stock perhaps 40,000 different part numbers to service our customers and given the range of units delivered the last 64 years, it's a challenge to stay "inventory relevant". How to keep exactly what is needed daily in our shelves. We supply 80% of the stuff people want and get another 10% from the local depot. Ergo, 90% of the customer demand but that leaves 10% which we locate and ship within 48 hours. Getting those missing parts — or countless others ordered on the phone — to the user is expedited by a shuttle service that runs four trucks a day, sending parts to 15 branches and 30 drop boxes for customers to pick up. We can provide parts for a 20-year-old D7 tractor quicker than I can get a part for my two-year old Infiniti. Shuttle service saves days.

Technology has three purposes: understand something better; achieve with more facility; do something better. Our technological or practical improvements are sought and employed to be used in our business which is to provide accommodation to the end user. And if we keep thinking and planning, we are at this task forever. If we stop thinking in order to just continue <u>doing</u>, we are marching to our doom. ■

Assumptions

September 2009

I have been a fairly intense Presbyterian all my life, and from early on knew the biblical stories, the history of Moses, King David, Nehemiah or Pontius Pilate; learned the Christian doctrine; a jillion scripture passages. And 75 or 80 hymns. One of them being a reference bridge for this essay, a folksy tune that includes the phrases:

"Give me that old-time religion,

"It's good enough for me."

People in 1931 (the year I was confirmed) never thought there were both "old time" and a "contemporary" religion. We assumed there was one Christianity based on the biblical account, which was divinely inspired and deserving of the utmost reverence. Moreover, like Moses' Code it was apodictic. No arguments, no alteration. Which happened to fit the normal pattern of the age because in those days we didn't argue with our elders; no one argued with the minister. Between the two, they did a lot of our thinking for us and were also infallible, leaving no wiggle room for alternatives, deviation or originality. Incidentally, this pattern was by now 1600 years old. It hadn't changed because those who tried to do so, by asking serious, often sensible but heretical questions, ended up as martyrs. The papal response to dissidents was the inquisition which obviated any discussion. Recall the Docetists, Anabaptists, Albigensians, the Waldensians and remember the late-lamented John Hus, Michael Servetus, John Wycliffe, Tyndale; all executed by the church for challenging doctrine, creed, tenet or teaching.

But efforts to suppress the truth and disregard the human intellect began running out of steam during the Florentine Renaissance when the House of DeMedici rediscovered and circulated Greek and Roman literature; sponsored the first secular art; encouraged (under Lorenzo) intellectual-philosophic discussion; saw Petrarch and Dante convert literature from Latin to Italian so more folks could understand it. Add next the Enlightenment Period; then rise of nation states, the printing press, and we have forces too broad for the church to manage.

A perceptive challenge to the purpose, origin and historic accuracy of the scriptures themselves was posited by one Julius Wellhausen in the late 1800's, pointing to implausibility, impossibility and inconsistency of biblical content. If faith is to be based on a solid foundation, careful study of the Old Testament proved much of the text was derived from unsound footings. Like the crazy concept of original sin; Lot's wife as a pillar of salt; Moses walking 2,500,000 people through a wilderness and oasis for 40 years; the sun standing still at Ajalon. There was too much fable and fiction. The frequent contradictions, contraventions of natural law, the huge amounts of material borrowed from pagan sources and outrageous exaggeration were impossible to accept as historic. Metaphor had become history. Since Wellhausen's time, add universal education, including new insight about our universe and its origins, decline of the patriarchal hierarchy, television and computers, diminishing church influence. In short a society vastly altered; smarter and committed to critical thinking; meaning careful analysis, search for facts; conclusions based on reason. If the theological quest is for the truth, then "that old-time religion" along with its Garden of Eden is in jeopardy. The tales learned at my Mother's knee collapse in the presence of improved scholarship, advanced epigraphy, archaeology, anthropology, and countless bits of data derived from other cultures.

But tantalizing enough along with myth and legend there exists a remarkably accurate reflection of the cultures, religions, peoples and dynasties in the biblical text. The world in which the Old Testament unfolded did exist. So when we excavated Shechem, behold — a Bronze Age settlement appeared with a huge altar complex where Abraham may have actually offered a sacrifice when he first camped in Canaan. We know Bethel, Hebron, Ai, Beersheba, Hazor and Jerusalem were already old when he arrived. Huzzah! The bible is corroborated! But we still have that snake, chatting with Eve while holding an apple in its mouth; folks living 969 years (Methuselah); Noah floating around with a boat full of animals for 14 months; a burro conversing in Moabite with Balaam or a God who never stops verbally ordering his heroes around. In all this I'm not pitching out the bible. I'm wondering mostly about what the text means, or meant, not necessarily what the language says. Why the exaggerated head count, flights of quail, fiery chariots, revival from the dead?

Well, maybe understanding what the bible is; how it got here might help. When I was 12, the answer was simple. God himself (this was before woman's lib) was the author, and he delivered his messages to selected teachers and leaders. The divine instruction, thus, issued told an ancient people what to believe; how to live; to organize their community; to deal with the problems of life. But a new theory, however, says "au contraire". The bible really began as tribal legends: an ancient people telling "family" stories, rehearsing early peregrinations and glorifying heroes. These oral tribal anecdotes, cultic laws, social customs and religious rituals fashioned their culture and defined their uniqueness. Seven centuries after the first tales (patriarchs), the stories were finally written down (1000 B.C.); though the story and the writing continued on into the Third Century B.C. In the course of one revision, an editor introduced a remarkable innovation, i.e. deity represented by a single god ... in a world of polytheism this was shockingly unique. Monolatry graduated to monotheism and became a distinguishing, differentiating characteristic. Subsequent editors added stories from their time; others included poetry, wisdom and genealogy, law and biography. Looks like there is a lot of mankind — men — in this evolution and less of God than we thought. The product went through endless revisions, picked up a lot of local color, folklore, creeds and codes. In the process the editors (priests) defined the God; made the Hebrews a divinely select, superior group bound to the deity in covenant; crediting said God with the creation and ongoing management of at least the Canaanite universe. (In one of the biblical passages Jahweh warned Hebrew troops invading Moab; they were moving out of his protection because <u>that</u> territory belonged to Chemosh, the Moabite God.) These tribal tales and legends were converted into a religious document by claiming all previous history was divinely ordained; took a millennium to fashion and provided us a deity who evolved from history itself.

All this was my Sainted Mother's "old time religion" imparted by the Lutherans and then the Calvinists. She — <u>and</u> both denominations — ignored Dr. Wellhausen and the discussion he provoked. Fact, a lot of people today do so as well. My mother was scripturally, doctrinally, creedly, theologically and historically ignorant, and it never bothered her for a minute. Her faith would surmount it all. ("Nothing is right or wrong, but my thinking makes it so.") She

believed it all happened the way it was written, and went into heaven, consoled and reassured by what it promised. Hilda just "knew" she was saved. (Since I'm into aphorisms: "When ignorance is bliss, tis folly to be wise.") The question is: "Did what she believe make sense? Was it the truth? Did it get her to heaven? If it didn't, what do we substitute?"

The bible is also a book about God and appears to present two versions of said God, one in each "Testament". The Hebrews viewed him like the other gods of the ancient world, i.e. totally anthropomorphic ... sees, hears, talks, gets angry, pouts and is forever unhappy with his people. He is depicted on the ceiling of the Sistine Chapel as Moses (and Mother) probably envisioned him: a benevolent, majestic, muscular figure stretching out his hand to bring human life (Adam) into existence. Great art! But is this how we really got here? Not according to contemporary scholarship. Well then, how does one depict God? Right answer is: He can't! God is "undepictable". But since we cannot have a religion without considering a creator, we shrink him to fit within the scope of the human intellect. If <u>I</u> had to depict the deity, I would also use an illustration. Not from the Vatican but a photograph from the Hubble Telescope, one which captures the galvanic character and the protean phenomenon of the infinite.

Because our world is not 6,013 years old as the bible suggests through the "begettings" in Genesis, arriving at Bishop Usher's date. Our <u>planet</u> is really 4.5 <u>billion</u> years and is not the center of the universe but a miniscule speck in a cosmos 15,000,000,000 years old and so vast no human mind can conceive it. Even if he defines it. A billion <u>bodies</u> in our galaxy, a billion <u>galaxies</u> in the universe ... so far. Vastness, pressures, speeds, mass and heat; configurations ever-shifting and in motion are all simply inconceivable. It's a little hard for me to accept Michelangelo's (or Moses' or my Mother's) God in view of this overwhelming, prodigious, gargantuan cosmic display. A God who has no jurisdiction in Moab could hardly create the whirling spheres and the incomprehensible regions of space and bodies impossible to measure or count. To deny the reality of God, however, is to deny the fact that we are here and this planet exists. Cogito ergo sum! The problem lies in how we now envision, define, interpret and view a creator; then what is our relationship to it? How can I possibly relate to this spiraling nebula cart-wheeling across the vastness of space? The frustration in things theological is the need to accept given doctrinal principles without proof (hard for a rational mind); to deal with elements we can't explain; to believe without knowing for certain. A phenomenon called faith. Put to a test when we examine the vastness and complexity of the universe and now know how it got here (big bang). But have to answer the question, "Why?"

We aren't going to resolve or conclude these issues and surely you are wearied to death with this excursus, so let me carry the issue of beliefs or convictions or assumptions into the secular sphere where we resort continually without batting an eye to believing what is <u>perceived</u> or assumed. Conclusions also based on theory or probability rather than fact. We elected a President last November on what he proposed or promised, on what he was going to do, not on what he has done. We are spending trillions of dollars to resolve hypothecated economic conundrums, <u>assuming</u> this will "get our economy going". Now we sit back to see what happens; if anything. We examine existing economic data, come to conclusions, then invest our money (if we have any left to invest) in a given fund. The outcome never assured or guaranteed. A lot of actions are based on what might happen but unlike theology, definitive future results will occur, specific and measurable. At which point the accuracy of our judgment is determined. The results alter or confirm opinion.

The same dynamic is inevitable and essential in the business — even the primitive tractor world. Assumptions concerning utility, production, costs, etc. precede purchase, but these are more certain because they are supported by empirical evidence, by case histories, production studies, guaranteed maintenance figures, trade-in values. Reason based on fact supports their decision. Machine deployment on the job quickly verifies or rebuts original assumption data. Perceptions are partner first to expectations, then to results. He who buys a CAT loader <u>believes</u> it will run flawlessly for 10 years and load 60 trucks a day. It takes a nanosecond on the job to see if what was perceived becomes fait accompli. Becomes a fact. At which point it graduates from perception to realization. Meaning, my opinion was correct. I assumed properly.

The Caterpillar world is not a theological realm but as a dealer we inherit a universal legend — assumption — established worldwide, for 84 years now, which most people accept. It says: "Forget the hype. Look at the record. CAT is the choice of experts, proven by market dominance." This mantra will induce customers as long as our experience in the field continues to prove our reputation. But that premise has to be proven day after day in unit after unit and holds steady so far. We succeed only if we help the user benefit. That sounds like promotional "sloganing", like: "We aren't in business for the dollars but here to help the other guy." Which ironically enough has a biblical ring to it. Says our main objective is assure success to owners. We are altruistic like the Salvation Army or the Red Cross. If the statement has some truth, it doesn't deny self interest. No one makes money on poor operators or dummies going broke or contractors who don't know how. By providing implements, knowledge and services that assure him success means we also succeed; and do so each time he comes back.

This analogy is going to be a bit strained, but we had an "old time" style that arbitrated our actions in my father's day. It gave him success and made him the Caterpillar dealer. But 64 years later we have had to revamp, alter, expand and equip our company enormously; 20 times the number of employees he had; 50 times the debt; 30 times the number of products; bigtime foreign competition. Machine sophistication with its power steering, automatic transmissions, 10,000-hour warranties, computer-controlled systems, GPS capability and you name it, all constitute a revolution not only machinery but in productive efficiency. But directing all this is a small piece of "old time" management my dad used when everyone knew everyone else; mechanics were content to make 65 cents an hour; the shop hoist was an "A-frame" with a chain pulley. Health insurance was simple: The hospital sent the bill; the patient wrote a check. What hasn't changed is "that old-time" commitment or attitude adopted in a different time by a different group that made him unique. It included quality product, in-the-field service, fair dealing and professional integrity, parts availability and superior workmanship. If we are committed to succeed in this endeavor, we are obliged to stay current in technology and system and innovation but to retain our "old time" personal and professional values. It's important to stay true to the code, not because we are that pious but because of necessity. It is impossible to do business with people who do not trust us. If we "live by the book", we keep our customer base. We deal with them as friends, providing a peculiar expertise they can't supply; exist to solve their machinery problems. Our creed or doctrine is providing proof to our promise, delivering results to he who uses our services, maintaining consistent contact, anticipating problems. Working with and for the owner. ■

2010

LXV ANNI (65 Years)

July 2010

Since this issue commemorates our 65 years as the Caterpillar dealer for 68 of 92 counties in Indiana, forgive me if I take a moment to reminisce a bit. Though it will be a solitary exercise! Reminds me of a broken-down ex-pirate in one of Masefield's poems, idling on the docks of Bristol or Plymouth, remembering former adventures and buried chests of gold, observing ruefully, "I'm last alive that knows it, all the rest have gone their way." I'm not lounging aimlessly on a dock but also observe ruefully, am the last of a crew that unfurled the Caterpillar flag on Gale Street 65 years ago. Not only are my colleagues gone, all my competitors have departed. History can be a winnowing process whose results are best seen in retrospect, noting the detritus of failed or fallen enterprise only occasionally glimpsing the trophy of those who have survived. The obvious query at this juncture might be: "How's come you —and CAT—are still here?" The answer is more than "brilliant management from its three Managers" (E.W., myself and Chris). The answer is sundry.

Reason for early success would have been the Caterpillar line. My Dad had been an Allis Chalmers distributor, competing with CAT … and with International, Cletrac, Case, John Deere, Clark Michigan, Hough and LeTourneau et al. He succeeded so ably against all comers; CAT wanted him in their camp, so when invited to join, he seized the opportunity. Caterpillar provided unarguably the best potential. It was "the standard" — worldwide.

A supporting factor in this union was my Father's reputation, every bit as good as CATs, gained through selling skills and personal character. Fred Johnston told me that before E.W. came to Indiana, the hostility among local dealers was so vitriolic they refused to sit at the same table together. He had to approach each of them, one at a time before they buried the hatchet and created an Indiana chapter of AED to protect their mutual interests. This was a prickly environment with some unbridled and exuberant characters. Events like the Purdue Road School or the annual contractors' conventions were distinguished by dealer suites, amply supplied with a lively traffic in booze; while business meetings rarely assembled a quorum. Add hotel brawls; all night parties; "one more for the road"; each a talisman of the era, typical of boom times. When the war ended, an economic resurgence slowly took shape, buttressed by an enormous amount of building to meet a 14-year backlog. Contractors were now both busy and profitable, so our world, too, was good! We may have em-

MacAllister Tractor Co., 1941.
E.W. MacAllister (on right).

MacAllister MACHINERY CO., INC.

MacALLISTER

ployed the free-drinks program, but with moderation, reflecting E.W.'s personal discipline and sense of decorum. Contractors — like the rest of us — have to trust and respect the folks with whom they do business. Character is demonstrated in who we are and in all we do. The fact that no one ever questioned my Dad's ability, his fairness and honesty added immeasurably to the Caterpillar name.

Maybe the third aspect in our story was negotiating the dramatic change which followed a long period of economic desuetude induced by "The Great Depression" and then complicated by four years of war. Between them they had locked our economic engine into established, treadmill patterns. The war, e.g. froze wages and prices; it controlled and allocated all production; minimized real estate or highway construction. When the restraint fell off in the late '40s, a spontaneous resurgence occurred, marked by endless suburban housing projects, a new complex called the shopping mall, requiring new roads and streets; add new manufacturing plants and factories; new churches, schools and hospitals. Following this a spate of toll roads and water conservation projects which segued in the '60s into 20 years of interstate construction. By the early '80s, however, all the steam was gone, replaced by an eerie, uneasy calm. The large-scale, helter-skelter earthmoving binge was over. Meaning, sale of big dozers, scrapers and motor graders — our bread and butter — floundered. The humongous paradigm shift with its moribund market knocked all our competitors out of the box; one at a time. "What do we sell now?" was the question. How about selling what people are buying? Ironically, that new opportunity happened in machinery CAT did not invent or even make. The hottest selling unit in early earthmoving in the '40s and '50s has been the two-wheeled, rubber-tired tractor-scraper unit, invented by R.G. LeTourneau. It was 1951 before CAT came out with its version of the same machine, called a DW21. The first rubber-tired loaders were made by Hough and Clark; the hydraulic track-type loaders were introduced by International and Allis Chalmers. The hydraulic excavator, the loader backhoe, off-highway truck, the skid steer et al were designed and sold by competitors. Truth is CAT even lagged in building big tractors (D9, D10, D11).

The largest one was first produced by Allis Chalmers who dominated the coal market with its HD21.

The secret, however, is not making the first unit, it is making the best unit. CAT's concept of quality, long life, ease of operation, and the worldwide dealer support system allowed us to invade these markets already covered…and ultimately dominate them. But before the toll road and the interstate highway market ended (and our opportunity diminished by 50-60%), Caterpillar said, "Guys, we are going to add to our product line and give you a new customer base. It will include truck engines, small tractors, backhoe loaders, blacktopping, agriculture, landfill compaction, commercial construction, etc." And a new pressure to nudge us into the rental business as well… Ugh! During this 20-year transition process, we were grudgingly, reluctant participants. None of us was dying to get into the backhoe business. Case and Deere created and owned the market. The truck engine business was dominated by Cummins. CAT plunged into the Ag market which was totally different marketing to a brand new cliental. We did not get excited about a line of little tractors or dozers; were edgy about excavators and groaned when they said "paving products". The issue, however, is never "how easy is it to handle; or how popular". It is what brings in more customers, sells more units, and generates parts and service volume. The ability to change courses, to flex and explore (like it or not) is a major reason we have negotiated the swings in the U.S. economy. To prove how important flexibility is to survival, ask the five major competitors we had in 1980 … if you can find them.

Another causative spinoff from the Late Great War was a burst of experimentation, engineering, research and technology to build a war machine, much of which continues onto this day … unabated, unrestricted. Behold the age of technology. Its failure to stop is kind of a nuisance. One never has the latest computer, camera, cell phone, Blackberry …

CAT Skid Steer 259B

CAT Backhoe 432E

whatever … very long because a new one "just came out". The result was drastic impact in modification of dealer systems – for accounting, communication, inventorying, troubleshooting, market analysis, Six Sigma performance, etc. But not everyone in business is capable, or willing, or can afford to move from "parked" to "80 miles an hour" in nothing flat. Our way of accommodating change and taking advantage of technology was employing "This Generation Management". My Father thrived at the dawn of our industry and like a couple hundred peers remained fascinated with a business which was shaping, molding and building America. Most started in sales … at J.D. Adams or Galion or LeTourneau, Russell, or Bucyrus Erie, LaPlant Choate, etc. to become business owners. Operations were modest in size; were person-oriented and included tramping out onto the construction jobs, checking on repairs in the shop, collecting slow-pay customers. They survived the mistakes of the manufacturer and the parsimony of the buyer. The year I was President of AED (1972), this movement had ballooned (and maybe peaked) to around 2000 dealers in America; a wide ranging pattern of success vindicating the American dream. But inheriting a common weakness: self-satisfaction, pride in their achievement, loving their companies the way they had made them. They genuflected to the status quo. "If it ain't wrong, don't fix it.

Suicidal advice! Means "don't change what you have." Unhappily, the "status" is never "quo". Beneath there is movement and pressure. To presume a model which works great now, will be adequate forever is fantasy because more than product lines change. Economic conditions, people, management styles, the nature of facilities, the world of communication and record keeping are elements "in progress". All have to react and respond to new conditions, stimuli, challenges, opportunities. Let's deal as much with "what will be", as we manage "what is". My Father's generation had justifiable satisfaction in what each had created (not inherited). Their model was smaller organizations; were familial in nature nurturing a sense of fellowship, fraternity and informality. So it's the team which has brought us success. When we get so big

we don't know each other, the dynamic changes. The more computers or systems replaced people, the less attractive the business became. The more delegation required, the farther removed is the boss from the action. I have known dealers who finally retired because the fun was gone, and they were into the smaller line of machines, ERISA, the ubiquitous computer (which they did not trust or understand); Six Sigma, OSHA, equal opportunity employment, the rent-to-rent business, EPA, five-year installment purchases, 403 CAT models, etc. It's now beyond my control. Not what I expected.

The result of success is growth. The resolution to handling what is newer and larger is simple. Let people familiar with the style and requirements of the current period, refit the company, so it conforms to 1991 (when Chris took over) (or 2010) rather than 1945. Policies and practices from my era are often irrelevant and totally impractical today. This generation needs to be using the guidelines or models employed by this generation. I cannot imagine my Dad owning a computer much less turning it on to send someone an assignment from home. He did his business face-to-face. He'd have disdained the computer, would be embarrassed because he couldn't understand it, and did not have the patience to learn how to use it. He'd find his own way, sans computer. But his effectiveness would be limited as a result. The facility of using systems to get things done better by using fewer people is crucial in writing today's success story, and this ratcheting up never stops. Our first computer (1964) required a room as large as my office (18 x 18) and cost $700,000 today. I'm valiantly trying to use a new Blackberry which cost $300 and does more "stuff", more quickly than that whole room full of boxes. Today's generation with today's technology, idiom, standards and norms needs to be managing today's challenge, and the record indicates they find the same fascination with the business, the same satisfaction and same adventure my Father did.

A fourth element in our story is staffing: the systems and standards and reputation that recruits and deploys top notch people. Hiring was intuitive in 1945; job interviews were chat sessions where one

1972— P.E.'s first AED Leadership Award.

maybe learned a third of what he needed to know about a job applicant. Why? Because managers never learned how to interview. It was assumed anyone can do it. They can. But to do it right requires planning and technique. Beyond that there were no job descriptions or departmental objectives back then. We didn't need them. We were selling dozers and making money, why worry? To start scrambling when market share or total sales sag, is too late (called "tail gunner management"). I learned "interviewing" from AED and realized to do it well required preparation; knowing what the job demanded; see if the experience or qualities the applicant had, dovetailed with what we needed. Then wondered about personal traits: hobbies, judgment, taste (newspapers, books), or favorite heroes, temperament, former employment; leadership roles in high school, college, church, etc. It's hard to blame an employee for his/her failure. The fault lies with the people who hired him/her and their lack of care in assuring this arrangement would fit. Chris carries this even farther. Major management applicants are interviewed by two other people and given a three-hour psychological test, which indicates whether this will work or not. Invaluable!

There is also the flip side to hiring and that is… firing. I remember my Dad's crew and what a neat bunch of people they were — faithful, dedicated, affable and cooperative, servicing a limited product line. But unhappily, marginally competent. I got a $5,000 bonus (double my salary) in 1946 (to buy more stock) when my Dad hadn't seen a financial statement for three months. The shop foreman was a wonderful guy and a fabulous mechanic, well respected by his guys but never heard of a "budget" or built one. With an eighth grade education, he would talk to CAT about fixing D7's or motor graders, but didn't talk long about a training program, initiatives to gain new business, long-range objectives or measuring performance in his own shop. Managing what he had (fixing) was done well; planning for excellence or future expansion was out of the question. Results are more important than congenial temperament. My guess is E.W. considered his affection for George more important than having the most efficient service operation possible. Again, we had a good reputation for repairing tractors. No sweat! But "today" is not forever. We do not achieve optimum proficiency with no defined job criteria or do super work with mediocre employees, no matter how loyal or well meaning. My Dad's weakness, and that of my brother, was their inability to fire anybody. Who likes the idea? Right! No one. But is it important and essential? Absolutely! Separating people who are not going to grow and excel is part of the package. The

P.E. and Chris MacAllister 2005, MacAllister Machinery Co.'s 60th anniversary.

manager today who allows marginal productivity puts himself in jeopardy, as well as a worker who can't deliver.

This infers that success is the reward for wiser management from smarter people — from more planning, more luck and more ingenuity than tending the status quo. We currently employ some 731 people and have six branches plus 15 rental outlets. There was no way of reaching this size with the organizational structure of 1945 or 1955. Can you imagine operating today with manual typewriters and yellow-page carbons; duplication via the mimeograph; pen and ink accounting ledgers; managers with high school diplomas; service truck is the trunk of your car; part orders to CAT once a week; all communication by mail, phone or face to face? The size and complexity, the variant of products, the number of customers, the correlation of branches and divisions all demand systems, protocol, structure and supervision directed by the best managers and people we can find. It takes far more intelligence, deployment of sophisticated systems, communication and continual fine-tuning than I ever had to contemplate or my Father could imagine. The objective isn't "status quo", but rather "What's next?" Although this is mostly about us, the reasons for the progress has to do mostly with the customer. The more ways we can help him in the management of his machinery fleet to minimize downtime, make machines more productive and give him the range of machinery options, the more he likes doing business here. Good service is not altruism, it's long-range security.

In closing this personal soliloquy, the past 65 years have been somewhat of an adventure. What the three managers had during this three-generation odyssey was never a lead pipe cinch. What each had was an opportunity, which if properly managed would lead to success. Caterpillar has allowed us to run our own show in such a fashion it delivers acceptable results, and each of us has known the contract provides the opportunity but it is contingent upon performance above and beyond that produced by our competitors. How we have performed has been different in each generation, and Chris' task now is to prepare the fourth MacAllister President with that knowledge, staffing, facilities, motivation and excitement to be equally fortunate and competent when his turn comes. ■

Product Differences

July 2010

The change in Caterpillar machines themselves the past 65 years has probably been as revolutionary as our changes in communication or air travel or auto design or the way we market groceries or gain our news. We began with three crawler tractors, three motor graders and two rubber tired tractor-scrapers (which almost no one wanted to buy). (They were four wheel units and not as agile as competition, though they lasted four times longer.) Crawler tractors were designed with transmissions similar to automobiles; meaning, three speeds forward and one in reverse with the facility to shift into any of the modes contingent upon need at the moment. They were steered by recourse to two levers, called steering clutches; one right and the other on the left. By pulling back the right lever, the operator disconnected power from the right track. Since the left track continued to function, it moved the left side around the powerless right track which was held more firm by applying the brake. Dozing all day, often a back and forward motion, meant hauling back one lever after another with each pass, an ongoing ceaseless exercise, developing enormous "abs" and "pecs". It was physical work. In contrast with today, our crawler tractors have automatic transmissions. No shifting. With hydro-steer capability and finger-tip control. (Ergo, no muscle building here.)

Augment this with GPS capability and it means the dozer now can utilize satellite control, giving it the capacity to establish the depth of the dozer blade so the cutting to grade is made on one pass, improving efficiency about 80%, cutting costs enormously and completing jobs much more quickly.

- The larger CAT models also are driven with a new principle called "high drive". Raised sprocket to keep the drive train in line and get it out of the mud.

- Motor graders now — seven — in number, once required recourse to eleven different levers to fully operate. Current models use two.

- CAT track type loaders called "Traxcavators" were mechanically operated with pulley and winch, raising the bucket up and down in a given fixed channel. It had no flexibility aside from moving the tractor itself. Clumsy, slow, poor visibility but able to run forever. Today, most loaders are rubber tired, with the agility of a bicycle. Easy to run, hydraulically operated buckets, ability to back drag; five different sizes (versus two in 1945) and again with finger-tip control. Enormously more maneuverable and versatile.

- A major design change was the method used to start a Caterpillar diesel engine. In the early years, we got it going though recourse to a "starting engine" ("a pony motor") mounted on the back of the diesel, which we cranked by hand to fire up, then engaged it with a flywheel which turned over the big diesel and induced it to fire. It took a long time before we came up with battery and direct start, but we finally made it.

- Bulldozers on larger tractors were all cable-operated attachments. Meaning a winch of sorts, front or back, with one end of cable attached to the blade, the other to a winch. The dozer blade was raised or

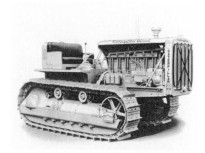

The Sixty Crawler Tractor was one of the first Caterpillar machines to be diesel-powered. It weighed 19,000 pounds and produced 50 drawbar horsepower.

The RD8, with 95 horsepower was introduced in 1935. Later the "R" was dropped and it became the famous D8. It reigned as power leader in the product family for 20 years.

One of the newer D8 models-it has more than three times the power of the original D8 and continues as a standard for earthmoving machines around the world.

lowered through winding or unwinding the winch. CAT's reason for cable was the fact it worked okay and hydraulics were not adequate enough to provide more efficient operation, despite the fact our competitors all used them. The element of productivity between the two systems was very small but ultimately better hydraulic pumps and larger pressures made the cable dozer obsolete.

- The advent of the hydraulic excavator and its increasing popularity is a major factor in today's market. In 1945 we handled Northwest shovels and draglines and maybe sold two a year. Cable operated; they ran forever but were limited in scope and versatility. Today, we have something like 25 models of hydraulic excavators, maybe most popular of products we handle (in terms of unit deliveries) because of their capacity and flexibility; a fact which probably changed the way contractors operate.

- The explosion of the line itself is the major revolution. We have added skid steer loaders, integrated tool carriers, a jillion excavators, the D3, D5, D9, D10 and D11 tractors, landfill compactors, wheel dozers, wheeled scrapers, articulated trucks, off-highway trucks (nine of them mostly for mining and quarry work), wheel loaders and skidders, feller bunchers (logging), soil compactors, asphalt paving equipment, asphalt compactors, cold planners and rotary mixers.

- We began with five salesmen; each guy with a large sales kit and each guy sold the complete CAT line plus Cedar Rapid Gravel Plants, Case Industrial Tractors and Mowers (but not very many), Chicago Pneumatic Compressors and Tools (not many of these either), the Northwest Crane and Shovel line, plus CAT's line of machines and engines. A good salesman had a lot to learn. He still does, but we have found specialists in given fields more effective. So there is a group selling Ag products; we have a crackerjack coal salesman; another who specializes in asphalt and paving stuff; some who sell the small line of equipment. We have our own engine section with its salesmen, and we have three or four guys who do used machinery.

- We used to pay salesmen on commission, i.e. they got 25% or 30% of the profit on the deal, ultimately that moved to a salary plus commission and expenses. Today, we do not pay a commission per sale, but our people are compensated on certain criteria and basically on the profitability of the company.

- Our markets are essentially the same as they were in 1945, broadened by adding different and newer lines (asphalt equipment or skid steers or hydraulic excavators). In 1945 markets were coal, construction, some public body, real estate development, an occasional landfill, aggregate, scrap yards, and a lot of pond construction and reclaiming of farm land; the latter two missing in today's scene. ∎

MacAllister salesteam at State Fair, 1947.
P.E. on left end and E.W. in the center.

MacAllister sales team, 2005.

Differences "Administrative"

July 2010

Since the theme for this issue is "65 years and still going", this issue looks back at where we have been and notes changes which we identify as elements of progress. Here are some random opinions of a general nature:

- Relationship with CAT in 1945 was maintained by only two Reps. One, the Service Rep, whose job was monitoring dealer performance in maintaining and repairing Caterpillar machines. Can we assure owners that we have an adequate shop and a qualified crew of mechanics to meet the need imposed by the product line? Another function and the most onerous was approving our warranty claims. The Rep had the final say on whether a given problem was indeed faulty in design or manufacture and if so, we were responsible for getting it fixed, and CAT for reimbursing our cost. The stickler here was a faulty machine was dealt with today, but we waited weeks after the decision on reimbursement. The Service Rep should understand field conditions, machine application, repair process, nature and character of CAT's products; where mechanical problems are showing up, etc. The weakness invariably being whether or not a given Rep knows enough about product problems, from his factory indoctrination and proving ground experience to make the right judgment in machine failure occurring both normally or in an application he hasn't seen before. Does he know as much as our guys? Will he make decisions based on fact or will he protect CAT?

- The second CAT figure was simply the Dealer Rep, or maybe Sales Rep, since he watched the rest of the operation and worked primarily with my Dad. The one I recall best was Winn Foster, an Illinois graduate, attractive, urbane, sharp, neat wife, and serious about this work and his dealers. One of his missions with us was sales force efficacy and in due course when I became Promotion Manager, worked with him not only on ordering endless direct mail pieces from CAT for separate markets and on special models, but ended up as well putting in a "Sales Control System". This was the sort of program that looked good in theory to those kibitzing sales coverage, and became mandatory. It required a fair amount of time to manage and ultimately proved of very little benefit. Every salesman had to write a call report on every sales call and send same into the office. My Dad had five salesmen and if each made four or five calls a day, he was reading 110 reports a week. Most salesmen hated the idea; did it because they had to, and I ended up recording the data. It did indicate a pattern of calls and did record a degree of salesman activity. Then it got so detailed, it began telling salesmen when to get back and see if customer "X" was "ready to trade by now". Come on! If you have salesmen who don't know when to ask for the order, no system in the world will fix that. We "sales reported" for years; found little or no tangible benefit and one day, unobtrusively, it quietly departed and never reappeared. Secret for successful sales force is having people smart

CAT carries over 400 models today.

enough to know who to call on, why and when. Machine orders, not an internal reporting system, reflect sales department success. Major challenge with CAT Reps, then and now, is understanding the nature of the dealer's market, the extent of the product line, the style and caliber of the dealer, competitive pressure and how he/she, (or CAT) can prove helpful.

- Biggest difference between then and now is selling a product line 30 times larger today than when we started. Add to that the fact that CAT carried the inventory in 1945-50. Peoria is only a half day away. Today, however, with a huge line of product it's the dealer who loads up. An obligation that means $100,000,000; more now than was needed then.

- Factory "support" programs these days are multitudinous; did not exist in 1945.

- Competition more intense because product differentiation which moved us into new markets where competition has been long established meant playing a lot of catch up. Selling telescopic booms or skid steers when competitors have been successful for years is dealing with new users who never heard of us.

- Competitive product quality is infinitely better than 1945 and, thus, our "edge" considerably smaller. Productivity, machine life, resale value, design features remain superior, but foreign manufacturers have increased product reliability and operation features.

- Conclude that it costs infinitely more — more capital, mostly borrowed — to run a dealership today, doing infinitely larger volumes. Pretax profits as a percent of sales, incidentally, are about the same.

- The first three decades we "owned" most of the parts and service business. Today, other people sell "will fit" parts, do major rebuild service. To pre-empt that, we now have 12 guys out there selling CAT parts and MacAllister service, monitoring countless fleets, advising owners on how to manage repairs…when to change or rebuild tracks, to rebuild "what" in an engine, to overhaul transmissions or hydraulics. Oil sampling is sort of the model. We take a sample each 250 hours that tells us by metal particles in the oils which components are wearing and the degree of wear. We can predict calamity and warn the owner when it's time to repair before failure. Point here is we find a lot more other-than-CAT parts out there, and there is a growing threat from people who want our repair business as well. We have no problem competing to earn business, but need to encourage our customers to include machine life and production, maintenance and repair costs as part of our competitive advantage by ignoring the true cost per hour or ton. One fails to consider factual reality. Up front savings are illusory; misreading costs may lead to unfortunate consequences.

- Initially, our customer base was 98% local; today with the concept of consolidated national accounts, mergers and acquisitions, a heck of a lot of our volume comes from people with operations here but headquarters elsewhere making for more competition and tougher bargaining.

- In 1945 the CAT product was pretty much "CAT"; meaning, they manufactured the engine, gears, hydraulic systems, dozers, tracks, etc. But for reasons of their own, today there are far more suppliers, building parts and components to CAT specs, so close quality control is more difficult.

- Government regulations and the "Green Movement" have adversely effected machine design. OSHA (1969) required that all of our machines be provided with rollover protective structures which means an indestructible cab wit each machine, adding to cost and also impacting

Doug Clark,
Vice President
of Operations

Jim Bernhardt,
Power Systems
General Manager

Dan Dayton,
Heavy Equipment
Manager

Jay Swearingen,
Rental Store/Light
Equipment Manager

Jay Shininger,
Ag Manager

design. (I testified in Congress when the OSHA bill was debated and learned more people died from bee stings or lightening than by machines rolling over on them. Even when it happened, it was mostly operator error; no one can prevent human stupidity.)

- Add to this the redesign of engines to minimize contaminating exhaust, a continuing process until one day any exhaust will be illegal. But constant diddling with engines adds considerably to the cost of the engine. The imminent modification is called "Tier Four" and means a 30% increase in cost to build. To prove what?

- We have fewer machine owners today than in the '40s and '50s when the state was boasting a jillion small contractors doing land clearing for farms, tiling, subdivision work, water conservation (ponds). There were also a dozen coal companies in 1945 and twice as many highway contractors. If we keep a customer "base" numerically, it is because we have added product to the line and found new owners: blacktop pavers, sewer people, hydraulic excavators, farmers, landscapers, golf courses, etc.

- CAT has long been represented overseas and manufactured machines abroad but has multiplied that aspect wondrously and given cheap labor costs and growing markets "over there", the pattern will probably continue.

- We don't rebuild as much of the machine as we used to … starting engines, cable control units, cylinder heads, starters, alternators, water pumps, compressors, etc.

- Major change, of course, is in the production and deployment of the computer in everything we do, which adds speed to the process, accuracy, clarity, dissemination of data; the ability for a given employee to do infinitely more.

- In terms of CAT "Reps" factory people who call on us, we are covered from hell to breakfast. As of today, we have 14 different people each trying to understand us and figure out how they can help. How they think they can help. In 1945 we had two. As an aside, Doug says the group today might be the brightest Reps we ever had.

- Quicker results. It took two weeks of manual effort to take off our monthly operating statement. Now it is four or five days.

- From one location to 16 as of now, keeping a presence closer to customers.

- Ten models then — 403 CAT models alone today.

Lest this go on forever, let me close with two more "differences". The first is the dominant role played by "systems", "instruments", "devices" et al which were once performed by individuals, persons. The computer is the obvious example since it is the most widely used and the most versatile in terms of performing given functions. It assembles data, does our parts ordering, does our accounting, provides status and updates, all a fingertip away; supplies statistical data to the salesman, serviceman, renter, switchboard operator, dispatcher, you name it. Our Rental Manager — and each of his stores — knows everyday the percent of utilization of each rental fleet — 4500 pieces. Gives the ability to move units between stores and put idle units in Muncie to work at Fort Wayne or Richmond instead of buying new units. This dynamic would be impossible without the computer, though it has become virtually indispensable, it has minimized personal contact; reduced the human input in most functions or actions. And contains a striking weakness: computers cannot reason so they cannot totally replace the person. I remember Martin Yager, our salesman at Fort Wayne 15 years ago, resisting voicemail. For a very logical reason: When a customer calls us, he expects to talk to a person; he wants someone to give him an answer dealing with his problem. He does not want someone "to get back with him" or redirect the call nor does he want to punch four buttons looking for a MacAllister human voice. He is seeking our wisdom and judgment or services. Of course, Martin held the fort as long as he was there, but when he left, we got computerized. But Martin had a point. We have done more things, more accurately and quicker, but has minimized human involvement, i.e. the personal touch that had been there before. Systems only partially replace people. I illustrate with an example while dealing with a local bank … where I have banked for a very long time. Said bank accommodates us with enormous capital to run our business, and they are very efficient, moreover, their people obey the rules.

I lost my wallet in January and with it all my credit cards. But I had a $700 check in my pocket-secretary and uneasy about walking around with no money, I stopped into my friendly banker to cash the check. I explained my dilemma: My credit cards and driver's license are gone. "Since I have been dealing with you-all for 40 years, since we put a million and a half dollars a day in your bank, how about cashing my check?" "Well, we need to have some identification". "I thought I explained that." We called the manager. He has rules too. He says, "Oh, I know who you are … but I have to see some identification." Hello! I can't believe this. No one wants to eliminate computers, but this tendency to eliminate personal judgment and resort to irrefragable abstraction is missing the point. The computer is to help us make decisions not preempt us. Our automation has its disadvantages. Computers cannot function beyond what they are programmed to do. Maybe some people are the same.

The closing difference is minimization of the impact made by the strong figure at the center as the power, the decisions, the controls and directions extend downward and outward. My Dad was the 500 pound parrot. The company was a reflection of "Mr. Mac". All departments did things the way he would have done them. He made the major decisions and the managers became lieutenants, carrying out his orders. It worked perfectly. He earned the CAT

Chris MacAllister, President and COO, 2010.

dealership. The style works great for the modest-size business but it becomes inhibiting and restricting when expansion occurs. Fact, it's our people who grow and expand the company through their efforts and ideas. The guy at the top ought to provide an opportunity for wider input and better ways to do more things.

In today's operations, the style and character of its President is pretty well understood and his objectives clear. The various departments operate within the guidelines which have been worked out. Understanding the company is not the product of one person but rather of 731 people. They are singing from the same hymnal, thanks to Doug Clark who directs the choir. Our rent-to-rent operation, one of the two or three best in the country is the product of Jay Swearingen. No way any of us on staff could have set up the system he is using. Our Engine Power Division reflects the management and intellect of Jim Bernhardt and has done so since he came aboard in 1980. Our Sales management is the model reconfigured by Dan Dayton; the Fort Wayne store is the product of Dennis Fawcett; and our Agricultural effort the brainchild of Jay Shininger. In each case the given manager has taken on an assignment in an existing entity and reshaped it in such a way it clicks like clockwork and is successful by all the existing performance criteria…market share, dollar volume profits, customer satisfaction and Caterpillar rating. Each manager and department are given components, defining the character of the company. It is their leadership, not that of the boss, that sets us apart and their expertise we count on to grow. ∎

Differences In Our Service Department

July 2010

Maybe an analogy to demonstrate the degree of change in our service operation will be to compare the mechanic's salary of 1945 with that of today and suggest the range of difference replicates the degree to which the operation has changed. When I came aboard in 1945, we still had wage and price controls. The top pay for a good mechanic was 65 cents an hour. But he got time and a half … almost a buck an hour … for overtime! Today, a qualified mechanic earns around $26 an hour. Purchasing power of the dollar makes comparisons difficult to compute but you can see there's an enormous disparity.

- Vehicles for a field serviceman changed a lot as well. "Then" it was the trunk of his automobile. Today's top-notch vehicle runs $80,000 with the larger ones costing maybe $120,000. Each is equipped with automatic hoist, with cutting torch, a compressor, maybe a welder or a generator, assorted lights, drawers and compartments for personal and special tools.

- In the shop our lifting or hoisting equipment began with an A-frame supporting a chain pulley; today, it's an overhead crane, electronically operated.

- Means for testing an engine or transmission overhaul in 1945 was to put either or both back into the machine and crank it up. Today, each is run on a dynamometer or test bench before reinstalling.

- To order parts for a shop job, one pulled out a parts book and went through the pieces he was replacing, then wrote up an order and sent it to the parts department. We graduated from parts book to microfiche, and today it has advanced to the computer. The mechanic sorts through the pictures and diagrams on his screen, selects parts number and orders parts directly, delivered to his job.

- Early on, a given mechanic could work on anything CAT made. He carried the tools he needed along in his car or truck (later on). If it were in the field today, there are so many different units, he checks the book and finds the tools he needs and takes those with him.

- A mechanic assigned to overhaul a tractor in 1945 went through each component one at a time and rebuilt the whole bloody thing. Today, we are specialized so that a torque converter comes out and goes to the converter bench; the engine goes to an engine rebuilder; the hydraulics to that expert, etc.

MacAllister service trucks in 1951 …

and the MacAllister service trucks today!

- Today, given the componentized nature of the machines, the component comes off and we pop an "exchange", sending the failed one to be rebuilt and then placed in the exchange inventory, saving days of time.

- Communication from the field originally came by finding a pay phone and calling in. Then we went to a truck radio. Today, it is by cell phone from the job.

- Each serviceman has a computer, which can be hooked up to one in the office where specialists can work with the field mechanic and see what he is looking in terms of malfunction on the given machine's computer screen.

- Troubleshooting originally was completed by listening, feeling, examining and a bit of luck. Today, a serviceman normally starts on a faulty unit, plugging said computer into the machine, and reads a string of data that informs him as to what might be going on. Sort of like the new dashboard in my car when a light pops on to tell me my rear tires are low, trunk is open or I need washer fluid.

- Service invoicing has also changed. It started early on with a work order, written up by the mechanic or foreman; then parts orders written up on a form and sent to parts, supplanted ultimately by the appropriate labor charges for the time spent by the mechanic. Same fundamentals except the field mechanic is dispatched by a central dispatcher, his assignment defined by a 'job writer"; the parts and labor hours recorded on the computer and the all pertinent detail then assembled into an invoice created by the service people.

Part of our obligation goes beyond fixing machines but working with the owner to get maximum production and performance from his machines. Our PSSRs help with that based on data collected and analyzed. They advise how to minimize downtime through a concept called preventative maintenance, managing the machine so it provides the utmost availability. Aided considerably by the computer once again. The new motor grader coming off the line today will have eleven computers on it collecting data, which will provide a history of the machine. It will record how many times the machine has over-heated, the number of times it has been shifted into reverse, the number of revolutions the crankshaft has made, the number of hours used, the number of miles traveled, etc. Knowing wear patterns, and wear-out points, we can estimate when to repair, i.e. when an engine needs rebuilding, transmissions are about to collapse, hydraulic systems need overhaul and proceed to react on the basis of that data.

This is far from a thorough account of the differences between the two periods, written by someone who can just barely change a light bulb but indicates, hopefully, that like the rest of the operation and like the industry, there is continual improvement and perpetual movement, all aimed at increased efficiency and, thus, increased productivity and profitability as well. ■

Parts Department Changes

July 2010

When my Father invited me to come to work for him in his new Caterpillar dealership (May of 1945), we discussed the nature of my employment (meaning he talked, I listened). I had a B.A. Degree from Carroll College and was still a Captain in the Air Corps where I had managed a crew of 45 guys for the past 40 months, taking care of the Armament Section of a Fighter Squadron. Not a lot of tractor experience but maybe some potential. Dad pointed out that I could start either at the top of the ladder or the bottom. In each case I had only one way to go in my career path. So he thought starting at the bottom was the best choice. "You will start working for Lee Henderson in the Parts Department" to which I responded, "Yes sir" and that was that. My claim to fame lies in being the only college-educated, stockchaser in a dealer parts department, in the state of Indiana. Maybe in the world.

Coincidentally, the three summers I was in college I had worked for Drott Tractor Company as … guess what … a stock chaser in the parts department. Putting parts in bins, filling orders for customers or service people by pulling parts from the same bins … packing and shipping orders each day, running to the factory to pick up parts. Not a complicated assignment.

Our inventories were managed in those days through a cardex system; each part we stocked had a card which fitted in a file drawer in a file cabinet, maybe 30 cards in single panel. They overlapped so all the part numbers were visible along with a description: 4A 233 … Fuel Filter … Bin 234; Rack A12…; Min 4 Max 16. The cards told what it was, where it was located in the warehouse and what the minimum and maximum numbers were. The CAT inventory control system is based upon historic usage. The rule being to stock a four-month supply of a given commodity (in my above illustration that is "16"). Each time we sell a part, we change the balance in the bin and when we get down to 4, it means we reorder to bring it back to 16. To initiate an order, we flag with a red tab. Once a week, on Friday afternoon, the manager sat down and flicked through the cardex panels looking for all the red tabs and then ordering what was needed for each part; pen and pad. The order went out to CAT by mail and a week later, we could expect a shipment from Peoria resupplying our bins as we had instructed.

- Once a year, the weekend of Thanksgiving, we had the whole company in the parts department taking a physical inventory to see how well the numbers on the cards conformed to the number we counted in the bins.

- Currently in our operation the computer is, of course, king. As we create parts orders for customers or the shop, the computer records the quantity ordered, resets balance in inventory, provides price, location, etc. and likewise orders from CAT what parts we need to keep a proper balance in inventory. All the accumulated orders processed by now from all our stores are forwarded to Morton (the major CAT depot), and the next day, the parts we wanted appear at the appropriate store to go to customers, or into bins. Order by noon, here next day!

P.E. working the parts counter back in the day.

Gene Cosler loading up parts to deliver to customers.

- There is a CAT Parts Depot in town and we took advantage of it, getting what parts we did not have from said depot twice a day. Today, we visit the depots six times a day, a round-robin ritual, providing hurry-up CAT service.

- We established a shuttle system where we dispatch parts nightly via two trucks to the branch stores and to major customers using 30 drop boxes, thus, giving them overnight service.

- All our branches are linked through computers so each can see the others' inventory and each can access parts within our system. Each store also has access to CAT depots across the country and can secure parts in a crisis from them as well.

- Inventories not only contain individual parts, but now include an endless number of exchange components, so a whole engine or torque converter can be supplied.

- Instead of counting all our parts at Thanksgiving time each year, we have a monthly rotation which defines certain areas of our inventory to count each month and by moving onto the next section, can cover the entire inventory each year. Inventorying is an ongoing routine.

- Instead of our customers coming in to order parts, aside from the phone, they can order parts on the CAT Store Front. They can also fax in orders or use the computer.

- We have added a NAPA store to accommodate customers who might need non-CAT parts.

- Where COD transactions were all in cash in the old days, today we accept credit cards.

- Instead of using parts books (which was the custom for 50 years), customers can go in the computer (store front), pull up the page they want and order from home or while sitting on a bulldozer.

- UPS and FedEx provides remarkable expedition in terms of getting parts quickly to us or the owners and is far more efficient than rail freight or bus service and far more universal.

Bottom line here is simply that given the number of products we now service, the number of different stores involved, the range of diverse customers, our charge has been drastically increased. Instead of adding 50 more people to shuffle papers as we process 742 parts orders a day, we have adopted computer-managed programs where we can facilitate the enormously expanded traffic and activity. Imagine the size of our cardex file today, supplying 403 models, involving the countless computations per day of "how much" of "what" to order, the tedium of manually leafing through cards and red tabs, all make the old way virtually impossible. Like the rest of our dealership, this area continually tries better to serve all parties involved: the user, Caterpillar, the employees and the owners.

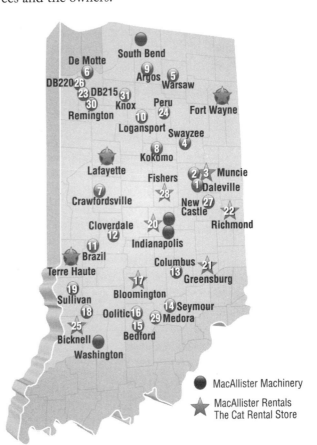

Map of MacAllister Drop Box Locations

P.E. received his MacAllister employee award for 65 years of service August 2010.

Plaque reads:
All your MacAllister teammates recognize the anniversary of 65 years of continuous service you have dedicated to MacAllister Machinery Co., Inc.

Thank you for assisting in the founding of the company, its initial success, assuming the President's role and leading the company after E.W.'s death and building the business through the 1950's, 1960's, and 1970's.

Thank you for also orchestrating an orderly transition to the third generation in 1991 and remaining connected and involved ever since. Your knowledge, experience, wisdom, conscience, reputation and perspective are invaluable!

P.E. MacAllister

Chairman of the Board 1952–Present
MacAllister Machinery Co., Inc.
(Dealer for Caterpillar Inc.)

CIVIC

Past President – Capital Improvements Board (100 million Convention Center & RCA Dome) (17 years on the Board)
Past Chairman – Marion County Convention & Recreational Facilities Authority
Past Board Member – Community Hospital Foundation
Past President – Indianapolis Opera Company
Past Board Member – Indiana State Symphony Society
Past Member – Board of Public Safety
Past Vice Chair – Edyvean Repertory Theatre Board
Past Member – President's Advisory Committee on the Arts
Past Member – Marion County Hospital Authority Board
Executive Director – "Conference on Cities" (An international symposium on urban problems in collaboration with NATO, held in Indianapolis, May 1971)
Past Chairman – Greater Indianapolis Republican Finance Committee
Campaign Treasurer – Richard G. Lugar Mayoral Election (1971)
Campaign Chairman – William H. Hudnut for Congress (1973)
Campaign Chairman – William H. Hudnut for Mayor (1975)
Presidential Elector – 1976, 1980, 2000
Chairman Emeritus – Indianapolis Parks Foundation Board
President – Indiana Opera Theatre
Vice President – Fine Arts Society (Classical Music Station) (39 years)
Member – Corporate Community Council Board
Member – Friends of Garfield Park, Inc.
Member – Greater Indianapolis Republican Finance Committee Board
Member – Guardian Home Foundation, Inc., Advisory Board
Member – Indiana Inter–Religious Commission on Human Equality
Member – Indiana Historical Society
Member – Indianapolis Committee on Foreign Relations
Member – Marion County Land Valuation Commission
Member – Opportunity Project of Indiana, Board of Advisors
Member – 2001 World Police & Fire Games, Executive Advisory Committee
Member – American Council of Learned Societies
Member – Indiana Broadcast Pioneers

CHURCH

Elder, Deacon, Trustee – Northminster Presbyterian Church
Past Moderator – Indianapolis Presbytery (Two terms)
Past Moderator – Synod of Indiana (1972)
Past Moderator – Synod of Lincoln Trails (1975)
Extensive Service – National, Synod, Presbytery Councils, Presbyterian Church
Chairman – Board of Trustees, Christian Theological Seminary (1972–1984)
Past Board Member – McCormick Theological Seminary

OTHER

Chairman Emeritus – Board of Trustees, Carroll College, Waukesha, Wisconsin
Past President – Associated Equipment Distributors (1972)
Past Chairman – AED Research and Services Corporation
Past President – Equipment Distributors of Indiana
Past Chairman – Vanderbilt Gulfside Condominium Association (1984–93)
Host – One–hour weekly television show, "On Site"
Chairman – Board of Trustees, American Schools of Oriental Research (Middle East Archaeology)

HOBBIES & INTERESTS

Public speaking, writing, the Old Testament; art, music (mostly classical); foreign travel
White wines – Alsace or German; Golf – 23 handicap... and wobbling!

NOTE

Mr. MacAllister is a prominent businessman and civic leader. He is an armchair authority on Old Testament. His book, "Tongue of the Nursling" deals with that work. He is knowledgeable in Greek and Roman history; is especially familiar with the Florentine Renaissance; wrote a series of essays in 1976 for AED's monthly publication on the Bi–Centennial and a second series in 1987 on the Constitutional Convention; is a member of the Board of the American Schools of Oriental Research, which monitors and authenticates archaeological excavation in the Middle East (this includes Syria, Jordan, Israel, Iraq, Cyprus, and sporadic digs in Egypt). He has received a Doctor of Laws Degree, Honoris Causa, from Indiana State University; a Doctor of Public Service Degree, Honoris Causa, from Christian Theological Seminary; and a Doctor of Humane Letters, Honoris Causa, from Carroll College. Along with C. Richard Petticrew, the two have created "The MacAllister–Petticrew Chair" of Old Testament Studies at Christian Theological Seminary. Mr. MacAllister has created "A Chair in Old Testament" at Carroll College. His lay understanding of the Bible was evident for 25 years when he preached summers, five or six times in Protestant churches. Mr. MacAllister's on–going love of opera has created the largest non–restricted vocal competition for opera singers in the nation (The MacAllister Awards), and ran for 22 years.

PERSONAL

Raised in Wisconsin
B.A., Carroll College, 1940
Five Years Air Force (Captain); 27 months overseas 1st Fighter Group
Married Rebecca Cochran 1945 (deceased 2001), 3 children
Married Fran Downing 2003

P.E. MacAllister (continued)

AWARDS

"Industry Leadership" Award – Associated Equipment Distributors, 1974

"Wings of Hope" Award – Wings of Hope, 1976

"Directors Award for Industry Leadership" – Indiana Contractors, Inc., 1982

"Service to Mankind" Award – Sertoma, 1984

"Board Member of the Year" – Republican Finance Committee, 1987

"Spirit of Life" Award – City of Hope, 1987

"Excellence in Education" Award – Tau Kappa Epsilon Fraternity, 1989

"Diploma of Honor" – Fine Arts Society for Service to the Arts, 1989

"Benjamin Harrison Award" – Columbia Club, 1989

"Certificate of Special Merit" – American Schools of Oriental Research, 1994

"Hoosier Heritage Night" – The Heritage Place of Indianapolis, 1996

Entrepreneur of the Year "Community Spirit Award" – Ernst & Young LLP, 1996

"Philanthropist of the Year" – Indianapolis Parks Foundation, 1997

"Distinguished Alumni Award" – Carroll College, 1998

"Indiana Academy Award" – Independent Colleges of Indiana, 1998

"Guardian Angel Award" – Children's Guardian Home, 2001

"Democracy Award" – Associated Equipment Distributors, 2002

"Indiana Business Hall of Fame" – Junior Achievement, 2002

"Arts Council of Indianapolis" – 2003

"Trustee of the Year Award" – Carroll College, 2004

"Spirit of Philanthropy Award" – Indiana University, 2005

"Sagamore of the Wabash Award" – Gov. Otis Bowen

"Sagamore of the Wabash Award" – Gov. Bob Orr

"Philanthropy Award" – Church Federation of Greater Indianapolis, 2005

"Presidents' Circle – Indiana University – 2008

"Michael A. Carroll Award" – 2008

"Whistler Award" – 2008

"Living Legends Award" – 2009